Psychological Assessment:
A Theory and Systems Approach

Psychological Assessment:
A Theory and Systems Approach

JAMES R. BARCLAY, PH.D.

University of Kentucky
Lexington, Kentucky

KRIEGER PUBLISHING COMPANY
MALABAR, FLORIDA
1991

Original Edition 1991

Printed and Published by
KRIEGER PUBLISHING COMPANY
KRIEGER DRIVE
MALABAR, FLORIDA 32950

Library of Congress Cataloging-in-Publication Data

Barclay, James Ralph, 1926-
   Psychological assessment : a theory and systems approach/
James R. Barclay.
      p.   cm.
   Includes bibliographical references.
   ISBN 0-89464-405-X (alk. paper)
   1. Psychological tests.   2. Psychometrics.   I Title.
BF176.B36   1990
150′.28′7—dc20   89-37230
                                                             CIP

10 9 8 7 6 5 4 3 2

Preface

This book represents an effort to understand and integrate the various components of psychological assessment into a conceptual framework. As a result it has turned out to be a formidable task that has stretched on for some years.

In part the book came into existence as a consequence of my enduring interest in assessment and teaching experience over thirty years. But the specific thrust towards clarification, classification and integration was related to the conviction that students of psychology need to understand the nature of assessment in more depth than provided by books on tests and measurements. So often testing becomes the answer to all assessment questions for psychologists. In short, just as in research methods there is a need for knowing about fundamental questions that relate to the logic of research over and beyond statistical tools, so in assessment there is a need to go beyond tests and techniques into the theoretical background of perception, empirical observation, and intuition.

This book focuses on assessment, not just testing but all those means devised and used by human beings to evaluate what is happening to them, where they are going, and what their goals might be. The primary purpose of this book is to develop a comprehensive philosophy of assessment; that is, to define the constructs developed in assessment, the tools used to verify constructs, and the methods of procedures designed to integrate findings. A second objective seeks to understand both the assets and limitations of the methods we employ in validating our information and suggests how we can integrate these methods into a coherent unity.

In order to facilitate these goals, the reader will find that each chapter is divided into sections that logically relate to the chapter itself. Within these sections certain declarative statements will be found that serve as a taxonomy and provide the reader with an organizer for each subsection of the book.

There are three levels on which understanding of this book can take place. The first will present the organizing statements. To understand what is meant by these statements, the text explanation follows. Finally to search out further information, the footnotes provide a base. Utilizing these three levels, the book should provide summary review for professionals, explanation for students, and further commentary for researchers in order to examine the underpinnings of both our methods of assessment and the tools used to verify or validate the data of assessment.

The book is not a substitute for a textbook on tests and measurements. In fact, it is assumed that students who will study this book have already completed a course in psychological testing and/or statistics. The book is designed for graduate students in psychology who are beginning the important task of trying to integrate interview data with group and individual tests, particularly as these methods of observation may lead to both a diagnostic evaluation and a treatment selection.

Frankly, as a professor, I looked for such an integrated book for years. Because I could not find it, I have attempted to write it myself. It has been a much more difficult task than I had thought possible since I found that assessment lacked a coherent theoretical foundation. As a result, many areas had to be probed and analyzed relative to the fundamental synthesis of methods and data. Consequently this book represents a personal conception of the integration of assessment methods and goals as they relate to the logic of hypothesis making. It is my conviction that the integration of assessment is an important skill for all students of clinical, counseling, and school psychology. The emphasis of the book is therefore on the common core of learning that relates to psychological assessment in general, rather than to the specific listing of techniques that may be applicable in certain specialties.

I am indebted to many hundreds of students who have studied these materials and who have offered helpful suggestions for clarification and amplification. I am also grateful for the comments and encouragement of colleagues who have offered many excellent critical ideas for the improvement of this book. I specifically wish to express a debt of gratitude to several mentors at the University of Michigan, Professor William Clark Trow and Professor William C. Morse, who by their example and encouragement many years ago enhanced my efforts to write this book.

James R. Barclay
Lexington, Kentucky

CHAPTER I

The Nature of Human Assessment

"In the field of observation chance favors only the prepared mind.
Indefinite expression is the best exponent of imprecise knowledge."

Louis Pasteur

This chapter provides an overview of the nature of assessment as a distinctly human process involving various forms of observation. Assessment is described as a process that includes the use of different methods, the identification of alternative procedures, the classification of phenomena observed within these alternative procedures, and the integration of methods and procedures into a typology for making inferences about human individual differences. The core components of good assessment are described as being based on reliable and valid observation, a careful and logical analysis of propositions derived from observations, and valid processes for the making and testing out of inferences. Inferences differ in their epistemological credibility. The targets of assessment are seen basically as referring to human skills within social criteria of effective human behavior.

ASSESSMENT AND SURVIVAL

An important question that students approaching the study of assessment might ask is "why is this necessary?" The reasons can be stated both from a nonprofessional and professional viewpoint. First, assessment is a naturalistic process that occurs all the time in human beings and it is valuable to understand how we make decisions on the basis of our assessment of a situation. Second, assessment is a survival skill in the sense that throughout our life decisions that we make, from crossing the street to getting married, are based on the assessment skills we have developed. Third, from a professional point of view, assessment is the key and distinguishing feature of the competencies of the psychologist. Whatever else a psychologist may do or be called upon to do, it is assumed that he or she possesses the skills necessary to perform an assessment of individual differences. By individual differences are meant all those genetic and acquired characteristics that distinguish one individual from another.

Assessment is a survival skill. Individuals depend on making good assessments of other people. Today as in the past the ability to interpret the behavior of others and to make the appropriate accommodations in one's own behavior that are necessary in differing circumstances is an important skill. Assessment requires adequate decoding of both verbal and nonverbal behaviors in others, the classification of those behaviors into various categories, and the ability to discriminate between categories. For example, when we meet a new person, we automatically "size up" characteristics. We observe body type, eye contact, verbal capabilities and relate these attributes to the time and place. Increasingly as we gain experience we also make inferences about future behavior, our own security, and what we should say or do. From our experience we have generated an entire set of such inferences based on empirical observation and these inferences are related to our own agenda of priorities. Thus, for example, if we meet a corpulent man at a cocktail party we may infer that he is excessively fond of food. If we subsequently note heavy drinking and reddened features we may infer that he has both a liking for and a possible problem with alcohol. If we observe this individual scanning the guests and seeking out influential people, we may conclude that he is enterprising and desirous of "selling something." Our inferences may be wrong! But they will most likely create some affective responses in us towards this individual. Moreover, if we have some ideas to sell ourselves, we will probably be very guarded in what we say to him.

Assessment provides an organizer for expectations. From early childhood on the task of discerning and evaluating the expectations and behaviors of others becomes an important personal and social skill. For many, the ability to discern what is expected and should be done in a particular situation is a means to accommodate to group criteria of effective behavior as well as the avoidance of punishment. Children often form judgments about each other on the basis of a set of questions: "Where do you live? what does your father do? what school do you go to? what grade are you in? what sports do you like best? what TV programs do you watch? how many gears does your bike have?" These questions establish social status and personal characteristics.

Assessment often implies causal attributions. The role of assessment has been an important component in the history of cultural evolution. For as long as humankind has lived in social groups, the assessment of individual differences has been a vitally important function. From the observation of individual differences came empirical descriptions of behaviors, and from these descriptions came causative explanations. As urban cultures developed, more sophisticated explanations led to theories of how behaviors were related to the physical energy system of the world (cosmogony) and how these characteristics determined or shaped personality. Virtually all early explanations of behavior were related to a correspondence between what was observed and what happened. Thus the concept of prediction of behavior was conceived and understood long before it was defined. Inferences were made about what was observed and what was believed to be causally related to those observations.

Early on, the empirical observations of behavior were categorized. One form of behavior was judged to be expressive of happiness, joy and love. Another form was indicative of sorrow, grief and unhappiness. Knowing how to read bodily responses and emotive responses was vital to survival. For it was from the systematic categorizing of responses vis-a-vis specific situations that early mankind could judge what constituted a secure and predictable response to an environmental stimulus. The chief needs of early man were for food, shelter and security. Thus, an understanding of how individuals behaved, how they separated roles and functions to meet the predictable needs of food, shelter and security was an assessment skill needed to survive.

Assessment is multifaceted. Modern times present these same basic human needs, but our culture has evolved into a complex technological network of systems and relationships. Assessment has expanded to much greater dimensions than those of earlier societies, or even the predominantly rural culture of the nineteenth century. There are needs for assessment in education, vocational planning, mental health, and many other areas of life. Moreover, we have many sophisticated tools for assessment, including not only a large repertory of tests, but also computers which provide for diagnostic testing of individuals, and the integration of great amounts of data. Thus both informal and formal assessment directly impinge on the lives of most human beings today in some way or other.

Assessment is a paramount skill of the professional psychologist. The study of assessment has often been hampered in recent decades by a number of factors. First of all, assessment has most often been identified as a term synonymous to testing. This is not the case because assessment includes a variety of methods other than testing itself. Second, as we shall examine in more detail in the next chapter, there has been an uneven use of assessment techniques in the related branches of psychology such as clinical, industrial, school and counseling. Third, there has been no real consensus as to how various assessment inputs can be integrated in terms of contemporary demands for accountability. Finally, there has been no integrative theory of assessment.

Unfortunately, testing and assessment have frequently been considered identical terms. Assessment is a generalized skill of evaluation, whereas testing is a specific psychometric technique that may or may not be relevant to assessment. It is because of the undue identification of the two terms assessment and testing that the well-known criticisms of testing have been extended to all kinds of assessment.

The inconsistent stance which exists between the several branches of applied psychology has been felt specifically as society becomes more aware of the systems approach to decision making, the use of the computer, and demands for psychological contributions to the assessment of performance competencies. The need for accountability demands that professionals understand the comprehensive dimensions of assessment, specifically as trait, state, and character determinations can be translated into viable and observable standards of competence.

The lack of a unified theory of assessment makes it difficult for psychologists to respond to the demand seen repeatedly in legal, business, and professional areas to know how psychologists make decisions and on what data these decisions are made. Some psychologists may reject all notions of trait characteristics and psychometric observations in favor of a strictly behavioral assessment. Others equally reject behavioral notions and vest their confidence in the interpretation of test scores and projective findings. Though criticisms have been directed towards clinical psychology for perhaps too high a reliance on intuitive and projective methods, and towards counseling psychology as often being deficient in assessment itself, the severest criticisms have been for educational and school psychology.

Assessment lacks an integrative theory. As a whole, psychology suffers from the lack of an integrative theory of assessment. In psychological practice there is very little agreement on the specific targets of the work to be done, a general but unfocused body of knowledge relating to the sources of problems, a glut of research with different premises, different methods, different instruments and equivocal outcomes. Moreover, there is very little consensus on what the functional components of assessment are, how they should be weighted, how they should be integrated, and what role—if any—diagnosis should play as an outcome of assessment. This is largely due to controversies between behaviorists and phenomenologists as to what are the relevant targets of assessment. It is also because most psychologists are thoroughly trained in the use of psychometrics to the virtual exclusion of other forms of assessment.

Assessment affects all phases of psychological thinking and practice. It therefore requires a systems approach for comprehensive understanding. With the accumulation of a vast repertory of alternative methods of assessment, i.e., interviewing, behavioral analysis, study of critical life episodes, neurological analysis, and psychometric tests, it seems both timely and necessary to relate assessment to a systems approach. This is particularly important to the student of assessment who enters this field without a recognition of the background. For all too often empirical, psychometric, and what may be termed intuitive methods of assessment thinking are confounded with competing theories of personality such as those propounded by psychodynamic theory, behaviorism, and humanism. Methods are clearly related to procedures for analyzing data; theories, on the other hand, relate to conceptual frameworks for interpreting data.

Because of the need for relating processes, method, goals, criteria of assessment, and conceptual frameworks of interpretation such as theoretical points of view, it is the general purpose of this book to develop a paradigm for assessment. Assessment is so broad a subject that theory alone does not suffice. A paradigm provides a philosophical rationale for the entire field and includes within it subsets of various theories. To illustrate the paradigm, a systems approach will be taken, examining each of the parts of assessment separately, and showing how they all are related.

Assessment can be viewed in a systems approach. In effect it is the goal of this book to apply a systems approach to assessment content and method. Ryan and Zeran (1972) have defined a systems approach as: "a disciplined way of analyzing as precisely as possible an existing situation by determining the nature of the elements which combine and relate to make the situation what it is, establishing interrelationships among the elements, and synthesizing a new whole to provide means of optimizing system outcomes" (p. 13). A system is viewed in definition as an orderly organization in which parts are seen to relate to each other in such a way that the validity of the total system is dependent on these functional relationships.

The concept of systems is not alien to current science. We know that the human body consists of systems which interact in maintaining the total body. Thus, the digestive process is not separated from the muscular system, nor is the circulatory system independent of the brain. Human beings also belong to social systems which can be identified in terms of the family as a primary one, and many secondary ones such as education, religion, social groups, and environmentally-related systems identified as neighborhoods, cities, states and countries. Moreover, we know from much recent research that the entire ecology of the world population constitutes a single system that is interactive with sea, air, and land masses. The possible effects of a "nuclear winter" have become probably the most important single deterrent to nuclear war. The prospects of a general elevation of temperature in our atmosphere may change fertile plains into deserts, submerge coastal cities, and make great changes in the ecology of our existence. To view life itself as a series of interactive systems makes sense. To view assessment as a series of methods which are united in some common goals also makes sense.

THE FOCUS OF HUMAN ASSESSMENT SYSTEMS

Human nature consists of a structural component and a control component. The two are related in a necessary, but not sufficient manner. In assessment the issue of human nature must be met head on, which is what this foundational axiom attempts to do. From the progress of psychological research it is apparent that there are two hierarchies that must be taken into consideration in understanding anything about human behavior. One is the structural hierarchy of the bodily systems, and the other is the control hierarchy that exists within consciousness and deals with both cognition and volition. Although it would take us too far afield to discuss all of the philosophical ramifications of the above statement, basically we are dealing with a Cartesian dichotomy: (1) the human body, that includes an extended measurable substance with component systems understood through biological science, and (2) an entity that we may variously call mind or ego that exists without substantive parts in the forum of consciousness.[1]

Biological science has described the body as a series of interactive systems proceeding from the minute to the gross. This configuration of systems is the structural hierarchy. In the course of modern science, the biological science method has been to study behavior, observe those physiological correlates which are concomitant with that behavior, trace such correlates to properties of the central nervous system, ultimately ending at the neuron and the electro-chemical foundations of neural activity. Thus biological study of the human body implies origins in the union of the egg and sperm that carry the minute hereditary components that specify both the sequence and range of the developmental process. From this primary beginning, the individual grows, various components appear, expand, and develop into a comprehensive interactive set of systems.

The structural hierarchy is complemented by a control hierarchy that exists within the forum or medium of consciousness. The upward hierarchical approach to understanding behavior stops at the threshold of consciousness. Consciousness represents a quantum leap from behavior. It is within the dimension of consciousness that the intellectual, social, and collective aspects of human life exist. As Jaynes (1973) wrote: "the intellectual life of man, his culture and history and religion and science, is different from anything else we know of in the universe. That is a fact. It is as if all life evolved to a certain point, and then in ourselves turned at a right angle and simply exploded in a different direction" (Jaynes, 1973, p. 9).

What Jaynes is stating is that consciousness is a dimension apart from the aggregation of cellular responses into behavior. No aggregation in the physiological sequence of human analysis can account for the emergence of consciousness. Consciousness is the unique forum for acquiring information through cognition, and making decisions through volition. To be sure, physiological constraints condition the nature of consciousness such as blood flow, intactness of cerebral conditions, hereditary factors, aging, senility, and other factors. In terms of causal explanations of altered states of consciousness, neurological substrata act as instrumental causes, not efficient causes. The body is a necessary condition for continued consciousness, but not a sufficient one. If the structural system were both the necessary and sufficient cause of conscious activity, then it would be impossible to explain "out of the body" memories. From the time of Cicero on, there have been many testimonies of "out of the body" experiences. Typically, these include observations after a car wreck in which the individual is observing what is happening from some vantage point other than the body.[2]

Consciousness as such relates to psychic phenomena. In the nineteenth century a great debate was initiated over whether psychology was a biological science or a science of consciousness. Considerable development has taken place in the biological arena over the past hundred years, but it is evident today that consciousness is still the *terra incognita* of psychology and that its analysis must proceed by the rules of careful logical analysis of the phenomena themselves rather than by fruitless efforts to tie neuronal activity to such psychic phenomena as thinking, willing, and choosing.

Consciousness is unitary, successive, based on perceptual representations and possesses no extension. To understand consciousness it is obviously crucial to identify the components that exist and operate within it. We cannot approach consciousness in the manner that we study biological phenomena for it has no extension. Rather it is based on representations derived from perception, is unitary, and successive in terms of a continual flow of mental phenomena. How then can one study consciousness? One approach is to examine how it functions and then logically deduce the nature of consciousness from its functions.

Cognition and volition are the two main functions that occur in consciousness. The major function of consciousness is to make decisions. It is therefore the forum in which decision making occurs. Within this forum or medium awareness, cognition and volition can be distinguished as entities or components. But these components are not equal. Awareness is a condition of both cognition and volition. Cognition serves as the conservator of information and actively seeks such information through observation and learning, and utilizes both short-term and long-term memory. Volition is then the component or entity related to the actual process of decision making.

In human beings, consciousness provides the forum for a control hierarchy that is inversely related to the structural hierarchy of biological systems. Rather than proceeding from minute elements to behavior as the structural hierarchy does, the control hierarchy extends from the top down. One can study the extent of power in the control hierarchy by identifying the entity or faculty that possesses the greatest amount of control. By logical inference, the greater the management control, the more central the component.

The two major components of the control hierarchy are cognition and volition. Cognition has biological referents in the structural hierarchy, specifically in intelligence, a largely inherited structural component. But it also includes attention, perception and judgment with subcategories of memory and imagination. Volition also has biological referents specifically in the emotions. Given the criterion of control as a means of evaluating, the relative power of these two faculties can be gauged in a common sense manner.

Volition is the dominant element in the control hierarchy. It is popular in recent years to assume that cognition has the central role in the control hierarchy. In part this has been due to an implicit judgment that knowledge leads to decision making. Problem solving, and cognitive behavior modification both tend to ignore the role of volition. Unfortunately, cognition does not hold the chief executive's seat in the control hierarchy. If it did, knowledge would determine behavior, studying philosophy would make one wise, studying theology would make one virtuous, and studying methods of problem solving would result in good decisions. Cognition serves in the human cabinet of control as the chief controller, i.e., the amasser and conservator of resources. It has the programmatic function of amassing the facts and intellectual resources for making decisions.

Volition, on the other hand, has extensive control over the nature and products of consciousness because of its very close relationship to emotionality. Moods have extension both in the structural hierarchy and in terms of time duration. Depression acts as an impediment to cognition. So does passion. States of tension within the biological organism not only can make their needs aware to the volitional faculty, but distort cognition. In point of fact, such needs can actually create imagery for bodily arousal. Regardless of academic controversies, the role of direct and subliminal arousal of emotions and hence to decision making, is constantly observable in advertisements, television and music. Subliminal appeals to volition through the emotions have a great role in selling liquor, automobiles, tobacco, vacations, and countless other items.

Even as emotions and bodily arousal can exert a great influence on cognition and volition in actual decision making, it is likewise true that volition itself can shut down bodily arousal by a variety of means. Once again, the necessary but not sufficient relationship between the structural and control hierarchies is apparent.

Volition is influenced strongly by temperament. If volition constitutes a major controlling feature in consciousness, then access to the characteristics that either impede or facilitate decision making is a target for psychological assessment. Using the same criteria as before, i.e., the spatial and temporal extention of control over the organism, one is led inexorably to the emotions. As has been illustrated earlier, one may liken the control hierarchy in human beings to that of a corporate board room. Volition is the chief executive, cognition is the controller, the emotions form the balance of the management team and temperament is the caucus leader.

Emotions are broad hereditary dimensions that are imbedded in what we have come to term temperament. Temperament is not a trait, in the sense that psychological testing defines it. Temperament is a comprehensive set of templates organized around hereditary dispositions that incline the individual to a given range of emotional activity. The major components of temperament as variously considered by Thomas and Chess (1977), Buss and Plomin (1975) and Strelau (1983) are: (1) energy-activity, (2) sociability, (3) impulsivity-control, and (4) emotionality. Hereditarily, these components themselves are part of a complex network involving excitation and inhibition as well as flexibility. In the East European perspective they represent indices of the "strength of the nervous system," i.e. the capacity to manifest energetic activity, to recover from unexpected circumstances and to alter focus and attention without perseveration.

Assessment focuses equally on structural and control systems in human behavior. As we shall see in later chapters, assessment must take into consideration all those biological components that regulate and control the nature of the human body. Thus sociobiological research, the research of biochemistry, analysis of brain functioning, behavioral analyses, and ecological components of human existence are all data bases for assessment. But in addition, the analysis of cognition, the developmental perspective of both fluid and crystalline components of intelligence, are foci of assessment. What is important in addition is the assessment of volition and temperament characteristics. No matter how we define the central entity of volition i.e. as ego or as will, much of human anxiety, conflict, and irrationality proceed from this aspect of the control hierarchy. It is likewise important to recognize that all of our self-report data comes through the forum of consciousness. This means in effect that all test results are filtered through perception and consciousness.

We have separated elements in the assessment system not to suggest that they exist as oppositional entities. But it makes sense to recognize that the control hierarchy, in a real sense, mirrors the structural hierarchy. Within the human brain the limbic system represents the very basis and core of the brain itself. Cognition is broadly related to the frontal lobes, though not exclusively. Damage to the frontal lobes may cause impairment or changes in personality, but often does not result in death. Damage or injury to the limbic system usually results in severe impairment and/or death.

Harre, Clarke, and De Carlo (1985) exemplify the relationship between the various components in terms of a mainframe depending on smaller regional microcomputers or minicomputer systems. Information is obtained from the satellite computers and forwarded to the mainframe. This information is needed by the mainframe. But commands and other information are also sent from the mainframe to the minicomputers. To understand the integrative process of human behavior, both the structural and control hierarchies need to be studied and assessed.

Not only are these systems the focus of our assessment efforts, but also it is imperative to recognize that the only major tool that we have to make such assessments is our own human perception. Thus, not only do we need to know where we are looking in the process of assessment, but we need to recognize that our very looking is through the use of our own bodily system. We ourselves are both the object and the method of assessment.

THE NATURE OF ASSESSMENT, APPRAISAL, AND DIAGNOSIS

According to Sundberg (1977), the term assessment first appears as a psychological term in the book *Assessment of Men* (U.S. Office of Strategic Services, 1948). It is thus a comparatively recent construct in psychology. Sundberg defines the assessment of personality characteristics as: "The set of processes used by a person or persons for developing impressions and images, making decisions and checking hypotheses about another person's pattern of characteristics which determine his or her behavior in interaction with the environment" (1977, p. 22). Sundberg believes that the process of assessment serves three major goals which are: image making, decision making, and theory building. Shertzer and Linden (1979) define assessment as "the procedures and processes employed in collecting information about evidence of human behavior" (p. 13).

Assessment can be defined as those procedures and techniques utilized by all people in an unsystematic way and by professionals systematically to evaluate individual differences and to relate those differences to alternative settings and problems. Assessment plays a crucial and consistent role in human behavior. The major function of the human brain is to organize experiences—interpreting them through the cognitive system and relaying them to the emotive system for reactions. In addition such perceptions are stored in memory. Thus every act of perception includes not only the cognitive interpretative transmission of what exists outside, but an affective affirmation of specific subjective meaning. Moreover, the individual conveys affective meaning to that perception virtually exclusively in terms of self-preservation and maintenance of human needs. Thus from early on in individual development, cognition and arousal interact with each other to provide meaning to perception. How individuals develop in a given environmental setting depends on their cognitive and temperament endowment, how susceptible they are to modeling, reward and punishment, and how they utilize past learning.

Appraisal constitutes a special form of assessment in which evaluation is generally formally related to value judgments. Shertzer and Linden suggest that the term assessment refers to the methods and measures employed, and the term appraisal is related to making value judgments. For example, the evaluation of how well a child is doing in achievement is often shaped by the judgment of whether he or she is on grade level in all aspects of achievement. Hence, the evaluation of a child's achievement in terms of achievement tests reported in grade-level norms may rightly be called an appraisal. This appraisal contains within it a value judgment that being on target is better than not being on target. For the most part, assessment almost always includes elements of appraisal.

Assessment is a naturalistic process employed with greater or lesser accuracy by each individual for purposes of self-protection and self-enhancement. Individuals from birth on continually evaluate the characteristics of the environment. Ordinarily with age, those within the range of normal intelligence come to accept a reality outside themselves with which they must come to terms. The perception of outer reality is never totally objective, even with considerable experience and education. The human brain (depending on its capacity for understanding and interpretation, neurological intactness, and level of emotional arousal) evaluates the ebb and flow of human experience almost exclusively in terms of personal needs, fears, and opportunities weighed against the effects of past learning and behavior. It is for this reason that the combinations of cognition, affect and past learning create such a nearly infinite number of human characteristics. Most human beings develop from these interactions a coherent function for executive decision making (referred to in modern terms as ego, and in older terminology as will). Most psychological theorists agree that this decision-making function has its origin in temperament components, but is heavily shaped by the influence both of cognitive learning and the environment. Very important to the development of his function in human beings is the self-assessment process that subjectively examines not only the consequences of behavior and thought, but the process itself.

The purpose of the self-assessment process is then initially self-survival and maintenance. Such surveillance is mandatory to make individual life secure and continuous. It is also extremely important in the development of control mechanisms in human behavior. To be unaware of one's tendencies and directions is a problem for many individuals because life in its various phases requires a continual monitoring of both thought and behavior and appropriate adjustments.

The functional processes of assessment and appraisal contain explicitly or implicitly judgments which are based on inferences. These inferences ascribe to others intentionality, causal relationships, and often affix values to assessment judgments. Though our own experiences in life (as well as those of others) could probably be categorized more objectively by tallying the frequencies of given behaviors in terms of time or place, it would appear according to Weiner (1974) and Frieze (1979) that cognitive and affective experiences are almost continually interpreted by an individual in terms of *post-factum* causal attributions. Success can then be attributed to personal skills and competencies or to luck. Failure likewise can be attributed to others who may "have it in" for us, or it may be ascribed to our own inadequacies (e.g., failure to study well enough for a test) or to just plain "bad luck."

Associated with such attributions are inferences about intentionality or motivation in others. If we are walking down a corridor, meet a colleague and say "good morning," we expect a greeting similar to our own. This is simply a matter of accepted reciprocal behavior. If we are ignored or frowned at, we may interpret this as a negative reaction towards us. We may also interpret the behavior in terms of other hypotheses such as: (1) he may have had an argument with his wife today and be in a bad mood; (2) he may be preoccupied. But we do interpret such behavior in any case. Should we accept the hypothesis that our colleague is negatively disposed towards us, and without justification, we may reciprocate the next time we see him by being aloof.

These inferences relative to causal attribution have a direct bearing on what has been termed expectations. Expectations are personal perceptions generated from ways that people treat us. They are often found to be related to sex, race, socioeconomic status and characteristics of our behavior as observed by others (Brophy & Good, 1974). They thus form a proximate basis for behaviors attempted, and mediate our conditional anticipation of the kinds of reinforcements we may obtain. Hence assessment and appraisal through a naturalistic process of inferring lead to a chain of expectations and behaviors which may or may not be realized and may or may not have a good foundation in reality. To a large extent it is very likely that negative patterns of thinking are at the basis of habitual self-devaluation, inability to take meaningful action in a situation, and lack of motivation.

Obviously, the connection between causal inferring and expectations is not one which has been clearly delineated by research. But the studies which have been done would suggest that causal inferring is probably an internal mechanism which is designed to integrate the results of feedback in the continual self-monitoring of the human system. The process which is experienced by all of us is in a naive way is the basis of the third element of assessment—diagnosis.

Diagnosis is a process of informed decision making. Diagnosis differs from the informal causal and motivational inferring that all individuals do. It can be applied to the analysis of an individual, to that of groups, to institutions and agencies and to environments such as is exemplified in the analysis of classroom climates or environmental "presses." When such diagnostic procedures are used with groups, institutions and agencies, the term evaluation is often used. Diagnosis, in its usual connotation, refers chiefly to individuals and to small groups such as families.

Typically, the process can be defined as follows: diagnosis is based on (1) the identification of present problems through client self-report, and psychologist findings from multiple methods of assessment which then result (2) in a set of inferences linking the individual to a classification system, and (3) hypotheses about alternate outcomes given one treatment or another (prognosis).

This definition contains a number of elements that need to be further explained. Diagnosis is a process of informed decision making. This means that diagnosis is performed by those individuals who have the appropriate academic and experiential background to make the requisite decisions. Diagnosis is related to client needs. This means that the focus of the decision making must be related to the needs and expressions of the individual who is the target of the process. However, such individual needs must also be evaluated within the entire range of assessment inferences. Sometimes, though a patient or client may present a specific focus on a problem, it may be that the psychologist will have or develop inferences about that problem not within the present knowledge of the individual. A good example of this process might be the case of a young male student who comes to a counseling center because of failing grades. An assessment of the situation may indicate that he is intellectually capable, relatively interested in his field of study, but depressed. The depression turns out to be related to loneliness which is most manifest on the weekends when his roommate is gone. Thus the plan of action developed relates to enhancing social skills, particularly with friends and female students.

Diagnosis involves classification. A third ingredient of this definition relates to the integration of the data as related to typology, etiology and causal inferences. A typology is a classification system for grouping various individual differences. There are a number of such typologies which exist in psychological studies. Some relate to physiological characteristics, others to test characteristics, and still others to classification systems such as the DSM-III-R (a psychiatric classification system). In some instances, typology may simply refer to a set of subjective criteria which an individual psychologist has determined. But in any case, the point is that the set of characteristics obtained by a psychologist is most usually referred to some kind of classification system.

Diagnosis is incomplete without a knowledge of etiology. Etiology means the sum of all factors which have contributed to the present status of the individual. Usually, such applications are very comprehensive. Thus, in looking at the etiology of a specific case of depression, one has to consider not only the medical history, but the socioeconomic background, the personal habits of the individual, marital and child relationships, and many other factors. All of these components interact with learned experiences to provide an estimate of the etiology of a specific problem. Naturally, the inferences made about the estimate of influence of particular factors in the behavior of an individual are purely and simply a matter of subjective integration. Though we certainly know how major forces impinge on an individual (of varying intelligence and susceptibility to emotional arousal), there is no method of weighting these influences at present. In research studies one can estimate the components which contribute to the total variance, but in actual life situations, this remains an unknown.

Prognosis of possible outcomes is a vital part of diagnosis. By the word prognosis is meant what might be considered the probable future outcomes for this individual. **Prognosis implies a kind of prediction**. This prediction may be related to the actual circumstances and etiology without reference to any future intervention, or may be made with regard to a specific set of interventions. One of the informal axioms which has governed this question of prognosis is that past behavior is the best guarantee of future behavior. This means in effect that the tendency of individuals with regard to a specific set of problems is most often explained by reference to what they have done in the past. Therefore, one assumes that a depressed condition will continue, or that a delinquent character disorder will persevere over time. In medical terms, prognosis means that an individual with high blood pressure, inordinate stress, too much consumption of alcohol, and too much smoking, may over time predispose himself/herself to a fatal heart attack or cerebral hemorrhage.

It is customary to estimate what may be the prognosis of the individual

WITHOUT intervention and also *WITH* intervention. Prognosis then refers to what are the expected outcomes or the predicted future for the individual with and without interventions. This is done primarily to aid the individual in the accomplishment of some goals that he/she considers of a high priority nature. Usually, clients will identify some particular criteria that are important to them. These kinds of goals are most important for the psychologist to identify in the diagnosis process. For diagnosis exists for the benefit of the individual client, and the process of arriving at such a set of decisions is important.

Diagnosis is meant to result in a treatment plan. Finally, the entire power of diagnosis is balanced in the ability to match the aggregation of inferences (as reliably and validly arrived at as possible), to a set of treatment experiences that will benefit the individual. This point is made here, although the question of matching assessment results to treatment alternatives is not a major focus of this book, but obviously, we should not go through the process of assessment without reaching some conclusions about the nature of possible treatments.

FURTHER ELABORATION OF DIAGNOSIS: A PROCESS PARADIGM

In order to understand how these elements of assessment, appraisal and diagnosis are used together, it is essential to consider what is the overall rationale of using them. The word paradigm literally means to "show side by side." What it has come to mean in today's language is a model or archetype which provides a rationale for action. A paradigm represents the clearest formulation of the core elements of a science—or for that matter of a philosophy. In the next chapter we shall deal more explicitly with the topic of how past and present paradigms have developed. In this overview chapter we should like to present some systems implications of what diagnosis means.

The definition of diagnosis cited earlier provides all of the functional elements which have been outlined in a systems model for assessment leading to diagnostic competency. Figure 1 provides the flow-chart which describes the systems model. Diagnosis in its etymological base is derived from the Greek verb, *gignomai*, which signifies a sense of becoming, growth, or a kind of birth.

In later Greek usage the word became converted to a verb *dia-gignosko* which could be interpreted as to perceive, to gain knowledge of, to mark, to discern between two or more things, to distinguish, to discriminate and finally to decide. Naturally, the noun from this then referred to the process of decision making with a distinctive futuristic focus, i.e., *diagnosis*.

The components of diagnosis can be described in terms of four elements:

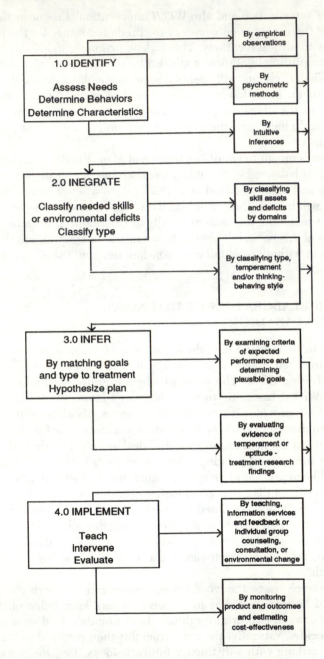

Figure 1-1 **Systems Model for Diagnostic-Treatment Paradigm**

identify, integrate, infer, and implement. Each of these elements is based on a solid knowledge of individual differences. Morevoer, all of these elements can be conceptualized as processes. **The first element is that of identification.** Identification consists of focusing on the problem of the client as verbalized. Though the presenting problem may not be the real problem, all assessment begins with the empirical evaluation of the verbal report of the client. (Note that I am using the term client generically here because the individual being evaluated may also be described by teachers, parents, and others). During the identification phase of diagnosis the psychologist brings to the interview a reservoir of psychological knowledge and experience that enables the professional to interpret the relationship of client needs and motivation. The psychologist can also obtain an estimate of the aspirations (goals of the client) and perceived obstacles, analyze the reality appraisal of the client in terms of self-reported solutions and plans, and identify the psychological support system which exists for the client in terms of family, peer, and community resources. To a large extent this information can be obtained from a systematic interview.

Once empirical impressions have been clarified (and it should not be thought that this can always be done in one brief initial interview), then the diagnostician needs to direct the attention of the client towards those specific behaviors which are the external linkages to problems. The frequency of behaviors, the settings in which they occur, the time of day, the specific antecedents and consequences which occur relative to the behaviors need to be carefully ascertained. In behavioral assessment terms this refers to obtaining a base rate of problem behaviors, often involving a simple tally of events such as, for example, the number of cigarettes smoked in a day.

After the problem has been empirically focused and behaviorally evaluated, it is then relevant to search for psychometric trait characteristics that may provide further information about the personality and temperament of the individual. Specific personality, achievement, intelligence, and vocational tests can then be administered for these purposes.

The second step in diagnosis is to provide an integration of the empirical, behavioral and psychometric data that have been accumulated. It is helpful at this stage to obtain estimates of the judgments of others about the client, provided that the client accepts such an evaluation. The crucial factor here is to integrate the characteristics of the individual into a typology or temperament cluster which makes sense in terms of a classification system. Since the question of classification of individual differences is one of highly contested alternatives, suffice it to state here that a classification system is needed that makes sense and can be utilized readily for planning the next stages of the diagnosis process. This matter will be discussed in much greater detail in a later chapter.

Step three in the diagnosis process is called inference. In the older psychodynamic model, prognosis was considered a separate process from diagnosis. Inference in this systems model refers to prognosis. Prognosis has in the past been an estimate of how an individual's characteristics relate to alternative treatments. This is still the medical model approach. Typically the diagnosis of the physician yields a pattern of characteristics that are suggestive of a specific disease. Alternative medical treatments are then reviewed in terms of how each of these treatments may affect the course of the patient's problems or disease. In psychological diagnosis, however, we are not dealing with functions of disease, but rather with learned behavior which is mediated by personality characteristics and environmental experiences. Our basic problem in step three is to determine how the characteristics of an individual can be related to the development of appropriate skills. Thus, given our knowledge of empirical, behavioral and psychometric characteristics, our effort to integrate these into a comprehensive multimodal and multitrait scenario, it is now our task to infer what alternative strategies may most effectively be employed to build the skills needed and desired by or for this individual.

To explain further, prognosis or inference making is strongly dependent on experimental research findings with alternative treatments. Unfortunately, in psychology it has not had that credibility in the past. In fact, prognosis has often been considered a separate step in the assessment process. However, because prognosis involves a judgment about what a person might do, given a set of goals, it has been included here as an integral part of diagnosis. Medicine is more adequate with prognosis because it has verified, through experimental methods, the consequences of alternative treatments. It is one of the important and crucial tasks of psychological research to add to the epistemological credibility of our treatment prognoses. Because of our inability to develop perceptive diagnostic information for the classification of individual differences we have not been able to obtain precise outcomes data. Thus it is probably at this point that the systems model proposed is weakest.

Obviously joined to prognosis is the problem of limited prediction. It is all too popular in psychological circles to assume that heredity times environmental factors equate to a prediction of human behavior. Generally, individuals with a scientific background assume that when we know the exact way factors of the environment and personality relate to each other, then an equation will be forthcoming to explain and offer a prediction relative to future behavior. Bandura (1978), however, has pointed out a very significant component to this equation, i.e. the effect of past learning. This has an important relationship to prediction which obviates the older scientific realism point of view that many natural or physical scientists have held. For example, Einstein thought that our inadequate knowledge of the laws of physics sufficed for stating why physicists could not chart the curve of an atom with accuracy. Einstein reasoned that once we knew all of the laws, then we could make absolute prediction. But Niels Bohr pointed out that in every case of measurement, the measuring instruments interact with the observations and are therefore not strictly speaking independent (D'espagent, 1979). Rather than accept the premise of determinism in behavior or that it is only a matter of time before we find out about all human laws of behavior, it would seem more appropriate for psychologists to recognize that individual behavior is always related to a set of perceptions on the part of the individual that include causal inferring. Thus, for example, if we have in mind influencing someone else and we are following a chain of logical inferences or hypotheses in this approach, we will most likely continue to do what we are doing if we meet with success and reinforcement for our thinking. If we do not, then we alter our thinking and make other contextual judgments appropriate to the feedback we are receiving. What can be said about this entire matter is simply that in our own personal thinking as well as in the professional process outlined above, we formulate hypotheses for action. Our method is our experience. Thus though we may infer the direction of behavior and consequences both for ourselves and for others, it is quite unlikely that human behavior is strictly related to a regression line. This fact has been aptly illustrated by the dictum that one can predict the behavior of most people most of the time, but not all of the people all of the time.

The fourth task in the diagnostic model is one of treatment implementation. Obviously the intended direction of the client in this matter is all important. As is indicated in the flowchart, the intervention needs to be monitored and evaluated. Since the entire process of identification, integration and inference is based on the best formulation of hypotheses needed, it may work or it may need revision. From the flow-chart it is apparent that a recycling may be undertaken at this point if the intervention is not succeeding.

In summary then, effective diagnosis: (a) begins with the identification of the problem. This procedure includes, but is not limited to, the initial interview and self-report of the individual or referring agent. It also includes the use of such psychometric empirical and behavioral observations as may be relevant. The problem may be in cognitive areas relating to thinking, in affective ones relating to emotional response, or in behavioral ones relating to social interaction with others. The clarification of the problem may be complicated by physical or biochemical disorders and symptoms, along with trauma or accident, and/or conditions which reflect heightened level of arousal in the individual. As a matter of fact in most instances of self-referred situations, clients are in a state of heightened arousal since individuals who seek help, be it for personal, social, cognitive, or vocational reasons are facing situations which have led them to seek outside help.

Subsequently (b) the diagnostician attempts to integrate the various empirical, behavioral and psychometric inputs into a system which allows for a classification of the characteristics of the individual. On the basis of such information, it is possible then to look at the goals of the individual in terms of needed skill development and match up personality characteristics with prognostic alternatives. Finally the treatment is implemented and monitored.

In summary, assessment has been described in this chapter as a naturalistic process used by all individuals to appraise reality. It is also a primary professional tool of the psychologist. Because assessment must not only be concerned with the physical structure of the human body and the systems within it, some aspects of it must also deal with physical assessment. However, because assessment also deals with intentions, cognitive processes, and emotional characteristics that involve adjustment, stress , anxiety , expectations, and attributions from the environment, it is necessary to consider the whole area of perception and awareness. Assessment is a system that involves much more than just testing, and concerns diagnosis and alternative treatments.

CHAPTER II

Observation, Logic, and Deduction

"Science is built up of facts, as a house is built up of stones, but an accumulation of facts is no more a science than a heap of stones is a house."

Henri Poincare

Chapter 1 discussed the functional components of the assessment process. But function is itself a necessary outcome of structure. It is the purpose of this chapter to deal with the cognitive determinants of assessment. These are: to observe carefully, to think logically, and to deduce validly. **There is no more rigorous task in psychological science than to make careful and logical inferences.** Assessment involves making judgments about facts, accumulating these judgments, and extracting from them their essential elements. From these elements basic descriptive properties can be determined. These elements and their properties then form both the bases for description of individuals (or groups) and the framework for developing a treatment plan when the elements are compared to alternative criteria of human behavior. The task of appraising the accuracy of our observations involves two major problems: one is to determine what constitutes reliable knowledge and the other is what establishes knowledge as valid?

THE NATURE OF RELIABLE AND VALID KNOWLEDGE

Observation is the primary basis of assessment. It is the instrumental cause or stimulus of perception. Perception is the distillation of sensations vested with meaning by the human mind. Meaning relates to inferences that are drawn from our perceptions. Perception includes not only the conscious awareness of feelings, ideas, and events both outside of us and within us, but also subliminal stimuli which are below our threshold of consciousness. What we perceive then becomes the basis of what we can know about the world outside of our own mind. Our problem in dealing with the relationship between our perception of external events and our inferences about them is how to judge the reliability of our perception.

There are conditions which qualify the reliability of our perceptions. Three of these are: (1) the focus and complexity of the observations relating to our perceptions; (2) the intactness of our neurological state; and (3) the progressive refinement of our perceptions through the process of learning. The reliability of our perceptions at any time in our life is related to these three components.

The accuracy of perception varies in relationship to the complexity of focus. It is easier to secure an agreement with others on a sample of leaves to be classified by color, shape and texture, than to find agreement over the perceptions of what happened in an argument between two people. Classifying leaves is relatively simple and straightforward. Classifying human process interactions is complex. It is because of the nature of complex perceptions that there are often disagreements about the facts which caused automobile accidents or other injuries.

Accurate perception presumes intact neurological functioning. A second condition which often threatens the reliability of perception is the condition of the brain itself. Perceptions can be distorted by a lack of neurological integration. What this means is that reliable perception requires a normal range of sensory integration including intelligence. Thus we do not expect marginally intelligent people to be as precise in perception as those with higher intelligence. Neurological integration also means that the brain be free at the perception time from strong emotional experiences, debilitating chemicals, excessive stimulation, and depressant drugs. Illness, conditions of aging, results of traumatic accidents or tumors (such as in cancer) also handicap and compromise the integrity of the brain. All of these components, separately or in interaction, potentially jeopardize the reliability of perception.

The accuracy of perception is refined through learning. Third, the accuracy and reliability of perception is constantly being refined through learning experiences. Thus, for example, a child may not be able to distinguish between a used cup and a clean one. But as experience accumulates, the used cup can be detected by recognition of the residual fluid in the bottom, or even by stains which are present in the dry cup.

Through learning we also come to doubt the reliability of our own experience under certain circumstances. Thus educated people recognize that their perception of an event may be colored by their own depression, inattention, anger, or bias. In addition, learning sometimes counters our own experience. We learn to distinguish between what is a true inference and an illusory one. For example, as I sit here working on the computer in my study, I have recently heard a cracking noise from the threshold leading into the family room. This room is adjacent to my study. Ordinarily, I would infer that someone is coming into the family room. However, because I know that I am alone in the house, and that this same phenomenon has occurred before on warm sunny days, I conclude that changes in the wood expansion of the threshold cause these noises.

In summary, reliable perception is based on the consensus of the perceptions of individuals who possess an intact neurological and psychological structure, who can agree on the focus of observations, and who have accumulated learning experience in judging perception. What emerges from this consensus is a tacit agreement on the correspondence which exists between an observed phenomenon and the inferences drawn in the act of perception. By analogy, if this process of correspondence could be related to the representation obtained by a photograph, then all photographs taken of a given object would have some basic similarities—some perhaps lighter, others darker. But they would represent accurately the phenomenon under consideration. By contrast, individuals with neurological disorders or any of the other handicapping conditions mentioned might present perceptions which are more like surreal paintings.[1]

Perception assumes a correspondence between what is observed and what is. The concept of correspondence is a key term in the establishment of valid perception. The working postulate that underlies all scientific perception is that of realism, or the philosophy that supports an external reality whether one is there to observe or not. The outer stimulation of reality creates a representation within the human mind that results in a perception. This perception is vested with a certain amount of meaning which is derived from inferences. Meaningfulness in terms of perception appears to be directly related to emotional states and task-order process. We invest perceptions with meaning when these perceptions relate to basic human needs, and later on when these perceptions are somehow connected to a cognitive task-order process. We often test the inferences we make related to perception before investing perceptions with meaning. We do this by checking with others. This is precisely what is meant when we say to others: "did you hear what I heard?" or "did you see what I saw?"

There is thus an implied social convention that presumes an isomorphic or equivalent relationship between the observation of external events and the corresponding subjective perceptual representations. The presumption of equivalence, though perhaps impossible of demonstration to some philosophers, is based on a set of social agreements relating to our culture and to the development of science itself. In summary, there is a linkage system between perception, inference-making, and meaning.

Sophisticated perception implies discriminatory inferences. This process of testing our perceptions is based also on our ability to discriminate between perceptions through learning. We arrive at this discrimination skill by observing the consequences of our inferences. Children learn to recognize subtle differences in teachers, knowing that such differences represent moods. Thus under one set of perceptions a teacher may be more indulgent and lenient, and at another time be quite demanding. Even some household pets learn to make such discriminations in perception. We once had a dog who came to the door to greet me everytime I came home. If I responded to him, he jumped up and down and showed his happiness to see me. If I did not respond to him, but simply put down my briefcase, he turned and went into the other room. These discriminations are based on learned experiences in testing inferences.

Discrimination in inferences is essentially a task shared in all scientific judgments. It is basically what is meant by developing clinical skills in psychologists. But often the conditions of reliable and valid knowledge as relating to inferencing are ignored. Thus, the differences between an inexperienced assessment student and the psychologist with scientific training is much like an example in a scene from a typical Sherlock Holmes or Agatha Christie novel. In such novels it is usual for even intelligent lay people to make inferences about the scene of a crime that are wrong. Even other professional detectives fail to see clues that are critical to solving the crime. It is the high degree of discriminant inferences manifested by Sherlock Holmes that leads to the uncovering of those specific clues that result in the solution of the crime.

Assessment is much like detective work. Inexperienced students often draw direct inferences from tests alone. They tend to accept the test scores at face value, without attempting to understand how these scores may be only approximations, and need to be integrated into many other sources of assessment information. It is perhaps because of this poor ability to discriminate that tests have been under such continual criticism in their use as criteria of personality constructs. The sources of difficulties in assessment are chiefly related to a too strong conviction that psychometric data are in themselves criteria of actual or potential behavior and that they represent the major objective means of determining personality traits and character.

Logical thinking is based on logical propositions. Whether we are concerned about the content of an interview or the interpretation of test results, the inferences of our observations are invariably translated into statements which we either make verbally or put into writing. These statements become declarative propositions. These propositions represent both declarative and logical relationships which must be tested. To ignore principles of logic in science, politics or assessment is shoddy thinking. For this reason, students of assessment must come to recognize that inferences drawn from either induction or deduction are based on principles of logic. The logic of statements (and the propositions and axioms upon which they are based) can be assessed through the use of the syllogism. Syllogistic reasoning is an old Greek discovery, but one that is as valid today as it was centuries ago.

To explain further, let us consider that at the very root of the correspondence assumption which governs the validity of our perception is a postulate of necessity. We perceive a tree as a tree because there is a necessary connection (albeit implicit) between that object with a trunk and extended limbs filled with leaves and bending in the wind, and the verbal definition of language we have learned as the concept of a tree. Thus a tree is a tree and there is an implicitly held judgment that there is a necessary connection between that object of our perception and the concept of what we have defined as tree.

However, let us proceed further. Suppose we look at a drawing of a tree and we make a set of inferences that the tree represents an individual's subjective view of reality. We are now faced with a set of inferences of a different nature. Before we can logically accept this set of inferences, i.e., that a picture of a tree is a psychological mirror, it must be demonstrated that there is a necessary connection between the statement: a tree is a tree, and the new one: a tree is a psychological mirror. In both instances the formal inferences made result in some premises. For example, in our regular perception of tree the logical process might be something like this:

(A) **Major Premise:** a tree is a woody perennial plant having a single elongated main stem with few or no branches on its lower part.

(B) **Minor Premise:** This is a woody perennial plant having a single elongated main stem with few branches on its lower part.

(C) **Conclusion:** This is a tree.

We are justified in making this conclusion because (A) represents a universal or general definition of what constitutes a tree, and (B) is contained wholly within the statement of (A). There is therefore, a necessary linkage between (A) and (B) which results in a necessary conclusion of (C).

However, let us take up the new premise. (A) All drawings of trees represent psychological mirrors of the drawer. (B) This is a drawing of a tree. Therefore (C) This drawing is a psychological mirror of the drawer.

In this set of premises, it is true that the minor (B) is included in the major (A), but for the conclusion (C) to be true, it is necessary that both (A) and (B) be true. We cannot make the conclusion from present evidence that (A) is true. Therefore the conclusion is false.

Inferences always result in implications, but the implications are based on structural relationships between premises. The relationships between premises (specified above as major and minor ones) must be accurate. The major premise (often also called the universal) must include all groups or individuals in the statement. In addition, the minor premise (often referred to as the particular statement) must be consistent with the major premise. Thus for example, in the following reasoning, there is a change in the minor which makes the conclusion invalid:

(A) **Major Premise:** All rabbits eat lettuce.

(B) **Minor Premise:** My wife eats lettuce.

(C) **Conclusion:** My wife is a rabbit.

The validity of our inferences is manifested when they are converted to propositions. These propositions express in formal language declarative statements. By placing them into formal propositions, the validity of the inferences drawn can be tested through the method of the syllogism. It is certainly obvious that all our perceptual inferences do not hold up to the validity of propositional analysis. Politicians often demonstrate this point of view. To argue, for example, that unlimited defense spending is necessary to preserve us from aggression as a major premise, and then to specify that an opponent wishes to limit defense spending, is to draw the conclusion that the opponent does not wish to preserve us from aggression.

Typically syllogisms can involve four kinds of statements: (A) The Universal Affirmative (All psychologists are diagnosticians), (B) The Particular Affirmative (Some psychologists are diagnosticians), (E) The Universal Negative (No psychologists are diagnosticians), and (0) The Particular Negative (Some psychologists are not diagnosticians).

These combinations can be put together in many ways such as AAA, OOO, OOE, etc. This process yields some 64 combinations. Major, minor and concluding terms can also be fitted in different ways and thus there are 256 combinations of which only nineteen are valid and useful.

What is perhaps more important is to recognize that this form of reasoning has some rules which are important in examining the logic of any proposition. Larrabee (1964) states these rules precisely: "Three Term Rule: Rule 1. A syllogism must include three and only three terms used throughout in the same sense. Distribution Rule: Rule 2. The middle term must be distributed at least once in the premises. Rule 3. No term may have a greater distribution in the conclusion than it had in the premises. Negative Premises Rules: Rule 4. From two negative premises, no valid conclusion can be inferred. Rule 5. If one premise is negative, the conclusion must be negative. Particular Premises Rules: Rule 6. If one premise is particular, the conclusion must be particular. Rule 7. From two particular premises, no valid conclusion can be drawn" (pp. 78–79).

In recent decades computer technology has been able to handle some of these propositions by evaluating whether a given statement can be judged true or false. This becomes a binary relationship of 1 for true and 0 for false. As can be seen from this brief examination of the validity of propositions, the estimate of the validity of factual judgments and the inferences they express is no easy matter. This is true in probing the validity of propositions in general, and it is specifically relevant in the matter of assessment.

In summary then, the reliability of inferential judgments in perception is based on the assumed correspondence between the perception of the viewer and the event which is observed in outer reality. This congruence is based chiefly on consensual evidence which exists between individuals of similar levels of training and ability.

The validity of our inferential judgments needs to be examined in terms of the logic of the propositions they reflect when couched in language. This is the keynote of validity. However, we shall see further extensions of this construct with particular regard to assessment in later chapters.

Assessment relies heavily on deductive reasoning. Though modern science has progressed beyond the deductive aspects of the syllogism, assessment is much more reliant on deduction than induction. Because the examination of human phenomena is so complex, it seldom can reach the levels of John Stuart Mill's canons for the inductive method. John Stuart Mill was a nineteenth century philosopher of science who made many profound observations about the nature of scientific inferences. For example, in Mill's canon of the Method of Agreement he stated: "if two or more instances of the phenomenon under investigation have only one circumstance in common, the circumstance in which alone all the instances agree is the cause (or effect) of the given phenomenon" (Mill, 1950, p. 215). It is obvious that seldom are psychological phenomena so precisely defined and ordered that this method of agreement could be used.

Recognizing the difficulties of the observation of psychological phenomena, after cautioning that one should always be aware of the relationship of physiology to brain functioning, John Stuart Mill suggested that one should rely on empirical observations to provide approximate deductive generalizations which could then be tested. These generalizations would then become the basis of a science of ethology (by which he meant something like the present day equivalent of personality). Mill stated: "The science of the formation of character is a science of causes. The canons of induction which ascertain the laws of causation can be rigorously applied to this subject. It is therefore, both natural and advisable to ascertain the simplest, which are necessarily the most general laws of causation first and to deduce the middle principles from them. In other words, ethology, the deductive science, is a system of corollaries from psychology, the experimental science" (Mill, 1950, p. 323).

Mill's statements are particularly relevant to the inquiry into the reliability and validity of observation in assessment, even though they were written over one hundred years ago. A modern paraphrase of Mill's ideas might be as follows: one ought to recognize the differences between the neurological factors of the brain and the conscious set of activities identified with "mind." Certainly one should recognize the connection between brain and mind, but not consider them identical. Nevertheless there is a close relationship between the physiological changes and psychological ones. The inductive findings as related to experimental physiology then provide a basis for drawing deductive inferences about mental phenomena. These deductions, though at first probabilistic may with further research approach the laws of other sciences. Valid inferences then must be grounded on experimental principles of psychology (e.g., laws of learning, and behavioral observations). Where different methods are utilized, the inferences from specific manifestations of behavior must be qualified by the reliability of the method.

EPISTEMOLOGICAL DIFFERENCES IN INFERRING

There are basically three levels of inferring which can be distinguished in the process of assessment. They can be classified as more reliable as they are closer to direct observation. We are thus more sure of those things we see and hear for ourselves than for the conclusions of others reported to us via hearsay. **The three levels of certitude associated with assessment are: (1) empirical, (2) psychometric, and (3) intuitive.** Both empirical and psychometric inferring can be further subdivided into structured and unstructured variations. Each of these levels of inferring involve assumptions about certitude or the extent to which we can put confidence in the reliability of inferences drawn from these various sources. Thus empirical observations can be casual or in terms of an interview, or structured in the sense of a behavioral analysis. Psychometric inferences can relate to the results of either group or individual tests which are highly structured and known as objective. Results are mechanically scored either by hand or by computer. Other psychometric tests are based on sets of inferences that reflect theories. These are more subjective in interpretation and are called projective tests. Intuitive inferences can be made in relationship to any form of empirical or psychometric observations. They are essentially leaps in drawing inferences which posit a connection between empirical or psychometric data that are best expressed as hunches.[2]

In general, inferences drawn from empirical observations are more accurate as they are focused or structured. Casual unstructured observations such as we all make in talking to others or watching people can be quite valid, particularly if they are confirmed by observations from a number of people (peer evaluations). A general goal of the structured approach, however, is to increase the accuracy of perception through a clear definition of the behaviors under consideration, the accumulation of base-rates of behavior, and the determination of precise relationships of antecedents and consequences. The greater specificity of behavior results in higher levels of credibility for inferences made, provided the technology is followed carefully.

Psychometric observations can be a reliable and valid addition to empirical and behavioral observations. They are, however, subject to specific problems in generalization and interpretation. By psychometric is meant the process of assessment that utilizes items or differential stimuli to elicit responses from the individual. For the most part in psychometric measures we are referring to tests or observations that have been developed using a process of standardization according to appropriate measurement procedures. Psychometric tests have been classified as objective and projective, group administered or individually administered. Tests of all kinds have been developed relating to cognitive, affective, personality, social and vocational domains, as well as to aptitudes and specific skill assessments. Tests usually provide normative data that help to provide an understanding of group tendencies and characteristics. They are most reliable and valid in their evaluation of group characteristics, and are less reliable and valid in their definition of individual characteristics.

The power potential for valid assessment of individuals rises as multiple measures (e. g. two or more tests) show similar characteristics, and as they are integrated with empirical observations. Naturally, tests are subject not only to the usual problems of reliability and validity in construction and development, but are subject to some special problems relating to response set (the tendency to respond in a given manner) social desirability (the tendency to place one's self in an appropriately socially desirable position) and acquiescence (which may be explained as the tendency to respond affirmatively or to agree with statements). There is likewise the problem that many tests are constructed with white middle class values in mind and are not therefore particularly accurate with cultural minorities.

Intuitive inferences are based on judgments drawn from empirical or psychometric data or a combination of them when these data are interpreted in terms of an *a priori* set of assumptions. These assumptions may reflect some general premises about the role of the universe in influencing human behavior (astrology), or the manner in which specific laws of nature influence human behavior and responses (circadian rhythyms), or how psychoanalytic theory is reflected in projective responses. In any event, the quality of these intuitive judgments is not only based on the strength of the observations, but more importantly on the validity of the assumptions underlying the interpretations. Intuition is a highly valued and important aspect of hypothesis making. It is inferential reasoning at its greatest extension. Thus, it is precisely because of the sometimes nebulous connection between specific observations and the intuitive conclusion, that it must be carefully subjected to logic and subsequent verification.

A good example of overextended intuition was the rash of books that appeared in the early 1970s about "gods from outer space." The concurrence of similar themes in the evolution of culture, the existence of pyramids in different parts of the earth, similarities in legends about creatures from outer space, all provide a set of deductive inferences which could be linked to an extraterrestrial colonization of the earth. The evidence is interesting, and perhaps even plausible (as described), but is it factual? Are there other explanations for these findings? Intuition is most helpful in generating hypotheses for further investigation; it is not a substitute for data collection or deduction.

The identification and integration phases of diagnosis become more valid as more methods of assessment are pooled. The use of multiple methods increases the overall reliability and validity of inferences made in the integration phase of diagnosis. Multiple inputs refer to the use of self-report data, unstructured and structured empirical observations, group and individually administered psychometric tests, possible physical tests, and the collection of ratings relative to skill functions, and accountability criteria of performance. Informal processes of diagnostic judgment making often have to be integrated on the strength and the skills of the clinician, but there are ways and means whereby alternative methods of assessment can be scientifically integrated and evaluated. One such method is the multitrait, multimethod approach identified and described by Campbell and Fiske (1959). This approach relies on the establishment of convergent and discriminant analysis. The rationale includes: (1) validating similar traits across methods to determine the extent to which a self-report method of measuring aggression agrees with empirical observations, group ratings or other methods, and (2) discrimination as a method of identifying differences between traits. Convergent validity occurs when similar trait measures correlate highly with others, and discriminant validity occurs when traits as identified across methods correlate negatively. For example, when measures of impulsivity as identified by self-report and by peer and teacher judgments correlate highly with each other and correlate negatively with measures of self-control across the same methods, one can conclude that there are a sets of measures which possess both convergent and discriminant validity.

Unfortunately, this excellent technique has not been utilized to any large extent in commercially available testing, in part because of the difficulty of obtaining both convergent and discriminant validity. What is important here is to note that even in the clinical diagnostic judgment process there should be an informal effort to determine the extent to which various observations in different methods lead to convergence in integration and inferences.

TARGETS OF THE ASSESSMENT PROCESS

A natural question at this point is to establish the targets of the assessment process. This is an important determination because many students have difficulty discerning what the targets of assessment are. One can proceed in assessment from very specific and molecular foci, to more global and molar ones. In the process the epistemological confidence changes. We can be more certain about very specific measurements such as responses, than about more global aggregations such as aptitude. Theoretically and logically, if larger entities are related to more molecular ones, there should be a relationship analogous to that between independent and dependent variables.

There is indeed a hierarchy of assessment constructs. This hierarchy extends from the smallest assessable unit, the response, to the clustering of responses in skills, the grouping of skills into traits, the organization of cognitive traits into what are called aptitudes, the organization of emotive traits into what is referred to as temperament, (though temperament tends also to subsume aptitude), and finally all of these units being integrated into what is called personality. Although personality is the most general overall classification, it is precisely in this construct that the influence of the culture and socialization process is most identified.

A comprehensive assessment involves all levels of the hierarchy. Though we may, for purposes of teaching, divide the levels into a hierarchical display, it is vital to remember that within human beings, all levels are integrated in a unitary manner. All levels of assessment can be considered dependent variables wherein neurological intactness, hereditary intelligence, and temperament dispositions are considered independent variables. This proposition means simply that assessment of empirically observable behaviors or psychometric findings reflect the central neurological structural system of the brain. Any disturbance, malfunctioning, or structural deficit tends to alter all parts of the integrative whole.

Learning interacts with both cognitive and emotional aspects of personality resulting in amplification, alteration or modification of original hereditary propensities. Although we are speaking here primarily of the individual, all environmental experiences are incorporated under the term learning. Thus, although formal learning procedures in school concentrate on the acquisition of information, the development of cognitive subroutines (such as in mathematics) that allow for the development of knowledge, memory, discrimination, and skills in the individual, it is likewise important to recognize that most early learning occurs through observation, social modeling, imitation and rehearsal. The impact of social settings, vocational careers, marriage and a host of other variables within the immediate and remote environment of the individual is also considered learning.

Personality is the most global construct to describe the individual. In the hierarchy identified in the figure, personality is described as the integrative whole of all assessment factors. It is thus a highly synthetic construct designed to present the total configuration of cognitive abilities and temperament dispositions as modified by learning. Such descriptions rely on empirical observation, psychometric findings, and often deal with more abstract entities associated with personality such as the "ego" or "self-concept."

The construct of temperament refers to a cluster of dispositions, heritable by nature, but modifiable to some extent in learning. Temperament is closely related to the biological components of emotion and relates to the manner in which individuals express energy and activity, their inclination to be socially-oriented or privately-oriented, the degree of personal control they manifest in relationship to the quest for basic goals and needs, and the manner in which they manifest their emotional responses. This aspect of human assessment appears to be closely related to the volitional control of human behavior. Constructs that are often associated with temperament are extroversion, introversion, excitation, inhibition, flexibility, field independence, and field dependence, and locus of control. Temperament may be assessed through empirical observations of the individual and by the use of selected psychometric instruments.

Cognition refers to the qualitative ability of the organism to learn and to adapt itself to changing circumstances. Cognition is closely related to both the biological components of intelligence and temperament. The emotional characteristics of the individual interact with the cognitive process to develop a store of memory information. Constructs associated with cognition are memory, (short-term and long-term), discrimination, aptitude, and achievement. Aptitude particularly represents a specialized set of competencies relating to abilities, such as verbal skills, mechanical skills, or social skills. In addition, the manner in which cognition interacts with learned inputs represents some complex variables that are often referred to as problem-solving ability or cognitive style. Although intelligence is often viewed as the primary focus of assessment relating to cognition, it is apparent today that biological intelligence is modified by learning and that an entire configuration of other components are involved with intelligence that relate to the nature of cognition. Cognition can be assessed through empirical observation as well as by a variety of psychometric tests.

Traits represent a coherent and fairly enduring cluster of characteristics relating to some specific aspect of temperament-cognitive interaction. Traits often manifest themselves in specific skills. Psychologists do not always agree on which units of assessment are most important. Many focus on traits, but traits assume a constant set of characteristics and many behaviorists think that the focus should be on states of the organism which are seen as temporary sets of characteristics related to perception and learning.

In modern times the concept of skill appears to be one that is acceptable to most individuals since elements of trait and state may be present in skill acquisition. In addition, the concept of skill can be connected to performance criteria of competency (something most desirable in current industrial, educational and business enterprises). Skill analysis, however, is related both to the necessary prior development of responses and to native predispositions which are in addition related to the higher-order constructs of temperament and intelligence. Consistent with the systems approach that guides this book, it is likely that a few higher-order principles, derived in large part from neurological and hereditary characteristics, provide the proximate ground or limitations for the development of traits in personality and skills in behavior.

The development of skills in individuals involves both the structural and control hierarchies in interaction, for skills represent ability as refined by learning. The concept of skill is a useful intermediate target for psychological assessment. For through skill analysis, one can arrive at the meaningful interpretation of the larger constructs in assessment. In short, the construct of skill can be viewed as the primary unit reflective of both higher-order components and learning.

SKILL ANALYSIS IN ASSESSMENT

A skill is a viable manifestation of the consequences of structure times learning. It provides a demonstrable focus for assessment which is related to performance and competency. It also incorporates the construct of response. A skill is a functional and observable response to environmental stimulation that reflects learning. **A skill can be defined as the functional capability of the organism to manifest a complex response to stimulation.** It is usually the byproduct or one of the manifestions of what we term aptitude. One can illustrate the relationship between skill and aptitude by looking at social interaction skills. These skills relate to the ability to meet another person to engage in reciprocal verbal and nonverbal behaviors that convey attending, responding and complementary interaction of an appropriate nature. The ability to manifest this skill in appropriate situations is part of a larger group of skills which may be subsumed under the construct of social aptitude. Social aptitude in turn can be considered an acquired or learned component of extroversion, a broader temperament type. Thus, skills have a relationship to temperament as well as to cognition through the construct of aptitude. Moreover, today there is an extensive recognition that human skills development is the target most appropriate for both prevention and remediation of problems.

Ordinarily skill assessment requires multiple inputs and therefore the reliability and validity of the assessment can be more readily demonstrated in external manifestations. Whether indivduals can readily identify social skills or not, they are conversant with those behaviors which they judge to be social in nature and can therefore make a reliable estimate. I refer here, not to one observation or self-report, but collective data from many sources.

There are a variety of clusters of skills. **Three major groups of skills are: sensory-motor, cognitive, and social-affective.** Skills are observable and functional manifestions of aptitude-learning interactions and can be classified in terms of their immediate function. Motor skills includes the use of gross and fine muscles in various activities extending from crawling to highly technical manipulations. Cognitive skills include accuracy of perception, concept formation, discrimination, memory, problem solving and reasoning as well as a number of specific cognitive skill functions relating to arithmetical, logical, language and speech processes. Social-affective skills relate to the display of emotional reactions, social relationships, the recognition and discrimination between coercive and reciprocal responding, personal care skills and socially appropriate behavior.

Motor skills mediate the development of cognitive skills. In accordance with general principles of human development it appears that motor perceptual skills emerge as a primary and early manifestion of learning. Learning itself is related to adequacy of nutrition, structural capacity, methods of presentation, reinforcement, environmental opportunity, and support systems. In addition learning is related to the emotional state of arousal, the judgment of meaningfulness and other factors. From the best knowledge available in developmental studies it appears that gross motor skills precede the development of fine motor skills, and that cognitive processes reflect such changes by qualitative changes in capacity for assimilating new information. Thus the development of motor-perceptual skills and eye-hand coordination appears to be a necessary level of functioning for the development of reading and writing skills. Later on, according to Luria (1973), the development of verbal and mathematical skills aids the brain in proceeding to higher order syntheses and integration required in symbolic production.

Harrow (1972) has identified a taxonomy of motor skills that extends from reflex movements through basic locomotor and manipulative movements to perceptual, compound, discursive and communicative movements. The exact extent to which each presumed lower segment relates developmentally to the next one has not been precisely established by research, but there is considerable evidence that the human organism early on interacts with its environment by extending its own capabilities, coordination, and synthesis of both perception and motor activities.

Affective and social-interaction skills have considerable effect on the elaboration and extension of cognitive skills. Affective skills are closely related to the arousal system of the brain. As we shall see in a later chapter, the distinction between cognitive and emotive systems in the human brain is arbitrary. However, the functions of the cognitive system are related to accuracy of perception, concept formation and symboling. Functionally, cognitive information is transmitted to the brain where it is acted upon by the emotional arousal system. A judgment of favorableness or unfavorableness results in emotional changes which are expressed in affective movements, thought, and behavior. Since fear, anxiety, and stress are basically related to emotional reactions involving basic self-protective mechanisms of the brain that are more closely attuned to the earlier evolution of the brain (e.g., the reticular activating system and associated mid-brain aspects such as the thalamus), it is apparent that high states of arousal preclude high levels of cognitive symboling.

Krathwohl, Bloom and Masia (1956) classified affective responses in a taxonomy. They view affective skills in terms of: (1) receiving or attending skills, that include awareness, willingness to receive; (2) responding which includes acquiescence in responding, willingness to respond and satisfaction in response; (3) valuing that includes acceptance of a value, preference for a value and committment; (4) organization, and (5) the constitution of a value complex. Bandura (1972) has likewise found these functional skills related to the ability to profit from modeling. Thus, attending, retention, rehearsal of the modeled event and social reinforcement are all related to affective conditions.

Cognitive skills through accuracy of perception coordinate motor-perceptual skills and affective social-value skills. Bloom et al., (1956) have devised a taxonomy of cognitive objectives. Their effort has become a classic in terms of the clarification of cognitive domain skills and tasks. In their taxonomy, objectives are classified basically under six major groupings: (1) knowledge of specifics and universals, (2) comprehension, including translation, interpretation and extrapolation, (3) application, (4) analysis in terms of elements, relationships, and organizational principles, (5) synthesis, and (6) evaluation.

In summary, then, skills are seen as functional units within larger groupings of aptitudes. Though one can distinguish arbitrarily between motor-perceptual skills, affective and cognitive skills, it is apparent that balance in the organism is required for the useful deployment of any form of skill display. Skills can be empirically observed, behaviorally measured, and psycho-

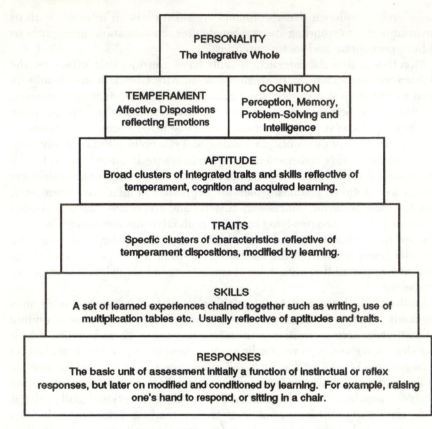

Figure 2-1 The Hierarchy of Assessment Constructs

metrically defined. Thus they become the viable primary goals of assessment and lead to the accumulation of information about the higher-order functions of both cognition and temperament and targets of assessment.

CRITERIA OF THE ASSESSMENT PROCESS

Criteria of assessment relate to what constitutes effective human behavior. Obviously, if we are going to assess behavior, traits, aptitudes, temperament or skills, we need to know how they relate to the criteria of effective human behavior, because in all instances, assessment must be related to some independent criteria. There are five models: (1) subjectivity, (2) normative behavior, (3) statistical conclusions, (4) cultural norms, and (5) heuristic performance standards. It is at this point precisely that the question of human values appears. For the observations we make, and the inferences we draw, are clearly related to the question of values i.e. what is good? and what is bad? What is conducive towards personal and social fulfillment and what militates against this goal?

The Subjective Model. Ultimately, the individuals themselves form the basis of adequacy of behavior in this model. Whether one takes the hedonistic position of Bentham that all behavior is fundamentally related to animal characteristics, or the altruistic position of Kant that all human beings should be treated as ends rather than means, a subjective judgment is involved that provides the individual frame of reference for behavior. Responsibility for behavior is ultimately a personal matter. The major religions even hold that conscience is the supreme arbiter of what constitutes right and wrong thinking and behaving in human beings. The extent to which the values of society are internalized depends both on the quantity and quality of experience, together with the ability of the individual to organize and synthesize such experience into a meaningful set of criteria for behavior. Thus one can argue that ultimately the criteria of human experiences are related to self-determined levels of competency, adjustment, and interaction. On the other hand to argue that all criteria of effective behavior should be and can be related exclusively to the level of self-gratification is not possible in a social culture.

The Normative Model. By normative is meant the provision of an exemplar to identify with and to compare one's personal behavior with a model. For the most part we refer here to religious authorities and models. The Christian religion with its direct reference to the person of Christ is an explicit example of this approach. Christians are exhorted to imitate Christ and to develop those attitudes, virtues, and characteristics which make them Christ-like. Similar comparisons can be made for Moses and the prophets for Judaism, Mohammed for Islam, Buddha for Buddhism, and Confucius for the Chinese cultural tradition. These individuals have become the cornerstones of many of the religious traditions of the world's cultures. The values exemplified by and the systematic training in the traditions of these moral leaders, provide the organizing set of values for many millions of people. Conversely, the normative criteria of what constitutes a good Christian, Jew, Muslim, Buddhist or Confucian, while exhorting to certain positive values, also provides the source of much conflict within human beings because of the disparity between lofty values, and the more naturalistic disposition to experience physiological and instinctual behavior.

The Statistical Model. The statistical model is a mathematical approach to behavior. Basically, it consists of determining the mode of human behavior in given circumstances, or at particular developmental periods. The use of statistical methods in terms of means, standard deviations, and ranges, are helpful to determine the characteristics of given populations. When the accounting of such characteristics is extended over a time line, actuarial predictions can be made. Moreover, these predictions can be modified in terms of mediating variables. Thus, for example, the probable life span of individuals can be predicted actuarially in terms of variables such as stress, smoking, excessive drinking, weight, family history, and other determinants. But plotting such trends, though they may provide characteristics of a statistical nature, does not alter the fact that such statistical trends also have to be balanced against normative cultural behavior. Though Kinsey and his colleagues may have indicated the high frequency of masturbation or premarital intercourse in adolescents, this statistical fact does not alter the impact of normative cultural or religious behavior which impinges on the individual.

The Cultural Model. Culture is a major source of expectations which form social norms. Culture refers to the sum of environmental and behavioral patterns that come to bear on the shaping and modeling of human behavior. It includes not only the process whereby certain responses are learned and assimilated, but also the important process of discrimination based on learned responses and anticipated responses within a given environmental setting. Children learn how to think about values and how to behave by observing models. The extent to which they benefit from such models is related to the individual's capability for attending to the modeled behavior, synthesizing it into a personal frame of reference, the ability to rehearse the modeled behavior either vicariously or in a real sense, and the consequences of that behavior in terms of reinforcement or punishment. Culture transmits patterns of behavior in a very systematic manner. Even as hereditary characteristics are transmitted through minute biological and chemical combinations which specify the direction, sequencing, and evolution of development, so culture as a mechanism operates for the basic purposes of: (1) making life more regularized, stable, predictable, and secure; (2) ensuring a food supply, shelter, and maintenance of life, and (3) regularizing the enjoyment of pleasurable responses and recreation.

Culture provides the great socializing and programming agent that transmits the impact of the social environment to the individual. The nature and quality of that programming is synthesized in the developmental pattern of the individual. There are many distinct similarities and differences between individuals in this accommodation-assimilation process. For example, even though all snowflakes are quite intricate and beautiful instances of individual differences, they are all hexagonal. By analogy, we may compare the socializing influences of culture to the technology of ice-crystal production. There is a basic set of values, behaviors, and thrusts that proceed from a cultural setting. But the variability of that assimilation and accommodation process is heavily determined by the basic cognitive-emotive structure of the individual.

The cultural transmission manifests itself typically through expectations. Very often it is not recognized by those who are involved in assessment and appraisal that criteria of effective human behavior are largely derived from the expectation systems of others. It is precisely here that we must look for an operational definition of what constitutes effective human behavior. And it is here also, that skills become the focal point.

Expectations become the proximate set of criteria that individuals must take into consideration as they attempt to manifest effective behavior. If a diagnostician wants to know what are the effective criteria of behavior in a school setting, the easiest method is simply to ask a teacher(s) who are the "best" and "worst" students. Once they have been identified it is easy to recognize both the personal-social characteristics of children who are meeting the criteria of effective human behavior and those who are not. Some years ago, the author used this very procedure with all the high school teachers of a large urban school district, grouping them by subject area, e.g., science, foreign languages, history etc. Since we had also administered a number of psychological, vocational, and achievement measures to the students, it was a comparatively easy process to compare students who amply met criteria of effective behavior with those who did not (Barclay, 1967). We used similar methods in surveying first job settings of graduates over the next year and found that by identifying successfully nominated job holders versus those who had been fired or left, or were doing poorly, we could ascertain clearly the criteria of successful job holding.

Expectations relate to thinking, behaving, performing, aspiring, and valuing processes. Though there are many sources of expectations, some of the chief ones are: (1) sex, (2) structural characteristics in terms of body form and build, (3) socioeconomic background, (4) age, (5) race, (6) religion, (7) educational level, and (8) role (i.e., parent, child, friend, etc.). These expectations are based on learned acquisitions from the culture. Thus in our culture, boys are expected by and large to be more aggressive than girls— and this behavior is tolerated. The extent to which a male is strong, tall, and handsome, provides initial positive impressions about character and personality and is directly related to favorable expectations. Verbal production, social interaction, race and religion, also provide other sets of expectations. Some of these expectations form themselves into stereotypic attitudes. Thus professors are thought to be absent-minded and unrealistic; undertakers are thought to be unctuous and soft-spoken; artists to be idealistic and erratic.

When such expectations are crystallized into a system, we can refer to that system as a "press". An environmental "press" is an organizational framework of expectations which exists for those who work or develop in a given environment. IBM is a good example of a business where there exists a coherent set of expectations for specific kinds of behaviors. The university environment is another such place. Astin (1965) identified a variety of college environments associated with various institutions of higher learning. Some are more sociable in their "press," valuing skills in interpersonal behavior, while others are more intellectual or enterprising. Even within the same university there are clear differences of environmental presses. Thus the characteristics to be manifested by a student in chemistry or physics may be in marked contrast to those to be expected and approved in art or music. High school teachers also tend to exhibit a derived institutional "press" by favoring student behaviors that are consistent with their subject-matter affiliation (Barclay, 1967b). Thus culture has both a pervasive general influence in shaping behavior and some specific forces which impinge on individuals by way of expectations and "presses." What is more important is that these expectations help to shape both success and failure experiences. Failure in academic processes leads to negative expectations by both the individual aspiring to academic success and teachers and peers. Failure in social interaction (e.g. being labeled a clown, dumb, fat, clumsy,) leads to avoidance of circumstances that call for social interaction such as dances. Though children from all socioeconomic conditions tend to enter school without too much discrepancy in their capacity for learning, somehow those who obtain negative expectations fall further and further behind. Moreover, as the pattern of failure multiplies, it spawns thinking which often relates the attribution of success to luck or chance, and the attribution of failure to others including institutions of learning.

Heuristic Criteria. In recent years, the emergence of a body of literature relating to criterion-related testing, performance objectives, and management by objectives has focused attention on the need to provide practical goals and guidelines for behavior. This approach has been part of a general systems effort to operationalize the goals of institutional learning or behavior in terms of practical objectives. The measurement possibilities from these developments have been considerable in that most often performance criteria of behavior provide some explicit suggestions for improvement or the meeting of such criteria. It is important to recognize that these more modern developments, are themselves only formal efforts to operationalize the expectations and "presses" of culture.

Summary. Assessment is a process which involves differing methods all based originally on empirical observation. The methods themselves involve naive or common empirical observation, structured behavioral and physiological observations, psychometric observations, clinical judgments and intuitive inferences. The linkage between basic empiricism and each of these methods is based on assumptions of correspondence between what is observed and what is. Thus assessment, no matter how objective it may attempt to be, is always related to the reliability and validity of human perception, logical analysis, and inferential judgment.

Each of the varying methods identifies phenomena which represent entities drawn from observations via inductive and deductive reasoning. In structured behavioral analysis these entities relate to competency and performance analyses and to behavior and skill manifestations. In psychometrics entities are identified which relate to psychometric properties of individuals or groups. In clinical process assessment reference is made to dynamic entities such as "ego" and the force of environmental characteristics such as environmental "presses." Finally, in the method of intuitive inferring, the entities are those variously associated with celestial cosmology, weather phenomena and magnetic fields and forces.

Once the content of each assessment method has been identified, then the next task is the classification of phenomena observed in each method. Phenomena within the methods are classified differently. For example, within the structured behavior analysis method, the manifestations of behavior are classified in terms of external criteria i.e., whether they are adequate to meet criteria of performance, skills or competencies. Physiological characteristics of the organism, including neurological ones, are judged in terms of intactness of operation.

Psychometric characteristics are classified in terms of statistical tendencies which often relate to factor analysis and profile analysis. Cognitive, emotive, attitudinal, and vocational characteristics need to be identified and discriminated for adequate understanding.

Observations drawn from clinical practice are often classified in terms of theoretical positions such as those of Freud, Adler, Jung and many others. Considerations about the force of ego strength, defenses, moral development, body language and somatotype are based on theoretical positions which approach the data of observation with a set of *a priori* assumptions.

Finally, intuitive observations employ a linkage between patterns of empirical observation of individuals and forces which exist in the form of weather patterns or magnetic influences. Very complex classification systems have been created to describe these forces as they impinge on human behavior and events.

The final question of assessment is how do these various methods of analyzing empirical observations in one format or another relate to each other? Most assessment book writers have not attempted to effect a linkage, rather suggesting that the methods of observation are unique systems. In point of fact many assessment book writers favor one form of assessment over another.

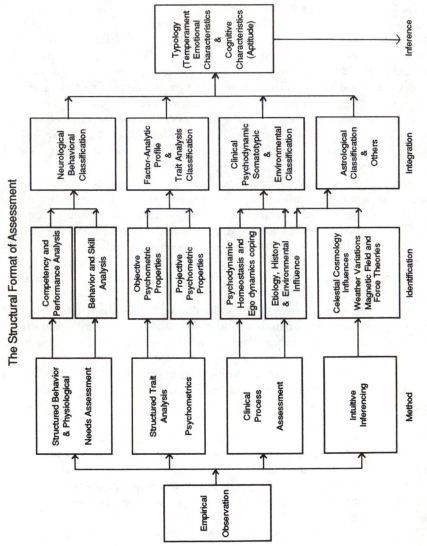

Figure 2-2   **The Structural Format of Assessment**

Some hold only for behavioral assessment. Others rely heavily and some-times exclusively on psychometrics. Still others favor clinical methods. For the most part, many who discuss assessment dismiss intuitive approaches as superstition. And yet this latter approach has existed intact for nearly 3,000 years and has more followers than any other form of assessment.

My own position in writing this book is dedicated to the proposition that each of these methods does contribute to a typology of integration—a unified theory of personality. To be sure, as I have indicated in previous figures, the reliability and validity of evidence must be carefully assessed in each of these methods. The accompanying figure provides an overview of the steps of identification, integration and inferring that can be used in assessment approaches.

CHAPTER III

Paradigms of Assessment: A Historical View

"There is a kind of truth in the history of a science which transcends the science itself. The history of a science as a kind of metascience is rarely seen by the individual scientist confined to his own specialty, for the very historical contexts that bestow significance on any discovery or specialty reach back in time to prior contexts, which in turn have been generated by still prior contexts. As we examine these matters, we are struck by a remarkable fact: the paths of these questions and contexts through time are not necessarily linear or logical"

(Jaynes, 1973a, p. ix).

This chapter focuses on the historical development of assessment. Assessment is regarded as an integral part of paradigms for viewing people in the context of culture. Three major paradigms reflect the growth of technological civilization. The first is associated with religious taboos and expiation and is centered on a cosmology of fear and superstition. The second paradigm developed by the Greeks is characterized by logical analysis and reason. The third takes its beginning in the fifteenth century with the development of contemporary science. The role of superstition, reason, and scientific inquiry in constituting paradigms of assessment is explored with the conclusion that the key to understanding assessment is found in an examination of the reliability of human observations and the validity of infererences drawn from these observations. Each of these paradigms has had social consequences for further cultural development.

THE HISTORY OF ASSESSMENT IN
THE CONTEXT OF CULTURE

All mature disciplines place considerable emphasis on the study of their origins and background. There are very good reasons for doing this particularly in assessment, for assessment is directly tied to the evolution of culture, specifically the philosophical and technological developments of culture. Assessment has always been one of the primary functions of those who seek to understand, predict, and control the world around them. Because these functional attributes of assessment are based squarely on conscious processes, the historical evolution of assessment covaries with the sophistication of human thinking. In this chapter we will discuss in some detail the history and background of assessment. This background is necessary to understand the role assessment has played in the development and advancement of culture and to recognize that much of the earlier thinking remains as a part or total explanation in the assessment of individuals. The history of assessment will not necessarily make an individual wiser, but it will provide a rationale for developing a perspective, through the understanding of the paradigms which have been used in understanding human phenomena and assessing them.

A paradigm represents the clearest formulation of the core elements of a culture, a philosophy, or a science. The word paradigm is of Greek origin and literally means "to show side by side." What it has come to mean in today's language is a comprehensive model or archetype which provides a rationale for a set of actions. According to Kuhn (1969) paradigms are rooted in the cosmology (theory about the nature of the universe) of the time period. This means that they attempt to explain the nature of humankind affirming certain beliefs about the conditions of human existence, the nature of inferences stemming from observation, and the meaning of human events.

Paradigms reflect the culture, level of technology, and thinking of a time period. They change gradually, rather than suddenly, and emerge as a relatively clear set of statements "only after persistent failure to solve a noteworthy puzzle has given rise to a crisis. Even then change occurs only after the sense of crisis has evoked an alternative candidate for paradigm" (Kuhn, p. 144). For example, Ptolemy's earth-centered paradigm that was the basis of the entire ancient-medieval world-view made sense in a day when the Roman Empire was the center of the civilized world. When the findings of Copernicus called this paradigm into question, there were not only some consequences for cosmological thinking, but considerable inferences drawn about the role of humankind. Thus shifting the earth from the center of the universe to a position as a minor planet in a minor galaxy resulted also in a shift in the view of mankind from the glory and center of God's creation to a physiological organism that had achieved consciousness. It also marked a change in the method of making inferences (e.g. syllogistic reasoning versus the experimental method), and external verification of data as against criteria of faith and logic.

THE NATURE OF CULTURE

People live in a social environment. They are constantly affected by the culture in which they live. This process begins at birth and continues throughout life. **By culture is meant the sum total of man's learned behavior in a social environment.** Culture defined in this way refers to the tangible, such as automobiles, toothbrushes, skyscrapers, and astronauts' space ships. It also refers to intangible behavior such as the wishes, hopes, fears, and ways of thinking. Culture includes the buoyant optimism of Americans to be popular in international politics, and it comprises also the hopes of the young African nations to develop a technological civilization.

Since all of us grow up in one culture or the other, we learn social behavior by a process of imitation and shaping which is, for the most part, unconscious. We behave in certain ways without really being aware that we are conforming with our culture. We learn our culture by living it. We do not inherit culture through our genes, as we inherit a tendency towards blue eyes or blond hair.[1] The manner in which a culture evolves as well as the purpose of that evolution are centrally related to the development of assessment, because assessment depends on certain working rules that also relate to culture. These rules are operationalized in expectations for predictable behavior called customs. And these customs become the actual criteria of effective human behavior.

Culture acts as a mechanism to provide stability and security in human needs. Our earliest customs were related to food-gathering, shelter, religious experiences, and the regulation of sexual behavior. It would appear that culture existed then as well as now to safeguard the human species in a specific locale. Behavioral expectancies relating to roles and functions in a social group are indispensable anchors for stability and security. Culture, therefore, is simply the code of behavior that grows up in a social group to maintain the security of the group in obtaining a continuing food supply and perpetuating the group.

Culture appears also to be governed in its complexity by its relationship to the harnessing of technology. Leslie White (1949) has analyzed culture in terms of the systematic utilization of energy through technology. White proposes the formula $E \times T = C$ (energy times technology equals culture).[2] White recognizes three stages in the development of culture. The first was the use of tools and language; the second was the discovery of agriculture. For better ways of cultivating land resulted in a whole train of social and technological advances, such as the smelting of metals, the development of the wheel, the plow, the loom, the invention of writing, and the organization of cities. A by-product of the development of technology was that as people could spend less time in agriculture (through the use of animals for plowing

Table 3-1   **Assessment and the Evolution of Technology**

12,00 BC? –6,000 BC?	6000 BC –3000 BC	3000 BC –1000 BC	1000 BC –1500 AD	1600 AD –1900 AD	1900–

Technological Developments of Culture

Tool behavior	Use of harness	Pictograms	Water power	Gears &	Diesels
Hunting	Wind Sails	Hieroglyphics	Pulleys	transmission	Generators
Fire	Invention of	Numerical	Mechanics	Steam	Automobile
Beginning	Wheel	notation	Chemistry	Electricity	Aircraft
Grain Culti-vation	Metal smelting	Pharmocopeia	Books		Radio
	Pottery	Medicines	Philosophy	Printing	Television
Domestication of Cattle	Solar Calendar		Dev. of	Gas Engine	Nuclear Power
	Orchards	Complex	Science	Machines	Computers
Art		Buildings	Military &	Trains	Micro-technics
		Horse riding	Mass Pro-duction		Space Flight
			Religion		
			Sophistication		

The Primitive Paradigm		*Rationale Paradigm*		*Scientific Paradigm*	
Animalistic	Priesthoods	Exploration of Nature		Medicine	
Ritual	Religious	Phenomena		Philosophy of Science	
Amulets	Sacrifice	Logic, Classification		Evolution	
	Divination	Temperament Theory		Clinical Studies	
	Ritual			Psychometrics	

Supernatural-Ritual-Warding off of Evil		*Naturalistic-Logical Homeopathic*		*Scientific Typology*	

Note: the above lists of developments are not all inclusive, but representative.

rather than human digging with sticks, etc.), there was more time for creative problem solving—at least on the part of some individuals. The third stage in the development of technology occurred in the late 1700s with the discovery of how to get power from heat. Although the Romans had gears, transmission factors, and the like, they did not have any real conception of how to obtain power from heat. Their main sources of energy were, aside from animal and human power, waterpower and, to some extent, windpower. During the period which began in the late 1700s, the systematic unfolding of the scientific method led to innumerable applications of technology. The introduction of steam, gas and later on internal combustion engines made industrial development possible.

Table 3-2   **Summary of Culture and Control Mechanisms**

	Primary Criterion Source	Secondary Criterion Sources		
Definition level	Culture as a series of historical patterns	Family as basic social unit	Peer group as another social unit	Law, custom, church, education, mass media, civil authority; specific control mechanisms
Operational level	Related to the enhancement and survival of the individual and group	Related to survival of the unit	Related to survival of a common age or interest level	Established by the culture to enhance and maintain the culture
	A coherent methodology developed by the group	A microcosmic control system reflecting the culture	A microcosmic control system reflecting the culture	Coherent methodologies devised by the culture for sustaining appropriate predictable behavior in the individual and group
	Related to the prediction and control of stable patterns of behavior	Related to the prediction and control of stable patterns of behavior	Related to the development of stable patterns of behavior	The development of specific sets of criteria for guiding and controlling individuals and groups
Behavioral level	A complex chain of behaviors that are shaped, sustained, reinforced, and extinguished by the group	A specific network of behaviors designed to sustain the optimum behaviors of male, female, and minor children	A specific network of behaviors formulated and designed to sustain the optimum behaviors of specific interest groups	
	Utilizing past experience and trial-and-error learning	Utilizing a series of learned behavior involving coercive and reciprocal behaviors	Utilizing a series of learned behaviors involving coercive and reciprocal behaviors	Utilizing reference to a series of criterion behaviors in learning

ANCIENT ASSESSMENT

When humankind emerged from the paleolithic period into the neolithic one (about 12,000 BC) people were living in tribal groups. The world around them was a violent and threatening place. They could not understand the roar of the waves, the thunder over the mountains, or the sudden occurrences of birth and death. They huddled in caves or other shelters, relied on burning fires for heat and protection, cast furtive glances into the darkness outside their shelter, and breathed sighs of relief for the daily return of the sun.

Through empirical experience people learned that certain behaviors seemed to have a pragmatic sanction for community survival. These behaviors were all related to the primary needs of food, shelter, and security. Children were taught to behave in certain ways. There was little room for the innovative and creative problem solver who suggested an alternative way of doing things. Nor was there much toleration for the individual who did not behave in the predicted and required way at the given time and place. During the period of tribal culture, it would appear that the major assessment processes involved were empirical observation, done in a sporadic and unsystematized manner, and intuitive leaps to attempt to understand relationships to the world and the unknown. Thus the two approaches which were taken in assessment relied on empirical observations and connections of these observations to religion and cosmic harmonies. Moreover, since medicine, psychology, and religion were all joined in most of the ancient societies, it is imperative to recognize that assessment had a much broader context than it does today.

Egypt and Sumeria. Sometime between 12,000 BC and 4000 BC, certain tribal cultures evolved into urban ones or civilizations. This change appeared to be related to the ability to settle down in certain areas where there was a plentiful water supply, rich soil for repeated crops, and access to trade. Two such areas linked to western culture were the valley of the Tigris and Euphrates rivers that became the setting for Sumerian and Babylonian culture, and the valley of the Nile River that was the home of Egyptian culture. Similar developments also took place in China and India about the same time. Urban cultures or civilizations soon made progress in all kinds of technology, architecture, and accumulated considerable traditions.

Much of our understanding about assessment in the ancient western world is related to records from Egypt, Babylonia, and the Bible. However, simultaneously in the Orient, and specifically China there were also developments occurring that reflect assessment concerns.[3] In both Egypt and Sumeria early tribal units had coalesced into larger political entities and finally into empires somewhere between 4000–3000 BC. The pharaohs in Egypt and the kings in Sumeria owed their allegiance to a panoply of heavenly gods and forces. Though the pharaoh was considered a god in himself, in Egypt and Sumeria, the various priesthoods became the repository of knowledge about religion, medicine, psychology, astronomy, astrology, writing, business and about everything except warfare itself.

Underlying the power of the priesthood was the belief system in both Egypt and Sumeria that the gods and forces of nature were arbitrary, sometimes capricious, and often antagonistic to each other as well as to human beings. Thus a major task of the priesthoods was to ward off evil before it occurred and to restore individuals to health after illness had taken place. The fact that the priest-physicians provided the rationale for the social order and safeguarded the secrets of both assessment and treatment of personal and social problems led to the concentration of much power in this group.

Urban culture or civilization resulted in the formalizing of early assessment and treatment rituals to ward off evil. Underlying the rationale of Egyptian and Sumerian religion was the basic assumption that there was a relationship between a priest's activities and the consequences to the individual. Originally, evil had been warded off by human sacrifice, but this practice was later replaced with the use of animals. In addition, a variety of other techniques were used. Divination was a particularly important component. If an individual had a problem, physical or psychological, or was about to make a trip, he could consult a specific type of priest who would kill a sheep, inspect the liver and provide a set of remedies or forecasts from this process. The movements of birds, snakes, other animals, and the birth of malformed infants all had a meaning which could be interpreted by the priests. There were also symbolic rituals. Some of these were elaborate incantations which involved eating or not eating specific foods; the use of amulets and charms in the form of necklaces, rings, pendants, medals, and figurines of gods and goddesses. In addition, an acute sense of physical and mental observations, a knowledge of drugs and herbs, and a considerable knowledge about weather signs, and star-planet influences developed.

In all ancient cultures, illness, either physical or mental, was considered to be related to devils or sin against cosmic deities. Thus for example, the Babylonians (successors of the Sumerians) attempted to learn what the specific evil was that infected an individual by reading lists of various problems to the patient. When the patient became visibly agitated, the priests noted the problem which had caused the reaction and this problem then became associated with the source of infection or sin. This was not unlike the modern lie detector technique.

The Egyptians were particularly advanced in their knowledge. They knew much about anatomy and used it in their mummification processes. In the temples were medical schools where diseases were catalogued and classified according to symptoms. From the evidence viewed in tombs, we are likewise

Table 3-2   **Characteristics of the Primitive Paradigm in Assessment**

Major Category	Subcategory	Explanation
Empirical Observation		- Naturalistic observation of individual differences attributing such differences to a variety of supernatural sources
	Orbisiconography	- Correspondence assumption that celestial influences are mirrored in individuals
	Divination	- Examination of entrails of animals, flights of birds, unusual happenings to diagnose the present and predict the future
	Medical-Psychological	- Observation of illnesses (physical and mental)
Ritual [Treatment]		- Methods of avoidance of evil or deliverance from evil [capriciousness of gods or personal sin]
	Amulets	- Objects which might be medals, figurines, hair or other parts of a human being which protect or create immunity from problems or under other circumstances create such problems
	Incantations	- Ritualistic ceremonies or recitations often accompanied with magical gestures, movements and behavior. These were sometimes used to create a spell and other times to remove one
	Sacrifice	- A ceremony generally designated to atone for personal or collective sin or transgressions against the gods. Initially involved human beings and later on animals
Medical [Treatment]		- Use or variety of remedies learned by trial-and-error
	Herbs & drugs	- Collection of extensive information about properties of various herbs and drugs
	Operations	- Experimentation with trephining, knowledge of splints mummification
	Psychological	- Temple treatments: rest, running water, diet, suggestion, and other features of ritual

led to believe that they performed surgery, used splints for fractures, understood much about the properties of various herbs, and even knew that the heart was the center of the circulatory system of the blood. From the Ebers papyrus of Egypt dating back several thousand years before Christ, we have a wealth of information about early medical science. This papyrus provides information about the variety of Egyptian medicines and drugs. Though a vast number of incantations are given to accompany some of the prescriptions, showing that superstitious and religious formulas were considered prominent factors in healing, there are, nonetheless, more than 900 prescriptions set forth. The writers of this manuscript knew and used at least one third of the medicinal plants and herbs listed in modern pharmocopeia. The ancient physicians also knew the benefits of rest, water therapy, and quiet. There is also evidence that some knowledge existed about the nature of hypnotism, dream interpretation, and suggestibility. This is documented from the Bible itself, where the priests demonstrated their considerable skills before the pharaoh by creating the illusion that a staff could be turned into a writhing serpent. In summary, the ancient priesthoods provided a combined religious, medical, and psychological assessment with a treatment center for the people of that day. The temples thus served as community medical and psychological comprehensive care centers for the ancients. Many different kinds of specialists occupied the temple. Some were concerned with divination and religious matters, others with astronomy and astrology, and still others with what we might term medicine and psychology today. But all of them were vitally interested in the analysis of human behavior, the nature of character, and means for predicting and controlling human behavior.

Empirical observation and intuitive inferences based on Chinese Cosmological Assessment. The most comprehensive ancient system for the assessment of individual differences using empirical information and intuition is that of the Chinese. In terms of time, it would appear that the Chinese system began to emerge about the same time as the urban cultures of Egypt and Sumeria were codifying their information. To what extent the cultures interacted is not known, but it is recognized that even in those early centuries there were caravans moving back and forth between the areas. The Chinese system is unique in that it exists still today and is estimated to be about 5,000 years old. It consists of a number of factors or parts—not all of which may be that old. However, the description which will be made here will include the system as it exists today.

The Chinese system is based on the assumption of a cosmological correspondence between the forces of life on the earth (ching) and human behavior. The Chinese system is complex, based on a variety of components that include weather cycles, the association of basic elements such as wood,

metal, earth, fire, and water with human characteristics, the careful observation of bone-structure, physiognomy, elements of astrology, and palmistry.
Assessment may include all or parts of these components, but is also based
on a careful examination of diet, exercise, and physical health.

Original determinants of health are thought to be related to planetary
influence within the specific set of coordinates occurring at birth. These factors
influence both the physical and psychological health of the organism. One
can determine imbalances in the body through an examination of the network
of pressure points within the bodily systems. Planets are also related to vital
organs or perhaps zones including the organs, and the cycle of years brings
about possible conjunctions, adverse relationships, etc. So the entire system
is one with a vast amount of correspondence between the "fate" of the
individual and the nature of the universe. However, such adverse circumstances can be countered by specific diets, appropriate exercises (Kung-Fu),
special herbal remedies, body position in sleep, and methods of contem-
plation.

The global Chinese approach to assessment includes first the astrological
cosmological computations, then selected use of palmistry and physiognomy,
and finally as needed (in cases of medical ailments and problems) the use of
further elements of physical analysis, i.e., pressure points, acupuncture, diet
and exercise. The system is complex, but it has been described in detail by
Porkert (1978), and the bases of physiological analysis, including pressure
points for massage, the use of acupuncture, and the burning of moxa on the
skin has been thoroughly analyzed by Lu and Needham (1980). Moreover,
for readers who are interested in the details of the actual method, Greenblatt
describes many interviews with Chinese fortune-tellers and some of the
methods they use in making inferences about individual futures (Greenblatt,
1979).

Though current Western techniques exist which probably have a lineage
nearly as ancient as the Chinese system (e.g., chirognomy or palmistry, and
astrology), little relationship is seen between these Western versions and
medical treatment. Thus, one of the major differences between the two
systems is that the Chinese system moves from assessment directly to a set
of prescribed treatments which include exercise, diet, herbal remedies, and
massage. Western systems, however, have included newer versions of these
approaches in the use of biorythyms and color analysis. To a large extent it
can be inferred that the origins of the Chinese and Western systems have
some common background.

Social Consequences of the Ancient Assessment Systems. There are some
long-lasting consequences which derive both from the Western and Oriental
approaches to assessment. The information and knowledge that the ancient
Egyptians possessed was transmitted in large part to the Greeks and later

to the Romans. Both elements of primitive thinking relative to warding off evil and formal elements of the Judaeo-Christian religious tradition influence much current human behavior. Primitive thinking lurks below the conscious level in most human beings. It is for this reason that medals, amulets and other items still retain their appeal even in an age of considerable educational sophistication. The heritage of the Jewish tradition was passed on to the Christian religion in large part. Since the Bible remains the great religious teaching of Christianity as well as contemporary Judaism, the promise made by God to reward those who keep His laws and punish those who do not, still remains a basic tenet in either the conscious or pre-conscious levels of much of Western thinking.[4] The correspondence between personal happiness and a meaningful life on the one hand, and concurrence with the laws of God on the other, remains a factor to be considered in both assessment and treatments. The situation is much more explicit in Chinese culture where the ancient system coexists with modern science, and there is no incongruity noticeable between acceptance of the assessment techniques and herbal remedies of the ancient system and the use of the modern system. Lu and Needham (1980) document much of the ancient medical treatment system with modern techniques, suggesting that perhaps the ancient system functions relatively well in coping with chronic problems, but not with acute ones. The great interest in Western medicine and psychology on the integration of the individual has also led to a renewed interest in Chinese techniques.

A direct consequence of the Chinese assessment system was its impact on the classification of individuals for civil service jobs. This system still has its residue in modern China and Taiwan where extensive examinations are required to enter universities. Dubois (1964) has pointed out that the Chinese have been utilizing assessment tools for over 3000 years. China reputedly established a kind of civil service examination about 1115 BC. This system continued with only slight modifications until about 1905. The system was based on the notion that a hereditary aristocracy was not the best way to perpetuate sound government. As a result, appointments to both local and regional control positions were based on a series of very severe examinations. Sample assessments were used requiring proficiency in the five basic arts—music, archery, horsemanship, writing, and arithmetic. Knowledge of a sixth area, skill in the rites and ceremonies of public life including the earlier discussed assessment skills was also necessary. Subsequently, with the introduction of Confucianism certain moral standards were also required relative to applied politics. Familiarity with the geography of the empire, civil law, military matters, agriculture and the administration of revenue were added.[5]

Ancient assessment techniques are still with us today. The Chinese system continues side by side with modern medicine and psychological assessment. So too do celestial cosmologies of correspondence that postulate planetary and meteorological effects on human beings. Nor are these characteristics limited to individuals without much formal education. What is apparent from a study of ancient assessment methods is that many valid inferences were made about herbs, medicines, and techniques. The inferences may have been correct, but for different reasons than were accepted in those days. The tradition of the use of certain herbs, roots, and nostrums for treating illness continues in many areas. As we shall see in later chapters dealing with empirical observations and inferences drawn from them, many old remedies appear to be valid in their approach.

What is less acceptable today is the view of the ancients about rituals warding off evil. But even so, how many times have most people today heard the injunction: "knock on wood." How many travelers on boarding domestic or international flights wear a medal or carry an amulet! Indeed, many individuals when bad things happen to them look for the causality of the event in their own short-comings or "sins." Though the external attributions of happenings are not now ascribed to a pantheon of animal gods, the thinking remains, if not on the surface, close to it. Perhaps the real explanation of why human beings continue to rely on amulets, believe in retribution for their sins, and fear unknown consequences for their behavior, is the fact that our thinking begins in very real concrete conceptions about reality which involve the idea that thinking can make it so. This thinking is subject to revision through the study of rational decision making and the study of science. However, learning new methods of problem-solving, reasoning, and scientific thinking does not eradicate the earlier tracks of thinking. Under stress, anxiety, and fear, human beings often revert to such earlier forms of thinking.

THE RATIONAL PARADIGM IN ASSESSMENT: GRECIAN-ROMAN CONTRIBUTIONS

In some measure the cultural development of a nation is always dependent upon geographical factors and climate. This was so in Israel as well as in Egypt and Mesopotamia. This dependence appears to have been a factor in Greek civilization too. Greece is a land of mountains and small valleys; it has few plains of even moderate size and no appreciably large rivers. The Aegean Sea which separates the mainland of Greece from Asia Minor is dotted with many small islands. Because of the numerous peninsulas and jagged sea coast, many of the interior valleys were not too far from a seaport, or at least had easy access to the sea. The climate was, and still is, rather invigorating, neither too cold in winter nor too hot in summer. Hence, with

Table 3-3   **Summary of Characteristics of Grecian-Roman and Medieval Rational Paradigm in Assessment**

Category	Sub-Category	Explanation
Empirical Observation		- Based on naturalistic factors and examination of etiological causes
	Clinical Observations	- Hippocrates, Galen & Roman encyclopedist
	Theories of Individual Differences	- Plato's tripartite model - Aristotle's definition of vegetative, sensory, perceptual, and abstract characteristics
	Causal Explanations	- Aristotle's explanation of being, potentiality, and causes and principles of learning (association, contiguity, etc.)
Intuitive Observations		
	Astrology	- Ptolemy's views on celestial mechanics and their influence on human behavior
	Christian Revelation	- Application of religious criteria in Scholasticism
Classification [diagnosis]		- Systematic efforts made to classify individual characteristics
	Category classifications	- Aristotle's explanation of being, potentiality & causes & principles of learning (association, contiguity, etc.)
	Bodily characteristics	- Hippocrates classification on humours
	Temperament classification	- Galen and the Roman encyclopedists
	Spiritual classification	- Medievalists utilizing seven cardinal sins
	Human Functions	- Galen studies in biology, brain, etc.
Treatment		
	Homeopathic Medicine Medical	- Hippocrates homeopathic medicine - Additions to herbal and drug pharmacopea of ancients by Greeks and Romans - Determination of pulse rate by Herophilus - Specific remedies for various illnesses - Continuation of minor surgery and treatment of broken bones - General development of treatments for chronic conditions
	Psychotherapy	- Treatment of Melancholia by Hippocrates - Greek temple and retreat methods - Medieval spiritual advising

these distinctive features of topography, one can see an admirable setting for a civilization based on rugged individualism. Without pressing topographical determinism too far, it is nevertheless true that Greece produced a civilization unique from the civilizations of the Near East that preceded it. This does not imply, however, that the Greek civilization was an indigenous one. Greece was in a peripheral relationship to the civilizations of the Near East with many good results. It was far enough away from the customs and mores of Asia Minor that the Indo-European invaders of the Balkan peninsula were not completely altered by the earlier civilizations, and it was close enough that the absorptive civilizations of Crete, the Phoenicians, the Hittites and others, transmitted some of the development of Egyptian and Sumerian thinking to Greek thought and culture.

The distinctive contribution of the Greeks to assessment is found in their method of evaluating phenomena from natural origins and causes rather than supernatural ones, the development of a core of empirical information about physical, biological and social sciences, and finally the development of a theory of psychology which included a philosophy of knowledge and a logic for classification.

HOMER AND THE SOPHISTS

Greek contributions to assessment are heavily related to developments which took place in philosophy and psychology. Unlike the Egyptians or Hebrews, the Greek gods were simply extensions of human characteristics. In the Iliad they are ghost-like creatures who talk to each other about mundane matters. Thus they do not in any way approach the awesome majesty of the Egyptian animal gods, or the supreme nature of the one Hebrew God. Considerable reflections on the nature of man are found in the works of Homer. For example, in battle scenes, the stress threshold is described by the Greek word *"thumos."* This word seems to represent the mass or emergency reactions known in modern physiology. According to Jaynes (1976), the *"thumos"* is seen as the force which impels the person to fight. It is not Ajax who is zealous to fight but his *thumos"*; nor is it Aeneas who rejoices but his *"thumos."* If not a god, it is the *"thumos* that most often "urges" a man into action" (p. 262–263). Another common observation is that related to the *"phrenes"* which is basically translated into lungs or respiration. The ancient Greeks recognized that changes in breathing reflected emotional surges. There was also a recognition of the role of emotion to the heart which was represented by the word *"kradie."* A coward in the Iliad is not someone who is afraid, but someone whose *"kradie"* beats loudly. The only remedy is for Athene to "put strength in the *kradie,"* or for Apollo to "put boldness in it" (Jaynes, p. 266). In addition to these constructs the word *"etor"* represented intestinal movements, such as the sinking feeling that occurs on news of a bad event or accident. And the word *"noos"* is representative of vision. But most interesting was the word *"psyche"* which was originally related to breathing and ultimately became synonymous with soul or spirit. These early empirical observations of behavior represented a tendency in Grecian thinking that led to the development of a rationale about reality and human beings which was not dependent on an explicit or implicit connection with a set of divinities. This explanation was that of philosophy. Beginning with Thales and his prediction from natural events of an eclipse of the sun on May 28, 585 BC, the Greek thinkers moved towards an observational explanation of the world order. This led to a quest for the universal substratum. Thales felt it was water, but his successors, Anaximander and Anaximines advanced the idea that the universal substance was fire and air, respectively. Later Empedocles was to name the four major elements, earth, air, fire and water. The quest led Democritus to state that the ultimate nature of the universe was determined by minute atoms! Finally, Aristotle posited the concept of "being" as the final substratum. This philosophical inquiry set the stage for the sophists who were characterized as a group of critically-minded opportunists. Not by plan or intent, but rather by the peculiar circumstances that existed in Greece, they proved to be very important in the development of a spirit of critical individualism. They accentuated the place of the individual in Greek thought and stressed the worth of personal ideas and goals over that of the collective state enterprise. The sophists frankly doubted the existence of the Greek gods and by asking questions, provoked considerable thought. They acted as yeast that produced the intellectual fermentation characteristics of the golden age of Athenian civilization.

Plato and Aristotle

No account of assessment theory and its evolution can ignore the contributions of Plato (427–347 BC). Plato outlined one of the persisting philosophies of Western culture in his description of reality, man, society, and education. This was the position of idealism. In effect, Plato accents the subjective and individualistic in man while his student Aristotle (384–322 BC) becomes the advocate of the philosophy of realism accenting the objective empirical and observable fact. It is here that we see for the first time both the philosophical controversy between the subjective and objective (later to be seen in the debates between Thomas Aquinas and Duns Scotus in the medieval period, John Locke and Gottfried Leibnitz in the seventeenth century, Herman Helmholtz and Franz Brentano in the nineteenth

Table 3-4   **Elements of Aristotle's Cosmology**

Nonbeing ──► Being

    Potentiality ────────────────────────────► Actuality

Material cause (cosmic dust)	Formal cause (the idea of the universe in the mind of the creator)	Efficient cause (the actualizing process of the universe by the creator)	Final cause (the purpose for which the Creator constructed the universe)

Sensation ─────────────────► Perception ─────────────────► Intellection
(particular   (recognition and   (abstraction of
individual   classification of   essential
sensations)   sensations by the   elements of
                               mind through internal   perception)
                               senses of imagination,
                               memory, instinct and
                               common sense)

│   │   │
▼   ▼   ▼

Undifferentiated   Creation of a percept   Universal idea
quantitative and   or image by the mind   in mind
qualitative thresholds
│   │   │
▼   ▼   ▼

Usual contact feeling,   This is John Jones   This is a man
pressure, etc.

Barclay, J. R., *Foundations of Counseling Strategies*, Krieger, 1978, p. 95.

century, structuralism versus functionalism in the early twentieth century, and humanism versus behaviorism in contemporary psychology).[6]

Plato's contribution to assessment is most evident in his work on psychology. Plato's conception of the vital principles of mankind show a striking foreshadowing of the later Freudian concepts of Id, Ego, and Superego. Tiebout (1952) wrote: "Plato, as we have said, presents in certain of his dialogues a medical psychology and what might be called an orthopsychiatric ethic. In his own thought, of course, this medical analysis is bound up with his second level vision of the nature of evil and the way of salvation. In his analysis of the nature, the health, and the pathology of the soul, Plato distinguishes three faculties or principles (*dynameis*) in the human psyche: the intellect (*noos*) or reasoning part (*to logistiken*), the contentious or willful part (*to thymoeides*), and the appetitive or desiring part (*to epitymetiken*).

The function of the rational power in the soul is to organize and control the other two powers. The proper function of this power constitutes wisdom or prudence (*sophia phronesis*). The reasoning part thus plays in Plato's system a role analogous to the Freudian ego" (pp. 155–157).

Plato extended his conceptualization of the forces in the individual to both political and educational applications. In politics, the three parts of the soul are represented by philosopher-kings (intellection), warriors (courage), and common people, (the belly). Education for each of these groups should be according to their predominant function.

Aristotle's entire approach was based on empirical investigation and possibly the results of experimentation.[7] Aristotle maintained that man's knowledge was dependent on sense knowledge. But he avoided the contention of Locke, made many centuries later, that the sum of all man's knowledge is based on sense experience. Aristotle believed that man had five principles of activity, or faculties. They were: (1) the nutritive principle, (2) the sensitive principle, (3) the appetitive, (4) the locomotive, and (5) the rational principle. He thus conceived man as a being possessed of a number of faculties and the soul as a vital principle of movement. The substantial attribute of the soul was the power to think and of course the ultimate abstraction of sense knowledge and digestion of sense data was ascribed to the intellectual faculty of reason. Aristotle considered sensation to be dependent on an alteration of phenomena. He maintained that it was the human mind that digested the data of experience and sensation. He likened sensation to some combustible material which was capable of burning, but required intellection for ignition. The sensation of external phenomena requires the presence of the intellectual faculty to recognize, synthesize, and establish concepts. Aristotle considered man's five external senses: hearing, smelling, sight, taste, and touch as primary avenues to discern motion and change. The intellect then employed four internal senses to analyze the input of sensation. They were: (1) memory, (2) imagination, (3) instinct, and (4) common sense. Through the process of intellection (and in virtue of it) the raw data of the senses were organized and classified and then referred to the internal senses where comparison with previous experiences were made leading finally to generalizations. Thus, in summary, Aristotle compared mankind's knowledge of external phenomena to the analogy of coming up from a dark basement into the full light of day. The first steps in the process of knowledge are sensory elaborations of phenomena. Subsequently, higher up on the stairs, the action of the internal senses is applied to elementary sensory data. Finally, the intellect of man digests the essential qualities of experience in the form of a universal and abstract idea.

As can be seen from this discussion, Aristotle's contribution to systematic scientific knowledge (based on empirical observation and generalization using the syllogism of logic) was a major breakthrough. His contributions were encyclopedic and in fact his works provided the first empirically based compendium of observational data subjected to logical analysis. He focused observation of human behavior on specific sensory modalities, identified functional entities of memory, imagination, common sense, intellection, emotions, and organized them into a framework for the interpretation of human behavior, thinking and acting. In addition, however, Aristotle made several other very important contributions. He maintained that all our thoughts and concepts could be interpreted in a number of categories. These categories were substantial forms or methods of our thinking about phenomena. They were: (1) substance, (2) quantity, (3) quality, (4) relation, (5) activity, (6) passivity, (7) place, (8) time, (9) situation, and (10) disposition. These categories are the classes of things or the framework created by the human mind to analyze phenomena. Related to this was his ability to classify being and nonbeing and functional attributes of being. These classification systems were used for many centuries and even formed the basis of Linnaeus's classification of living creatures by phylum etc. many centuries later.

One final contribution of Aristotle can be cited in his analysis of causality and learning. He postulated that there were four major causes of events. These four constituents of reality explain the ways in which one thing or agent influences another thing or agent. The classes of causes are: (1) material, (2) formal, (3) efficient, and (4) final. All being is composed of matter and form. Matter is described as the prime stuff of the universe. It is undetermined and unresolved until united with form which is the determining factor. The universe can thus be consider a cosmic organization in which these four causes are acting on matter. The material cause is the raw stuff of which everything is made, e.g., in modern terms—atoms; the formal cause is considered the exact form which determines the shape or construction of the matter into determinate being; the efficient cause is the active force of construction; and the final cause can be considered the ultimate purpose for which the other causes were utilized.

Causality as explained by Aristotle is still a source of problems in scientific thinking. Rychlak (1977) has argued very convincingly that one of the major flaws in modern scientific explanations is the identification of the formal and efficient causes as one and the same thing. This identification of formal and efficient causality is most pronounced in scientific positivism. For formal causality is the actual plan or approach that is taken in a project. For example, if one is playing chess, the material cause can be identified with the actual chessmen; the formal cause with the game plan in the mind of the player; the efficient cause with the moves made, and the final cause with the object of the game to checkmate the opposing king. **With regard to the study of assessment it is appropriate to point out that the material cause of assess-**

ment can be the bits and data of observation, the formal cause is the organizing plan of those who teach or do assessment. This includes organizers and classification systems. The efficient cause is related to the actual means and methods of assessment which are used, and the final cause is related to effective prognosis and treatment.

One other contribution that Aristotle made to assessment theory is to enunciate principles of learning which explain how events are related to each other in a sequence. He spoke of the laws of association of ideas and stated that ideas are associated by (1) reason of contiguity in space or time, (2) similarity, and (3) contrast. These laws of the association of ideas were used for many centuries, and were revived by Hartley in the eighteenth century. In addition, Aristotle recognized the basic concepts of reward and reinforcement as conditions of learning and suggested that the transfer of learning took place much in the same way that a body was built up by exercise. He believed that the mind of man could be exercised by an appropriate curriculum and that training of mental powers could thus be accomplished. So in effect, Aristotle was the author of the mental discipline theory of learning that still exists today.

Hippocrates and Medical Science

The Greeks, in accordance with the principles of empirical observation which they had in part inherited from Egyptian and Babylonian medicine, held the conviction that disease was part of the order of nature and that its progress could be watched and cured by natural means. In the 5th century BC Hippocrates earned the title of "Father of Medicine" by attempting to separate the ideas of a natural medical science from religion. He was the first to teach that some diseases clear up best if very little is done by the physician. He also believed that medicine must be separated from magic. Interestingly enough, Hippocrates compared a physician to the helmsman of a ship. In easy weather there is little skill needed, but in a storm it takes all of the skills of the helmsman to save the ship. Similarly, he remarked that in medicine some things are well enough left alone, but in serious problems then all of the know-how of the physician is required.

According to Hippocrates the most important practice of medicine was clinical observation itself. He drew conclusions from texture, change of complexion, voice and the like. Hippocrates' attitude toward treatment was characterized by one of the famous sayings attributed to him: "our natures are the physicians of our diseases." He admitted that medical skill at its best could never be more than a supplement to the healing power of nature. He strongly opposed the careless use of drugs, and his own prescriptions were relatively few in number. He attached great importance to diet which he said should be full in winter, but more sparing in the summer. Sedentary people were advised to eat less than active workers.

He also recognized the importance of rest, hot baths, and soothing music in curing individuals. These latter influences were known for many centuries before Hippocrates and were also ascribed to Asclepius who reputedly founded temple establishments for individuals needing rest and recuperation. These sanctuaries often made use of running water, tinkling bells, and a variety of techniques which bordered on hypnosis and suggestion.

Hippocrates was one of the earliest physicians to attempt to build a classification system that encompassed both medical and psychological characteristics. This system was based primarily on empirical observation, but it also made reference to the four basic elements of Anaximander. The classification system that Hippocrates developed was one that came out of crises. It was consistent with philosophical thought that human reality was made up of polar opposites and reflected a cosmic order between individual life and the universe. Thus, Anaximander believed earlier that the major constituent elements of the universe were four: fire, air, water, and earth. Hippocrates and the philosopher Empedocles developed the rationale that life was based on vital fluids, the body being the form and basis for the circulation of these fluids. These fluids were affected by four qualities of matter: heat, cold, dryness and moisture, and disease was considered a result of a fluid becoming too hot or too cold, too dry or too moist. Antiquity knew the red fluid as blood, the yellow fluid as bile, and the whitish fluid as secretions from the nose and lungs. Finally, a black fluid, another form of bile, was discovered adding to the complement of four fluids corresponding basically to the four elements of the reality, air, fire, water and earth. As Peters has written: "Considering first the physical structure, we find the basis is the four elements: air, fire, water, earth. To each of these substances corresponds a quality called dry, hot, moist, or cold: and again in correspondence with these a humour, namely blood (warm) phlegm (cold) yellow bile (dry), black bile (moist). Health is defined as a right mixture of these; disease is consequently a disturbance of the relations, usually expressed as a change of ratios" (1965, p. 57). In addition, these dimensions were also considered to reflect male and female polarities and were associated then as well as now with astrological signs (Diamond, 1957). Hippocrates came to an obvious conclusion as Jones remarks that:"Even the most superficial observer must notice: (a) the animal body requires air, fluid, and solid food; (b) too great heat and cold are fatal to life, and very many diseases are attended by fever; (c) fluid is a necessary factor in digestion; and (d) blood is in a peculiar way connected with life and health" (Jones, 1923, p. xlvi).

Given that chest troubles and malaria were two of the most common diseases in ancient Greece, it is reasonable that Hippocrates should have identified certain humours (actually in his thinking a kind of force) related to health and disease. Hippocrates believed that illness was a consequence of a fundamental imbalance. Thus much of his diagnostic and treatment abilities related to treatment by opposites. Cold was treated by heat, dryness with moisture. Various kinds of diets were suggested such as gruel or thin soup for individuals with stomach trouble. Again, Hippocrates noted that as a common cold became pneumonia, the discharges from the body increased. Recovery was characterized by gradual diminution of discharges. Hippocrates identified many illnesses, including plague, colds and pneumonia, malaria, coma, tuberculosis, and what he called melancholy. Interestingly enough he maintained that fevers were not infectious, but tuberculosis was. He also identified pervasive and continuing depression as a kind of disease which he called melancholy. The term probably referred to any kind of physical or mental depression of prolonged duration.

The earliest treatment procedure is found in Hippocrates' use of homeopathic methods. **Homeopathy is based on what might be called the law of opposites.** What is meant by this is that a disease or problem can be treated by opposite methods. Thus, for a fever one attempts to reduce it by means which may be successful. For a chill, one utilizes warmth. Applying the paradigm to psychology, one way to treat the problem of depression is by attempting to get the individual to become more socially involved. In more recent times, the practice of homeopathic medicine has included the idea that a disease is treated by a set of procedures or drugs which in a healthy person will bring about the same symptoms. Thus if a drug creates schizophrenic reactions in a normal individual, homeopathic medicine would suggest that this drug has the power to counter such characteristics in a schizophrenic. The modern approach to homeopathic medicine is not popular today, chiefly because of its views that one treats a medical problem by procedures which attack the etiology of the problem. But a distinction must be made between what was more recently held, and what was held (albeit with some confusion) in the ancient world. Ancient and medieval treatments were clearly homeopathic in nature. For example, depression was often treated by residency in a temple where running water and the sounds of chimes and music could be joined to rest and dietary control. Even before Hippocrates, Egyptian priests were said to glide between the sleeping and whisper suggestions about good health in their ears. The basic principle involved was the older homeopathic approach in the sense that illnesses were treated by opposites. On the other hand, the more recent approaches (from the eighteenth century on) founded on similarities, certainly has a basis in the idea of immunization for illness. Thus polio is prevented by a polio innoculation.

Hippocrates recognized the relationship of diet to habits of adjustment and mental health. He urged his associates to observe closely the habits of regularity which individuals showed. He noted that irregular body functions or habits were often signs of problems. In addition, the early Greek therapists also invoked a cycle of treatment which was known as metasyncrasis. Patients were given various exercises to do on different days and their diet was varied also. Thus seafood was prescribed one day, and on another day beef. Some of Hippocrates' successors also became very adept at relating pulse rate to health. Herophilus of Alexandria learned to count the human pulse with the aid of a water clock. This was about 300 BC (Luce, 1970, p. 8). In summary, Hippocrates enunciated a set of empirically derived principles for medical assessment and treatment. He recognized consistently the relationship between mind and body, and developed guidelines for what constitutes an homoeopathic approach to medicine.

Galen and Further Developments

From the contributions of the thought of the Greeks there is a vast proliferation of knowledge which takes place in the next three or four hundred years. Space does not permit a full examination of the development of engineering skills, the collection of libraries and the vast building programs of the ancient world of Rome. The Romans had a passion for organization and collection of data. Thus from the writings of Varro (116–27 BC), Celsus (25 BC–? AD), Pliny (23 BC–79 AD) and Galen (131–200 AD) there is a considerable amount of information. These four individuals are known as the Roman encyclopedists because they summarized whole branches of knowledge as then known. For example Varro wrote nine books on grammar, dialectic, rhetoric, geometry, arithmetic, astrology, music, medicine and architecture. Celsus wrote an encyclopedia of medicine, diagnoses, treatments, and classification of diseases. Pliny's contribution was chiefly in natural history.

Galen was the greatest redactor or summarizer of medical and psychological information available at the height of the Roman Empire. Though Galen was a biologist and primarily a student of anatomy, his status at that time led to an undue reliance on his reputation. In point of fact, Galen's reputation was so great that it remained for Vesalius to overcome it in the Renaissance. Galen's specific contributions were first in anatomy where he described the brain, and particularly the *rete mirabile* (a network of blood vessels at the base of the brain). However, it took well over thirteen hundred years to determine that Galen's observations were probably derived from examination of the brain of an ox rather than a human being. This *rete mirabile* was important for Galen because he believed it was in this area that the vital forces of nutrition mixed with the spiritual—particularly in the ventricles of the brain.

Galen systematized the first theory of temperament. Another contribution, which may have been more significant in terms of assessment psychology was that of expanding on the basic elements of Hippocrates' theories combining the four elements of fluids theory into a series of temperaments. Four major temperaments emerged from his theories in which an inclination to a given temperament is dependent on the particular preponderance of element mixes. Galen's four major temperaments were melancholic, choleric, phlegmatic, and sanguine. Each of these temperaments represented a series of naturalistic or empirical observations that had been made about individuals. Galen provided the first systematic classification system for the analysis of personality. The melancholic individual was considered to be moody, sober, and reserved. The choleric was restless, aggressive, and excitable; the phlegmatic was passive, peaceful, and calm; and the sanguine was sociable, outgoing, lively.

The temperament theory of personality classification has remained a central feature in the evaluation of human behavior down to the present. It was used extensively in the medieval period as a basis for what was termed spiritual counseling. The medievalists began a system of assessment, chiefly for determining candidates for the priesthood, that considered temperament a biological template, and character the results of temperament times learning. Utilizing the seven cardinal sins (pride, anger, envy, lust, gluttony, sloth and avarice), they determined how individuals with different temperaments might behave relative to these universal tendencies (Backus, 1969; Tanquery, 1930). A considerable amount of expertise was developed from medieval times down to the present in terms of what might be called "character" analysis. This had obvious relationships to the question of spiritual advising, but also to many books and studies which were done in the nineteenth century relating to character as the result of biological temperament modified by environmental forces and learning.[8]

The medieval stance towards the temperaments was also endorsed by others in more recent centuries. Immanuel Kant maintained a categorical point of view that every person could be assigned some dimension on this categorical system. Wilhelm Wundt discussed these types from the polar dimensional point of view, labeling one dimension slow-quick and the other strong-weak. He wrote (1903): "The ancient differentiation into four temperaments arose from acute psychological observation of individual difference between people . . . The fourfold division can be justified if we agree to postulate two principles in the individual reactivity of the affects: one of them refers to the strength, the other to the speed of change of a person's feelings. Cholerics and melancholics are inclined to strong affects while sanguinists and phlegmatics are characterized by weak ones. A high rate of change is found in sanguinists and cholerics, a slow rate in melancholics and phlegmatics" (pp. 637–8). In addition, Pavlov believed that central neurological processes of cortical excitation and inhibition together with the balance or motility of the nervous system, were responsible for the differences in the Galen temperaments. It was essentially the exploration of temperament differences that led to the discovery of classical conditioning in salivation in dogs (Strelau, 1983). Recently, Eysenck and Rachman (1965 p. 16) have reported the results of correlations of traits based on modern factor analysis studies by Guilford, Cattell, and Eysenck and consistent with the old Galen model.

Given the noteworthy developments in knowledge, one might wonder why the Romans did not become a technological civilization over and beyond what they achieved. The example of Heron may shed some light on this problem. In the first century AD the Greek physicist Heron developed a pneumatic pump which worked well and was used in ancient fire protection devices. He was also known to have invented a primitive electrical battery for use in silver plating. In addition, he developed a working steam engine which he used as a toy. Heron had the fundamental knowledge of pneumatic pumps, electricity, and steam power. However, this knowledge did not result in any technological breakthrough. The knowledge was simply not needed in a culture depending on slave power. It was put to use to hoist the thrones of Byzantine emperors up into the air before gaping barbarians—later on. Thus, the ancient world was quite knowledgeable in many areas, but there was no enterprising or business stimulus for the use of these techniques.

In summary, the rational paradigm related to assessment was developed by the Greeks and completed by the Romans. For the first time empirical observations were described, clarified, and used as a means for developing a theory of individual differences. The consequences of this approach led to a classification system based on logic, body temperament, and human functions. Treatment plans were developed for both medical and psychological problems based on empirical observation and integration of limited success or failure with various approaches. The key construct in both medical and psychologial treatment was based on a naturalistic homeopathy and treatment by opposites. The rationale for this approach was based not only on natural events, but also some intuitive judgments relating human welfare to celestial mechanics (astrology) and later on in the medieval period to faith. A practical analysis of character and temperament emerged in the medieval period which had considerable influence during the centuries leading up to the present.

THE EVOLUTION OF THE SCIENTIFIC PARADIGM IN ASSESSMENT

Modern assessment built upon the rational paradigm in assessment which has just been discussed. However, as Kuhn (1969) has pointed out, paradigms relating to human nature or assessment do not change suddenly. New paradigms emerge "only after persistent failure to solve a noteworthy puzzle has given rise to a crisis. And even then it occurs only after the sense of crisis has evoked an alternative candidate for paradigm" (p. 144). It is the failure or sense of failure of one paradigm which long before it topples and gives way to the next one, that leads to the new one. For example, it was the development of rationality in the Greeks, their practical agnosticism towards the traditional gods, the search for cause-effect relationships in natural phenomena which gave rise to the rational paradigm in assessment. So likewise, when the Ptolemaic earth-centered system of Roman civilization no longer squared with new findings in astromomical science in the Renaissance, then little by little, the entire Roman-Medieval paradigm of humankind began to break down. A scientific paradigm replaced it, but not all at once and not in the sense that rationality, logic, and causal relationships were abandoned.

Paradigms often emerge from the thinking of prominent figures. Integral to the development of the scientific paradigm in assessment is the relationship expressed between various key paradigm givers in psychology. Psychology existed from the Greeks on as a part of philosophy. It was only in the middle of the nineteenth century that efforts were made to separate psychology from philosophy. Thus the evolution of the scientific paradigm in assessment is related to key individuals in psychology as well as certain basic movements. Table 4 presents a list of individuals who have served as paradigm givers to psychology in general and to assessment in particular. The development of the scientific paradigm in assessment is related to the development of the scientific paradigm itself. Six important movements relate to this development: (A) the substitution of mathematics for the syllogism as the basic tool of science; (B) the reification of mathematics in philosophy as the philosophy of science; (C) increased interest in the physiological nature of human beings; (D) the development of evolutionary theory; (E) the development of psychophysical studies; and (F) the emergence of psychometrics.

Mathematics and the Development of Science

Medieval developments that led to the flowering of scholasticism and the origin of the universities were triggered by a number of factors. One most important was the inheritance of Aristotle from the Spanish Saracen culture. It was the reintroduction of Aristotle to Europe that led to the great contributions of Aquinas in scholasticism. Along with Aristotle, there was a great enhancement in mathematical knowledge which came also from the Saracens in the form of algebra. Galileo and Copernicus used mathematics to make inferences about the nature of the sun, the planets and the earth. Mathematics did not counter logic as such, but it became the tool for iden-

Table 3-5 Representative Paradigms Relevant to Scientific Development

Theorist	Description of Human Nature	Method	Classification System	Sociocultural Implications for Change
Aristotle 3rd Century BC	Hierarchical synthesis of five principles of activity: nutritive, sensitive, appetitive, locamotive and rational.	Empirical observation and logical deduction.	By faculty characteristics and levels of activity.	Indeterminist with emphasis on formal causal thinking and rationality. Goals of life related to moderation of lower impulses and *cultivation of reason*.
Hippocrates 5th century BC	A sentient-rational creature composed of a blend of substances and dispositions subject to differing states of physical and mental health.	Empirical observation and logical deduction.	By bodily composition of fluids e.g. blood, bile, phlegm etc. & by homeopathic inferences.	Indeterminist with emphasis on determination of characteristics, diagnostic judgments relative to moderation of food, stress, and other characteristics which tend to disturb bodily balances, *Moderation of health*.
Aquinas 13th Century	An individual composed of body (as described by Aristotle) and soul as defined by the Catholic tradition.	Empirical observation, & use of the syllogism for both reason and revelation.	By faculty characteristics of Aristotle and temperament characteristics of Hippocrates as related to the development of habits of moral virtue.	Indeterminist with emphasis on moderation of human characteristics in relation to the moral and religious criteria of the good life, *Moral growth and development*.

Table 3-5   (Continued)

Theorist	Description of Human Nature	Method	Classification System	Sociocultural Implications for Change
La Mettrie 18th Century	A physical machine not qualitatively different from other animals.	Empirical observation of the laws of nature (same for animals & mankind).	Physiological characteristics only. All distinctions due to hunger, sexual drive, thirst, and basic physical conditions.	Deterministic based on laws of nature, the logical extension of the thinking of Descartes, Locke and Condillac *Understanding and control of human behavior.*
Helmholtz 19th Century	A physiological machine to be explained exclusively through the laws of physiology.	Experimental verification of the specific characteristics.	Descriptions and explanation of sensory organs in terms of enervation.	Deterministic based on experimental evidence. *Understanding & healing.*
Wundt 19th Century	A sentient, thinking and moral individual.	Empirical and experimental methods with particular emphasis on psychophysical parallelism and reaction-time experiments.	Characteristics of Temperament following Hippocrates-Galen Model, related to the classification of mental characteristics via a mental chemistry.	Indeterminist because of strong Lutheran background emphasizing structured elements of conscious life. *Understanding of conscious processes.*
Freud 19th–20th Century	An animal socialized by culture, instinctively aggressive, hostile and self-aggrandizing.	Empirical-intuitive methods.	By balance between conscious (secondary process) and unconscious (primary process) mechanisms.	*Deterministic, understanding and control.* Change is reflected only by accommodation to mechanisms determining behavior. Consistent with 19th century positivism and evolutionary theory

Table 3-5 (Continued)

Theorist	Description of Human Nature	Method	Classification System	Sociocultural Implications for Change
Testing Model Late 19th & 20th Century	A biologically based social organism possessing a variety of trait characteristics some judged socially positive and others negative.	Empirical-psychometric methods using assumption of normal distribution of characteristics and average deviation.	Implied correspondence between test results and internal characteristics. Individuals classified according to traits.	*Deterministic, understanding and control.* Implied relations between traits characteristics and constitution. *Use of testing to classify, separate, segregate and control consistent with social Darwinism in economics and politics.*
Skinner 20th Century	A neutral-passive biological organism with innate reflexes and needs.	Empirical-experimental methods using various schedules of reinforcement, deprivation and punishment to encourage desired behavior and eliminate undesired.	Correspondence between behavioral responses and learning. Individuals classified in accordance with social criteria of adequacy, deficits, or maladaptive responses.	Deterministic viewing behavior as learned responses to environmental stimuli. *Use of approach to understand & control behavior.*

tifying major postulates about the nature of the universe to which logic could be applied. Therefore, in a very real manner, the core problem in the development of the new paradigm was whether the major premises of science should be based on logic derived from faith in the past, or from mathematical observations.

A knowledge of mathematics constitutes the proximate basis for both measurement and logic. One of the earliest inventions of urban culture was a set of measurements. Standard measurements were closely related to technological growth in civilization for they made it possible to determine both the quantity and value of objects. It was important, for example, not only to determine how many cows or pigs were owned, or how much grain was stored in warehouses, but how to equate these animals and commodities with a value either in trade or in precious metals such as gold and silver. Thus we find the Sumerians, Chinese, and Egyptians all developed systems of measurement. The Greeks and Romans proceeded to geometry and some notion of advanced procedures beyond addition, subtraction, division and multiplication. The Arabs continued still further into the development of algebra, and Leibnitz, possibly through contact with Chinese ideas, introduced the method of calculus to science. Perhaps the greatest continuing use of mathematics was found from Greek civilization onward in applications of astronomy, meteorology, and astrology.

The concept of number represents a symbol of extension. The central concept of mathematics is number. Numbers in measurement are symbols to represent quantitative or qualitative differences ordinarily calibrated against some standard. Thus one of the English and American units of measurement for distance, the mile, had its origin in Roman times when the mile was defined as a thousand paces by Roman legionnaires (*millia passuum*). Day and night were calibrated by the rising and setting of the sun. Time and its measurement led to intensive study of the planets and stars. The Chinese, Egyptian, Sumerian, Mayan, and Greek civilizations all invested considerable effort in the study of astronomy. Mathematics was an indispensable tool. All these efforts were important because they made it possible to predict the coming of various seasons, the specification of times for planting and harvesting, and indeed times for taking voyages by sea as well as times to stay home because of expected bad weather. From early beginnings to estimate the parameters of land, or bushels of grain, numbers came to represent a symbolic and isomorphic relationship with dimensions of height, weight, size, and other physical measurements. Indeed, some individuals such as Pythagoras, believed that the secrets of the universe were found in numbers. and began the study of numerology. In a very real sense the creation of numbers represented an effort to comprehend reality and to extend a certain control over that reality by measuring its dimensions and

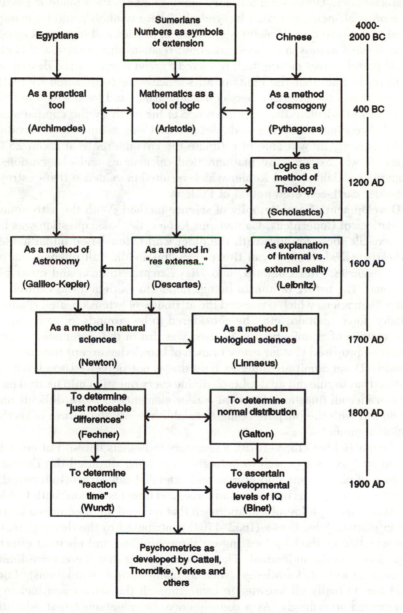

Note: these are representative individuals only.

Figure 3-1 **The Evolution of Psychometrics**

characteristics. Developing a theory about numbers then made it possible to express elements of reality in symbols. These symbols could be manipulated to examine causal relationships both in physics and in logic. Logic, in turn, formed axioms and theorems about relationships. Eventually Galileo could postulate that nature itself reflected a grand mathematical design, and Kant could state that the limits of all science were constrained by mathematics. It was the interface between mathematics and logic which led Eratosthenes to calculate the circumference of the earth by the comparison of sun dial readings at Cyrene and Alexandria. Using geometric observations and reasoning, he was able to estimate the circumference at about 25,000 miles. It was likewise the mathematical calculations and observations of Copernicus, Galileo, and Kepler which resulted in evidence that destroyed the older earth-centered notion of Ptolemy.

Development of a philosophy of science method. With the astronomical revelations of Copernicus, Galileo and Kepler, the basic question was how to reconcile these findings with the older world view based on faith. René Descartes (1596–1649) began this process by dividing all phenomena into two categories: "*Res Cogitans*" and "*Res Extensa*" (human and other phenomena). The nature of human beings he left to Faith and the Church. All other phenomena which possessed the attributes of extension, i.e., quantity, quality, force, motion, etc., he considered to be grounds for examination. The method of examination he devised was that of the systematic doubt in which he proposed that for every branch of knowledge except theology, one should: (1) not admit anything as true that is not perceived so clearly and distinctly as to rule out all doubt; (2) divide every question into natural parts; (3) consider all questions from the easier elements to more difficult ones; (4) do this with the purpose being to establish firmly the nature of truth in logical argument.

Thomas Hobbes (1588–1679), a secretary to Francis Bacon, but not influenced by Bacon's approach to inductive reasoning, disputed the Descartes division of phenomena into human and extended categories. Influenced by Newton's conceptions of matter and force, and from discussions with Galileo, he enunciated a philosophical approach that reduced all phenomena to matter in motion. John Locke (1632–1704) contributed to the development of the scientific method by focusing on the controlling and eliciting effect of experience on the individual. Though recognizing that there were limited intuitive aspects of knowledge (such as mathematical foundations), Locke held that virtually all knowledge came through the senses and had to be interpreted accordingly. As a consequence, he maintained that education could and did make the vast difference in most individuals.

These philosophical observations had much influence on the development of the philosophy of the scientific method. A number of implicitly held postulates which really guided researchers from that time on were a by-product of English Empiricism, i.e., the systematic doubt or distrust of previous knowledge; the postulating that all phenomena could really be considered matter in motion through forces; and that knowledge of the appearances and substances underlying these appearances could be known only by sensory processes of careful and repeated observation.

Continental philosophers did not completely agree with English Empiricism. Gottfried Leibnitz (1646–1716) disagreed with Locke's contention that all the contents of the mind were obtained from sensory experience, retorting to Locke that this was true except for the mind itself! Moreover, Immanuel Kant (1724–1804) ruled out psychology as a discipline that could be investigated by scientific method because it dealt primarily with mental phenomena which were not characterized by extension.

CHAPTER IV

Scientific Assessment and Professionalism

With the establishment of the scientific paradigm and the weakening of restrictive influences from the Church and State, there was a quickening of research on anatomy, physiology and particularly the brain. The study of comparative physiology was one of the contributing factors to the development of the theory of evolution. Interest in heredity, cultural anthropology, and measurement converged to develop psychometrics and statistics. Finally, within the setting of the New World, these developments all provided a basis for an objective approach to assessment. From this task, the emerging discipline of psychology became associated with an important new role in society, that of evaluation and placement.

THE STUDY OF PHYSIOLOGY

The emergence of empirical observation as a method and mathematics as a basis for determining laws of structure and function led to increased emphasis on the study of physiology. With the unprecedented emphasis on empirical observation, and the overturning of the ancient cosmology of the Ptolemaic system, a simultaneous thrust was applied in physiology. During the middle ages the study of the human body and physiology was very limited. Students were allowed to witness the dissection of a male only twice and that of a female only once. The authority of Hippocrates, Galen, and the Roman encyclopedists remained the last word in physiology. However, in the Renaissance explorations of the anatomy of the human body became more pronounced, even though they had to be covert and in some instances performed on corpses. Vesalius (1514–1564) dissected the human body and published drawings of what he found. He also learned that Galen had not dissected human bodies and particularly brains, but rather those of oxen. Harvey (1578–1657) in 1616 discovered the circulation system of the blood.

Botany became a part of medical science. Above all, physicians began to search for the material causes of disease.

Though in the sixteenth and seventeenth centuries, researchers in both astromomy-physics and medicine were careful not to attack openly the doctrine of the soul, in the eighteenth century such caution was discarded. Julian La Mettrie (1709–1751) published in 1748 a small book entitled: *Man a Machine*. La Mettrie denied the need for, and the existence of, a theological soul, and throughout his writings he attributed all behavior to mechanistic principles. For example, he wrote: "The human body is a machine which winds its own springs. Nourishment keeps up the movements which fever excites. Without food, the soul pines away, goes mad, and dies exhausted" (La Mettrie, 1943, p. 93). La Mettrie cited physiological and anthropological reasons to prove that man is not qualitatively different from animals, and he used his ability and training as a physician to show, rather grandly, how knowing will long remain unknown to the physician. As Boring wrote: La Mettrie is important because, taking an extreme position, he became a signpost for a trend—the trend toward materialism away from spiritualism, the trend toward the mechanistic and physiological interpretation of the mind" (Boring, 1950, p. 214). Ultimately, La Mettrie's model of a human machine was used by Lashley in a very similar analogy—that of a machine built on reflex response principles. It also leads quite sequentially to the construction of the electronic brain in the computer.

The writings of La Mettrie and others such as the Abbe Condillac (1715–1780) who used an analogy of a statue rather than a machine, influenced much experimentation related to the brain. Francis Joseph Gall (1758–1828) began with exploration of the brain and identified gray and white matter in the brain. He also did much comparative analysis of brains of children, the elderly, animals, and brain damaged individuals. Gall did much good work in the comparative analyses of human and animal brains, but he was influenced by the idea that various characteristics of individual differences could be ascertained by evaluating bumps on the head. The logic of this explanation was that bumps on various sectors of the skull reflected differences in the brain itself. Some knowledge was available at that time about localization of some brain functions, and the generalization that these functions could manifest themselves on the surface of the brain was one that Gall made. This study became known as phrenology. Gall identified 27 zones which corresponded to faculties. Thus individuals with bulging eyes were thought to be inquisitive, and those with large cerebellums extremely sexual.

Unquestionably, Gall's specific applications to the brain in phrenology were also part of a larger movement in which the physiognomy of individuals was seen to represent internal character (Johann Kaspar Lavater 1741–1801). To be sure there is a natural tendency in all individuals to assess others somewhat by their physiological characteristics. Thus, in folklore, individuals have been described as possessing "a shifty eye," or "an irresolute chin." This method of assessment became the focus of the Italian criminologist Cesare Lombroso (1836–1901) who maintained that criminals could be identified by their physical characteristics (which he considered degenerate).

Although there would seem to be some relationship between physiognomy and personality (as we shall see in a later chapter), unfortunately, Gall drew some inferential conclusions about the nature of brain functions and faculties, and their influence on external aspects of the skull, that were soon abandoned. However, what he did was to accentuate further the study of specific empirical impressions about the physiognomy of individuals that led to a heightened attention to such physiological details.

Hypnotic suggestibility and its discovery led to efforts to cure mental disturbances and to theoretical inferences about the nature of psychic phenomena. Another movement that heightened the sensitivity to empirical observation began with an increased interest in attempts to heal individuals who manifested psychological problems. During the ancient periods of assessment, phenomena which we might term today as "psychotic" or at least extremely "neurotic" were often associated with transgressions against God. This idea continued explicitly into medieval psychology where witches were burned at the stake, and mental deviancy was ascribed to the devil. A remedy for this problem was seen in increased religious devotion, and in instances where the problems were great, exorcism (or the religious casting out of devils) was used.

But just as empirical observation had supplanted theological reasoning and tradition in other areas, so the continued problem of mental illness became a focus of empirical methodology. During the eighteenth century, a priest Johann Joseph Gassner (1727–1779) came under scrutiny for a process that he practiced. When an individual suffering from problems was brought to him, he utilized a form of exorcism to command the evil spirits to depart. If they did not, he concluded that other procedures were needed and he therefore commanded the symptoms to move around to other parts of the body or to manifest themselves in less destructive methods. Gassner came under attack, and in an inquiry set by the Prince-Elector of Bavaria in 1775, a physician from Vienna, Franz Anton Mesmer (1734–1815) testified and demonstrated that he could cause the same phenomena as Gassner. The technique he used was basically hypnotism, though Mesmer attributed the effects to what he called animal magnetism. Mesmer, over a long career, developed a method of treating mentally ill or at least severely neurotic individuals. What this method entailed was the use of a specially designed room where patients sat around a tub filled with iron filings. They also had rods which led into the filings that they could grasp. With the aid of music (sometimes using Franklin's glass harmonica that created bell tones from rubbing glass), his appearance in long flowing robes, and a series of induction like statements, Mesmer obtained all kinds of results—even though he charged very high fees for his services. Though Mesmer remained convinced to the end of his life that there was some kind of magnetic influence, and later on he though it flowed chiefly from him to others, his contributions—even in the contemporary society of those days were scoffed at. He was, for example, condemned by a special commission that included among its members Lavoisier the chemist and Benjamin Franklin.

Though many explored the ideas of Mesmer, it was Jean Martin Charcot (1825–1893), director of the famous Parisian hospital Saltpetriere, who formalized the techniques of hypnosis. Charcot was at a hospital where there were many different kinds of neurological and psychological problems. He used a variety of techniques, but came to identify hypnosis as a method that could provide a number of specific changes in individuals. Many other professionals by the later decades of the nineteenth century were also using the technique. Charcot was not a theoretician. It was therefore Freud and others who explained some of the theoretical foundations of what was occurring in hypnotism.

EVOLUTIONARY THEORY

The emphasis on studies of human beings through physiology was an effort to determine by scientific (or perhaps quasi-scientific) procedures components which resulted in the determination of human differences. The impact of determinism on human variability gained considerable power through the enunciation of the evolutionary theory of Charles Darwin (1809–1882) and the genetic studies of Gregor Mendel (1822–1884). The summary conclusions that most educated people made from the evolutionary hypothesis and the influence of genetics on growth and development was that human characteristics had evolved from lower creatures by a process of selective breeding and environmental influences. When Herbert Spencer (1820–1903) applied evolutionary theory to social classes and social behavior, it was a logical consequence of this thinking that just as the most capable of species continued to evolve through biological genetic selection, so those individuals with more capability rose to the top of social class and social power.

The evolutionary hypothesis lent credence to the idea that one could evaluate individuals by their physiognomy. Thus efforts were made to assess individuals on the basis of physical characteristics as Lombroso did. But there were also efforts to evaluate individuals on the basis of skull characteristics. A typical approach was to fill skulls with pebbles or sand and then to note the cubic content of skulls. Efforts were made to suggest that criminals, Negroes and apes had smaller cranial content than Caucasians. But these efforts were ambiguous in their findings. In addition, the evolutionary hypothesis formed a good bolstering argument for the continuation of slavery, since proponents could argue and did that the Negro was inherently inferior to the Caucasian. As we shall see later on in this chapter, the evolutionary hypothesis, joined to physiological determinism from genetic sources, became a set of postulates which enabled a number of American psychologists to utilize testing as a means of discrimination between "desirable" and "undesirable" elements in the population.

Psychoanalytic thought as developed by Sigmund Freud was an effort to apply evolutionary thinking to psychic phenomena. Sigmund Freud (1856–1939) had a tremendous impact on the development of psychology in general and in clinical observation particularly. Although much of his thought has been translated into specific areas of psychotherapy, he has also influenced the areas of philosophy, history and literature. Freudian theory expanded the nature of empirical observation to include inferences about dynamic states or problems drawn from observation via intuition.

Freud's life spanned 83 years. Educated within the tenets of the Helmholtz school of physiological psychology, he abandoned this approach, though he always recognized the importance of physiology in accounting for psychological characteristics. His studies with Franz Brentano, the teacher of Husserl and Stumpf, provided him with an approach to intentionality which is both confirmed in his writings and in recent analyses of influence relationships (Barclay, 1959; Stanescu, 1971). Freud's study and residency with Charcot also taught him a great deal about the potential effects of hypnosis. On his own Freud developed a system for treating a variety of mental illnesses and problems. He asserted that mind was a mechanism for the direction of free-flowing energy into channels. He maintained that consciousness was only a part of mental life and that all behavior was purposeful and meaningful, taken in the context of tension reduction and the bipolar goals of seeking pleasure and avoiding pain. His model was in point of fact based on neurological brain characteristics and asserted that morality, as well as stress, and psychological defenses, were created by the mind in response to social acculturation.

What is important particularly to assessment is that he enunciated a series of principles about empirical observation that influenced the entire field of clinical observations. Freud essentially expanded the correspondence assumption of assessment. This assumption had in the past suggested an isomorphic relationship between what was observed and what was really present in an individual. Freud did not deny this assumption, but altered it to suggest that the correspondence was also between what was observed and what was hidden in the unconscious or preconscious of the individual.

Freud maintained that all behavior was goal-centered and intentional in nature. However, the goals which were sought in many instances were not consciously known to the individual. Thus it was important for the observer, particularly the clinical observer, to recognize that the behavior of the individual and the goal-seeking of the individual were symptomatic of deeper needs and perhaps repressed experiences. Freud enunciated a theory of human behavior which included the following major points:

1. Mind is an apparatus for the reduction of free flowing energy from unstable to stable forms.

2. The psychic apparatus is modeled on the reflex arc. Socialization alone has forced the psychic apparatus to either disguise or repress certain major thrusts of the organism.

3. All psychic processes, contents, and thoughts of an individual life are meaningful and their meanings are mutually and intimately related.

4. Most of human thinking and behaving is related to what is termed "primary process." This is a frank and explicit seeking of pleasure in every way possible and an avoidance of pain.

5. Through the process of acculturation the "primary process" yields in part to the "secondary process" which represents the best interests of the individual under the duress of restrictions by culture. This secondary process is therefore associated with ego.

With these major assumptions about human behavior, it was then quite important to intuit what was meant by specific acts of behaving or thinking. And so Freud developed a comprehensive theory about the nature of the unconscious and how instinctual drives were developed, gratified, and controlled. Freud's alteration in the correspondence assumption was of tremendous impact on clinical observations. Nor were his influences limited to his own system and followers. Freud's ideas were at least argued, if not accepted by Alfred Adler (1870–1937), Otto Rank (1884–1939), Carl G. Jung (1875–1961) Karen Horney (1885–1952), Harry Stack Sullivan (1892–1949), and Albert Ellis (1913–). The entire psychoanalytic system in various areas and ways, along with many modern variations and developments, came to recognize strongly that all behavior was symptomatic, and that even illnesses were symptomatic of different kinds of problems. A very comprehensive, but dated, summary of the research and assumptions and principles related to clinical observation is found in Otto Fenichel's book: *The Psychoanalytic Theory of Neurosis* (1945).

Nor was clinical interpretation of empirical experience limited to this form of observation. An entire host of testing instruments, based roughly on psychometric principles, were developed which were termed projective devices. In these testing instruments, such as sentence-completions, drawings, and interpretation of ink blots, the principles of Freudian psychology were applied with the idea that the psychometric production of the individual should be interpreted in terms of underlying dynamics that had to be intuited rather than accepted at face level.

BEHAVIORAL CONTRIBUTIONS TO EMPIRICAL ASSESSMENT

Behavioral interpretations of empirical observation narrowed the range of acceptable observations to specific limited categories of antecedent stimuli and consequent responses. Although early analyses of behavior had included some reference to learning (such as in Aristotle's principles of contiguity, contrast and similarity), a particular thrust towards the simplification of learning principles developed in the first two decades of the twentieth century. This was the movement known as behaviorism. **Behaviorism basically contracted and delimited the principle of correspondence, whereas the Freudian influence expanded it.** This approach in the United States was spearheaded by John B. Watson (1879–1958). Watson was educated in the traditional introspective approach to psychology which was prevalent in the United States at the beginning of the century. But influenced by the studies of the Russian physiologist Ivan Petrovitch Pavlov (1849–1936) in the discovery of the conditioned response, he enunciated this theory in his presidential address to the American Psychological Association in 1915. In the next five years he developed an approach to behavioral analysis of emotions and infants which had a tremendous effect on child-rearing throughout the 1920s and 1930s. Unfortunately, Watson was involved in a scandal in 1920 at the Johns Hopkins University where he was both a professor and chairperson of the department. He entered the advertising business and became identified with business from then until his death.

Others were also greatly influenced. Edward Lee Thorndike (1874–1949) applied many ideas of Watson to his own thinking about stimulus-response bonds in the cortex, and developed three principles of learning: the law of exercise, the law of effect and the law of readiness which were widely applied in education. But the great contemporary influence on the expansion of behaviorism is due to the impact of B. F. Skinner (1904–1990) who through his studies of operant conditioning and his research which continued up to the time of his death had become most heavily identified with behaviorism. In many ways, the behavioral approach has been modified to contemporary social learning theory as represented by Albert Bandura (1925–) and others too numerous to mention here. Behavioral learning theory has had a great influence on school psychology, and a moderate influence on counseling and clinical psychology. Essentially, from our viewpoint of surveying the historical development of assessment, the contributions of behaviorism are focused on a precise limitation of empirical observation. Whereas early empiricism tended to accept what was subjectively observed as an indicator of what existed, and Freudian developments expanded empirical observation to include intuitive judgments about what was inferred, behaviorism carefully and systematically defined the elements of empirical observation which were to be used in making judgments about assessment. These were responses. The response of the organism was seen as a viable observable event which could be directly related to antecedent stimuli. By a careful analysis of the quantity of responses as related to antecedent stimuli, it was then possible to determine a base-rate of behavior. Social learning theory, in more recent years, has tended to modify this position between stimuli and responses, by suggesting that some mediation and self-determination appears to be present in the equation (Bandura, 1978). The impact, however, of behavioral thinking has been very strong on the definition of what constitute legitimate targets for assessment through empirical observation.

PSYCHOPHYSICAL STUDIES

Psychophysical experiments in just noticeable differences led to efforts at the quantification of internal phenomena. The measurement of psychic entities and the development of psychometric theory had their origins in the nineteenth century. German physiological and psychological thought was central in the emergence of the new method. Three movements can be distinguished. The first was the physiological approach of Herman Helmholtz (1821–1895), who as a student and in conjunction with other colleagues vowed once and for all to remove spiritualism from psychology and make it a branch of physiology. He specifically related the explanation of the human mind to physiology and believed that all mental activity could eventually be explained by reliance on physiological methods. Thus, it is not surprising that Helmholtz spent a considerable amount of his professional life examining sensory processes in terms of vision, hearing, taste, and other sensory modalities. The method was basically that of physiology. Second, there was a movement towards the logical analysis of empirical observations of perceptual phenomena, for all German psychologists did not share the radical physiological approach of Helmholtz and his colleagues. Franz Brentano (1838–1917) was the leader of this movement asserting that psychology could become a science by careful empirical observation of perceptual phenomena. Though Brentano maintained that the method of philosophy was the method of science, he strongly advocated a focus on the perceptual properties of human life, and therefore carefully defined the nature of psychic phenomena. He did not disagree at all with the experimentation in sensory processes, but emphasized that the key features to an understanding of human behavior were vested in the act of perception and not in sensation. From such systematic empirical studies Brentano believed certain principles could be generalized which would aid psychology in becoming a science. His work expressed in *Psychologie vom Empirischen Standpunkt* (Psychology from the empirical viewpoint, 1924) influenced the development of Gestalt psychology through his student Stumpf, was instrumental in the development of psychoanalytic theory by Freud who was also his student, and contributed to Husserl's phenomenology (Barclay, 1971). A third point of view which represented a middle-ground between the Helmholtz approach and the Brentano empirical method was that of psychophysical parallelism.

Gustav Theodor Fechner (1801–1887) proposed a psychophysical parallelism which postulated a relationship between mind and body. Fechner argued that sensation itself could not be measured, but that it is possible to observe whether a sensation is present or not, and whether one sensation is greater than, equal to, or less than another sensation. However, because it is possible to measure the stimulus values which create a given sensation, it is also possible to note the differences between sensations.

Reaction-time studies provided a viable method for equating internal changes with responses to external stimuli. Wilhelm Wundt (1832–1920) used these methods and other physiological ones to focus on reaction-time studies (RT). The RT studies were seen as a crucial method for the experimental investigation of mental activity. According to Bringman and Bringman (1980), Wundt distinguished five separate events or processes which occurred in a reaction. "First the stimulus was conducted from sense organ to brain; second the stimulus was perceived, or entered into the range of consciousness (Blickfeld); third, the stimulus was apperceived, or entered into the focus of consciousness (Blickpunkt); fourth, the will acted to initiate a motor movement; and fifth, the movement occurred to produce a reaction" (p. 194). Because it was difficult to do a direct measurement of these processes, a method of subtraction was used to infer RTs. Three methods were devised. The first was the simple RT experiment. The subject reacted as fast as possible to the presentation of a visual stimulus. This was termed by Donders the "s" reaction. A second arrangement, called the "b" reaction, was the multiple choice method. Two stimuli (say, white and black) randomly alternated, each associated with a specific response (say, right hand to white, left hand to black). A third arrangement, the "c" reaction, or simple choice method, randomly alternated two stimuli but only one was associated with a response. Subtracting the simple RT from the multiple choice RT represented the length of time for the subject to discriminate between stimuli and make a choice of response. Subtraction of the simple RT from the simple choice RT, on the other hand, represented the time for the discrimination alone, since the subject did not have to choose between responses. Thus, it was hypothesized to be lengthened in the simple choice experiment over the simple RT experiment only by the addition of a time interval required for the discrimination of which stimulus was presented. This subtraction of the "a" reaction from the "c" reaction gave the absolute recognition time"(Boring, 1950, p. 150).

Wundt accumulated a vast amount of experimental data utilizing this method and instrumentation which he and his students developed to measure RTs. Wundt's influence on the development of an eventual science of psychometry was unparalleled. J. M. Cattell who was one of his students sought early on to study individual differences via this method. Wundt's American students were J. M. Cattell, E. W. Scripture, E. B. Titchener, G. M. Stratton, and R. Pintner. In addition, H. Munsterberg, one of Wundt's German students, also spent many years in the United States and developed some of the first scales to measure vocational aptitudes. The dissemination of method and influence through doctoral students is amazing. Thus Wundt's six American-placed students were the mentors of R. M. Yerkes, K. Dunlap, B. T. Baldwin, R. M. Elliot, R. S. Woodworth, W. F. Dearborn, E. L. Thorndike, V. A. C. Henmon, C. E. Seashore, W. B. Pillsbury, M. Bentley, O. L. Bridgman, J. W. MacFarlane, and D. G. Patterson. These individuals in turn had as students an entire second generation of professors such as C. Louttit, K. Spence, L. V. Carmichael, C. L. Hull, J. McVicker Hunt and others too many to name. Thus from the reaction-time experiments and the physiological laboratory of Wundt, virtually the entire impetus for the extension of reaction time experiments to the observation of units of measurement in attitudes, and self-report measures was accomplished.

STATISTICAL CONTRIBUTIONS AND PSYCHOMETRICS

Statistics applied to measurement theory provided an objective basis for evaluating individual differences. To the last decades of the nineteenth century assessment was confined to empirical observations of individuals or groups, the use of some form of classification system, and a typology derived from that classification system. During the last decade of the nineteenth century, statistics became a major contributor to the development of psychometric theory. Statistics became the tool for the development of a new approach to the measurement of individual differences. The responses which individuals made to an inventory or to questions could be standardized and evaluated along criteria determined by statistics. Psychometrics then became a "scientific" method of evaluating individual differences through responses.

Statistics is said to have been begun by the Belgian mathematician Adolph Quetelet (1796–1874) who applied the theory of Laplace and Gauss about the "normal law of error" to human measurements. Measuring a number of French army men, Quetelet found that their heights were distributed in a bell shaped curve. Sir Francis Galton (1822–1911) applied Quetelet's findings to the distribution of genius, and an associate of his, Karl Pearson (1857–1936) enunciated the formula for correlation in 1904 and 1912. Along with statistics as a tool, evolutionary theory played a large part in the development of psychometrics. Sir Francis Galton was Charles Darwin's cousin. Galton was most impressed with the theory of evolution and encouraged Darwin in many ways. Galton had a wide range of interests and activities, but one of his primary contributions to the development of psychometry was his study of heredity. It was the subject of his most celebrated book *Hereditary Genius* (1972). In this work he argued that hereditary factors were the root cause of most variability in human beings. Galton argued in his work that the classification of human abilities and talents was related to the law of deviations from an average. Galton studied the distribution of grades in a university setting, looked at the distribution of natural ability characteristics over populations, and examined the actuarial data of percentage of gifted children derived from gifted parents. He concluded that the definition of the range of "average" can be determined by looking at the average deviations (we tend now to use the standard deviation instead) from the mean. He also developed the concept of correlation (though it was his associate Karl Pearson who provided the formulae). Galton developed this concept, now represented as "r" as a method of evaluating the relationships between specified ranks of kinship. As he states : "It had appeared from observation, and it was fully confirmed by this theory, that such a thing existed as an index of correlation; that is to say, a fraction, now commonly written r, that connects with closer approximation every value of deviation (from the median) on the part of the subject, with the average of all the associated deviations of the relative as already described. Therefore the closeness of any specified kinship admits of being found and expressed by a single term. If a particular individual deviates so much, the average of the deviations of all his brothers will be a definite fraction of that amount; similarly as to sons, parents, first cousins, etc. Where there is no relationship at all, r becomes equal to 0; when it is so close that Subject and Relative are identical in value, then r = 1. Therefore, the value of r lies in every case somewhere between the extreme limits of 0 and 1" (in J. R. Newman, 1956, II, pp. 1170–1171).

With methods of reaction time and the development of experimental psychological methods, the discovery of methods of evaluating the distribution of characteristics and statistical techniques for handling and interpreting such data, it was only a matter of time before psychometric integration in terms of test items and scales emerged. At the turn of the century and in the beginning decade of this century, Alfred Binet (1857–1911) and his colleagues (Victor Henri and Theodore Simon) in France, conceived the idea of creating norms for certain developmental tasks in accordance with age levels. This method formed the basis of the individual intelligence test which Terman later on put together as the Stanford-Binet. An implicit assumption of the method was that an individual's mental ability could be measured by comparing the level of mental development with the chronological development and out of this came the formula for the intelligence quotient I.Q. = 100 times the product of Mental Age divided by Chronological Age.

The Binet test was introduced into the United States in the latter portion of the first decade of this century. It was used by Goddard to screen immigrants to the United States, and soon became a standard tool for the assessment of intelligence. Moreover, it was seen as a scientific procedure for such assessment. About the same time or shortly before, written tests had become more popular for the assessment of achievement than oral examinations. Although such examinations had been typically graded on scales ranging from 1–5 as in the case of the Reverend George Fisher, an English school master, it was J. M. Rice who popularized the written test as an objective measurement of achievement. The real credit for the development of group testing and the systematic application of psychometric theory must be given to James McKeen Cattell (1860–1944). The son of a college president, he went to Leipzig in 1880 where he became an assistant to Wilhelm Wundt. Cattell sought to study individual differences through reaction-time studies. Wundt was looking more for similarities and general laws, but permitted Cattell to go in this direction for his dissertation. After completing his work in Germany, Cattell came back to the United States where he established the first psychological laboratory at the University of Pennsylvania (1888–1891). It was here that he wrote and published the keystone article of psychometric theory entitled: "Mental Tests and their Measurements." This article appeared in *Mind* (1890). Subsequently, Cattell moved to Columbia where he founded a new laboratory and remained until 1917 when he was fired for urging Congress during the war to respect the rights of conscientious objectors. Almost simultaneously with Cattell's article on psychometric measurement, Joseph Jastro developed some fifteen tests at the University of Wisconsin (1892) and Hugo Munsterberg, (another of Wundt's students), developed some tests for children from his laboratory at Harvard (1891). Subsequently, in 1904 Edward L. Thorndike (a student of Cattell's) published the first book dealing with mental and educational measurements. He made one of the first applications of statistical methods in education. Cliff W. Stone, a pupil of Thorndike, published the first standardized test in arithmetic, the Stone Arithmetic Test, in 1908. Subsequently, with the onset of World War I, efforts were made to provide a paper-pencil equivalent of the individual I.Q. test. The Otis Tests began at this point.

Yerkes, Thorndike, Seashore, Angell and many other psychologists found the need for the assessment of the fitness of soldiers a ready-made opportunity for large scale studies of mental and physical characteristics.

During the 1920s many hundreds of group tests appeared. Some survive to this day and others have disappeared. Not only were group tests developed to measure achievement and intelligence, but others were created to measure personality, interests and physical abilities. Thus the psychometric method had been devised to assess individual characteristics in accordance with an implied correspondence between responses on items and mental states, abilities or capacities. With the development of more psychometric measuring instruments, more statistical studies were also forthcoming. Pearson developed the analysis of variance procedure in relationship to agriculture studies in the 1920s. Thurstone produced the first major effort at factor analysis in the 1930s—a task which took him and his students nearly a year to complete and which now can be done on a high speed computer in a few moments. For the most part, however, statistical analysis depended chiefly on relatively simple procedures such as the determination of measures of central tendency, correlation, simple tests of statistical analysis of difference (T tests and F tests) until the advent of the high speed computer. The reasons for this were that all statistical computations had to be done by hand using a calculator. Calculators at first were heavy and cumbersome machines that were expensive to purchase. Small sample statistics tended to be the chief mode of psychological research. With the advent of the computer it was possible to analyze many thousands of cases on an almost unlimited number of variables with techniques that had been too difficult to do earlier. Analysis of variance became a routine procedure, particularly two and three factorial analyses of variance. Analysis of covariance emerged as a variation on this approach with many other new techniques both in parametric and nonparametric procedures. With advanced technology subsequent developments took place in psychometric sophistication and statistical analysis.

EVALUATION AND THE SOCIAL CONSEQUENCES OF ASSESSMENT: PSYCHOLOGY EMERGES AS THE "SCIENTIFIC" AUTHORITY ON ASSESSMENT

With the advent of testing in the early decades of this century, psychologists had a tool for assessment which placed applied psychology in an important position. Nonetheless, decisions had to be made about how to use these tests, how to integrate them with other data, and what role evaluation played in the whole matter. Evaluation in recent decades has become a separate branch of assessment relating to how systems perform. There are many approaches to current assessment, but in its most general sense evaluation compares some set of standards to actual performance. These standards may be arbitrarily set up or may be arrived at via some consensus of those who are involved in the evaluation. Evaluation can be politically motivated, or it can be concerned with certain questions, but it is virtually always value oriented (Madaus, Scriven & Stufflebeam, 1983). A large number of evaluation studies rely on quantitative methods of making an assessment, and this usually translates into the use of testing. Testing in the sense of objective psychometric measurements became the most usual method of making an evaluation. The desire to evaluate, however, predates the method of psychometry, and in a very real sense the need to evaluate explains the rapid and unprecedented technological development of testing. Evaluation in the nineteenth century became a part of general growth of efforts to reform education, the hospitals, welfare laws and working conditions. One of the earliest efforts at evaluation in the United States was that of Horace Mann and the Boston Board of Education in 1845. Though Cambridge had adopted the use of essay examinations to evaluate students previously, it had been the common practice of all universities from the middle ages on to evaluate students by oral examinations conducted by a panel. Because Horace Mann wished to be able to evaluate the headmasters of various schools, one way that he thought this could be done was by the use of essay examinations. Later in the century, education was another primary focus of such efforts. For example, J. M. Rice attempted to discover whether the study of spelling for longer periods of time resulted in greater learning and retention. However, testing itself became a viable and ostensibly objective method for evaluating performance in many areas. Testing became the scientific means for appraising individual differences. Thus, great efforts were made for the assessment of individual differences prior to the First World War and immediately thereafter.

The basic focus of applied psychological practice in the earl 1900s was related to being a specialist in assessment. The development of the Simon and Binet scales in Paris was quickly assimilated into the mainstream of American culture. Certainly, Simon and Binet could not have guessed the enterprising potential of their technique (and in point of fact they cautioned against its use as an absolute criterion of intelligence). In the United States four factors have to be taken into consideration: (A) the nature of psychology programs; (B) the impact and belief in Social Darwinism; (C) the immigration movement; and (D) the expansion of public education. All of these factors played an important role in the development of applied psychological services.

Characteristics of Early Assessment Practice. In the early decades of this century, the universities of the United States made an important contribution to the development of assessment technology. This was not because there were many of them, or because training programs existed, but rather that the psychologist professors were a closely-knit elite group who governed access to education in psychology. It should be pointed out that in most instances in those days psychology was still considered a branch of philosophy and housed in those departments. There were only a few major universities and most of them had one primary psychologist with a number of assistants, much in the model of the European University. Experimental methods were being introduced from Europe, largely in the model of Wundtian studies, but also with much emphasis on introspection and the analysis of personal conscious phenomena. Individuals such as William James, John Dewey, Edward Bradford Titchener, William R. McDougall, and Edward Lee Thorndike were among the key psychologists in this country. Within the small circuit of academic psychology, most of the professors were known to each other, and their students formed a rather elite circle of colleagues. The impact of German psychology and physiology was very strong, and this was also mediated by the English tradition of Alexander Bain, Herbert Spencer, Lloyd Morgan, and J. M. Baldwin. With the increasing need for expanding public education and for providing specific kinds of training for different types of individuals, testing in terms of intelligence assessment, achievement and vocational placement became very important. Testing was an important concept in the expansion of John Dewey's ideas about education, and particularly those of Edward Lee Thorndike.

Evolutionary theory, and particularly Spencer's Social Darwinism had a strong influence on the thinking of that day. Testing became a tool for placement and control of selected groups. An early conclusion about psychometric testing was that it provided an objective means for making evaluative judgments. Unlike many of the typical concerns about introspection and consciousness, it had some practical consequences for psychologists interested in advancing the cause of psychology or social issues. It was therefore used under many circumstances to provide evidence that a certain approach was "right" or "wrong," or that a movement ought to be "changed" or "corrected." Many of the early evaluation studies inspired by the technology had political or other motives (Madaus, Scriben et al., 1983). Taking a cue from evolutionary theory, instincts and irrational urges were considered to be common properties of both man and animal. In the early 1890s G. Stanley Hall enunciated his recapitulation theory in which he postulated that a child in the process of development recapitulates the whole history of man. These ideas joined to the philosophy of the scientific method advocated by John Stuart Mill, and the social thinking of Herbert Spencer, formed an approach to social evaluation and action which postulated that just as man's biological evolution was guided by laws of the survival of the fittest, so social evolution, and progress towards wealth and the good life, came to those who by virtue of inheritance and effort came out on top. Scientific method, and particularly the use of testing in evaluation provided the means for both assessing what needed to be changed and how it could be changed.

This thinking was appropriate to the United States whose origins had been as a frontier relying on pragmatic problem solving. It was particularly actualized by the flood of immigrants in the last decade of the nineteenth century. The immigration movement of the 1880s and 1890s brought thousands of immigrants from Southern Europe and Asia Minor. Although these immigrants provided cheap labor for the increasing economic marketplace, there was concern about their specific cultural patterns differing from those earlier immigrants of Irish, German, and Scandinavian origin. The concern was that they might affect traditional American values in a negative way. When Binet's test became available, a number of psychologists became interested in it as a means of assessing and classifying individuals. Lewis Terman at Stanford, Robert Yerkes at Harvard, and Henry Goddard in New Jersey were three proponents. Kamin (1975) states that these three pioneers in the testing movement shared a number of common sociopolitical views which included Social Darwinism and eugenics. Thus Terman in discussing the "Menace of Feeble-Mindedness" (Terman, 1917, p. 7) wrote: "Only recently have we begun to recognize how serious a menace it is to the social, economic, and moral welfare of the state. It is responsible . . . for the majority of cases of chronic and semi-chronic pauperism. Organized charities . . . often contribute to the survival of individuals who would otherwise not be able to live and reproduce . . . If we would preserve our state for a class of people worthy to possess it, we must prevent, as far as possible, the propagation of mental degenerates, the increasing spawn of degeneracy." **Thus it is apparent that a theme present in Terman's thinking is that there could not be social equality without mental equality.**

Henry Goddard was taken with this problem and believed also that there could be no social equality for people of different mental abilities. In 1912 the U.S. Public Health Service invited Goddard to Ellis Island to apply the new mental tests to the arriving immigrants. Kamin remarks: "Goddard reported that based upon his examination of the great mass of average immigrants 83% of Jews, 80% of Hungarians, 79% of Italians, and 87% of the Russians were feeble minded" (Kamin, 1975, p. 319). On the basis of such findings Goddard was able to report that substantial numbers of undesirable immigrants were turned back. Robert M. Yerkes then with this background collaborated in the testing of nearly 2,000,000 draftees in World War I. The National Academy of Sciences then published findings about the recruits indicating that blacks scored lower than whites, that recruits from Latin and Slavic countries were low and that Polish recruits did not score significantly higher than blacks (Kamin, 1975, p. 320).

The work of Terman, Goddard and Yerkes was really coalesced in a book by Carl Brigham, then Assistant Professor of Psychology at Princeton (*A Study of American Intelligence*, 1923). Brigham reanalyzed the army data on immigrants and found that immigrants who had been in the United States 16 to 20 years before testing were as bright as native-born Americans. Those who had been in the country only for a few years were virtually feeble-minded. What this seemed to indicate to Brigham was the superiority of immigrants who had come from northern Europe (Scandinavia, Germany, etc.), and the inferiority of those immigrants from Latin, Slavic or Asian backgrounds. A logical conclusion for him was that there were racial differences in ability, though a more obvious one would have been that the earlier Scandinavians had accommodated to American culture due to their longer stay here. Brigham appears to have been instrumental in the passage of new and restrictive immigration quotas in 1924. Moreover, quotas were set at levels of the census of 1890 (before the greatest immigration from southern Europe). Kamin (1975) remarks that these laws were in part responsible for the curtailing of immigration to the United States during the Nazi persecution. Another by-product of these findings related to the passage of permissive or mandatory sterilization laws which could be applied to individuals identified through the new scientific process of testing as mentally defective. Given the vagaries of diagnostic judgment today, it is a very sobering consideration to think of what happened to many individuals certified as mentally defective in the 1920s. Naturally, as the children of these immigrants crowded into the cities of the United States, it became necessary to consider new approaches to education, reserving traditional education for those who could benefit from it, and developing "training" programs for others. Terman referring to the poor test performance of a pair of Indian and Mexican children wrote: "Children of this group should be segregated in special classes. They cannot master abstractions, but they can often be made efficient workers. There is no possibility at present of convincing society that they should not be allowed to reproduce . . . they constitute a grave problem because of their unusually prolific breeding" (Terman, 1916, p. 6).

Special testing clinics and facilities became an agent of social reform. Although some of the attitudes expressed by the pioneer users of intelligence tests may seem quite racist today, they were actually concerned about many social issues. It was believed that education facilities could be related to the needs of various groups. Thus Thorndike believed that children of lower intelligence should have a different kind of education, and he even believed that the education of males and females should be different. The testing movement also coincided with considerable interest in mental health, the reform of welfare laws, and the recognition of the need for vocational testing and advising. One way this need was met was to establish local clinics for testing purposes. According to Gray (1963) there were 220 cities in the United States with special classes by 1911. And many of the children in these classes were tested in accordance with the rationale and thinking of Goddard, Terman, and Brigham.

Although the views and attitudes of some of these early leaders of testing may seem extreme and prejudicial today, readers should recognize the very different background and thrust of these psychologists. In the minds of many of the highly educated people of that day democracy was essentially an elitist system in which knowledgeable and financially responsible individuals would make decision for the masses. Blacks could not vote in the South, and women everywhere had no vote. Moreover, the great flood of immigrants created foreign-speaking ghettos in most of the large cities. Severe religious conflict existed between Protestants and Catholics particularly in the development of education. Cultural traditions were involved in education and a heavy proportion of the later immigrants were Catholic rather than Protestant as most of the Scandinavians were. Though Goddard had many negative findings to report from his studies of immigrants at the beginning of this century, the same and worse attitudes had been shown towards the Irish in Boston fifty years earlier. Egalitarianism was definitely not a realistic component in American society at that time. The example of the French Revolution indicated to most educated leaders and statesmen that the outcomes egalitarianism were chaos, political disaster, and economic failure. It has been by a slow and deliberate process over 70 or 80 years (many times characterized by violence and civil disobedience) that blacks' and women's rights have come to be recognized, and that barriers to civil rights have been removed in most of the legal areas, if not in the hearts of Americans. Finally, it ought to be recognized that early thinking about the nature of intelligence as measured by intelligence tests, despite the warning of Binet, tended to consider the I.Q. as a measure of intellectual potential. The joy over having a tool that provided some kind of an objective index of intellectual functioning, overwhelmed the caution that ought to have been associated with such measurements. Those who popularized the tests of intelligence and used them, frequently tended to generalize beyond the information they had.

THE DEVELOPMENT OF PROFESSIONAL IDENTITIES AND MORE CRISIS

Subspecialties in psychology developed in response to special needs, professional training programs, and certification criteria: the development of clinical psychology. The political origin of the use of testing in the United States was followed in recent decades by a series of continuing expansions wherein psychology attempted to define itself in terms of clinical practice, and to apply itself to a number of specialties such as school and counseling psychology. One of the first efforts to systematize the functioning of the psychologist in assessment procedures was that of Williamson and Darley at the University of Minnesota (1937) who developed a paradigm for using interview and test data to provide a diagnosis-prognosis-treatment model. They also grouped common problems of students (since their focus was on student personnel services) around topics such as: (1) personality problems, (2) educational problems, (3) vocational problems, (4) financial problems, and (5) health problems. To be sure earlier efforts had been made to systematize the use of clinical testing procedures, but the application of the various intelligence tests, e.g. the Stanford-Binet and the earliest version of the Wechsler tests, the Wechsler-Bellevue, was slow in developing.

After World War II, there was a great need to organize and standardize the applied professional areas of psychology. This was crucial because universities did not have programs which were defined by national criteria and the press of many veterans into education made it imperative to organize the disciplines better. The Boulder Conference was called in 1949 to define clinical psychology as a professional discipline.

Though there had been considerable growth of tools in psychology such as the projective technique of the Rorschach, modifications of the original Wechsler, and many other techniques such as word-association procedures, sentence-completions, most of the interpretive rules for these instruments were obtained by what could only be called "clinical intuition" often learned by clinical apprenticeship. At the same time there had been massive expansion in the use of measurements in education extending to all kinds of achievement and intelligence tests as well as aptitude tests. The integration of these assessment devices was not spelled out in any specific way other than efforts such as those of Williamson and Darley who attempted to identify the kinds of problems which students had and how various sources of information could be put together. Bordin also at this time attempted to identify the sources of problems which ought to figure in while attempting to arrive at a diagnosis (1946). He felt that five categories could be established: (1) dependence problems, (2) lack of information, (3) self-conflict, (4) choice anxiety, and finally (5) no problem—which was a catch-all category. Pepinsky (1948) also refined the Williamson categories and Bordin categories as a model for clinical counseling. The major problem, however, was to determine how these devices and methods could be utilized in clinical psychology. Since much of the focus of clinical psychology was on psychotherapy and assessment was seen as an ancillary means to determining the course of psychotherapy, a considerable emphasis in the Boulder conference was on this topic of psychotherapy. So Raimy (1950, p. 93) could describe the entire psychotherapy process as: "an undefined technique applied to unspecified problems with unpredictable outcomes. For this technique we recommend rigorous training."

What Raimy was unquestionably considering in this statement was the variety of individualistic inputs which must be weighed and interpreted in terms of clinical decision making. Unfortunately, the specific criteria for decision making were in part inherent in the nature of tests such as projective techniques, and in part acquired under the tutelage of other clinicians. In a very real sense one of the problems of early clinical psychology was related to deciding what epistemological weighting should be given to empirical data, psychometric data, and intuitive data derived from projective assessment. The position of the clinical psychologist was heavily related to psychotherapy in mental institutions, veterans hospitals, and clinics associated with medical facilities. The specific role fixed for the clinical psychologist in these settings was as an expert in assessment, and particularly in the use of individual diagnostic techniques. Over a period of several decades since the Boulder Conference, the establishment of Division 15 in the American Psychological Association, the implementation of APA accreditation programs and the development of the diplomate status, has tended to provide a consistent framework for the training and evaluation of clinical psychologists.

School psychology had a functional beginning early in the century, but was formalized in the 1950s as the practice of clinical psychology in the schools. From the evidence that over 220 cities had clinics for the assessment of children within the first decade of this century, it is apparent that most of the early psychologists functioned as school psychologists. As was the case with clinical psychology, the specifics of training programs were very haphazard. Individuals often learned about tests on the job, and even the Binet tests could be administered (and were) by ancillary staff. The definition of clinical function which resulted from the Boulder Conference certainly influenced the Thayer Conference which was convened in 1954 to determine the nature of school psychology. At the Thayer conference the school psychologist was described primarily as the clinical psychologist in the schools. As a consequence the definition of psychotherapy practice was transferred intact from clinical psychology to school psychology. The rapid formal growth of school psychology has been noted by Meacham and Trione (1967). In 1950 there were 519 school psychologists in the United States. By 1960 the number had grown to 2,836. By 1980 there were approximately 17,000 belonging to the formal APA Division 16 organization or the larger National Association of School Psychologists (NASP).

School psychology has grown through formal state certification laws, the initializing of university training programs, and the requirements of PL 94–142 dealing with the rights and needs of special education children. For the most part school psychologists are still held mainly to the testing of children for placement in special education or the coping with problems of a behavioral or emotional nature. In the last few decades many legal decisions have been made by courts which have changed the functioning of school psychologists drastically. School psychology leaders urge the wider use of school psychologists, the implementation of more consultation and evaluation procedures, and a focus on psychoeducational interventions. A recent plenary conference of school psychologists at Olympia, Wisconsin, focused on future scenarios of school psychology practice, but without any firm directions enunciated. Perhaps the most drastic change is in what constitutes the client of the school psychologist. In the past the client has most often been seen as the individual child. But today, it is apparent that not only the child, but the classroom, the teachers, administration and parents are all part of the larger system of education. Though recognition of this role has been long in coming in terms of administrative awareness, the school psychologist is more and more viewed as a learning expert in the education system rather than an individual clinical therapist in the schools.

Counseling psychology emerged out of a merger of the earlier vocational counseling function, counselor-education programs, and professional interest groups. Counseling psychology has been a relatively new development in professional psychology. For a number of decades counseling psychologists tended to have a vocational psychology affiliation and to be identified with this area. This influence stemmed from the work of Frank Parsons in developing vocational assessment counseling. In addition, many of the present counseling psychology programs had at least part of their origins in the counselor education programs which were initiated after Sputnik in the mid-1950s. Congress, stunned by the Russian accomplishment, believed that American children needed more guidance and counseling, specifically in technological and scientific fields. It enacted the National Defense Education Act which led to the establishment of hundreds of counseling programs geared initially to the training of masters' degree school counselors, and later to doctoral level counselor educators. For the most part, unlike clinical and school psychology training programs, the counselor education programs deemphasized the role of assessment. The reason for this deemphasis was that in the 1950s a significant break-away from the traditional format of psychotherapy occurred with the publication *Client-Centered Therapy* (1951) by Carl Rogers. Rogers denied the value of diagnosis at all, suggesting that it created negative expectations in the counselor and imposed labels on the client. Eventually, the Rogers indictment of diagnosis extended not only to individual tests, but to all measurement instruments. As a consequence, testing was viewed as antithetical to holding "unconditional positive regard" for the client. Rogers believed, much as Rousseau had believed several hundred years earlier, that the negative expectations of society were the sources of many problems in individuals. Rogers also believed that tests produced negative expectations, and therefore he could see no real use for them. He argued that through a supportive and accepting stance from a counselor, individuals could solve their own problems. Though it is unlikely that Rogers ever held that no measurement should be used at any time, this was the message accepted by the proponents of the so-called nondirective therapy. In the twenty years after Rogers broke with traditional psychotherapy, a variety of alternative systems grew and swept across the country.

Tacitly, many professional psychologists who had in-depth training in testing believed that if masses of teachers needed to be trained for guidance counseling in a few months (such as in the summer NDEA Institutes) or over a year, probably teaching them to listen and be supportive was the best possible tactic. Approaches such as those of rational-emotive therapy, Adlerian counseling, transactional analysis, and Gestalt therapy had little or limited use for any kind of product diagnosis, though transactional analysis utilized a kind of simplified psychoanalytic process evaluation (Shertzer and Stone, 1980). Newer movements such as existentialism emphasized process development, even denying the value of *a priori* human structure as a determinant in problem or crisis analysis (Barclay, 1971d).

In addition, in the 1960s there was a revival of behaviorism triggered in part by the work of B. F. Skinner, but more directly related to the social learning and behavior modification approaches of Wolpe, Mischel, Bandura and Krumboltz. Behavior modification had little use for traditional psychometric or empirical measures. As a consequence, most counseling programs (certainly those in counselor and guidance training) tended to deemphasize the role of diagnosis. Other than trait-factor approaches and eclectic ones in which detailed analysis was unimportant, Shertzer and Stone (1980) assert that of 22 known counseling theories only two make even limited use of testing—not to speak of diagnosis. Moreover, with the emergence of counseling psychology programs in the last decade or so, there has been a kind of eclectic effort to build a bridge between the more traditional clinical programs and the more group-measurement oriented counselor education programs. Counseling psychology particularly has suffered from an identity crisis as it has emerged as a speciality focusing on normals rather than abnormals, positive trait utilization rather than negative deficit coping, and process rather than product outcomes in therapy.

Counseling psychology has also a Division in APA (Division 17), but this division was established later than either clinical or school psychology. Moreover, the guidelines for accreditation of counseling psychology programs are comparatively new by comparison with those for clinical programs. One of the major problems that confronts counseling psychology has been one of identity and discrimination between clinical on the one hand and school psychology on the other. It has also been very difficult to separate the technique-oriented tradition of guidance from the thrust of counseling psychology. Holland (1982) pointed out with regard to counseling psychology that there is a wide range of opinion about goals, that publications lack cohesiveness, and "mirror confusion about disagreement." He indicated that the actual work of the counseling psychologists is at variance with any old or new definition of role. According to Holland a definition for today would be "We work anywhere, we use almost any technique (parenthetically, if you will provide a workshop we will also add new techniques to our resources), and we will serve any and all populations" (Holland, 1982, p. 8).

This brief summary of professional development in this chapter has focused chiefly on the role of assessment. Unfortunately, the role of assessment in these three specialities is not yet adequately defined. Much of the control of what psychologists do is related to those agencies and institutions that pay for services. Clinical psychology is particularly dependent on psychiatric classification systems and psychiatry. School psychology has been severely reined in from the work of learning consultation in the schools to focus on legislative mandates to test special education children. Counseling psychology has not yet determined whether students in this field need to be trained in assessment in identical or different ways from clinical psychologists. But the reality of internship placements, where counseling psychologists are expected to know and be able to use the same methods as clinicians, together with recent thinking in professional psychology, have tended to favor a common core of testing and assessment work for all professional psychologists.

THE ATTACK ON TESTING

Testing has come under attack by many different groups during the past twenty years. Even the traditional use of group tests for the measurement of achievement and aptitude characteristics came under tremendous attack in the early 1960s. To be sure some real flaws had been found in tests in terms of personality prying and experimental studies which were not sound. However, the entire testing movement was attacked as biased against minorities and ill-advised. In some instances testing was seen as a communist plot to subvert the morality of youth. Others saw it as an instrument of "progressive education." Though psychologists attempted to put the record right by answering the more absurd charges and citing the cultural basis of testing and need for care in test analysis (Barclay, 1968b), the problems continued. Some counseling psychologist educators attempted to point out the dangers to counselors who over-extend themselves on the basis of incomplete data or a preoccupation with morbidity rather than positive aspects (Brammer and Shostrum, 1977). But there were some in the very ranks of counseling psychology who argued that the marriage between testing and counseling had not and would not be meaningfully consummated (Goldman, 1972). Thus generations of psychologists being trained for clinical, school, or counseling practice have found the situation of systematic training in assessment and diagnosis extending from complete rejection, to reliance only on psychometric instruments of unquestionable validity and reliability, to a kind of eclectic and clinical intuitionism.

Testing developed into a gatekeeper role in American society. Testing became big business in the last forty years. Virtually every person in the United States has had to take standardized tests in achievement and intelligence. Tests are required for entrance into all universities and colleges. Tests are required for qualification in all of the professional schools, both on the entry level and on the certification level. Tests are used in the military. They are used in industry. They are used in government. And many times in all of these settings they have been misused, misinterpreted and considered to be absolute measures of talent, ability, or whatever. More recently, testing results have been used to indicate that education at all levels is doing a poor job. As a result, it is no surprise that the use of tests as an exclusive "gatekeeper" function for admission to higher education, specialized professional programs, and as a criterion of effectiveness has been increasingly condemned.

Court decisions have modified and restricted the unlimited use of testing. The political turmoil over the consequences of testing in the United States has been followed in recent decades by a series of continuing legal decisions and legislative efforts which have brought sustained pressure on psychologists in every area and specialty. Some of the landmark decisions are very important to assessment. The case of *Brown v. Board of Education* (1954, U.S. Supreme Court) was a crucial one since this decision emphasized the right of all children to an education, regardless of race. The importance of this decision is that for the first time education became a right of the child in all states. The Constitution says nothing about education being an "inalienable right." Education for generations was a matter of state entitlement, and very often various states simply declared a handicapped child ineligible for education and excluded the child from further education. The case of *Hobson v. Hansen* (1967 District of Columbia) was related to minority children who were not provided adequate education through a process of homogenous grouping or tracking. This procedure was declared illegal. In the decisions of *Arreola v. the Santa Ana Board of Education* (1968 California), and *Diana v. California State Board of Education* (1970, California), it was mandated that minority children could not be placed in special education

settings without the full participation of parents and comprehensive evaluation, and that where such evaluations were done, they must utilize a primary
or native language rather than English. Another important decision was that
of *Larry P. v. Riles* (1981, California). In this case it was argued that there
were a disproportionate number of black students in classes for the mentally
retarded and that such placements resulted from standardized tests (including group and individual intelligence tests). The judgment of the court was
that such tests could not be used in California to place black children in
special classes for the mentally retarded without court authorization for the
use of specific tests. Questions of due process for minorities, the validity of
tests used in testimony before the courts, and education of the handicapped
are just a few of the areas in which there have been extended controversies
about psychological practice and its consequences.

In summary then, it has been our intent in this section of this chapter to
provide the reader with some background information on why the question
of assessment has had such a varied reputation. The arguments have been
presented that the very concepts of assessment and diagnosis have had a
mixed background and evolution. Tests have been viewed by many unedu-
cated people and also by some of those who use them, as supreme criteria
of ability, intelligence, personality, and competence. Moreover, with the
breaking-away of Rogers from traditional psychotherapy, there have been
many and varied efforts to popularize psychotherapy (not indicated here as
a bad feature at all) but which have involved process approaches that do not
utilize testing or assessment except in minor ways. Finally it has been the
argument that testing itself had a background which was strongly shaped by
Social Darwinism and "gatekeeping" functions.

ASSESSMENT AND THE NEED FOR A NEW PARADIGM

In the past two chapters we have traced the evolution of assessment paradigms from primitive thinking to rational inference to scientific judgments.
As one paradigm gave way to another, there was a period of crisis in which
the paradigm was viewed as inadequate. We are currently in a state of crisis
relative to the existing nineteenth and early twentieth century paradigm.
There are some substantial reasons why the current paradigm is inadequate:
first, the current paradigm is largely based on a positivistic-evolutionary
determinism in which hereditary and environmental components are viewed
to interact in a necessary and efficient causal relationship. The consequences
of such a paradigm lead to testing, classification and placement. Testing then
becomes a tool for classification, placement and control. If there is a necessary and efficient causal connection between hereditary and environmental
components, then what will be will be. It is for this reason that Rychlak

(1977) singled out the efficient causal relationship as a critical flaw in the current scientific paradigm. It is also because of such thinking that there is a basic pessimism about preventive interventions (Albee, 1982).

A second fault of the current assessment paradigm is that rests too heavily on psychometric testing. We are currently fully aware of the fact that empirical methods, psychometric findings, and intuitive judgments need to be integrated in some comprehensive manner. In addition, there is a tremendous amount of interest and desire on the part of education, industry, the military and many other professional sources to identify skills, competency, and performance characteristics of individuals. These latter assessment characteristics are not identifyable in a one-to-one correspondence with psychometrics.

Third, with the tremendous advance in computer technology, there has been an unprecedented development of computer scoring and interpreting programs for psychological tests, interview data, and more. Most of the scoring routines of these programs are correct, but the inferences they make are often wrong and labeling in their content. A contributing factor to the poor or outright wrong inferences drawn in these programs (as well as in individual usage) stems from the fact that most test users think that all trait characteristics exist on an equal basis, or at least that the chief way to interpret a test is based on a profile analysis (which generally treats all test variables as equal). This approach is used, for example, by Millon (1981) in his rationale for several new personality assessment instruments. The alternative approach is to view traits as related hierarchically to other major factors or components. In the chapters which follow, there are some major assumptions made about assessment. It is hoped that these assumptions will contribute to the development of a new and relevant paradigm for assessment. They are as follows: first, a new paradigm of assessment must be built on an indeterminist position relative to the effects of heredity and environment. In addition, both the structural and control hierarchies in human beings must be considered as valid foci for assessment. What this means is that insofar as assessment theory is concerned, the nature of the structural endowment, the effects of learning, and the control hierarchy of cognition and volition must be considered in human assessment. To take this approach to assessment is to state that behavioral responses are important, but not the sole components of assessment. In like manner, what may be inferred relative to ego states, conscious or unconscious goal-seeking, must be related to empirical observation as well. To believe in an absolute determinism either on the part of behavior or unconscious factors is to close the door to preventive interventions.

Fourth, a new paradigm of assessment should consider the classification of dimensions rather than categories, with the recognition that many indi-

Table 4-1 **Selected Notable Events in Recent Assessment History**

1860–1900

Adolph Quetelet applies "normal law of error" to human measurements.

Wilhelm Wundt initiates reaction-time experiments in Leipzig.

Gustav Theodor Fechner proposes a method for evaluation of psychophysical parallelism.

James McKeen Cattell establishes first testing laboratory in the United States at the University of Pennsylvania. He also publishes first definitive article on mental tests and their measurement.

Joseph Jastro and Hugo Munsterberg develop tests for children.

Francis Galton initiates scientific study of individual differences in hereditary studies of genius.

Franz Brentano asserts that the proper object of psychological investigation is perception rather than sensation.

Sigmund Freud develops method of psychoanalysis based on physics model of brain. He defines mind as mechanism for channelizing free flowing energy in terms of socialization.

1901–1920

Karl Pearson enunciates formula for correlation.

Theodore Simon and Alfred Binet develop first calibrated individual intelligence test for screening mentally retarded in Paris.

Goddard and Terman popularize the use of the Stanford-Binet modification of Simon's and Binet's test.

Edward Lee Thorndike publishes the first book dealing with mental and educational measurements.

Clifford W. Stone publishes the first arithmetic achievement test.

C. G. Jung develops a word-association test for the exploration of unconscious phenomena.

Psychologists use the Army Alpha and Beta for the first widespread evaluation of army recruits in W.W.I.

Over 220 cities have testing centers and classes for special students.

The U.S. Congress passes restrictive immigration quotas based on testing data & testimony of psychologists.

1921–1940

Herman Rorschach publishes *Psychodiagnostics* describing the use of ink blot analysis for personality assessment.

J. M. Cattell establishes the Psychological Corporation for the development and marketing of tests.

Achievement school batteries proliferate.

E. K. Strong publishes the first test for evaluating vocational interests.

Table 4-1   (Continued)

Moreno develops the technique of sociometry for evaluating social interactions.

Edgar Doll develops the Vineland Social Maturity Scale to evaluate the social characteristics of mentally retarded students.

David Wechsler develops the first individual intelligence test based on statistical inferences.

Fisher proposes the statistical procedure of analysis of variance based on agricultural studies.

Henry Murray and others develop the Thematic Apperception Test.

Lauretta Bender introduces the Bender-Visual-Motor Gestalt Test for assessing maturation, brain damage, and personality.

Thurstone develops and demonstrates the technique of factor analysis.

1941–1960

Educational Testing Service is formed.

The army studies on the assessment of men reflect advances in assessment methods.

Paul Meehl and L. J. Cronbach propose concept of construct validity and multitrait, multimethod data analysis. Cronbach particularly stresses role of testing in decision making.

Guilford suggests three-dimensional "Structure of intellect".

H. J. Eyesenck provides evidence of the existence of broad temperament groupings of introversion and extroversion based both on physiological studies and psychometric ones.

Hathaway and McKinley develop the Minnesota Multiphasic Personality Inventory.

First organizational conference of Clinical Psychology held at Boulder.

First organizational conference on School Psychology held (Thayer Conference).

U.S. Congress passes N.D.E.A. Act supporting extensive training of counselors throughout the nation.

Carl Rogers attacks the use of testing and diagnosis as detrimental to individuals.

1961–1985

Entrance examinations such as the American College Testing Program and the Graduate Record Examination used in a widespread manner throughout the United States.

Behavioral assessment and performance assessment methods are developed.

Criterion-referenced tests are posed as an alternative to norm-referenced ones.

Herbert Walberg and J. R. Barclay provide first testing methods to evaluate classroom climate.

J. Royce indentifies superstructure of cognitive and emotive characteristics based on invariant factors.

Table 4-1   **(Continued)**

Eugene Glass develops theory and method of meta-analysis to make inferences about large numbers of studies.

Federal court decisions restrict the use of testing in many ways.

Systematic development of expectation theory and attribution theory influence motivation in assessment.

Computer technology for administering and scoring many intelligence, achievement, personality, and vocational tests is developed. This first occurs with regard to large mainframe computers and is extended to use of microcomputers.

viduals at times show irrational and abnormal behavior. Further such an approach to assessment should be related to the development of hierarchies of personal and social traits and performance competencies with the recognition that a variety of approaches or methods may converge on meaningful characteristics not only for assessment, but for preventive interventions.

Last, a new paradigm should be committed to merging psychometric, empirical and behavioral-performance characteristics in a comprehensive technology which is both parsimonious and susceptible to treatment alternatives. Most particularly such a technology should provide evidence of the nature of inferences made, and should be committed to an ever-increasing set of studies to document the reasonableness and efficacy of such inferences.

CHAPTER V

Empirical Methods of Observation

Motto said to be in letters of gold on the walls of Pavlov's laboratory outside Leningrad: "Observation and again observation."

This chapter focuses on the nature of empirical observation, distinguishing between unstructured, behavioral, and clinical types of observation. Each of these adds further dimensions to the task of seeing and classifying phenomena. From these observations and the mind's ability to categorize them come the inferences which provide the grist for the logic of assessment. The assumptions that alternative theories bring to interviewing reflect varying foci on the interview process. Knowing such assumptions enriches the total impact of theory on interviewing.

INTRODUCTION

Anyone who starts on a trip usually has a plan of how to proceed, what roads to take, what signs to look for, and what sequence will lead to the destination. This plan of action represents a kind of cognitive map which is developed to make traveling most economical and direct. Cognitive planning or mapping also takes place in a number of other circumstances. If, for example, I need a particular kind of sheet metal screw for something I am putting together, I know where to go in the garage and how to search for what I want. In life it is helpful to have a plan for a variety of situations. Thus, for example, if I am sent into a room to get "something," just anything will do. But if I am sent into a room to get a white box, then I have something specific to look for. However, if the room is filled with white boxes, then it is helpful to know that the particular white box I need has a red mark on it. In assessment, there are a variety of goals that relate to the process. In the first chapter, the hierarchy of assessment constructs was mentioned. We can look at responses, skills, traits, aptitudes, temperament components, and cognition. All of these relate to the assessment of individual differences. In addition, there are many effects of past experience, home conditions, environment, and learning that affect the entire process of assessment. Because assessment constructs are organized in a hierarchy, it is helpful in the process of developing skills in assessment to keep that hierarchy always in mind.

In this chapter the focus will be on interviewing and what has been termed empirical observation. It should be noted, however, that the use of empirical is in the older sense of that word. Empirical in much of contemporary psychological language means based on observation or experimental design data. It thus often includes any data that relate to scientifically observable phenomena. In the sense that it is used in this chapter and elsewhere in the book, it is concerned more specifically with perceptual data obtained by direct observation rather than testing data.

The first part of this chapter will explain the nature of empirical observation and the various levels of sophistication involved in behavioral, phenomenological, and clinical observations. A second portion of the chapter will deal with the interpretation of problems and concentrate on the problem identified together with some assumptions about interviewing and integration of information.

TYPES OF EMPIRICAL OBSERVATION

There are three types of empirical observations. The first is what we have referred to as unstructured, the second is behavioral, and the third is clinical. Both behavioral and clinical observations are structured in the sense that they bring to the observational setting some specific *a priori* limitations or assumptions.

Unstructured or Common Empirical Observations. By far the most common form of observation is unstructured. In some instances this has been referred to as naive observation, though terming it naive is erroneous. Our very survival as human beings depends on our ability to observe, and by no means can it be considered naive or simplistic. By "common" observation is meant the conclusions which we ordinarily infer from sensory experience, perception, and the entire residue of our memory and learned skills. Typically this form of empirical observation has been faulted for problems of observer focus, bias, and interpretation. Regardless of the conditions which may hold for one person's observations of another, the consensus which comes from many individuals observing another usually results in a high level of congruence. Moreover, since most individuals in observing others do so over a period of time, the observations then become more reliable as they are extended and repeated.

Structured Behavioral Observations. Structured empirical observations are those which are delimited by a specific set of assumptions about the nature or interpretation of observational phenomena. This is often the approach that is taught by behaviorism. Behaviorism postulates that a considerable portion of behavior is the product of learning. In very concrete ways responses of the organism lead to consequences which may be reinforcing or punishing. From the research which began with John B. Watson, developed further under B. F. Skinner and many modern researchers, the basic targets of behavioral observation are responses and stimuli. Antecedent stimuli or events are looked at carefully in terms of how they relate to responses of the organism, and then to the consequences that the organism experiences. Thus for many behaviorists, the approach is summarized in the ABC paradigm: antecedents, behavior, and consequences. However, rarely do those advocating the behavioral approach or the social learning approach limit their observations absolutely to this paradigm. The paradigm is the focus, or to use a Gestalt term, the field, but other observations, which can be compared to the ground, are also made.

The intent of this deliberate restriction of empirical observation is to determine what is called a base-rate of behavior. By carefully counting behavioral events along with their consequences, it is possible to obtain a frequency of events or behaviors that constitute a base level of such behaviors or events. For example, if an individual is concerned about cigarette smoking, keeping an accurate self-record of the number of cigarettes smoked in a day may provide objective data about the frequency of smoking. Likewise if an individual complains of being depressed, having this person keep a record of times, days, and locations when depression occurs may provide information very helpful to further assessment. Thus a college student may indicate that he feels most depressed on weekends when his roommate has gone home.

Behavioral approaches to empirical observation stress the focus on the ABC paradigm because it is directly related to the questions: where? when? how often? and with whom? These questions can be answered more directly by behavioral techniques and often after a complete assessment of these questions has been completed, some clear inferences exist as to the question why? Moreover, the accumulation of base rates of behaviors, either through a self-report, or by observations from others, such as peers, has been found to relate quite well to psychometric observations. The relationship between repeated observation of behavior and psychometric traits has been documented by Epstein (1980) in three studies where he examined correlations between behavioral data and psychometric findings. He found that the correlation between specific psychometric traits with behavioral observations, carefully made, increased directly in proportion to the number of observations made. Thus after a number of days of such behavioral observations, correlations with psychometric traits reached the magnitude of the 70s or 80s in many instances. Empirical observations taken only once by one individual may not correlate with psychometric dimensions at all, but taken by the same observer over a period of time, and using carefully determined behavioral ratings, they often show strong relationships. Likewise, when many individuals observe another, there are results which generally show the similarity of observational conclusions between individuals.

Clinical Empirical Observations. In contrast to the behavioral focus that tends to restrict empirical observation to specified responses and stimuli, clinical observations concentrate more on the interpretation of responses, or dynamic inferences about what lies behind the responses in terms of ego control, volition, utilization of cognitive resources, and environmental influences.

Clinical inferences often drawn from insights derived from phenomenological thinking and Freudian theory expand the range of observations. Clinical observations often postulate that behaviors are symptoms of underlying problems. Clinical observations seek to infer from behavior, by both verbal and nonverbal manifestations, the underlying problems. If all behavior is purposeful, meaningful and goal-oriented, (even though individuals do not know what the purpose is, and the meaningfulness must be interpreted in terms of unconscious dynamics by others), then observations must not be restricted to stimuli and responses.

The clinical argument is that to analyze responses without inferring a causal relationship to other dynamic forces and goal-seeking behavior is to miss the message the responses are really providing. Behaviorists and social learning theorists tend to believe that making interpretations beyond the nature of the response itself is seldom warranted (Bandura and Walters, 1963). However, there is no unimpeachable evidence that either behaviorist or clinical interpretations are absolutely correct. **A reasonable compromise practiced by many therapists is to deal first with the symptom as the problem utilizing the behavioral format, and then only if this does not seem to provide results, to proceed to longer-term therapy focusing on clinical dynamics.**

The three approaches that have been outlined here represent some of the ways that individuals approach empirical observation. But it should be recognized that, in all three approaches, the intentionality and purpose of the observer interprets the phenomena of observation. As was said succinctly hundreds of years ago by Spinoza, Paul's conception of Peter tells us more about Paul than Peter (Ratner, 1927, xiv). Unquestionably, even in so-called "common" or unstructured empirical observation, individuals attend to what concerns them most, and infer what they believe to be the fact from the event. Behavioral methods aid in making a precise focus to observation, but once again, the interpretation in terms of learning theory has to be constantly assessed against the other dimensions which may be important. For example, Bandura (1978) has pointed out the importance of the mediation of self-concept or self-competency in the selection of reinforcers desired. In the situation of an individual who has used drugs and desires to break the habit, self-determination then becomes the efficacious component which (despite previous learning and reinforcing experiences) can overrule the desire for reinforcement of this type.

Clinical expansion of empirical observation also has both its positive and negative aspects. On the one hand, it is most likely that behavior is meaningful and goal-oriented. The opposite is to state that it is meaningless and random. But it is possible that the trained clinician may project his or her own problems on to the interpretation of the empirical data. Thus, for example, a psychologist may see sexual problems in almost everything a client says. And a social worker, who has been healed by a physician treating her for thyroid problems, may suggest that every child she sees needs to be checked for thyroid deficiency.

No value judgment is expressed here about the comparative merits of these approaches. All three have an important role in assessment. In point of fact, if any value is to be associated with this discussion, it would be that a competent diagnostician ought to be aware both of the assets and liabilities of all three approaches and be able to use each of them as needed.[1]

CONTRIBUTIONS OF PHENOMENOLOGICAL THEORY TO EMPIRICAL METHODS

Theories which explain the functioning of personality are based on an organized effort to analyze the consequences of empirical observation. Constructs are formed which are usually the logically derived inferences from observed behavior. As indicated in the first chapter, the criteria which aid in the formation of these constructs are replicability and prediction. Thus the inferences drawn from empirical observations are based on the extent to which individuals show a consistent set of replicable responses to stimulation and the extent to which these behaviors do predict other behaviors in the future.

Phenomenological Thinking and Empirical Observation. Phenomenological thinking attempts to clarify science by the analysis of common experiences. Phenomenology is characterized by an effort to "bracket" or understand common language in more profound ways. It is best explained as the process of conceptual clarification and deals chiefly with an effort to understand everyday language and experience (Heider, 1958, p. 4). Because our everyday contact with other individuals is guided by our perception of them, it is appropriate to look at what generalizations can be made about such contacts and experiences. There are three leading exponents of phenomenological thinking as applied to the psychological processes of experiential observation. Although they are not the only contributors to this field, their writings are particularly lucid and serve to exemplify some major conceptual approaches to observation. They are: Fritz Heider, Kurt Lewin, and George Kelly. Fritz Heider (1896–1988) received his Ph.D. from the University of Graz in Austria. He taught at the University of Hamburg and at Smith College in the United States and was a professor at the University of Kansas from 1947 until his death. He was associated with many proponents of the Gestalt theory of perception, and particularly with Kurt Lewin. A major contribution by Heider to the phenomenological theory of perception and observation is *The Psychology of Interpersonal Relations* (Heider, 1958). Perhaps the key feature to Heider's thinking relates to the correspondence assumption in human perception. Heider maintained that the correspondence assumption should be expanded to reflect the entire perceptual field. He suggested that the classical ideas of correspondence should include all kinds of experiences for every contact between a person and the environment as directly experienced. Behavior and thinking are based on what Heider terms a naive realism, which suggests that common axiom of "what you see is what you get" or to put it another way common perception is generally a reliable estimate of what actually exists outside the human mind (Heider, p. 22). Heider is not concerned with the implications of the unconscious, but rather consciousness itself, which he defines as the exposure of the self to the outside world (p. 27) and consists of raw perceptual material that is organized by the individual (p. 25). The consistency of human interactions is squarely based on the development of a coherent network of expectations derived from experience. Personality traits themselves have their foundations in this common experience because it is the consistency of such individual characteristics as perceived by others, despite the irregularities of experience, that leads to the construct of trait.

Inner feelings provide the map or template for external behavior. Heider believed that inner feelings were in part generated from external social interaction. Social perception as related to the interaction of two individuals was conceptualized as "a process between the center of one person and the center of another person, from life space to life space" (p. 33). The degree of intimacy of contact between two people thus depends on the situation, how long they have known each other, and on individual differences (p. 57). This interaction also depends on affective responses which include overt motor reactions, eye contact, and subjective interpretation of verbal concepts. Thus meaningfulness is related to a host of interpretations, not the least of which is the understanding of language which differs from time to time, place to place, and between individuals. Intervening variables must be assumed in any kind of interaction between individuals. Heider states that they consist of a hierarchy of meanings and evaluations which can be compared to a system of interlocking concepts or schemata (p. 58).

Though much of Heider's formal writing postdates that of Kurt Lewin, he was closely related to Lewin, and there is some evidence that his ideas influenced Lewin. Heider aided in the translation of some of Lewin's work from German to English.

Kurt Lewin (1890–1947) was immersed in the considerable intellectual ferment that spawned the birth of Gestalt psychology. Marrow (1969, p. 17) cites contemporary witnesses that Lewin was first a psychologist and then a philosopher, indicating that Kohler, Koffka and Wertheimer were primarily philosophers and then psychologists. Lewin studied with Carl Stumpf who was director of the Psychological Institute at the University of Berlin. After obtaining his Ph.D., he taught at the Psychological Institute and became well known as a teacher with a vital message. He traveled extensively to Great Britain, Japan, Russia, and the United States. After the Nazi takeover in Germany he left and took a position at Cornell. Subsequently, he taught at the University of Iowa, and his last years were spent in attempting to launch the center for Group Dynamics at M.I.T. where he died suddenly on February 11, 1947.[2]

Perhaps Lewin's influence was felt most directly on all those students or colleagues who later translated his ideas into their own variations. Marrow provides a list of 51 individuals (1969, p. 260) who participated in one way or another in Lewin's topological seminars. Some of these colleagues and students developed portions of Lewin's ideas and added new ones of their own. A few representative names from the list of individuals who worked with Lewin are: Roger Barker, Jerome S. Bruner, Malcolm Cartwright, Richard Crutchfield, Fritz Heider, Sigmund Koch, Jacob Kounin, Ronald Lippitt, Boyd McCandless, Gardner Murphy, Lois Barclay Murphy, Robert Sears and E. C. Tolman.

The dynamic nature of Lewin's theories and action research ranged over the entire field of what is now known as social psychology. He saw learning in the context of an interaction between the person and the environment, and, true to Gestalt psychology, he attempted to look at the total picture, to view the impact of cognitive reorganization through insight and understanding, while examining how people change. His major ideas relate to learning, perception, affective movements as related to cognition, the impact of knowledge on thinking, characteristics of change, and process development.

Learning is an interaction between the person and the environment.

Lewin postulated that behavior could be expressed by the formula: $B = f(PE)$. In this formula the psychological behavior (B) is the result of an interaction between the state of the person (P) and the perceived impact of the environmental situation (E). Unlike environmentalists who attribute much of the personal state to situational characteristics (Mischel, 1968), Lewin believed that the state of the person comprised not only genotypic characteristics related to constitutional theories of personality, but also momentary states of the organism such as anxiety (Lewin, 1935a, p. 71).

Perception is the key variable in determining behavior. In a manner similar to that expressed by Heider, Lewin also saw perceptual processes as providing a map to corresponding behavior. Perception as conceptualized by Lewin was not a passive reactor to experience, but a dynamic intending force of the individual continually seeking out from the range of experiences new ways of formulating roles, values, and freedoms. Moreover, it was not possible, in Lewin's topology, really to separate the cognitive, the affective, and the social dimensions of human behavior. All were affectively toned by qualitative characteristics of the environment, whether that environment be one of supportive facilitation and growth, or negative repression and hostility. As Benne (1976) has stated in commenting on this principle: "The world in which we act is the world as we perceive. Changes in knowledge or changes in beliefs and value orientation will not result in action changes unless changed perceptions of self and situation are achieved" (p. 35).

Affective learning does not necessarily correlate with cognitive learning. Lewin and Grabbe (1945) expressed this principle in a number of ways. They suggested that changes in sentiments do not necessarily lead to changes in cognitive structure, and also that a lot of first hand experience does not necessarily create correct concepts or knowledge. In the first instance, changes in attitudes are not sufficient to change either cognitive or social behavior, but rather these changes must be sparked by perceptual reorganization leading to social rehearsal and exercise. In this way, some correspondence between affect and cognition can take place.

Correct knowledge does not necessarily result in the alteration of false perceptions (Lewin & Grabbe, 1945). Though unquestionably well-designed experiments may aid in the development of appropriate social perceptions and interpersonal relationships, Lewin was painfully aware that cognitive understanding of correct principles could be held by individuals at the same time that they held false impressions or perceptions about either themselves or others. Thus, for example, one might have an excellent cognitive understanding of the principles of moral behavior and ethical responsibility, and yet operate with stereotypic prejudices. This cleavage between thought and behavior is well documented in Nazi Germany where many people who had the cognitive understanding of human rights and responsibilities allowed themselves to acquiesce to the genocide of the Jews. It is likewise applicable to the condition of blacks as a minority race in this country. What Lewin was recognizing was that studying philosophy does not make one philosophical; studying theology does not make one a morally good person; and obtaining a Ph.D. in psychology does not necessarily result in adequacy and competency in coping with human behavior.

Change is a function of responsible involvement in appropriate social contingencies. Though Lewin did not recognize fully the linkage between social perception and self-perception (Benne, 1976), he did point out that specific experiences were necessary to bring about personal growth and integration as well as changes in value systems. According to Benne (1976), subsequent experiences in group therapy, or organizations such as Alcoholics Anonymnous, and efforts to change prejudices in police and industrial organizations, have demonstrated that the reconstruction of an individual's action-ideology is related to the extent and depth of involvement in the examination of his/her own operating values relative to others. "Lacking this involvement, no objective fact is likely to reach the status of a fact for the individual, and no value alternative is likely to reach the status of a genuine alternative for the individual and therefore come to influence his social conduct"(Benne, 1976, p. 37).

The processes governing the acquisition of the normal and abnormal are fundamentally alike (Lewin & Grabbe, 1945). Lewin's position here focuses on classification methods. For all too long there has been a cleavage between what is considered abnormal and normal. Classification systems have by and large focused on the abnormal, implying that the normal is simply absence of abnormal symptoms. Benne believes that there is a class-theoretical thinking process in which many classify individuals by labeling them "pathological," or "criminal." Such classification systems relate to precategorized forms of thinking which, according to Lewin, are determinants to action and methods of behavior (expectations in our more modern terminology) (Lewin, 1935, p. 27). Lewin recognized that the person-environment interaction could produce amoral as well as moral behavior, self-deprecation as well as self-esteem. He thus reasoned that one of the first goals in the reeducation or rehabilitation of individals was a change in the classification system operating in the minds of others. As Benne has remarked, "field-theoretical thinking about people and the processes of their reeducation keeps a focus on the reality of concrete persons in their actual manifold relationships and situations and does not let abstract classifications of persons prescribe the mode or manner of their differential treatment" (1976, p. 32).

George Kelly (1905–1966) was born in Kansas and obtained his Ph.D. at the University of Iowa in 1931. He taught at the University of Maryland, spent twenty years at Ohio State University as director of clinical training, was a president of the American Psychological Association, and also president of the American Board of Examiners in Professional Psychology. In 1965 he moved to Brandeis University where he assumed the Riklis Chair of Behavioral Science. He died in 1966 leaving behind much unfinished work.

Kelly can be classified with the phenomenologists because his contribution lies directly in this area. However, as Kelly himself reported, his ideas seemed to be classifiable in every category: "Personal construct theory has also been categorized by responsible scholars as an emotional theory, a learning theory, a psychoanalytic theory (Freudian, Adlerian, and Jungian— all three), a typically American theory, a Marxist theory, a humanistic theory, a logical positivistic theory, a Zen Buddhistic theory, a Thomistic theory, a behavioristic theory, an Apollonian theory, a pragmatistic theory, a reflexive theory and no theory at all. It has also been classified as nonsense, which indeed, by its own admission, it will likely some day turn out to be. In each case there were some convincing arguments offered for the categorization, but I have forgotten what most of them were. I fear that no one of these categorizations will be of much help to the reader in understanding personal construct theory, but perhaps having a whole lap full of them all at once will suggest what might be done with them" (Kelly, 1966).

Kelly through his teaching and personal contacts has provided some major guidelines for the interpretation and understanding of human cognitive and emotional processes. He referred to his own system as personal construct theory, and he believed that a construct was an operational explanation for individual meaning.

Human behavior is moderated by subjective constructs which are defined as bipolar value systems which filter the ebb and flow of experience. Kelly believed that personal constructs could not be compared to scientific concepts as such, but are the essential elements that determine the behavior of individuals. In a real sense, then, he suggested that personal constructs are similar to the maps or templates that explain behavior (earlier identified by both Heider and Lewin). The basic constructs of Kelly's system are one essential postulate and eleven corollaries:

A. FUNDAMENTAL POSTULATE: A person's processes are psychologically channelized by the ways in which he anticipates events.

B. CONSTRUCTION COROLLARY: A person anticipates events by construing their replications.

C. INDIVIDUALITY COROLLARY: Persons differ from each other in their construction of events.

D. ORGANIZATION COROLLARY: Each person characteristically evolves, for his convenience in anticipating events, a construction system embracing ordinal relationships between constructs.

E. DICHOTOMY COROLLARY: A person's construction system is composed of a finite number of dichotomous constructs.

F. CHOICE COROLLARY: A person chooses for himself that alternative in a dichotomized construct through which he anticipates the greater possibility for extension and definition of his system.

G. RANGE COROLLARY: A construct is convenient for the anticipation of a finite range of events only.

H. EXPERIENCE COROLLARY: A person's construction system varies as he successively construes the replications of events.

I. MODULATION COROLLARY: The variation in a person's construction system is limited by the permeability of the constructs within whose range of convenience the variants lie.

J. FRAGMENTATION COROLLARY: A person may successively employ a variety of construction subsystems which are inferentially incompatible with each other.

K. COMMONALITY COROLLARY: To the extent that one person employs a construction for experience which is similar to that employed by another, his psychological processes are similar to those of the other person.

L. SOCIALITY COROLLARY: To the extent that one person construes the construction processes of another, he may play a role in a social process involving the other person (Kelly 1963, 103–104).

Kelly's entire system was based on this postulate and the corollaries derived from it. Basically, he suggests that the anticipation of events in the act of perception is the way we map our thinking and behavior. Our ability to do this is based on our intelligence and experience, and particularly in the manner in which we can infer predictive behavior from past behavior. Individual differences affect the act of perception, as well as select different sets of memory events; thus we are not equal in our ability to anticipate or analyze phenomenal events.

On the basis of our constitutional characteristics, our learning and experience, we organize a system which is unique to ourselves and involves polarities of "good and evil," "happy and sad," "strong and weak" value judgments which are implicit in our very thinking. We make choices on the basis of these implicit values, determine alternatives in thinking and action that best represent our interests and apply these choices to a restricted set of events.

In terms of change, an individual's ability to change varies as he/she successively predicts outcomes, as he/she is capable of modifying approaches, and can integrate potentially or actually conflicting construct systems. Further, in terms of communication, two individuals tend to be more understanding of each other as they identify and communicate similar psychological processes, and can be involved in possible change based on this communality.

In summary, Kelly's system of personal constructs provides an important and viable approach to the interpretation and understanding of empirical observation. It also provides some important guidelines for assessment, counseling, and therapy.

CONTRIBUTIONS OF BEHAVIORAL THEORY TO EMPIRICAL OBSERVATION

The behaviorists have always taken a more radical approach to empiricism and have looked chiefly at responses in terms of learning. Through a process of classical and operant conditioning they have postulated that human behavior is shaped by reinforcements and punishments. For the most part in the past they have not seen the necessity of positing internal-external correspondences which relate to physical and mind entities.

The effects of learning necessitate a shift in the Lewinian paradigm to include learning as an eliciting component in each of the major interactions between behavior (B), environment (E), and personality (P). In the last decade some modifications have taken place in the behavioral approach, and particularly in social learning theory, and the development of a cognitive-behavioral approach. These changes have been noted as a softening of the rather iconoclastic approach to assessment which was typified by Mischel (1968). In recent years, Mischel has acknowledged the validity of utilizing personality tests (Mischel, 1975), and has indicated that self-report methods do yield data similar to both clinical judgments and certain test data (1981). Thus it is apparent that some integration of behavioral methods with other forms of assessment is taking place. Mischel has also been concerned with the process of translating self-report contingencies into competency planning via a method of hypothetical inferences i.e., "if . . . then."

A cognitive emphasis in behavioral approaches has also been observed in the works of Donald Meichenbaum. He affirms that cognitive assessment depends primarily on the subject's self-report and that this approach needs to be effected through open-ended discussions and the use of self-report inventories. (Meichenbaum and Cameron, 1981, p. 5). Meichenbaum has also been interested in the development of explanations of what he calls meta-cognition or the variables and rules which govern subjective processes.

Cognitive structure variables, particularly as they exhibit rules and constructs about thinking and behaving become a legitimate subject of behavioral analysis. This heightened interest in explaining how the subjective reacts to the laws of behavioral learning has led Albert Bandura to reaffirm, in modified social learning terms, much of what Lewin and Kelly expressed earlier. In a 1978 article, Bandura looked closely at the earlier phenome-nological tenets. He admitted that extreme behaviorism tends to see the environment as the instigating force "to which individuals can counteract" (p. 344). But he then points out that individuals create and activate their own environments as well as selecting the kinds of reinforcements they wish to receive.

Bandura points out that past learning experiences dispose the organism to certain tendencies. Though Bandura concedes that environmental influ-ences can be resisted and even changed through dissatisfaction with con-sequences of behavior, suggesting that internal responses are probable rather than determined, he shifts the problem of determinism to the inner forum of what he calls "interlocking determinants" (p. 346). As a consequence, cognitive structure becomes a legitimate target for behavioral analysis. Ban-dura states:"In social learning theory, a self system is not a psychic agent that controls behavior. Rather it refers to cognitive structure that provides references mechanisms and to a set of subfunctions for the perception, evaluation, and regulation of behavior"(p. 348).

In summary, behavioral approaches to empirical methods have become more attentive to the nature of human reasoning as manifested through self-report. The extension of behavioral interests to the analysis of the inner forum of perception and experience does not signal an abandonment of the basic tenets, but rather is an effort to determine how individuals respond to environmental stimulation, reinforcement and punishment, and what par-ticular combination of characteristics can be found in the analysis of self-report.

PSYCHODYNAMIC CONTRIBUTIONS TO EMPIRICAL ASSESSMENT

Though the influence of Freudian theory has continued to impact on psy-choanalytic conceptions of development, it is totally wrong to assume that psychoanalytic theory has remained fixated at the level of "little Hans," even as it is grossly inadequate to believe that behavioral theory stopped with Watson's case of Albert, Skinner's pigeons, or Harlow's monkeys. Theory which is dynamic continues to grow. Much of earlier psychoanalytic theory focused on the nature of the unconscious and how it impinged on conscious-ness. Although this aspect of psychoanalytic theory as well as the emphasis on the formation of defense mechanisms remain as constants in psychoana-lytic theory, contemporary approaches have been much more concerned with the development of the ego.

Contemporary psychodynamic theory focuses on functional needs, de-velopmental and moral stages, and the role of the ego. Four major contributors to the general field of psychodynamic theory have added to the known clinical characteristics of interpreting behavior in the interview. These contributors have focused chiefly on analyzing the developmental process and the manner in which this process impacts on the coherent expression of self, known in psychodynamic terms as the "ego" or in the more general descriptor of self-concept. However the executive functions of the control hierarchy are described, psychodynamic theory is chiefly concerned with an analysis of the interaction between human control functions, human needs, problem solving, and moral decision making. It is thus less specific in focus, more concerned with the bridge between developmental stages and psychological adjustment, and consequently more tending towards the use of inferences to describe these stages. We will concentrate on this aspect here.

Abraham Maslow, Eric Erikson, Lawrence Kohlberg, and Jane Loevinger have made great contemporary contributions to the understanding of the processes of how human development in the context of the environment shapes and elicits internal mapping. Maslow (1970) turned his attention to the classification of fundamental human needs positing that human development was contingent on the meeting of these needs. Eric Erikson examined stages of psychosocial development (Erikson, 1968), Jane Loevinger has examined the processes which are involved in ego development, and Lawrence Kohlberg (1976) has researched extensively the stages of moral development.

Each of these researchers has made a contribution to knowledge in describing how human needs interact with the development of internal mechanisms. Maslow described basic human needs as being arranged in an ascending hierarchy. Each level is important to the next. Thus the satisfaction of basic physiological needs relates to hunger, thirst, sexuality, and drives which are inherent in the human being. Safety needs come next and include housing, and freedom from fears. Love needs are at the third level and include the need for affection, companionship, and human relationships of intimacy. Subsequently, there are self-esteem needs and self-actualization needs. Though it is comparatively easy to specify the needs at the lower end of the hierarchy and to identify them from empirical interactions, the needs relative to self-esteem and self-actualization are somewhat less easy to define because they are more contextual depending on the individual's own lifestyle.

Erikson (1959) has attempted to determine the basic social tasks of individuals over a series of stages. He identifies eight stages which include: infancy, early childhood, play age, school age, adolescence, the young adult, adulthood, and mature age. For each of these stages, Erikson sees some fundamental tasks which need to be addressed. For example, the fundamental task for infancy is the establishment of basic trust versus basic mistrust. For early childhood the task is autonomy versus shame and doubt—a task which reflects the growing consciousness of self and the need for individuation and autonomous functioning. For the preschool and elementary school ages, the tasks relate to initiative versus guilt and industry versus inferiority. Adolescence is a time of identity crisis and the task is one of working out a proper identity versus identity confusion. In the young adult, there's the problem of intimacy versus isolation, the need for establishing intimate relationships and the attending consequences from that effort. In adulthood, the major task is one of generativity versus stagnation, a time when productivity and task-orientation as well as parenthood have to be balanced against other human needs. And finally, in mature age, there is the need for coming to terms with integrity versus despair, as many individuals find that the "yellow brick road" of future hopes, expectations, and desires does not extend forever.

Kohlberg (1976) has attempted to look at the moral development of individuals. Kohlberg describes moral development as occurring in three hierarchical levels: preconventional, conventional and postconventional. Within each of these levels he discriminates two stages. Thus in the preconventional level he identifies stage 1 as heteronomous morality, which is essentially obeying rules to avoid being punished. Stage 2 is a kind of individualism in which moral rules are equated with what is fair and a kind of contract or equal exchange. In level 2, the stages are mutual interpersonal expectations, which break down to holding the "golden rule," and to developing a social system and conscience. In the latter stage there is the need for a recognition that laws and rules are made for the well-being of all people and can only be broken under certain extenuating circumstances. Level 3 is the most difficult level to discriminate between stages. Kohlberg sees stage 5 as a state of social contract, utility, and individual rights, and stage 6 as a quest for a universal ethics based on principles. In both of these stages higher-order processes and integration are needed.

Whereas Maslow looked at the overall broad stages of human needs and Erikson and Kohlberg viewed human tasks and moral development in terms of developmental stages, Loevinger (1976) has dealt more directly with the mechanism for internal identity which is most likely central to all of the others. Loevinger focuses her developmental stages on the gradual unfolding of the ego. Whatever may be the theoretical descriptions of the ego as a mechanism, it is surely of great importance to human development. The ego is considered the psychological mechanism of integration. That mechanism has as its fundamental task the coordination of basic individual human needs with the pressure of moral and social criteria that operate in human socialization. It functions as the great arbiter of experience, sensing, feeling, intuiting, and attempting to organize, chart the flow of expectations and

Table 5-1   **Examples of Maslow's Needs Applied**

Needs	Home or Interview Manifestations	School Manifestations
Physiological Needs	*Poor nutrition* Inadequate food Reliance on junk food	Hunger, apathy Lack of supervision in eating
	Poor health Chronic medical and dental problems without care	Health problems noted: running nose and ears, uncorrected vision, dental decay
	Inadequate sleep Inability to attend Chronic tiredness	Falling asleep in class, listless, tired, apathetic
	Inadequate housing Lack of heat, water, electricity, gas, toilets	Frost bite, uncleanliness, soiled clothing
	Inadequate clothing Poor, soiled or inappropriate clothing for the season	Soiled, dirty or inappropriate clothing for peer group and/ or season
	Substance abuse Excessive use of alcohol, tobacco, drugs	School manifestation of alcohol, drugs, excessive smoking. Inability to attend and lack of motivation
Safety Needs	*Broken homes, foster homes*	Anxiety, fear reactions
	Family or marital discord	School problem behavior
	Child abuse, spouse abuse Bruises, unexplained damage, broken limbs	Bruises, broken limbs and unexplained damage to person of child.
	Unsafe neighborhoods, Fear of robberies, violence, rape, etc.	Fears of going home or coming to school, fear of peers
	Sexual exploitation Sexual abuse, incest	Unusual behavior towards sex, overt sexual behavior in school
Love and Belongingness Needs	*Lack of stable mature relationships with others*	Underachievement
	Domineering father or mother	Overachievement

Table 5-1 (Continued)

Needs	Home or Interview Manifestations	School Manifestations
	Overprotective parents	Problems with peers and/or teachers
	Parental rejection or preference for other siblings	Problems in self-competency and group interaction
	Punitive, hostile, coercive interpersonal relationships	Fears, problems in self-control
	Extreme ethnocentric values Excessive competitiveness Anomie, lack of community or social identification	Problems in cognitive motivation Problems in attitude and discipline Stealing, truancy, antisocial behavior
	Instability Frequent family moves History of parental incarceration	Attendance at many schools Failing achievement and repeats, lack of friends and academic motivation
	Lack of Intimacy Inadequate adult role models, sexual exploitation Promiscuity, repression, sexual deviations	Many and varied manifestations often resulting in lack of learning achievement appropriate to ability, phobic reactions, isolation and loneliness.
Esteem and Self-Actualization		
	Conditions of isolation and alienation. Conditions of stress and anxiety. Conditions of guilt and hostility.	
	Conditions of restriction and lack of reinforcement.	

Note: The above examples are meant to illustrate conditions of deprivation and are not all-inclusive.

demands into some kind of coherent framework (though this framework may contain many discrepant constructs as Kelly has stated, inconsistent affective-cognitive relationship as Lewin has pointed out, and be subjected to the influence and changes of learning as Bandura has stated). Loevinger believes that there is an eight stage developmental sequence discernible in ego maturing. From earliest stages the ego develops as a presocial and impulsively reacting mechanism to the demands of reality. It is self-centered and self-determined. Subsequently, in the next stage where the superego begins to assert itself as the internal "momma," the ego becomes preoccupied with problems of being caught, and thus tends to externalize blame and act in a way that is basically opportunistic. The third stage involves conformity to external rules, and the feelings of shame or guilt for breaking them. The fourth stage is typified by a differentiation or discrimination of norms and goals. The fifth and sixth stages show development towards the internalization and individualization of ideals and personal goals through conscientiousness and individual responsibility. The last two stages focus on autonomous functioning and integration which bring personal needs and social responsibilities into a new perspective.

The efforts which have been made by these theorists represent a kind of meta-theory derived chiefly from empirical observations and focused by psychodynamic constructs of personality theory. Since many of the on-going explanations are based on empirical observations and particularly process comparisons, these theories are fundamentally empirical rather than psychometric. As can be observed from the brief descriptions of the systems of Maslow, Erikson, Kohlberg, and Loevinger, they overlap on many functional stages of human development. Though they cannot be absolutely related to each other, there are sufficient similarities at given stages to try to group them in a common figure.

It should be emphasized however, that movement or placement on one hierarchy does not necessarily imply correlative placement on another hierarchy. The reader should then recognize that the meeting of basic needs does not imply certain levels of ego development. Nor should placement at one or the other levels of Erikson's task stages necessarily relate to a given stage of moral development in Kohlberg's schema. In point of fact, it is probable that the discrepancies between values, ego integration, and needs may result in the stress, anxiety and frustration which can often be found in human interviews.

In summary, psychodynamic theory in the broad sense has turned to the developmental process which occurs in interactions between constitutional factors of the individual and the impact of the environment. No reputable theorist today doubts that hereditary and environmental factors interact in the process of human development. There are, however, a number of issues which are really not yet resolved. One of these deals with the question of whether human development proceeds chiefly from *a priori* structure variables downward to specific behaviors, or whether it involves the accretion of specific responses, as shaped by learning, upward into the development of cognitive principles of operation. Another issue concerns the extent that motivation towards goal-seeking behavior is conscious or unconscious. A third issue focuses on the qualitative characteristics of the core base of self

Table 5-2   **Integration of Developmental Stages, Needs and Ego Development**

Maslow's Needs	Erikson's Stage Tasks	Loevinger's Ego Development	Kohlberg's Moral Development	Summary Outcomes
Self-Actualization (Creativity) Higher Order Integration of Meaningful Experiences	Integrity vs. Despair Generativity vs. Stagnation	Autonomous Integrated	Post-Conventional 6. Universal Ethical Principles 5. Social Contract	Discrimination Toleration of Ambiguity Conceptual Complexity
Self-Esteem (Prestige, Status) Sense of Personal Competency, Meaningful Work Relations	Industry vs. Inferiority	Individualistic	Conventional 4. Social System & Conscience	Distinguishing Internal from External Life Control, Responsibility
Love (Intimacy) Personal and Social Relations with Others	Intimacy vs. Isolation Initiative vs. Guilt	Conscientious Conformist	3. Mutual Interpersonal Expectations	Differentiation of Norms and Goals Conformity to Expectations
Safety (Security) Home Security, Stability, School Safety, Freedom from Personal and Psychological Abuse	Autonomy vs. Shame	Self-Protective	Pre-Conventional 2. Individualism Instrumental Purpose Mutual Exchange	Conceptual Simplicity Fear of Being Caught External Locus of Control Opportunistic
Physiological Nutrition, Shelter, Clothing, Sexuality Freedom from Substance Abuse	Trust vs. Mistrust	Pre-social Symbiotic Impulsive	1. Heteronomous Morality	Stereotyping Conceptual Confusion Autistic, Exploitative

Note: These stages and needs are not to be considered as proceeding systematically up the hierarchy. They are broad indicators of progress and may show considerable variation.

identity, whether referred to as self or as ego. Crucial in the discussion of this latter question is whether the executive and coordinating function of self-identity has some limited freedom of choice or whether it is determined by outside factors or even internal ones.

SOME FUNCTIONAL POSTULATES OF OBSERVATION

One of the important goals in discussing empirical observation is to relate it to the process of assessment. Generally empirical observation is the basis for interviewing. Interviewing encompasses many dimensions. Emphasis in recent decades has been to view the interview as a first step in a counseling process involving change. A number of counseling psychologists have extracted from the entire range of theories outlined in the previous sections some important elements which they believe represent functional postures towards interviewing.

Three somewhat similar but also slightly different approaches can be distinguished. The first of these approaches was enunciated and has been continually followed up by Robert R. Carkhuff (1969a, 1969b). Carkhuff has developed a model for helping other people through counseling. He believes that human growth and development must be viewed as embracing simultaneously physical, emotional and intellectual factors. He also sees the role of the counselor (helper) in a crucial relationship with the client (helpee) as a means to change. He has developed a number of postulates for guiding the process relationship.

Secondly, George M. Gazda (1971, 1975, Catterall & Gazda, 1978) has incorporated much of what Carkhuff uses, but has made original contributions to the process of group therapy utilizing similar ideas about helper-helpee relationships, concentrating more on the development of assessment approches, and recently attempting to identify target personal, intellectual, and social skills which can be utilized as competency goals in the change process.

The third approach has been one which attempts to integrate elements of other functional approaches to counseling process with a general social learning theory cast in a systems model. This is the work of William H. and L. Sherilyn Cormier (1979).

With the recognition of the contribution of the various theories discussed earlier and the functional approaches cited above, the following general postulates are presented to summarize an approach to empirical observation.

Every cultural background is of primary importance to those living in it. Cultural background and experience are important factors in every empirical assessment situation. They form a series of patterns and behaviors which shape human conduct. Valid empirical observations take into consideration the client's background, family and setting. A specific understanding of different cultures and subcultures is imperative if one is to work with individuals with any degree of acceptance and rapport and to derive from those contacts valid empirical information. For example, the extended family kinship system and the value it serves in rural Appalachian culture may often be incomprehensible to a dweller in a large city. The conditions of minority groups such as blacks or Mexican-Americans is often not understood by those who live and work in a majority culture. Differences in religion and nationality can also provide differences in outlook. Thus, for example, new immigrants such as those from Vietnam need to be understood in terms of their culture. Assertive behavior which some counselors might wish to see in their clients is alien to many cultural groups. Competitiveness is not a trait which one often finds in American Indian or Eskimo families. The ideals, goals, and values of a cultural group, early training habits, outlooks towards life and the whole pattern of familial nurturance, influence the thinking and behavior as well as aspirations of individuals living in that culture.

A knowledge of the specific conditioning or learning to which an individual has been subjected often provides inferences about ideas or motives not logically connected. All of us are influenced by the history of our developmental background. Therefore, through the dialogue with the counselor or through structured questioning, the history of the individual, background experiences, relationships towards parents and siblings is gradually established. Certainly there are many components which contribute to the development of an individual. Early traumatic experiences such as death of a parent or caregiver, physical or psychological abuse, continued negative experiences in school could affect vocational goals, or the choice of a husband or wife. In many instances individuals are not fully aware of how these experiences have related to their present-day motives and behavior. Self-fulfilling prophecies are often implicitly held and they shape behavior. Perhaps a child is told that he is just like an uncle who had many problems. This statement is retained in his unconscious and acts as a force on his development. Or perhaps a woman feels she will not live any longer than her mother. Upon reaching the age when her mother died, she goes into a rapid decline and dies within the year. These experiences together with the socioeconomic background of the family, intellectual ability and opportunities available within the environment are factors which interact with individual behaviors and motives. At the present state of our knowledge, the mode of this interaction cannot be judged to be logically apparent, but the empirical analysis process can provide inferences about what might be the relationships.

Behavior is symptomatic, purposeful, and in response to inner needs and strivings. It is virtually a psychological axiom that all behavior has meaningfulness to the individual. This does not suggest that behavior is necessarily understood by the individual. Nor does it suggest that the connections between a set of behaviors and certain conscious goals should be immediately evident to either the client or the observer. Though cognitive and affective components exist in each individual's thought process, it is a delusion to think that they are equally balanced or that they are understood comprehensively by individuals. According to many phenomenological and psychodynamic theorists human needs and desires are often deeply rooted in unconscious processes, or at least processes which are not immediately accessible to consciousness. On the other hand, bodily responses and emotive reactions rather than verbal output often express the deeper unconscious reactions to situations which are not evident, or only marginally evident in the cognitive processes of the individual. Certainly many individual attempts at problem solving are bungled efforts to bring some order out of relationships between human needs, which may not be recognized on a conscious level, and culturally sanctioned goals.

The best guarantee of the future behavior of an individual is the record of past behavior. Certainly this proposition is a common sense one in that something like it is often heard. It is not intended to be a fatalistic one, but rather to indicate, based upon the major sources of personality theory that thinking and behaving do not radically change unless there are compelling personal or social reasons for the reorganization of cognitive mapping and the subsequent investment in new behaviors. What this suggests to the psychologist is that without interventions of some kind, i.e., changes in the pattern of thinking, a recognition of one's own needs, imagery, or changes in behavior, it is most likely that individuals will continue in a pattern of behavior which they have established. If we consider both the manner in which changes concern social involvement (Lewin), or the crucial nature of the "helper" in the special counseling relationship (Carkhuff), or the role of negative reinforcements and consequences on the self (Bandura), then it is evident that behaviors as well as thinking tend to follow a homeostasis based on the past experience and learning.

Cultural patterns of acceptable behavior are often transmitted via expectations. These expectations on the part of others, first from parents and siblings and later on from peers and teachers, provide a set of implicit cultural guidelines by which the individual comes to recognize criteria of effective human behavior. With consequent efforts to meet these expectations, reinforcement or punishment often occurs. The pattern of behavior which an individual manifests is thus the overt method of analyzing the manner in which the individual has come to terms with environmental expectations.

The expectations which psychologists bring to interview or counseling situations must be understood in terms of their own emotional and intel-

lectual understandings. Crucial to this proposition is a recognition on the part of the psychologist of the logic of inferencing which takes place in subjective life. Psychologists in making inferences based on empirical assessment must be very careful to recognize their own biases and to make sure that what they are observing has a reality basis in the individual being assessed. Psychologists can be influenced by their own prejudices unless they are careful in their assessment. The chain of logic which is delivered by a client in response to the analysis of his/her own problems is often faulty due to impaired emotional perception or the existence of conflict between needs and reason. For psychologists to recognize these empirical connections in others, it is indispensable that they recognize them in themselves. As Socrates said long ago the first task of wisdom is "to know thyself."

Constructive alterations or changes in either thinking or behaving depend on satisfying experiences. What is meant by this is that change in individuals comes about only through a positive activation of their own abilities and desires. Thus scolding, recrimination, or lecturing are hardly methods which can be interpreted by a client as positive and satisfying experiences. Nor can implicit disapproval be viewed positively by a client. Therefore it is imperative that the resources of the clinician elicit the positive skills of the client to make changes in behavior or rethink fundamental constructs. This has to be done at the pace and level of the client's understanding and willingness to change. Moreover, the clinician needs to understand that all changes and all efforts to change must be fitted to the special characteristics of the client. There are fundamental reality considerations which are present in the lives of most people. These include the necessity of work, living situations which cannot be changed, and personal problems which have to be addressed in the context of the individual.

In summary the foregoing postulates provide a frame of reference that is important for those who would use empirical observations as a method of assessment. To be sure they represent inferences drawn from personality approaches. Because they agree largely with major approaches to personality and constitute operating modes of regarding empirical observation, they have been expanded here as generalized rubrics which may guide the clinician in the effort to gain maximum reliable and valid information from empirical observations.

CHAPTER VI

The Clinical Interview

"Our task (clinical assessment) is in some way similar to measuring a floating cloud with a rubber band—in a shifting wind."
Edwin S. Schneideman, (1966, p. 7)

Although one can outline the various approaches to the interview, the implications of what the interview means are strictly a matter of clinical interpretation. Data can be accumulated using basic common sense and phenomenological criteria, or in terms of behavioral technology, but the interaction between interviewer and client results in the formation of hypotheses about the individual and how he or she has come to this point in time. Much information is available to the keen observer, provided that observer can understand what is being said and what message is proceeding from the process itself. Clinical wisdom does not occur as a result of reading books alone, but comes from the practice of assessment under varying conditions, problems, and supervision. This chapter attempts to summarize some of the major clinical perceptions that can be gleaned from the interview process. The interview for assessment purposes must be separated from the counseling approach. Clinical interviewing is a form of assessment. Counseling may or may not include such information.

FUNCTIONAL OBSERVATIONS IN ASSESSMENT INTERVIEWING.

In the previous chapter the background of research relating to behavioral, phenomenological and clinical observations has been summarized. Since it is difficult to expand the various approaches all at once, it is appropriate here to identify functional targets of assessment that can occur in the process of interviewing.

Rapport Building. Most clients come to psychologists because of a problem. When a client is referred by an agency or by someone else, there is often a notable lack of cooperation or motivation and an unwillingness to become involved. Under these circumstances special patience must be shown by the clinician. Usually clients who come on their own are more motivated to change. Where individuals are referred for a specific reason (a court assessment, a premarital evaluation), motivation may or may not be as great as from individuals who are come on their own.

Some psychologists distinguish between a counseling session and an assessment one. This is a distinction that often reflects a particular counseling theory. Many counseling approaches do not systematically employ an assessment thrust. Others reflect a specific psychodynamic, behavioral, or other approach. Regardless of theoretical approaches, if one wishes to utilize assessment information to provide the best understanding of the individual, it is useful to recognize that interviews can be structured in such a way as to provide maximum relevant information. This can be done in an unobtrusive manner which does not impair the quality of an initial counseling relationship.

In the initial stages of discussion it is most likely that a common base or rapport will be established through a discussion of the weather, a recent sports event, or some other topic of mutual interest. This process takes place informally whenever individuals meet and begin to relate to each other. Implicitly there is an intention to establish some working relationship between two people and usually this involves neutral and nonprofessional issues, the recent basketball scores, or some other topic that can be talked about as a means of establishing a common base of relating. Usually this phase of the initial interview is termed "rapport building." Once rapport is established it is usual for the client to identify the reasons for coming in the form of a problem. This may not occur where individuals are referred by agencies or others. In either case a problem is usually identified by the client. Where clients do not readily identify a problem, usually psychologists ask them. The client may say something like this: "I have come to see you because I have a problem with my children." Or the clinician, after a pause may say: "How may I be of assistance to you?"

Problem identification is often contingent on rapport. Though usually both the client and the psychologist wish to reach a stage of problem exploration as soon as is feasible, it is very important to establish first some kind of personal relationship. One cannot proceed to major issues if there is a disagreement on rather fundamental ones such as the weather, or basketball scores. Thus, the rapport building of the initial phases of the counseling communication is directed at the establishment of one basic fact: Do we have enough in common relating to overall human concerns in this community to proceed further?" Logically what this boils down to is a question on the part of the client about the clinician. "Does this clinician have enough human qualities and interests in the same things that I do to trust him/her with my problems?" Though an interview might conceivably proceed beyond this stage even if the client and the clinician disagreed about the weather, the basketball scores and other common factors of potential agreement, it is unlikely.

Problem Determination. Initial problem identification may or may not be the real problem brought to the interview by the client. There is no comprehensive list of problems that may surface in an interview. Through careful listening, the interviewer can often identify what might be the problem focus of the client. Sometimes, however, the problem initially voiced by the client may not be the actual problem. For example, students coming to a counseling center often approach counselors with the presenting problem that they want "to talk about their grades." This is a reasonable motive for wanting to see a counselor, particularly one in a educational setting. But often as the discussion continues about that specific problem, it becomes evident that the grade situation is a function of other problems. For example, the client's girl friend has left him or is pregnant. In the latter situation perhaps parents have cut off financial support. Now the problem focus changes and by common agreement it can be so determined. A host of other problems are voiced. There is a lack of interest in the major field, a sense of frustration, a fear of failure, loneliness, anger and conflict. So in the process of discussion, the initial reason for coming, i.e., grades, may change to a problem of "What am I going to do now that my girl friend is pregnant and I am failing my courses and have no financial security?" So likewise with adults, presenting problems may not be the real ones. Thus an early identified problem relating to husband-wife relationships may initially focus on arguments over money or lack of mutual respect. But the real problems which may be later identified are related to a mid-career crisis, or something quite different.

Initial observational assessment begins with a helper/helpee analysis of the problem area. In the approach to this phase of problem identification it should be clear to the psychologist that his/her stance is as the helper in a helper-helpee relationship. Thus it is important to demonstrate to the client that you are a warm, thoughtful, and kind person. Not all psychologists are such, but the contention of Rogers that empathy and an accepting non-judgmental stance is crucial to therapy is something that is universally recognized. In addition, it is important not to foreclose too soon on the nature of the problem.

Some of the areas that often constitute the problem focus in interviews with students of all ages are: academic problems, failing grades, inability to study, insufficient motivation, lack of time or money, problems with recall, and similar concerns; and vocational decision making or the process of matching one's own aspirations, skills, and abilities to jobs or occupations that are related and self-fulfilling. In addition, there is the problem of coming to terms with the environmental demands of various occupations.

A number of problem areas common to all elements of society appear to relate to interpersonal conflicts with family members, teachers, supervisors, or peers. Specific problems may also occur as a subset of each of these areas such as marriage conflict, sexual inadequacies, abuse of drugs and alcohol, and a variety of other topical foci.

In many instances where interpersonal problems are noted, there are also intrapersonal problems. These often revolve around conflicts within the individual, the resolution of oppositional tendencies, irrational thinking, i.e., to believe that everyone must love a person for everything he or she does, or that some ideas are so wicked that they cannot even be thought. Obviously, in some instances there is a pervasive sense of guilt, of doom, or of depression. In other instances, individuals are faced with the reality of having transgressed either legal or moral codes or both, and this becomes a problem focus—such as in corrections assessment.

A final group of problems involve aging and illness. Our society is one that is growing older. More and more individuals not only survive to retirement, but find themselves confronted with problems relating to second careers, retirement, and new life styles. Others face problems of illness both physical and mental. Finally, the problems of death and dying are now recognized as very important ones. This is not a comprehensive list of all problems that one may encounter in the assessment interview, but it does include a large number of areas that surface in common experience with assessment.

A crucial factor in the determination of a problem area is to secure helper/helpee agreement on the problem. The interviewer generally can do this by rephrasing the problem in many possible ways to make sure that this is the client's actual concern. In some instances, many problems surface in an initial interview. Where this occurs, a technique that helps is to summarize all those that have been mentioned and to ask the client to prioritize them.

Clarification of the Problem Through Behavioral Analysis. Behavioral analysis sharpens the focus on the problem and provides inferences regarding the extent and situational characteristics of the problem. The best and most direct method of both clarifying the problem and determining specific situational relationships to client discomfort is through behavioral analysis. Three techniques often used are: (1) behavioral observations either by client recall, or systematic efforts at self-observed behavior; (2) observations by others (such as peers, friends, spouses and family); and (3) behavioral inventories or schedules.

From the behavioral point of view, the problem can and should be explored further by asking a series of questions that attempt to focus the problem

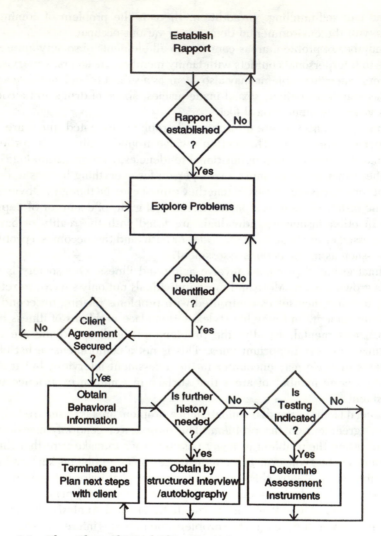

Figure 6-1   **Flow Chart of Initial Client Interview**

more specifically. Thus if a client indicates that her central problem is un-popularity, the interviewer pursues this idea operationally, asking the client to break it down into specific behaviors which occur. When this is done, an effort is usually made to determine with whom, under what circumstances, how often, at what times of the day or night, these events occur. The focus on the problem then becomes more specific by giving examples of what is happening and under what circumstances.

The one question that is usually not too relevant at this point is to ask "why" is this happening. In many instances individuals come for counseling because they cannot answer this question, and in the early stages of assessment it often results in lengthy detours.

A second component of the behavioral examination is to ask the client to describe what is happening both in his thinking and his body when events related to the problem are occurring. Specifically, what is sought here is to determine how cognitive and emotional aspects of the individual are affected by the events noted in connection with the problem.

The behavioral approach lends itself to the identification of deficits in skills. This in itself is helpful in clarifying a focus for further assessment and/ or intervention by determining whether there is a deficit, inability to perform some behavior or act, or a maladaptive response that reflects inadequate learning. A behavior is judged to be adequate if it is presumed to meet the needs of the individual within the context of environmental situations. If it is deficient, it represents a lack of ability or learning, and if it is maladaptive, the presumption is that a form of learning has taken place that needs to be modified (Ciminero, Calhoun, & Adams, 1977, p. 71).

A considerable and impressive literature has been assembled utilizing the behavioral approach to assessment and psychotherapy. Bergin and Garfield (1973) summarize a vast number of studies. Bergan (1977) indicates how the system can be utilized by consultants. Barclay (1971a, 1971b) has explained how the system can be integrated into more effective school psychology practice. Nay (1979) and Lazarus (1976) make behavioral practices the core of assessment. Ciminero, Calhoun, and Adams (1977) detail both general methods and specific applications to problems of anxiety, substance abuse, sexual behavior, social skill development, and psychotic behavior. Behavioral schedules provide an index of reinforcing or non-reinforcing activities associated with a setting or condition. Aside from direct observations either by others or by the self, another form of assessment that helps to outline the parameters of problems is the behavioral survey. This is a device, similar to an inventory, but not standardized, that attempts to determine a hierarchy of items or events related to a specific condition. Cautela (1981a, 1981b) has developed a number of these surveys that provide additional information about target problems. In one volume (1981a) he provides schedules that would be helpful for the evalution of organic dysfunctions, such as base rate information relating to arthritis, asthma, cancer, cardiac problems, headaches, hypertension, stress, pain, and other physical complaints. This volume would be of great help to assessors who are working in medical-related facilities or private practice. The second volume (1981b) deals more with general problems that typically might be observed in counseling, school, or clinical psychology. For example, he has surveys for adolescent needs, children, school reinforcement, marital reinforcement, parent reinforcement with children, physical appearance, aging, exercise, recreations, types of reinforcers, sexual reinforcement, social reinforcement, vocational reinforcement and many other areas. Behavioral techniques, including the survey approach, provide specific information about the nature of the problem identified. Very often, the survey itself provides a focus on the problem by determining in a rough manner a kind of hierarchy of fearful or distasteful or liked activities.

CLINICAL ASPECTS OF THE INTERVIEW

Problems and behavioral analyses are placed in context by the analysis of the life history of the individual. The life history of an individual helps considerably to understand the impact of environmental factors on both problems and behavior. There are various approaches to life-history assessment. Although counseling, clinical, and behavioral theories agree on the value derived from an analysis of self-report into thematic areas of life history, they disagree on the focus and methods which should be used. Three general foci can be distinguished: (1) a phenomenological indirect approach to accumulating background information; (2) a clinical direct approach using a structured set of interview questions; and (3) a behavioral approach that tends to focus on specific complaints or problems and explores the etiology of those complaints or problems. In addition to differences in focus, there are also differences of opinion as to methods. Methods can involve the use of assessment questions within the interview, or the completion of a structured interview assessment system (sometimes using a computer program), or the writing of an autobiography outside the context of the interview.

Psychologists who have been trained in counseling psychology generally do not believe that the gains obtained from a structured assessment interview outweigh the damage which accrues to the development of a positive rapport with clients. In general accord with the phenomenological point of view they seek to learn about the background of the client by indirection, by probing gently and naturally about statements made in the natural course of the interview sessions. This is a position taken by Brammer and Shostrum (1968).

Others such as Rim and Masters (1974) and Nay (1979) believe that history factors may provide hypotheses or inferences about present behavior. The extent to which such a history is developed through a series of structured questions is an issue which clinicians tend to favor and counselors oppose. The arguments in favor of the formal structured interview are: (1) clients can be prepared for this and an explanation of the relationship of their background history to their present complaints can be drawn; (2) relevant factors contributing to the present problem can be more quickly identified; and (3) modes of client thinking and problem solving can be evaluated. The analyses of such interview data have been found to relate to external criteria of behavior, and to psychometric profiles (Gottschalk and Gleser, 1968). More recently they have been related to categories of the DSM-III (Stangl, Pfohl, Zimmerman, Bowers, & Corenthal, 1985). In this latter study 160 questions grouped under 16 sections such as self-esteem, level of social interaction, and dependency, were administered over a 90 minute period to 63 individuals. Two ratings of the interview data were obtained for each subject with reliability of classification being .79. There were also significant relationships observed between DSM-III categories and the MMPI.

The behavioral approach neither holds for the indeterminate focus of most counseling theorists, nor for the structured approach of the clinician. Since behavioral therapy is related strongly to specific complaints or problems, the general approach is to investigate the somatic and psychological reactions associated with the specific set of responses or behaviors involved. This does not mean, however, that past history is ignored, but rather that the rationale provided by the client in response to the specific targeted problem is judged to be the most relevant area for further investigation. Thus Ciminero, Calhoun, and Adams (1977) agree that such information is relevant and needed. What they do not agree with is that information relevant to therapy can be acquired either by indirect accumulation, or by intensive exploration. They suggest rather that the focus be on the remote antecedents of the complaint or problem behavior.

With regard to method there are alternatives. If one does not wish to take the time for asking many assessment questions, then it is possible to obtain much valuable information either by a structured set of questions to which the client responds after the interview, or by the use of an autobiography which requests that the clients provide a history of their background. The autobiography often is an excellent opportunity for the client to evaluate his or her own background, but it should contain some structured questions in order to guide the responses of the client. In recent years structured psychosocial histories have been developed which can be filled out by a client using a microcomputer. One of these is a psychological/social history by Rainwater (1983) which directs a client through 91 questions that can involve multiple responses. The program also provides an opportunity for the client to "ear mark" certain items where the client would like further discussion. After the client completes the questionnaire, a report is produced and specific areas which might require further discussion are noted for the psychologist.

There are some real advantages to such a structured computer approach. First of all it does not take valuable interview time but can be done independent of that interview. Second, it provides a common structure for dealing with many clients. Third, it suggests to the psychologist areas that might be probed further, and fourth, it gives the clients an opportunity to identify areas that they would wish to pursue further. Finally, most individuals are familiar with these types of surveys from visiting medical doctors' offices.

Because there is no clear consensus on how history and background information should be obtained, in this section we shall simply outline the general areas which are usually contained in such an analysis. The clinical aspects of an interview are based on inferences which are made relative to the functioning of the individual. In general, the psychologist wishes to ascertain what are the cognitive, social, and emotive functioning levels of the individual. Given the effect of nurturance and cultural background on an individual there are some specific areas which are known from much past experience in the field of counseling and clinical psychology to apply to the individual's functioning. These are: childhood history and family relations; education together with interests, hobbies and activities enjoyed; sexual adjustment; religion and values; and vocational areas. Each of these areas relates to a fuller understanding of the individual.

Childhood History and Background. The quality and characteristics of early background are important determinants in the development of an individual. Even in prenatal development the nurturing process of the individual is extremely important. This is why pregnant women are requested to stop smoking and drinking alcohol, not to use drugs except as prescribed, and to eat nutritional meals. Very often the above components are related to level of education and socioeconomic status. Bowes and Gintis (1973) in a study of level of economic achievement have pointed out the close and significant relationship of parental learning, I.Q., and academic achievement to economic opportunity. Families possessing a higher level of education and who hold higher paying jobs tend to live in more affluent neighborhoods, and tend to be more achievement and learning oriented. The modeling they may provide for their children, and the enriched setting tends to provide more opportunities for environmental stimulation of development. Conversely, a low level of socioeconomic background, constant moves, dependency on welfare and/or the imprisonment of one of the family members, usually has a negative effect on later development. If there has been a divorce or separation, or if the individual lived with only one parent, the quality of life may be impaired. On the other hand, sometimes this type of adversity may result in increased task-orientation and achievement. It is therefore important to ascertain the extent to which the individual client had a secure or relatively stable childhood. Attitudes towards father and mother often surface in such discussions. Ratings of the characteristics of mother and father in memory often have a direct relationship to the self-concept of the individual, with positive self-report being related to positive patterns of nurturance, and negative self-report being related to inadequate or aversive patterns of nurturance.

Birth order is associated with certain differences. Another important factor is to determine whether the client was the first-born child, an only child, or one of later siblings. Bradley (1982) has summarized literature relating to birth order. Though birth order is only one of a number of multidimensional aspects of family life, it does appear from a number of research studies that there is a preponderance of attorneys, congressmen, astronauts, physicians, teachers, and nurses who are first-born children. In addition, a number of researchers have found a linkage between intelligence and primacy of birth (Zajonc, 1976). Bradley has also related primacy of birth order to higher school performance.

Being a second, third, or later child makes a difference in terms of relationships with parents and other siblings. Parents make comparisons which are felt as very important determinants in individual behavior. Thus if the first born child is doing well in school and the second one is not, it is usual for parents to point that fact out. Sometimes a last child is different from all the others simply because of a resistance to being influenced. Certainly, there is a natural competitiveness between siblings for attention from the parents. From what has been theorized for the greater achievement and task-orientation of first born and only children, it may well be that parents lavish much more attention and concern on only or first-born children than they do on later ones.

Injuries or traumatic experiences affect the individual in multiple ways. Another important component in early childhood analysis and developmental history in the family is to determine the extent of accidents, hospitalizations, and other traumatic episodes. Severe diseases and chronic health conditions also play a part in this area of investigation. The reasons for this are related to physiological and mental functioning. Traumas, ingestion of toxic substances, accidents, and diseases all can impair both neurological intactness and mental functioning. Also grouped with this set of factors is any injury that occurred in birth. In addition, conditions which may impinge on the family setting should also be noted such as a history of mental retardation or state hospital commitment, criminal incarceration, child abuse, incest, and inordinate use of drugs or alcohol. Since drug usage is virtually epidemic in our society, this is an important area for concern and examination. All of the above factors can lessen the capability of the individual for achievement and the maintenance of stable and productive patterns of behavior. Most particularly these components as they impinge on the brain and central nervous system lessen the ability of the individual to solve problems successfully. As we shall see in the later section, a considerable number of these factors do relate to the needs assessment of the individual.

Education, Hobbies, Interests. Education, hobbies, and interests reflect both genetic components and socioeconomic status. Another area for further information is to determine the extent and quality of education attempted and accomplished. Education is an important personal determinant in the lives of most individuals. Access to higher education depends on the completion of high school or its equivalent. Success in higher education depends on habits of personal discipline and task orientation. In this sense it is tied into both temperament and cognition components. A discussion of early educational experiences, relationships with peers and teachers often provides illustrative examples from the individual's life about the success the individual had in coping with the stress of task-order achievement, grades, interpersonal relationships and career determination. It is often possible to determine what kinds of expectations parents, teachers, and peers had for the educational potential of the individual. From this analysis it is often clear how the individual viewed the experiences. In some instances such experiences may have led to further striving and effort, and in others blame for failure can be observed as being related to school authorities and teachers. Overall dispositions towards learning and the attribution of success and failure are key empirical factors in the development of temperament characteristics.

It is often helpful to ask the individual what kinds of studies were liked best and liked least. Often the studies liked and/or disliked have a relationship to hobbies which individuals pursue. Virtually always it will be found that individuals like those subjects in which they had success and disliked those subjects in which they had failure. The extent to which individuals had hobbies such as stamp collecting, coin collecting, model building is related to internal characteristics of discipline and achievement. Conversely, virtually exclusive preoccupation with sports, social activities, popular music, automobiles, and motorcycles is related to externality in personality. To be sure, many individuals show interest in both sets of activities, but the most important factor is to determine how extensive these activities were. Barclay (1966c), in a study of junior high students, found that interest patterns, specifically hobbies, music, and athletics were related to patterns of social acceptance by other students. Children with a higher interest in reading, stamp collecting, model building and similar activities often came from higher socioeconomic backgrounds. They were frequently seen by other children as "thinkers" rather than "doers." On the other hand, many popular children or leaders were highly interested in peer-oriented activities such as popular music, popular magazines, etc. Children from lower socioeconomic backgrounds participated less in athletic contests or school sponsored clubs and tended to be more interested in television. Some of this, of course, may be related to the fact that children from lower socioeconomic backgrounds often had more part-time jobs and needed money more than some of their "thinker" and "leader" colleagues, and thus had less time for other activities.

Religion and Values. The nature of religious training and background has an influence on values development. Formal religious or cultural instruction often influences the development of values. Western society by and large accepts explicitly or implicitly the Judaeo-Christian set of ethics. In Judaism there is a wide range of manifestations associated with congregations and specific religious exercises; some are very strict in observing dietary laws and specific religious garb as well as education. Others are more informal and really relate to a kind of cultural influence that indirectly permeates life and family affairs. Christian churches tend to divide themselves into evangelical and traditional forms. Some churches have a firm doctrine of literal interpretation of the Scriptures with a high reliance on direct correspondence to specific rules. Others tend to be more oriented towards collective and individual problem solving of moral responsibility. In addition, in some communities a specific religion can be the predominant one. In other societies, Islam forms a basis with a number of varieties of expression. In China, Confucianism plays a nonreligious, but moral-ethical role in the development of thinking. Specific religious training can be either a factor in the development of positive personal and social habits of responsibility or a deterrent if it is the source of unreasonable guilt, anxiety, and ritualism. Such determination can usually be made from the interview.

Sexual Development. Human sexuality is a life-long need. It forms the basis of intimacy and affection. More than any other area this is one that individuals may resent probing. Experience with other human problems, however, would tend to substantiate that patterns of sexual adjustment are often involved in the other problems of the individual. Attitudes towards the opposite sex, the extent of familiarity in social contacts, the attitudes of and formal training given by parents, the question of personal sexual preference and experiences both within and outside of marriage, are all factors that may relate to the effective functioning of the individual. The extent to which this area should interface with others in counseling and assessment is based on topic relevance, client willingness to share information, and good taste and judgment on the part of the clinician.

Vocational Directions. The attainment of a satisfying work relationship is an important personal task. Without question, much of the personal success of individuals is related to their ability to obtain and maintain a satisfactory career. Career selection is a process which begins in the elementary school, extends through junior and senior high school, and becomes specifically focused in the post–high school period when decisions have to be made either to attend a college or technical school, or to seek employment. The college years when individuals are forced to make decisions about majors and courses of study can be particularly stressful. Career determination, as Holland (1966) has pointed out, is part of a total plan that involves the scrutiny of personal assets and liabilities, preferences and interests, as matched against opportunities and academic achievement. In a very real sense, the socialization of the individual, the extent of education, personal interests, hobbies and preferences, the modeling effect of siblings and parents, and the availability of appropriate information and work experience all converge in vocational decisions. In addition, from studies of vocational thrust and the press of the environment, it appears most likely that temperament dispositions and cognitive style are critical components in making a good vocational choice. In contemporary society, problems relating to dual career marriages and other contributing factors such as the decision to have children, often complicate vocational planning or career evaluation. Not the least of modern-day problems is the growing need for advice and aid in mid-career changes and aging, because more and more people are living to retirement and beyond. In summary, empirical methods of interviewing can be used to provide considerable relevant information about the socialization and learning background of the individual. Such information should typically focus on the nature of the home and background, siblings and birth order, illnesses, trauma, and other factors which could involve intact neurological and/or mental functioning. The pattern of education, hobbies, religion, sexual experience, and vocational directions are also very important issues in assessment. It is likewise relevant to ask the individual about goals and aspirations, and what kind of planning has been made towards the future.

TEMPERAMENT ANALYSIS

Temperament characteristics can be estimated from empirical observations in the interview. In the first chapter temperament was defined as a comprehensive set of templates organized around hereditary dispositions that incline the individual to a given range of emotional activity. One of the central foci of the approach to assessment outlined in this book is the evaluation of temperament. Temperament is associated with affective ways of viewing reality. Because it is tied so centrally to mid-brain activities (i.e. the limbic system) it can directly affect both the reticular-activating system of arousal, and the cognitive system of knowledge retrieval and analysis. One of the problems with temperament is that there is a residue of older ideas associated with the construct. Thus for many decades of this century, there was a reluctance by researchers to use the word. However, in recent years there has been an increasing recognition of the importance of temperament in the analysis of human behavior. A round-table discussion including a

Table 6-1 Estimate of Temperament Characteristics from Observation Using a Bipolar Continuum

	Energetic Persistent Competitive Active	Sociable Affiliative Nurturant Outgoing	Controlled Compulsive Ritualistic Inflexible	Emotional Arousable Excitable Rapid Responses to Stimulation
Definitely shows characteristics of this pole				
Tends towards characteristics of upper pole				
Tends towards characteristics of lower pole				
Definitely shows characteristics of this pole				
Classification	Lethargic Non-Persistent Non-Competitive Passive	Private Self-Sufficient Autonomous Inward Oriented	Impulsive Acting-out Unpredictable Uncontrolled	Unemotional Calm Cool Slow Responses to Stimulation

Note: inferences drawn from observational data in the interview can be utilized to estimate the individual's position on these four temperament characteristics.

majority of American researchers in this field (Goldsmith, Buss, Plomin, Rothbart, Thomas, Chess, Hinde and McCall, 1987) examined the major constructs of temperament. Their first conclusion was that the construct is helpful despite the inability to define precisely how it interacts with environmental influences. One reviewer pointed out that we have no final definitions of intelligence either, but we accept it without hesitation. Another conclusion was that temperament included elements of activity (energy, intensity, vigor and pace of movement in both speech and thought, but not their contents), reactivity in terms of approach or withdrawal from stimuli, emotionality, and sociability. A third conclusion was that the origins of temperament were in biological predispositions, but the extent to which this was true was not agreed upon. Finally, there was a recognition that there was a higher degree of stability manifested in temperament expressions through the life span than for other features of personality.

Operationally, the characteristics of temperament that can best be distinguished in an empirical observational mode relate to four elements: (1) energy-activity, (2) sociability-affiliation, (3) control-impulsivity, and (4) emotionality.[1] These four elements can be evaluated empirically by examining the entire range of observations in the interview. They are few in number and easily identifiable. Each of them can be considered on a continuum that involves bipolarity, i.e., the element at one end represents the characteristic, and the one at the other end represents the opposite characteristic. Table 6-1 provides some guidelines for judging these characteristics. Energy and activity are associated with drive, persistence, leadership, and competitiveness. They are also most often associated with intelligence. On the opposite pole, there is a lack of effort, passivity, a follower mentality, and a non-assertive stance. Indicators of this set of characteristics can be found in learning, hobbies, and extracurricular activities. Individuals high in energy and drive are often field independent, like activities that require a great deal of energy such as sports, or even intense self-directed tasks such as building models or collecting stamps and coins. Being high in energy and activity does not necessarily indicate the construct of extroversion. Many private people or those tending towards introversion are also high in energy and activity. What is most differentiating between high energy people and passive ones is the extent to which the former finds all kinds of activities and thrusts in life. Individuals low in energy and drive are more field dependent, tend to wait for others to initiate activities, and often are not very effective in the ways they use their abilities.

Sociability-affiliation can be observed as a tendency towards needing people, liking social situations, providing others with nurturance, and being outgoing. On the opposite pole, characteristics may relate to being a private person, being more self-sufficient, and enjoying solitude. In extreme situations, the highly sociable-affiliative person simply cannot be satisfied unless he or she is involved in a host of activities with other people. Boredom sets in when the highly sociable individual is at home without anything to stimulate activity. For this reason, highly sociable individuals tend to watch more television, listen to the radio longer, and engage in activities that explicitly pull them away from solitude. On the contrary, individuals at the opposite end of the continuum may be very private persons who have a few good friends, but who are basically self-stimulating and self-oriented. To a large extent, this characteristic is reflected in how individuals arrange their own personal resources. Highly sociable people focus on outward relationships to keep themselves stimulated. Highly private people focus on inward relationships, since they often find their own level of excitation sufficient to keep themselves stimulated.

Control-impulsivity represents a continuum related in part to what has been referred to in Chapter 1 as volition. Both extremes of this characteristic can provide problems to the individual. The overly-controlled individual tends to be compulsive and ritualistic in following rules (either of his/her own making or of others). Gratification of basic desires is often postponed indefinitely. Rigidity of outlook is often reflected by over control. On the other hand, impulsivity is observed by acting-out behavior, immediate seeking of gratification of impulses, and unpredictable behavior. A balance between control and impulsivity appears to be associated with reasonable ego control and flexibility. Thus individuals who are neither excessively controlled nor impulsive often manifest the ability to direct their resources towards interim goals, to make a reasonable deferring of impulses, and to be flexible in adapting to alternative situations.

Emotionality is often associated with the display of affective responses. Fear, anger, physiological arousal, and excitement are posited at the high end of the emotionality continuum. The relationship of the autonomic nervous system and facial and skeletal-muscle responses are strong. Thus the emotional person tends to be easily aroused and explosive in nature. On the other end of the emotionality continuum, individuals tend to be slow to anger, show moderate arousal characteristics under circumstances that might elicit higher levels of response, and generally show a "cool" demeanor to situations calling for some form of emotional response.

To be sure, these four components of temperament are not truly independent of each other. Thomas and Chess (1977), Buss and Plomin (1975) and Strelau (1983) indicate initial connections between these components. All researchers indicate that these initial tendencies are modified gradually by socialization, observation, modeling, selective reinforcement, and self-determination. Nonetheless, identifiable patterns tend to emerge that are related to these categories. For example, extreme extroversion often involves high energy-activity, high sociability-affiliation, low or moderate control, and moderate to high emotionality. Extreme introversion might involve likewise high energy-activity, low sociability, high control, and low emotionality. Again, individuals who may be low on energy-activity, but high on sociability, impulsivity and emotionality can manifest all kinds of personal problems. Stable and unstable behavior patterns include various combinations of these temperament characteristics. A more precise description of these characteristics is dependent on more rigorous research in terms of statistical analysis and psychometric characteristics. For this chapter's purpose, suffice it to state that the major components of temperament can be estimated from a review of problems, a detailed analysis of behaviors associated with those problems, and observations drawn from life history and expressive movements.

COGNITIVE FUNCTIONING

Cognition involves the entire information-processing aspect of brain activity. We are typically dependent on psychometric findings to evaluate cognitive ability, but this is not a necessary factor. Empirically, we all observe others day in and day out. We make judgments about how intelligent they are from a variety of sensory clues that we obtain from interacting with them. Specifically, we consider verbal fluency, knowledge of abstract constructs, and social competency to be external manifestations of intelligence. Individuals who have a good vocabulary and who can describe their own problems in a range of verbal concepts usually represent a higher rather than lower level of intelligence. Where excellent immediate and long-term memory is joined to this, that is another indication of higher rather than lower intelligence.

Just as biological and genetic tendencies specify the nature of temperament, so biological and genetic tendencies underly the nature of cognition. Nor is it easy to separate cognitive aspects from temperament ones. Obviously cognition plays a role in the specific interaction that exists between intelligence and temperament. But for the purposes of this chapter, a distinction is being made simply from a focus point of view.

From an observational outlook, academic achievement is a good, but not necessarily accurate, measure of the use of intelligence. Individuals who have done well in school, i.e., who have received superior grades both in classroom and achievement tests, usually have a better cognition system. In addition, individuals who have a higher socioeconomic status as related to the achievement of their parents and their personal background, may have had a culturally enriched childhood. For adults, cognitive functioning and intelligence specifically can be estimated from achievement level and vocational status.

Generally, a rough estimate of intelligence can be formed from the occupational level of the client. Hartlage (1973) indicates that senior professional people such as executives of large corporations, senior statesmen, and senior university professors generally have an I. Q. of 130 and up (i.e., falling within the superior range). Other professionals such as physicians, acountants, chemists, engineers, dentists and college teachers he estimates fall within the 120–130 I.Q. range (though obviously there is no ceiling indicated here). People in college graduate level positions, supervisors, production managers, nurses, school teachers, pharmacists, etc., are in the 110–120 I.Q. range, while skilled tradesmen, electricians, licensed practical nurses, policemen, machinists, secretaries and opticians are in the 100–110 I.Q. range. Semi-skilled individuals such as firemen, painters, hospital orderlies, carpenters, bricklayers, timekeepers and file clerks fall in the 90–100 range, and unskilled laborers below that. Naturally, these are estimates made from general occupational and educational levels and should be employed with caution. Where there are questions about cognitive functioning, and vocational problems, further and more accurate clarification of characteristics can be made via the use of appropriate testing.

Coping style often provides an index of how effectively cognitive abilities have been utilized. Coping style refers to how effective individuals have been in solving their own problems. Often, it is not a matter of abstract intelligence that detracts from such problem solving, but rather the interaction with a host of temperament and environment components. Lazarus (1976) sheds considerable light on the analysis of the coping process in his discussion of what he calls THE BASIC ID. Lazarus uses the term as a mnemonic device to aid the user in recalling the elements of his system. This acronym refers to Behaviors, Affect, Sensation, Imagery, Cognition, Interpersonal, and Drugs. Lazarus views each of these areas as modalities. Naturally, he does not believe that they have a separate existence as such, but that they are all interconnected.

Lazarus defines behavior in terms of the overt verbal and motor characteristics of the individual. As we indicated earlier in the analysis of behavioral approaches, the components of intensity, frequency, and duration of behaviors are important in terms of the analysis of whether an individual's display of behavior is adequate, excessive (maladaptive), or deficient. Affect is considered a concomitant emotional response related to anxiety, frustration, rage, severe depression, etc. Lazarus feels that it is important to ascertain the self-report of individuals relative to these emotional movements. Thus an inquiry into what makes an individual respond in these ways is deemed very important.

Sensation mediates many of the higher-order processes. Some individuals block their own sensations and in some instances problems relate to basic sensory modalities, i.e., vision, audition, etc. The role of psychological characteristics in the development of psychosomatic disorders is thus acknowledged in the assessment process. Imagery is considered a very important component in assessment. Obviously imagery is related to affect and historical content. But it is well established from hypnosis and allied procedures that imagery in the sense of conjuring up images of memory items or fantasy desires is highly related to actual behavior. Thus the description of a luscious steak when an individual is hungry can serve to elicit responses in the organism including salivation. The same kinds of memory characteristics apply to sexual fantasies and behavior. Adequate sexual performance may even require a certain level of fantasy operation.

Cognition refers to the process of perceptual representation, concept formation, and symbolic activity unique to the individual. The role that cognition plays in the maintenance of both aberrant attitudes and values as well as healthy ones is something that Ellis (1962) has repeatedly detailed. Unquestionably thinking in terms of guilt, inability to behave, constrictions from outside including social pressures, do influence the behavior of the organism and serve often to inhibit the development of adequate behavior. The existence of irrational thinking is something that Ellis has defined as a cause of much human suffering. Thus the distinctive ways in which an individual thinks about reality are a vital component in eliciting change. For this reason many of those who have subscribed to psychodynamic theories of behavior have recognized the importance of identifying patterns of thinking that cause irrational discrimination in affect, subsequent depression, anxiety, and stress.

Interpersonal relations often serve as the arena in which most of the foregoing categories are galvanized into action. The role in which the individual finds himself/herself in terms of earlier family relationships and sibling influence, the present and past experience in marital relationships, and relationships to others in the domain of work and vocational fulfillment, are very important. The extent to which self-report of the individual on these matters agrees with objective and external observation is, of course, an important determinant in the course of therapy and/or treatments.

Illegal drug use is important in the total coping of some individuals. Today drug abuse is epidemic in many segments of the population. These drugs in almost every instance serve as a means of trying to cope with stress, anxiety, responsibility, and other factors in human socialization. Not only are specific pharmacological drugs used in this way (tranquilizers, "uppers," "downers"), but also alcohol, marijuana, cocaine, and narcotic substances are utilized for the same purposes. The fact that most of these drugs alter states of consciousness, increase or decrease levels of cortical arousal and inhibition, and affect both attention and judgment in reasoning is an important component in evaluating coping style.

All of the components which Lazarus has defined as ingredients into the assessment process of coping bear directly or indirectly on what have been termed defense mechanisms. Frustration, anxiety, and stress over failure to meet a conscious or even unconscious set of goals are often seen in three typical constellations of coping mechanisms. These may be identified as aggression, avoidance, and indecision. Aggression can be noted in typical patterns of behavior which result in increased volume of force, reddening of features, evidence of hostility, projection, and displacement. Where direct increase of force through violence cannot be sanctioned, indirect aggression can lead to the undercutting of competitors by "damning with faint praise," displaced emphasis, innuendo and the like. Aggressive responses can often be cloaked by apparently sweet behavior towards a likely victim.

Where aggression is ruled out as a means of defensive coping, individuals often turn to avoidance. Avoidance can take the form of physical withdrawal or running away from a situation, or psychic withdrawal in which there can be a continued preoccupation with daydreams or apathy. Often performance without ego involvement ("I'll do what you say, but when I fail it is your responsibility") is another form of withdrawal. Another form of avoidance is simply denial which has been relegated to the role of repression, an unconscious mechanism that psychoanalytic theorists see at the base of much mental disturbance.

Defensive operations are in themselves a kind of rough index to cognitive capabilities. The more elaborate they are, the more cognitive in nature, the more probable that an individual is capable of higher cognitive functioning. The defensive manuever often reflects the more mature approach to problem solving (as contrasted with increase of force or avoidance). However, it can also result in a host of other mechanisms in which the individual is caught up in an endless cycle of attempts, withdrawals, and frustrations. Sometimes this approach takes the form of compensation or substitution. Thus overeating is seen as a compensatory mechanism. Reaction formations (the embracing of a set of causes or values which may be essentially desirable to the individual such as arguing violently against sexuality, smoking, drinking, and the like) is another of these compensatory mechanisms. Rationalization is often an effort to reorder basic goals and to alleviate tension by changing goals. Finally devaluation of self-esteem is often a by-product of this approach.

The examination of typical sensory modalities utilized and defensive reactions employed aid the assessor in making a judgment about coping style as related to needs assessment, moral functioning, and ego functioning. Cautions need to be taken, however, to make sure that judgments of assessment are not made by quick intuitive leaps. Valid assessment depends on multimodal inputs.

EVALUATING THE VALIDITY CONDITIONS OF EMPIRICAL ASSESSMENT

Evaluating the validity of the client's perception is a key factor in assessing empirical observations. One of the major tasks of the clinician in the empirical assessment process is to determine the validity of the client's perception. By this is meant the extent to which the perception of the client agrees with reality factors in the personal or social environment. This is really a key factor, because all judgments concerning a client are related to judgments about the competency and validity of the impressions proceeding from the client's verbal and nonverbal behavior. Perception is indeed a kind of "open window" on the thinking of another. It is the conscious avenue to

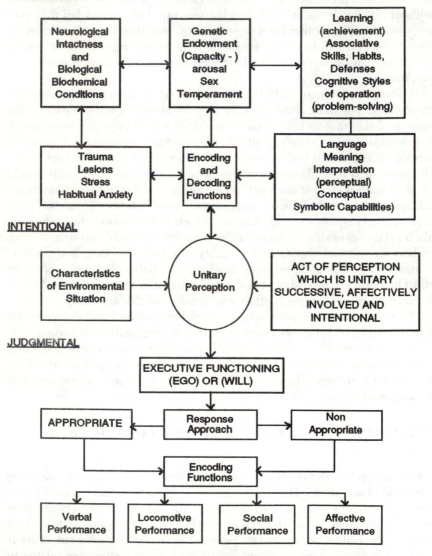

Figure 6-2 **Interaction Between Model Components**

the private world of brain functioning that exists in each of us. And it is in perception that the entire physiological and psychological state of the organism is both reflected and transmitted through simultaneous reactions of the human body. To explain the kinds of influences which can impact on the individual and thus create faulty changes in perception may be helpful at this point. The behaviors of individuals which we observe in their speech, eye contact, and body movements are reflective of a number of interacting components. Each of these will be discussed separately, but it should be recognized that they interact.

Genetic Structure. By this is meant the hereditary endowment of the individual. Obviously, this can only be estimated since so many factors have impinged on and interacted with it. But intelligence or lack thereof tends to show through either as enhanced by a variety of interactive factors or lessened by similar interactions. The same judgment applies to temperament characteristics related to the emotional system of the individual.

Neurological Intactness. By this is meant the extent to which the brain and nervous system together with other systems of the body are providing the proper physiological and structural basis for homeostasis. Any arbitrarily determined capacity of a system (such as abstract, motor, and social intelligence) is essentially a potential to be realized in actual performance. Though the brain is quick to adapt and often provides alternative methods of circumventing problems in the neurological area, failures in this area are bound to have an effect on the quality and integration capabilities of perception. Thus it is important to recognize that trauma of any kind (blows to the head, accidents, military wounds, etc.), could be related to diminished capability in attention, coordination or production of logical thinking and problem-solving. In addition, the effects of aging and certain illnesses such as Alzheimer's which may impinge on the nature of neurological intactness are also factors to be considered.

Biological and Biochemical Conditions. Closely related to problems of neurological structure are those of the basic biology and biochemistry of body processes. Much evidence is present today that altered mental states may be related to specific biochemical, hormonal and biological malfunctions. For example, a deficiency in lithium is seen as a possible cause of debilitating prolonged depressions such as Abraham Lincoln and Winston Churchill appeared to have had. Certain depressant and stimulant drugs have different reactions on extroverts and introverts (thus for example, introverts tend to become more extroverted via depressants such as liquor, and extroverts become more introverted through the use of stimulants) (Powell, 1979). Moreover, the habitual effects of alcoholism or substance abuse are likewise known as agents which interact with brain tissue and create damages or alterations in both perception and behavior. Thus it is important to determine in the interview whether an individual is on medication or has been on medication. If discussion of alcohol or substance abuse takes place, it is important to ascertain just how much of either or both have been used and their probable effect on perception. The estimate of use of either alcohol or drugs is usually far below what has been actually consumed. Thus an admission to one or two alcoholic drinks per day is usually an acknowledgment of far more.

Learning. Unquestionably a large portion of perceptual output is the consequence of learning. Patterns of speech and thinking are reflective of the experience of learning. When the condition of the organism is influenced by neurological or biochemical problems or stress, undoubtedly the past influence of learning is also affected. Useful to an estimate of impaired functioning is an assessment of the discrepancy between the level of background, education and previous achievement attained, and the level of current functioning. When there is either a gradual or sudden increase of loss of jobs, decrease in income, and decrease in personal responsibility (not associated with retirement, of course), then there are good reasons to hypothesize that an impairment exists. Sometimes such sudden decreases in personal efficacy reflect a brain tumor or other cerebral conditions.

Decoding-Encoding. Decoding is a term referring to the process whereby incoming sensations are analyzed in the act of perception. Encoding refers to the process whereby perceptions are interpreted within the individual and reactions manifested. The manner in which a client interprets the responses of the counselor is a process of decoding. The total input available to the client from listening and watching the counselor is analyzed in the action of perception and is invested with meaning of some kind. Thus if the client perceives the counselor as being sympathetic, understanding, and empathic, this meaning is usually conveyed to the counselor from the interpretation of the client's behavior. Products of the autonomic nervous system of the client together with verbal responses then provide another set of data for the counselor to decode.

It is important to realize that all the factors we have been discussing interact and affect the unitary act of perception. In the transactions of communication there is a rapid and simultaneous exchange of decoding and encoding procedures taking place between two individuals. And it is precisely on the skills that the counselor or clinician possesses in decoding the perception of the client that judgments are made about internal states of the client.

Output. The process of reasoning and thinking which occurs by virtue of the encoding-decoding process usually results in some kind of action. The quality and characteristics of that action reflect the interpretation of perception, the judgment of meaning, and the executive response. Thus the integration of reality forces is shown by the quality of the response. Naturally, stress states influence this response and the content. Thus it is the interpretation of both verbal and nonverbal cues provided by the client that gives the psychologist an insight and understanding into the quantity and quality of verbal production and thinking associated with client needs and affect. It is the analysis of this production which provides insight into the state of ego integration, defenses, and moral development. Skills in this area require not only knowledge of all relevant components, but also training in the recognition of their implications for adequate human functioning.

In this section of the chapter the topic of the evaluation of personal functioning has been discussed in some detail. The reasons for this are related to estimating how well an individual is capable of coping with problems. The process of human life is replete with a continual flow of problems that need to be addressed and solved. Problem solving and coping ability can be severely hampered by any one of the components described in this section. Assessment should lead to a plan, particularly if it is related to a form of counseling, guidance, or therapy. This involves problem determination, behavioral analysis, explanation of environmental factors, observation of temperament and cognitive components and especially the notation of those conditions that may hamper the implementation of such a plan. In recent years it has become clearer that neurological, drug, and aging factors can severely handicap the individual's ability to cope.

EXPRESSIVE MOVEMENTS

Body movements externally display internal states of emotional involvement. Body movements are based on an inference of correspondence between mental states and physiological responses. A very ancient and impressionistic basis for empirical assessment is close observation of body movements. For centuries people have recognized that both cognitive and emotional states are subject to correlative expressive movements in behavior. In point of fact it is said that the body does not lie. An old adage states: "What you are thunders so loudly in my ears that I cannot hear what you say." Whereas in behavioral observations the inferences drawn are to learning, in the observation of body movements the inferences are often made to assumed body-mind correspondences.

Expressive movements according to Wolff (1943) are movements of an automatic nature that may be reflected in gestures, facial expression, gait, writing, drawing, and many other personal manifestations. Basically, these movements, gestures, or facial expressions, represent the thought processes of the sender. Cuceloglu (1967) presents a theoretical model of comunication via facial expression that conveys feelings. It is an encoding process for the subject and a decoding process for the observer. For example, a client speaks of an episode in his/her life; while speaking, the client's expressive movements encode (transmit) the inner emotional experience. Trembling, breaks in voice transmission, downcast eyes, efforts to wipe away tears, all encode to the observer the message of intense grief and emotional reaction. The process as judged by the assessor becomes a decoding one in which a set of interpretations or inferences are made. What the client experiences as an emotional episode is encoded in that way, and the reactions which are internal are transmitted via expressive movements. The psychologist or assessor then decodes the information and responds. The psychologist's responsive feelings are in turn encoded by his or her own expressive movements and subsequently decoded by the client in terms of support, lack of support, or other feelings.

There are a number of functional interpretations which can be made from expressive movements. However, it is not always easy to make such inferences. Birdwhistell (1970) theorizes that as many as 5,000 bits of information may be transmitted between two people in one minute. The structure of this process has been analyzed by a number of researchers. For example Mehrabian and Ksionsky (1972) attempted to discern the major categories which influenced judgments of social behavior as related to nonverbal communication. Utilizing 256 undergraduate students and 22 confederates, they analyzed both verbal and nonverbal responses between students and clients recruited for that purpose. Through the analysis of video and audio tape recordings their results suggested that affiliative relationships are connected to: (1) the number of positive statements made per minute; (2) the percentage of duration of eye contacts; (3) positive verbal content and head nods; (4) head and arm gestures made per minute; and (5) the pleasantness of facial expression.

Osgood (1966) has pointed out that there are similarities between semantic categories of judgment such as potency evaluation, and nonverbal modes of expression. Tompkins, (1962) found that the primary facial muscles and affects are universal to mankind and are most clearly related to: (1) expressions of interest-excitement; (2) enjoyment-joy; (3) surprise-startle; (4) distress-anguish; (5) fear-terror; (6) shame-humiliation; (7) contempt-disgust, and (8) anger-rage.

Cuceloglu (1967) said, however, that students of facial expression must distinguish between the basic system level (physiological-emotional response) and the content. Individuals in different cultures express contextual differences in nonverbal communication that may relate to closeness to each other, modes of expression and other factors associated within a specific culture. The decoding process is subject to many considerations that are both system reflective and contextual. For example, a lifted arm may serve to reach for an object or offer a greeting, or it could be a gesture of aggression, or defense. One must study specific gestures and movements in terms of both context or symbolic significance (such as in psychoanalytic theory). Some generally accepted interpretations of nonverbal communication responses are grouped together in the following figure.

Wolff (1943) indicates that extreme inhibition, depression, and elation can be detected by a combination of expressive movements. For example, extreme inhibition is often characterized by nervous jerking and reflexive movements, as well as withdrawal movements, repetitive ones, and gestures of anxiety, such as scratching, eyelid fluttering, finger gnawing, clenching hands, and wringing of hands. Depression is often represented by slow motor or verbal speed, hiding gestures, hesitation, indecision, face-mask expressions, and a slow gait. Elation is reflected by quick movements, expressions of joy, smiling and shouting.

Another form of expressive movement is graphology. **Graphology is a term that refers to handwriting analysis.** Although graphology can also be considered a projective technique, it often occurs in an interview, if an autobiography is written by the client. In addition, with projective tests such as the *Thematic Apperception Test*, sometimes the client writes out interpretations of the pictures, and in this sense handwriting does provide some clues as to current mental states. Handwriting analysis has been for a long time a part of European training programs in clinical psychology. Until very recently, courses in graphology were required in European clinical training programs, and were accorded the same or greater respect as specific projectives such as the *Rorschach*.

Graphology has been of interest to psychologists for a number of centuries. Purportedly, it started with an effort to analyze handwriting by Camillo Baldi, an Italian scholar and physician in 1622. According to Crumbaugh (1980), it was practiced as an art rather than a science by Goethe, Poe, the Brownings, Leibnitz, Balzac, Dickens, and many others. Alfred Binet who originated the first intelligence tests used handwriting analysis to test personality and ostensibly could distinguish successful from unsuccessful persons by their writing with an accuracy of 61 to 92%. Other psychologists who were interested in this area were William Preyer at the University of Berlin, Ludwig Klages who developed the term "expressive movements" and N. M. Bunker who in 1929 coined the term graphoanalysis. Graphoanalysts have an international society, work or consult in business and industry, vocational counseling, in mental health clinics and hospitals, and in forensic investigations (for more information, see Roman, 1961, Singer, 1969, and Crumbaugh, 1980).

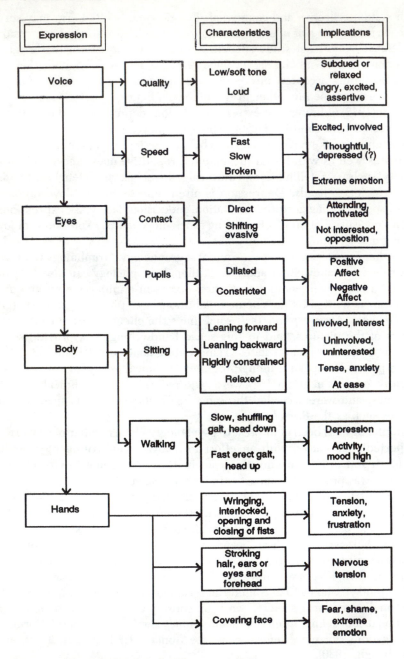

Figure 6-3   **Representative Body Characteristics**

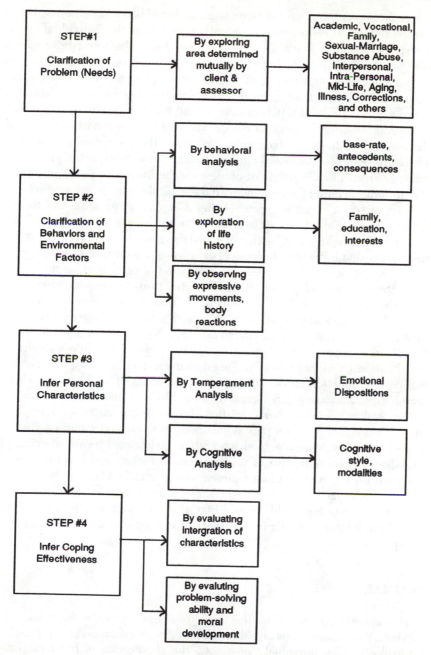

Figure 6-4 **Steps of the Empirical Assessment Process**

Graphology is based on the same logic as that of body movements. Handwriting is seen to represent a systematic encoding of the individual's characteristics. As the individual's mental and emotional characteristics undergo change, there are subtle but distinct changes in handwriting. Thus graphology is the interpretation of the decoding process of the individual's encoded responses, and represents an alternative method of evaluating expressive movements. It is particularly helpful within the context of the functional and behavioral aspects of the interview, if the client wishes to provide the assessor with an autobiography written in the individual's own hand. There are both functional and clinical aspects to the interpretation of handwriting. From a functional point of view handwriting is responsive to states of deterioration under the influence of old age, alcoholism, drugs, and extreme anxiety, or stress which is overwhelming. Graphology goes beyond the immediate functional inferences to a set of clinical inferences that include the intuitive. Graphology looks at the form and movement of handwriting. Movement is divided into characteristics of expression, coordination, speed, pressure, tension, and direction. The interpretation of vertical expansion is said to relate to self-display, and claim in status (thus those individuals who perceive themselves as high in status tend to use more and more grandiose forms of writing, and particularly with regard to their signature). Horizontal expansion is interpreted as a demand for elbow room and freedom. A smooth coordination reportedly manifests integrated processes, while a disturbed coordination unintegrated ones. Speed characterizes the tempo of somatic and psychic functioning, while pressure is an index of vital energy. Heavy markings relate to impulsivity and a strong libido, while light ones tend to reflect weak or irresolute characteristics. High tension (constricted as opposed to free-flowing) indicates a poor adjustment to stress and strain or physical anxiety, and low tension a good integration. A leftward trend in writing is considered to be indicative of introversion, passivity, and femininity with emphasis on the past and inner dimensions of reality. Conversely, a rightward trend is seen as extroverted, active, masculine, future-oriented and relating to the outer world. In addition to these characteristics, the style, size of the letters, and alignment, margin, and signature are all subject to interpretation.

SUMMARY

This chapter has reviewed the major components in the assessment interview. Four major steps are identified: (1) the clarification of the problem by exploring the individual's needs; (2) the clarification of behavioral and environmental factors by an examination of actual behavior and life history noting expressive movements and body reaction; (3) the determination of personal characteristics both as they relate to emotive and cognitive components; and finally (4) an evaluation of the individual's ability to cope, particularly as there may be constraints on such coping through neurological or other factors that mediate such efforts.

CHAPTER **VII**

Psychometrics and Inferencing Methods

"Test theory has had few major ideas. I can list only five: 1. the decomposition of obtained scores into true and error components; 2. the duality of psychophysics and psychometrics; 3. the notion of unidimensionality; 4. the idea of test validity as theoretical equivalence, usually called construct validity; 5. the scaling ideas derived from various item chacteristics curve models. Apart from the first, these ideas have been hesitatingly and unconfidently applied" (Lumsden, 1976, p. 251).

INTRODUCTION

Modern assessment is heavily dependent on psychometric methods. In recent years there has been much criticism of the internal focus of psychometric theory, suggesting that test makers are more concerned about eking out meaning from items and scales rather than constructing tests which have relevant meaning (Levy, 1973). In this chapter we shall attempt to survey the rationale of psychometric assessment and the variety of techniques which have been developed in terms of the inductive and deductive processes involved. **This chapter does not intend to be a substitute for a course textbook in psychological testing such as Anastasi (1976) provides, or as a forum for reviewing the characteristics of specific tests as evaluated by the** *Mental Measurement Yearbooks* **(Mitchell, 1985) or** *Test Critiques* (Freyser and Sweetland, 1984). It is assumed that most readers will be familiar with tests, and will know that specific reviews of tests can be found in the above cited sources. The thrust of this chapter is to provide a background in the nature of psychometrics as applied to testing, to relate such a background to the various levels of assessment, with specific focus on traits, aptitudes, temperament, and cognition, and to present the specific assets and liabilities of testing as a central component in assessment.

In Chapter 2 the historical development of mathematics and its relationship to psychometry was outlined. **What mathematical theory was to science is what psychometrics has become to assessment.** In both instances the ability to quantify forces, vectors, and characteristics through mathematical means has been an extremely important tool. Psychometry has become so central in assessment because it purports to provide an objective basis for describing the characteristics of individuals, groups or environments. It does this by converting measureable dimensions into indices that reflect a mathematical quantity. It is easy, then, to equate a person's interest patterns, achievement, and personality to those objective quantities. However, both in the philosophy of science and in the theory of assessment, mathematical quantification can become the tail that wags the dog. Test results or computer printouts are not the efficient cause of conceptual theory, but rather a by-product of construct development. Where there are sound and solid constructs, well implemented in psychometric theory, there are good tests. Where there is a lack of conceptual thought, there are poor tests.

THE NATURE OF PSYCHOMETRICS

The psychometric method is an approach to the measurement of mental or physical characteristics which is considered objective. Psychometric methods are considered objective because they are based on a scientific approach to the measurement of characteristics as contrasted with the subjective aspects of the interview or empirical observations. The differences between psychometric observations and empirical observations is that the former are assumed to be based on an objective method of making observations and the latter are viewed as being related specifically to the limitations of clinician observations. A test then represents (through the use of psychometric methods) an objective measure of some aspect or sample of behavior (Anastasi, 1976, p. 23).

Psychometric observations are dependent on both inductive and deductive reasoning procedures. The psychometric process is one that starts first with a basic construct. This may be arithmetic achievement, sociability, or one from a variety of other areas. The question addressed psychometrically is how to understand and conceptualize this basic construct in such a way that it can be examined. Typically this is done by clearly defining the construct and then developing a series of items that are believed to describe that construct. Note that we do not start with several items first, and then try to find out what they refer to, but we start with as clear a concept of what it is we are attempting to measure as is possible, and then develop items that are believed to relate to that construct.

We often arrive at the nature of the construct itself from empirical observation, or even intuition. The point is that the basic ingredient of all

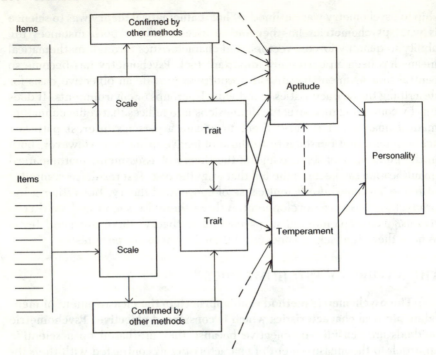

Figure 7-1 **Hierarchy of Assessment**

testing is the development of good items. From items, scales are developed. Scales represent a grouping of items that relate to a specific construct. Psychometric methods strongly emphasize the method of induction. However, they do not exclude the use of deduction. The distinction is that in the initial development of items and scales, the inductive method is followed. Subsequently, in the analysis of common sources of variance, a deductive and extracting procedure is used. In this section of the chapter we shall discuss first the inductive procedures and then the deductive ones.

In Chapter 1 the hierarchy of assessment terms was specified. These terms are important in understanding the inductive procedures of psychometrics. They range from the smallest unit of response, to skill, to trait, to aptitude, and finally to temperament, cognition and personality. Psychometric methods can be used in most of these areas. It should be noted, however, that ordinarily psychometric methods begin with the creation of items. Scales that measure traits or aptitudes are composed of all related items.

The measurement of responses in psychometric theory can refer to answers given to a testing stimulus or to latency in responding. Although the term response refers to an observable behavior in empirical observations or interviewing, it is also used in psychometric theory to represent a response to an item. In computerized testing the time it takes for the subject to respond to the item can be measured. This approach is often called response latency and may indicate either resistance in responding or difficulty level in responding. Items are grouped into scales, and scales form parts of a test. Although some tests involve or include only one scale, it is more likely that there are several scales which measure different things. Some individuals tend to equate a test with a trait, but the distinction is not automatic. **A trait, such as impulsivity, sociability or dominance, MAY be associated with a scale or even a test. However, a trait needs to be confirmed by multiple methods.** Some of the methods whereby a trait can be established include agreement between empirical and/or behavioral observations with a psychometric scale, the use of autobiographical data to document specific characteristics observed over a long period of time, and the use of factor analysis. For example, sociability as a trait may be indicated by a high score on a specific scale or scales of the *California Psychological Inventory*. It might be said to be confirmed by a personal history in which sociable outgoing contacts with other people appear to be the rule. It could also be confirmed by observation of the individual in a social setting. Although sometimes the term skill is used interchangeably with trait, this is not a consistent use of that term, since skill as defined in the first chapter is an observable ability that reflects learning and the performance of multiple responses. In this context, skill does not have a viable psychometric equivalent, but is rather inferred from a group of traits. Very often, a statistical procedure called factor analysis is used to clarify the nature of traits. A trait is identified by a factor analysis of either items or scales of a test. The product of such a procedure yields entities termed factors. These factors, particularly if they are replicated many times through independent studies, are often identified as traits. This is the case with tests, such as the *Sixteen Personality Factor Questionnaire* in which the factors are referred to as traits.

Basic or fundamental units of measurement can be grouped to form larger assemblies of traits and characteristics. The concept of aptitude refers to the grouping of assemblies of traits which relate to motor, vocational, and academic-cognitive characteristics. **The term aptitude generally is viewed as the product of factor analysis when related to cognitive abilities.** Factor analysis has been one of the chief ways to define multiple cognitive aptitudes (Anastasi, 1976, p. 15).

The concept of temperament refers to the grouping of assemblies of traits, specifically in hierarchical order, that relates to emotional, motivational, and affective characteristics. The terms aptitude and temperament often provide a source of confusion in the minds of students because they are viewed as equivalent with traits or even scores. The concepts of aptitude and temperament both represent higher-order aggregations of traits. Traits are established by multimethod verification and from a psychometric point of view are usually based on a set of scale dimensions reflective of the trait and initially derived from items that are used in scale determination. Thus, for example, if we state that an individual has high mechanical aptitude, it would usually mean that he would have a pattern of vocational interests similar to Holland's outdoor-mechanical cluster of characteristics and the occupations which he has coded as being related to that aptitude area.

With regard to the construct of temperament, this notion also consists of the aggregation of traits, but inclines towards the total aspect of the individual, specifically emotional characteristics and patterns of extroverted or introverted behavior. It is then in the determination of cognitive aptitudes and temperament characteristics that the aggregate of responses, scales, and traits build up to provide a basis for deductive inferencing. Ultimately, behind the total scaffolding of assessment constructs are the primary biological and hereditarily-linked components of intelligence, emotions, and cortical processes of excitation and inhibition (Eysenck and Rachman, 1965). The final construct, that of personality, includes the highest organization of psychometric characteristics and reflection of environmental stimulation and learning. It is the most abstract level of all. Most test publishers provide information based on scales. Some of the major tests however refer to scales, traits, aptitudes, and temperament dimensions as equivalent terms. This leads to considerable confusion in the minds of those who attempt to deal with these tests. For example, the *Differential Aptitude Test Battery* refers to its components as aptitude scores, and the *Myers-Briggs* and *Taylor Temperament* inventories refer to their outputs as temperament dimensions. Sometimes those labels may be correct, but more often they are not.

Generally, the position which will be taken in this chapter is that the scale is the basic unit of psychometrics and it is composed of items. Traits MAY legitimately be based on scales, provided there is multimethod justification for this judgment. Aptitude refers to a cluster of mechanical, social or cognitive traits closely related to intelligence and learning, and temperament to a cluster of emotional traits closely related to central cortical processes as mediated by excitation and inhibition.

FUNDAMENTAL ASSUMPTIONS OF PSYCHOMETRICS

The first and foremost assumption underlying psychometrics is that if a construct can be defined in terms of observable performance and behavior, it can be measured. From the older psychophysical procedures and reaction-time studies it was evident that individuals differed in relationship to their ability to respond to stimuli. Cattell's derivation of the reaction-time studies of Wundt was to apply this to the measurement of individual differences. Thus intelligence could be inferred from the rapidity and accuracy of responses to stimuli.

A second assumption relates to another axiom in correspondence, i.e., that there are correspondences between mind-body states and psychometric outcomes. This assumption is similar to the correspondence between perceived reactions and internal states which is a major assumption of empirical observations. What this means is that test scores are assumed to correspond with mental traits and states. Psychometric theory basically assumes that there is a correspondence between what is observed in testing and the extent or quantitative characteristics of mental or physical functioning existing in the individual. Thus a high score on a test scale which measures impulsivity is assumed to correspond to a tendency of that individual to act in impulsive ways. Naturally, there are many conditions which must be satisfied before one can justifiably agree to the correspondence assumption. Test items must be valid indicators of the trait with empirical foundations, the test must be adequately constructed with acceptable reliability and validity criteria, and the circumstances relating to testing including the environmental context and personal attitudes of the testee all play an important role in whether the correspondence assumption is justified or not. Finally, the test must be administered under standardized conditions with standardized scoring.

A third major assumption is that most measures of ability, traits, and/ or performance are distributed normally in the population. This means that, given any identifiable construct in achievement, aptitude, temperament, personality or interests, it is assumed that there is a normal distribution of these characteristics, provided there is a large enough sample drawn randomly from the population base. The characteristics of individuals can then be described, utilizing measures associated with the mean, mode, median and standard deviation, as well as with the use of a variety of standardized scores such as stanines, z scores, T scores and the like which facilitate comparisons of individuals among tests. An individual's score or scores then represent points on a continuum related to a population.

It is important to realize, however, that this assumption applies to large unselected populations. If a restrictive criterion is used or applied to a given population, this can decrease the variability in the target group. For example, if one examines the mental abilities of entering freshmen at a rural multipurpose educational institution, there is more likely to be a wider range of abilities than for freshmen entering a highly selective Ivy League institution. The consequences of a restrictive set of criteria on a college population often decreases the ability of admission tests to predict grades or other academic accomplishments. This is the reason why predictions of accomplishment for

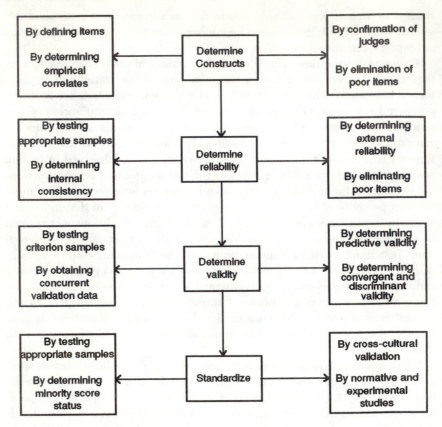

Figure 7-2   **Representative Tasks in Psychometric Development**

graduate students from admission tests are often insignificantly low. The same restrictions can also apply to populations or groups who have similar emotional or temperament traits.

A fourth assumption is that trait characteristics represent clusters of attitudes and behaviors which are consistently maintained over long periods of time. This assumption has been verified by numerous studies tracing trait characteristics over periods of 20, 30 and even 40 years (see Block and Haan, 1971, and Conley, 1984).

PSYCHOMETRIC CONSTRUCTION

The construction of psychometric scales is dependent on the nature of the phenomena to be categorized. In the development of the psychometric method a number of rules were established. These rules are in part related to the kinds of data that one may be attempting to measure. For example, virtually all measurement data used in connection with psychometric instruments fall into one of four categories: (1) nominal or categorical, (2) ordinal, (3) interval or (4) ratio scales. The nominal or categorical scale is one in which there are characteristics, or qualities without any sequential order. Thus, we may consider sex, eye color, marital status, or race as examples of nominal data. The ordinal category refers to a process of ranking individuals on some variable. Thus we may assign first, second, third, and fourth places in a spelling contest to John, Mary, Elizabeth, and Paul. In this kind of a scale there is no concern about the absolute distance between the rankings, but simply the sequencing of such ranks. Interval data requires that there be some kind of scale or range of scores which can be identified. Thus, points earned on a final examination can be used as illustrative of interval data. Ratio data requires a criterion or reference point. Thus the measurement of individuals' heights has reference to a scale of measurement. Fiske (1971) has pointed out that each of these methods requires more and more specificity. Nominal or categorical data analyses requires only that individuals be assigned to various categories or bins. Ordinal data calls for the specification of a rank and interval data requires the development of a set of steps or intervals (which most often are postulated at equal units of measurement). Ratio scales not only include the above characteristics but also require reference to a criterion. Generally most education and psychological studies seem to concentrate largely on ordinal and interval data analyses, though sometimes the assumption that differences in individuals can be made on an interval basis is not strictly consistent with the task at hand.

Construct Identification. The construction of a psychometric index or scale begins with a clear idea of what the goals of measurement are. Unquestionably this consists of defining a construct carefully and clearly. The procedure further mandates separating or dividing the goals with precision and as much previous knowledge as is possible. If one's goal is to measure achievement, it is necessary to specify what kinds of achievement are being addressed and to consider already known information about developmental levels. If one is examining personality characteristics, then it is appropriate to define very carefully the construct(s) under consideration. For example, one might utilize Murray's needs system as a frame of reference for developing certain constructs. Though all psychometric indices begin with clear construct formation, there are different ways that individuals go about doing this. However, some of the major ways that indices are created include: (1) developing a pool of items which represent the trait or characteristic under consideration (often by pooling the impressions of a group of knowledgeable individuals); (2) placing the items under the scrutiny of a group of judges (knowledgeable individuals in the particular field or discipline) and asking them to make discriminatory judgments as to which item fits with alternative categories; (3) examining the consistency of judges' opinions and throwing out those items on which there is not considerable interjudge agreement; (4) trying out the revised items on a general population of individuals for whom the items are appropriate; (5) trying out the items on individuals who may be empirically consistent with the constructs under consideration (such as trying out items purporting to evaluate the extent of depression on known depressives); (6) eliminating poor items either from the general population testing or the special group testing or both; (7) examining scales for internal consistency and/or test-retest reliability; and (8) establishing cross-validation by correlations with other tests known to possess high reliability and validity or with other methods such as interview data, peer nominations, or behavioral observations.

Validity and Reliability. One of the first and foremost characteristics of a good psychometric index is validity. **Validity refers to the qualitative judgment that the index provides sound descriptive data for decision making.** The focus on good decision making is the precise contribution which psychometrics makes to assessment (Cronbach and Gleser, 1965). In point of fact, if tests are not reliable and valid measures of individual differences, and even if they are, but are not related to improving decisions about alternative classifications, descriptions or treatments, then they are useless in assessment.

Validity begins (and some say may really ends) at the construct stage which we have just described above. Without good and careful conceptualization of just what is meant by the construct or constructs under consideration, it is unlikely that one can have a valid index. Typically, one can look at the content of the index or test, the relationship to effective criteria of human performance, and agreements obtained by comparisons with other instruments. In addition, the extent to which the index provides both convergent results with other methods of assessment or other tests and discriminant differences is one of the strongest aspects of the consensual approach.

By content validity is meant the extent to which a series of items or scales reflect the subject matter or task at hand. If one is looking at spelling achievement, then there should be an array of spelling terms, procedures, rules and methods which are consistent with the learning process, developmental stages in that process, and what is actually taught. So likewise, in the determination of the content validity of a personality trait, it is important to identify those behavioral traits or characteristics which are closely identified with a trait—such as sociability or impulsivity. Content validity can often be established in part through the use of expert judges, or comparison with existing instruments. However, caution has to be taken with this latter approach to content validity because sometimes repeated generations of instruments can be developed based on assumed content validity since similar items are used. The establishment of such content validity or consensual validity (often referred to as concurrent validity) can be considered a case of psychometric incest, particularly if correspondence with behavioral or other observational techniques is lacking.

Criterion-referenced validity virtually always involves the situation of prediction, and often relates to observable independent judgments. Though prediction in an absolute sense is most likely an impossible goal, given the contextual way in which individuals make decisions (see Chapter 1), a certain amount of predictive validity is indispensable in a valid index or test. Thus academic achievement tests in high school should be predictive of college entrance examinations, and vocational interest profiles should show some relationship to the characteristics of individuals who have been successful in a given occupation. Similarly, personality tests which purport to measure introverted or extroverted behavior should show some relationship to behavioral measures of these characteristics.

There are a variety of means that can be used for assessing the extent of criterion-referenced validity of an index or test. Many of these are related to performance in personal, academic, or social settings. Performance that is particularly relevant and appropriate is often judged to be a competency. Thus, many schools and organizations are moving towards the development of performance criteria that specify characteristics of competency. **Generally, criteria of psychometric validity should be relevant to the task, independent of the test itself, reliable and pragmatically applicable.** For example, if we are looking at performance in a higher education setting as a criterion of validity for an achievement test, we might find that the achievement test under consideration has a much higher prediction of grades and other performance data, such as awards, activities, etc., at a regional state college than at an Ivy League institution. Though we have selected a relevant criterion reference for our achievement test, the restricted range of admissions at the Ivy League institution would result in a lowered predictive correlation where the wider range of talents and abilities in the local state college would result in higher correlations. So likewise, in a particular business one set of behaviors may be desirable, but not transferable to another organization. Thus, it may be the modal form of behavior at a large corporate office for executives to wear three-piece suits and provide a low profile image. At other offices this same set of expectancies are not operative. Care must be taken in choosing criteria for prediction of testing results to select those criteria which are usually considered typical characteristics. This has been the general approach of those vocational tests which have attempted to estimate the probability of success for a given individual based on the similarity of the individual's profile to successful individuals in that occupation.

Validity can be assessed also by the extent of agreement with another set of measures which measure the same trait or characteristic. This is referred to as concurrent validity. Concurrent validity is the most common method of establishing validity because it usually results in correlations between indices or traits or scales on test 1 with test 2. Obviously this is a way of establishing validity provided that the second test has construct validity. More important is the approach outlined by Campbell and Fiske (1959) using convergent and discriminant validity. The basic contention here is that a trait as measured in method 1 (let us say through self-report) should correlate highly with the similar trait as measured in method 2 (for example peer ratings). So likewise, there should be a discriminant validity shown by negative correlations on opposing traits such as a comparison of sociability-affiliation with hostility-alienation in the two methods. If the trait measures are accurate and valid ones, then there should be significant positive correlations between similarly conceived traits, and significant negative correlations between opposing traits. In short this method of convergent and discriminant validity analysis tends to document the accuracy of a trait construct. This method can also be applied to different approaches to assessment utilizing behavioral observations, test data, peer nominations and the like. Though ideal in its conceptualization, the method detailed by Campbell and Fiske has been difficult to apply. One of the most important aspects of validity lies in the interpretation of the validity correlation. Typically, those who design tests wish to see high validity correlations with content, criteria, and concurrent approaches. There are many tables which refer to the extent to which various correlation coefficients relate to the identification of different percentages of the population. But in some instances a prediction of 10 to 20% above chance can be useful. Thus a test designed to determine the characteristics of depressed individuals who need medication versus psychotherapy, if it distinguishes at a level of 10 to 20% above chance allocation, is better than no test at all. So likewise a procedure in education which enhances the learning of a part of the school population above the chance level is worth trying out. The primary purpose of testing is to improve decision making and this often relates to estimates about the effectiveness of alternative treatments. Ultimately, psychometric indices, based as they are on the assumptions of normal distribution of characteristics, provide both descriptive information about individuals and aid in providing relevant information for decision making. The extent to which certain indices or scales possess sound descriptive and predictive characteristics depends largely on the purpose of the assessment device in the hands of the professional. For example, Rosenthal (1982) illustrated this problem by discussing the impact of a drug which had a correlation of .40 with survival in a given illness. Prior to the drug's introduction there was a 50/50 chance of survival for individuals who contracted the disease. The drug correlated at .40 with survival. When one squares the correlation of .40 one arrives at 16% of the variance. Adding this to the 50% chance survival leads to a 66% chance of survival with drug usage. This represents a significant contribution to healing, though the correlation is low by statistical standards.

Reliability is another required attribute of a good psychometric index. Reliability is an extremely important characteristic of good psychometrics. In fact, some have argued that if a psychometric index is not reliable then validity concerns are of little use. This opinion has some merit and might have dictated that the discussion of reliability precede that of validity. Another view suggests that if a test scale is truly valid, it will most likely possess good reliability. Thus I have preceded the discussion of reliability with an analysis of validity.

Usually reliability refers to internal consistency of items or to test-retest correlations. In the first instance, internal consistency is directed towards the extent to which individual items agree with the total scale. This can often be determined by Kuder-Richardson formulae or by Cronbach's alpha procedure (see any standard measurement book for these formulae). The examination of the internal consistency of the index or scale thus provides the psychometrician with an opportunity to either delete or add new items which will increase the overall internal consistency of items. The second approach to reliability often involves the use of parallel forms which are correlated with each other or test retest correlations. Generally, reliability refers to the extent to which there is consistency between observations over time. Reliability then assumes that ordinarily there is a consistency between the stimulus value of the items of a scale and the response of the individual. Naturally, there are many situations which can occur that will militate against reliability in individual cases or even in group administrations. Thus extraordinary events (a fire, riot, etc.) or individual conditions of health, mental status, physical ability, classroom conditions, fatigue, and a variety of other factors can militate against good test retest reliability. To a large extent, the use of equivalent forms is advisable rather than test retest procedures. In summary, both validity and reliability are important judgments relative to the construction, use, and interpretation of psychometric indices. They are essentially the value standards of certitude associated with making inferences or judgments about individuals or groups based on psychometric methods.

DEDUCTIVE INFERRING FROM PSYCHOMETRIC SCORES

Through the use of statistical procedures such as factor analysis tentative principles of meta-theory can be parsimoniously obtained. This proposition states that statistical methods can provide a basis for establishing parsimony of factors (i.e., reducing many trait names to a set of fewer integrative constructs), and through these methods to infer some tentative suggestions for building a meta-theory of individual differences. One of the chief functions of the procedure of factor analysis is to obtain what might be called scientific parsimony. The task here is to learn what common sources of variance may unite certain items or scales. This has been an important task in psychometrics because after the First World War many tests were developed that named all kinds of traits. Early efforts were made to understand aspects of personality through the development of specific scales (Bernreuter, 1935; Cattell, 1946; and Edwards, 1954). By 1953 French reviewed some 70 studies and found no less than 450 trait names referring to some test scale or other. He attempted to unify them in certain ways and came up with a list of 50 general factors (French, 1953). What was particularly difficult was to attempt to equate what one test author meant by a scale called aggression with what another test author might mean by a similar scale.

Though the primary ingredients of psychometric scales derive their power from the adequacy of the constructs defined, the precision of the items devised, and the reliability of the scales thus created, further statistical methods have aided in the deriving of deductive inferences from scales. Many users of tests consider scale scores to be the final products of a test. In many instances scales are treated as equivalent to traits. But there is evidence that a scale should not be considered equivalent to a trait unless it is quite clear that the scale in question can be verified by other methods as well. Tryon (1979) has succinctly detailed the errors that psychologists continually make by considering test scores of scales to be measures of traits. A trait is usually something broader than simply a test score. Ideally, it should be related to empirical and/or behavioral observations utilizing other methods.

Statistical procedures have aided researchers to develop a more adequate conception of the psychometric trait through the use of factor analysis. Moreover, the problem of equivalence of methods has also been addressed via the multimethod, multitrait matrix. In this section, we would like to expand on the matter of deductive inferring from psychometrics by a brief consideration of factor analysis and multitrait, multimethod procedures. Factor analysis is a method which extracts from a number of scaled scores or similar inputs common sources of variance (items may be used, but scale scores that have already met the criteria of internal consistency are the more usual candidates). These common sources of variance may then be considered the structural scaffolding supporting a finite number of scale score inputs. Harman states (1968, p. 145) that as a method factor analysis addresses itself to the study of interrelationships among a total set of variables, no one of which is selected for a different role than any of the others. In some sense all variables in such a study are construed to be dependent with the independent variables being the new hypothetical constructs called factors. As one of its results, factor analysis actually leads to linear regression of each of the observed variables on the factors.

L. L. Thurstone (1935) made the advance which was lacking in the work of Spearman. He came to recognize that the factor analysis of correlation matrices required much more sophisticated matrix algebra. Thurstone set about to learn these procedures and apply them to the problem of factor analysis. In 1935 he published *Vectors of the Mind* and in the next few years developed his own *Primary Mental Abilities Battery* in which he maintained that there were seven such factors: N, numerical ability; V, verbal ability; S, spatial-visualizing ability; M, memory; I, induction ability, and D, deduction ability. As Carroll remarks: "the importance of the PMA battery was that it brought into general awareness the concept of discernible mental ability factors" (Carroll, 1982, p. 60). What is difficult to realize today is the laborious nature of these computations before the use of mechanical calculators. This was the case with much of Spearman's early work. By the time Thurstone was working on the problem, mechanical calculators were available. Even so, it took Thurstone several years working with a large group of graduate assistants to do what a high speed computer can now do in seconds.

There are currently a number of approaches to factor analysis, but one common and popular one is the principal-factor solution. This method needs to be conceptualized from a geometric point of view. Harmon states: "Just as a set of N values of two variables may be represented by a scatter diagram of N points in the plane of the two variables (as axes), so more generally the point representation of n variables may be conceived as one point for each of the N individuals, referred to as a system of n reference axes. The loci of the swarm of points of uniform frequency density are more or less concentric, similar and similarly situated n-dimensional ellipsoids. The axes of these ellipsoids correspond to the factors in the principal-factor solution" (Harmon, 1968, p. 151). In short, what Harmon is saying is that it is very important for the researcher to conceptualize factor analysis in terms of geometric characteristics. The most popular solution is one or two dimensions. But others that involve three dimensional solutions are also possible and available.

Factor analysis begins with the calculations of correlation coefficients between all of the variables. Then factor 1 is selected as the component which explains the most variance or communality in the set of variables. After the residual correlations of the variables with this factor score are obtained, the procedure selects factor 2 which is the component that now explains the

Table 7-3 **Representative Theorists and Their Conclusions from Factor Analysis Studies**

Author	Topic	Structural Components
Thurstone (1935)	Primary Mental Abilities	Numerical, Verbal, Spatial-Visualizing, Memory, Inductive Ability, Deductive Ability
Cohen (1968)	Psychological Theories	Subjectivity-Objectivity, Holistic-Molecular, Experimental-Clinical, Qualitative-Quantitative, Biological-Social, Dynamic-Static
Eysenck (Eysenck & Rachman 1965)	Galen's Temperaments	
	Melancholic	Moody, Anxious, Rigid, Sober, Pessimistic
	Choleric	Touchy, Restless, Impulsive, Aggressive, Excitable
	Phlegmatic	Passive, Careful, Peaceful, Controlled, Reliable
	Sanguine	Extroverted, Sociable, Outgoing, Responsive
Royce (1973)	Cognitive Structure	Perceiving, Conceptualizing, Symboling
	Affective Structure	Emotional Stability, Emotional Independence, Extroversion-Introversion

most variance (which is left) after the removal or extraction of factor 1. This procedure continues until all of the variance is accounted for, or a certain arbitrary criterion is reached (two usual ones are to specify a given percentage of variance such as, for example 75%, or to specify an eigenvalue level such as any factor at or above 1.00).

This approach, since it is illustrative of the process, provides an example of factor analysis, but there are many other factor analytic solutions such as the maximum-likelihood approach, orthogonal multiple-factor solutions, and the oblique multiple-factor solution. Their use is determined by the theoretical nature of the research problem and the personal preference of the researcher. Each process poses its own constraints on the interpreting of the overall meaning of the discovered relationships.

One of the major uses of factor analysis in assessment is related to the principle of parsimony mentioned earlier. From factor analysis it is possible to take a set of raw scale scores, and develop composite factor scores for individuals using the Z score or T score as a basis of comparison. This has many great advantages. For example, suppose a battery of 30 scales are administered to 1,000 individuals. To be sure, these 30 scales themselves could all be converted to T scores, but using 30 scores to describe an individual makes this task virtually incomprehensible. But through factor analysis it is learned that the 30 scales really can be converted to six factor scores—and these hierarchically arranged in terms of weighting. When this is done, the computer program can generate a six factor score profile for each of the 1,000 individuals. Thus, factor analysis leads to the development of a parsimonious and scientifically deduced structure which presumably underlies a given set of psychometric scales.

There are many other applications of factor analysis that are relevant to researchers in assessment. To name three: (1) it has been used as a method of confirming logical-conceptual frameworks; (2) it has been used as a method of deducing primary structure characteristics underlying intelligence and personality variables; and recently (3) it has served as a source for the development of a meta-theory about individual differences.

Factor analysis can confirm logical-conceptual frameworks. Two examples of the confirmation of the logical-conceptual framework can be related to factor analysis. For example, the author in the late 1960s (Barclay 1968a) postulated a model to explain the range and dimensions of counseling theories based on an analysis of how they fit in terms of two sets of bipolar dimensions (existence versus essence and subject-orientation versus object-orientation). This was purely a logical-empirical analysis not based on any kind of statistical approach.

In 1968 also, but after the writing of the Barclay monograph, Coan (1968) reported on a factor analysis of the ratings given 54 major theorists by 323 psychologist correspondents who at one time or another had taught the history of psychology. Six factors emerged from this analysis. Factor 1 appears to be subjectivity versus objectivity (note the similarity to Barclay's object versus subject pole). Factor 2 appears to be related to a·pattern of holistic, totalistic or molar approaches versus an elementaristic, atomistic or molecular one. Factor 3 contrasted experimental with clinical methods and factor 4 was a methodological one characterized on the positive pole by content that lends itself to quantitative treatment rather than procedures less readily permitting such treatments. Factor 5 appears to be a dynamic versus static continuum and factor 6 a contrast of biological (i.e., structural) versus social or functional-environmental influences. Thus through this procedure Coan established a meta-theory framework for the explanation of the components which appear to explain variability in content, focus, and method in psychology. Parenthetically, it substantiates the subject-object orientation of Barclay's (Coan's factor 1) logical model, as well as the structural-functional dimension (Coan's factor 6). What this illustrates is that sometimes deductive inferring, not necessarily based on known inputs, can be substantiated by factor analytic methods.

Another example of the confirmatory nature of factor analysis relates to the Galen model. Recall from Chapter 2 that Immanuel Kant, Wilhelm Wundt, and Ivan Pavlov all believed in the validity of the older Galen model of personality. However, their belief in this model was based on different reasons. Kant believed in it because of his views about categorical structures and character analysis. Wundt and Pavlov believed in it because they held a theory of cortical excitation and inhibition, with different effects found in personality related to socialization. They could not prove the actual theory (although Pavlov did work in conditioning that he felt related to the validity of the temperament groups—see Strelau, 1983). Eysenck, however, by a factor analysis of personality characteristics did document the validity of this categorical classification. Thus, one use of factor analysis is to confirm logical analyses. What occurs basically in factor analysis is a geometric plotting of variables in two dimensional space or sometimes in three dimensional space. This procedure can document the validity of empirical observations or logical analysis.

Factor analysis can aid in determining the primary structure characteristics of larger constructs such as intelligence and temperament. Factor analysis can serve as a basis for defininition of meta-theory about individual differences. This requires the establishment of a set of invariant meta-factor characteristics across valid factor analytic studies to provide a nomological network for the organization of individual differences. One of the questions which arises from the studying of various factor analytic explanations is to determine how these several studies may contribute to a larger and more generalizable conception of the hierarchical organization of individual differences. The works of Cronbach, Guilford, Cattell, and Eysenck have added to an understanding of the organization of specific areas of individual differences. Royce (1973; Royce and Mos 1979), has attempted over several decades to develop a multisystem approach to describe individual differences. This system is based on the invariant characteristics found in the other systems. In other words, Royce searched the evidence found in other factor analyses for the existence of still more primary components based on characteristics which were found in all or most of the other systems.

Royce has done a tremendous amount of work in the development of a nomological network to explain both cognitive and affective development as well as the interaction between the systems. His model is based on the work of Eysenck, Cattell, Guilford, Thurston, Vernon, Gagne, Vandenburg, and others. His formulation of first order, second order and third order structures represents a kind of super framework which may exist for the explanation of individual differences.

Royce concludes out of his analyses that both the cognitive and affective systems are composed of clusters of traits which combine in specific ways in individual differences. Thus in the cognitive area, he sees the third-order factors most generally related to the tasks of perceiving, conceptualization and symboling. Likewise in the affective system the major components are emotional stability, emotional independence, and introversion-extraversion.

Two further observations are important here about the Royce theoretical framework. First of all, it is important to recognize that the development of basic skills, in what Royce terms the first-order factor skills, is both a function of capability as derived from hereditary transmission, and an interaction with the quantity and quality of environmental stimulation variously associated with cultural "press" in the transmission. The cognitive system is more susceptible to such environmental transmission (possible because it is more closely associated with more recent evolutionary developments in the brain) whereas the affective system is less susceptible to environmental influence. The manner in which specific skills are developed and their relationship to the higher-order syntheses has been discussed at length by Buss and Royce (1975) in an analysis of the ontogenetic origins of development. Whether it is a process whereby original latent characteristics are gradually differentiated, or a process in which specific skills build up to definable superstructures is not known at this time.

An example may help to clarify this matter further. Let us suppose that two children could be born with identical genetic characteristics and one is reared in rural Guatamala or Yucatan in an area dominated by Mayan culture. The other child, let us say, is raised in Brooklyn, in a Jewish culture. It is probable that survival and adult-sanctioned social learnings in a jungle environment might result in rapid progressive differentiation of cognitive characteristics related to eye-hand coordination, spatial excellence, and superiority in physical-motor skills. On the other hand, it is probable that in Brooklyn, the emphasis would be on the development of verbal and reasoning skills. This progressive differentiation would take place in cognitive development, with performance being the actually achieved competency or set of skills manifested through social modeling and reinforcement, and capacity being the rather arbitrary theoretical range specified by genetic structure.

Though such cognitive differentiation appears to be highly influenced by environmental elicitation (as is for example the superiority of most Native American and Inuit cultures to Anglo ones in spatial relations and spatial memory skills), there is less evidence available to demonstrate that the affective or emotional system is subject to such marked differentiation. Strelau (1983), for example, believes that temperament characteristics would exist even in the absence of socialization. To be sure, cultural expressions of emotionality may be related to specific environmental influence, but if researchers such as Zajonc (1979) are correct, the emotional components of personality are more closely related to lower and earlier portions of the brain concerned with self-survival and therefore more fundamental in their expression and less malleable to environmental programming.

In concluding this section on factor analysis, it is extremely important to point out that factor analysis is a tool. It can help to provide a parsimonious structure for explaining test scales if the scale ingredients are carefully developed and documented for their statistical validity and reliability. Pawlik (1973) has pointed out that many times naive researchers approach the use of factor analysis as a method of making scientific sense out of garbage. This is what is called the "shotgun approach." Simply throwing items together, administering batches of such tests and other devices to large groups of individuals, submitting them to factor analysis, and expecting a scientific miracle of definitive structure to appear is nonsense. The first rule of failure in factor analysis is "garbage in-garbage out." Thus, the first real requirement in the use of factor analysis is to have a well grounded theoretical position reflected in scales that have been carefully developed item by item for construct validity. Failure to do this invalidates everything from this point on.

Sound factors result from sound preliminary research and conceptualization. Dust bowl empiricism may possess some merits, but it seldom generates conceptual thinking. What it probably does better than anything else is to illustrate what does not work. On the other hand, sound development of factors provides a basis for further research and conceptualization as Cattell (1966) has remarked.

Before leaving this section there are some important caveats which need to be directly stated about factor analysis. For the optimum use of factor analysis there must be a consistent and logical theory for the selection of items, scales, and hierarchies of skills, which go into the factor analysis. Moreover, this selection process must be examined for validity and reliability meeting acceptable standards BEFORE factor analysis is used. It should be noted carefully that though factor analysis results in statistically relevant subdivisions of functions and traits (grouped under the general rubric content of factors), these statistically derived entities should not be considered as necessarily corresponding in an isomorphic manner to the physiological structure of the brain. Though the brain (as we shall see in a later chapter), appears to be organized in a hierarchical manner, such a hierarchy in the brain is a functional one and not a structural one. In statistical analysis, the basic approach is one of linear relationships in various geometric planes. Our present understanding of the functioning of the brain simply does not posit such a linear model of relationships. Therefore, one should be extremely cautious in placing some kind of absolutistic value on the entities of factor analysis as such. Another caveat is related to the outcomes of factor analysis. Obviously one is not going to see a factor moving around in actual life. Interpretation of factors is one of the important tasks of individuals who utilize the procedure. Factors should aid us in making more relevant decisions about individuals. To do this, one must verify the multimethod equivalence of factors, and their relevance for explaining alternative postulated treatments. Ultimately, the value of Royce's work must be demonstrated in some kind of treatment outcomes based on appropriate decision-making theory. Thus the ultimate test of factor analysis is the parsimony and utility of the constructs thus derived for facilitating and improving decision-making skills. Without this essential follow-up, the whole process is useless.

ADVANTAGES AND DISADVANTAGES OF PSYCHOMETRICS

The psychometric method summarized in this chapter has been an important feature of assessment since the beginning of this century. It has made it possible to survey attitudes, abilities, personal characteristics, and many other aspects of human beings in an objective manner. It has therefore allowed psychologists and educators to develop better descriptions of human beings utilizing the method of psychometric appraisal. Rather than simply interviewing or observing individuals and drawing conclusions from this method, it has been possible not only to measure the characteristics of individuals, but to compare their scores with those of others. It is therefore a major tool in arriving at accurate descriptions of individuals or groups.

On the other hand, there are certain very real problems with the use of psychometrics. The major one is that many psychologists, most educators and virtually all people who have only passing contact with tests tend to think that test scores represent some absolute value that is clearly a part of the individual's character or personality. Test scores have assumed an inordinate role in assessment in recent decades. They have become the single most important aspect of assessment in the minds of many. They have become extremely important in the placement and selection of individuals in educational and business settings. Those who use the inferences drawn from psychometrics should bear in mind what Cronbach argued some 25 years ago (Cronbach & Gleser, 1965), **that tests should be used to aid in decision making.** Once the basic psychometric method is understood, it is clear that inferences drawn from tests, particularly for individuals, are less valid than inferences drawn from large groups. Psychometric scores can be of considerable aid in the assessment of individual differences, but they should always be used with caution.

CHAPTER VIII

Cognitive and Personality Measurement

In this chapter various areas of assessment will be outlined in terms of what can be obtained through tests. This chapter is not designed to be a comprehensive treatment of all tests, but rather is meant to provide the reader with a description of major tests that exist and what their general function has been in assessment. In many areas of testing, such as intelligence, thousands of books and monographs have been written. To attempt to present a comprehensive survey of all this work would be impossible within the constraints of this book. Some of the major and representative tests which have been used for some time will be noted. They are cited, however, because of their stature in testing. There are many other tests designed for a variety of purposes which could have been included.

ASSESSMENT OF ATTITUDES

Attitudes reflect responses to contextual stimuli that involve more or less enduring dispositions towards evaluation. One of the most common uses of psychological indices is to assess the characteristics of attitudes. Attitudes usually refer to a rather consistent or enduring set of evaluations about some object or situation. These attitudes are the product of learning as reflected by both the social context of the life of an individual and the interactions which take place with constitutional characteristics. The concept of attitude has also been applied to semantic evaluation of language meanings, particularly by Osgood (1957) in his use of the semantic differential. According to Shaw and Wright (1967) attitude measures are methods of indirectly measuring systems of belief, motives, concepts, and opinions. All are derived from more basic cognitive and emotional processes which presumably are tapped via the rating process. Shaw and Wright explicitly detail the grounds for an assumed correspondence between attitude measures and influences in the choices and preferences of the person taking the test. They suggest that the stimulus value of a particular item elicits needs related to a drive state (p. 6), that attitudes are a function of past learning (p. 8), and that they are relatively stable and enduring (p. 9). They also suggest that attitudes are almost always a product of social interaction (p. 10).

Attitudes are generally measured via psychometric methods of scaling responses. There have been a number of methods used for scale construction in attitude measure. One of the chief problems which has existed from the beginning is knowing how to evaluate the various points expressed regarding an item. Thurstone (1929, 1931) first formulated a procedure for weighting evaluations of an attitude by having judges place items relating to an attitude in 11 categories which were then so weighted (i.e., 1–11). When the final items are selected each represents a numerical point ranging from 1–11 and respondents are asked to check those statements with which they agree. This provides a weighted set of statements from which a summary score can be obtained. Unfortunately, this is a time-consuming process and is not often used today.

Rensis Likert in the 1930s developed perhaps the most popular approach to attitude measurements. Basically this approach involves a five point continuum from strongly disagree to strongly agree which can be applied to virtually any type of attitude. The assumptions underlying this approach really suggest that a rating of a 1 or 5 represents a high degree of affect, 2 and 4 a moderate affect and 3 a neutral position. A variation of this approach is one that has been proposed by Guilford (1959) which involves a seven point continuum in which the rater evaluates himself/herself on a scale that is designed to provide greater personal discrimination. Each point on the scale is related to a numerical value. An example of this is: How serious minded is he or she?

7. Takes everything as if it were a matter of life and death.
6. Ordinarily serious and conscientious about things.
5. Slightly on the serious, conscientious side.
4. Neither serious nor unconcerned.
3. Slightly on the relaxed and unconcerned side.
2. Ordinarily unconcerned and carefree.
1. Seems not to have a care in the world (J. P. Guilford, 1959, p. 142).

These three approaches to attitude measure are the most popular ones used today, though there are other contributions to the theory of attitude measure such as the scalogram approach of Guttman (1944, 1947). "This method is based upon the idea that items can be arranged in an order such that an individual who responds positively to any particular item also responds positively to all other items having a lower rank. If items can be arranged in this manner, they are said to be scalable. In developing an attitude scale, a number of monotone items about the attitude object are formulated, the set of items is administered to a group of subjects, and their response patterns are analyzed to determine whether or not they are scalable. With N items requiring only agreement or disagreement, there are 2N response patterns that might occur; if the items are scalable, only N + 1 of these patterns will be obtained. The relative nonoccurrence of deviant patterns allows the computation of a coefficient of reproducibility:

$$\text{Rep} = 1 \text{ minus } \frac{\text{total number of errors}}{\text{total number of responses}}$$

where an error is any deviation from an ideal pattern. Theoretically, Rep. is equal to the proportion of responses to items that can be correctly reproduced from the knowledge of an individual's score. If Rep is 90 or better, the items are said to be scalable" (Shaw & Wright, 1967, p. 25).

Two other techniques which have enjoyed a mixed popularity, (in the sense that they were more used a decade or two ago than at present) have a relationship to attitude ratings. They are the Q sort techniques devised by Stephenson (Stephenson, 1953) and the semantic differential (Osgood & Suci, 1957). In the Q technique an individual is given a pile of cards which contain words, phrases, or other descriptive characteristics and is asked to sort them into piles in accordance to subjective criteria. For example, the criteria could be most like me, much like me, somewhat like me, not very much like me, quite different from me, and very unlike me. Osgood's semantic differential examines the attitude towards words or concepts using evaluative bipolar adjectives such as good-bad, pleasant-unpleasant, serious-flippant and many other combinations. The concept is measured along three dimensions of meaning: evaluation (good-bad) potency (strong-weak) and activity (fast-slow). Many concepts have been analyzed via this technique and a lexicon exists for individuals who wish to use various common words in the English language which provides them with an analysis of their evaluative, potency, and activity levels.

A vast number of rating scales have been developed and used. Generally, these evaluation of attitudes scales do not possess the most rigorous reliability and validity studies characteristic of many of the more sophisticated instruments. For readers who are interested in examining both the quality and quantity of such attitude measures, the book by Shaw and Wright, *Scales for the Measurement of Attitude*, McGraw-Hill, 1967, is an important compendium of attitude measures. There are seven chapters which relate to social practices, social issues and problems, international issues, abstract concepts, political and religious attitudes, ethnic and national groups, significant others, and social institutions. Several hundred instruments are discussed with summary data on reliability and validity.

ASSESSMENT OF INTELLIGENCE AND ACHIEVEMENT

The concept of intelligence is a hypothetical construct which reflects the aggregate or global capacity of the individual to act purposefully, to think rationally and to deal effectively with the environment, (paraphrased from Wechsler's definition in Matarazzo, 1978b, p. 79). Perhaps there is no other construct in psychometry that has obtained more study and analysis than that of intelligence. From earliest times humankind recognized that some individuals were more capable of solving problems and dealing with their environment effectively. Both Aristotle and Aquinas recognized the paramount role that intelligence played in leadership. The first century educational theorist, Quintillian, suggested that teachers ought to be able to identify aptitudes in learners and alter educational instruction to provide for these differences. He also apparently recognized that little might be done absolutely about intelligence, but that aptitudes could be increased and strengthened through learning (Snow and Yalom, 1982, p. 503). The Chinese devised competency tests to describe intelligence many centuries before the Christian era (see Chapter III).

In modern times, the actual development of psychometric tools to measure intelligence was specifically focused by Simon and Binet. They wished to be able to differentiate normals from the mentally retarded. So they developed a series of test items which were grouped empirically in order of difficulty. Using a criterion of pass-fail, they applied these tests to varying age groups and found that it was possible to determine the presumed cognitive functioning of an individual by the number of subtests passed within a given age group. Obviously their reasoning was based on Galton's postulate that human abilities were distributed normally in the population.

Intelligence is largely hereditary in origin, related to problem-solving ability, and affected by learning and socialization. The concept of intelligence is applicable to many aspects of assessment. First of all, it is recognized that intelligence for the most part is a global factor influencing all parts of human life. Most of intelligence is hereditary. Though various theorists differ on how much is hereditary and how much is related to learning and socialization, the consensus is that at least half of the manifestations of cognitive abilities are related to heredity. Furthermore, the relationship of I.Q. scores within families that are biologically related is about three times as great as that within adoptive families (Scarr & Carter-Saltzman, 1982 p. 792 and p. 860). On the other hand, intelligence appears to be strongly related to learning ability, intellectual organization, and information processing, and these characteristics are related in part to the enrichment of socialization derived from the family and society, and the quality of instruction (Snow and Yalom, 1982). There are dispositional tendencies and adaptive processes embedded in the construct of intelligence. In some of the original research on factor analysis, Spearman distinguished what was called the "g" factor and the "s" factor. He meant by this the general component of intelligence and those specific components which might be applicable to a certain person. Later, both Cattell and Guilford came up with ideas about how certain aspects of intelligence appear to be inherent in individuals, while others are adaptable to learning, but according to Sternberg and Salter (1982b) most of these earlier ideas are flawed in some way and further research is needed.

The assessment of intelligence relates to the classification of individuals who may be mentally retarded, normal, gifted, creative, or even genius. So it has widely been accepted, but not without controversy, that intelligence is a major factor in success in education, business, science, and nearly every aspect of human life. For the most part, the largest portions of populations in any country fall within the normal ranges of intelligence. In every country, however, there are also those who are mentally retarded or extremely defective in intelligence, and also a substantial corps of individuals who are gifted or creative. All gifted individuals are not necessarily creative, but creativity is generally confined to the upper and middle levels of intelligence. Intelligence manifests itself in early and sometimes precocious development of language skills, in generally superior motor and coordination skills, and often in advanced social skills. It is thus a dimension which underlies all human behavior whether it be in the cognitive, motor, or emotional domain.

Intelligence in the biological sense and I.Q. tests are not equivalent concepts. One of the besetting tendencies in the assessment of intelligence is to equate it with the measurement of I.Q. There is considerable evidence that I.Q., even as achievement test scores, can be improved by coaching, rehearsal, and test-specific learning. In addition, intelligence and achievement tests very often judge intelligence by testing in areas relating to abstract reasoning, memory and recall rather than what has been called social intelligence. In other words, an intelligence test does not isomorphically correspond to the biological substratum derived from heredity, any more than a temperament test taps into the biological substratum of emotion. It is an artifically contrived mechanism for inferring intelligence from certain tasks or responses.

In contemporary usage, intelligence tests can be classified as individually administered or as group administered. The origin of intelligence testing was related to individually administered inventories. These today are used by psychologists who are specifically trained in their usage. Alfred Binet began the systematic study of intelligence in his work of the 1880s with studies on associationism. Later on he also studied mental organization in terms of consciousness, perception, and a host of other variables. During the 1890s Binet and his colleague Victor Henri developed a series of items which were grouped under the categories of memory, images, imagination, attention, comprehension, suggestibility, esthetic appreciation, moral sentiments, muscular force, force of will, motor skills, and visual judgment. Through the efforts of Theodore Simon, a physician, these series of tasks were tried out on mentally retarded children at the Salpetriere and a variety of other children in the primary schools of Paris. The first scales were organized and tested out in 1905 and then the scales were revised in 1908. They determined that an item was appropriate for the given age level if 60–90% of normal children passed it. In the next few years they revised the scales further and the result was the 1911 scale.

The work of Simon, Henri, and Binet in the development of a method for measuring intelligence was a giant step towards the development of psychometrics in general and for the analysis of intelligence in particular. From the accumulation of a series of tasks designed for varying age levels, they inferred that intelligence itself was a function of direction of thought, discrimination, and capacity. They thus used an inductive procedure to ferret out characteristics of intelligence by reference to age norms. It was then a comparatively easy further judgment to scale intelligence to a ratio involving mental age and chronological age.

The scales were introduced to the United States about 1906 with the application made to the identification of mentally retarded at the Vineland Training School in New Jersey by Goddard. As was indicated in the fourth chapter, Goddard also made use of the system to evaluate the characteristics of immigrants. Considerable usage of the scales was made possible by the extension of a variety of clinics around the country to assess mentally retarded children and adults. In 1911, Lewis Terman produced the first American translation of the Binet scales, and in 1916 he and his associates at Stanford University published a revision called the Stanford-Binet. The use of the scales expanded all over the United States and subsequent revisions and standardizations occurred in 1937, 1960, 1970 and 1986. Specific details of the development of the Stanford-Binet can be found in the book by Jerome Sattler (Sattler, 1980) and The Manual by Thorndike, Hagen and Sattler (1986).

The early success that was accorded the Stanford-Binet appeared to foreclose on further development. Moreover, many of the American psychologists who were identified with the Binet scales felt that they did a sufficiently good job at assessing intelligence and did not seem inclined to change the scales. Many American psychologists ignored the caveat that Binet had made about placing too much confidence in the subtests themselves and judging that the product of the test did indeed equate with intelligence.

Others, however, saw some problems with the Stanford-Binet, particularly the failure to discriminate between verbal and performance components in the I.Q. as separate scores, and the fact that the I.Q. was geared to chronological age and had to assume a ceiling in early adulthood. Thus David Wechsler, as chief psychologist at Bellevue Psychiatric Hospital, began to develop a psychometric test which had more properties than the Binet scales. He was concerned that there were nonintellective factors in intelligence also, and that the age I.Q. index simply did not work well for adults. Wechsler felt that it was necessary not only to look at a number of abilities, but also at how they were combined or integrated by such factors as needs, drives and motivation. As a consequence, he developed the *Wechsler Bellevue Scales* which later became the *Wechsler Adult Intelligence Scales (WAIS)*. Wechsler divided intelligence testing into verbal and performance components. In the verbal component he included subtests of information, comprehension, digit span, arithmetic, similarities, and vocabulary. In the performance section he included picture arrangement, picture completion, block design, object assembly, and digit symbol. A verbal and performance I.Q. was estimated from actuarial studies. In addition a total I.Q. was obtained. Much of the benefit derived from the Wechsler Scales was related to the clinical clues obtained from the manner in which individuals approached the task and their reaction to frustration. As a consequence, the Wechsler scales gained in acceptance simply because they provided more than the basic I.Q. of the Binet scales. The *Wechsler Intelligence Scale for Children (WISC)* was developed in 1949. The range of the Wechsler scales was thus extended downward to five years of age. Subsequently, in 1967 the *Wechsler Preschool and Primary Scale of Intelligence (WPPSI)* was marketed. This was standardized on children from four to six and one/half years of age. There are now new versions called the WISC-R, the WAIS-R and the WPPSI-R. Each of these revisions has been important in bringing the tests up to date by removing outdated items or adding items which appear more relevant.

During the decades of the 1920s and 1930s a vast amount of development took place with group objective tests which were directly or indirectly related to the Stanford-Binet as the criterion. The first major group intelligence test was developed by Otis, Yerkes, and others during World War I and was called the *Army Alpha*. Other pioneers in intelligence and achievement testing were Thorndike, Kuhlmann, Pintner, and Cattell. Munsterberg earlier had produced aptitude tests around 1913, and Seashore created a test of musical talent about 1915. Thus out of the development of an individual

test of intelligence with the aspects of age grouped norms, an easy trans-
ference was made to the group academic achievement tests, aptitude tests,
and subsequently personality tests.

Some of the most popular and extensively used cognitive assessment instruments are: The *California Short Form Test of Mental Maturity (CTMM)*
(California Test Bureau) appropriate from kindergarten through college
which yields three scores: (1) language I.Q., (2) nonlanguage I.Q., and (3)
total; *The Cognitive Abilities Tests (CAT)* which provides separate scores for
verbal, quantitative, and nonverbal sections and was combined with the *Iowa
Tests of Basic Skills and Tests of Academic Progress (Houghton-Mifflin)* and
is appropriate to a range from preschool to grade 13; *The Cooperative School
and College Ability Tests (SCAT)* which also yields verbal, quantitative and
total scores and is appropriate for grades 4–14, (Cooperative Test Division,
Educational Testing Service); and *The Henmon-Nelson Tests of Mental Ability, Revised Edition* which is appropriate from grades 3–14 yielding three
scores—verbal, quantitative, and total (Houghton-Mifflin Co.). There are others, but these intelligence and ability tests are representative of those for
assessment in the intelligence domain.

**Achievement tests are most often geared to grade levels, much in the
same way that I.Q. tests have been referenced to cognitive competency at
a given age.** They also provide grade-referenced scores for subareas within
subject matter such as reading, arithmetic, and language. Often within such
areas there are subarea scores. Thus, for example, in the *California Achievement Tests (CAT)* reading achievement includes reading vocabulary and reading comprehension while in arithmetic, there is arithmetic reasoning.
Language covers both the mechanics of spelling and of English usage. *The
California Achievement Tests* are appropriate from lower primary grades up
to advanced levels in high school and above (California Test Bureau-McGraw-
Hill). Another common achievement test is the *Iowa Tests of Basic Skills
(ITBS)* (Houghton-Mifflin). This test is likewise multidimensional and focuses
on skills. It is appropriate to grades 3–9. *The Iowa Tests of Educational
Development (ITED)* consists of nine subtests and begins where the ITBS
leaves off. *The Metropolitan Achievement Tests* (Harcourt Brace Jovanovich)
are appropriate from primary levels of kindergarten through the 9th grade.
The SRI Achievement Series (Science Research Associates) is designed for
grades 1–9 and also provides separate scores. Finally, the *Stanford Achievement Test Series* (Harcourt Brace Jovanovich) goes from the primary level of
the 1st grade through the 9th grade. All of these tests are taken by children
using optically scanned answer sheets and are analyzed by high speed computers. Most of the group intelligence tests range from 30 minutes to 1½
hours. The achievement tests are much longer and often range from 5 to 7
hours in length. Given the repeated use of these tests for virtually all children

in the public schools, it is amazing how many millions of hours are spent by children in such assessment.

Another form of cognitive assessment is aptitude tests. For the most part the word "aptitude" is used rather loosely. Anastasi (1976) points out that the term aptitude really was an artifact derived from factor analysis and referred to a cluster of abilities or skills of a basic cognitive nature. Most of the tests so designated attempt to evaluate higher-order clusters of skills. Two examples of aptitude assessment are the *Differential Aptitude Test Battery* and the *General Aptitude Battery. The Differential Aptitude Test Battery* is available for grades 8 through 12 (Psychological Corporation). It provides separate scores for verbal reasoning, numerical ability, abstract reasoning, clerical speed and accuracy, mechanical reasoning, space relations, spelling, and sentences. This battery takes from 3 to 4 hours. *The General Aptitude Test Battery* is produced by the United States Employment Service. There are nine subtests which were based on the nine factors determined by Thurstone's method of factor analysis. The battery can be given in about 2¼ hours and it is often used for job matching or selection. The subsections of the specific tests are name comparison, computation, three-dimensional space, vocabulary, tool matching, arithmetic reason, form matching, mark making, place, turn, assemble and disassemble. It includes a number of items and skills relating to manual dexterity.

Two other forms of testing for achievement should be mentioned here. One is highly traditional and the other is a new approach to the assessment via psychometrics designed to measure competencies or attainment of performance criteria. The first is the college entrance battery which is essentially the evaluation of advanced achievement. Two major systems are in common usage: The American College Testing Program (ACT) which originates in Iowa City, Iowa, and the Scholastic Aptitude Test (SAT) of the College Entrance Examination Board (CEEB) which is processed in Princeton, New Jersey. Both of these examinations are used in colleges and universities throughout the country to assess the characteristics of entering freshmen. Not only are the tests reflective of regional norms, but they can also provide to the institution and to the student comparative ranks and standings at particular institutions. Generally, the ACT tends to be used in a wide variety of multipurpose colleges and universities and the SAT with more restricted or specialized colleges and universities. In addition, achievement-type tests such as the Graduate Record Examination (GRE) are used for admission to graduate school, and others such as the Medical College Admissions Test (MCAT) for admission to professional schools (medicine, dentistry, law, etc.). These examinations are used to restrict entrance into graduate studies and into specific professional curricula.

In recent years, with the advent of criterion-referenced testing, a number of test publishers have begun to produce such tests. Each of the major test companies has entered this market. Thus Houghton Mifflin has a *Customized Objective Monitoring Service, Reading and Mathematics* for grades 1–8 in which elementary and junior high schools identify items to be used from banks of items. Science Research Associates has a *Diagnostic Test in Reading and Mathematics* available for grades 1–6, together with a *Mastery Evaluation Tool* for kindergarten through grade 9. California Test Bureau/McGraw-Hill has a number of instruments relating to a bank of items and tests which can also be used by elementary and secondary school customers such as a *Prescriptive Mathematics Inventory* and a *Prescriptive Reading Inventory*. Most of these assessment instruments are relatively new but are relevant to criterion-referenced trends in school assessment. In addition, many states have developed their own competency-based systems of evaluation.

Group administered objective tests for the systematic measuring of intelligence, achievement, and aptitude have been widely used in the United States. Because testing in elementary and secondary education is mandated in every state and because tests are used for college entrance, graduate school admissions, and for many specialized training programs, there are differing views about their use. On the one hand testing has been attacked as limiting the access of certain segments of the population to higher education or professional programs. And yet, the requirements for specific sets of skills and aptitudes in given professions and various schools have been met either adequately or well by the means of various screening tests. Some criticize tests as being biased against certain minorities, but the record of the major testing companies has been quite good in their efforts to revise tests continually, and to follow good standards of test construction and validation. In addition, there is mounting criticism of the practice of mass testing of children in elementary and secondary education every other year or so, without using the test results for diagnostic teaching. Typically children are tested in the late winter or early spring and often test results do not return until late in the school year or during the summer. Of course, the testing companies have difficulty handling so many millions of tests in a short time, but they urge schools to use the tests diagnostically. Unfortunately, many schools only use the tests as a criterion of whether the particular grade or classroom within a grade or school or district is on target.

Very often school districts and even state testing coordinating offices draw conclusions about schools based on the average percentile or grade equivalent score. Since the data are based on individuals, the drawing of conclusions about classes or schools is essentially wrong—like comparing apples and oranges—but it is continually done. Thus in some instances one can only wonder whether the major purpose of cognitive assessment from the local school administrative point of view is simply related to vanity. In summary, there are mixed opinions on the value of mass testing in the cognitive and achievement areas. Much of the criticism should be directed at the use made of the instruments and the timing, not the construction and design of the tests.

PERSONALITY TESTS AND INVENTORIES

Psychometric methods have been applied to personality and emotive characteristics of individuals in similar procedures to intelligence and achievement measures. With the development of intelligence, achievement, and aptitude tests, it is not surprising that personality tests and inventories were also created. Personality as a concept or term is ambiguous, partly because, like the concept of intelligence, there are many possible meanings and connotations. Generally, test constructors have tended to identify traits that are emotionally related, rather than cognitively associated with personality. **Personality really represents the total of both cognitive and emotive factors in the individual as altered by the process of socialization and learning.** Cognition and temperament each represent the original hereditary components of personality. Behind cognition is intelligence, and behind temperament are emotional components. Intelligence tests (particularly individually administered ones) are often used to estimate personality characteristics or changes in personality, such as deterioration of functioning, identification of learning problems, and to provide clinical information on personality characteristics (Anastasi, 1976). In addition, there are relationships between reflective abilities in problem solving and impulsivity that have been noted (Baron, 1982). In the same manner, personality tests often provide insight into basic levels of intelligence.

It is because personality connotes the sum of all measurable traits and characteristics as influenced by learning and socialization, that in this book, cognition and temperament have been viewed as discrete, but interacting, components of personality. Snow and Yalom (1982) point out that the two major components are complex interwoven multivariate progressions (p. 516). For practical purposes then, this section will deal with what has been termed personality testing, but with the hope that the reader will ascertain the basic emotional anchor of these tests. As is true with the group achievement, intelligence and, aptitude tests, individually administered personality batteries paved the way for group ones. The role was not as pronounced because many of the individually administered personality tests focused on psychometric standardization only as a second priority with clinical interpretation being the first priority. Though it is true that many individually administered personality tests do have reliability and validity data attached to them, group personality tests followed the lead of intelligence and achievement testing more closely than did individual tests.

Over a number of years, with hundreds of correlational and research studies being done, three major group personality assessment instruments have emerged as most accepted. They are: *the Minnesota Multiphasic Inventory (MMPI), the California Psychological Inventory*, and *the 16 Personality Factor Test.*

The Minnesota Multiphasic Personality Inventory (MMPI) has probably been used more in clinical and counseling-related situations than any other group personality assessment instrument. The test was developed by Starke Hathaway, a psychologist and J. Charnley McKinley, a psychiatrist. It was first published in 1943 and some of the standard references on the test are those published by Hathaway and Meehl (1951), Welsh and Dahlstrom (1956), and Dahlstrom and Welsh (1960). The test consists of 550 items which are answered by true, false, or "cannot say." The individual form of the test used cards which were placed in stacks, but it is more common today to use the group form with an optically-scanned answer sheet. There are nine clinical scales which are: (1) hypochondriasis (Hs) which deals with abnormal concerns about health; (2) depression (D); (3) Hysteria (Hy) which appears to be related to repression; (4) psychopathic deviance (Pd) which appears to be related to certain character disorders, brooding, anger, and continual resentment; (5)masculinity-femininity (Mf) which appears to be related to stereotypic ideas about sex role; (6)paranoia (Pa), a mental condition of thinking one is persecuted or being suspicious of others; (7) psychasthenia (Pt), which is generally associated with anxiety; (8) schizophrenia (Sc) which covers a broad range of items; and (9) hypomania (Ma) which relates to irritability, hyperactivity, and other items. There are in addition, other scales that relate to social desirability, the extent to which the individual is attempting to put himself/herself in a good perspective, a lie scale, and others which have been formed from the original scales.

Although the original standardization of the MMPI was completed largely with a Minnesota population and was therefore somewhat localized in nature, subsequent re-analyses were done to improve the content of the scales (Wiggins, 1969). Nonetheless, there were still outmoded items within the scales such as reference to playing "drop the handkerchief". There were also some items relating to religion that offended many individuals who belonged to church groups.

Over a period of years extending from 1982 until 1989 a total re-standardization of the MMPI was completed. Old items were scrutinized, and new items were tried out. Samples of individuals for the standardization were drawn from various geographical locations within the United States, representing both minority groups and sex and age differences in an appropriate manner. Uniform t scores were also computed. Out of this effort the older scales were updated, sharpened in content, and a new set of content scales were developed (Butcher, Graham, Williams and Ben-Porath, 1990).

The fifteen new content scales reflect a more modern clinical theoretical framework, rather than the older Kraepelin approach which had been in vogue when the original MMPI was developed. With internal improvement and modification of the original scales, together with the development of fifteen contemporary scales, the MMPI-2 (as the revision has come to be known), is a much more sophisticated and comprehensive instrument than before. The fifteen new scales are grouped into four content areas. They are: (1) internal symptomatic behaviors (anxiety, fears, obsessiveness, depression, health concerns and bizarre mentation scales); (2) external aggressive tendencies (anger, cynicism, antisocial practices and Type A behavior scales); (3) negative self-views (including a low self-esteem scale); and (4) general problem areas including social, familial, work and treatment (family problems, social discomfort, work interference, and negative treatment indicators scales).

The MMPI-2 is a very new contribution to the assessment literature. One of the major problems facing researchers is the question of how comparable are the old and new versions of the test. Duckworth (1990) compared the scores of 85 college students who took both versions. Her conclusions after examining the results are that there may be significantly different results drawn from the two versions for the same person. In some instances the scores are virtually identical, and in others there are significant discrepancies. She therefore believes that caution should be exercised in using research based upon the MMPI-1 to interpret the MMPI-2.

The California Psychological Inventory (CPI) (Gough, 1964) consists of 480 items which are responded to by "true" and "false." About half of the items were taken from the MMPI, so it also provides a set of measures related to the MMPI for those who might wish to use the inventory for counseling or clinical assessment. The CPI consists of seventeen scales concerning social, dominance, psychological-mindedness, and styles of achievement dimensions. Two scales which are often singled out as contributing something unique are the achievement by conformity (Ac) and achievement by independence (Ai) scales. The CPI scales fall into categories which make them easier to intepret and understand than the MMPI. Considerable work was done on the CPI to differentiate areas. It has a second-order factor analysis which provides overall analysis of temperament characteristics and styles. The CPI is appropriate to individuals who are 17 or older. The completion of the inventory takes about 45–60 minutes (Consulting Psychologists Press Inc.). Computer scoring services are also available from different sources. The main differences between the MMPI and the CPI are that the accent on the CPI is not on pathology, but on normal behavior, the construction of the scales is more congruent with modern statistical approaches, and it has known relationships to vocational dimensions such as the *Holland Vocational Preference Inventory*. The CPI is also reviewed extensively in Buros (1972).

The Sixteen Personality Factor Test is another instrument which has had considerable usage and has been applied to many varying problem fields such as clinical assessment, vocational interests, and the assessment of special area interests. The instrument was developed by Cattell and has had a number of alternative versions for the high school and elementary areas. Thus the *High School Personality Questionnaire (HSPQ)* and the *Children's Personality Questionnaire (CPQ)* are two spin-offs from the *Sixteen Personality Factor Test*. Testing time for the 16 PF is 45–60 minutes and it has had a number of current uses such as the matching of husband-wife profiles for marriage counseling (Institute for Personality and Ability Testing). Recently, Krug (1981) has provided a method for analyzing and reporting the second-order factor structure of the *Sixteen Personality Factor Test*.

Krug's manual is a valuable addition to the psychologist's repertory because it not only provides data for institutionalized patients and normals, based on over 17,000 cases, but also provides a wealth of data on vocational interests and patterns, together with other scales relating to sociopathy, psychopathy, etc. *The Sixteen Personality Factor Test* has one of the best factor structures in group testing. The chief reason is that various scales in the test show negative correlations with each other, whereas in many other group tests there are virtually no negative correlations between scales. This is important from a discrimination point of view since a scale which measures ego control ought to by construct definition correlate negatively with another one measuring impulsivity. *The Sixteen Personality Factor Test* is also available in a computer-scored form and can be ordered from the Institute of Personality Assessment Testing, Champaign, Illinois as well as from a variety of other publishers.

Two other popular personality tests often used for research are the *Omnibus Personality Inventory (OPI)* and the *Personality Research Form*. The former has items drawn from the MMPI as well as the CPI, and is often used for college students. Testing time ranges from 50 to 70 minutes and it is marketed by the Psychological Corporation. The latter test, the *Personality Research Form*, yields a number of scores which are appropriate for research and is generally suitable for college students. It takes approximately from 40 to 70 minutes to administer (Research Psychologists Press Inc.).

There are, in addition, tests which relate to temperament identification. Temperament is a construct which we shall discuss at great length in a future chapter. Suffice it to state here that by temperament is meant a cluster of dispositions which narrow the absolute range of variability in human beings. These tests attempt to identify those dispositional characteristics which aid in understanding the individual. Three of these are: *The Eysenck Personality Inventory (EPI)*, the *Myers-Briggs Type Indicator* and the *Barclay Classroom Assessment System*. *The Eysenck Personality Inventory* (Educational and Industrial Testing Service) takes about 10–15 minutes to administer and is appropriate from grade 9 upwards. It is based on the extensive research which Eysenck has done with his system of interpreting human behavior. At the core of this system is the construct of extroversion-introversion. Thus Eysenck's inventory attempts to identify the predominant pattern of preferences of the individual on the extroversion-introversion continuum. In addition, there is a neuroticism-psychopathy continuum and a lie scale.

The Myers-Briggs Type Indicator (Consulting Psychologists Press) takes approximately 55 minutes to administer and is appropriate from about grade 9 through adults. It is a test which attempts to identify overall characteristics of individuals. In this effort, the test provides a comparison between introversion and extroversion, thinking and feeling, sensing and intuition, and judgment vs. perception. Based on Jungian constructs the test looks at styles of behavior, much as aptitude tests attempt to capture basic skills of individuals. Much research has been done to identify the characteristics of medical students, health related professionals, and other groups to determine the predominant patterns of thinking and perceiving. The Myers-Briggs is essentially an assessment tool to determine predominant modes of responding to stimulation from the environment.

The Barclay Classroom Assessment System (BCAS) is a multitrait, multimethod approach to the measuring of individual differences in the elementary classroom (Western Psychological Services, 1983). It takes about an hour to an hour and one half to administer and involves self-report, peer sociometric judgments, and teacher ratings. It is appropriate to children from grades three to grades seven. From the multiple inputs, factor scores are obtained which characterize children by type of preference for various activities and involves locus of control dimensions. Thus, via a multimethod, multitrait factor analysis six basic temperament types are identified. The system is designed to provide a technological tool for teachers, counselors, administrators, and psychologists who are interested in the early identification of children with learning disabilities, social and behavioral problems, and gifted or creative children. The output of the system is strictly by computer integration and report since the complexity of the system requires computer analysis and judgments.

Vocational interest testing assesses the characteristics of an individual in relationship to established patterns of interests shown by professionals in ecific fields. Perhaps of all the assessment dimensions in personality or related areas, vocational assessment is one which is used most. Even those counseling theories or systems which do not rely on tests much at all do use vocational inventories. Generally, vocational assessment has been done by determining the interest patterns of individuals and matching their individual profile with groups of professionals or other vocational groups who are in that occupation. First of the major tests in use today in point of historical origin is the Kuder series. There are three current series, *the Kuder Form D* or what is known as the *Occupational Interest Survey*, the *Kuder Preference Record-Vocational*, and the *Kuder Form E General Interest Survey* (Science Research Associates). These interest surveys provide comparisons for individuals on a variety of occupational and professional categories via preferences indicated in outdoor, mechanical, scientific computational, persuasive, artistic, literary, musical, social service and clerical groups. Some versions can be handscored and others are computer scored. Depending on the version used the instrument can be administered to grades 6 and upwards to adult.

A second major system which is used in many settings is the *Strong-Campbell Interest Inventory (SCII)*, the *Strong Vocational Interest Blank for Men Revised (SVIB)* and the *Strong Vocational Interest Blank for Women, Revised* (SVIB) (Consulting Psychologists Press Inc.). This instrument has been used widely and has undergone several major revisions. In the SCII new scales have been added which included a General Occupation Theme based on Holland's research (1966) and some Basic Interest Scales. So the SCII contains a much more sophisticated set of analyses than the SVIB alone. The instrument takes anywhere from a half hour to over an hour depending on the version used and it is appropriate to individuals 17 and over.

Another popular inventory, the *Vocational Preference Inventory (VPI)* (Psychological Assessment Resources), is based on the research of John Holland. This inventory consists of a number of occupational titles and provides scores relating to a typology based on outdoor-mechanical (realistic), investigative (intellectual), social, conventional, enterprising, and artistic preferences in occupations. It also provides an evaluation of self-control, masculinity, status, infrequency and acquiescence. Holland has also developed a profile for what he terms the *Self-Directed Search* which is an effort to provide direct information back to an individual without the intermediary of a counselor interpreter.

Two other instruments which are used for more specific vocational purposes are the *Minnesota Vocational Interest Inventory (MVII)* (Psychological Corporation) and the *Ohio Vocational Interest Survey* (OVIS) (Harcourt Brace Jovanovich). The former takes about 45 minutes and can be administered to high school and adult males for purposes of nonprofessional vocational interests, and the latter takes about 80 minutes and is essentially a high school vocational interest inventory.

There are, in addition to personality, temperament, and vocational interest inventories, a number of other measurement devices which can be broadly grouped under this category. Some of them are specific to values such as the *Study of Values*, Third Edition (Houghton-Mifflin) which looks at six value types such as theoretical, economic, aesthetic, social, political, and religious values, and the *Survey of Personal Values* (SPY) published by Science Research Associates which provides six scores relating to practical mindedness, achievement, variety, decisiveness, orderliness, and goal-orientation.

Personality and vocational tests are widely used in all kinds of settings and employ the profile analysis. This entails examining high and low scores. Much research has also been done in looking at the profiles of certain types of mental patients and classes of individuals successful in various occupations or professions. Sometimes profile analysis needs to be done by the psychologist scoring the test, but in most of the more commonly used group personality and vocational tests the profile analysis is done by computer. Naturally, the interpretation of the profile analysis of personality tests and vocational ones relies on inferences to translate a pattern of test scores into written language. This requires such a degree of caution that in most instances computer reports speak in tentative terms. As we shall see later on in the chapter, it is very important to determine the conditions of the test-taking and the individual taking the test, as well as the reliability and validity of the instruments.

From a critical point of view, it is fair to state that there are major differences of opinion about the use of structured group personality and vocational tests. The criticisms do not focus so much on the standardization of the instruments, as on the question of how reliable the profiles are. Behaviorists tend to see the output of these tests as related to learned attitudes and temporary states of the organism. They believe that such instruments should be viewed as temporary analyses and not as permanent characteristics of the individual. Mischel (1968) took this position earlier, but has tended to recognize more or less enduring dispositions in recent years (1975).

On the other hand, the majority of psychological test users believe that these tests measure relatively enduring traits of the individual. Though there may be changes in certain scales, it is believed that individuals tend to represent themselves in similar ways over time. This has been documented over a period of 30 years by Block (1975). Perhaps the most critical point of all is the application of such tests. If they are more closely related to state conditions, then they are not as valuable as predictors of future behavior.

On the other hand, if they do represent relatively enduring trait characteristics, they may be used judiciously to advise individuals in terms of adjustment goals and vocational objectives.

PSYCHOMETRIC PROJECTIVE TECHNIQUES

Projective techniques are individualized administered personality tests that infer structural or dynamic entitites from the production of responses given to indeterminate stimuli. George Kelly once wrote: "When the subject is asked to guess what the examiner is thinking, we call it an objective test; when the examiner tries to guess what the subject is thinking, we call it as projective device" (Kelly, 1958, p. 332). Projective techniques represent a set of inferences, in part based on psychometric properties, and in part based on the interpretation of the clinician in accordance with a set of *a priori* assumptions about meaning.

Under this heading is included primarily what are termed projective techniques, although to some extent the analysis of interviewing also involves making inferences about meaning. Projective techniques are included in this section because they do use psychometric methods such as the computation of means, standard deviations, and profile analysis. There is also the comparison of target criterion groups. However, the clinical interpretation of responses to stimuli presented to a client involves a theoretical set of assumptions about what constitutes the meaning of those responses. There is therefore a considerable amount of intuitive inferring which takes place in the use of such techniques.

The status of projective testing and usage in the United States today has been recently surveyed by Piotrowski and Keller (1984). They sent out questionnaires to 113 APA approved programs in clinical psychology and received 80 or 71% back. They found that less than half of the programs required one course in this area, nearly half of the programs anticipated decreased usage of projective tests, while objective test use would be increasing. Of all the projective tests which were being used, the five which received the most nominations were the *Thematic Apperception Test* (85%), the *Rorschach* (83%), *Sentence-Completions* (53%), *Human Figure Drawings* (26%), and the *Bender-Gestalt* (17%).

Piotroski and Keller point out that the decline in the use of projective techniques may stem from the fact that orientation of most of the programs (62%) was eclectic, with a behavioral orientation of some kind favored by a minority (15%). By contrast only a small fraction of programs expressed a psychodynamic orientation (4%). The increase in the eclectic and behavioral orientations contrasts considerably with the heavier psychodynamic approach after World War II and the Boulder Conference in 1949. Given that the programs themselves are less insistent on the use of such techniques, and that they are usually taught in broad survey courses, it is understandable that students seldom obtain the depth of clinical knowledge necessary for their extensive use. On the other hand, graduating students often find that their employers in either state hospitals or comprehensive mental health clinics require substantial competency in the administration and interpretation of these techniques.

Projective techniques as a formal aspect of assessment date only from the beginning of this century, but informally it has been reported that even the ancient Sumerians used them. For example, the Sumerians employed a version of the word-association technique to identify the particular devil which was bothering a person. They would pronounce a list of stimulus words and watch reactions. When the patient became agitated, they would note the word and relate it to the devil which was bothering him. The term projective comes from the Latin verb *projicere* which literally means to throw or cast forward. It thus represents in assessment a method for determining the dynamics of the inner world. By responding in a certain manner to a word association, or sentence-completion, the inner workings of the mind are revealed. In similar manner, the method in which an individual draws a picture of a person is also thought to represent certain imagery about male and female roles, parents, etc. Word associations and sentence-completions are examples of more structured projective techniques. On the other hand, the drawing of a human figure, the interpretation of a picture, and the interpretation of inkblots are examples of unstructured techniques.

Freud used the term projective in its earliest contemporary sense to describe defense mechanisms and exemplify his conception of the unconscious determinants of behavior. "The projection of inner perceptions to the outside is a primitive mechanism which for instance also influences our sense-perceptions, so that it normally has the greatest share in shaping our outer world. Under conditions that have not yet been sufficiently determined even inner perceptions of ideational and emotional processes are projected outwardly, like sense perceptions, and are used to shape the outer world, whereas they ought to remain in the inner world" (Freud, *Collected Papers, IV*, p. 187). Freud believed that it was possible to deduce the nature of conflicts, basic needs, and the pattern of psychological development from neurotic behavior and thinking. He basically assumed that individuals did not know what they thought they knew and that the underlying conflicts of human beings could reveal themselves both as themes in dreams and as forces underlying symbols. Though Freud himself was not involved in development of projective techniques, he believed that content about the unconscious dynamics of life could be obtained by elaboration of dreams and the peculiar association of ideas which they revealed. Others drew conclusions from his general theoretical approach. Jung, for example, developed one of the first word-association techniques, and Hermann Rorschach developed the interpretation of ink blots to a fine technique, in part as a result of Freud's thinking.

More recently, both Erikson and Loevinger have looked at the development of the ego as a process which could be understood through projective techniques. Rapaport (1946) describes the nature of projective techniques by suggesting that projection is similar to the projection of an image by a movie camera. He believes that the test protocol acts as the picture on the screen, the film as representative of personality, and the movie projector as the technique. But it should be pointed out that the representation projected by the client and the interpretation by the clinician indicate something more akin to an impressionistic painting than a photograph. First of all, there are the assumptions which underly the very theory of projection, and second, it is evident that the judgments of clinicians on projective test data are not only based on these assumptions and some psychometric properties, but also on inferential judgments which at worst are highly subjective and at best are intuitive.

There are literally hundreds of projective devices and tests developed on the theory of projection. By and large these devices can be classified structurally by the nature of the stimulus presented to the client or subject. Word associations and sentence-completions are more structured (and hence more amenable to clear classification), while inkblots, picture drawing, picture interpretation, and figure interpretation are less structured and therefore more imprecise in classification. In the following section a brief description of some major instruments will be written, but individuals interested in a more complete survey of such techniques should consider reading the book by Anderson and Anderson (1951). This book, though now primarily of historical interest, provides a comprehensive overview of a number of techniques and summarizes earlier research.

Word-Association and Sentence-Completion Techniques. The word-association approach is one of the oldest of projective techniques. It was used by Galton and Wundt and also by Kraepelin. Jung used a list of about 100 words which he chose to represent common emotional problems. Kent and Rosanoff developed a list of words (1910) and Tendler (1945) modified their scale using 25 words. Tendler reported that adjective-noun responses were more characteristic of neurotics and individualistic responses were characteristic of psychotics. He worked out a table of percentile scores on the basis of results with 240 cases to reveal the level of contrast (normal), individualistic (psychotic), and adjective-noun (neurotic) responses. The basic classifying rationale for scoring words is derived from psychoanalytic theory which suggests that normal well-adjusted individuals will make responses to a stimulus word which bear a conventional conceptual relationship to the stimulus, whereas bizarre responses reflect intrapsychic conflict, disturbances in the interpretation of reality, unfulfilled needs, or sources of conflict.

Sentence-Completion Tests. More representative of this form of projective testing (because it is more used) are sentence-completions. Originally sentence-completions were used primarily to assess intelligence rather than to evaluate personality, but it was soon evident that such tests were tapping personality characteristics and they were thus correctly classified as projectives. Rohde and Hildreth in 1939 published a variation of the sentence-completion test which was used earlier by Payne (Forer, 1950). The purpose of their test was to develop an instrument which would have the advantage of other projective techniques, but which could be readily used in schools and other institutions. Forer advocated the use of the third person in his format, but Rohde and Hildreth used the three basic forms: (1) first person singular, (2) third person plural, and (3) third person singular. Many studies have been done with sentence-completion techniques. Some versions have attempted to interpret responses in accord with need-press dimensions from Murray's rationale. During World War II, the sentence-completion technique was used widely by army psychologists (Hutt, 1945, and Holtzberg, 1947). Perhaps the most widely used sentence-completion test is the one that Rotter (1950) marketed with versions for school-aged children. Though most such instruments provide some reliability data, the general approach to validation is rather arbitrary. Criteria which are used in evaluating such responses often relate to popular and bizarre responses as well as to the interpretation of personal and social pressures and conflicts felt by the client as interpreted by the clinician.

Drawings. Another popular projective technique relates to drawings that individuals make. This has been particularly popular with school psychologists (Harris, 1963; Goodenough, 1926; Machover, 1953). The basic rationale here is that a drawing represents an interpretation of the individual, perceived life-space and problems. Thus color, form, lines, shade areas, the placement of the figure on the drawing paper, the sex of the figure, the size of the self figures in relationship to parental or authority figures, and the balance of form and details in relationship to age, are all important considerations. Most of the manuals relating to the interpretation of drawings have criteria for estimating intelligence as well as psychodynamic problems. A variation of picture analysis and sentence-completion has been developed by Rosenzweig (1948). His approach (*the Rosenzweig Picture-Frustration Study*) was designed to aid in research concerning reactions to frustration. There are a number of cartoon-like drawings representing incidents in everyday life. The client is asked to write a reply that would be made by a second person and the records are interpreted on the assumption that the client's response is a projection of what overt reactions he or she would make in a similar situation.

The Thematic Apperception Test. One of the most unstructured projective techniques which has been used for many years is the *Thematic Apperception Test*. This test first appeared in 1935 and has had widespread usage by psychologists ever since. The test was developed along with a theory of personality by Henry Murray. It consists of a set of 20 pictures with alternate ones appropriate for males and females. The general rationale of the test includes the assumptions that the needs of an individual together with emotional overtones are reflected in the interpretation of a picture stimulus. Murray believed that behavior consists of several functional levels. The first and more peripheral layer of behavior relates to verbal exchanges which are expressed or shown. A lower level of such functionings is revealed through ideas, wishes and the elaboration of stories about the pictures. Murray did not suggest that all of the needs of an individual will express themselves in relevant stories or elaboration of pictures, but he did believe that responses to these picture stimuli will reflect some of the outstanding needs of the individual.

Murray's system of picture analysis places considerable emphasis on the content of the stories which are analyzed in regard to forces seen as related to the "here and now" and forces related to the "press" of the environment. A need is a construct which represents a brain condition or deficit that is translated into verbal messages as an unsatisfactory condition. A "press" represents the force of a specific or generalized environment, and a "theme" is the interaction of the hero's need (as derived from the explanation given) and the environmental "press." Thus when all the themes derived from the picture interpretation or stories reflect sadness, frustration, and unhappiness, a logical interpretation is that the client is experiencing these feelings. A variety of scoring systems exist for the *Thematic Apperception Test*. Murray himself placed heavy emphasis on the content analysis, but this almost requires a recording and a detailed scrutiny of the output. Bellak (Murstein, 1963) attempts to analyze the T.A.T. in terms of 10 factors which are: (1) the main theme, (2) the main hero, (3) the main needs of the hero, (4) the conception of the environment, (5) the nature of parental, contemporary, and junior figures (6) significant conflicts, (7) the nature of anxieties, (8) main defenses against conflicts and fears, (9) severity of the superego as manifested, and (10) the integration of the ego as it manifests itself.

The T.A.T. has been used by many psychologists for decades. Unfortunately, according to Murstein (1963), the vast majority of studies show poor or mediocre reliability estimates. Another minor problem today is the fact that many of the figures in the pictures are represented in clothing or in situations which are approximately 50 years old. Perhaps the pictures ought to be updated, much in the way that some elements of the Stanford-Binet have been modernized. But on the other hand, some may object to this procedure as changing the basic stimuli of the pictures.

The Rorschach. *The Rorschach Inkblot Test* is perhaps the most unstructured and controversial of all projective techniques. Esteemed most highly by some clinicians it has also been equally condemned by others. Though thousands of studies have been done with it, there is still not a clear indication of the extent of the reliability and validity of the system and how it agrees or disagrees with other assessment methods. It is in a classification by itself. Rickers-Ovsiakina, a Rorschach authority, had clearly outlined the situation: "The problem of the reliability of the Rorschach is a many-faceted problem. The Rorschach must like all instruments of study demonstrate its reliability, but it should demonstrate it through methods which take into consideration the peculiar characteristics of the Rorschach" (1960, p. 377). With regard to validity she states that the Rorschach "has no status apart from the methodological orientation of the group that is evaluating it. It is a Fugue, it is an endeavor of the past; as a Chorale it is an effort in the timeless present; and as a Prelude it is an exploration, the fruits of which lie largely unknown in the future. By the canons of test analysis, the Rorschach Technique as a whole has been shown at present to have neither satisfactory validity nor invalidity" (p. 36).

What is being expressed here is a concept which occurs frequently even in recent literature on the Rorschach, that it is an instrument *sui generis* (of its own category and classification). It stands with no real peers to evaluate it. Thus it appears to be much like faith: if one believes, the products are of great richness and the depth of meaning is of great value. If one does not, the results seem meagre for a large investment of time and effort. The test was originally devised by Hermann Rorschach, a psychiatrist who lived near Zurich during the 10 years when he worked on the test. Rorschach began the development of the system at a time when Gestalt psychology was being popularized in Europe. Rorschach was familiar with free-association techniques and therefore conceived a projective technique which would use as its stimulus an inkblot to tap depths of personality. The test itself consists of 10 inkblot designs printed on white cardboard. The blots are all centered and are presented in the same order. Five of them are gray in varying shades. In figures 2 and 3 bright red blotches are present, but no other color. Figures 8, 9, and 10 have mostly colored blotches. The order of presentation is not varied because it is held that this is an important factor in the diagnosis. According to Rorschach the three main dimensions which are tapped in the technique are: (1) conscious intellectual activity, (2) the internalized emotions, and (3) dimensions of internal emotional activity. Researchers in the Rorschach technique tell us that the test provides an integrated pattern of the total personality, that its very complexity defies analysis in accordance with traditional testing methods, and that the test stands as an unique instrument.

Modifications, changes and efforts at psychometric standardization have taken place with the Rorschach. Though one major problem with the instrument has been the variety of scoring procedures introduced by Beck, Klopher and Kelly, as well as Piotrowsky, more recently Exner (1974) has attempted to integrate various elements of different scoring into his own system. Exner, more than any modern researcher, appears to have reacquainted many new psychologists with this old technique. There have also been many efforts to standardize responses. These include the Harrower and Steiner *Large Scale Rorschach Technique* (1944, 1951) and the *California Test Bureau S-O-Rorschach Test* (1958). Each of thses systems attempted to use a multiple-choice format for determining and scoring responses. But these efforts apparently did not bear long-range fruit. On the one hand, the multiple-choice format seems to offend the purists who believe that the Rorschach cannot be so categorized, and on the other hand, the standardizations did not result in the intended validity and reliability which other researchers looked for.

In the 1970s a massive effort was mounted by Holtzman (1972) to develop an inkblot test using many different blots. This system was based on the same theory, but required new blots and a new format. This effort did not seem to reach critical mass as a new instrumentation of an old technique. In recent decades research with the Rorschach seems to have slackened. Dana (1982) in a book on projectives chiefly cites studies from the 1950s, 1960s, and some from the 1970s.

The Bender Gestalt. The final instrument to be mentioned in this survey is the *Bender Gestalt Test* (Bender, 1946). This is a perceptual motor test which is widely used and consists of nine geometric forms or designs each drawn in black ink on a piece of white cardboard of about postcard size. The client is presented with each of these designs sequentially and asked to copy them as well as is possible on a sheet of unlined paper. The interpretation of the test is again related to dynamics which are reflective of Gestalt psychology of perception, and more recently related to neurological inferencing. Koppitz (1975) has summarized recent research with the instrument (1963–1973) and discusses the variety of uses as a test of visual perception, motor coordination, higher-order neurological integration, and personality. In addition, the many applications to learning disabilities, mental retardation, and emotional problems are discussed. The Bender is a popular instrument used with children in school psychology practice.

Projective techniques are very difficult to evaluate critically in terms of psychometric procedures. The main reason for this is that there are really

	Surveys	CTMM	CAT	SCAT	DAT	ACT	CEEB	MMPI	CPI	16PF	Myers-Briggs	BCAS	SVIB	VPI	MVII	OVIS	Study of Values	Tennessee	Piers-Harris	Coopersmith	Sociometry
Academic Achievement		X	X	X	X	X	X					X									
Achievement Style									X												
Adjustment	X							X	X	X		X									X
Body Image	X							X		X											
Cognitive Aptitudes				X	X	X							X								
Control								X	X	X		X									X
Creativity	X								X	X		X									X
Depression	X							X	X	X		X									X
Delinquency								X	X	X		X									X
Dominance								X	X	X	X	X									X
Interest Patterns	X											X	X	X	X	X					
Intelligence		X	X	X					X												
Leadership											X	X									X
Physical Skills	X											X									
Problem-Solving	X				X	X	X														
Quantitative Skills		X	X	X	X	X	X	X													
Self-Concept									X									X	X	X	
Self-Sufficiency								X		X											
Self-Competency												X									X
Self-Discipline									X	X											
Sociability								X	X	X	X										X
Social Power												X									X
Temperament										X	X	X									
Values	X																X				
Verbal Skills		X	X	X	X	X	X	X													
Vocational Interests												X	X	X	X	X					

Note*: There are many other tests which also measures these areas. These
are cited as representative ones.

Figure 8-1   Selected Areas of Assessment and Some Representative Tests Appropriate for the Area.

very few common denominators to evaluate them according to a unitary classification system. Each one has its own script and set of assumptions. Perhaps the real problem is listing them as a process form of psychometrics. Though many of the instruments have accumulated reliability and validity data with use, they are often limited: first because psychometric method studies have been applied post-hoc to techniques that did not originally consider psychometrics important, and second because the instruments have relatively low levels of data relating to "normal" individuals.

One critical question which is still unanswered is whether it is more valid or valuable to obtain information by indirection and inference rather than by a direct approach. For example, behaviorists believe that sexuality and sexual characteristics can be ascertained more directly through the measurement of sexual arousal to various pictures than inferring sexual content from the interpretation of inkblots. No easy answer can be forthcoming to the problems of projective techniques. For those who believe, criticism is invalid. For those who do not like them, results of projective devices are reduced to subjective intuition. Perhaps the only viable criterion is one that relates to determining what the techniques offer either by way of cumulative variance with them over and above other assessment procedures, or the insights which they provide regarding information for therapy change, or for treatment. Here again individual clinicians differ.

THE ROLE OF TESTS IN ASSESSMENT

Tests are an important aspect of assessment by providing both general and specific information about individual differences. By virtue of the manner in which tests tap specific responses of individuals, it is possible to gain a considerable knowledge about many aspects of attitudes, intelligence, achievement, personality, and vocational preferences. It is, however, important to recognize that testing results are subject to many possible sources of error as we have mentioned earlier in the chapter. It is imperative that the users of tests recognize that test results are always conditional and tentative. If there is any one cause for abuses with testing, it must be ascribed directly to the strong tendency of students of psychology and even psychologists who have completed their studies to consider test results as absolute indicators of personality, achievement, etc. The greatest error made with regard to the use of tests is to assume greater validity than they possess. This is often in part because testing courses attempt to cover large numbers of tests, dealing with basic properties of reliability and validity without teaching students how these tests should be used. In addition, the error variance that occurs within testing itself is seldom taken into consideration adequately, and the fact that tests often reflect middle-class values and may therefore be prejudiced against certain minorities is also a problem.

The three principles important in developing skills in test assessment are: (1) **learn a few tests well;** (2) **obtain a global overview assessment of the individual before looking at specific problem areas; and** (3) **consider testing as one of the assessment strategies that leads to a treatment.**

Learn a few tests well. By this suggestion is meant that selected tests should be studied in terms of their construction, reliability, validity, and usage. In this chapter a number of those tests which have been used for some time are described. Ordinarily, these tests have been well constructed, and have survived the test of usage. The products of most major test companies usually meet criteria of good reliability and validity. In addition, it is always possible to look up test reviews in the *Mental Measurement Yearbooks* (Mitchell, 1985) or *Test Critiques* (Keyser and Sweetland, 1984). However, there is one major caveat about these test reviews. Virtually all test reviews are written by individuals who attempt to examine all possible facets of reliability and validity. Thus, even well-accepted test instruments have surprisingly negative reviews. In many instances, the reviewers have only looked at the test manuals and other literature sent to them. They often have not had a personal experience in using the test they review. To a large extent this is the situation with the *Mental Measurement Yearbooks Test Critiques.*

By and large, major test publishing companies attempt to develop and market their products in accordance with the *Standards for Educational and Psychological Testing* (American Psychological Association, 1985) developed jointly by the American Educational Research Association, the American Psychological Association, and the National Council for Measurement in Education. Thus a detailed reading of the manual of the specific test comparing the results of the manual with the standards developed by APA may be most helpful in arriving at a conclusion about a test. Although testing companies may tend to accent the positive about one of their tests, it is likewise true that the *Mental Measurement Yearbooks* tend to accent the negative. Since virtually no test has ever obtained a completely clean endorsement by reviewers in the *Yearbooks* it makes sense to take these reviews with a proverbial "grain of salt" and to consider the actual use of the test in assessment procedures. Ultimately, the personal evaluation of a test is dependent not only on good construction, but utility in assessment. This is often a personal matter stemming from usage.

Obtain an overview of the individual before looking at specific problems. In the matter of assessment it is very important to obtain an overview of the individual's characteristics before looking at specific problem areas. Very often, students or even other faculty ask something like "what's a good measure of depression?" They have even asked questions like "how can changes in paraplegics' nutrition be measured by personality tests?" The answer is that it all depends. There are some good scales which measure specifically depression, or locus of control, or a number of other traits. But the question of assessing depression is clearly related to the total personality. Depression is not an independent variable in itself, but rather the consequence of certain personality characteristics challenged by a set of environmental and/or biological conditions. It is therefore more important to view depression in the context of the total personality.

Consider testing as one of the processes of developing a treatment plan. Although testing usually results in providing both descriptive characteristics and predictive ones, for the most part psychologists are interested in knowing how tests relate to the development of a treatment plan. This means in effect that it is necessary for us to know how a given set of personality, temperament, or achievement variables relate to what we might conceivably do in attempting to provide some growth and development for an individual or a group of individuals. This task is at the very core of assessment itself. The topic will be pursued further in a later chapter, because developing a treatment plan is not specifically determined by test results.

ABUSES OF PSYCHOMETRIC TECHNIQUES

There have been many unwarranted uses of psychometric techniques and many abuses of testing. Most of the problems that have occurred in testing stem from the misuse of tests. Some of these misapplications stem from inadequate knowledge of the purpose and function of psychometrics, lack of recognition of both internal and external threats to validity, and the use of testing results as a criterion of trait characteristics. The extensive use of psychometric instruments in present day culture often obscures the real purposes for such usage. Psychometric instruments should serve as scientific estimates of characteristics of individuals. Their major purpose is to furnish a standardized and objective aid to decision making. The decision making is often about how an individual will do in a certain situation, or what are chances of success in an academic or vocational direction. The primary source of information is that obtained in the empirical interview. Tests then may provide additional assistance in understanding how the individual is functioning. Tests never have been intended to be a substitute for individual decision making. Thus the first question which assessors should ask is this: does this particular technique add something to what is known about an individual in order to arrive at a good decision? Tests should not be used simply because everyone expects it, or because there is money available for testing. Tests should provide relevant information regarding cognitive or emotional characteristics, a variety of vocational interests and educational accomplishments.

Tests should never be used as criteria in themselves. Because tests frequently have been used explicitly or implicitly by psychological personnel as CRITERIA, there have often been problems in identifying intelligence with an intelligence test, personality with a personality test, or vocational skills with a vocational test. Tests usually constitute a legitmate and logical sample of attitudes, skills or achievements, but should not be considered criteria in themselves. Often when tests are used as criteria there are serious problems with the interpretation of scores made by minority groups who score uniformly lower on some basic intelligence and achievement tests. Though there is a broad assumption that traits and characteristics are distributed normally in the population, a variety of possible errors can creep into test interpretation when tests are used to assess cultural minority groups, or are applied in ways for which they were not designed. Thus, in recent decades there has been much criticism of testing in terms of racial bias, sex bias, and socioeconomic bias. These biases occur because many tests were standardized chiefly on white middle-class individuals, or were focused chiefly on male interests (such as the vocational inventories), and did not sample sufficient numbers of individuals from lower socioeconomic backgrounds or of both sexes. However, some of the solutions are not always acceptable. For example, some researchers have stated that separate norms ought to be established for blacks and whites. This would also, presumably, include Hispanics and Orientals. Since socioeconomic background is important also, then norms should be established for higher socioeconomic groups, middle socioeconomic groups, and lower socioeconomic groups. So in effect, to be perfectly consistent with this approach we ought to have norms for at least four different racial groups and three different socioeconomic groups. If sex differences are not taken into consideration, this yields a set of 12 separate norms. If sex groups are taken into consideration, we have 24 separate norm groups. This is a common problem faced by the construction of separate norms for minority groups. Logically, if one is to accept the validity of measuring groups only against their own constituency, then one ought to have at least 12 sets of separate norms and most likely 24. This is the problem which faces individuals who create tests which are related to specific minority groups. For example, Williams (1972) argued that blacks should be evaluated against their own norms. He then constructed a test for blacks based on street culture concepts. This was called the *Black Intelligence Test of Cultural Homogeneity* (BITCH). There are no published data as to its relevance as an intelligence test, and Matarazzo and Wiens (1977) found that it does not correlate with the full scale WAIS or any of its eleven subtests. Thus, one should look carefully at those techniques or combination of other valid approaches which are somehow accommodated to cultural minorities.

A better approach may be to make some accommodations to standard instruments. Mercer and Lewis (1979) developed an instrument entitled the SOMPA for measuring intellective, perceptual-motor and adaptive skills in children. This instrument uses a variety of other tests to evaluate children from multicultural backgrounds and also makes adjustments depending on sociological differences. Although the process does allow for some accommodation to cultural norms, it is a lengthy one for busy school psychologists, and some reviews have criticized the system for technical reasons and practical utility (Reschly, 1982; Reynolds, 1985). However, Mercer and Lewis attempted to find a way to measure individual differences, to accept the differences which exist, and to plan some interventions to do something about them.

Some researchers feel, nonetheless, that making adjustments in standardized psychometric tests or developing separate tests for minorities actually confirms the opinion of those who believe that minorities are inferior. For if separate tests are required, and separate norms need to be computed, it is obvious that the means and standard deviations of subgroups differ, and the only way this problem can be solved is by separate tests or separate norms. For decades now tests have been criticized on many other accounts than minority bias. Severe charges have been lodged against psychologists, counselors, and school personnel because of both uses and abuses of tests. Earlier protests were directed at the inappropriate use of tests, such as the administration of the MMPI in schools (Barclay, 1968b). There have been those who have considered testing as part of a Marxist-Communist plot to undermine education. In addition, the suspect reliability and validity of projective techniques, often used in the past as a basis of clinical expertise, have prejudiced authorities against the validity of other psychometric procedures. There have been many abuses of testing both by using inappropriate tests in situations where they are not called for, and by using tests themselves as the criterion of educational progress (such as with achievement tests).

In all too many situations, psychologists have tended to use test scores and profiles as absolutes, or as the explicit or implicit gatekeepers to opportunity (as in specialized admission tests). Though a reasonable argument can be made for admission tests into colleges and universities, when they are the exclusive basis for admission or rejection they can be very poor indicators. What is being suggested here is simply that tests not be considered the ONLY basis for judgment of admissions. Personal interviews, autobiographical data, and references often add considerable information of value.

Some years ago Martin Gross (1962) published a book entitled: *The Brain-watchers*. Page after page of information is provided about the use of aptitude testing and projective techniques by big business. Example after example is provided to illustrate the techniques used. He suggests that school counselors are woefully untrained in testing procedures and often use tests to find something to talk about with a student. What Gross wrote nearly 30 years ago is still often true in the use of testing. Unfortunately, part of the problem is how testing is taught to students. Testing is often taught in much the same way that individuals walk through a museum. They look first at one picture on a wall and then another. Tests cannot be used adequately by individuals who just look at a test descriptions in a textbook. They must be understood through study of manuals, experience in both taking and administering the test, and experience in integrating the test with other indicators of assessment in the process of test interpretation. Tests must be understood as scientific instruments which attempt to improve the quality of decision making about specific situations. Thus the criterion which is implicit behind all testing is that of what constitutes adequate human behavior. We have discussed earlier the assumptions of psychometric methods and the need to consider carefully both reliability and validity factors in the acceptance and use of tests.

In addition, it is important to recognize that even when test instruments are carefully standardized, there is still what is called the standard error of measurement. This means that there is a built-in-error of measurement in any test. The true score of an individual may be anywhere from 2 to 10 points other than the obtained score. Thus it is imperative for users of tests to recognize the standard error associated with obtained and true test scores. When multiple scores are obtained for individuals such as in an achievement or personality test where there are many scales, the extent of error that may be present is potentially great. There are reasons for this error factor. Conditions which are not susceptible to control such as the personal feeling of the child, the conditions of the testing situation, or actual mistakes in scoring and interpretation, result in this error of measurement. For example, the 1960 revision of the Stanford-Binet Intelligence Scale has an error of measurement of approximately 5 I.Q. points. This means that a child who obtains an I.Q. of 95 could have a true I.Q. falling anywhere between 90 and 100. Similar problems exist in all achievement, personality, and vocational tests. The standard error of measurement also relates to another problem, i.e., what is called regression towards the mean. This simply means that one testing result may be either low or high. On another testing of the same instrument children who scored low may tend to obtain a higher score, while those scoring high may obtain a lower score. Sometimes for many reasons individuals may simply be more accurate, or guess more correctly. So likewise, they may feel more like taking the test and putting more effort and motivation into it. In any event, the standard error of measurement and the concept of regression towards the mean are factors which all test users must take into consideration.

All of these problems accent the difficulties which exist in relationship to careful test usage. Testing is simply an objectivized method at arriving at decisions about the characteristics of individuals and groups. Its essential characteristic therefore is related to its value as an objective method of decision making. It is very important, however, to recognize that tests tend to describe the characteristics of groups better than of individuals. So a test of any kind is more valid for groups than for individuals. We can be more sure of describing groups of individuals than we can in describing an individual within a group. Individuals may miss or answer correctly different items within scales and yet come out with similar scores. Generally our tests are constructed so that they yield scale scores on the basis of correct items as compared with the theoretical template. But in many ways, the items which individuals indicate they are not interested in or which they reject provide us with as much information as those items they choose.

Criteria of effective human behavior are contextual: test data should be interpreted in a goodness of fit relationship with heuristic criteria. The final problem to be discussed here is the criterion one. Tests are so often and in so many ways used even by professionals as criteria. **Criteria of effective human behavior cannot be established either by canonical fiat of religious or political groups or by normative data from a test standardization.** The determination of what constitutes adequacy of human behavior must be derived from the set of expectancies which exist in certain circumstances and from the subjective perceptions of the client. Both expectancies and subjective perceptions are most often a by-product of the cultural tradition and environmental "press." What constitutes good and acceptable behavior in one culture is not the same in another. Thus, for example, American frankness of expression can often be considered rude in Chinese culture, even though no such intent was manifest. The Chinese tendency to decline large portions, or additional portions of food, may result (in American cultural settings) in hunger on the part of the Chinese visitor. Not only culture in this broad sense must be considered in arriving at criteria of effective human behavior, but also the specific vocational differences that occur in normal life. Psychologists often work for different clients. Whether they work for governmental institutions, academic ones or business, they usually know quite explicitly what are the criteria of admission, promotion, success, etc. Therefore, tests often have sets of scores which translate these expectancies into concrete facts. Though one can argue whether the criteria of admission, promotion, retention, etc. are just and adequate, the fact is that such criteria exist and most often the task of the psychologist is to determine if a given individual meets these criteria. Moreover, if prospective students or employees want to be admitted, or hired, they need to be advised that certain criteria need to be met. However, psychologists can and should look at the objective evidence of test data, together with many other factors, before making a final judgment.

In addition, the implicit criteria of a job or academic setting also need to be taken into consideration. I refer to those intangible attitudes which we term expectations. The expectations for behavior as an accountant may differ considerably from those for an artist. The same personality or intelligence or vocational profile is not indicative of adequacy of judgment or behavior in both circumstances. The criteria of school expectations are those implemented by teachers, peers, and parents. However, no claim is made here that those heuristic expectations can be judged to be accurate criteria of behavior for a given individual. Thus the criteria may be too difficult, too biased, or may reflect other circumstances which are not beneficial to the individual. So the determination of what constitutes an effective set of criteria for human behavior must be determined by the demands of expectations, the capacity of the individual, and the history of past experience. It is in this perspective that psychometric data can help to provide valuable insight and understanding both to the clinician and to the client. Though there are many criterion references for judging adequate behavior, cultural determinants as related to basic human needs constitute the major referent. However, in all circumstances the cultural referent must be related to the contextual demands, the client's implicit or explicit goals, and courses of behavior which are both possible and realistic. In short, in the use of psychometrics there is no substitute for informed knowledge and understanding.

CHAPTER IX

Self-Concept and Self-Competency

Perhaps no other construct has been examined in more detail than that of self-concept. A conservative estimate of studies reported in Wylie (1961, 1974) and Uhlenberg (1972) would be 3000. Though some notable reviews have been done by Wylie (1961, 1974) of the instruments and methodology used in self-concept research, there is no readily available estimate of the effectiveness of treatments to alter or enhance self-concept.

The purposes of this chapter are: (1) to provide a clarification of the nature of self-concept and its ramifications, (2) to explore the covariates of the construct, and (3) to outline a multisource basis for evaluating self-concept.

In the process of developing this review we shall also look at some of the most prominent instruments employed to measure self-concept, and provide some suggestions for the assessment of self-concept in contextual settings. The major thrust of the review will be directed towards school age children and adolescents. Moreover, we shall not dwell on extreme pathological situations, but be mainly concerned with the range of problems that relate at one time or the other to most individuals.

Though the emphasis of the chapter will be directed towards the analysis of instruments utilized in intervention efforts, the pervasive interest in self-concept research and the consensus of its importance to personal life style and happiness have resulted in a maze of methodological approaches that are not always consistent with the theoretical basis of the construct or the design of adequate studies utilizing this construct.

THE NATURE OF SELF-CONCEPT

Self-concept is a construct that refers to the perception of the individual by himself or herself. Sometimes other terms are also used to describe this construct. One of these is self-esteem or self-regard, and another is self-competency. Self-esteem is basically a ramification of self-concept and a

211

suggestion that the positive aspect of self-concept is a good self-regard or esteem for one's abilities and characteristics. For the most part, studies relating to self-concept have used the terms self-concept or self-esteem rather interchangeably. **Self-competency connotes something different. It provides a somewhat more behavioral approach to self-concept inferring that competency is related to self-perception and social feedback,** and that individuals who view themselves as competent are identifying behavioral components that are more easily observed or confirmed than internal value dimensions that are less susceptible to direct and empirical observation and confirmation.

A review of studies in the correlational stream of psychology indicates that self-concept is a popular topic for doctoral dissertations and masters' theses. Uhlenberg (1971) reviewed no less than 758 self-concept studies done during the years 1959–1969. Wylie (1961) reviewed the existing literature to 1961 and subsequently extended her review in another decade (1974). Her original review contained over 900 references and the revised edition probably doubles this amount. In addition, Wells & Marwell (1976) provided a comprehensive overview of methods, instruments, and theories, Mitchell (1985) reviewed them in the *Ninth Mental Measurements Yearbook*, and reviews are found in Keyser & Sweetland (1985) that provided in-depth reviews of the major instruments. The Chicago Board of Education (undated mimeographed compendium) listed 54 instruments that purport to measure self-concept, many of which possess scant reliability or validity data. Virtually every new issue of *Psychological Abstracts*, and every professional conference or convention contains at least one "new" instrument that claims to measure self-concept.

Unquestionably all of this research activity means that a great number of researchers and students of human behavior believe devoutly that self-concept/self-esteem/self-competency is a most important construct for the explanation of human behavior.

THEORETICAL BASES

Self-concept is primarily related to phenomenological theory, i.e., personality theory that places much emphasis on the perceiving organism and the manner in which perception is created. In comparatively modern times Brentano spearheaded the development of a perceptual school of psychology that reacted to the physiological basis of the Helmholtz school of psychology that dominated much of European psychology in the late nineteenth century.

The issues at that time joined specifically on what were the proper phenomena or subject matter of psychology. The Helmholtz School, dominating Berlin and Vienna psychological studies, maintained that sensation was the

proper phenomenon of psychology and that all human behavior would ultimately be interpreted through proper studies in physiology. Brentano insisted that the act of perception was the key phenomenon and developed
an entire method for the study of psychology as an empirical science based
on perception. In a very real sense the chief argument centered on the
nature of perception itself with Wundt hoping to develop a quasi-experi-
mental and empirical science of mental phenomena utilizing a chemistry
model of association, arguing that sensations were put together in an asso-
ciational chemistry that could result in appropriate equations for mental
imagery or thought. Brentano concentrated more on the development of a
methodology for evaluating internal acts of the mind in what was later to be
called "Act Psychology." He maintained that psychology itself, its laws, the
fundamentals of thinking and logic that undergird the very scientific method,
was a function of perception, and that no explanation of sensory data even
through neurochemical reactions would suffice to explain the synthesizing
and coordinating characteristics of human perception. Brentano, through
empirical evidence and reasoning, suggested that perceptions are the basic
phenomena of psychology.

Perception, Brentano suggested, was not like a photograph but more like
a painting. A photograph and a painting reveal similar characteristics, but
there are also paintings which include special insights, accents, and even
surrealistic distortions. The act of perception then was the subjective impressionistic translation of the events of sensation moderated at once by the
internal needs of the perceiver and the contextual characteristics of the
environmental situation.

Brentano also indicated that there was always an affective tonality involved
in the total aspect of perception. Though the act of perception was itself
unitary, transitory, and passing, it involved both an object relationship to
external reality and a similar one to internal needs. Thus, for example,
suppose an individual is dining in a beautiful restaurant, listening to chamber
music, enjoying an excellent cuisine and fine vintage wine in the company
of friends. This is obviously a pleasurable perception programmed by a
variety of sensory inputs. However, if a person intensely disliked now enters
the setting and takes a table nearby, the total configuration of that perception
can change.

From Brentano's initial discussion and elaboration of the characteristics
of internal perception, other theorists went further. Freud elaborated in
detail a psychology explaining how the ego develops from the primitive id
and how the superego likewise develops from the id and early identification
with parents. Over four decades Freud studied human psychic development,
and engineered a theory about the nature of unconscious, the interaction
between primitive pleasure-seeking tendencies and reality constrictions of

socialization. More than anyone else, Freud assimilated much of the philosophical and logical-deductive reasoning of his teacher, Brentano, and expanded Brentano's seminal ideas into an inclusive system of psychoanalytic theory based on case studies and to some extent empirical observation. Freud's impact on psychology, and particularly the aspects of psychology relating to human development, personality, and psychopathology, has been enormous as Gardner Murphy has noted (Murphy, 1949).

Other indirect influences on the development of the basis of self-concept theory have come through the phenomenological studies of Husserl, Meinong, Heidegger, and in more modern times Heider and Kelly in this country. Phenomenology represented more accurately a methodology for attacking complex internalistic problems than a coherent philosophy as such. In fact, phenomenology was considered by many who understood it as a kind of meta-philosophy embracing scientific exploration as included by logical-positivism and addressing itself equally to dimensions such as space and time. Ash Gobar (1968) has provided a detailed synthesis of how this phenomenology as originated by Brentano and greatly expanded by his student Edmund Husserl influenced the French school of psychological studies, particularly in terms of naturalistic observation and child study. Most representative of these approaches today in the United States are the studies of Fritz Heider (1958), and George Kelly (1955). Heider has studied the nature of social perception, and Kelly's theory of interpersonal constructs falls directly in the mainstream of phenomenological thought, building on the implications of self-concept for conditional "if" assumptions that govern and reinforce much anticipated behavior.

From still another source, Gestalt psychology, a genuine emphasis was placed on the unitary nature of perception in terms of a gestalt or configuration. Though Kohler and Koffka both provided frameworks that lent themselves to the development of interpersonal theory, it was Lewin in his field theory who was most popularized. Lewin suggested that people and environmental contexts had valences—similar to chemical properties—thus providing a formula $B = f(P \times E)$, or behavior is a function of interaction between the person and the environment.

Unfortunately, the theoretical origins and background of perception theory were largely unknown to most American psychologists or students of psychology. Much of phenomenology and Gestalt psychology was viewed as a kind of "modern day scholasticism." Further, though virtually everyone accepted the validity of the Gestalt psychology contentions, it simply did not produce the research development needed to continue it as a viable force in psychology. Lewin's form of Gestalt psychology appeared to be most influential in the development of a number of studies relating to democratic versus authoritarian discipline.

Both Rogers (1950) and Maslow (1954) provided a popularization of the notion of self-concept as an important component in perception and interpersonal behavior. Rogers borrowed heavily from many other sources such as Freud, the existentialists, and Snygg and Combs (1949) in the development of his own position. For example, Johnson in studying the origins of Rogers's thought wrote to Rogers and learned from him that he had been told by students at Chicago that he was an existentialist. He indicated he had been influenced by Snygg and Combs's theories. Johnson wrote to Combs about the matter, and was told that it was Donald Snygg who had engineered most of the phenomenological components. Johnson then wrote to Snygg who indicated that his own phenomenological thought had been chiefly influenced by Brentano (Johnson, 1961).

Maslow contributed to the development of self-concept by relating it to needs. He referred to "D" needs (deficiency or basic ones), and "B" needs which are "becoming" ones. Deficiency needs include (1) physiological needs, (2) safety and security needs, (3) love and belonging needs, i.e., being accepted and accepting others, (4) esteem and respect for self and others' needs. These are basic needs that are required for any real development of the individual. "B" needs are (1) information about one's environment, (2) understanding with comprehension and some kind of a moral or religious system, (3) beauty, with esthetic appreciation and a development of one's innate talents, and (4) self-actualization or the ability to handle problems relating to conflict, anxiety, frustration, sadness, hurt, guilt, and conscience along with creativity.

Self-concept, then, emerges as a major aspect of phenomenological theory with convergent aspects supported by psychoanalytic and field theory developments. The self-concept represents as Yamamoto (1972) has described it a composite, but imperfect representation of self that relates to social interaction in a crucial way, to socioeconomic classification, family forces, expectations, failure, unconscious dynamics, social power, and communication (Yamamoto, 1972, pp. 2–20). Though self-concept is central to human psychological development, how it can be measured and changed is still controversial.

THE MEASUREMENT OF SELF-CONCEPT

There are many instruments that purport in one way or the other to measure self-concept. The majority of them rely on self-report and some are based on needs or deficits in self-competency. The interview and behavioral evaluations can shed much light on self-perception. Many of the projective techniques tap dimensions of personality that would be related to self-concept. However, the *Rorschach* specifically, and to a lesser extent the *The-*

matic Apperception Test, tap forces of personality that are more clinically attuned to the complexity of personality, but at the same time rely more heavily on specific training and clinical interpretation. Q-sort techniques, in which ideal and real self-portrayals have been contrasted, provide a greater specificity of clinical attributes associated with depression, anxiety, social interaction and the like, but call for alternative decision points in subjects that often result in difficult choices.

Most popular are those instruments that are presented to the subject in a paper-pencil format and call for responses in terms of "yes" or "no," "true" or "false," or some Likert-type scaling in which the individual is asked to judge how like himself, or different, a given statement might be. Other instruments utilize a semantic differential format or adjective checklists to ascertain self-concept. These instruments are more commonly used because they call for a minimum of clinical interpretation, can be utilized by a variety of professional and semi-professional staff, and possess ease of scoring. There are a number of instruments that purport to measure self-concept in this latter sense.

During the last decade, and specifically in the 40 or 50 studies reviewed by the author in the last few years, the majority of the studies tend to rely on the *Tennessee Self-Concept Scale* (Fitts, 1964; 1965), the *Piers-Harris Children's Self- Concept Scale* (Piers, 1969), and the *Self-Esteem Inventory* (Coopersmith, 1967). *The California Psychological Inventory* (Gough, 1956) and the *Personality Orientation Inventory* (Shostrum, 1968) are also quite popular with adult or older groups. Many doctoral dissertations and the conclusions drawn by the writers have hung on the reliability and validity of these instruments; at least experimental treatment effects judged by these test criteria depend strongly on such considerations.

The Tennessee Self-Concept Scale is evaluated by Crandall (1973), Bentler (in Buros, 1972, p. 151) and by Wylie (1974). Bentler criticizes the many overlapping scales that correlate highly with the *Taylor Manifest Anxiety Scale*, questions the diagnostic procedures used for clinical applications, and suggests that the question of its advantage over the simpler *Taylor Manifest Anxiety Scale* should be considered. Crandall (1973) commends the Tennessee for its construction, and the fact that research data are centralized by Fitts the author and reviewed consistently. He suggests that research tends to support some convergent and predictive validity. Another problem noted by Crandall is the fact that all five areas tapped tend to correlate highly with each other. The majority of these problems are cited in recent reviews as well. Wylie (1974) is more negative. After reviewing a number of studies with the Tennessee she concludes: "My conclusion is that no justification can be offered, either from *a priori* analyses in terms of acceptable methodological criteria or from a survey of empirical results to justify using this scale rather than certain others which are available or better ones to be devised in the future" (Wylie, 1974, p. 236).

The Piers Harris Self-Concept Scale is also reviewed by Crandall, Bentler (in Buros) and Wylie. Crandall notes that it possesses convergent, discriminant and predictive validity, that it is well constructed, but finds fault with the extent to which self-esteem is purported to be related to peer and teacher judgments. He also points out that there is little work available to show the relationship between self-esteem and behavior (Crandall, 1973, 73–75). Bentler's review (Buros, p. 124) suggests the need for further factor analysis and some revisions of the manual. Wylie (1974), reviewing the available studies, concludes that the Piers-Harris "seems worthy of further research and development" (Wylie, 1974, p. 180). In recent reviews, the Piers-Harris appears to have had further development and some of the earlier problems are no longer relevant.

The Coopersmith Self-Esteem Inventory, though very popular, was not reviewed by Buros in 1972, although a considerable number of studies had been reported. Both Crandall and Wylie fault the inventory on several points chiefly because no systematic work has been done on the scale and there are high correlations obtained with social desirability. Moreover, Wylie indicates it is difficult to know details about the standardization. Wylie concludes her review of the Coopersmith by stating: "It is obvious, then, that Coopersmith's research cannot appropriately be used to support the construct validity of his self-esteem inventory as a measure of self-regard because the research is uninterpretable for all the reasons mentioned above" (Wylie, 1974, p. 173). She does hold out some hope for the use of the Coopersmith. "Altogether, the state of development of this inventory and the amount of available information about it do not make it an instrument of choice for self-concept research on child subjects. If further research and development were to be undertaken, this conclusion might be modified, depending on the results of such research" (Wylie, 1974, p. 177). The review by Adair (Keyser & Sweetland, 1985) is more positive and points out that Coopersmith spent many years researching the nature of self-esteem.

As mentioned earlier, the CPI (*California Psychological Inventory*), and the POI (*Personality Orientation Inventory*) have also been applied to a number of studies with adults or senior high school students. Crandall's review of the CPI is favorable, based on the excellent construction and evidences of convergent, discriminant, and predictive validity (Crandall, 1973, pp. 97–99). His review of the POI is mixed and suggests the need for more internal consistency, and convergent, discriminant, and predictive validity studies (Crandall, 1973, pp. 140–141). Perhaps the major caution against the latter two instruments is that they are not designed specifically as self-concept instruments. On the other hand they represent approaches to the measurement of personality that may provide a more adequate discriminant profile of the consequences of self-concept.

The reviews of the three major instruments for the assessment of self-concept as described by critical review sources, taken altogether, are quite negative and pessimistic. Perhaps this is because these instruments are being compared to other personality instruments such as the MMPI, the CPI, and the 16 PF. On the other hand, there is a flat recognition that a considerable amount of the total variance of these instruments is related to social projection or what has been termed social desirability. Perhaps it is untenable to seek reliability and discriminant validity in a self-concept measure that may be so susceptible to fluctuations of mood and affective relationship towards the classroom situation. That this may be the case was documented by Steger (1975) in a study where he administered the *Piers-Harris, the Tennessee* and the *Barclay Classroom Climate Inventory* to the same sample of fifth and sixth graders and then factor analyzed the results. The Barclay instrument yields six multitrait and multisource (self, peer, and teacher ratings) factor scores which are qualitatively different from the self-report data of the *Piers Harris* and *Tennessee* instruments. He found that 52% of the variance for the males (N = 60) and 50% of the variance for females (N = 57) was accounted for by the various scales of the *Tennessee* and the *Piers Harris*. This common factor appears to be social projection. The Barclay did not load at all on the first factor. The other two factors were social-extroversion and energy. *Tennessee* variables did not load appreciably on any of the other two factors, but the *Piers Harris* did show loadings of around .50 on the energy factor for girls. This study appears to be supportive of the critical evaluations expressed regarding the *Tennessee* and *Piers Harris*, and confirmatory of the social projection or social desirability influence that exists in the use of these self-report instruments.

The Barclay Classroom Climate Inventory (Now known as the Barclay Classroom Assessment System) is a multi-source, multi-trait system for evaluating classroom climate variables with elementary school children (Barclay, 1977). It has one component that relates to self-competency. This component concerns skills such as being able to run fast, or play a musical instrument. The rationale developed by the author (Barclay, 1977) indicated that the self-competency items were derived from Holland's theory (1966) of vocational development and personality and therefore reflect perceived competencies in artistic, intellectual, social, and enterprising areas. Research has indicated that self-competency judgments in various trait areas do show a relationship to corresponding peer support or lack thereof. Thus, it would appear that the measurement of self-concept as such should be referenced to environmental support systems such as peer and teacher judgments. Though discrepancies occur between input sources (and are in point of fact significant indicators of underestimating and overestimating children and therefore useful in terms of classification), the multi-trait, multisource factor analysis and loadings thereof or over 5,000 children show appropriate trait correspondence for self, peer and teacher components (Barclay, 1977; Tapp & Barclay, 1974).

Indirect Measures of Self-Competency. Two other approaches that relate to the measurement of self-concept are the measure of deficits or problems, and the measurement of needs. *The Student Adjustment Inventor* (Barclay, 1979, 1988b) and *Stephenson's Q.- Sort Technique* (Stephenson, 1953) are instances of the first approach, and the *Edwards Personal Preference Schedule (EPPS)* (Edwards, 1953) and *Adjective Check List (ACL)* (Gough, 1960; Gough & Heilbrun, 1980) are examples of the second method.

The *Student Adjustment Inventory* was derived in part from the self-competency scales of the BCAS. Seven scales were developed for problems expressed by individuals in the areas of self-competency, group interaction, self-control, verbal skills, energy and persistence, cognitive motivation, and attitude towards school. It has been utilized with upper-elementary, secondary and college freshman students as well as with prisoners to determine self-reported problems. Studies with it have indicated significant correlations with the BCAS factor scores over a three-year period. Significant negative relationships were also obtained between problem scores and achievement as well as with other personality variables (Barclay, 1979b, 1988b). Although the separate problem scores are not independent of each other, the test has been found to be useful in determining a specific set of strategies of intervention for a child or a group. It has recently been made available on microcomputers by Metri-Tech in Champaign, Illinois with suggested treatment strategies related to severe problem areas.

The Q-sort technique is another approach to the measurement of self-concept. This technique was initially presented by Stephenson (1953) and reviewed in 1980. It was very popular in the decades following its introduction because it appeared to relate to phenomenological approaches to therapy consistent with Rogers's approach. Basically, it consists of a series of cards that are sorted by an individual into categories which might include "most like me, very much like me, somewhat like me, neither like me or not like me, not much like me, hardly at all like me, not at all like me." The cards themselves might represent any sort of statement such as "a real social person," or "acting foolish in the classroom," or "I tend to make up my mind quickly." Some idea of the extent to which this technique was used and researched can be obtained from the review of Brown (1968) who cited 580 references. One of the most popular Q-sorts was designed to be used by professionals in rating others (Block, 1961).

Although the technique is flexible, easily adapted to many circumstances

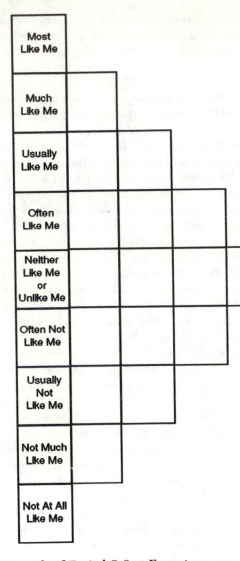

Figure 9-1   **Example of Typical Q-Sort Format**

and has been used a good deal in therapy situations, a recurring problem exists in the methodology and techniques for analyzing the results. Some individuals disagreed with Stephenson's forcing individuals to categorize statements in a normalized distribution. Cronbach (1956) believed such a forced distribution was "treacherous" (p. 176). However, in view of the many studies completed since his remarks, it is unlikely that the forced distribution has much significance in analyzing outcomes. The technique has been broadly applied into many areas such as in communication theory, sociology, education, and industry where it has been a prototype of group processes designed to solve problems and elicit creativity.

Two other approaches have related self-concept to both need statements and adjectival ratings. *The Edwards Personal Preference Schedule* (Edwards, 1953) is an inventory of 210 pairs of statements framed so that individuals must agree or disagree with them. The inventory is based on personal needs such as affiliation, autonomy, dominance-succorance and order that are drawn from Murray's approach to personality (Murray, 1938). The instrument has been widely used both in personality assessment and efforts to determine the needs of various occupations, though there are more negative reviews of it than of the other major personality tests.

The final method that has been applied to self-concept and self-report research is that of the adjective checklist. This approach consists of presenting to individuals a list of adjectives as descriptors of personality and having them rate either others or themselves. Barclay in the *BCAS* (1983) used adjectives for teachers to rate children, and Gough (1960) and Gough and Heilbrun (1980) in the *Adjective Check-List (ACL)* have developed 37 scales to evaluate individuals. One of the chief problems with adjectival descriptors is related to meaning. Words differ in their meaning to different individuals and this is a limitation of the adjective descriptor method.

CRITERIA OF SELF-CONCEPT CHANGE

One of the problems related to the measurement of self-concept or self-esteem has been that of determining an adequate criterion for the evaluation of the validity of self-concept measures and changes associated with treatments. Evaluating the consequences of treatment in terms of criteria of "adjustment" or "insight," Wylie (1961) indicates that **adjustment criteria** are so inconsistent from one study to the other that one cannot posit a direct effect (Wylie, 1961, p. 235). Reviewing 19 studies purporting to utilize the **criterion of insight** she concludes that the results are so ambiguous as to fail to result in any definite conclusion. Often tests that measure self-concept are used as the criterion themselves, throwing the ultimate proof of change back on the stability and validity of the instrument. With regard to overall changes as a consequence of "therapy" Wylie states: "We cannot say at present what different kinds of criteria or improvement in therapy may correlate with improved self-regard" (Wylie, 1961, p. 182).

Unfortunately, it is difficult to establish a relevant and independent criterion measure for a construct so diffuse as self-concept or self-esteem.

Traditionally, self-concept researchers have attempted to deduce the effect of self-concept by attempting to identify the amount of variance associated with a given measure of it. "Let us see how much of the variance in ss behavior we can account for on the basis of variance in ss self-report responses or instruments A, B, C. We shall offer an interpretation of our findings based on the assumption that self-report responses correlate with other behaviors because ss phenomenal fields are tapped by our measures A,B, C, and have determined ss behaviors on x, y, z" (Wylie, 1961, p. 8). Wylie points out that though proportions of variance may be accounted for in this manner, the theoretical formulations which have been used are often vague and inadequate. There are problems of establishing construct validity indices, controls have not been adequate, and there have been wide differences from study to study in hypotheses, types of subjects, instruments and procedures, lack of controls for other sources of variance, and the simple fact that self-concept may be heavily related to measures of social desirability or social projection and therefore to situational contexts (Wylie, 1961, p. 274).

In 1974 Wylie published an updated edition of her original work. Though this volume contains much additional material, particularly in reference to more recent studies and instruments, her conclusions of 1961 still appear to hold. She sees a lack of proper refinement and elaboration of the nature of self-concept (1974, p. 316), an inability or at least a failure thus far to define the usefulness of theories regarding self-concept (p. 323), and some question as to the relevance of continuing or justifying research along the same lines and with the same instruments. (In light of this observation, it is relevant for readers to review any volume of *Psychological Abstracts* and simply count the number of studies relating to self-concept and self-esteem. Thirty to forty references appear in each issue). On the other hand, she sees some improvement in the recognition for documenting convergent and discriminant validity, avoidance of the use of more esoteric and undocumented instruments, and some general understanding of the complexity of the methodological problems entailed in self-concept or self-esteem studies.

Even so, Wylie concludes her evaluation by stating: "In any event, after a thorough overview of publication on these more fully studied instruments, I have had to conclude in the light of modern methodological standards and such evidence as is available, that use of a number of these instruments should be abandoned. Others may prove useful for research in their present form, pending the kind of work that is really indispensable, namely starting from scratch to develop new instruments, using all available conceptual and methodological refinements in instrument development" (Wylie, 1974, p. 325).

Recognizing the problems identified by the reviews of Wylie, Crandall, Buros, Mitchell, and others it is our intent now to look at some studies that have been completed, and to evaluate the consequences of their impact. Further, it is our special purpose to look at the variables that apparently covary with self-concept or self-esteem, and to determine what may be the moderating or mediating influences presumptive of causal variation in self-concept measures.

RELATIONAL CHARACTERISTICS OF SELF-CONCEPT

Physical Characteristics and Body Image. There are a number of different meanings associated with body image. Certainly it is a complex phenomenon to deal with because it is experienced and internal, by comparison with other phenomena that are "out there." Certainly it is an empirical fact that we all make some judgments about others associated with their body type and characteristics. Sheldon (1952) examined this in considerable detail developing a primary index to classify somatotypes using the height of the individual divided by the cube root of weight. Sheldon made a number of inferences about personality characteristics of individuals associated with somatotypes. Unfortunately the wealth of information collected by Sheldon did not seem to lead to a viable framework for further analysis. With recent developments in research technology, Sheldon's approach might be a fertile field for multivariate analysis.

Wylie (1961) in reviewing body image studies quotes research that would suggest the relationship of body image to pubic signs and physical development. Rothfarb (1970) indicates that physical exercise is a concomitant variable related to more autonomy and self-confidence. Kirkendall and Gruber (1970) cite a number of studies that suggest strongly the relationship of body coordination and intellectual development as measured by Cattell's *Children's Personality Questionnaire, the High School Personality Questionnaire, the Kuhlman-Anderson IQ,* and *the Stanford Academic Achievement* scores. Thus a relational effect between physical motor capabilities, structure and body image seems defensible and highly plausible.

Moreover, it is most likely that these same physical characteristics affect others differentially, keying and triggering expectations and affective movements of liking or disliking. Kehle (1972) asked 93 white and black teachers to rate the psychological reports of a number of children where pictures of the children (considered good-looking versus ugly by independent judges) provided one stimulus for evaluation. In addition, the level of intelligence, socioeconomic level of the father, race, and sex of the child provided other independent variables. Based on the systematic variation of the variables, teachers checked adjectives to describe a fictitious essay of the child, and the child's characteristics. Kehle found many significant main effects and interactional relationships that substantiate the fact that body characteristics, sex, intelligence, race, and socioeconomic status all had effects on teacher expectations.

Though research in this area is far from exhaustive, particularly as it may relate to self-concept, there is considerable observational support and evidence for the concept that physical structure, beauty, and handsomeness may predispose others to act more favorably towards subjects possessing these attributes than towards those who are obese, ugly, uncoordinated, or poorly coordinated. Moreover, there are developmental differences between males and females in school that often affect teacher expectations and peer choices. The early maturing female student with well-endowed secondary sex characteristics is often viewed negatively by teachers and sometimes by peers. On the contrary, the early-developing male is often accorded some special attention, particularly as voice lowers, beard appears, and physical structure approaches more adult male standards. What is said for fast maturation as a source of expectations can likewise be said for slow maturation. The boy who does not evidence outward signs of secondary sex characteristics when his peers do, or is small, or overweight as in frequent prepubertal stages of development, may feel inferior and be affected by an adverse body image. Similarly, girls who fail to develop secondary sex characteristics in contour, breasts or the onset of menses, also suffer from these problems. Thus it would appear that self-concept is affected by physical structure and characteristics, both as it relates to the intuitive perception of the individual and as it relates to the expectations and level of reinforcement provided by others.

Sex Differences. Though there are obvious physical differences, and some rather highly suspected psychological differences, due to sex, the evidence regarding the effect of sex on self-concept or self-esteem is not clear. According to Wylie's review (1961) males tend to have a higher ideal stereotype of self than females. Beemer (1971) found that females tend to have a higher self-concept in middle childhood and preadolescent years, but not in adolescence. Using a sample of 4,941 children and adolescents, Beemer reported that physical and affectional components contributed most to self-concept in middle childhood, but the peer group was a very important contributor to self-concept in adolescence, a fact that could be associated with the much greater preoccupation with sexual characteristics in adolescence.

Flammer (1971) suggested that sex role identification was associated with self-esteem in preschool children. Boys who had a high sex role identification tended to have a higher self-esteem than those with a lower sex role identification. On the contrary, preschool girls with a low sex role identification tended to manifest a higher self-esteem. Barclay (1974) found that in terms of self-competency estimates, boys routinely score higher than girls—though possibly this may be related to the inclusion of some competency items of an outdoor mechanical nature that may be judged by girls to be less appropriate for them. It would thus appear that sex differences as measured by self-concept instruments may be an artifact of either social desirability or sex-role competencies. In the former case, females may be more attuned to social expectations, and in the latter case, competency skills that somehow merge into sex-related projections may alter self-concept scores.

Developmental Trends. There seems to be some evidence for a generalized decline in self-concept or self-esteem over school years. Soares and Soares (1971) found this to be so in their use of a semantic differential technique for evaluating self-esteem. Barclay (1974) in the evaluation of trends from the second through sixth grades by sex and race found a generalized decline in self-competency (based on data from 123 classrooms). A Japanese study (Kikuchi, 1968) also found a general decline of self-concept from elementary to secondary levels in pupils.

The effect of socioeconomic class on this developmental decline is inconclusive. Brady (1972) found that self-concept appears to increase positively by ages for both boys and girls from upper or upper middle SES settings. It tends to be stable for the middle-middle group and to decline for lower middle and lower SES subjects. However, both Soares and Soares (1972) and Trowbridge (1972) found, contrary to Brady's study, that lower SES children tended to have a higher self-concept. Thus, the evidence for developmental trends suggests a decline and some influence of socioeconomic level on changes one way or the other. It does not seem unreasonable to associate higher self-esteem with a more enriched environment and affluence. At the same time, the decline in self-concept, self-esteem or self-competency may reflect a more realistic assessment of skills, a maturity in symbolic levels of abstraction, moving away from the enactive and iconic states (Bruner, 1963; 1966), or a transition from the concrete operations to formal operations levels of Piaget (1952).

It would seem reasonable to suggest that increased language usage, the emergence of an internal locus of control, and enriched home support may encourage the growth of positive self-esteem, while increasing demands from school, the internalization of failure experiences, and competition for grades may discourage it. This seems to be supported by the fact that longitudinal studies of subjects assessed in the first and second grades as well as later on in the fifth and sixth grades indicate a low stability for self-concept (Trickett, 1968) and a much higher prediction derived from peer-ratings and teacher judgments (Barclay, 1974).

Racial Characteristics. As far as the author could ascertain, there is no real evidence for significant differences or main effects ascribable to race as such for self-concept and self-esteem. Where differences have been found, culture and socioeconomic status appear to be interacting with race. Lefebvre (1971) found some differences between racial groupings, but these appeared to be mainly related to SES. Soares and Soares (1971) observed differences for disadvantaged versus advantaged. Laryea (1972) did not find significant results in achievement x self-concept x race interactions. Barclay (1974) found a tendency towards lowered self-competency in blacks, but the factor of SES was not controlled. Wu (1975) contrasting Chinese with American children in the same grades found that Chinese subjects, male and female, had about the same self-competency scores, and that American females viewed themselves as more competent than their Chinese counterparts. However, Chinese subjects tended to rate themselves higher on artistic-intellectual interests and competencies and were seen as more introverted and withdrawn generally than American subjects. A study of Anglos, Blacks and Spanish-American children in Corpus Christi showed some preferences for higher social competencies in Spanish-American children (Barclay, 1972). A detailed study of all graduating seniors in the Oakland, California schools on Grade-Point Average, the CPI, Holland Scales and a battery of interests contrasting white, black, Oriental and Spanish surnamed subjects indicated few significant differences at higher socioeconomic levels for racial groups, but highly significant ones at lower socioeconomic levels (Barclay, 1967). It would thus seem that race by itself does not indicate differences in self-concept or self-esteem, but rather the effects of expectations and environmental conditions interacting with race.

Socioeconomic and Parental Transmission. Self-concept, self-esteem, and self-competency appear to be related directly to socioeconomic levels of parents. Wylie in a review of earlier studies concludes (1961) that children's self-concepts are similar to the view of themselves which they attribute to their parents. Hollander and Marcia (1970) found that children perceiving their parents to be peer-oriented tend to be peer-oriented themselves. Felsenthal (in Yamamoto, 1972) suggests that parents transmit an entire set of values right from infancy on relating to stimulation of the child in affectivity and language modes. This is consistent with Bruner's views (1963; 1966), and Piaget's approach (1952) as well as that of Vygotsky (1962) where language development is seen as an integral component in the development of body image, control over reality, and the natural progression from enactive or preoperational stages of development to symbolic modes. Hess and Shipman (1965) confirm this fact indicating that middle class mothers use more verbal information and encourage problem solving more than lower class mothers. Miller (1971) found that suburban mothers (as compared with the inner city) tended to show a greater quality of empathy related to self-esteem of their children. On the contrary, the self-esteem of inner-city black children was strongly related to the maternal evaluation of their children. Bilby (1972) and Gabel (1971) found that student plans were mediated by parental attitudes and self-concept. Bledsoe and Wiggins (1973) indicated that adolescents who reported their parents understood them had better self-images. A similar finding was made also by Gecas (1972). Systematic variation in self, peer, and teacher scores were found related to paternal occupation by Barclay, Stilwell, and Barclay in a study of 1600 Corpus Christi youth (1972). Personality and interest characteristics of Oakland seniors (Barclay, 1967) appeared to be mediated primarily by socioeconomic class with fewer significant differences observed between upper-class whites, blacks, Chinese and Spanish-Americans than might have occured by chance, but with very significant differences occurring in the lower class contrasts. Housing and its adequacy appear to be significantly related to self-concept and achievement as determined by Lewin (1970), and the extent of mobility and self-concept for military children indicated that mobility was a factor in lowered self-competency, more instability, etc. (Wooster & Harris, 1972). Thus, of all the major determinants to self-concept, outside the immediate social context, it would appear that socioeconomic status is a major component, particularly as it interacts with sex differences, race differences (as culturally defined in terms of advantaged and disadvantaged criteria), and developmental trends.

Personality and Interpersonal Aspects. Another chief component in self-concept, self-esteem, and self-competency is the impact of interpersonal relations. Wylie in reviewing these relationships (1961) suggests that persons chosen in sociometrics tend to be more similar to notions of ideal self. Richmond and White (1971) indicate that activity is a component in peer relations connected with self-esteem. Barclay and Elton (1975) found that multi-method factor analysis showed that self-competency was related to teacher expectations and peer support systems. Further analysis of second-order factors of the BCAS also indicated the manner in which self-competency, peer support, and teacher expectations appear to covary in terms of basic temperament characteristics (Barclay, 1978).

A host of studies support the fact that teacher expectations moderate self-competency for children (McGee, 1972; Mason, 1972; Brophy & Good, 1970, 1974). A Canadian study (Schludermann & Schludermann, 1970) evaluating 328 college freshmen indicated that a high real self-concept is significantly correlated with self-control, tolerance, and good impressions. Canty (1970) looking at the characteristics of high self-esteem individuals viewed these same individuals on the MMPI and CPI, finding that high self-concept individuals show less pathology and more normal behavior. High self-concept individuals tend to have a better sense of humor according to LaChance (1972), and tend to show a more generalized ability to modify their self-image as a consequence of feedback from significant others. Individuals with a high self-esteem tend to be less anxious in a stress situation, particularly boys (Lekarczyk & Hill, 1969), and overall are more flexible, more capable of being attuned to social exigencies, and less rigid.

Wylie suggests that there is a very strong component here relating to individual differences. "There is some limited evidence to suggest that there are consistent individual differences in the tendency towards overestimation, underestimation, and accurate estimation across a variety of traits" (Wylie, 1961, 316). Cotler and Palmer (1970) suggest that intrinsic personality traits and external contingencies moderate social reinforcement. Barclay (1976) in a review of external-internal locus of control studies and characteristics of temperaments obtained from BCAS analysis of self, peer, and teacher inputs concludes that there are at least four major combinations of factor characteristics that relate to self-competency variance as a function of peer and teacher support systems. In summary, there appears to be considerable evidence indicating the role of social support systems in peers and teachers as being another important determinant of self-concept. These support systems interact with developmental trends and SES components in a complex matrix that is related to self-competency, and views self-competency (if not self-concept and self-esteem) as a direct consequence of SES and school reinforcement systems.

Achievement. Several studies suggest strongly that self- competency is a component in achievement. The direct causal relationship is not that strong, but rather it helps to view self-competency, self-esteem and self-concept as by-products of SES and school support systems that do influence or interact with achievement. Kifer (1975), for example, suggests that achievement itself is a determinant of good self-competency or self-concept. Hamachek (Clarizio, 1969) presents evidence for a significant relationship between immature self-concepts and reading disabilities in third and sixth grade students. He also reviews studies that suggest underachievers are more immature and unstable than achievers. This was found also by Krupczak (1972). Children who engage in independent study regarding their homework were found to be more able in academic tasks and liked themselves better (Earl, 1971). Various courses of study and school environments concerning academic, vocational, and terminal courses of studies appear to show a relationship to level of self-concept (Takacs, 1973). In addition, study of school children grouped according to ability into different tracks indicates a lower self-concept in lower ability tracks (Weiner and Weiner, 1972). Children with lower self-esteem appear to be more susceptible to persuasion (Wylie, 1961), and from what we know about susceptibility to modeling and reinforcement, we might suggest this to be the case also with these behaviors (Bandura & Walters, 1963). Field dependence as mediated by situational feedback or failure information lowers self-concept (Brauer, 1970). Binder, Jones, and

Strowig (1970) found that for 12th graders self-expectations, self-concept of ability, was significantly related to aptitude and GPA. Finally, Crandall in interpreting five studies about self-esteem indicated that self-esteem is positively related to coping ability and optimism (1972).

The Effects of Treatments. Self-concept, self-esteem and other measures of self-involvement have been used in many studies as a dependent measure of the effectiveness of various treatments. Wylie reviews studies that were done earlier utilizing criteria of adjustment and "insight" as measures of change. In discussing the former criterion she notes that the construct of adjustment has been used as a global criterion to refer to: (A) degrees of diagnosed pathology, (B) behavior ratings and instruments related to teacher, authority or peer judgments presumably relevant to adjustment, (C) observable behaviors viewed in interaction, (D) projective test scores presumably related to adjustment, and (E) scores obtained on instruments presumably measuring self-concept or self-esteem.

Summarizing a number of studies completed with various criteria of adjustment, she suggests that studies comparing psychotics to normals on self-concept measures are ambivalent in their outcomes, and that studies looking at neurotics versus normals tend to demonstrate that neurotics devaluate themselves (Wylie, 1961, pp. 215–216). In summarizing studies that purport to effect change with various treatments utilizing self-concept measures as a criterion of adjustment, Wylie suggests that there are some relationships under certain circumstances between self-concept measures and teacher judgments (Wylie, 1961, 221), but that adjustment measures are so inconsistent, so subjectively determined, that one cannot posit a direct relationship in change to a treatment (p. 235) even though there appears to be some relationship between self-acceptance and acceptance of others based on a review of 21 studies (p. 240).

The use of "insight" as a criterion does not fare much better. Again, "insight" is a difficult criterion to define and means many things to many people. It often refers to: (A) adjustment as determined by some personality variables associated with understanding or inferred from it and as measured by self-report methods, external observers, diagnostic opinion, scores compared from interval 1 to interval 2 on some pre-post comparison; (B) defensive behavior inferred from the subjects' responses on nonprojective or projective techniques used either directly or indirectly; (C) the ratings of therapists (in which therapist competency, bias, and self-involvement may be contamination factors); or (D) success in a vocation. Wylie in reviewing 19 studies concludes that the results are ambiguous and are often related to problems concerning the intensity of the treatment, the validity of the measurements used, the failure to observe behavior over longitudinal time periods, the unknown relationship to behavioral correlates, poor or ineffective data analysis, imprecise treatments, and failure to control for significant other variables.

In recent years there has been a tendency to favor more behavioral treatments in the evaluation of efforts to change self-concept. Nonetheless, the instruments for measuring self-concept remain chiefly those based on self-report exclusively. Treatments have been generally related to (1) feedback procedures both to subjects, teachers, parents, and others in an effort to change expectations, (2) social training modeling and reinforcement procedures utilizing significant persons such as teachers, peers, parents, and (3) environmental change procedures in which entire environments were altered or an attempt was made to alter them.

Feedback procedures involve giving information back to subjects and helping them to do something about that information. Sallade (1973) provided self-knowledge and essay assignments related to that self-knowledge over a 15 week period to a group of fifth graders and found that the information feedback and essays increased self-concept. Stern (1972) utilizing feedback and measuring self-concept and locus of control found that feedback greatly influenced low self-concept externals. Subsequently, in descending order he found that feedback was most effective used with low-self-concept internals, high-self-concept externals, and least with high-self-concept internals. Felker and Thomas (1971) and Felker and Stanwyck (1971) provide evidence that self-initiated verbal reinforcement after an academic task tends to support growth in positive relationships to self-concept. Barrett (1968) after feedback of test results to students found that students characterized by high self-regard made more accurate estimates of their interests and aptitudes. A near feedback mechanism is described by Earl (1971) as the practice of independent study. In this study 85 boys and 75 girls who practiced independent study tended to like themselves more and be more academically able. On the contrary, with negative feedback the results appear to be related to lowering self-esteem. Glazer (1972) found that for both approval dependent and approval nondependent subjects the results of negative feedback (1) increased antagonism towards the experimenter, (2) decreased self-esteem, and (3) made the subjects less defensive. Thus, there appears to be some evidence that feedback information, provided by teachers or others to subjects, particularly if this feedback is designed in some way to maximize and effect operant levels of responding by the subjects themselves, and after success experiences, tends to effect positive changes in self-concept. On the other hand, the results appear to be mediated by external-internal locus of control constructs that suggest that some individuals are more susceptible to that feedback than others.

Studies utilizing social training, modeling and reinforcement techniques have also shown results. Bidwick (1972) identified 36 seventh and eighth graders who had self-control problems and asked them to choose someone in the school who might be able to help them. They chose 18 teachers, but named no counselors. These teachers over a semester met with individual students for 20-minute conferences each week. As a consequence there was a significant increase in the self-concept of the target students. Trowbridge (1972) found that teachers who had had training in creativity tended to foster higher self-concepts in children. Other approaches have employed peer training in terms of tutoring and selective feedback, and parent training. Bouchard (1971) reports that peer group teaching via eight specific objectives in group learning affected significant increase in self-concept. Conway (1972) trained the parents of disadvantaged sixth graders in behavior modification techniques over nine training sessions and found significant gains in achievement and self-concept of ability on posttesting scores. Parent groups and training procedures have also been used by Stilwell (Stilwell & Barclay, 1979) in an attempt to raise self-competency of subjects. In one effort, parents of children who had such problems were invited to attend planned training sessions. The comparative effectiveness of those parents who chose to attend as against those who did not was inferred from posttesting changes in self-competency on the part of those children whose parents attended. Obviously, a by-product of training is the development of specific skills in parents, teachers, and peers, where they make efforts to develop skills in others. So training itself may have greater effects than can be readily measured by self-concept instruments. The immediacy and relevancy of contact that subjects have from peers, teachers, and parents appears to be more spontaneous and less contrived. This may be a real factor in effectiveness. On the contrary, counselors are one step removed from the academic or home experience. Though obviously there is some influence on students, Bidwick (1972) indicated that no problem students chose a counselor for help in problem areas, but 18 teachers were so named. Though counselors attempted in several studies to increase self-concept via group procedures, the results were insignificant. Higgins (1972) did not obtain results looking at self-concept measures as a criterion, and Speisman (1973) with the Carkhuff model and systematic training in human relations succeeded in developing better interpersonal relations in students, but the same subjects did not increase their self-concept.

Some attempts have been made to change environmental circumstances. Boyko (1970) assumed that experimental discovery methods of learning would be more effective in raising self-concepts than traditional didactic approaches. He obtained insignificant results. Geisler (1968) reports that compensatory education succeeded in producing a higher self-concept and higher GPA for students in the program. Systematic use of art experiences is also reported by White and Allen (1971) as being instrumental in raising self-concepts. On the other hand, considerable interest and efforts, including architectural changes and designs, have been made for the concept of "open" education with the avowed notion that such "open" education will increase achievement, affective interaction, and generally be more advantageous to students. Unfortunately, this has not been demonstrated. Ruedi and West (1973) find equivocal results. Longitudinal studies by Barclay, Covert, Stilwell, and Scott (1975) and Cunningham (1975) indicate that the "open" school has some negative side effects. In the former study, it was found that teacher expectations as a predictor of achievement decreased significantly and were supplanted as predictors by peer nominations. A higher frequency of suspected problems in group interaction and self-control areas seemed to be evident, and self-competency estimates did not appreciably improve. In the latter study Cunningham found significant multivariate differences in achievement and personality variables between the two schools, favoring the traditional over the "open" environment.

The review of the literature about self-concept suggests strongly that self-concept is related to a number of internal and external factors. Sex, past achievement, physical characteristics, home environment, level of aspiration, and social interaction all relate to perception. Nor can one state that good characteristics in a majority of these components can be strictly gauged as additive in the sense that the better each of these characteristics may be, the better the overall results in self-concept. For hereditary components and environmental ones do not interact in a linear manner. Some children or adults who seem to be in ideal conditions will still be depressed in their self-concept. Others who are beset with adversity may have very sound self-concepts.

Though many techniques have been used to improve self-concept, there is no clear proof that any particular one does so in a permanent fashion. It is more likely that self-concepts related to self-competency, and that the ability to perform well in environmentally related tasks is a condition for positive self-regard. Situational constraints influence self-concept or self-regard. When things are going well, one tends to have a higher self-regard. When things are going poorly, one tends to have a lower self-regard. Given the situational influences, there still seem to be responses related to the temperament-aptitude characteristics of the individual as Wylie has inferred. Frustration may lead to aggression in some individuals, but not in all. Success may lead to elation in some and depression in others. Thus, in summary, there are no clear guidelines for the treatment of self-concept in a precise prescriptive manner, particularly if one ties such measures strictly to environmental influences.

What do exist are some major approaches that have a general effect on the development of a healthy and viable self-concept or self-esteem. These influences are felt through environmental conditions. We may identify them as: (1) positive expectations, (2) feedback, and (3) social interactions. Two major sources of expectations and behavior associated with such expectations are those of teachers and parents. One of the first strategies to be employed in raising self-competency is the development of a set of positive expectations towards the individual. Operationally, this means being concerned, smiling, and communicating both verbally and nonverbally. It is the development of a helping approach to the child's problems. This is obviously easier said than done. Life consists of many and varied circumstances which are not always conducive to a positive regard towards others. However, in the case of individuals who need support and help to develop self-competency skills, a change in expectations, a positive regard, and the encouragement to try out new skills (minimizing mistakes) are imperative. In effect teachers and parents should set realistic goals for accomplishment and make a special effort to provide to individual children an opportunity to make mistakes without negative comments. Probably the fear of mistakes and the fear of social disapproval play an important deterrent role in the development of self-competency.

Closely allied with the change of expectations is the use of personal and social reinforcement. For maximum results reinforcement should be administered verbally or nonverbally as soon as possible after the accomplishment of a desired behavior. Finally, negative expectations and disapproval should be eliminated as far as it is possible. Minimizing disapproval does not mean that parents and teachers should accept all forms of disruptive and deviant behavior without discipline or negative reactions. There are times when such negative reactions are appropriate and necessary. But the continued attitudes of negative expectations should be terminated. The change from negative to positive expectations can be most helpful with children who have had a history of dependency or failure. The development of positive attitudes and expectations towards others can be enhanced by feedback. So often both home and school circumstances tend to foster a critical attitude towards others. Implicitly, the feeling is that one elevates one's own self-competency and self-esteem by denigrating others. This may in part be a consequence of a misplaced ethnocentrism, or a result of the learning process where so often failure serves as a criterion of self-esteem. Stilwell (1975) developed a procedure for developing positive attitudes towards others in the classroom. Each morning every child drew a name out of a box. The name was that of one of the children in the classroom. Each child had a notebook with his/her name on it. The individual drawing a specific name would then take the child's notebook and write something positive about the child in the notebook. It might be related to dress or action, or anything the writer might wish to indicate. The teacher also participated in this process. This procedure was empirically evaluated as being quite effective in changing attitudes from a negative outlook to a positive one.

When tests are administered, it is helpful to the individual who took the test to receive positive feedback. This is true of achievement and teacher-made tests as well as other inventories. Barclay (1979) analyzed the computer feedback provided by his BCAS testing program to children. Some 200 children wrote letters to the computer in response to the computerized letter they received about their own behavior. The responses of these children indicated how eager they were to receive feedback—even from a computer. Though information and feedback are important in self-understanding, they are often not sufficient. For once there is some cognitive understanding of a problem, it is important to provide a model of appropriate behavior. Thus, for example, in learning how to play basketball, it is not only necessary to understand what the game is all about, but to practice and improve one's ability to shoot baskets, fake, and play the game. This learning is done by observation of others, modeling, feedback, and positive reinforcement for growth. The same analogy applies to social skills.

An effective means of helping certain children in their self-concept of academic and motor-social skill areas is the use of peer tutors. Very often individuals whose characteristics are related to dependence and who have a history of failure in learning and/or social processes can be helped by peer tutors. The effects of such peer tutoring are multiple. First of all, the tutee learns necessary skills that may be acquired through individual attention. Also, the tutor by reason of the effort helps to organize his/her own learning. The notion of tutoring is not a new idea, but one that was present early in first attempts at public education through the Lancastrian system in which a teacher instructed a number of students who then formed groups to instruct others.

Because much of the inadequacy of self-esteem is derived from situational and environmental conditions, perhaps the greatest single method of providing a healthy self-competency is through changes in the system itself. Carkhuff (1969), Gazda (1973), and Gordon (1974) have developed training packages for both educators and parents which attempt to aid in coping more effectively with decision making, responsible personal and social behavior, and self-esteem. Each of these systems' approaches to developing human relation skills has been field tested and applied to educational settings.

The major arguments of this chapter may be summarized as follows:

1. Self-concept is a popular construct, expressing inadequately a concept that combines at once the intentionalistic nature of organizing perception and environmental fluctuations in support systems.

2. Measures of self-concept and self-esteem are largely simplified modi-

fications of more sophisticated personality measures. They are strongly influenced by social desirability and social projection.

3. The theoretical basis of self-concept theory is shallow; criteria of evaluation are often based on insight or adjustment judgments difficult to replicate across samples.

4. The construct of self-concept appears to be affected by the physical structure and capabilities of the individual, sex differences and expectations, developmental contingencies, socioeconomic level of parents, personality characteristics, including specifically locus of control and achievement-motivation.

5. An examination of treatments involving change in self-concept seldom, if ever, takes into consideration the majority of factors known to influence self-concept as indicated in the foregoing conclusions. Thus the effects of treatments (even when well defined and lasting for a period of time) are unclear and not replicable.

6. From the literature surveyed, it would appear that changes in expectations, positive reinforcement, feedback, modeling, peer tutoring, and the development of human relations skills in groups of teachers and parents are treatment techniques that will aid children in developing positive estimates of their own self-competencies and self-esteem.

7. It is most likely that part of the confusion about the outcomes of self-concept measures is related to the fact that self-concept (self-esteem, self-competency) may be directly related to temperament components.

The complexity of the problems associated with the construct of self-concept, self-esteem, and self-competency could lead one to a rather pessimistic conclusion. When considerations of deficient theoretical conception, methodological inadequacies, and the complexity of other variables associated with self-concept are examined, the picture darkens even more. Add to this the variability and inconsistency of treatments, and the ambiguity of outcomes, and one could easily dismiss the total area as a wasteland for research. This is not really the case because despite all of the above problems, self-perception is an important dimension to personal and social mental health. As researchers become more precise in the evaluation of characteristics of individuals, obtain more knowledge about what these perceptual phenomena really mean and how they relate to goals of behavioral and attitude changes, perhaps a clearer pattern of treatments will emerge.

CHAPTER **X**

Sociometry

THE NATURE OF SOCIOMETRY: AN OVERVIEW

Sociometry is a method of discovering and analyzing patterns of friendship within a group setting. Its primary asset to assessment is that it provides both an independent source of individual assessment based on peer perception, and an indirect, but powerful, estimate of one of the chief sources of psychological support, i.e., peer reinforcement.

The earliest literature on sociometry was provided by Moreno in a book entitled: *Who Shall Survive* (Moreno, 1934). Moreno in developing the specific technique of sociometry saw it as a branch of a larger science which he called "socionomy." Moreno believed that sociometric patterns of choice reflected a profound set of process values that continued to influence individuals throughout life. He believed that such values could be altered and that, by enhancing them, individuals assumed power positions not only for themselves, but as related to others. These power positions could be evaluated as negative or positive. For example, Moreno and Moreno (1976) suggested that Hitler exemplified the process of negative leadership evolution. Hitler started as a disillusioned isolate who seized upon negative issues stemming from the First World War and galvanized the hate and avenging tendencies of a nation. On the other hand, Roosevelt, proceeding from a patrician background, focused on national survival issues and created his power base in this manner. In effect, Moreno believed that sociometry was an indispensable method for evaluating the effect of individuals in a group and what he called the social atom. He believed that the technique had profound possibilities for education and mental health.

Moreno's ideas were distilled into various definitions of the nature of sociometry. A survey of 200 users led to this definition of sociometry as "the field that should be concerned with the quantitative treatment of every kind of inter-human relation and particularly with those involving the expressions

236

of preference or rejection of other members of a group with respect to a choice situation" (Bjerstadt, 1956). On a more practical level Barclay (1966a) defined sociometry "as a method for discovering and analyzing patterns of friendship within a group setting" (p. 1070).

Another very important component in the development of sociometric techniques was the confluence of Lewinian field theory with the mental health movement. This event that took place in the 1950s had a great impact on the then small profession of school psychology. At the beginning of the 1950s, according to Meacham and Trione, there were only 519 school psychologists operating in the United States (Meacham and Trione, 1967). Even by 1960 the total number had only increased to 2836. In those days, psychologists who operated within the schools were much more social-psychological consultants in a variety of educational and mental health roles and had much freedom to contract with administrators regarding their tasks. Many new or beginning school psychologists came out of graduate programs steeped in Lewininan ideas and modified psychodynamic theory. Most did some individual testing, but in addition, there was a considerable emphasis on personal and social adjustment.

The theories that guided this approach were vested in both the postulates of Lewin (1935; Lewin & Grabbe, 1945) regarding the importance of assessing the environment, and the contributions of psychodynamic thought to learning theory (Dollard and Miller, 1950). This approach emphasized the propositions of Lewin, i.e., (1) that learning is an interaction between the person and the environment; (2) that perception is the key variable in determining behavior; (3) that affective learning does not necessarily correlate with cognitive learning; (4) that correct knowledge does not necessarily result in the alteration of false perceptions; and (5) that change is a function of responsible involvement in appropriate social contingencies (Lewin & Grabbe, 1945).

In terms of learning theory itself, the bridge made between psychoanalytic constructs and learning theory by Dollard and Miller (1950) led to a view of learning that could best be described as the mental health approach. This position, highly compatible with Lewinian theory, recognized both the need for viewing individuals as responsible persons characterized by motivation and intentionality, and the conditions of change as determined in environmental contingencies. A key emphasis then for individuals working in situations where change was desirable was to assess the quality of the environment. This involved evaluating perceptions and looking specifically at the social support systems that existed in such settings.

Far more scholars were associated with this movement than can be identified here, but some of them were: Eli Bower, Boyd McCandless, William Morse, Merle Bonney, Leon Festinger, Jacob Kounin, Ronald Lippitt, and

Norman Gronlund. Lewin's influence was great on these individuals, and three of them, McCandless, Kounin, and Lippitt, did their own doctoral work with Lewin.

From the 1950s on, a rapid series of applications of social evaluation as a technique used to operationalize the tenets of Lewinian thought developed. Heider (1958) urged that phenomenological thinking be used to clarify the nature of human interaction through the acceptance of common experience. Kounin (1970), Kounin and Gump (1961), and Kounin, Gump and Ryan (1961) examined the influence of teachers on the misconduct of children. Morse (1965) focused on intervention techniques that could be used by counselors in fresh-air camps and by teachers. Redl and Wineman (1952) explored the establishment of controls from within for the aggressive child (1952). It was reasoned that if much variability in human behavior was due to unfavorable group interaction, then it was important to evaluate the quality of group interaction and specifically to identify those forces of individual differences that interacted both as negative factors and positive ones in individuals and in groups. The bottom line to much of this research was that both children and adults cannot learn either cognitive knowledge or affective skills without being free from external conflict or internal problems. The mental health movement was designed to create freedom, to develop personal responsibility, and to reeducate.

Assessment was important to determine what kinds of individual or group procedures could be used to reeducate both individuals and groups. Sociometric techniques evolved as one means to measure the complex relationships identified by Lewin and Grabbe. Most of them were related to the development of a variety of methods that could be used to estimate the individual's status in a group situation. Several individuals who pioneered work in this technique in the field of education were Merle Bonney (1943a, 1943b; Bonney & Powell, 1953), M. L. Northway (1952), Norman Gronlund (1951, 1955, 1959), Ned Flanders (Flanders and Havumaki, 1960) and E. Amidon (1963). Although many of these applications were in the field of education, the technique was also used in the military, industry, and business to predict a wide variety of personnel problems (Mouton, Blake & Fruchter, 1955b; Hart & Nath, 1979).

A further elaboration of sociometry as a technique extended research into the area of mathematical models. For example, Coleman (1961) analyzed in diagrams cliques in the Elmtown High School. Later, Hunter (1978) and Langeheine (1978) both provided extensive inquiries into the algebra of predicting consistency in individual and group choices and the development of theorems for illustrating these models.

Although a good deal of research was done during the 1940s, 1950s, and 1960s, this research was heavily directed at social processes and mental hygiene goals. It focused chiefly on descriptive analyses, was not always precise in defining phenomena investigated, and was generally unaware of the newer statistical techniques popularized in the 1960s. It was enhanced greatly by the use of computers in the 1970s. The focus of much of the research was on groups; for example, the identification and contrast of groups of children identified as under-achievers, or socially maladjusted, with other groups of children. It therefore had an appeal to those who would improve the overall quality of education for all children rather than concentrating on a few children with many difficulties. Today, in contrast, school psychological services appear to be designed for the few rather than many.

In the 1970s and into the 1980s, sociometric studies fell into decline. There are a number of reasons for this. First of all, the influence of Rogerian approaches to counseling denigrated the use of all tests, and towards the end of the 1960s the growing popularity of behavioral techniques tended to deprecate all nonbehavioral methods of assessment. Sociometrics were included in this condemnation even though sociometrics were very consistent with behavioral approaches and could be used as a criterion for selected reinforcement procedures (Barclay, 1967). Second, the emphasis on mental health, focusing on internal changes of responsibility, that had been the keystone of Lewinian ideas, gradually declined and disappeared in favor of direct methods of external behavior change. Thus, techniques which were designed to increase motivation, to reorganize thinking, and to build personal character were abandoned in favor of response manipulation. Even references to the construct of motivation tended to disappear. For example, there are only a small handful of references to it in the *Handbook of Research on Teaching* (Gage, 1963), and only one reference to it in the *Second Handbook on Teaching* issued ten years later in 1973 (Travers, 1973). Third, with the passage of PL 94–142, the emphasis in school psychology was directed specifically at special education problems rather than generic mental health ones. Moreover, the increased flow of judicial and legal decisions reflected negatively against experimental studies within the educational setting. Legalistic restrictions and the mounting requirement for continuous retesting of children already assessed year after year led to a clear injunction to focus on "safe techniques and methods." Fourth, those individuals who had had some experience with sociometrics realized that there was a great deal of work that had to be done to develop sociograms and manually score these data. Norms were difficult to ascertain and to generalize. Many of those who used sociometrics found them difficult to score, time consuming to analyze, and could not see any relationship to what strategies of intervention might be associated with their use. Although sociometric data could and were scored by computer analysis, those who used the technique either found out about such developments too late or were not aware of their potential.

Perhaps the greatest single problem with sociometric data has been the lack of a comprehensive theory about the meaning of the phenomena. The emphasis on sociometrics as a technique led to its virtual dismissal by school psychologists and school psychology trainers. Because it was theoretically underdeveloped it was not seen as a tool with possible consequences for learning and human development, particularly as both are mediated by the environment. Its value as a means of devising psychological interventions is virtually unrecognized today, as is evident from Shapiro (1987) who found only three nonbehavioral interventions cited out of 597 intervention research articles published between 1981 and 1986. All the rest are behavioral in orientation.

In summary, sociometry had its origins in the work of Moreno. The primary preoccupation of researchers in the early decades was with alternative techniques to measure sociometric data. With the decline of the mental health movement (broadly associated with Lewinian field theory and psychodynamic theory), and the advent of behavioral technology as a basis for assessment, sociometrics have declined in usage. In addition, when school psychologists became more involved in the assessment of special educational students as contrasted with the earlier emphasis on the overall mental health needs of children, individual analysis became the overriding specific interest of most school psychologists.

THE NATURE OF THE SOCIOMETRIC METHOD

As a method, sociometry is important in determining specifically the psychological support system that exists for individuals in an environment. No other technique possesses the power potential for accurately assessing the quality of reinforcement that flows from individuals in a group setting to other individuals in that setting. Within many settings where individuals must remain (as for example, in the school placement or in a job that must be held), the judgments of peers are felt by their attitudes of liking or disliking of others in that environment. Within the school setting any student's psychological support system is derived from two main sources: the peer group and the teacher. Thus, if knowledge of the psychological support system is to be obtained, sociometry possesses the power to provide this information. As we shall see from the research to be discussed, psychological support systems do not correlate highly with academic achievement or teacher judgments.

During the first decades in which sociometric methods were developed, a natural focus was on both the characteristics of the method itself and the reliability and validity of the results. Within the field of education there were many variations of the technique. Most of them were intended to identify global friendship patterns. These patterns could be obtained by seeking positive and negative choices. For example, a child could be asked to identify those children who were considered friends either in work or play, and conversely those who were not liked.

Although there were many varieties of sociometric techniques developed, the most common approach was to ask children to identify children with whom they would like to play and work. For example, a *Manual of Sociometry for Teachers* (Smith, 1951) at the University of Michigan recommended the following format for use with elementary children:

I. Boys and girls, this is a choosing exercise that will help me to find out which boys and girls in our room work and play best together. Think about each of the questions below and answer them by writing the names of the children you choose. Answer the questions just as honestly as you can; no one else will look at your answers so be sure to write the person's name that you really want. Please do not mention your choices to any one else. Write the names of the children with whom you would like best to play any of the games that we know. There might be several so write the names of any you would really like.

    1.----------------------------
    2.----------------------------
    3.----------------------------

II. Now, write the names of the children with whom you would like best to work or make something—any work that we do. Again there might be several so write the names of any you would really like.

    1.----------------------------
    2.----------------------------
    3.----------------------------

In an example of this method, the classroom teacher would end up with 22 child reports to be examined with 6 choices from each child, for a total of 132 choices. Choices would then be recorded on a matrix.

The tabulation of the matrix is done in the following manner: (1) each child's choices are registered in the matrix; (2) Arabic numerals are used to identify play choices, with 1, 2, 3 indicating first, second and third choices; (3) Roman numerals are used to identify work choices, with I, II, III indicating first, second and third choices. The output of this system can then be diagrammed into a configuration.

What is done to determine this configuration is to draw a series of circles in which the central or smallest one represents those children with the most choices. In typical sociometric terms these are the "stars" of the class, or in our preferable terminology, these are the children with the greatest "psychological support system." The other circles represent children with decreasing levels of choices, and the outer circle represents those children who have the fewest choices, in this case, those with only one or two choices. These are children who have a poor psychological support system. If a child receives no choices at all, the term used to identify this child is "isolate." Mutual choices can be diagrammed by searching the individual choices. Other terms derived from such diagrams are "clique" where a small group of children choose only each other, and "cleavage" which often represents groupings by sex, or sometimes by race and/or social status. The term "rejectee" refers to individuals who receive many negative choices. Since no negative choices were made in this example, there are no "rejectees."

From this analysis it is apparent that in the early decades of work with sociometrics many individuals were discouraged from using the technique simply because of the time consumed in collecting the data, tabulating it, and then creating a sociogram. Once it was completed, few school psychologists and virtually no teachers knew what to do about the results. There were many reasons for this hiatus between assessment and intervention. First of all, the terminology of the older system was descriptive of the configuration. It makes much more sense to evaluate the positions of these children in terms of the qualitative characteristics of their support system, than in terms of "star," "isolate," "rejectee." Second, the emphasis of much of the earlier research was exploratory and descriptive. Assessment of characteristics then often stopped at the point of correlating specific sociometric indices with achievement, intelligence, personality, or many other forms of assessment. Third, it was only in the 1970s and later that the concept of intervention as a set of experiences designed to decrease maladaptive behavior and augment prosocial behavior became known. It was largely due to the influence of behavioral techniques that this necessary sharpening of intervention focus took place.

Barclay in the mid-1950s, working with a suburban Detroit school and wishing to utilize both sociometrics and teacher ratings as a rough screening procedure, developed a simplified method for obtaining some of the sociometric data. He asked students a general positive and a general negative sociometric question. Rather than use names, he provided a form with numbers on it and had the teacher write the name and number of each child on the blackboard or give the child a listing of names and numbers. His instructions were:

"All of us like some people better than others. On the board is a list of the names of boys and girls in your class, with a number before each name. Who are your best friends in this class? Who are the boys and girls with whom you most like to work and play? Circle the number that goes with your friends' names. You may choose as many or few as you want."

The negative question was couched in this form. "As we said before, all of us like some people better than others. Using the numbers next to this, circle those numbers that go with the names of boys and girls with whom you would rather not play or work. Again choose as many or as few as you want" (Barclay, 1964).[1]

Scoring of this sociometric instrument was comparatively simple. The total number of positive choices could be easily obtained and so could the total number of negative choices. To obviate negative values an arbitrary mean of 50 was assumed. The sociometric index for a given child was then the total number of positive choices minus the total number of negative choices with an assumed mean of 50. Thus if Joe received 10 positive choices and 4 negative ones his score was 56. If Susan received no positive choices and 12 negative choices her score was 38.

Because this approach was developed in a school system and employed for a number of years as a screening device for consultation, a teacher rating was also asked for (Barclay, 1964). It was reasoned that the two major sources of within-class reinforcement and modeling came from peers and teachers. However, teacher ratings were known not to correlate that highly with the social skills of students (Gronlund, 1951, 1959; Bonney, 1943a, 1943b; Bonney & Powell, 1953). The Barclay teacher ratings were made on a five-point scale extending from excellent to poor on the following components: (1) overall emotional adjustment, (2) social maturity, (3) depression, (4) aggression, (5) security, (6) stability and (7) conduct. The teacher ratings then yielded scores ranging from the highest of 35 to the lowest of 7.

The results of these two sets of ratings were then combined on a grid of nine cells where sociometric ratings were plotted on the vertical axis and teacher ratings on the horizontal axis (see Figure 10-1). These cells were helpful in obtaining an overall view of the child in the classroom. Cells 3, 5, and 7 fall along the correlation line. Cell 3 has a population of children highly accepted both by teachers and students. Cell 7 is the most negative and represents the area where both peers and teachers have rejected or ignored the individual. Cell 1 contains those individuals who are leaders among their peers, but who may express values or skills not appreciated by the teacher. Cell 9 is the converse of cell 1. Individuals here have strong teacher ratings but poor peer ratings. These children might typically be viewed as teacher "pets."

Out of these studies done in the practical crucible of school experience, Barclay learned three things: (1) norms could be developed for a particular school setting using the simplified scoring procedure outlined earlier, (2)

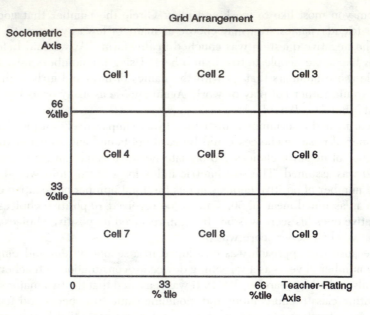

Figure 10-1   **Barclay Teacher-Peer Grid**

teachers found the grid arrangement useful in understanding children and were interested in learning what they might do about a given child, (3) sociometric data and teacher ratings combined in this simple format provided a basis for consultation.[2]

RESEARCH WITH EARLY VERSIONS OF SOCIOMETRY

A considerable amount of research was done with the simple sociometric method. Because there were so many versions of simple sociometric tests, studies were often method specific. Nonetheless, a considerable body of research was developed in reliability and validity studies.

One of the first concerns with sociometry was to determine its reliability. Although many forms of reliability studies were undertaken including: (1) interpretative reliability (i.e., identification of position on the sociogram over time), (2) internal consistency (or split-half), (3) equivalent or alternate forms, and (4) test-retest, (or stability over time), some methods seem to have been used more than others. Lindzey and Borgatta (1954) favored using graphic results to confirm the relative position of individuals within the sociogram. The split-half method was used but criticized by Gronlund as having no special significance. The alternate forms method involved administering several sociometric questions to the same group at the same time and then correlating the results. Although Kerr (1945) found general correlations between eight sociometric questions that referred to different activities, and Gronlund (1955) found a high degree of relationship between the resulting sociometric status scores obtained from three general sociometric questions of work, play, and seating arrangements with five choices allowed on each, there was evidence that correlations between sociometric questions was specific to the activity described. Thus children may identify certain peers as most popular for attending a party (possibly because the family is wealthier and can afford such a party), but they may choose some one else as a friend to study with.

The most frequently assessed form of reliability has been test-retest. Mouton, Blake, and Fruchter (1955a) summarized in detail 27 studies on the consistency of choice status found by test-retest methods. They concluded that the results indicate choice status of the individual remains consistent over the time he or she is evaluated by others. Gronlund (1959) also reviews many studies and states that he finds substantial agreement of the stability of sociometric status among adolescents. He suggests that over time intervals, those of less than a week, coefficients of approximately .90 might be expected; over several weeks, correlation coefficients of .80 are indicated and for time intervals between 8 and 20 months, coefficients of approximately .60. Barclay (1956) in a one-year follow up of over 2500 elementary children found that a correlation of .70 existed in sociometric status. This was true even though most of the sample had moved from elementary schools to a junior high school.

Where sociometric questions are related directly to specific skill areas such as intellectual, mechanical or social skills, Barclay (1974a) found that there were pre-post correlations over the course of one academic year of .58 to .77 for artistic-intellectual peer choices, .57 to .64 for outdoor-mechanical choices, .66 for social skill choices, .65 to .71 for enterprising and leadership choices, .50 to .67 for group reticent and shy nominations and .58 to .70 on group disruptive and acting-out nominations.

In summary, the research suggests that there is a tendency for sociometric correlations to decline as the time span between tests is increased. Results based on general criteria are more stable than those based on specific criteria. Composite sociometric scores based on several criteria (i.e., work and play) tend to be more stable than scores based on a single sociometric criterion. The use of a limited number of sociometric choices such as five positive choices or three positive and three negative tends to yield higher reliability results than either an unlimited number of choices or simply one or two.

Finally, extreme sociometric positions such as leadership, rejection and isolation tend to be more stable than sociometric ratings in the moderate range (Gronlund, 1959, pp. 152–153).

Many validity studies have been completed. The construct validity of sociometric choice is held to be valid by definition. Jennings (1950) contends that the sociometric test is not an indirect measure of other behavior, but rather a sample of actual behavior and as such is directly meaningful and need not be validated by relating it to an external and independent criterion. He feels that if each individual discloses his or her preferences on the test in an honest way, the test is valid. On the other hand, even if biases exist—such as in racial discrimination—the reality of these impressions are valid indicators of what is actually happening in a given environment.

Concurrent and predictive validity is the most popular approach to the meaningfulness of sociometry. Mouton, Blake, and Fruchter (1955b) reviewed 44 studies on the validity of sociometric test scores in educational, industrial and military settings and found that sociometric scores agreed with many outside criteria of performance. Table 1 groups a number of representative studies relating to the validity of sociometric choices. These studies indicate that sociometric phenomena have been correlated with social worker and psychologist ratings, mental health ratings, and teacher ratings. They have shown a relationship to personality tests such as the *California Test of Personality*, the *High School Personality Questionnaire*, *the Rorschach*, the *Kvaraceus Delinquency Proneness Test*, and other measures of perception such as the *Id-Ego-Superego Test*, and the *Ellis Visual Designs*, motivation and self-concept tests, and a variety of achievement and intelligence measures.

Sociometric indices have also been related to distinctive interest patterns, the socioeconomic status of parents, and behavioral observations in the classroom. They have been related to military status, have been predictive of dropouts in the school, have been used in experimental studies as criterion measures, and appear to have enduring longitudinal and predictive validity in terms of a variety of criterion measures of effective human behavior.

Sociometric choices have also been used with adults. An example is the work of Smith (1967) in analyzing the peer support system of 583 college students, 521 nursing students, and 324 high school students. Smith used 42 adjectives, all of which had polar connotations and asked each student to nominate five of their classmates who met the one alternative and five who met the polar opposite. This format was used along with achievement tests, the *Edwards Personal Preference Schedule*, and High School grade point to predict first year achievement (for the general college students only). He found in a regression using the above predictors and first year grade point as the criterion that peer ratings accounted for 68% of the total variance;

Table 10-1   **Summary of Older Validity Studies**

Area or Criterion	Author(s)	Findings
Mental Health	Bedoian (1953)	Low status children lower on mental health ratings.
California Test of Personality	Bedoian (1953) Barclay (1964)	Significant differences between high and low sociometric status.
High School Personality Questionnaire	Guinouard & Rychlak (1962)	High sociometric status significantly related to intelligence, self-confidence, enthusiasm and acceptance of group rules.
Rorschach	Tindall (1955)	Significant relationship between social acceptance and protocols.
Kvaraceus Delinquency Proneness Test	Barclay (1964)	Correlation between sociometric status and delinquency proneness—.53
Id-Ego-Superego Test	Barclay & Barclay (1965)	High sociometric status significantly higher on ego scores; significantly lower on impulsivity.
Ellis Visual Designs	Barclay & Barclay (1965)	High sociometric status significantly higher on perceptual organization.
Teacher Ratings	Gronlund (1955, 1959); Barclay (1964)	Low positive relationship between sociometric status and favorable ratings.
Achievement & Intelligence	Gronlund (1959) Barclay (1964)	Low positive relationships between achievement and sociometric status.
	Miller (1956)	Superior students most often chosen, followed by average and retardates
	Gallagher & Crowder (1957)	.45 correlation between I.Q. & social status.
	Barbe (1954)	Bright children choose friends with slightly lower I.Q.s.
Self-Concept & Self-Competency	Barclay (1974)	Group sociometric choices significantly related to self-competency scores.

Table 10-1 (Continued)

Area or Criterion	Author(s)	Findings
Interest Patterns Vocational Interests Hobbies, TV etc.	Barclay (1966c)	Sociometric status related to differential interests in many areas with popular more interested in TV & Sports.
Industrial, Military, Business	Mouton, Blake & Fruchter (1955)	Review of 44 studies show advantages for high status individuals in all areas. Sociometric status clearly predictive of performance.
Prediction of Dropouts from School	Kuhlen, Collister (1952); Barclay (1966b)	Both longitudinal studies (involving over 1400 ss) indicate low sociometric status children significantly more prone to drop out.
Sociometry as a Criterion for Experimental Change	Amidon (1963) Dineen, Garry (1963) Kranzler, Mayer, Dyer & Munger (1966); Barclay (1967)	Efforts to change isolate behavior (Amidon); classroom cleavage through seating (Dineen & Garry); use of reinforcement and modeling to change social status.

academic aptitude tests accounted for 19%; high school grades for 13% and the Edwards for 0%. One adjective alone accounted for 55% of the variance. That was "quitting." Similar factor structures were found for nursing, college, and high school students. These factors were Agreeableness, Extroversion, Strength of Character, Emotionality and Refinement, with Strength of Character being the strongest factor.

FURTHER DEVELOPMENTS AND THE BARCLAY CLASSROOM ASSESSMENT SYSTEM

In an earlier section, I indicated the method used to modify sociometric techniques and to combine them with teacher ratings in a grid. Over the period from 1955 to 1968, this basic technique was used on a number of studies. I would like to summarize them here briefly because they relate to the development of a more comprehensive system of data analysis for elementary children.

Using the grid method described earlier, Barclay and Barclay (1965) found a significant relationship between lack of social acceptance by peers and teachers in third grade students and measures of impulsivity. Barclay (1966b) in a follow up of 949 children tested originally in 1959 and again in 1963 found that 54% of the female dropouts from school and 65% of the male dropouts had been located initially in the cell of maximum rejection (cell 7). This study confirmed what Kuhlen and Collister (1952) had found about predicting school dropouts from the sixth and ninth grades by use of sociometric indices.

Again, these cells were compared for patterns in class interests, television viewing habits, music listening preferences, study preferences and habits and hobbies for 1,777 elementary and junior high school students (Barclay, 1966c). It was found that significant differences in preferences accompany high and low social acceptance in the classroom.

Several other studies addressed the quality of the environmental conditions expressed by overall averages of teacher ratings and peer ratings for 70 classrooms. Male elementary school teachers tended to have overall lower mean peer ratings and showed lower ratings for children than did female teachers. Young female teachers tended to rate boys the highest and foster the most positive peer interaction, and older female teachers were most positive towards girls (Barclay 1966d).

Davis (1967) found a significant correlation between scores for 445 students tested in the 7th or 8th grade by Barclay and retested in the 10th grade. Drawing random names from the various cells she presented teachers with the names of 100 students. Teachers confirmed independently of either the pre- or posttesting results the social acceptance status of students. Kennedy (1969) found the system helpful in relating referrals to a mental health facility. Finally, the system was used as a criterion for initiating planned interventions, selective reinforcement, and modeling procedures, and change of teachers in three classes. The effect of these interventions could be assessed in terms of the social acceptance of students (Barclay, 1967; Forsythe and Jackson, 1966). Perhaps the most important feature of this latter study was that the cell arrangement of the teacher-peer grid provided a direct criterion measure for selective behavioral and intervention techniques.

From the research cited earlier, it was apparent in the mid-1960s that sociometric data analysis was valuable in providing a global analysis of the social acceptance of individuals in the classroom. Sociometric phenomena, arranged in a number of different ways, manifested reliability indices. It was further evident that sociometric indices had a broad but significant relationship to a host of factors such as achievement, intelligence, personality, and other measures of personal and social effectiveness. In addition, it seemed clear that whatever was involved in sociometric choices, it covaried with a number of personal interests in hobbies, music-listening activities, sports, etc.

It became evident to the writer then that the sociometric index was a global factor reflecting a host of cognitive and emotional variables. In pilot studies with children, it was evident from interviews that they had rather specific behavioral criteria in mind when they indicated why they liked or disliked someone. These criteria focused specifically on skill competencies. Children who were popular had considerable skills—not always in every area—but in specific areas. Running fast, coordination, and catching were skills related to athletics. Study skills, learning quickly, and verbal abilities were related to intellectual skills. Similar arrays of skills could be identified for artistic, enterprising, disruptive, and reticent behavior. Discussions with John Holland (1964) suggested that certain kinds of skills were associated with competencies. Further it was most evident that the parental occupations and education had major effects on children's interests, affective style, and aspirations.

In the mid 1960s the earlier Barclay technique was developed into a system to include peer nominations in specific skill areas that encompassed outdoor-mechanical skills, artistic ones, intellectual skills, enterprising, social and conventional competencies. There were 28 sets of nominations altogether. In this system the general friendship criterion was abandoned in favor of a set of specific skill criteria. Thus for example, rather than identifying their specific friends for work and play, children were asked to identify children "who could run fast" or "who got their work done on time," or "who could sing real well." In addition, the negative question was dropped. Along with these peer nominations, there was a self-report section in which children rated their own skills on the exact same skill competencies as peers used (thus providing a comparison of self-reported skills with peer evaluated ones for each individual). A teacher evaluation component was based on adjectival ratings. Preliminary studies with the new system eliminated poor items, and refined the three sources of evaluation as specifically related to reticent children and disruptive children (Ferris, 1968; Stickel, 1968).

However, the task in assessment had doubled and tripled and it was evident that this kind of assessment could only be done by computer analysis. Through the assistance of the Stanford Research Institute and specifically Richard E. Snow of Stanford University, a computer analysis system was devised for analyzing the data. Though the process in the late 1960s was highly cumbersome by comparison with present methods, it did provide without any doubt a model for future development.

With the introduction of a multimethod and multitrait system for analyzing the psychological support system of children, it became evident that the system was far more than a sociometric device. The system was focused specifically on skills. Skills were defined as the external observable behaviors of individuals as related to either cognitive or affective domains. Many further modifications of a technical nature were made to the system including the integration of standardized achievement scores to the total inventory to provide a set of algorithms for making decisions relative to both cognitive and achievement components.

The reporting of all of the research that went into this system by the author and by others is too tedious to discuss in this book, but is reported in detail in the *Manual of the Barclay Classroom Assessment System* (Barclay, 1983a). A listing of the most important research studies with a brief explanation is provided in Table 10-2.

What is most important is that the BCAS system is a form of artificial intelligence in which data from self-report, peer nominations, and teacher ratings are integrated with standardized achievement scores to provide a set of algorithms for making decisions. The interpretation of the data and its conversion into sensible useful language terms was an important part of this process, because it was apparent that the convergence of methods and the comparison of traits could not be done by visual inspection. The criteria for statements were empirically evaluated by discussions with teachers and by behavioral observation methods (Barclay, Stilwell, Santoro & Clark, 1972). The details of these procedures are presented elsewhere for those interested (Barclay, 1988b). However, some examples may be helpful here. A poor psychological support system is judged thus: a significantly low score on positive peer ratings and an absence or low number of positive teacher descriptors with the inclusion of some negative teacher ratings. When these conditions are met, they lead to a computer judgment that the psychological support system of the child is poor. Many peer ratings of shy, reticent behavior joined to similar judgments by the teacher in selecting key reticence adjectives leads to the computer judgment that the child is probably reticent and shy. The output therefore provides readers with a comprehensive diagnostic view of a specific child in a specific environment.

The research that has been done with the system not only provides descriptive characteristics of the individual, but pinpoints areas for teacher, principal, elementary counselor, or school psychologist concern. Some of the interventions suggested are obvious. If peer support is good and teacher support poor, then an obvious judgment is to increase teacher support. If a child is shy and reticent, then a counselor or school psychologist may use this information to work with the teacher or parents to devise appropriate strategies of intervention.

The computer analysis of the data suggests strategies of intervention for reticence, for increasing peer or teacher support, for verifying impressions that a given child is disruptive or gifted, and for alternative learning strategies. Based on research with alternative treatments in an aptitude-treatment paradigm and using effect size scores as pre-post measures of change, it also provides interim hypotheses (for further evaluation) about what kinds of curricula or counselor interventions may work best with different children

Table 10-2   **Selected Research with the Barclay Classroom Assessment System**

Area or Criterion	Author(s)	Findings
Convergent & Discriminant Validity	Tapp & Barclay (1974)	Multi-method, multi-trait study.
	Barclay (1983a)	Systems comparison with Bennett findings (1976).
	Barclay & Wu (1980)	Comparison of Chinese and American versions of BCAS and validity of factor scores across cultures.
	Barclay (1974c)	Consumer reactions to use of BCAS.
Diagnostic Characteristics of Children	Barclay, Stilwell & Barclay (1972)	Relationship of socio-economic status of father to BCAS data.
	Barclay (1974b)	Relationship of seven different problem areas compared across three districts by age and sex.
	Ferris (1968) Stickel (1968)	Analysis of reticent children and discrimination from disruptive children.
Behavior Analysis	Barclay, Stilwell, Santoro & Clark (1972)	Results of behavior analysis of 700 children over ten days in relationship to BCAS data.
Special Education	Kehle & Guidubaldi (1978); Barclay & Kehle (1979)	Discusses EMR & LD placements of 115 Ohio classrooms using BCAS and negative effect of mainstreaming.
	Barclay, Phillips & Jones (1983)	Development of an index for identifying gifted from the BCAS with 75% accuracy in discrimination against individual tests.
Systems & Change	Barclay (1974a & 1974b)	Discusses district-wide analysis and identification of target areas for intervention.
	Stilwell & Barclay (1976, 1977, 1979)	Experimental interventions in affective domain using the BCAS.

Table 10-2 (Continued)

Area or Criterion	Author(s)	Findings
	Barclay, Covert, Scott & Stilwell (1975)	Three-year follow-up of behavioral, open, and traditional curricula assessed by the BCAS.
Temperament and Prevention	Barclay, (1983b)	Meta-analysis of six different approaches to change using the temperament x treatment paradigm.
	Barclay (1983c)	A prevention approach utilizing school or district-wide screening.
	Barclay (1987)	Analysis of the relationships of various tests to super factors of temperament.
	Barclay (1988a)	Analysis of the basis of temperament.
	Barclay (1988b)	Use of the computer as a prevention diagnostician.
	Barclay & Barclay (1986)	Applications to early childhood & kindergarten.
	Cohen (1983)	Temperament as a causal factor in attributions.

(Barclay 1983b). In summary, the system was designed and researched to provide overall screening of elementary children based on self, peer and teacher judgments. But in order to obtain this information, all children must be tested, even though not all reports require interventions. A set of decision-rules specify the grouping of data for individuals and groups, the determination of whether a child's problems are primarily related to achievement or personal-social developmental areas or both. Examples of some of the decision paradigms were illustrated in a previous article (Barclay, 1983c).

In summary, the BCAS system was devised as a multimethod multitrait system for evaluating children within a group setting, looking at how they feel about themselves, how others feel about them and how the teacher views them. In addition, basic standardized achievement data is a supplementary but important entry by teachers. By scanning the introduction to the printouts, school psychologists can immediately identify children who may need either further observation, classroom consultation, or additional testing.

THE TEMPERAMENT BASIS OF SOCIOMETRICS

The progress of investigations into social learning aspects of personality, behavior modification patterns, the influence of heredity on environmental variations, recent research on monozygotic twins, and many other collateral lines of research has come more and more to focus on temperament. There is a growing recognition that underlying interview data, psychometric scores, and even intuitive inferences about behavior, is a set of templates, largely hereditary in origin, that manifests a continuing influence on individual reactions towards environmental influences. These dispositions tend to manifest a parsimonious but universal base for human behavior as identified in a variety of studies using different methods.

The recognition of this situation has been marked by an increasing interest in the construct of temperament and efforts to define the nature of the construct. For example, a round-table discussion including a majority of American researchers in this field (Goldsmith, Buss, Plomin, Rothbart, Thomas, Chess, Hinde, and McCall, 1987) examined the major constructs of temperament. Some of their conclusions were: (1) the construct is helpful despite the inability to define precisely how it interacts with environmental influences. (One reviewer pointed out that we have no final definitions of intelligence either, but accept it without hesitation.) Another conclusion (2) was that temperament included elements of **activity**, energy, intensity, vigor and pace in both speech and thought, (but not their contents), **reactivity** (in terms of approach or withdrawal from stimuli), **emotionality**, and **sociability**. A third conclusion (3) was that the origins of temperament were in biological predispositions, but the extent to which this was true was not agreed upon. Finally, (4) it was recognized that there was a higher degree of stability manifested in temperament expressions through the life-span than for other features of personality.

Elsewhere (Barclay, 1988a), temperament was described as forming a basic typology for classifying individual characteristics on a meta-theory level. Temperament has been viewed as a coherent grouping of hereditary dispositions primarily related to the limbic system of the brain which tends to serve as a template that restricts the total possible range of behavior for an individual. This restriction of the range of behavior is the by-product of interaction with learning, thinking, reactions to stimulation, and responses to arousal and stress. Thus individuals evolve a specific style of behavior which is recognizable by others.

What is most important about the construct of temperament is that it is biologically anchored and perhaps more closely related to the emotional characteristics of individuality, i.e., the limbic system, than to cognition. It appears to be more directly related to survival and is therefore manifested specifically in the strength of arousal, and the duration of arousal. Contemporary research on these biological aspects of temperament has been developed chiefly in England through the studies of Eysenck and others (Powell, 1979), and more recently by Strelau and other Eastern European researchers (Strelau, 1983).

One can look at the evidence for temperament from many sources. There are logical, empirical, and psychometric studies of temperament. Temperament theory is as old as Hippocrates and Galen. It is seen in the work of Carl G. Jung and even Wilhelm Wundt. It has been the focus of empirical studies by Thomas and Chess, and Buss and Plomin (Barclay, 1988a).

In addition, second-order factor analytic studies suggest common elements that are found in tests that are empirically based (CPI), factor based (16PF) and physiologically based (*Strelau Temperament Inventory*). Further evidence is obtained from studies of the brain both within England and in Eastern European countries, and particularly as related to differential reactions of introverts and extroverts to stimulating and depressant drugs. Finally, there is evidence that temperament plays an important role in aptitude-treatment interactions designed for specific educational or psychotherapeutic treatments (Barclay 1988a).

The convergence of many lines of research relating to temperament suggest strongly that it is a very important component in the assessment of personality, that it is specifically related to emotional aspects of the individual. Thus levels of arousal, speed of arousal, and duration of arousal to stimulation are seen as primarily governed by hereditary components.

Given the composite nature of the BCAS, evidence has accumulated over a period of years that the BCAS is actually measuring, at a meta-theory level, temperament characteristics. These temperament characteristics are derived from what may be called, for lack of a better term, naive human perceptions.

How was this judgment reached? Through two sets of research: first through factor analyses of the BCAS that indicate proximity of BCAS primary and secondary factors to accepted components of temperament, and second by some specific studies relating sociometric nominations to indices drawn from the *Strelau Temperament Inventory* (Strelau, 1983), an inventory based primarily on physiological studies with temperament.

The first set of evidence linking temperament to sociometric studies is related to a series of factor analyses done over a period of years on the BCAS. Barclay (1972) factor analyzed 23 of the BCAS scales using samples of 1,938 males and 1,768 females. Analyses were done separately by sex and contrasted two methods of factor analysis: (1) principal axis with varimax rotation, and (2) multimethod factor analysis devised by Jackson (1969) to control for method variance. As was expected, in the principal axis method, self-report scales, peer-nominations scales and teacher-rating scales formed separate factors.

The multi-method factor analysis of Jackson (1969) appeared to be the most valuable one for determining how the three sets of inputs related to common factors. In this procedure, within method variance is minimized in favor of between method variance. From this procedure six multimethod, multitrait factors emerged: task-order achievement, impulsivity, reserved-internality, physical energy, sociability, and enterprising-dominance behavior. Each of these multisource factors has an analogue to primary studies done by others with temperament.

A second-order factor analysis of these multi-method and multi-trait factors led to two factors, energy and sociability. When these components were reduced to vertical and horizontal axes, a grid emerged wherein individuals could be placed in terms of the values of their first-order factors. Some 64 combinations of the first-order factor scores have been plotted and these are depicted in the manual of the BCAS.

In order to illustrate the hierarchical development of the overall system, some figures and tables have been prepared. Figure 10-2 provides the final output of the system (or typology) indicating the loading of the second-order factors of energy and sociability on the type. The four quadrants represent four types of children who through many analyses have been characterized as thinkers, leaders, followers, and agitators. These terms are not used in any pejorative labeling sense, but rather as summary descriptors of types of behavior perceived by peers and teachers and by unique personal attributes in self-report. In addition, it should be pointed out that there are two other groups of children who represent solid citizens of the classroom and are positioned in the middle of the grid.

What is important to recall here is that no child is ever placed in one of these quadrants by one method alone, but is classified by factor loadings that represent subtle but important contributors to this typology. This fact is an important consideration in terms of both interventions and outcome evaluation studies. The results of a number of studies indicate that interventions must be type specific and evaluations must focus on changes in the type, not changes in the classroom. When changes do occur, particularly on factor scores, they reflect not only self-report changes, but changes in peer acceptance and affiliation, and changes in teacher attitude.

Tables 10-3 and 10-4 provide a schematic interpretation of what specific scales load on the factor scores. These are reported on the left side of each subset figure of the table. On the right side of each are reported other variables that are associated with this factor as drawn from research with another alternative system.

A word of explanation should be provided relative to the components on the right side. One of the most convincing validation sources for a system such as the BCAS is comparison with another similar system. In 1976 Bennett in England collected data on a number of children. He used achievement tests, the *Junior Eysenck Personality Inventory* (Eysenck, 1965), self-report data, teacher ratings, and a sociometric device. In the sociometric measure, Bennett asked students to nominate those peers who were most like or least like a series of descriptions of behavioral stereotypes (e.g., "the children that I most often work with"). From all these data, Bennett identified eight cluster types which show a considerable degree of construct convergence with the BCAS types (Bennett, 1976).

Given the similarity between measures and groups, the results of the two systems were compared using rho correlations of rank. There were many significant correlations (the full tabular accounts of these are reported in the Manual, Barclay, 1983a, pp. 94–95). The similarities between types of students identified, similar personality factors in the two systems, and mean gains in achievement, provide a unique kind of construct validity and evidence for the generalizability of temperament characteristics as the essential ingredients of descriptive categories across culture and measures (Bennett, 1976).[3]

The examination of the overall typology and hierarchical structure of the BCAS provides ample evidence that the core ingredients of the system relate to temperament. The second-order factors of energy-activity and sociability are similar to those identified by Strelau (1986) and are discussed at length in the chapter on temperament.

A second source of evidence that sociometrics have a direct relationship to temperament characteristics is found in two preliminary studies. The origin of these studies came from the result of a search to find any other set of indices that would correlate strongly with sociometric data. Certainly one of the obvious constraints with the use of the BCAS is that all children in a given classroom must be tested to obtain scores from the sociometric portion of the system. Research from the manual indicates that the sociometric component of the BCAS provides a hefty portion of the variance accounted for by the total instrument. To dismiss this portion of the system would severely limit the diagnostic characteristics of the system. But to retain it means that all children in a class need to be tested—even if concern is only over one or two.

Although previous research (Gronlund, 1959; Barclay 1983a) confirms that general sociometric indices are related to a host of other variables at a low magnitude (including intelligence, achievement, and social status), a plausible research question is this: do sociometric indices show appropriate relationships to measures of temperament? To explore this question, BCAS scores were correlated with some measures of excitation, inhibition, and mobility derived from Strelau's temperament inventory (Strelau, 1983). In Strelau's inventory excitation reflects a major component of the nervous system which is characterized by the level of energy and activity manifested by the individual. Inhibition reflects the extent to which the nervous system restricts the flow of energy and activity, and mobility indicates the ability to shift from one activity to another. In addition, it is possible to obtain a ratio of excitation to inhibition by dividing the former by the latter (E/I). A high ratio score 1.25 suggests a much stronger excitation tendency than inhibition whereas a score of .75 suggests emotional characteristics dominated by inhibition.

In one study the *Strelau Temperament Inventory* and the *Barclay Classroom Assessment System* were translated into Chinese and administered to a sample of 176 fifth and eighth graders in Taiwan. The Strelau excitation scale showed significant positive correlations with self-competency skills and overall group peer nominations and was related negatively to group disruptive nominations. Mobility was observed as significantly related in a positive manner to both self-competency skills and attitude towards classroom experience. By far the most important and highest correlations were obtained using the Ratio of E/I. Correlations significant at the .01 to .002 levels were found between the ratio score of the Strelau and all major sociometric indices of the BCAS. Although this was done with a sample of Chinese children, earlier research has shown a high degree of similarity between American and Chinese students on the BCAS (Barclay & Wu, 1980). What this suggests strongly is that high sociometric scores (associated with leaders) correlate significantly with high ratio scores (1.25 and above), and low sociometric scores (associated with reticent, withdrawn or isolated individuals) tend to be associated with low ratio scores (.75 or below).

Preliminary findings of research currently under way (Doll and Barclay 1988) with some 60 elementary children in Wisconsin show similar relationships. The children were administered both the BCAS and a new child's version of temperament analysis based on the Strelau scales of excitation, inhibition, and mobility. The relationships appear sufficiently strong to provide regression equations for predicting the multitrait, multimethod factor scores of the BCAS using the derived Strelau scales.

What appears to be significant about this ongoing research is that the only substitute for sociometric inputs thus far assessed by the author is found in Strelau-type scales.

In summary, the primary and secondary factor structure of the BCAS and specific correlational relationships with temperament measures define major sociometric phenomena as part of the temperament makeup both of the observer and the observee. How friendship patterns are perceived, it would

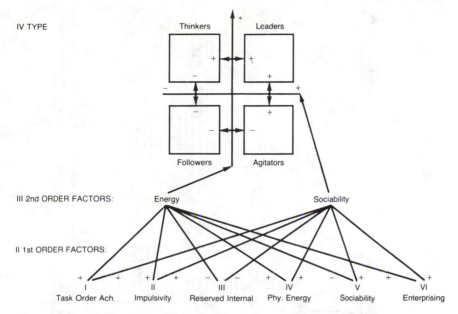

IV TYPE

Thinkers   Leaders

Followers   Agitators

III 2nd ORDER FACTORS: Energy   Sociability

II 1st ORDER FACTORS:

I	II	III	IV	V	VI
Task Order Ach.	Impulsivity	Reserved Internal	Phy. Energy	Sociability	Enterprising

Figure 10-2   **First and Second-Order Components of Temperament**

seem, is an important early skill. We learn early to assess whether people are friendly or unfriendly, predictable or unpredictable, similar to ourselves, or not. Hart (1980) explains this in terms of a universal need for affiliation. Wainwright (1980) maintains that we make those judgments based on movements, i.e., spontaneity, verbal styles, nonverbal communication, kinesthetics, the chemistry of speech production, and facial expressions. However these judgments are formed, it is clear that they do relate to energy, activity, sociability, and inhibition in ways that in temperament terminology reflect central nervous system components, and in terms of Lewininan ideas represent "valence."

Though clearly more research is needed before this proposition can be unequivocally accepted, it is highly likely that the persistent research power of sociometrics in predicting and assessing human behavior lies squarely in the fact that it represents a popular and common method for assessing temperament.

PERSISTENT PROBLEMS WITH THE USE OF SOCIOMETRICS

Although it is apparent from this review that sociometrics provides a powerful independent and supplementary source of assessment of children, and one that adds substantially to the variance in measurement received from

Table 10-3 Scale Loadings on BCAS Factor Scores I–III

Factor I

Primary and Associative Components of Factor I Task-Order Achievement as Contributors to Second-Order Factors of Energy and Sociability

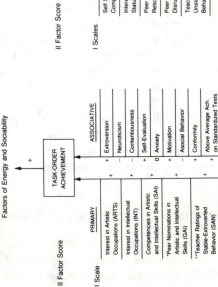

II Factor Score: TASK-ORDER ACHIEVEMENT (+)

I Scale

PRIMARY		ASSOCIATIVE	
Interest in Artistic Occupations (ARTS)	+	Extroversion	+
Interest in Intellectual Occupations (INT)	+	Neuroticism	–
Competencies in Artistic and Intellectual Skills (SAI)	+	Contentiousness	–
*Peer Nominations in Artistic and Intellectual Skills (GAI)	+	Self-Evaluation	+
**Teacher Ratings of Stable-Extroverted Behavior (SAN)	+	Anxiety	0
		Motivation	+
		Asocial Behavior	–
		Conformity	+
		Above Average Ach. on Standardized Tests	+

*Predictive of Nelson Reading Test and ITBS Scores
**Predictive of Stanford Reading Scores
NOTE: 0 = No loading or correlation: + means is associated with or has a significant loading on this factor: – sign the opposite.

Factor II

Primary and Associative Components of Factor II Impulsivity as Contributors to Both Second-Order Factors of Energy and Sociability

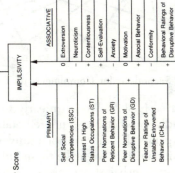

II Factor Score: IMPULSIVITY (+)

I Scales

PRIMARY		ASSOCIATIVE	
Self Social Competencies (SSC)	–	Extroversion	0
Interest in High Status Occupations (ST)	–	Neuroticism	–
Peer Nominations of Reticent Behavior (GR)	+	Contentiousness	+
Peer Nominations of Disruptive Behavior (GD)	+	Self-Evaluation	–
Teacher Ratings of Unstable-Extroverted Behavior (CHL)	+	Anxiety	+
		Motivation	0
		Asocial Behavior	+
		Conformity	–
		Behavioral Ratings of Disruptive Behavior	+

NOTE: 0 = No loading or correlation: + means is associated with or has a significant loading on this factor: – sign the opposite.

Factor III

Primary and Associative Components of Factor III Reserved-Internal As Contributors to Second-Order Factors of Sociability and Energy

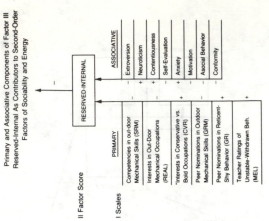

II Factor Score: RESERVED-INTERNAL (–)

I Scales

PRIMARY		ASSOCIATIVE	
Competencies in out-door Mechanical Skills (SRM)	–	Extroversion	–
Interests in Out-Door Mechanical Occupations (REAL)	–	Neuroticism	+
*Interests in Conservative vs. Bold Occupations (CVR)	+	Contentiousness	+
Peer Nominations in Outdoor Mechanical Skills (GRM)	–	Self-Evaluation	–
Peer Nominations in Reticent-Shy Behavior (GR)	+	Anxiety	+
Teacher Ratings of Unstable-Withdrawn Beh. (MEL)	+	Motivation	–
		Asocial Behavior	–
		Conformity	–

*Negatively Predictive of Stanford Arithmetic and Language Scores
NOTE: 0 = No loadings or correlations: + means is associated with or has a significant loading on this factor: – sign the opposite.

Table 10-4 Scale Loadings on BCAS Factors IV–VI

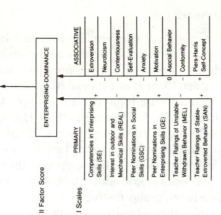

Primary and Associative Components of Factor IV Physical Activity as Contributors to Both Second-Order Factors of Energy and Sociability

II Factor Score → PHYSICAL ACTIVITY (+)

I Scales	PRIMARY		ASSOCIATIVE
	Interests in Intellectual Occupations (INT)	+	+ Extroversion
			− Neuroticism
	Interests in Social Occupations (SOC)	−	− Contentiousness
	Interests in Conventional and Clerical Occupations (CONV)	−	+ Self-Evaluation
			−− Anxiety
	Peer Nominations in Outdoor Mechanical Skills (GRM)	+	+ Motivation
			− Asocial Behavior
	Peer Nominations in Reticent-Shy Behavior (GR)	+	+ Conformity
	Peer Nominations in Disruptive Behavior (GD)	−	
	Teacher Ratings of Stable-Introverted Behavior (PHL)	+	

NOTE: 0 = No loading or correlation; + means is associated with or has a significant loading on this factor; − sign the opposite.

Primary and Associative Components of Factor V Sociability as Contributors to Second-Order Sociability and Energy Factors (1)

Energy (+) + Sociability → SOCIABILITY

II Factor Score

I Scales	PRIMARY		ASSOCIATIVE
	Competencies in Social Primary Skills (SSC)	+	+ Extroversion
			− Neuroticism
	Interests in Status Occupations (ST)	+	+ Contentiousness
	Peer Nominations in Artistic-Intellectual Skills (GAI)	+	+ Self-Evaluation
			− Anxiety
	*Peer Nominations in Social Skills (GSC)	+	+ Motivation
	Teacher Ratings of Unstable-Withdrawn Behavior (MEL)	−	− Asocial Behavior
	Teacher Ratings of Stable-Introvert Behavior (PHL)	+	+ Conformity
	**Teacher Ratings of Stable-Extroverted Behavior (SAN)	+	+ Above ave. Ach. on Standardized Tests

**Predictive of Nelson Reading and ITBS scores.

**Predictive of Stanford Reading scores.

(1) Loadings on second-order factor of Energy-Activity are reversed

NOTE: 0 = No loading or correlation; + means is associated with or has a significant loading on this factor; − sign the opposite.

Primary and Associative Components of Factor VI Enterprising-Dominance as Contributors to Both Second-Order Factors of Energy and Sociability

II Factor Score → ENTERPRISING-DOMINANCE

I Scales	PRIMARY		ASSOCIATIVE
	Competencies in Enterprising Skills (SE)	+	+ Extroversion
			− Neuroticism
	Interest in outdoor and Mechanical Skills (REAL)	−	− Contentiousness
	Peer Nominations in Social Skills (GSC)	+	+ Self-Evaluation
			− Anxiety
	Peer Nominations in Enterprising Skills (GE)	+	− Motivation
	Teacher Ratings of Unstable-Withdrawn Behavior (MEL)	−	0 Asocial Behavior
	Teacher Ratings of Stable-Extroverted Behavior (SAN)	+	− Conformity
			+ Piers-Harris Self-Concept

NOTE: 0 = No loading or correlation; + means is associated with or has a significant loading on this factor; − sign the opposite.

teacher judgments and self-report, it is equally true that it is hardly ever used in school psychology. Nonetheless, there is a resurgence of interest in sociometrics in early childhood: specifically in preschool and kindergarten age children. Not too long ago there was a special issue of the *Merrill-Palmer Quarterly* (1983, 29) devoted to the topic (see for example Coie & Dodge, 1983; Dodge, Schlundt, Schoken & Delugach, 1983; Hymel, 1983; Ladd, 1983; Rubin, & Daniels-Beirness (1983), and Cairns, 1983).

The reasons for the limited use of sociometry have been outlined earlier. These include also: (1) failure to read child development literature by school psychology researchers; (2) ethical considerations; (3) the generalized distrust of school psychologists for group testing instruments; and (4) the lack of an operational rather than theoretical priority on prevention.

Ethical issues of sociometry were never felt to be problematic in earlier decades, though most users believed that negative questions should either be very carefully worded or omitted. However, in the last few decades there has been an increase in caution for the use of personality tests with school students. Parents, society, and the law have all looked at such tests as an invasion of the rights of students and parents.

Where do sociometric phenomena fit in this issue? Specifically is the sociometric device a personality probe designed to establish pathology? Unquestionably, the response is what the specific sociometric item seeks. For the most part sociometric indices do not tap personality traits in the sense of a test inventory, but they can be used to generate relevant temperament data that relate to personality. Relative to general friendship or dislike questions, Cairns (1983) views the issue in terms of what is gained and what is lost by certain techniques. He does not believe that children should be encouraged to make up semipublic "hate lists" or "slam books" for whatever reason. But he points out that failure to use the sociometric question may deprive us of some very important information about social structure. Certainly, this view is consistent with much earlier thinking where the sociometric technique was used to determine what kind of a peer support system exists for an individual in a group setting. Cairns suggests that there is "frightfully little empirical information" on what are the effects of sociometric studies on students and teachers.

There is some information about the effects on students relative to the sociometric technique. Ratiner, Weissberg, and Caplan (1986) conducted a study of 32 sixth graders two months after an assessment battery that included a class sociometric rating scale. Each individual was interviewed about his reactions to these measures. Specifically they examined the students' reactions to the sociometric measure, the degree to which ratings were discussed among classmates, and what might have been the differential impact of sociometric testing on popular and unpopular children. Contrary to their expectations, they found few negative reactions to the sociometric ratings. "Many of the students remembered the sociometric ratings and reported that the measure was discussed afterwards. However, only 3 of the 32 subjects liked the sociometric the least of all the measures. None of these students mentioned ethical or social considerations such as the potential negative effects of giving or receiving low rating. Additionally, there were no significant differences between popular and unpopular classmates in the tendency to dislike the sociometric measure. Overall, these findings alleviate some concerns about the potentially negative effects of sociometric testing, but several clinical and research issues remain to be investigated" (Ratiner, Weissberg, & Caplan, 1986).

Barclay (1974c) amassed reactions about the feedback of information derived from the BCAS to parents and teachers. From studies done in several settings where parents viewed the computer reports of their children, many positive comments were obtained about the importance of this information. Teachers have found the reports very useful in conducting case-conferences with parents and have rated workshops on the use of the system highly.

Teacher and parent feedback suggests that sociometry can be helpful in providing relevant social information and temperament data about children. The reports that are generated from the computer analysis can avoid any negative connotations. Second, sociometric data does not directly probe into personality, but results in information that can provide insight into support system and temperament. Third, the information thus obtained is helpful in a number of ways for determining teacher, counselor, or school psychologist interventions and in consulting with parents. Finally, the essential question is: can such valuable data be obtained without sociometrics? At present it appears that sociometrics provide data of unique value and strength. Although the ethics question is not completely resolved, it does appear that if sociometric data are used without negative references, they are not identical to personality testing, and they can provide good feedback to all concerned. In short, they provide unobtrusive measures of individual functioning that have many direct applications to strategies of intervention.

A reason for the underuse of sociometric techniques is the general decline in the diagnostic use of group tests by school psychologists. Because of the emphasis on individual testing and behavioral assessment, the reservoir of group tests that are or could be used in the school setting to facilitate programmatic planning and intervention by school psychologists are often ignored. This may be because school psychologists view group tests as possessing less relevance for their work. It is more likely that they do not consider how the testing program of a district ought to be implemented into a systems approach for the early prevention of psychological problems.

To be sure, the time constraints on school psychologists make it difficult to become involved in a systems approach to the assessment of individual differences, but if such a goal is part of the school's agenda, and particularly if prevention is viewed as an important across the board goal for all children, then the use of group data as a preliminary screening vehicle is imperative. While achievement and intelligence tests are frequently administered in most schools, virtually no schools include other measures of emotional and temperament adjustment. If prevention of psychological problems is a goal of the school effort, as it should be, group tests and interpretation by computer methods are a resource that school psychologists ought to consider seriously (Barclay, 1983c).

Peer nominations are clearly one set of multiple observations that can and should be used for amassing the evidence needed for intervention strategies. Peer data furnish an analysis of the psychological support system available to a child that cannot be obtained in any other manner, and this information is vital to determining whether a child needs intervention planning. Insofar as peer nominations also relate to temperament diagnoses they represent a doubly important means for prevention as well as remediation.

This chapter has reviewed sociometry as a theory and method of measuring social relationships within a psychometric framework. The conclusions are: (1) sociometric choices covary and are related to a number of personality group measures and individually administered instruments; (2) sociometric choices are strongly related to ratings by social workers, psychologists, military personnel, industrial and educational ratings of efficiency and competence; (3) sociometric choices are moderately related to the structure of intelligence and achievement tests; (4) there are positive correlations between measures of motivation and self-concept or self-competency and to socioeconomic status; (5) sociometric choices are strongly related to behavioral observations of children in the classroom; (6) sociometric ratings taken with other assessment inputs can provide a computerized assessment of temperament with many implications for strategies of intervention; and (7) preliminary studies with temperament (as derived from sociometrics and without its use) strongly suggest that temperament is a mediating variable for planning alternative educational and curricular interventions either as a function of remedial or preventive approaches.

CHAPTER XI

Sources of Individual Differences: Brain and Environment

"Operatio sequitur Esse" (Old Scholastic Axiom)
"Function is a necessary outcome of structure."

In the previous chapters the various methods of assessing individual differences have been outlined. This chapter focuses on the sources of these individual differences, i.e., brain and environment. Though the brain and environment are critical in specifying the nature of individual differences, their interaction with learning is usually mediated and known to us through variations in cognition and motivation. This chapter will concentrate first on a clarification of the constructs of cognition and motivation. Second, the brain and human structure components will be discussed in terms of methods and instruments of assessment. Third, the influence and measurement of the environment will be outlined. Since these larger influences on specific assessment data involve changes in many dimensions simultaneously, the classification of them is more complicated and difficult. An old dictum states: "when the tide rises all boats float upwards." The converse is also true. Core components of cognition, motivation, and environmental influences act as the tide in individual differences and have an indirect but important influence on all other aspects of assessment.

Cognition and motivation are large constructs that involve many interactive components. Behind cognition is intelligence and behind motivation is arousal. Both are related to essential brain characteristics in their initial formation and hence to the mechanisms of heredity, but they are both continually modified by the effects of the environment. Because brain structure and environmental forces not only shape and modify cognition and motivation, but also are determinants of all those classification systems enumerated in the previous chapter, this chapter will outline some of the major factors that need to be addressed in attempting to understand cognition and motivation.

Cognition and motivation are the functional action terms which represent a process. Cognition is derived from the Latin verb *cognoscere* to know. Motivation is a by-product of the Latin noun *motus* motion. The process of cognition or knowing reflects intelligence, which in turn specifies characteristics of sensory apperception, and perception. Behind the process of motivation lies arousal which appears to be the major determinant to motivation. To understand either cognition or motivation it is necessary to conceptualize each as involving both biological-brain characteristics and environmental stimulation. To assess and to classify characteristics of cognition and motivation it is imperative to view them within the overall context of hereditary and environmental interactions.

COGNITION

Cognition is an action word referring to the way individuals process information. In a very real sense it is what happens between the perception of a stimulus and the response to that stimulus. Cognition provides meaning to the act of perception. Functionally, cognition is the process of encoding of perceptual data. It involves information processing, the attending activity, the acquisition of learning, and the storing of such information in both short-term and long-term memory. All of the processes of perception, memory-recall and learning represent qualitative changes which influence the act of cognition in problem solving and in the development of those critical facilities which we associate with "insight" and "creativity" (Sternberg and Salter, 1982).

Cognition deals with information processing, the quality and quantity as well as accuracy of representations in perception, and can be viewed from the perspective of learning theory, communication theory, linguistics, and human development. Some learning theorists view cognition as the end product of much learning. Others such as Piaget believe that there are structural schemata or components which systematically evolve over the course of development via assimilation and accommodation.

When cognition is subdivided into related parts there are theories about how sensory, visual, auditory and speech perception develop. In all of these considerations, the characteristic of attending-responding behavior plays an important role. In addition, the ability to recall previously learned material through short-term and long-term memory contributes to the effectiveness of cognition. Finally, the relationship of all of the above components must be clarified in order to understand the process of problem solving, the social contexts of learning, and the consequences of experience on the formation of self-competency.

Cognition implies a structure. That structure Royce (1974) defined as a multidimensional and organized subsystem of processes which subsume perceiving, thinking, and symbolizing. Central to all of these components is intelligence which acts as the great sharpener of experience, and the interpreter of the quality of perception through the conveying of meaningfulness in what is happening. In an earlier chapter we have reviewed the efforts of Binet and his colleagues to associate intelligence with sensory-motor items, the work of Galton in exploring the hereditary effects of genius, the expansion of the Binet test in the United States by Terman and Goddard, and the development of a series of subtests by Wechsler which relate intellectual performance to a normal curve distribution for scores on the total test. Over the years, the Stanford-Binet and the various Wechsler tests have remained the most popular sources of the measurement of intellectual functioning, but they are by no means the only ones used. Buros (1972) in the *Mental Measurements Yearbook* has listed over 121 tests of intelligence. This listing of Buros is indicative of another aspect of the nature of intelligence: it correlates to some extent with almost every other known measure, i.e., personality tests, spatial-motor characteristics, achievement, sociometrics, self-concept, human drawings, and projective elaborations.

What then is the relationship of intelligence to cognition? The response must be pervasive and yet elusive. There have been literally hundreds of efforts to define intelligence. Both Spearman and Thorndike alluded to the fact that intelligence was conceptualized to be what intelligence tests measure. Nor have the more sophisticated efforts to factor analyze the results of intelligence testing been that explanatory. There have been efforts to explain the major residual of intelligence by a general factor and a special factor (Spearman). There have been many factor analytic studies which altogether strongly support the multidimensionality of intelligence.

Perhaps Wechsler (1939) made the clearest definition of what intelligence is. He stated that "Intelligence is the aggregate of global capacity of the individual to act purposefully, to think rationally, and to deal effectively with his environment" (p. 3). Without doubt the fact is that we do not observe intelligence, we only observe intelligent behavior in individuals as we observe them, chiefly in the process of cognition that involves problem solving, inference making, and creative solutions to living.

From the point of view of classification, it is apparent to those familiar with testing that we classify the attributes of intelligence by a variety of verbal and performance tasks. These have included the traditional sub-areas of information, comprehension, arithmetic, similarities, and vocabulary as well as digit-symbol, picture completion, spatial relations, picture arrangement, and object assembly. However, our knowledge of evaluating specific problem-solving abilities and performance compentencies is closely related to interaction with emotional characteristics as well, and these emotional characteristics are often observed in functional approaches or reactions to the test tasks.

MOTIVATION

The term motivation is an inferred construct that is made by observers in a given set of environmental conditions and individual behaviors (de Charms, 1976). It has been considered traditionally as a key variable in the understanding and treatment of individual differences. References to the concept of motivation in a standard educational research work on teaching are notably few. There is only one reference to it in the *Second Handbook on Teaching* (Travers, 1973), and a small handful of references in the earlier handbook published a decade before (Gage, 1963).

The dearth of actual references stems from the fact that motivation is a complex variable. Generations of psychological researchers have viewed the term from alternative points of consideration. Three concepts, however, contribute to an understanding of the construct of motivation: (1) **arousal which focuses on the historically relevant development of drive times habit and organismic homeostasis** (Pavlov, 1927, Hull, 1943) and the more recent work of Bandura (1969, 1972) as referenced to modeling; (2) **achievement-motivation which has been related to success in competition relative to a standard of excellence and conditioned by internal perception** (McClelland, Atkinson, Clark & Lowell, 1953; de Charms, 1976); and (3) **expectation which has been variously defined as the perceptual focus related to the bridge between internal needs and external forces that mediates the behavior of the individual.** This construct has been variously explored by Atkinson (1964), Barclay, (1970), Rosenthal and Jacobson (1966, 1968), Mason (1972), and Brophy and Good (1974).

Motivation involves social consciousness. The review of research directions relative to the construct of motivation and its consequences indicates a sociological perspective across time. Buss (1975) suggests that the direction of psychological research is strongly channelized by social consciousness. Thus "social existence may determine social consciousness" (p. 989). This contention appears to be true for the historical evolution of research relative to motivation. The early research into motivation was exemplified by forays into neurological-physical domains and infrahuman subjects. This approach was consistent with the general Lockean and American political tradition, the social evolution theory of Spencer, and the cultural anthropology of Tyler. The early learning approach and efforts to probe the organismic continuity seemed consistent with a "pragmatic cultural climate that emphasized competition, quantitative growth, and a single standard of evaluation" (Buss, p. 994).

Arousal explanations of motivation constitute a major traditional approach to motivation. Historically, the first considerations about the concept of motivation were centered on the behavioral construct of arousal. The original focus was on neurological correlates of learning behavior, but in recent decades, though this area continues to be important in terms of neurological developments, there has also been a specific emphasis on social characteristics. Berlyne (1967) in reviewing the research with arousal, identifies some of the major conclusions thus: (1) considerable differentiation takes place relative to the effects of structure and function within the reticular activating system viz., specifiation of at least three different kinds of arousal identified as autonomic, electrocortical, and behavioral; (2) the generalized law of effect has been revised to include not only rewards operating through contingency mechanisms, but also expectancy, incentive, and positive-feedback mechanisms; and (3) the determinants of arousal are viewed in terms of psychophysical and ecological variables" (pp. 1–22).

Of particular import for the study of individual differences is the determination of components of arousal which have been identified as related to both the **speed and duration of cortical excitation and levels of inhibition.** The examination of these components of arousal have played a central role in both British and Eastern Bloc psychological research and have been considered very important to the determination of temperament. Since we shall discuss temperament and this research as related to temperament in some detail in the next chapter, suffice it to state here that a key component of arousal in motivation concerns temperament differences.

Arousal can be viewed as directly stimulated from sources both without and within the individual. Hebb's analysis of imagery (1968) suggests strongly that **imagery is a physiological correlate of sensory input, central excitation, and motor output**. Control of a voluntary nature of arousal appears to be possible. Considerable extension of the voluntary control of arousal and reinforcement is found in the works of Homme (1965), Thoresen & Mahoney (1974), and Mahoney & Thoresen (1974). These studies, plus the mounting research with biofeedback methods, demonstrate a recognition in psychological studies of the importance of cognitive structure variables in the control of arousal. **Social observation and modeling also affects arousal.** Bandura has explored the effects of observational learning and modeling relative to the motivational process. He has felt that arousal is related to observational learning wherein "observers organize response elements into newer patterns of behavior at a symbolic level on the basis of information conveyed by modeling stimuli" (1972, p. 39). Given the absence of lesions and gross structural defects in the brain, Bandura reasons that the modeling process can be explained through four stages: (1) **attention** in which the distinctiveness, affective valence, complexity, prevalence, and functional value of modeling stimuli are evaluated against the sensory capacities, arousal level, perceptual set, and past reinforcement history of the observer; (2) **retention** which includes symbolic coding, cognitive organization, symbolic and motor rehearsal; (3) **motor reproduction processes** which are specified through physical capabilities, availability of component responses, self-observation of reproductions, and accuracy of feedback; and (4) **motivational processes identified with vicarious and external reinforcement and self-reinforcement.** In summary, then, the arousal approach to motivation has progressed from a direct behavioral approach dominated by studies of the effects of external reinforcement, to a more complex interplay between imagery and arousal, examination of psychophysical correlates and recognition of the role of self-reinforcement and self-control of arousal states, and finally the effects of social modeling.

The concept of achievement-motivation focuses more on the internal executive characteristics of the organism in task pursuit. It holds more of a bridge between the act of perception itself and the understanding of the goal-centered or task-oriented behavior associated with organismic needs. The role of needs was defined by Murray (1938) and extended into studies with the *Thematic Apperception Test.* Maslow (1954) identified a hierarchy of needs that included: physiological, safety, love and belonging, esteem, self-actualization, and desire to know and understand. McClelland (1965), McClelland and Altschuler (1971) and de Charms (1976) have identified and developed approaches to working with the task-ordered behavior termed achievement-motivation. De Charms has related much of this research to a consideration of intrinsic and extrinsic control within the classroom setting, shaping the concept of achievement-motivation into a forced dichotomy of control systems.

Fundamental to the construct of achievement-motivation is the notion of an intrinsic self-rewarded consistency in task-orientation. Heckhausen (1968) in an extensive review of achievement-motivation research states: "motive arousal is an interactive product of motive and various conditions, circumstances and/or constraints of a presently given situation or setting. Secondly, motive has to be regarded as an organized system with a fairly high degree of cognitive complexity made up of generalized expectancies" (p. 104). Motivation appears to be related to coping mechanisms for dealing with (1) fear of failure, and (2) internal versus external control of reinforcement. "Fear of failure extends from the least threatening situation of working at home alone, to the most threatening one of competing with several other individuals in front of a large audience" (p. 123).

The more threatening the potential effects of embarassment or failure, the greater the risk for the individual in pursuing a task-orientation. Heckhausen believes that a number of studies with different instruments tend to substantiate the fear of failure hypothesis relative to achievement-motivation. Concerning the internal-external control of reinforcement, Heckhausen does not feel that the evidence is so clear. He does conclude that "people with low perceived responsibility for their own successes and failure are not decision optimizers who set realistic goals in the service of scrutinizing their competence and of getting correct opinion about their ability" (p. 129). Consistent with the internal-external hypothesis of control is the more recent work of de Charms (1976) in which he ascribes external control to those who feel like "pawns." He provides evidence that perceived locus of control does influence outcomes in achievement motivation.

Naturally, an inevitable question about these findings on motivation is the source of that "organized system which tends to react with consistency in human behavior." For, as Heckhausen comments, achievement-motivation is viewed not as behavior in search of an approval reinforcement, but something that is frequently **manifested for its own sake** (p. 132). Heckhausen believes with Crandall, Katkovsky and Preston (1960) that the origin of the achievement-motive is somehow developed from ontogenetically earlier motives. Very likely this early manifestation comes both from genetically inherited tendencies and from the desire to please parents. From a very early age there are some children who possess the capability of inducing their own emotional arousal and reinforcement as a consequence of behaviors surmounting certain difficulties. Summarizing a number of studies relative to socialization in the family and the development of the achievement-motive, Heckhausen concludes that task-oriented parental styles of behavior and warm emotional reinforcement for accomplishment tend to promote high achievement-motivation in their sons. This finding is not dissimilar to Baumrind's research on parenting styles and social responsibility of children in schools. She found that the authoritative family structure, rather than the *laissez faire* or authoritarian one, more positively fostered social responsiblity in school age children (Baumrind, 1971).

Ausubel (1963) has also related achievement-motivation to contexts in both the family and the school. His theory of meaningful cognitive learning argues that **the development of intrinsic motivation is partially related to the effectiveness of developing meaningful receptor learning.** Building a case for receptor learning in which the total content is presented to the learner in final form, he maintains that this approach is the predominant one used from arrival at a mature stage of development, or in Piaget's terms the keystone of the stage of formal operations. Adequacy of learning, as determined by readiness of the subsuming organism, organizer presentation, and logical meaning, is itself a prime factor in the development of subjective meaning-fulness and intrinsic motivation. Adequate teaching maintains Ausubel, is a mighty factor in continuing and reinforcing intrinsic motivation.

Expectations are described as the products of perception. Perception in this context is seen as the combined interaction of cognitive factors with emotional styles within an environmental setting. More specifically, expectations are commensurate with level and operation of intelligence, inherited and acquired levels of arousal, and accuracy of perceptual representation. Expectations provide the intermediate act of the human mind that leads to the development of constructs about the nature of reality and plans for individual behavior. Explicitly or implicitly, the message from much recent research in classroom learning appears to be centered on the importance of expectations between teachers and pupils.

Illustrative of the more popular view of expectations are the observations of Bloom and Rosenthal and Jacobson. Bloom (1968) wrote: "Each teacher begins a new term (or course) with the expectation that about a third of his students will adequately learn what he has to teach. He expects about a third of his students to fail or to just get by" (p. i). Through such expectations grounded in the school policy of grading, beliefs about poor home conditions or low I.Q., the teacher enters into a series of relationships which more or less confirm expectations.

Rosenthal and Jacobson (1966, 1968) built a case for the role of expectations in the classroom. Despite methodological flaws in their 1966 study, it is still impressive (Snow, 1969). In this study all children in three classes at each of six grade levels were administered a verbal test of intelligence. The teachers of a randomly selected group of one-fifth of the children were told that these particular children revealed themselves to be late academic bloomers and that great academic strides could be expected during the ensuing year. The following June, the same tests were readministered and the results were compared with the earlier assessment. It was found that while children in the control group gained well in I.Q., the special group made astounding gains. Brophy and Good (1974) point out, however, that the Rosenthal and Jacobson study provided product data but no process data.

A comprehensive process explanation of how expectations are generated has been enunciated by Mason (1972). Mason postulates that there are nine steps to the expectation process. The first one of these is the introduction to the teacher of specific information about the child such as race, sex, and physical appearance. This information may be nonspecific and obtained from records, verbal communication, and/or observation. The second step then is the generalization of this specific information to the character of the individual student. Here the teacher's attitudes and internal belief system come to bear on the specific information. For example, a teacher who has come to believe that lower class children, black children, or low intelligence scoring children cannot achieve well forms an appropriate generalization. The third stage is the assigning of specific traits to children based on the generalizations reached in the second stage. For example, because a child is black and not very intelligent, the teacher may expect poor mathematics and science achievement. In the fourth stage the teacher demonstrates differential expectations for the behavior and achievement of children based on expectations. In the fifth stage the child and teacher interact. The teacher behaves towards the child in accordance with his/her expectations, and the child perceives the feeling tones and reacts accordingly. In the sixth stage, the results obtained by the teacher from the child are evaluated. Most often the results confirm the set of expectations. In the seventh stage, the teacher weighs the relative significance of his/her initial impressions plus the consequences obtained. Here the teacher may either (1) give credence to the original expectations, (2) form a new set of expectations for the child, or (3) blend earlier and later perceptions. In the eighth stage the teacher then either modifies the set of expectations or intensifies them on the basis of experience. The final stage results in teacher-assigned grades or other criteria of evaluation.

Brophy and Good (1974) in an extensive review of the concept of expectation and studies relating to it indicate that, in general, expectations serve as a "self-fulfilling prophecy." Though they reference this statement primarily to teachers, there is evidence that the statement is applicable not only to school settings but to other kinds of situations. Thus for example, in the movie *One Flew over the Cuckoo's Nest*, the manner in which inmates reacted in a mental institution was a direct consequence of the way they were treated by nurses, doctors, and other attendants. In a situation like a mental institution where the "expectations" are for crazy behavior, people live up to the expectations. It was also delightful to witness a scene in the movie where a whole busload of inmates leave the institution and go to board the boat of one of the resident doctors. Here they are introduced to the attendant who watches over the boats as "Dr. Smith" or as "Dr. Jones" and they demonstrate very plausibly the expectations which are held for such professionals.

Known sources of variation in expectations are related to: (1) socioeconomic status, (2) race, (3) sex, (4) student personality, (5) physical attractiveness, (6) seating arrangements, and (7) achievement characteristics including intelligence, writing, and speech patterns (see Brophy & Good, 1974, pp. 1–30 for a full discussion of these components). Lower socioeconomic status tends to be associated with lowered intelligence and social skills (Coleman, 1966). Minority race membership often relegates children to lowered status in their own views and those of others (Clark and Clark 1947, 1955).

Socialization roles for the sexes indicate that boys are more often harshly criticized while girls are talked to in conversational terms. Boys are more likely to receive poorer grades than girls, and girls tend to have more favorable attitudes towards school (Brophy & Good, pp. 13–14). Yet by contrast, female school teachers often treat adolescent boys who are maturing ahead of their classmates with more positive expectations, particularly if they are handsome and dominant. Conversely, they watch with suspicion the adolescent girl who matures ahead of her classmates.

Expectations also interact with personality and social status. Gronlund in a review of the older sociometric literature (1959) and Barclay (1982) have provided a number of examples drawn from the literature and from research programs that overwhelmingly indicate that peer choices are influenced by expectations. Behavioral ratings of 700 children in classrooms done over a 10 day period by substitute teachers identified behaviors that could be classified as introverted, extroverted, disruptive, and attending, properties which were clearly associated with psychometric indices of peer and teacher expectations (Barclay, Santoro, Stilwell & Clark, 1972).

Personality, race, intelligence, social status, and physical attractiveness were all found to be contributing sources of expectations in teacher evaluation of students (Kehle, 1972). Kehle presented 94 teachers in an inner-city school district with a psychological report, a picture of a child (black or white, male or female) and an essay supposedly written by the child. In addition, the socioeconomic status of the child was identified by three alternative paternal occupations. Using a multivariate design, Kehle found many significant interactions. Attractiveness appeared to be a key factor in association with intelligence. Another was socioeconomic status as determined by the father's occupation. The latter finding confirmed what Barclay, Stilwell, and Barclay (1972) found in a multivariate analysis of peer ratings and teacher judgments utilizing Holland-type codes for paternal occupations (Holland, 1966a). Both peers and teachers expected less from lower socioeconomic class children than from middle and upper class children. The status (and/or presence-absence) of the father in the home was an important determinant to the psychological support system of expectations for the child found in the classroom. Even seating arrangments in classrooms reflect expectations. The brightest, most eager, and often most task-oriented children cluster in the front and center of the classroom, whereas those children with lower status tend to sit on the sides and in the back.

It is apparent from this discussion that a host of variables are involved in the formation and maintenance of expectations. All of these variables include naturalistic and subjective classification systems that individuals, perhaps in a virtually unconscious manner, covertly assimilate into their own perceptual framework. Built into the process is the paramount need to protect oneself from fearful situations. This self-protective mechanism then leads to reactive responses in social behavior or task-order achievement. Success itself often generates more success, while failure results in a tendency to withdraw from further efforts.

Attribution Theory. In recent years, largely as a result of efforts to evaluate the construct of locus of control and expectations, reasons have been advanced for interpreting the interaction between motivation and environmental conditions. This has led to a body of research focusing on attributions, which appear to be one of the major ingredients of expectations.

Attribution theory suggests that individuals ascribe causal inferences to the consequences they perceive for their behavior. Attribution theory deals with the construct of inferred causality, suggesting that individuals habitually make judgments about why they have failed or succeeded. The earlier studies in locus of control attempted to divide such attributions into either an internal responsibility for one's own behavior and success/failure, or projection of such responsibility on "luck" factors, or an external source of responsibility over which the individual had little or no control. Weiner, Frieze, Kukla, Reed, Rest, and Rosenbaum (1971) proposed a model for looking at attributions of success and failure which focused on four causal modes of thinking: (1) ability, (2) effort, (3) luck, and (4) task difficulty.

Attribution theory has advanced the idea that causal thinking is central in terms of shaping behavior. It is well known that causality is the most difficult question to respond to in assessment of individual differences and behavior (either for others or ourselves). A much clearer and accurate assessment often results from concentration on questions such as what, where, and how often. Nonetheless, it is probably accurate to state that no one makes decisions based exclusively on these base-line measures. More often than not, the subjective evaluation of what causal circumstances entered into the situation influences the course of thinking and/or behavior.

A recent emphasis of attribution theory has been on the question of achievement. Specifically, how does an individual interpret success or failure? Early in the educational experience tests are introduced. Children learn to succeed or to fail. Frieze (in McMillan, 1980) states that failure and success experiences are directly connected with the affective system. Success generates a feeling of happiness and failure one of unhappiness. These feelings are directly related then to arousal in the sense that we have discussed earlier in this chapter. But along with such arousal are the constructs of internality, externality and intentionality. **Internality refers to personal attributions of trying hard and having the ability or capacity to do the task. Externality refers to persons or events outside of the control of the individual, and intentionality refers to the extent of control or deliberate motivation behind the event.** For example, an individual who passes a test well may often ascribe his performance to a combination of internal events such as capacity and effort.

Effort itself is usually internal and intentional. Thus, if an individual thinks or knows he/she has the ability, but fails to study hard (effort), then the attribution of failure can be ascribed to that fact (although it is possible that attribution may also be made to a bad test or other factors). For example, if there was not a sufficient effort made, and the test itself was very difficult (with many peers also flunking), then the attribution might be made partially to lack of effort and partially to the difficulty of the task. However, if there was knowedge that the test maker "had it in" for the group, then external intentionality or bad faith enters into the situation and the failure can be ascribed largely to the external source.

Frieze (1980) summarizes some general principles that have been derived from attribution research. (1) "There is a general tendency for outcomes attributed to internal factors to produce stronger affective reactions than those attributed to external factors. (2) Those successes attributed to ability or effort produce more pride than those attributed to luck, the teacher, or ease of task. (3) Effort attributions (which are always internal and intentional) tend to produce especially high rewards. (4) Happiness and pride are seen as common affective reactions to any type of success although there is much less pride if the outcome is believed to be caused by other people or by luck. (5) Lack of ability attributions lead to feelings of incompetence and resignation; lack of effort is associated with guilt" (Frieze, 1980 pp. 47–48).

What appears to be emerging from the research with attribution theory is a partial explanation of how failure and success experiences are integrated into the operational motivation and goal-seeking behavior of the individual. When individuals continually fail and those failures are attributed to stable internal causes, then this leads to a sense of depression and helpless resignation (Frieze, p. 49). A cognitive dissonance exists in the individual who may believe he/she possesses the ability and effort, but cannot achieve. This could certainly explain much of what has been termed "apathy" in students or, in older professionals, "burnout."

It may also be a significant factor in the readjusting of one's goals and occupational aspirations. If one aspires to enter medical school, but cannot pass the prerequisite courses, then aspirations may be lowered to another field, and the process goes on until one finds something congruent. This is of course where environmental "press" intersects with individual aspirations and success-failure experiences. An individual in a collegiate curriculum where the environmental "press" is for memorization, strong academic performance, and precise knowledge must manifest these characteristics to be successful. Where personal and social needs for partying and fun take precedence, the consequences (even for able students) result in failure. Of course, many differences exist in the whole question of individuality and attribution theory. For example, individuals who believe their success is due more to internality reasons (such as ability and effort) tend to have a higher self-esteem (Frieze, p. 56). Sex differences appear to be present also. Men of high achievement attribute more of their success to their own effort and failure experiences to lack of effort. Women, according to Frieze, tend to underestimate their performance early on in the educational setting whereas men tend to overestimate their performance (Frieze, p. 56). Blacks tend to make more external attributions of success than do whites (Frieze, p. 59).

Obviously, individuals do discriminate between attributions of success and failure. Within subject matter differences, if one is successful in history and social studies, and poor in science and mathematics, this fact tends to promote an interest in the areas of success. With even broader connotations is the situation where an individual finds no area of success at all. It is easy to understand how he or she might reject the school system and seek to find some kind of success experiences even in deviant and illegal activities. And it is also easy to understand how such failure experiences create apathy and distaste (as well as distrust) for these culturally imposed criteria of adequate behavior. Thus when an individual has come to believe that reality factors are subjectively impossible to achieve, then the escape into the euphoria of drugs becomes a plausible alternative.

The classification and organization of motivational and cognitive components in individual behavior is one of continual interaction between dimensions and forces of the human brain and environmental influence. **Cognition and motivation mutually restrict or enhance each other. A lower level of cognitive ability tends to allow motivation factors of arousal to shape behavior into more primitive response categories, while a higher level of cognitive ability tends to amplify the range of emotive responses.** Thus complexity of cognitive abilities, reflecting intelligence, tends to partition more primitive emotional responses into more sophisticated ones, and allows for further discrimination and elaboration in the range of responses. Expectations and the achievement motive both are reflective of differences in the qualitative sophistication of cognition, and subsequent mediation of emotional levels of arousal. The consequences of behavior or performance which have been identified here in terms of attributions, are then instrumental in the further development of expectations and the achievement motive. The following figure attempts to diagram these relationships in terms of either the limitation or enhancement of cognition of such responses.

In summary, this section has discussed cognition and motivation as the functional attributes of intelligence and emotive arousal. Considerable emphasis has been placed on the derivatives of the interaction between cognition and motivation that have been described by research in terms of

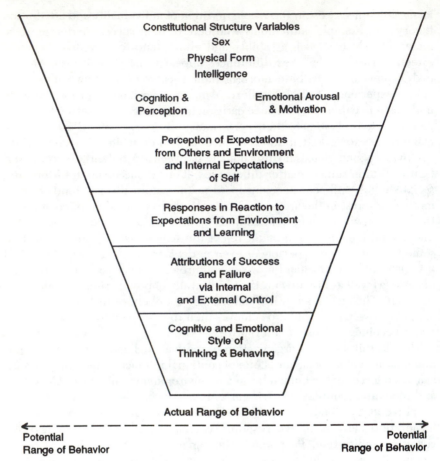

Constitutional Structure Variables

Sex

Physical Form

Intelligence

| Cognition & Perception | Emotional Arousal & Motivation |

Perception of Expectations
from Others and Environment
and Internal Expectations
of Self

Responses in Reaction to
Expectations from Environment
and Learning

Attributions of Success
and Failure
via Internal
and External Control

Cognitive and Emotional
Style of
Thinking & Behaving

Actual Range of Behavior

Potential
Range of Behavior

Potential
Range of Behavior

Figure 11-1   **Relationship between Constitutional Characteristics, Expectations and Attributions**

expectations and attribution theory. No effort has been made to identify the specific components of motivation that can be attributed to intelligence. But it is suggested here strongly that expectations and attributions in motivation are obviously conditioned by the quality of cognition. And cognition involves intelligence. Thus with higher cognitive capacity, there is more variety in the elaboration of expectations and attributions; with lower cognitive capacity there is more stereotypic expectations and less variety in attributions.

Because expectations and attributions provide fertile examples of the interplay of cognition and motivation, it is the strong opinion of the author that they provide the most direct basis for a classification of cognitive and motivational functions. **Unfortunately, there are no standardized inventories of either expectations or attributions.** However, as will be seen in a subsequent chapter, there are strong indications that attributions reflect different temperament characteristics, and thus attribution theory may provide a fertile research field for investigating the relationships between heredity and environment in specific circumstances. What appears to be reasonable is the assumption that attributions are nested in a matrix of cognitive-motivational interactions with environmental press. If research bears this out, they may be the most directly interpretable consequence of this matrix of intereactions.

SOURCES OF INDIVIDUAL DIFFERENCE: THE BRAIN

Some years ago Fenichel in writing about the relationships of organic and psychological factors wrote: "whenever a connection between an organic symptom and a mental conflict is encountered the first question must be: has the conflict produced the symptom or the symptom the conflict? No doubt there is sometimes a vicious circle of symptom and conflict perpetuating each other" (Fenichel, 1945, p. 261). Fenichel summarized the psychoanalytic literature around some of the basic theoretical contributions of Freud. Though in recent decades there has been intensive conflict between the behaviorists and the psychodynamic theorists as to whether symptoms should be treated as actual problem behaviors (behavioral opinion) or as clues in the search for underlying causal linkages (psychodynamic opinion) it is very likely that this point has tended to obscure a major contribution of Freud, i.e., the linkage between organic processes and brain chemistry on the one hand and the manifestation of mental problems on the other.

It is the purpose of this section of the chapter to advance the argument that the brain organizes reality in accordance with biochemical characteristics. These characteristics are of course influenced by environmental stimulation, but it will be argued that modes of thinking and data processing are subject to properties of the brain which are heavily determined by genetic components. The relationship between brain processes and thought-behavior patterns is not questionable. No knowledgeable theorist will deny such a relationship. Reactions between psychological problems and physical states have been documented for obesity (as a disturbance in which excessive body size becomes the expressive organ of conflict), ulcer, and colitis (as an organismic response in reaction to basic physiological needs of reception, elimination and retention), rheumatic and arthritic conditions (as a response to unconscious tendency to suppress movements), respiration problems (as a physiological response to anxiety), headaches (as a symptom of inner tension), circulatory and heart conditions (as related to the blocking of external discharges of emotions), hypertension (as related to tension between a general readiness for aggression on the one hand and a passive-receptive desire to get rid of the aggressiveness on the other hand) (Fenichel, 1945, pp. 241–261). Moreover, depression has been related to one or more biochemical, and biophysical reactions to mental grief (Beck, 1967; Flach and Draghi, 1975) and schizophrenia has been seen as an interactive illness with biochemical factors and hereditary-environmental components (Meehl, 1962). Obviously, all theorists are not willing to concede that the case is documented in all of the above categories. There seems to be a widespread agreement that brain-mental interactions occasioned by conflict in perceptual and emotional areas is a source of many psychological problems—the solutions to which may indeed be seen by manifestations of coping methods which have been learned. It would be valuable for the advancement of science if it were possible by some means to determine the exact etiology of interactions between psychological and physiological states. However, it does not appear likely that this will occur in the near future. Probably one must look to the nature of the human brain for explanations of what we can know and reasons why we have problems in understanding behavior.

The Human Brain as a Magnificent Organizer. "The brain is a conglomeration of specialized tissue whose job is to assist the organism in its quest for self-survival and self-reproduction" (Powell, 1979, p. 2). In this statement there are several concepts important for understanding the brain. First of all, by the brain is a conglomeration is meant a heterogenous grouping of specialized tissues. These tissues and neurons are governed by electrochemical excitation and possess chemical properties which aid in the transmission of impulses both to the brain (afferent) and from the brain (efferent). Second, the various groupings of brain tissue as one can identify in terms of frontal, parietal, occipital, temporal lobes, or in terms of brain stem, midbrain, and cerebral cortex, or hemispheres (right and left) have multiple functions. Though it is definitely known that certain portions of the brain are related to sensory, motor, affective, and coordination responses, it is likewise believed today that these areas are parts of functional wholes. Thus, Luria (1973) believed that not only do certain areas of the brain relate to particular basic functions, and this is crucial in the brain stem and mid-brain areas, but also that more complex processes are involved that require the integration of a number of differing components of the brain.

Luria distinguishes primary, secondary, and tertiary zones within the brain that help to explain coordinating functions. Primary zones tend to be related to specific modalities such as visual, auditory, or body sensory information. Each of these zones is composed largely of cells which respond to certain modes of stimulation, but there are other cells which tend to respond to other stimulations. These latter cells, Luria suggests, are related to what is termed cortical tone, something most likely specified by aspects of the reticular activating system located in the brain stem. Secondary zones are adjacent to the primary ones and are related to the integration of various assemblies of cells. Tertiary zones are still more remote from the primary ones, but serve as sources of integration of information across sense modalities. They generally are areas that lie at the borders of the parietal lobe (where they integrate sensory-bodily responses) with the temporal lobe (where auditory responses are integrated) and with the occipital lobe (where visual responses originate).

As we shall see later, the **brain itself can be looked at in terms of specific neurons, assemblies, systems, and higher order integrations, but many of our inferences about the actual relationships are based on indirect evidence.** We can be quite certain that the brain not only functions relative to specific areas with known cell responsibilities, but also functions in regard to higher order activities in ever widening and larger interactions. It is precisely this physiological model which we believe should be considered in relationship to psychological functioning. For even as the biological and biochemical components are drawn together in a functional relationship which appears to be contextual to feedback information, memory records, and past reinforcement, so a parallel can be drawn to psychological phenomena which appear to have some isomorphic relationship to the biochemical bases of human behavior.

The development of the frontal lobe in man and the resultant problem-solving abilities through conscious perception reflect increased responsibility for behaviors not possible through instinctual guidelines. The word conglomeration has still another meaning relevant to our discussion of the function of the brain. In higher-order mammals (apes and particularly man), the frontal lobe of the brain is quite large by comparison with the more ancient aspects of the brain. From what is known about the ontogenetic origins of mammals, a very complex chain of DNA specifies characteristics of organization, development, and behavior. But in man, the increasing complexity of the environment required the evolution of the ability to make situational decisions, and decisions which could not be referred to instinctual regulatory mechanisms alone. The brain stem and midbrain, for example, coordinate all systems relating to arousal and switch from parasympathetic reactions to sympathetic ones in the autonomic nervous system. Thus, with more complex decisions needed, the newer cerebral cortex developed to coordinate through consciousness more elaborate cognitive processes.

These further developments, however, did not abrogate the earlier brain functioning, and it is for this reason that we can refer to the brain as a conglomerate. Unlike situations in technology where we discard an older form when a newer and more effective form appears, (for example, in transportation, moving from human locomotion, to horses, to automobiles), the brain continues to employ both more primitive and higher-order functions, very often simultaneously. Thus the brain, to continue the analogy, still employs the horse and buggy mechanisms but also learns the use of the internal combustion engine.

This very fact that more primitive aspects of the brain function along with more advanced ones explains, with comparative ease, the question of why human beings with sophisticated cognitive abilities have not yet shown similar ability to channel their primitive levels of emotional arousal appropriately. The concepts of territoriality and fear of invasion appeal directly to those most primitive aspects of our brain, namely, the affective-arousal system. As a consequence, despite our advanced cognitive technology, we exist in mortal fear of universal annihilation, simply because we have not yet learned how to control the basic passions of the emotive system.

It is because of the primary nature of affect as related to arousal and survival (basically matters of biological inheritance), and the redundancy of connections within the brain, that the position stated earlier of affective priority in human thinking and behavior has been strongly postulated in this book. With this kind of priority, it is likewise evident that the brain does function with survival and self-reproduction as primary fundamental processes specified by the goals of heredity and elicited by situational components in perceived reality.

The affective system of the brain, including sensory-motor segments, is predominantly under the influence of hereditary mechanisms. The cognitive system is partially under the influence of hereditary mechanisms and the values and styles systems are predominantly under the influence of environment. In the past it has been fashionable to debate the relative influence of heredity versus environment in brain functioning. For the most part this was an argument joined chiefly to determine the amount of variance attributed to heredity and the amount to environment. For example, Jensen (1969, 1970) argued that genetic transmission accounted for 80% of the variation in I.Q. scores; Jencks (1972) stated that about 45% of such variation related to genetic components, 35% to environmental sources, and 20% to assortative mating (the notion that like individuals tend to mate and therefore provide a certain impetus to their combined genetic thrust). These estimates were based generally on overall brain functioning as directed towards the I.Q. This seems to me a rather specious argument. It is apparent that behavior is an interaction between the two, but the emphasis here is not so much on heredity as a limiting and constraining factor, but rather as a component that is less apt to change. In this line of reasoning, we are following the points of observation which Royce and Powell have made (1979), rather than earlier discussions on the matter.

Some clarification of this point may be valuable here. Walsten (1979) defined heredity thus: "Heredity is a property of an individual organism in relation to its parents and its offspring. Heritability is a property of a population of organisms. Heritability expresses the extent to which variability of some measurable characteristic of individuals comprising a population is attributable to variations in the heredities of the organisms" (p. 426). And Royce and Powell stated: "a heredity dominant factor is a primarily genetically determined dimension with a developmental curve which is highly resistant to environmental effects. It is statistically definable in terms of relatively small variations from the genotypic curve despite attempts to introduce environmental effects" (Royce & Powell, 1979, p. 16). Though both definitions overlap, it is apparent that the Royce and Powell one stresses the impermeability of those structures chiefly under the influence of heredity. Two important concepts should be mentioned at this point, that of genotype and phenotype. **Generally, genotype is the particular assembly of genes possessed by the individual, while phenotype represents the expression of individual genotypes under environmental influence.** It is thus apparent that the genotype and environment are the only two major contributors to phenotypic characteristics such as weight, motor speed, and I.Q. Thus, environment means the sum of all other components that affect the phenotypic characteristics of the individual. Royce and Powell gave the following definition: "an environment dominant factor is a dimension with a primary environmentally determined developmental curve which is relatively uninfluenced by hereditary effects. It is statistically definable in terms of a relatively large variation from the genotypic curve as a result of attempts to induce environmental effects" (Royce & Powell, 1979, p. 17). Obviously the last word on interactions between heredity and environment has not been written. But there is a good deal of research which has looked at the relationship between these components in terms of behavior, and thus more remotely in terms of brain functioning. Most of the research has had to look at *post-factum* data because it is not possible to experiment with human beings, and a great deal of it has centered on specific differences obtained in monozygotic and dyzygotic twins, and/or other family similarities. Similarities and differences can be estimated by a coefficient of heritability. (See DeFries, Kuse, and Vandenberg, 1979, for a full summary and discussion of research and methods related to this concept.)

Royce has summarized research studies relating to hereditary effects on the cognitive and affective systems. Separating four major systems within the brain, i.e., sensory-motor, cognitive, affective and values systems, Royce asserts that the hereditary effect is very strong for the sensory-motor system, and for elements of the cognitive system including verbal comprehension, spatial relations, and word fluence; moderately strong in other cognitive areas such as memorization, perceptual speed, inductive reasoning, and number factors, and weakest for such cognitive factors as associative memory, verbal fluency, and ideational dimensions.

In the affective system Royce believed that there is evidence of strong hereditary influence on 25 of the 30 factors identified with affect. The strongest evidence relates to introversion-extroversion, emotional stability, and independence, and the subareas of fearfulness, surgency, escape, territoriality, avoidance, and autonomic balance. The value system Royce feels is derived from an interaction with the three other systems and the environment and is thus quite heavily influenced by environmental opportunities.

In summary, Royce believed that the cognitive system of man is approximately 31% influenced primarily by hereditary factors, while the affective system is 83% influenced by hereditary factors. Royce's work in searching for invariant factors of various factor analytic studies was particularly noteworthy in this area simply because he distilled evidence from many different systems of statistical analysis. His estimates of heritability therefore are based on inferences drawn from the works of many other researchers. If Royce was correct on the evidence presented for the various systems of the brain, then it is evident that the primary focus in human behavior should be directed to those elements of the brain which are most determining in their influence on total behavior functioning. This places the area of most concern with the affective-emotive system. Brain functioning is related to temperament-personality characteristics of individuals as compressed in thinking and behavior.

It is obvious that brain function is related to thinking and behaving. Powell (1979) states: "if the role of the brain is to organize and if personality traits are organizations (or a product of organization) then it is inconceivable that personality is not ultimately a function of the brain" (p. 2). Again he states: "With complexity there must also come variety—more and more possible ways of organizing input mediation and output Individual differences in how effector response patterns (behaviours) are organized are linked together to form superordinate dimensions and individuals can be placed at various points along each dimension or trait. The position of any person on a trait somehow reflects the strategy he or she uses to cope, live and ultimately survive. **In other words personality traits reflect the way that individuals are organized**" (p. 2).

Brain functioning can be described in terms of four levels. One of the chief problems in relating personality dimensions to brain functioning is that the brain operates on this variety of levels. Many of these levels have no access to what we term consciousness. Actually, **consciousness may be only a higher order manifestation of brain functioning which has evolved as a response to the increasing complexity of human behavior.** Powell's (1979) four general levels of brain function are:

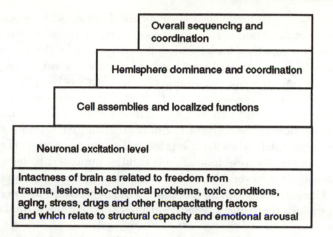

Figure 11-2   **Differential Levels of Brain Functioning**

1. The level of excitation of tissue or neuronal characteristics governed by chemical properties and cell activities.

2. The level of intactness of cell groups underlying particular psychological functions (e.g., including effects of brain lesions in different areas, or the level of activity within certain systems such as the limbic or ascending reticular system).

3. The manner in which groups of cells underlying a particular psychological function are physically distributed within and between the two cerebral hemispheres, as for example, the distribution of language functions in degrees of lateralization or nuclear grouping within one hemisphere.

4. Features of brain processing that involve higher-order processes though they may involve specific cortical areas, do not appear to be restricted to specific locations in the brain. Examples of this concept relate to levels of cortical inhibition and excitation, relationships to temperament dimensions as measured on standard personality tests, and relationships to aspects of intellectual functioning.

The four levels of brain functioning are interrelated. All levels influence to some degree the remaining levels. Thus, the chemical-electrical capacities of the neuronal assemblies are dependent on specific balances of potassium and sodium, deficits of which can occur through a variety of reasons including infection, trauma, lesions, nutritional problems, and tumors. These characteristics in turn effect the interaction between the reticular activating system (which monitors thresholds of arousal and alertness), the limbic system (dealing with emotional responses) and the frontal lobes (where higher order cognitive processes are thought to originate). In addition, the manner in which specific psychophysical systems are distributed between the two hemispheres of the brain is related to specific characteristics of motor, sensory, affective, cognitive, and social skill deployment by the organism.

The extent of interdependence between various sectors of the brain in relationship to problem-solving abilities has recently been explored by Giannitrapani (1985) who in a unique study related the results of the Wechsler Intelligence Test for children to EEG patterns of 103 children from 11–13 years old. By focusing on certain frequencies of the EEG alpha amplitude and frequencies obtained for 16 points located on various sectors of the brain, he found that specific problem-solving abilities appeared to be correlated with brain activity in several lobes and in both hemispheres in a simultaneous manner. Giannitrapani concluded that to relate specific problem-solving functions exclusively to one lobe or hemisphere of the brain is fundamentally erroneous.

The formal cause of human behavior is the action of the brain in responding to enviromental stimulation. In this statement, it is posited that the human brain is the formal cause of behavior. This is a distinction that is very important. For many years there have been those who have considered the environment the efficient cause of human behavior. **This is not really the case, for the brain can and does reject stimulation from the environment under certain circumstances that it chooses.** Rychlak (1977) has examined the thinking of scientists from the seventeenth century on relative to scientific causality and finds that the substitution of efficient for formal causality has been in effect for some centuries.

What is meant by this is simply that the brain is the ultimate decision maker. It is important to recognize that the decision-making process of the brain is influenced and elicited but not compelled (except in the obvious cases of duress and/or physiological-psychological incapacity). It is the brain that is the formal cause of behavior, formulating (often on an unconscious or preconscious level), those behaviors, moves, and strategies which somehow fit into the purposes of survival and enhancement of the organism.

It is precisely in the formal causality of brain decision making that alternate levels of arousal and inhibition exert their influence. Thus, the manner in which different individuals conceptualize their formal causal intentionality is a function closely related to the affective system, and therefore highly influenced by hereditary factors.

The fact that much of this formal causal intentionality may not be on a conscious level of self-knowledge is demonstrated by the concept of what is termed assortative mating. Assortative mating often occurs on the basis of phenotypic traits, suggesting that individuals select each other because of similarities in genetic, physiological, or psychological traits. Thiessen (1979) sees this as a kind of sociobiological perspective which obviously is being filtered through not only conscious perception but unconscious determinants (or at least determinants which seem to be partially below the threshold of consciousness). Thiessen postulates that this behavior is done implicitly to strengthen the gene commonality for offspring. There is considerable agreement between mates (particularly those who endure) relative to age, weight, ethnic status, and intelligence, somewhat on the order of correlations between .50 to .99 (Thiessen, p. 203).

The whole process appears to be done first on a broad window filter of socioeconomic, ethnic, and religious characteristics. Second there is a medium-sized window based on general intelligence, attitudes, and beliefs. And third, there is a narrow window which reveals highly specific morphological and personality traits (p. 203). Thus, assortative mating illustrates not only the implicit design of evolution on a sociobiological base, but the meaning of a formal intentionality that places the brain, both by reason of inherited and learned characteristics as the executor of behavior.

A conceptual linkage can be described as the relationship between structural capacity (organization) and interactions with environmental stimulation. This system includes in hierarchical order the concepts of stimulus-response, skill, trait, aptitude, temperament, and personality. Just as the interaction of brain operations can be hierarchically ordered in terms of functional processes, so a conceptual linkage system can be described to express a similar hierarchical level. This conceptual system involves the constructs of response, skill, trait, aptitude, temperament, and personality. Each of these constructs represents ever-widening systems of thinking and behaving.

The sequencing of these constructs is analogous to levels of brain functioning. For just as higher order brain functionings cannot take place without adequate electrochemical excitation and inhibition in nerve cells and tissues, so likewise traits and aptitudes depend on primary stimulus-response learnings which have become habituated into skills and habits. Even as deficits may be present in certain portions of the brain without seriously impairing overall functioning, so likewise certain failures to acquire needed skills may not absolutely handicap the overall functioning of the personality.

A child learns to respond to words as the first step in the sequence of verbal skills. Later the child develops a set of skills in stringing words together to make a sentence and communicate. Still later the child may develop a particular trait of verbosity becoming word facile. This trait, joined to rapid reading skills, may then constitute an aptitude for verbal-visual learning. This aptitude along with others forms a basis for a temperament style which includes rapid decision making, accuracy of reality appraisal in judgment, persistence in tasks undertaken and other aptitude characteristics. Finally, the cluster of temperament characteristics forms the basis of what we term personality.

MEASUREMENT AND CLASSIFICATION OF
BRAIN FUNCTIONING

The complexities of the brain are reflected in efforts to measure its functioning. One can distinguish between direct and indirect methods. Direct methods involve the measurement of internal rhythms such as the alpha, beta, zeta rhythms of the EEG, specific tracing of neural impulses, blood supply and blockages through arteriography (in which a radioactive substance or dye is introduced to the brain, and computerized axial tomography. The latter involves scanning sections of the brain to determine functioning of various sectors and components and has undergone rapid development in recent years.

Considerable research has been done specifically with the EEG. The EEG is an effort to measure gross synchronization of synaptic potentials and their circulation of impulses in closed self-reexciting chains. This is done by the placement of electrodes on the scalp and the recording and amplification of minute scalp electricity. Essentially, it is theorized that neuronal activity can be related to mental processes (Eccles, 1951; Nunez, 1981).

Over the past few decades many studies have attempted to relate core areas of temperament characteristics such as level of cortical excitation and inhibition, to alpha rythyms. Some of this research relates to the effort to establish a relationship between temperament dimensions and EEG. These studies have attempted to verify the contention of Eysenck (1957) that extraverts tend to have a high cortical inhibition and introverts a low cortical inhibition. According to Broadhurst and Glass (1969): "high cortical inhibition is thus equated with low activity of the reticular formation and hence with low EEG arousal and high alpha activity. Extraverts, with high cortical inhibition would be expected to show more elevated amplitude and increased prevalance of alpha activity than introverts, low in cortical inhibition" (p. 199). Representative studies on this problem (Becker-Carus, 1971; Deakin and Exley, 1979; Gale, Coles and Blaydon, 1969; Gale,Coles, Kline and Penfold, 1971; and Gale, 1983) have generally (but not always) supported Eysenck's theories. However, Gale points out (1983) in a review of some 30 studies relating the EEG to extraversion that all may be criticized (1) on the basis of comprehension of the theory underlying the studies; (2) on the definition of personality in a very unsystematic manner; (3) on the manner and methods of administration and interpretation of the EEG results; (4) on the basis of sampling and scoring vagaries; and (5) on the basis of statistical analysis. These objections, conceptual and methodological, have been admirably overcome by Giannitrapani (1985) who in a very careful study of 83 children 11–13 years old in Oak Park, Illinois, eliminated cases representing pathology, standardized administration procedures, utilized computer technology in recording alpha frequencies and amplitudes, and documented quite clearly the relationship of EEG alpha activities in certain ranges to specific measurements of intellectual functioning. This study indicates that intellectual characteristics as measured on an intelligence test of the calibre of the WISC are related to specific sets of frequencies and amplitude variations within different lobes of the brain. From his study, tentative conclusions can be made about both specific central areas involved in particular subtests, as well as the interrelationship between various lobes and hemispheres in many activities.

For the most part, however, psychological assessment has utilized indirect methods. Much of the approach to brain functioning has been stimulated by pathology. Some years ago, psychologists were willing to settle for vague indicators of "brain damage" usually derived from subtest discrepancies in individual testing, anomalies of the *Bender-Gestalt* or *Porteus Mazes*, and the use of other techniques such as the *Archimedes Spiral* (which made inferences regarding brain functioning from the absence of spiral after-effects).

To a large extent early work tended to search for the specific effects of localized lesions or problems with the effort to determine whether there was a specific area of brain malfunctioning or a generalized deterioration. Another approach has considered the principle of multiple determination. "Behavioural deficits are defined in terms of impaired test performance. But impaired test performance may be a final common pathway for expression of quite diverse types of impairment" (Kinsbourne, 1972). Walsh (1978) points out that the inferences drawn from the Digit-Symbol subtest of the *Wechsler Adult Intelligence Test* may relate to visual perceptual, oculomotor, fine manual motor or mental functions, thereby providing no ready discrimination between sources of problems.

In general psychological tests which have attempted to evaluate brain functioning have utilized the normative approach that is typical of most psychometric testing, i.e., obtain comparison data between various categories of individuals and develop norms. From such research Wechsler developed a deterioration quotient (Wechsler, 1944) in which some subtests were considered to be ones relatively impervious to cerebral impairment and others were considerably more susceptible to brain problems. These were termed the "Hold" and "Don't Hold" tests. Those that held up were: Vocabulary, Information, Picture Completion and Object Assembly. Those labeled "Don't Hold" were: Similarities, Digit Span, Digit Symbol and Block Design. According to Walsh (1978) there have been more unsatisfactory results with this index than satisfactory ones.

Other instruments for assessing brain damage or impairment are more sophisticated such as the *Halstead-Reitan Battery* (Reitan 1966). It is beyond the scope of this brief survey to discuss the merits of each of these approaches, but there is some consensus that the *Halstead-Reitan Battery* provides a reliable impairment index.

Another approach to the assessment of brain functioning was initially developed by Luria through a clinical examination of specific functions that relate to certain lobes of the brain. This was a clinical approach characterized by a successive number of sieves or branches which tended to associate difficulties with a specific region of the brain such as parietal or frontal lobes, or with one or the other hemisphere. Recently, the Luria approach has been integrated into a psychometric base by Golden, Hammeke, and Purish (1984). This battery is called the *Luria-Nebraska Neuropsychological Battery* and has been viewed as sensitive to the identification and diagnosis of specific functions such as motor, memory, receptive speech, and hemisphere origin (among many others).

Neuropsychological assessment is a specialized area of assessment which calls for considerable additional training and experience. As is evident from this brief discussion, the classification of brain functions either as they relate to cognition or motivation is a complex matter. For not only must the question of lesions, hemisphere balance, memory, and sensory-motor functions be considered, but problems associated with benign and malignant growths, impaired blood supply, aging, and effects of drugs need also to be taken into consideration. It is evident that the quality of cognition and problem solving, the interplay with emotional arousal characteristics which we observe in behavior, is strongly conditioned by an intact brain. Problems of brain functioning exacerbate all kinds of personality and social relationships.

From the brief review of the dependence of cognition and emotionality on central brain functioning, it is apparent that the human brain is a marvelously complex mechanism in which there are both specific and global functions. The primary role of cognition and emotionality in human behavior has been shown to relate to a hierarchy of cells, specific cortical areas, hemispheres, and interactions between them. The measurement of aspects of cognition and emotionality has been attempted by both direct and indirect means. Increasingly with more precision in biophysical measurement as indicated by the recent work of Ginnitrapani (1985), assessment research may be able to establish more firmly the connections between psychometrically derived characteristics and central cortical functioning.

THE ENVIRONMENTAL "PRESS"

The concept of environmental "press" refers to the total of environmental and cultural factors which come to bear upon the shaping and molding of individual behavior in a given setting. It includes not only a process whereby certain behavioral responses are learned and assimilated, but also a process of discrimination based on learned responses and anticipated responses within a given environmental setting. For example, children learn how to behave in relationship to aggression. Sometimes fathers suggest they fight; other times they are taught to arbitrate their differences. As they grow older, they learn to filter out the various stimuli in a situation and adjust to them by what they judge to be an appropriate response.

Socialization and Cultural Patterning. The effects of socialization lead to massive differences in attitude, cognitive efforts, and emotional manifestation. Unquestionably the entire process of socialization has a tremendous and lasting influence on the development of individual differences. Cultures differ in many subtle ways in the manner that they socialize infants. In Western societies like the United States there is much emphasis on the nuclear family, where a child is usually raised by a mother and father. In Eastern societies on the other hand, such as China, there is great emphasis on the extended family, with a child not belonging so much to the nuclear family, but being a part of a larger familial group that includes grandparents, uncles, aunts, etc. In Western society, great emphasis is placed on independence training, while in Eastern societies there is great emphasis placed on the subordination of the individual to the group.

Historically, factors in our environment have given rise to many of these procedures of socialization. For example, in the United States the impact of the frontier, the kinds of people who came here to a wilderness setting that was often isolated and dangerous, the movements of people from East to West, the largeness of the country, and the need for small families to be independent and provide for themselves is in marked contrast to the Eastern society of China where families have lived in the same area and under the same cultural rubrics for two thousand years or more. All of this shows in the transmission of the culture. Even from very early infancy, the socialization process differs markedly. American parents generally attempt to convince their children to show control of toilet functions by a verbal process, but Chinese mothers condition their infants by placing them in appropriate positions for voiding and simultaneously whistling. Chinese infants will sit quietly in small, wheeled playpens adjacent to their parents' shop on the street for hours without venturing from these containers or even crying. American infants would not tolerate such confinement. In the schools, Chinese students are taught to conform to group expectations. The greatest source of punishment is to be "shamed" by teachers and made to stand at their seat for their failure to recite correctly. In American society, some of this attitude is present, but the peer group generally acts at variance with educational authority, rather than in conformity with it. In all cultures, however, our earliest mental reactions are not verbalized, but we feel a wide range of emotions before we can think. This emotional aspect of our personality is formed very early and continues to develop throughout our life. Our earliest shaping of behaviors comes from the affection or lack of affection which our parents and particularly mothers have for us. The tender episodes of nursing, cradling, fondling and singing to the child convey a sense of security and well being to the child and aid in the development of both cognitive and social responses. On the contrary, children also learn to react to anxiety, implicit or explicit rejection, hostility and inconsistency of treatment. All of this treatment is a direct consequence of the programming effects of the environment. Attitudes, emotions, and feelings are derived from the shaping effect which is continually going on around us and to us. We are, in a very real sense, what our parents and society make us. To paraphrase the statement of a popular anonymous poem, "if a child lives with criticism, he learns how to condemn others. If he lives with tolerance, he learns how to be tolerant; if he lives with fairness, he learns what justice is; and if people like him, he learns to like others."

The cultural transmission also results in differential patterns of socialization for males and females. Certainly there are many known differences between males and females. A few of these refer to biological characteristics (as we shall see in the next section) but the majority are related to socialization. Maccoby and Jacklin (1974) have surveyed thousands of studies, and have documented many of these differences. Concretely, the process of socializaton discriminates between the expectations which are formed for male and female infants. In Western culture for many decades, boys have been allowed to do things that girls should not. Differences in modeling, the way aggression is allowed, forbidden, or tacitly encouraged, is very discriminatory between the sexes. In other cultures, for example, that of China, great preference is given to males as against females, because females when married become actively a part of another family system. Such differences are mentioned here as a formal and intentional by-product of the socialization process.

Invariant and Variant Factors in Human Development. The terms invariant and variant refer to the degree or extent to which components in human development are subject to change. **By variant is meant modifiable,** and by **invariant is meant relatively impermeable** in structure or characteristics. Any consideration of human development and classification systems must consider what factors or components of this process are invariant, moderately variant, or highly variant. Kuo (1967) states that any attempt to understand the epigenesis of behavior must take into consideration five categories: (1) morphological factors, (2) biophysical and biochemical factors, (3) stimulating objects, (4) developmental history, and (5) environmental context. From the point of view of categorical classification, the only real invariant categories relate to morphology, but practically speaking, the effect of the cultural transmission as viewed through the quality of housing, the environmental enrichment or deprivation, the intelligence and achievement, as well as the socioeconomic status of the family, represent a set of categories which interact continually with morphological factors and learned responses. The morphological factors are important because all human development proceeds from the initial structural endowment. Moreover, because of human assortative mating, individuals of similar intelligence, socioeconomic status and achievement-learning tend to marry each other thereby reinforcing the genetic thrust.

Socioeconomic status, intelligence, achievement through education, and economic success are in part associated with the morphological factors and in part associated with the specific eliciting aspects of the cultural environment. In effect, what seems plausible is to suggest that from the almost infinite range of individual differences, there is a zone or limited range specified by hereditary factors. The impact of the eliciting environment is both to restrict that hereditary zone and to reinforce certain aspects of it through a process of positive and negative reinforcement and learning experiences.

Further clarification of Kuo's categories may be relevant for the sake of better understanding. By **morphology, Kuo is referring to basic hereditary components that specify the sequence and structural elements that relate to development.** The morphological structures of the limbs, for example, determine the mode of locomotion; the oral structure determines the modes of eating and drinking. Ultimately, we are dealing with the hereditary prototyping of development. By **biophysical and biochemical is meant the basic energy system of the body, the intactness of its structure and the concomitant level of functioning.** To a large extent this category is nested with morphology, but not completely so, since accidents or other factors (such as substance abuse or aging), can impinge on the biophysical and biochemical elements of the individual. Though not explicitly mentioned by Kuo, sex classification is another important component in the structural elements, since there is evidence that sex does alter certain biochemical elements of the body and that certain areas of the brain (e.g. Wernicke's area) reflect sex differences. For example Buffery and Gray (1972) state that lateralization of the brain is more extensive in women than men and therefore accounts for their better functioning in language tasks while men do better in spatial ones. Witelson and Pallic (1973) also found that the temporal plenum (broadly identified with Wernicke's area) was larger in female than male neonates. By **stimulation is meant not only the quality and quantity of stimulation, but the perceptory apparatus in its ability to observe, react, imitate, and rehearse behavior** (as noted by Bandura, 1972). By **developmental history**

Table 11-1 **Invariant and Variant Categories of Ontological Development According to Kuo**

Category	Description
I. Morphology (invariant)	Structural endowment, genetic combinations, theorized capacity, and genetically related intactness of neurological structure.
II. Biophysical-Biochemical (largely invariant)	Functional homeostasis of bodily processes, chemical-physical thresholds, and characteristics associated with sex. (Obviously, the ongoing processes are related to nutrition, aging, and other chemically induced and traumatic or infectuous agents, but we are viewing this component from a single observational standpoint and do not frankly know the extent to which homeostasis in individuals is dictated by genotypic components.)
III. Stimulation (variant)	The large extent of sensory stimulation with variations related to socioeconomic status, groupings etc., leading to specific gradients of arousal in the organism.
IV. Developmental History (variant)	The specific sets of environmental experiences that are characterized by "environmental press" as they have been integrated into structure variables of the brain, and can be recalled through memory processing.
V. Environmental Context (variant)	Specific contingencies of behavior and thinking as related to a specific situation.

is meant the entire sequence through time of the interaction between the invariant category of morphology and all of the other dimensions. Finally, by **environmental context is meant the entire range of situational variables relating to specific circumstances.**

The complex interaction of developmental factors is not necessarily quantitatively linear in individuals. There is no simple regression line to explain human variability in individuals. Thus, possessing an enriched neurological structure in the sense of a high-order intelligence, joined to an enriched cultural experience, and high levels of sensory stimulation does not guarantee optimum development in a given individual. In our society there is a continual effort to imply that environmental enrichment will increase the level of human functioning. Obviously it does in many cases, but not invariantly so. Cronbach and Snow put it this way: "The idea that environments and heredities can be rank ordered still confuses thought. Thus when an heredity times environment interaction is invoked, e.g. to explain differences and similarities in twins, the layman usually thinks of a ranking of heredities and a ranking of environments, whose merits combine multiplicatively as well as additively. Interaction is thus interpreted as merely the mutual reinforcing effect of two pushes in the 'good' direction. This view is more wrong than right. Genetics has established a multi-variant conception of environments and of heredities and recognizes that the ecology that benefits one genotype blocks the development of another. A similar complexity is required in thinking about social environments" (Cronbach & Snow, 1977, p. 10).

Socioeconomic Class. Socioeconomic class, intelligence, and achievement through education are the functional attributes of culture and constitute the main effects of the shaping-molding forces of family, society, and economics. Even as cultures differ in their general thrust of socialization, so within a given culture the socioeconomic level of parents and the years of formal education provide considerable impact on the individual. Families differ in their living circumstances, the availability of family enrichment factors such as books on hand, wealth, quality of vacations, recreation, music, art, and many other characteristics. These characteristics are distributed largely in accordance with the educational level of the parents and their economic success. We tend to classify such characteristics in American society by lower, middle and upper classes, though many times other groups are identified such as lower-middle, middle-middle, and upper-middle. Specifically, the socioeconomic class background and years of education have a great effect on the income of the individual. These factors also have clearly been identified with one aspect of the development of intelligence (the environmental component associated with specific learnings—see Cattell, 1946).

The interactive nature of these forces has been well illustrated by Bowes and Gintis (1973) in a monograph where they discuss these relationships in terms of income. They present a series of expectancy tables which compare two or more sets of variables in terms of possible outcomes. The data from which they draw their conclusions and tables were collected by the U.S. Census Current Population Survey in 1962 referring to Anglo males aged 25–34 from nonfarm backgrounds in the experienced labor force. These data were used in their report because whites represented then the dominant labor force and the group into which minority groups and women would have to integrate to realize the liberal ideal of equal opportunity, and hence to whose statistical associations these groups would become subject (Bowes and Gintis, 1973, P. R. 296–4). A second source of information was related to childhood and adult I.Q. from a 1966 survey of veterans by the National Opinion Research Center and the California Guidance Study.

Bowes and Gintis maintain that though I.Q., social class background, and education contribute independently to economic success, I.Q. is the least important. They define socioeconomic background as a weighted sum of parental income, father's occupational status, and father's income where the weights are chosen so as to produce the maximum multiple correlation with economic success. There are a number of significant conclusions which Bowes and Gintis obtained from their statistical data. First of all they found a direct correlation between adult I.Q. and economic success of .52. Thus in effect, I.Q. is predictive of economic success and accounts for approximately 25% of the total variance on economic success. Second, they looked at the relationship of years of schooling to economic success and found that the correlation is .63 accounting for approximately 36% of the total variance on economic success. Third, they found a correlation of .55 between social class and economic success which is almost the same as the correlation between intellectual ability and economic success. Fourth, when they looked at the differential probabilities of attaining economic success for individuals of equal adult I.Q., but differing levels of education, they concluded that the strong association between level of schooling and economic success is because economic success depends both on cognitive capacities and access to schooling. Both of these components tend to be associated with those individuals who either by personal motivation or selection gain access to higher training or education. They do not believe that cognitive skills alone are all important, but rather must include other emotive characteristics and skills that appear to be a by-product of the experience. In effect they state: "schooling affects chances of economic success predominantly by the noncognitive traits which it generates, or on the basis of which it selects individuals for higher education" (296–7).

This information ties very strongly with the discussion earlier in this chapter on the manner in which environment, through the expectations of others, and individualistic attributions of behavioral consequences by the person interact with economic success (and the reinforcement that goes with it). Other research supports these views. An unpublished study by Barclay and Soldahl (1966) found that success of vocational graduates of the Oakland, California Public Schools was directly related to their emotional and personal-responsibility characteristics. It has also been supported by the longitudinal follow-up of the effects of Head-Start programs by Lazar and Darlington (1982) from the period of 1965–1976. Lazar and Darlington reach the following conclusions: "(1) Children who attended programs were significantly more likely to meet their school's basic requirements. Controlling for family background factors and initial ability, program graduates were significantly less likely to be assigned to special education classes and less likely to be retained in grade than were controls. (2) Children who attended early childhood programs surpassed their controls on the Stanford-Binet intelligence test for several years after the program had ended. There was no evidence that the programs differentially raised the I.Q. test scores of some subgroups of children (differing on sex, initial ability, and family background). There was some indication that program graduates performed better on achievement tests than did controls. (3) In 1976, children who had attended early education programs were significantly more likely than were controls to give achievement-related reasons, i.e., positive and internal attributions, such as school or work accomplishments, for being proud of themselves. Older program graduates also rated their school performance significantly better than did controls. (4) Program participation also affected maternal attitudes toward school performance and vocational aspirations relative to those of the child" (Lazar and Darlington, 1982, abstract). In summary then, it would appear that I.Q., years of schooling, and socioeconomic class all contribute to the development of specific skills in individuals which relate to the accomplishment of economic success. The core of these skills appears to be related to years of schooling, which in turn appears not only to be joined to successful accomplishment of grades and achievements, but to a group of noncognitive skills, presumably closely related to personal attribution of success, i.e., self-worth and persistence.

THE MEASUREMENT OF ENVIRONMENTAL "PRESS"

As previously stated, environmental "press" refers to the set of expectations which characterize a given cultural setting. The concept of environmental "press" was initiated by the work of Pace and Stern (1958). They found that the learning conditions and expectations varied in the secondary school setting. Subsequently, Thistlethwaite (1959, 1960) and Holland (1958, 1959, 1966a, 1966b) found that personality dimensions were also involved relating to vocational aspirations. Barclay (1967a, 1967b) applied some of Holland's findings to the elementary and secondary school setting and found that already in the elementary school there were differential "presses" (1967a). In the secondary setting (1967b) Barclay found that the desired personality characteristics for foreign language students were quite different from those for art and music students. In point of fact students needed to adjust their own skills and abilities in a discriminatory fashion to teachers in different areas. The extent to which they were able to do this, in part, affected both the expectations of their teachers and the extent of reinforcement they received from their teachers. These findings were found to be true in a variety of other studies such as those by Walberg (1974), Anderson (1968, 1970), McIsaac (1974) and Spuck (1974). The most practical demonstrations of such techniques were made by Astin (1965) for measuring the college-university environment, and Moos (1978) for the junior high school and senior high school environments.

Astin (1965) devised an environmental assessment technique which he applied both to students and to colleges and universities. Six major characteristics of entering freshman classes were identified: Intellectualism, Estheticism, Status, Leadership, Pragmatism, and Masculinity. Astin obtained data on entering freshmen at 1,015 colleges and universities to obtain standard scores for each institution on the six freshman input factors plus some other institutional data. These results expressed as T scores made it possible to compare 5/6 of all the colleges and universities in the United States. It was apparent from looking at Astin's data that universities and colleges could be described in terms of these dimensions. Thus one institution might be very high on intellectualism and another very high on pragmatism. In addition, colleges and departments within universities could be looked at as exhibiting differential environmental presses within the institution.

Astin's studies clarified one very important consideration in the assessment of environments, i.e., the identification of a rather systematic social-affective-cognitive set of behavioral criteria (derived from expectations) relating to what constitutes effective human behavior in the collegiate or university setting. For by a process of student-faculty interactions on a variety of cognitive, social and affective dimensions, a tentative "goodness of fit" relationship could be established. Thus students within the high school could begin to make not only subject-matter choices, but the selection of institutions and programs which best fit their own personality characteristics and needs. His system provided direct help to both students and counselors (should they care to use them or learn how to use them), for a match between student characteristics and curricula within environments.

Moos (1978) has made a more limited contribution to the secondary classroom climate (limited because it is not based on national data such as Astin's). He has summarized a chain of research that he and his colleagues have done relative to the development of a profile of secondary classroom climate (1978). Utilizing a classroom environment scale that measures the social perception of students and teachers, Moos developed a cluster analysis technique on 382 junior high and senior high school classrooms. He found that control-oriented classrooms differed from innovative classrooms on a number of dimensions. The dimensions he identified were: Involvement, Affiliation, Teacher Support, Task-Orientation, Competition, Order and Organization, Rule Clarity, Teacher Control, and Innovation. He also looked at a variety of student satisfaction measures and expected grade outcomes in the various classroom setting. What appears to be lacking in Moos' system are the prescriptive suggestions as to what might be done, given the diagnostics of his classroom system.

Specific Methods of Approach to Environmental Measurement. One specific direction that has been taken with regard to the measurement of environments is that of assessing what has been called the classroom climate. Classroom climate is an aggregate term referring to the general psychological support characteristics for individuals derived from a specific learning context. One of the realities of learning in educational settings is that it most often takes place formally in groups. Analyses of the classroom climate are comparatively recent. Though teachers have somehow intuitively evaluated classroom settings for as long as education has been formalized, efforts at determining good affective and cognitively conducive environments are very recent. In fact, for much of the history of formal learning the business of cognitive transmission has been the only consideration. What is connoted by classroom climate may seem obvious at first, but it is really much more than a good physical environment. It is really an ecology in which not only are physical characteristics of the environment important, but also psychological ones of support and risk-taking.

Three approaches can be identified relative to studies with the concept of classroom climate: the **focus on incidental individual differences** wherein various psychometric, achievement, behavioral and teaching behaviors are viewed as exerting an influence on learning outcomes viz., self-concept (Wylie, 1961, 1974; Wells and Marwell, 1976), peer choices and sociometry (Gronlund, 1959; Barclay, 1966a, 1966b, 1966c, 1966d), achievement and teacher-societal characteristics (Bush, 1954; Coleman, 1966); (2) **focus on aggregate compositions** where climates are characterized on various dimensions of environmental "press" exemplified in the previously cited work of Pace & Stern (1958), Astin (1965), Moos (1978), Eash and Waxman (1983), and Gottfredson (1984); and finally (3) **focus on aptitude-treatment interactions** represented by the work of Cronbach & Snow (1977), and Barclay, (1974a, 1974b, 1983a, 1983b).

Incidental Approaches. The first approach that was made to the evaluation of the classroom climate may be termed incidental because it focused on individual differences. It is characterized by observations either via psychometric devices, behavioral methods, or some combination thereof. Many thousands of studies have been completed involving classroom settings. Typically some achievement, personality, intelligence or interest test is given to a classroom group. One or more instruments or methods may be used. The results are summarized, dichotomized, and a generalization is made to the classroom climate based on the results. The prevalence of this approach was documented by a literature search done by the author on the subject of classroom climate in 1984. Over 138 entries occurred for the year 1973 alone! These studies utilized a variety of assessment instruments, analyzed results on a continuum extending from impressions of process to multivariate statistics, and generalized findings based on two or three classrooms as well as on samples in excess of 5,000 students.

There are some notable problems associated with this approach to studies of measurement of classroom climate. First, they grossly underestimate the complexity of the ecological setting they are attempting to measure. They deal with several observational or psychometric instruments which may describe the modal pattern of individual differences, but do not approach the problem of interaction. Second, they often use instruments which are either correlated with each other or are quite susceptible to situational bias as such. For example, many studies focus on self-concept measures which are unreliable or invalid. Wylie, after extensive reviews of the topic of self-concept, states that there is a notable lack of rigorous theoretical development, and that most of the instruments should be abandoned or reworked from scratch (Wylie, 1974, p. 325). Other studies may employ process observations which are subject to high inter-observer reliability bias, and cannot be applied from one classroom setting to another. Third, a fundamental error occurs time and again in describing the classroom climate as the aggregate of individual differences found on a few instruments. This same error is perpetuated constantly by school districts as they describe achievement characteristics of schools by aggregating individuals and arriving at some mean percentile score. It is the old problem of describing oranges in terms of apples. Classroom units are themselves the unit of measurement and any generalization relative to that unit must be based on normative studies of such units. Finally, these studies seldom lead to differential prescriptions that can be utilized for instituting educational treatments and preventive interventions.

Aggregation Studies. The studies of Astin, Pace and Stern, Walberg and Moos, Eash and Waxman, and Gottfredson represent efforts to identify relevant student characteristic and environmental support factors across classroom groups. These researchers subject their inputs to a variety of statistical methods including cluster analysis, factor analysis, and multiple discriminant analysis, resulting in a typology that characterizes classroom climates and environmental presses through a kind of profile analysis. The aggregated profile appears, in most instances, to provide a sound measurement index that typifies the classroom climate in general. For example, Eash and Waxman (1983) in an instrument entitled: *Our Class and Its Work* provide eight scales to evaluate the climate through the self-report of students from grades 3–12. These scales relate to instruction, enthusiasm, feedback, instructional time, opportunity to learn, pacing, structuring coments, and task orientation. Gottfredson (1984) has developed an inventory, The Effective School Battery, that includes both a student survey and a teacher survey. For the students there are 13 scales relating to a number of relevant dimensions such as self-concept, belief in conventional rules, and school effort. Teachers fill out a survey consisting of 7 scales. This system cannot be scored by hand but must be scored by the publisher.

One of the problems with these approaches, however, relates to the question as to what to do, given a significant deviation from the entity mean. Most researchers are not interested particularly in the question of remediation and treatment, but rather in the reliability and validity of their descriptive analyses. Very likely Astin's research showed the most perceptive approach to this problem, for he provided both individual data and institutional data. Thus the individual could ascertain how his/her characteristics would fit with the environment to be considered. Given intact climates, treatments designed to change that environment may have marginal effect on some individuals and maximum effect on others. But the moot point is that no treatment will equally affect and change all individuals in a given environment.

Aptitude-Treatment Interactions. An alternative approach to the measurement of the classroom climate builds upon the research findings from these earlier studies but goes further. This is the aptitude-treatment interaction. Cronbach and Snow (1977) have made the most extensive recent review of the literature and problems associated with the aptitude-treatment interaction. The ideas behind the model are simple: identify relevant discriminating individual differences as they relate to aptitude for learning or change; then identify relevant discriminating treatments; finally match the aptitudes and treatments in a context that is sufficiently long in duration to effect results and measure the results adequately. From the interaction with personality, it is particularly relevant to studies of individual differences in classroom settings.

The aptitude-treatment model is particularly valuable in considering effects from either the environment, or personality, or interaction effects from both components. Barclay has applied this approach in a classroom setting **to infer peer-teacher support variables for individuals** (1971, 1980, 1982, 1983a, 1983b). This approach results in temperament-treatment interactions. Since we have already discussed this system, it is relevant here only to point out that Barclay utilizes measures of environmental press drawn from teacher ratings and peer evaluations to estimate characteristics of the individual in that environment rather than to estimate the classroom climate as a whole. What may be concluded from Barclay's studies is that measures of environmental support for specific individuals are valid descriptors of those individuals and can be deduced from environmental factors.

The incidental and aggregation approaches to measuring classroom climate are both somewhat faulty. In the first instance, as we have seen, there are many instruments simply picked out and applied to groups of children. Whether these instruments have any direct relationship to relevant environmental variables is often not ascertained. In the second instance, where relevant variables may have been identified, as in the instrumentations of Walberg and Moos, the findings result in a profile of classroom variables based on classroom means. These data may indeed be quite relevant and valid for classroom unit comparisons, and researchers could conclude on a distribution of such classroom units that given units are significantly below or above the mean if there were real differences obtained. The moot point

Table 11-2   **Holland's System for the Classification of Major Fields and Personality and Environmental Types**

Personality orientation	Relevant major fields	Characteristic personality and environmental type
Realistic	Engineering, forestry, physical education.	Asocial, conforming, frank, genuine, materialistic, persistent, practical, stable, thrifty, uninsightful.
Investigative	Architecture, biological sciences, mathematics, pharmacy, philosophy, physical sciences.	Analytical, curious, independent, intellectual, introspective, introverted, passive, unassuming, unpopular.
Social	Education, nursing, physical therapy, social science (general), sociology, social work, speech correction.	Friendly, helpful, idealistic, insightful, persuasive, responsible, sociable, tactful, understanding.
Conventional	Accounting, business, business education, economics, library science.	Conforming, defensive, efficient, inflexible, inhibited, obedient, orderly, persistent, practical, prudish.
Enterprising	History, hospital administration, industrial relations, political science, public administration.	Acquisitive, ambitious, dependent, domineering, energetic, impulsive, optimistic, self-confident, sociable.
Artistic	Art and music education, English, fine arts, foreign languages, literature.	Complicated, disorderly, emotional, imaginative, impractical, impulsive, independent, intuitive, nonconforming, original.

in this matter is that the data thus obtained are relevant only for comparison of similar groups. It says nothing about the individual within the environmental situation.

Barclay's rationale on the other hand approaches the question of environmental press from the point of view of the individual. By aggregating the number of peer nominations in various skill areas or deficit areas, it is possible to determine the extent of a psychological support system available to a given child in a specific environment. By asking teachers to select from an array of positive and negative adjectives those most characteristic of each child it is possible to determine indirectly what are the expectations of the teacher for each child. It does not take much sophistication to recognize that when one child receives 75 nominations from his peers that this child possesses social power in that setting. Moreover, when a child receives no positive nominations and many negative ones, it is likewise possible to conclude that this child has a lack of a support system. Likewise, with teachers, when a teacher checks fifteen positive adjectives regarding one child, and ten negative adjectives about another, it is entirely possible to deduce that she does not favor the second over the first. When these two sources of evaluation are placed together, they provide a direct input into assessment of the individual which is drawn from the classroom environment.

By utilizing peer and teacher inputs as direct indicators of environmental press it is possible to obtain a valid indicator of what the expectations are for individuals within that specific environment and obtain relevant diagnostic information for making suggestions for psychological interventions. When a child has a lack of positive peer support and much negative attribution is identified, a logical recommendation is to devise some method of increasing this child's support system from peers. If the same negative findings are found from the teacher ratings, there is ample reason for meeting with the teacher and discussing ways and means of increasing teacher support and positive expectations.

In summary, a logical critique exists both of those systems which attempt to evaluate classroom climates by any combination of available tests, and of those which aggregate relevant variables, but simply classify a given class on the basis of its means. Such approaches have very little utility since they simply provide a class profile and do not suggest how changes might come about. The summing up of individual attitudes towards a teacher or a subject matter does not reflect individual differences. In all candor, there is no such thing as a classroom climate. There are attitudes of maybe thirty children towards each other, towards the tasks they engage in, and towards the teacher who organizes and either rewards or punishes them. To use environmental variables meaningfully with relevance towards remediation and intervention, one must look at the individuals in the environment, not the results of all individuals summarized across variables.

THE MEASUREMENT OF ADULT ENVIRONMENTAL PRESS

Explorations into the psychology of career choice have identified a series of dimensions which are related to basic personality characteristics. Many of the same kinds of processes that have been described for the classroom climate have been applied to adult environmental components. One popular approach has grown out of the work that has been done with vocational assessment and classification.

Vocational assessment was one of the first major thrusts of the counseling movement. Extensive accounts of the historical development of the vocational assessment movement have been written by Strong (1943), Darley and Hagenah (1955), Crites (1969), Campbell (1971), and Holland (1966a, 1966b, 1971). In general the approaches to the measurement of career needs and assessment is done via interest inventories and the classification of those interests into a system. Some of the notable inventories which have been developed are the *Strong-Campbell Vocational Interest Blank, the Kuder Preference Record, and the Holland Vocational Preference Inventory*. Such a volume of research has been published on all of these instruments that one cannot doubt either the value of the systems or the research associated with them.

There have been problems, however, relating to the question of how classification should be done. Roe (1956) compared the results of her own classification system to the previous work (and factor analyses) of Vernon, Thurstone, Darley, Strong, Kuder, and Guilford. She believed that the systems devised by these various researchers could be classified under eight major organizers: (1) service occupations which were concerned with social service, people-oriented and gregarious in nature; (2) business contacts which were similar but related also to persuasive and enterprising approaches; (3) organization interests with an administrative and clerical focus; (4) technology which was identified with science, and thing-oriented tasks rather than people-oriented ones; (5) outdoor which focused on occupations and interests of an outside nature; (6) science which was similar to technology; (7) general culture which was more language, verbal and literary minded, and finally (8) arts and entertainment which focused on aesthetic expression, musical, and language display (Roe, 1956, p. 148).

John Holland (1966b) in a number of studies with the Vocational Preference Inventory has developed a classification system which appears to be most parsimonious in its factor analytic structure and appears to have a more generalized application to personality theory. The Holland classification system (Holland, Viernstein, Kuo, Karheit, & Blum, 1970) identifies six main categories: Realistic, Investigative, Artistic, Social, Enterprising, and Conventional.

Holland's basic theory classifies the primary interests of an individual in relationship to the frequency of occupations chosen or interested in, as indicated in his inventory. **The realistic category relates to outdoor and mechanical skills** with a high degree of technical competency associated with this choice. **The investigative (sometimes also referred to as intellectual) category tends to be associated with intellectual and scientific interests** and is often also associated with considerable emphasis on internality and interest in ideas. **The artistic classification is related to the performing arts such as music, sculpture, art, drama and the like. The conventional category is often associated with clerical jobs, attention to detail,** and is often found in both secretarial and accounting skills. **The social category is generally an** extroverted one relating to human services and performance in the arena of social relationships. Thus elementary teaching and counseling are seen as typical examples of primary interests associated with this area. **The enterprising category has to do with jobs that offer leadership potential and domination over other people.** Law, the role of judges, military leadership, and administration seem to be closely allied with this classification.

Basically, Holland theorizes and demonstrates from research a close relationship between personality and vocational choice. Individuals go through a process of attempting to match their own interests and characteristics with those occupations which appear to meet their needs. Thus in vocational assessment and counseling, one major task is to determine the characteristics of individuals, along with their goals and personal competencies. By examining personal characteristics and the expectations of various job fields, an individual can begin to make a "goodness of fit" judgment that can guide higher education or technical education thrusts.

Without a doubt, the environment of the home and the entire socialization process help to facilitate this process of vocational selection in junior high school or senior high school. As mentioned earlier, the environmental press of colleges and universities is such that students can match their own goals and needs in vocational areas to schools in higher education that are consonant with these needs (Astin, 1965).

What is perhaps more important beyond the personal classification system of vocational interests is that environments do exert a series of expectations on those who live in them. Thus, even in the college and university setting, it is very clear that the expectations held in the study of chemistry may be quite different from those held in the study of art. Professors who teach chemistry are often enamored with ideas and have been selected by their colleagues as individuals congruent with a specific thrust of teaching and research which focuses on the assimilation and memorization of elements, formulae, etc. Professors in art, chosen by their colleagues because they are also congruent with that thrust may be quite different in personality and demands on students.

What exists in the university also exists in the home, the school, and in the occupational market. For Holland's general theory is related to the concept that individuals because of their personality and their characteristics in relating to the several major environments of their life develop a set of skills and competencies, together with value preferences, that impel them towards specific vocational goals. To be sure hereditary factors are involved which are buried within academic and socioeconomic index factors of parent-child relationships. Thus in a large scale study of 127,125 students entering 248 four-year colleges, Werts and Watley (1970) found that these college students tended to be outstanding in areas of their fathers' occupational skills.

Thus the sons of scientists tend to win science contests. Moreover, Nichols and Bilbro (1966) in comparing 498 identical and 319 fraternal twins on the California Psychological Inventory and Holland's Vocational Preference Inventory, found that identical twins were more similar on virtually all measures than were fraternals.

The origins of such preferences appear to be in the elementary school and are focused in the secondary school. Barclay, (1967a, 1967b) found that preferences of a Holland nature existed in the elementary school setting and could be used as a vehicle for the development of social skills (1967a). Moreover, in an extensive study of the Oakland Public Schools (Oakland, California) it was found that teachers in specific fields such as foreign languages, science, and mathematics expressed a preference for students who were congruent with the basic expectations of that field. Moreover the field thrust itself was closely identified with university fields in the same area (1967b).

Vocational classification categories can also be used to describe the major expectations and limitations of occupations. What is applied to individuals in this matter is also related to the fields of occupations themselves. Skills required in commercial businesses and banking may not be the same ones required in becoming a forestry service expert. Order, competency, and business acumen may be required in certain companies such as IBM, but not so required in others. Thus occupations exert a series of expectations on individuals. In some businesses, dressing neatly in three piece suits is a requirement for executives. In others it is not. The requirements are generally delivered in the form of a set of specific expectations. Individuals who work and live in that setting are expected to meet the established requirements. The process of determining both what are the requirements of the job situation and whether the individual can live up to them—and be happy and satisfied in meeting human needs—is a big developmental task for maturing.

PERFORMANCE EVALUATION

Many modern approaches to environmental assessment and change employ management by performance objectives. By far the most popular approach to the evaluation of organizational and business climates is what has been termed management by objectives. This approach focuses on identifying the needs of a business or company, surveying attitudes of workers and management towards these needs, and then establishing them as a set of objectives. In this modern effort to identify the elements of a successful business or operation, many techniques are available. The techniques generally fall under the category of performance evaluation, and there are many evaluation models which can be related to this task. Perhaps the most common one is a performance discrepancy model which involves identifying the goals and objectives of a group (or several groups), reducing these objectives to performance statements, and then determining how individuals within the organization meet these objectives. An interesting and promising example of this approach in personnel selection has been developed by Krug (1984) in the *Adult Personality Inventory*. In this instrument, a set of criteria can be developed by a group in business to select applicants. If the business group is looking for an aggressive sales manager, it can identify the traits it is looking for and applicants can be screened against these criteria. The process is done completely by means of microcomputer analysis. Currently, Barclay and Krug are using this technique with the University of Kentucky medical school to identify the characteristics of medical students most related to surgery, psychiatry, pathology, etc.

The process of doing this ideally involves all levels of management as well as those working in the organization. Typically a set of performance goals is identified, attitudes towards them, and perhaps management policies in implementing them are collected, and a discussion or exchange technique is used to define the characteristics desired. In addition, personality characteristics can be identified for individuals who serve in key positions. Other factors such as the amount of stress generated from a position, or methods of providing systematic relaxation and exercise, are also examined. Thus environmental press has become a very real goal of assessment in every segment of our society. The popularity of these procedures can be illustrated from manuals published listing hundreds of firms which specialize in all kinds of evaluation and training programs (see for example, *The Trainer's Resource A Comprehensive Guide to Packaged Training Programs*, Amherst, Massachusetts. Developmental Press, 1981 which describes 322 such programs developed around 13 major areas such as sales training skills, management development skills and competencies, supervisory skills, communication skills, etc.).

SUMMARY AND CRITIQUE

In this chapter the focus has been on some key variables that are highly complex in their nature. We have identified the two major ones to be cognition and motivation. Each of these functional modes of performance is based on hereditary factors of intelligence and emotional arousal. Cognition and motivation interact with each other and with the environmental "press" over a continuing period of time which covers the developmental life-span. Expectations drawn from specific circumstances lead to attributions of success and failure which appear to be the most concrete integrative outcomes of individual differences and environmental press. Efforts to evaluate individual differences within environmental settings have led to the development of methods of evaluating environments.

The application of assessment to both brain functioning and environmental settings leads to complex generalizations about individuals. The matter of vocational appraisal is an excellent example of the complexity of assessment at the highest level. Far from being able to categorize an individual simply by comparison of his or her vocational similarity to target criterion groups, it is apparent that vocational assessment includes a host of embedded cognitive, motivational, personality and environmental factors. Vocational assessment then is a good example of higher-order inferences drawn from assessment data. In this chapter the major by-products related to the complexity of hereditary-environmental interactions have been summarized. Assessment in the past did not take into consideration the direct focal pressures which environments placed on individuals who live in them. As a result, though such presses were indeed recognized informally, there was little effort to assess their impact in a direct or indirect manner. Both cognition and motivation are key factors in human task orientation. Environments, in schools or in businesses, play an important role in providing the systematic psychological and social support system for individuals living in them. They thus have an indispensable role both in the assessment of human needs and goals, and in the happiness or sadness which comes from living in a specific environment. Not the least important factor in all of this is the fact that today microcomputers of all kinds can provide a listing of objectives either for school or business, and can organize assessment data and analyze progress towards such objectives. This development obviously indicates the direction of the future.

CHAPTER XII

Classification

"Classification is a contrivance for the best possible ordering of the ideas of objects in our minds; for causing the ideas to accompany or succeed one another in such a way as shall give us the greatest command over our knowledge earlier acquired and lead most directly to the acquisition of more " John Stuart Mill

This chapter will discuss one of the most difficult topics in assessment, i.e., classification of psychological phenomena. It is difficult because it deals with the problems of integrating alternate assessment inputs. Classification is described as a means of ordering the content of assessment into discrete areas. This chapter will discuss the methods and criteria used in classifying a variety of psychological phenomena, including observation, empirical methods, psychometrics, and specific other approaches such as for mental illness.

INTRODUCTION

In the previous chapters attention has been focused on the methods of assessment. Empirical observations and psychometric methods have been discussed. In this chapter the focus will be on the content of assessment. Specifically, there are two questions: (1) how can assessment data be classified according to various methods, and (2) what are the criteria used in each of these methods? This leads to another question: how can we integrate multiple sources of assessment data?

Classification is the second function of diagnosis. In the first chapter of this book the role of diagnosis was discussed as it relates to decision making. A model was provided which consisted first of identification, then integration, third, inference, and fourth, implementation. In the first chapter it was also indicated that no matter how assessment phenomena were identified, a truly crucial question was to determine how they were classified.

309

The reasons for this relate to goals of assessment itself. Assessment is used for a variety of reasons other than description of characteristics. **The major motives for assessment are to improve placement, formative evaluation, diagnostic decision making and summative evaluation.** By placement is meant the determination of whether the characteristics of an individual are congruent with a given setting, such as admission to a college or university curriculum, or advancement to a specialized group for training purposes. In addition, some assessment is concerned with formative evaluation or arriving at judgments about how well a given process or training program is proceeding. By far the most consistent use of assessment is for diagnostic decision making in terms of some specific set of problems. In this sense assessment plays an important role in modifying or identifying the specific targets of an intervention which will be most appropriate to the characteristics of the individual on the one hand, and the goals or targets desired on the other. Sometimes summative assessments are done in order to provide an overall intensive view of an individual with regard to possible future placements.

In all of these aspects of assessment a critical component is the function of classification. For it is through the classification of alternative content of assessment that one can employ the placement, formative, diagnostic or summative aspects of assessment. Classification then becomes a primary and indispensable component of assessment needed for effective integration of assessment results, as well as the selection of treatment alternatives.

THE NATURE OF CLASSIFICATION

Classification is the process of grouping the elements of assessment in a coherent and logical relational framework. The purpose of this grouping procedure is both descriptive and diagnostic. It is descriptive since it orders elements together or separately as components related to some set of criteria. It is diagnostic because assessment itself is a tool relating to intervention. Classification provides the summative differences which are applied to distinctions between individuals and/or groups. The classification of phenomena, whatever they be, is an effort at systematic understanding. This has been arrived at via the positing of linkages between sets of observations. From the origin of humankind it is evident that man has classified weather phenomena, seasons, stars, animals and human characteristics. **Classification has its origin in the construct of regularity and predictability.** Because certain events or behaviors appear to occur with regularity and therefore with predictability leads to inferences that they are part of a pattern, or are thought to be in someway connected causally. On the basis of regularity and predictability a search is made for logical elements which are similar or dissimilar. Finally, the formulation of these elements in a classification system leads to scientific testing and verification. So at the very core basis of the concept of classification is the grouping of characteristics by certain common or uncommon elements. The basis of this grouping has its foundation in regularity and predictability.

The classification of assessment phenomena relies on inferences of causal relationships between the manifestation of an assessable response and what it corresponds to. There are three categories of inferences derived from classification: logical, scientific, and intuitive.

Several important ideas are stated above. First of all, the postulate of correspondence underlies all assessment. It was noted earlier in the chapters on empirical observations and psychometric ones that the correspondence postulate is extremely important. Basically what this postulate holds is that there is a correspondence between what we observe and what is. This applies to both empirical observations and psychometric ones. Naturally, the extent to which the correspondence postulate can be held in specific sets of assessment data is dependent on the consensus of many individuals who have examined the phenomena as carefully, logically and scientifically as possible.

A second aspect of this definition is that classifications need to be verified logically, scientifically, and experimentally. This means simply that the classification system employed must be logically sound, but correspond to scientific information, and must provide results of an experimental nature which verify the classification system.

Aristotle devised a rationale for classification systems based on the identification of essences. Aristotle developed the first major rationale for classification of phenomena when he suggested that items to be categorized should be grouped by their functional properties. These included the characteristics of quantity, quality relationship, action, reaction, place, time, and situation. These properties could then be grouped by similarity and dissimilarity. Aristotle reasoned that the functioning of the properties of a person, item, etc. was a by-product of structure. **Though structure itself might not be observable, it was possible to deduce the nature of the structure from the functioning of properties.** From observations of people, things and weather, certain consistent characteristics led to inferences about how people behave, what kinds of stresses could be placed on materials, and what kind of weather might be expected. As we have seen in the discussion of Hippocrates' medical treatment, knowing how to classify physical ailments was important to treatment. Just as important to an architect is the classification of building materials by durability, strength and design features. Thus phenomena were classified by Aristotle in terms of inherent structural characteristics which he derived from continued observation of functional properties. The basic tool which Aristotle used was that of logical analysis of observational data. Aristotle's system has effected the development of science. It has been used for well over 24 centuries and is really related to the notion that classification must include categories which though they may relate to each other in certain ways (e.g., quantity, quality etc.,) are basically constituted by reason of essential characteristics.

Modern classification systems often classify both essential characteristics and hierarchical extension or generalizability of categories. This process is noted in the work of Linnaeus (the Swedish classifier of botany and zoology) in that he created a hierarchical system in such a way that groups or families of closely related species or genera had certain elements in common. Thus, the further one moves towards the major general categories of his system, the more tenuous the overall set of relationships, while at the specific end of the system there is a much more inclusive set of relationships.

A good modern example of the combination of structural elements and hierarchical development in a classification system is that for chemistry devised by the Russian chemist Mendeleyev. He arranged the chemical elements in the periodic table according to their weights and predicted (because of the regular properties and characteristics) the existence of the elements gallium, scandium and germanium before they were discovered. Here the logic is based first on the ascending order of atomic weights beginning with the lightest element hydrogen which has an atomic weight of one up to the heaviest man-made element. But in addition, Mendeleyev also saw that in this order certain characteristics appeared over and over again. Thus he grouped certain elements by families. For example, lithium, sodium, potassium, strontium, and magnesium can be grouped into a family, and so can fluorine, chlorine, bromine, and iodine into another.

The two scientific classification systems which have been outlined above meet certain basic criteria. First of all, categories in the system are logically inclusive by reason of structural properties and characteristics. Second, the categories are parsimonious in the sense that they contain only the number needed to explain the phenomena classified. Third, the categories are comprehensive in that they include all phenomena so classified. Fourth, there is a hierarchical development in the classification phenomena ranging from more general to more specific components. Fifth, the documentation of the classification system is based on experimental evidence which includes the predictability of phenomena as described in the classification system, particularly with regard to alternative treatments.

The classification of assessment procedures in psychology is far more difficult than the classification of living organisms or of chemical elements. **Nonetheless, the principles of good classification criteria apply to assessment phenomena. We seek both to infer structure itself, and to arrange our inferences in an hierarchical system.** All assessment starts with the analysis of the human body. We want to know how it works, why it works, and what it can do. In order to search out the answers to these questions we can observe it directly by looking at structural aspects of the body itself or indirectly by looking at process products which proceed from the body. Direct observation on the empirical basis leads to classification of bodily characteristics. We can describe the characteristics of fat people, thin people, and athletes. Direct observation on the physiological and biological basis (through measurement of blood pressure, brain functioning, EEGs, and brain scans, plus a host of other biological measures) provides us with a knowledge of the operating functions of systems. Indirectly, we can examine the products of communication through empirical analysis of interview data and the characteristics of responses, either to behavioral stimuli or written and spoken test stimuli, through psychometrics. From the array of direct and indirect methods, empirical and physiological-psychometric, we come to an understanding of the essential properties of human beings. From the classification of those properties we can infer the structural characteristics of individuality, and draw conclusions about the hierarchical ordering of these properties.

There are, however, some complicating factors to this scenario as sketched. First of all learning and environment continually interact with functional properties of the organism and to an extent not truly clear may alter structural components of the organism. Secondly, when assessors depart from the clearly verifiably empirical and psychometric-physiological methods of measuring functional properties of the organism into the intuitive realm of inferring causality, the results are not as clear. The reasons for this are that intuitive inferencing, whether in projective techniques or in other areas such as astrology, relies on a set of assumptions about the nature of structure that are based on theoretical tenets not always aligned with scientific thinking.

CLASSIFICATION OF BODY STRUCTURE AND FORM

Empirical assessment has often been based, at least in part, on bodily and physical characteristics. Some of the classification approaches to this form of assessment are very old. They include: (1) the classification of body build and form; (2) relationships assumed to exist between such body characteristics and ways of behaving and thinking; and (3) inferences made to cosmic forces. Bodily structure and form have been judged to be related to dispositions of personality, tendencies towards physical ailments, and conditions and type of mental disorder. In Chapter III we discussed both the Chinese system of assessment and that based on the Hippocrates-Galen model. Ancient civilizations believed that people differed in accordance with their physiological characteristics. Thus the older system of Hippocrates and

Table 12-1 The Classification of Assessment Data

Approach	Focus	System	Unit of Assessment	Criteria	Typology	Bases of Inference	Application
Empirical	Structural	Body-Build Physiology	Height/Weight Configuration Interview Data	Behavior Illness Psychiatric Classification	Ectomorphy Endomorphy Mesomorphy	Clinical (much) Statistical (some) Actuarial (some)	Idiographic (some) Nomothetic (some)
		Physiology Biochemical Biophysical [Circadian]	EKG, EEG, Various Scanning, Blood Pressure, Temperature, Other units	Diagnostic Criteria Related to Functioning	Adequate vs. Inadequate Normal vs. Pathological	Clinical (much) Statistical (much) Actuarial (much)	Idiographic (much) Nomothetic (much)
Empirical	Functional	Interview Data	Process Interaction	Cognitive Affective Verbal & Nonverbal Output	Adequate vs. Inadequate or Deficient Normal vs. Pathological	Clinical (much) Statistical (some) Actuarial (some)	Idiographic (much) Nomothetic (some)
		Behavior Analysis	Response [Performance]	Adequate vs. Inadequate	Adaptive Maladaptive Deficient	Clinical (much) Statistical (much) Actuarial (much)	Idiographic (much) Nomothetic (some)

Table 12-1 Continued

Approach	Focus	System	Unit of Assessment	Criteria	Typology	Bases of Inference	Application
Psychometric	Structural	Cognitive Emotive Personality Interests Vocational	Item, Scale Trait, Aptitude Temperament Factor	Standard Deviation Norms	Profile Dispersion & Analysis	Clinical (much) Statistical (much) Actuarial (much)	Idiographic (much) Nomothetic (much)
Psychometric	Functional	Cognitive Emotive Personality	Responses	Constructs (Norms)	Profile Dispersion	Clinical (much) Statistical (some) Actuarial (little)	Idiographic (some) Nomothetic (some)
Intuitive	Structural	Cognitive Emotive Personality Interests Vocational	Configuration of planets, houses at moment of birth	Positive and negative aspects	Positive and Negative Influences Profile Analysis	Clinical (much) Statistical (some) Actuarial (little)	Idiographic (?) Nomothetic (?)

Note: values expressed under categories of bases of inference and application are those associated with the methods of assessment and not indicative of criteria of validity.

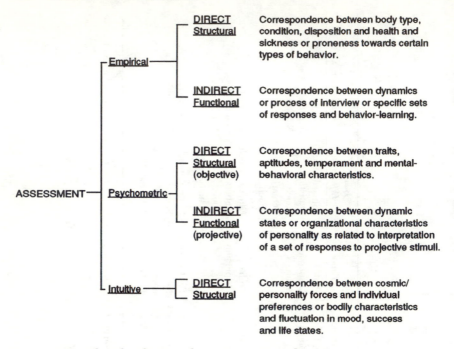

Figure 12-1   The Classification of Assessment Procedures

Galen identified a typology of individuals along two basic poles, stable-unstable behavior, and extroversion-introversion. A stable extrovert was called sanguine. Unstable extroverts were termed choleric. Stable introverts were identified as phlegmatic, and unstable introverts as melancholic.

In the medieval days, specific kinds of characteristics were associated with these types. Hock (1950, pp. 13–14) describes the fundamental character-istics of the temperaments (as derived from medieval spiritual counseling theory) thus:

> The choleric person is quickly and vehemently excited by any impres-sion made; he tends to react immediately, and impressions last a long time and easily induce new excitement. The person of sanguine tem-perament, like the choleric, is speedily and severely excited by the slightest impression, and tends to react immediately. But the impression does not last; it soon fades away. The melancholic individual is only slightly excited by any impression received; a reaction does set in at all or only after some time. But the impressions of the same kind are repeated. The phlegmatic person is only slightly excited by any impres-sion made upon him; he has scarcely any inclination to react and the impression vanishes quickly. The choleric and sanguine temperaments

are active. The melancholic and phlegmatic temperaments are passive. The choleric and sanguine show a strong tendency to action; the melancholic and phlegmatic did not.

These conclusions, summarized into a psychopathology explanation by Barta (1952), had a direct relationship to early efforts to classify psychological phenomena in the late nineteenth and early twentieth century typologies of Kraepelin. Individuals appear to be disposed towards certain kinds of mental illness as related to their temperament type. This meant that behavior was type-bound. Thus sanguine types tended towards manic behavior, cholerics towards paranoia, phlegmatics toward hebephrenic schizophrenia, and melancholics towards depressive problems. Actual physiological characteristics of individuals also formed a basis for classification. We have seen earlier (Chapter 2) that the Chinese use physiognomy as one of their methods of assessment, evaluating the size, dimensions, and bone structure of the body, and particularly the face (see Sidney L. Greenblatt in Wilson, Wilson and Greenblatt, 1979 for a contemporary discussion of this process). Similar developments occurred in the West with the development of Gall's system of phrenology. And though the bizarre aspect of phrenology was discounted, during the nineteenth century there were many interesting explorations into the nature of empirical classifications of physiognomy (see for example John Caspar Lavater's "*Essays on Physiognomy Designed to Promote the Love of Mankind*" 1855). By the last decades of the nineteenth century and the first two decades of the twentieth century, physiognomy had become a kind of applied art of assessment which relied selectively on scientific support from physiology and evolutionary theory. Some of the basic assumptions were: (1) that all form has meaning; (2) that the form of the body and particularly the face was indicative of characteristics or faculty traits of the mind; (3) that mind itself informed the entire body rather than just the brain; and (4) that there was a hierarchical evolution of the form of the bodily structure of human beings in accordance with the evolution of higher mental faculties.

Form was viewed as having an interpretative relationship to innate dispositions derived from heredity and the consequences of character development through environmental influences, learning, and faculty usage. Thus the external form of the body and particularly the head and face, though constrained initially by hereditary components and dispositions, showed continual modification that corresponded to internal character development. The body itself was seen as being coextensive with the faculty of mind and thus the properties of mind and character could be perceived directly in the face of individuals. Mind itself appeared to include not only certain innate dispositions related to racial characteristics (which were viewed from an evolutionary point as a restriction of the range of potential character development), but to reflect the consequences of learning and behavior. In short, character, strengths and weaknesses manifested themselves in constantly changing dimensions of facial components.

The complexity of such analysis was illustrated by Stanton (1920) in the publication of an encyclopedia of physiognomy. She divided the face into five regions which included: (1) domestic, moral, and social character traits (the mouth and chin); (2) artistic and literary traits (the lower nose); (3) executive characteristics (the upper nose and eyes); (4) mechanical and practical characteristics (the eyebrows); and (5) mathematical and reasoning traits (the forehead). Stanton draws at length on geology and evolutionary theory to document her approach.

> The five subdivisions of the human physiognomy illustrate the progression or development of the human body and mind as they rise from the vegetative up to the thoracic, through the muscular to the bone and brain systems. They also illustrate the geological progression of the world, also the evolution of the animal organism from the first animal organ and feature up to the perfected human face and the perfected human being. There is a wonderful beauty and harmony attending Nature's progress, and the careful student of natural laws can readily trace this coeval evolution of the several departments of Nature's domain by reference to the sciences of physiognomy, geology, and the evolution of man. . . . As evolution advanced the lower animal organism to greater development and perfection, other facial features and mental faculties were developed, and accordingly we find in the most developed races of man a perfected forehead and nose. With the perfection of these features we observe the accompanying higher faculties of Conscience, of Reason, and ability for Art, Science, and Mechanics; Conscience is exhibited most decidely by the development of the width of the bones of the chin. . . . (Stanton, 1920, 292–294)

Stanton illustrates each of the characteristics identified at length and provides pictorial illustrations of many famous people on whom she has completed physiognomic analyses. Stanton was not alone in the study of physiognomy. Her encyclopedia is filled with diagnostic inferences but virtually no support from the writings of others (except as she gleans a comment from Haeckel or Maudsley or Cicero). It goes without saying that there is not a shred of scientific research to document her diagnostic classifications. But in the beginning of the twentieth century, the new statistical techniques together with a better understanding of human development led researchers to seriously establish a linkage between some of the more salient physiological characteristics and personality types. Caesare Lombroso believed that physiognomy did manifest personality and moral characteristics in individuals and that it was possible to distinguish between criminal and law-abiding persons by an examination of their physical characteristics and particularly their faces. Degeneracy was thought to be present in ugly people with receding chins, shifty eyes, malformed bodies etc. More scientific studies began with Naccarati (1921) who found correlations of about .23 between body build characteristics and intelligence. Ernst Kretschmer then attempted to correlate psychiatric characteristics to body build and temperament.

Efforts are still continuing to follow-up on Kretschmer's work. For example, Uhr, Thomae, and Becker (1969) and Thomae (1973) report data of a longitudinal nature. Some 1,500 children born in four West German towns in 1945–1946 were examined in nine successive years and some of the follow-up research continued into the 1970s. One set of physical measures employed Kretschmer's body-type categories of leptosome, (Sheldon's ectomorph), athletic (mesomorph) and pyknic (endomorph). Those children who consistently showed poor health were found to be mostly pyknic (heavy-set) in body type. Another study by Sundqvist (1975) used Kretschmers's typology on 110 female and 86 male students with an average age of 20. Weak relationships were found between psychological characteristics of these individuals and the typology.

The most comprehensive objective and research-oriented set of studies of bodily characteristics is that related to the work of William H. Sheldon, a medical doctor who collected data on body characteristics of thousands of men and women during the 1940s and 1950s. Sheldon used a combination of photography of bodily characteristics and intensive interviewing and ratings to arrive at a classification of individuals. Essentially Sheldon believed that the type of bodily structure covaried with a number of preferences and characteristics of individuals. He did some limited actuarial studies of individuals and made inferences on clinical, psychometric and to some extent intuitive bases of assessment.

In 1954 Sheldon, Dupertuis, and McDermott published the *Atlas of Men* in which individuals could be classified according to their height and weight. They found three major types: **endomorphy** (characterized by roundness and softness of the body, central concentration of mass, predominance of abdomen over thorax, smoothing of contours, overall short neck, small bones, soft and smooth skin); **mesomorphy** (characterized by squareness and hardness of the body, rugged prominence, massive musculature with thoracic volume dominating over abdominal volume); and **ectomorphy** (characterized by linearity, fragility, delicacy of body, thin arms and legs and dry skin).

Bodily characteristics appear to be related to dispositions of personality, type of mental disorder under stress, and actuarial survival data. Sheldon over a period of years and with the assistance of many colleagues collected data on body characteristics such as height and weight, and through an interview-observation and rating technique calculated the temperament type of individuals based on this procedure. He first calculated the index of height and weight over a cube root procedure which provided a numerical code that could be located on a larger plot of characteristics. This code was also related to a rating scale of 60 characteristics. He also provided a shorter version which included 30 characteristics. Each of these characteristics was rated by a knowledgeable observer on a seven-point scale. According to Sheldon the frequencies of these ratios were based on 600 such evaluations. Sheldon grouped the ratings for endomorphs under the general heading of viscerotonia or characteristics which reflected a central gut disposition. For mesomorphs, he reasoned that their characteristics would be more related to body form and shape and thus he termed this heading as somatotonia. Finally for ectomorphs the appropriate heading was cerebrotonia which reflected the idea of brain and cerebral dominance. Thus for endomorphs the prevailing disposition was one related to the gut, for mesomorphs, it was the form of the body, and for ectomorphs it was brain.

The individual who did the assessment used observation and interview skills to rate the client on each of the traits under all three categories. A seven-point scale was used which was calculated on the basis of the following set of categories: (1) extreme antithesis to this trait; (2) the trait is weakly present; (3) the trait is distinctly present, but falls a little below the average; (4) the individual falls just about half way between the two extremes—he is slightly above the general average in the trait; (5) the trait is strong, although not outstanding; (6) the trait is very strong and conspicuous approaching the extreme; (7) extreme manifestation of the trait. Sheldon estimated that based on 600 ratings the approximate distribution of such body-trait characteristics was 4% for category 1, 15% for category 2, 29% for category 3, 29% for category 4, 15% for category 5, 6% for category 6, and 2% for category 7.

Once the ratings had been done, Sheldon stated that the cumulative score for each of the major characteristics (viscerotonia, somatonia, and cerebrotonia) could then be calculated by the translation of raw scores to numerals. Characteristics of endomorphy (viscerotonia) were based on ratings of the following characteristics: relaxation in posture and movement, love of physical comfort, slow reaction, love of eating, socialization of eating, pleasure in digestion, love of polite ceremony, sociophilia (indiscriminate amiability), greed for affection and approval, orientation to people, evenness of emotional flow, tolerance, complacency, deep sleep, the untempered characteristic, smooth easy communication of feeling, extraversion of viscerotonia, relaxation and sociophilia under alcohol, need of people when troubled, and orientation toward childhood and family relationships. Thus for example, if the total ratings of this set of traits was between 89–105, the numerical code for the individual rated would be 5.

Characteristics of mesomophy (somatotonia) were: assertiveness of posture and movement, love of physical adventure, the energetic characteristic, need and enjoyment of exercise, love of dominating, lust for power, love of risk and chance, bold directness of manner, physical courage for combat, competitive aggressiveness, psychological callousness, claustrophobia, ruthlessness, freedom from squeamishness, the unrestrained voice, Spartan indifference to pain, general noisiness, overmaturity of appearance, horizontal mental cleavage, extraversion of somatotonia, assertiveness and aggression under alcohol, need of action when troubled, orientation toward goals and activities of youth. The sum obtained on these traits could then be converted to a numerical index.

Characteristics of ectomorphy (cerebrotonia) were: restraint in posture, movement, tightness, physiological over-response, overly-fast reactions, love of privacy, mental overintensity, hyperattentionality, apprehensiveness, secretiveness of feeling, emotional restraint, self-conscious motility of eyes and face, sociophobia, inhibited social address, resistance to habit and poor routinizing, agoraphobia, unpredictability of attitude, vocal restraint and general restraint of noise, hypersensitivity to pain, poor sleep habits, chronic fatigue, youthful intent, manner and appearance, vertical mental cleavage, introversion, resistance to alcohol and to other depressent drugs, need of solitude when troubled, and orientation toward later periods of life.

On the basis of these ratings, which Sheldon admonished should be done over a period of time, a three digit code could be obtained. Thus, a 1-3-7 would represent an individual of very high ectomorphy, and a 5-5-5 might be someone like Henry VIII. A very sluggish overweight person might be coded 7-4-1. Sheldon also believed that psychiatric problems were correlated or related to somatic typology. Thus for the category 2-7-1, Sheldon believed that mental disorder, if it occurred, would be directed towards aggressive responses and disorder with manic euphorial reactions.

Sheldon's observations have not been regularly applied to many areas of psychological assessment, but one area in which they have been applied is to the area of juvenile delinquency. Sheldon and Eleanor Glueck amassed considerable evidence indicating a relationship between body type and delinquency proneness (1956). Their conclusions were based on many comparisons of delinquent (as adjudicated) and nondelinquent children. They provided evidence, chiefly by chi square analyses of frequencies of observed behavior and characteristics, that some relationship exists between the mesomorphic type and individuals who get in trouble with the law.

The Gluecks suggest that the mesomorph characteristics are probably associated with problems relating to the law because their physique provides them with traits which under pressure of unfavorable sociocultural conditions disposes them to more energetic reactions against the environment (Glueck and Glueck, 1956, p. 270) while endomorphs are less likely to manifest such reactions. Some criticisms can be voiced against the Gluecks' conclusions in terms of a total explanation of delinquency since their observations were chiefly based on bodily characteristics and frequencies of specific behaviors. However, the newer evidence relative to expectations and attribution theory was not known at the time of the Gluecks' research. The extent to which body type predisposes individuals to seek prowess in athletic or at least physical competitive activities rather than task-oriented intellectual ones might be a logical direction for further research.

Research continues with Sheldon's system. Hartl, Monnelly, and Elderkin (1982) published a 30-year follow-up of youth initially identified as delinquent with impressive actuarial evidence of the relationship of morphology to behavior. Lester (1976) explored preferences of college students for various Sheldon categories and found that many wished to be more somatotonic and less cerebrotonic. He also explored the question of whether physique and temperament differences may account for psychological disturbance, but found rather that the two dimensions were related to each other in terms of psychological problems. The Russians have also looked at the relationship of Sheldon typology along with other measures to the strength, equilibrium, and mobility of the nervous system. Belous (1968) found that elements of Sheldon's system and Eysenck's approach to temperament loaded significantly on two major characteristics of nervous system components, e.g., extroversion and introversion.

Perhaps the best summary judgment relative to the value of physique characteristics occurs in a review by Eysenck (1970) in which he examines the evidence for a relationship between physique and personality. **He concludes after reviewing a number of studies that there is a relationship of the order of .30 to .50 between ectomorphy in body build and introversion.** He also believes that the evidence supports in a general way the relationship of body build to predisposition in mental disorder. Thus the ectomorph appears to be more susceptible to neurotic problems and schizophrenic disorders while the endomorph appears to be more predisposed towards manic disorders.

In summary, body classification was developed further by Sheldon et al. to provide a tentative system which utilized both structured empirical observations, physiological measurements, and some actuarial data wherein mesomorphs were seen as militating towards aggressive disorders, ectomorphs towards schizophrenia and paranoia, and endomorphs towards withdrawal and inadequacy reactions. What Sheldon appeared to infer was that bodily formation and characteristics had a basic relationship to temperament type which Eysenck confirmed, and towards basic patterns of physical health and illness.

In this section an outline of efforts to evaluate the structural characteristics of human beings in terms of their body has been described. Throughout the ages assessment has been focused on individual bodily differences. Though Hippocrates and Galen employed bodily characteristics to classify illnesses, both mental and physical, the development of scientific thought led first to phrenology and later on to physiognomy. **Unfortunately, though physiognomy made some passing references to scientific findings, much of physiognomy tended to identify prototypic Grecian models as idealized and perfected human beings.** The tie in to evolution then led to the natural conclusion that whites were more developed than blacks or orientals because of their "superior" form. **This became a natural justification for racist thinking and was certainly behind the rationale of Nazi Germany in destroying millions of "undesirables."** On the other hand, most clinicians do recognize that judgments about personality and character are made through bodily analysis. Body build, voice, looks are all aspects of form which do influence initial and perhaps lasting expectations. The work of Sheldon was a serious attempt to utilize somatic classifications in a scientific manner. His contributions may have been vastly underestimated given the current emphasis on holistic medicine and the influence of temperament on the regulative nature of human behavior. Sheldon believed that genotypic templates shaped the phenotypic behavior of individuals. As the obvious and most central tool of intelligence and cognition, the human form was strongly influential on modes of receptivity to arousal and consequent patterns of emotionality. He amassed considerable evidence in favor of his ideas, and the Gluecks in their massive study of delinquency found confirmation for the central hypothesis of genotypic influence.

BIOCHEMICAL AND BIOLOGICAL CLASSIFICATION

By far the most utilized form of empirical assessment has been that of biochemical and biological measurements associated with the scientific method. These methods have been developed primarily in medicine and have essayed to evaluate the condition of the human body. In general all of the instruments which have been developed for measuring various states or conditions of the physiological organism are calibrated to a classification system which focuses on a range of normal responses and responses which for one reason or another are considered deficient or abnormal either in quality or quantity.

Representative of major indicators of bodily status are body temperature, pulse rate, blood pressure, brain functioning as determined by the electroencephalographic method (EEG), heart functioning as determined by the EKG procedures, and galvanic skin responses which monitor fluctuations in a constant low voltage current. Specialized tools and techniques are employed in every area of human biological assessment. In addition, a vast literature documents the relationship of biochemical factors in the maintenance of normal or abnormal behavior. Schizophrenia has been associated with dysfunction in the dopamine system, and amphetamines have been related to the development of schizophrenic-like symptoms. Fluid electrolyte balance and neuronal membrane permeability have been associated with affective disorders. Ribonucleic acid (RNA) has been associated with biochemical facilitation of long-term memory, and various protein synthesis abilities have been related to positive mental health. The effects of depressant and stimulant drugs, alcohol, smoking, and other hallucinogenic drugs have all been associated with brain system performance as well as bodily health and deterioration (Kaplan, Saddock and Freedman, 1980, *1*, 208–211).

What is more important is that these various measures and findings have been integrated by computer technology to provide comprehensive diagnostic tools. A good example of this is computerized axial tomography which depicts the condition of a portion of the brain or the body. This procedure is better in many ways than the older (and still utilized) arteriography in which radioactive isotopes were injected either into the carotid artery or through the heart. Through the integration of multiple physiological and biochemical measures, medicine has reached a high degree of specificity in terms of assessment of the bodily organism. This brief section has simply provided tribute to this scientific effort and its accomplishments. Moreover, as we shall see later on, there is a considerable amount of information relating psychological states to alteration in biochemical or biophysical factors. One other point that needs to be included briefly here is the fact that medicine also recognizes the nature of circadian rythms in human behavior. Diurnal, weekly, and monthly cycles exist in human beings which have been thoroughly noted. This has been amply documented by Kaplan, Sadock, and Freedman (1980). We shall discuss this matter further later on in this chapter.

The detailed analysis of the biochemical and biophysical characteristics of the human body provides a model of assessment practice. Medical science has made such great strides in treatment through better and more comprehensive diagnoses of the human condition. **Though the knowledge of these many techniques is rightfully the domain of medicine, from such studies psychological tools relative to biofeedback have been developed for measuring aspects of responses.** These advances in turn have been a consequence of good instrumentation, longitudinal outcomes of treatment, and continual refinement of assessment procedures. What still remains is to determine the relationships of physical health to mental problems, thought production, and what may be called the human mind in its limited extension to brain functions or in its extended connotation to the entire form of the body. Though there is clear evidence that physical conditions affect mental health and vice versa, there is still much that needs to be done by way of psychological contributions to this area of human classification.

BEHAVIORAL CLASSIFICATION

A second form of empirical assessment is based on functional responses. Here the focus is on the immediate interpretation of what happens in a specific individual's behavior. In keeping with the behavioral approach, the set of measurements is related to an individual's behavior, without any reference to whether such behavior can be used as a normative measure for groups. For the behavioral approach tends to view behavior as the result of learned states, not relatively enduring traits.

The behavioral approach focuses on directly observable characteristics classified by deficit, adequacy, or maladaptive learning experiences. The behavioral approach makes some major assumptions about classification and assessment. First of all, it dismisses generally the idea that traits and characteristics of individuals have a consistent and persistent reliability in their manifestation. Thus, the behavioral approach is against the "trait" hypothesis. Second, the behavioral approach stresses the impact of situations on individual differences and believes that the classification of characteristics should be related to dimensions of socially observable behavior. Third, the behavioral approach ascribes the vast majority of individual differences in behavior to acquired or learned characteristics. Fourth, the behavioral approach generally rejects assumptions of unconscious determination and deep-seated internal conflicts which can be identified only through a process of inference and reliance on psychic mechanisms which are not observable. In effect, the rationale of the psychodynamic theorists that a form of maladaptive behavior is a symptom of a more basic problem is rejected in favor of accepting the symptom as the problem behavior. The differences which exist between typically psychodynamic and behavioral clinical diagnosis have been clearly outlined by Eysenck (1967, p. 11).

The behavioral classification system is essentially related to the determination of three questions: (1) is the behavior manifested adequate? (2) is the behavior manifested maladaptive? and/or (3) is there a deficiency in what would constitute effective and adequate behavior? The criteria of what constitutes adequacy (effectiveness) are related both to the cultural setting of the individual, as well as to personal satisfaction and happiness in that setting. Thus the judgment of whether a behavior is adequate or not is a matter which must be established by the dual reference to cultural criteria of effective behavior and personal satisfaction. Once this has been established, the question of whether the individual is manifesting a maladaptive form of behavior (i.e., behavior which has been learned and is counterproductive with goals of cultural or personal effectiveness), or whether the individual has simply failed to develop adequate skills in the specific area designated (i.e., does not possess social interpersonal skills where they are desirable) becomes relatively easy to ascertain. Thus, for example, if a condition of classroom learning is related to a general rubric of staying in one's seat, then habitual "out of seat" behavior represents a maladaptive form of behavior (which is often maintained simply through reinforcement which the child gains from teachers by getting out the seat). Adequate behavior would be considered to stay in the seat and raise one's hand for attention and recognition.

In many instances, a two-fold strategy is devised, to counter the maladaptive habit of getting out of the seat and learning to stay in the seat or gain attention (and or reinforcement) through recognition in the seat. Thus the behavioral approach gives careful attention to the exact characteristics of behavior manifested, concurrent emotional states of arousal and reactions, and the quality and quantity of social reinforcement provided. It is therefore most important to determine the specific antecedents which occur prior to a behavior and the consequences that follow. A considerable and impressive literature has been assembled utilizing the behavioral approach to assessment and psychotherapy. Bergin and Garfield (1973) summarize a vast number of studies. Bergan (1977) indicates how the system can be employed in psychological consultation. Nay (1979) and Lazarus (1976) both provide complete descriptions of the behavioral approach and how it fits with other kinds of assessment. Research in behavioral techniques has been particularly fruitful because it has defined responses of organisms as the primary focus for evaluation and change in psychotherapy.

Responses are viewed basically as the dependent variables in assessment and as an evaluative criterion of change. Global assessment techniques that simply relate to perception are thus seen as contributing very little to the questions of assessment, classification, and treatment. Direct stimulus variables which relate to response modes (and concomitant arousal conditions) are seen to be more effective an unambiguous than indirect ones. For example, the appropriate stimuli to assess sexual arousal and propensities can be assessed (such as pictures, movies, etc.), rather than responses to inkblots (Adams, Doster and Calhoun, 1977). That this approach has contributed substantially to a knowledge of deviant and normal sexual behavior and to cures is apparent from the extensive review of the topic by Barlow (1977). The basic rationale of the behavioral approach then is to focus on the most unitary aspect of human behavior, i.e., the response. And the classification of human behaviors is thus related to various categories of responses. Adams, Doster, and Calhoun address the problem of classification for diagnostic assessment pointing out the need for a taxonomy of basic responses. Behavioral classification is based on categories derived from motor, perceptual, biological, cognitive, emotional and social responses. The integrity of the central nervous system and the role it plays in human behavior is also accented.

Another feature of the behavioral approach is related to the vast array of instrumentation which the behavioral researchers have developed to measure responses in human behavior. The development of such technical devices speeds up the ability of psychologists to measure relevant dimensions of human behavior. Though a considerable portion of the behaviors measured in this manner must be accomplished in laboratory situations, the role of self-report and measurement of base rates of behaviors which occur in social interaction, such as events of social interaction with coercive or reciprocal outcomes, can be evaluated through the use of wrist counters and careful efforts at observer evaluation.

The research with behavioral assessment and therapy has been immediately verifiable, succinct, and clear because of the definition of both problem behaviors in terms of learned responses, and the immediate treatment related to such responses. To be sure, the criterion of success in behavior therapy relates to the changes of maladaptive behavior to adaptive behavior and the development of positive adaptive behaviors from a point where there were deficit behaviors in the past. The ingenuity of the approach has also been extended to adapt to many other areas, which have traditionally been considered very complex, such as the role of self-monitoring, self-determination, and self-treatment (Thoresen and Mahoney, 1974; Mahoney and Thoresen, 1974).

Behavioral classification approaches are simple, straight-forward and relatively easy to classify in terms of maladaptive, deficient, and adjustive criteria of performance. Behavioral techniques have had a rather bipolar reception in psychology. On the positive side, behavioral theorists have argued that behavior is largely shaped by environmental factors and that it is the organism's tendency to learn which makes learning theory a viable source for the explanation of behavior. Second, a considerable amount of evidence has documented the power potential of behavioral techniques for effecting change in human behavior. Third, the outcomes of behavioral analysis and treatment are clearly intelligible and understandable in terms of specificity of analysis and treatment. Behaviorists have focused on the "what," "where," "when," and "how often" of behavior rather than the nebulous "why." Fourth, behavioral approaches have avoided the rather foggy constructs of psychodymamic behavior, and have treated symtoms as problems. All of these factors have contributed considerably to the power of psychological assessment and treatments.

On the other hand, initially, behaviorists were extremely arrogant in their claims for what behavioral techniques could do. With the introduction of behavioral therapy and assessment in the 1960s, sweeping indictments were made of other forms of assessment (Mischel, 1968). However, there was a subsequent amelioration of such indictments over the decade of the 1970s. (Mischel, 1975, Bandura, 1978). This change in attitude has been due in part to a recognition that behavioral techniques will not remedy basic structural deficits, as for example with extremely autistic children (Lovaas, 1973). In addition, there has been an increasing recognition that behavioral learning is still largely consciously monitored by the self in its choice to accept or reject such learning experiences (Bandura, 1978). There has also been an increasing recognition that behavioral assessment techniques do correlate highly with psychometric traits, provided that there are repeated behavioral observations (Epstein, 1979). Thus there has been a moderation of the original iconoclasm of behaviorism with a recognition that self-report methods and psychometric characteristics do have some relationship to behavioral data, particularly if repeated measures are made of behavioral or self-report characteristics. Thus, the initial great assertiveness of behaviorism as the only valid technique has been modified by the behaviorists themselves who recognize some of the deficiencies of maintaining behavioral changes without subsequent and lasting cognitive reorganizations to fill in for the gap of immediate reinforcement, and by therapists who have attempted to integrate both traditional and behavioral methods in a multimodal approach (Lazarus, 1976).

In summary, behavioral methods have become a very important aspect of assessment. They function on the specificity of behavior of individuals, call for behavioral documentation of psychometric characteristics, and provide an important and indispensable set of tools in the repertoire of any psychologist concerned with assessment and treatments. The healthy skepticism which behavioral measures and techniques generate about other approaches, and the experimental evidence they provide of change as a consequence of treatment are mighty forces in aiding psychology to use assessment to better the quality of treatment.

EMPIRICAL FUNCTIONAL CLASSIFICATION: INTERVIEWING

Functional aspects of thinking, feeling, judging can be classified through content analysis of interview data. Content analysis often leads to inferences about the nature of structural characteristics in traits and/or character analysis. The classification of interview data has been a difficult area of research. Basically, the intent here is to evaluate the verbal and nonverbal production of clients in such a way that a content analysis can be obtained. This content analysis then provides clues to presenting problems, coping styles of behavior, the strength of dynamic internal mechanisms such as the ego, and suggestions for further treatment. The task which faces researchers who wish to code interview data is formidable because it entails detailed analysis of the content of an interview, the development of categories of classification, and the integration of that data into some kind of a diagnostic profile. Though many efforts have been made for such classification, two systems will be discussed in detail in this section of the chapter. They are the system divised by Gottschalk, Winget, and Gleser (1969), based on the research of Gottschalk and Gleser (1969), and the system of Lorna Benjamin (1974, 1977; McLemore and Benjamin, 1979).

Content-Analysis and Communication. Gottschalk, Winget and Gleser have developed a method for analyzing the communication that takes place in an interview. **They hold that language, spoken or written, reflects learned behavior just as maze running and lever pushing behavior does** (Gottschalk and Gleser, 1969, p. 9). The method they propose is that the subject of the analysis talk five minutes in response to purposely ambiguous statements. By analyzing the content of the production they believe that it is possible to evaluate affect and emotional response. "The essential feature of affects is that they are quantitative feelings of varying intensity about which the individual has various degrees of verbal articulateness or discriminatory capacity, these depending on the relative amounts of awareness he has about these feelings and drive states" (p. 13).

Gottschalk and Gleser have applied the analysis of content to anxiety, outer directed hostility, inner directed hostility, ambivalent hostility, and social alienation. Each component is given a weight which is then summed up. Gottschalk and Gleser provide considerable evidence from studies that they have done relating their scales to various dimensions of test results such as the *16 Personality Factor Test* and the *Thematic Apperception Test*. They have also found significant relationships to psychophysiology and psychosomatic analyses.

A major problem with this type of analysis is the need for careful examination of content. However, with improved computer technology, and particularly the technology of audio classification of interview data by a computer, it may well be possible to have individuals speak to a computer and have the data analyzed in a reliable manner.

Interpersonal Diagnosis. Another approach to the content analysis of interview data is represented by the work of Timothy Leary (1957) and the more recent contributions of Lorna Benjamin (Benjamin, 1974, 1977; McLemore and Benjamin, 1979). Though for decades psychiatrists and psychologists have made judgments on interview data, it was Timothy Leary (1957) who attempted to develop classification schema for the evaluation of interpersonal phenomena. Leary believed that diagnosis could be related to five levels of personality: (1) public communication, (2) conscious communication, (3) private perception, (4) unexpressed significant omissions, and (5) values. Leary developed a classification system for interpersonal behavior which identifies 16 mechanisms or reflexes. In addition, Leary and Coffey (1955) showed the hypothetical relationships between such categories and psychiatric diagnoses. In each of the variable codes they indicated what type of maladjustment was expected and what psychiatric classification was appropriate.

Benjamin, drawing in part on the Leary method and an extensive review of literature, developed a system entitled the structural analysis of social behavior (SASB). Utilizing correlational and factor analytic studies as well as empirical tests, she developed a system which looks at others, self and intrapsychic characteristics along the horizontal axis of affiliation and the vertical axis of interdependence. This system allows for the classification of opposite behaviors, complementary ideas and antitheses in the sense that the model prescribes what behavior to enact in order to draw out the opposite of what is at hand "For example, if someone is diverting and misleading the therapist (a form of hostile power), the antithetical behavior would be 214" (McLenore and Benjamin, 1979, p. 23).

Benjamin's system has been repeatedly refined and has been extensively validated. Probably one of the most essential contributions of Benjamin's system is the extensive use of mathematical verification through the use of Markov chains, and the verification of psychodynamic and psychoanalytic constructs.

The theories of Leary, Gottschalk, and Gleser, and Benjamin are sophisticated efforts to quantify very important dimensions of process involved in interpersonal communication. Since these systems require extensive training of individuals and the collection of considerable amounts of data, fundamental questions exist about the usability of these systems in terms of extensive application in the field. Benjamin has attempted to reduce the original complexity of her system to usable components. However, it remains to be seen to what extent her excellent nomological network will be introduced regularly into the repertory of psychologists and psychiatrists. One most promising element to her system is the provision of alternative approaches to treatment based on the polarities of constructs identified.

PSYCHOMETRIC CLASSIFICATION

The classification of psychometric phenomena is the function associated with diagnostic judgment making that is most often associated with the term classification. In Chapter VII psychometrics were discussed at length and different types of tests were described. From that chapter it may be recalled that tests are often used as objective measures of traits. In general tests are classified in terms of normative criteria and summative pattern analysis. In the first instance, tests are standardized on large populations of individuals who are deemed by the test makers to be representative of the target group or groups for which the specific test is appropriate. In the second instance, a profile of test scores, or traits, or factors, is provided that is then applied cumulatively to identify conditions that allow for a comparison of pattern analysis.

Normative or criterion-related classification is representative of virtually all tests. For example, intelligence tests may be classified by overall I.Q., or by subareas relating to verbal and performance sectors. Even more minute analysis of specific scales can be done. The overall conclusions classify individuals into a variety of categories ranging from extremely intelligent to mentally defective. The normative criterion here is the distribution of intelligence within the representative and standardized population data. In the area of achievement testing, scores obtained can be looked at both in a total score conclusion or by subtest categories.

Criteria here are often related to age and grade norms, and the results of classification provide an analysis of where a given individual may be in relationship to age and grade norms appropriate to the achievement criteria.

Personality tests such as the CPI, the 16 PF Test, and the MMPI provide the measurement of a number of trait characteristics. Some of these may be considered positive prosocial traits and others less so. In these tests and other similar ones, such as temperament inventories, individuals are assessed in comparison with various criterion groups. In most tests the criterion group consists of a broad spectrum of individuals across ages who constitute the basic normative group. In some personality tests, however, alternative set of criteria may be identified such as in-patient groups in a mental hospital, drug addicts, and various pathological groupings. The MMPI is a test that if most often used to determine the presence of pathology. Thus, the results are often classified in terms of psychotic, neurotic or undifferentiated. Some tests such as the *Millon Clinical Multiaxial Inventory (MCMI)* (Millon, 1981), were designed specifically to aid in clinical screening, and norms are related to clinical populations.

Vocational tests such as the Kuder series, the *Vocational Preference In-*

ventory, and the *Strong-Campbell* tests are generally geared to normative populations within specific categories of occupations. They provide a comparison of an individual's attitudes, preferences, and other interests with those of groups of individuals within the ranks of professional workers or blue-collar workers. To some extent they also provide a measure of environmental press or congruence with a set of expectations existing within a given environment.

Self-concept measures are generally normed to populations within the normal setting, and provide a classification of self-concept, self-esteem, or self-competency by comparison to the distribution of scores in the group. Sociometric measures, though often not so well standardized, provide a measure of the psychological support that exists for an individual within a given environment such as the school situation or a work-setting.

Projective techniques such as the *Rorschach*, the *Thematic Apperception Test*, and the *Bender-Gestalt* provide classifications that are based on a specific theory of personality in terms of intrapsychic dynamics, unmet needs, or perceptual organization. For the most part, the normative data for these techniques are more pathological-oriented than normal based. The interpretation of these tests then requires not only a valid test administration, but a high degree of intuitive judgment as to the meaning of findings.

Profile analysis is the second approach to psychometric classification. In most tests the assumption that traits are distributed normally in the population has led to the further conclusion that test traits should be looked at as equal variants in the structure of personality. This premise has led to the development of the profile approach to analysis. Virtually every test that has more than a few scores relies on the profile for the description of the scores in a summative way. This profile has been further used to compare the results for an individual with some criterion group. In many instances the highest and/or the lowest scales are coded to represent peaks and valleys on the profile. This system has been implemented by the MMPI, the 16 PF, the VPI, and other tests. A variety of systems have been developed, specifically with the MMPI, but the most popular one is a two-digit code related to the highest and second most high scale. The 16 PF **presents** high and low scales in a similar manner, but indicates them in terms of the letter of the scale. *The Vocational Preference Inventory (VPI)* also uses high scales as a set of digits reflecting primary vocational interest.

In some tests the coding structure is integrated into a typology of classification. This is the case with the *Myers-Briggs Type Indicator*. In this test the individual's scores are classified into four sets of dimensions: extraversion-introversion, sensing-intuiting, thinking-feeling, and judgment-perception. Individuals can then be classified by a four letter code that represents the predominant score on each of these comparisons. Thus the code ISTJ represents an individual characterized by introversion, sensing, thinking, and judging, and the code ENFP classifies an individual as extraverted, intuitive, feeling, and perceptive.

Krug (1981) has developed a comprehensive type classification for the 16 PF Test. Using the four second-order factors (introversion, anxiety, tough-mindedness, and independence) he obtained stanine scores for over 17,000 individuals. He established a coding system that assigns a 1 to stanines 1–3, a 2 to stanines 4–6, and a 3 for stanines 7–10. Every individual can then be classified by the four second-order factors in some combination of 1–3. Thus the code 1-1-1-1 would mean that an individual falls within the 1–3 stanines on each of the second-factor scores, i.e., introversion, anxiety, tough-mindendess, and independence. Some 81 types can be distinguished and Krug provides an index not only of what proportion of each type can be classified in terms of a psychiatric diagnosis, but also in terms of normality. He includes normative data for each type relating to career themes, clinical scales, and leadership-creativity categories.

Barclay (1983) in the BCAS also has a coding system to classify individuals. The coding system expresses relationships between self, teacher, and peer group, as well a profile representative of temperament categories. The first three digits represent normative judgments based on the standard deviation. The first digit is a letter from A to E. A = high self-concept, low peer support; B = low self-concept, low peer support; C = average self-concept and average peer support; D = high self-concept, high peer support; and E = low self-concept, high peer support. The second digit of the code is a number 1–4 that represents behavioral dispositions. The number 1 is related to self, group, and teacher judgments that reflect unpredictable and acting-out behavior; the number 2 reflects judgments from the same sources relative to predictable and sociable behavior; the number 3 represents unpredictable withdrawn behavior; and the number 4 predictable but internal-oriented behavior. The third digit is another letter code from F to J and represents various combinations of peer-teacher support in a similar manner to the first letter.

Finally, another numerical digit may range from 1–64 and represents a specific profile with six temperament classifications. In addition, in some cases the letter R or D or X is added to the classification code representing reticence, disruptiveness, or both categories. Thus the code A-1-G-22 would describe a child who has a high self-concept, tending towards unpredictable and acting-out behavior, with a poor support system from both peers and teacher. This child would also fall within a temperament grouping characteristic of high energy, and introversion. If the letter R appears, it would suggest that this child cumulatively (i.e. by all three inputs) is considered reticent.

Coding systems that take profile analyses and convert them into a higher-order classification can be very helpful in interpreting the total structural characteristics of tests. The MMPI and 16 PF have been applied to DSM-III categories, but without much success. To be sure, learning the coding system for each instrument requires a considerable familiarity with the test and the manner in which scales or factors interact. Sometimes such an effort is difficult for individuals, but code books exist that can provide this information for users. Code systems are most helpful to clinicians who wish to grasp the essential characteristics of an individual in quick fashion. For example, the BCAS code is complex, but it provides in summary fashion the relationship of self-concept, peer and teacher support systems, along with disposition, presenting classroom problems and temperament characteristics.

CLASSIFICATION OF ABNORMAL, PATHOLOGICAL OR DEVELOPMENTAL DISORDERS

Thoughout this book there has been a deliberate attempt to focus on the variability of human behavior within normal manifestations. The view that has been expressed implicitly, if not explicitly, is that human behavior—whether classified as normal or abnormal—develops from the same sources. Two basic views can be taken regarding the assessment of abnormal from normal behavior. One regards abnormal, pathological or deviant behavior as extreme variations within basic human dimensions. The other tends to see such manifestations as meeting a criterion of abnormality. The dimensional approach suggests that individuals under the constraint of biological, environmental, and developmental stressors can and do manifest abnormal, pathological, or deviant behavior. The second approach can be termed a categorical one in that it reflects the cumulation of symptoms and characteristics that lead to inferences about abnormality, pathology, disease, or disorder. In part, these approaches are reflective of paradigms of assessment as discussed in the second chapter. The dimensional approach represents the newer paradigm of indeterminism, based on assess, treat, and reassess, viewing abnormal behavior as an extreme variation of normal behavior. The categorical approach is reflective of the positivistic paradigm of test, classify and place that tends to assume a difference in fundamental characteristics or structure.

The most popular classification system for abnormal behavior is a categorical system identified with the American Psychiatric Association (DSM-III, 1980; DSM-III-R, 1987). This is not a psychological classification system, but is one that psychologists need to utilize because it is associated with virtually all the financial support for psychological assessment found in private practice or institutional practice. The American Psychiatric Association since 1952 has published four glossaries of descriptions of diagnostic categories for mental disorder. The first one appeared in 1952 and a major revision took place in 1968 with the appearance of DSM-II. This latter compendium was in part based on the International Classification of Diseases. A third revision occurred in DSM-III which appeared in 1980, and further revisions took place that resulted in DSM-III-R in 1987.

With each revision, more distinctions are made relative to diagnosis. Another revision is anticipated in the 1990's which will be DSM-IV. The DSM systems in their progressive revisions represent the most widely known and used classification effort of psychiatry to distinguish normal from abnormal behavior and to provide a systematic approach to such efforts. Because clinical psychology often is tied closely to psychiatry in terms of collaborative work and medical payments, the DSM systems need to be considered seriously.

When DSM-III was introduced, a multiaxial approach was developed. This included five axes: Axis I, mental disorders except personality disorders and specific developmental ones; Axis II, personality disorders and specific developmental disorders; Axis III, physical disorders and conditions; Axis IV, psychosocial stressors, and Axis V, highest level of adaptive functioning during the past year. The multiaxial framework of DSM-III is a departure from earlier codification efforts. It recognizes that diagnostic classifications as such are always related to physical functioning (Axis III), and to stress factors (Axis IV), as well as to the extent of adaptive functioning (Axis V). All of the foregoing are demonstrated empirically in the behavior of the individual, judged primarily on a medical physical examination, interview data, ability to maintain a job or consistent task orientation, and ability to function adequately in family or social settings. A particularly important addition of DSM-III were decision trees that graphically analyzed the kinds and intensity of various reactions that needed to be considered for the meeting of criteria for a given categorical diagnosis.

In DSM-III-R a number of refinements, clarifications, and additions were made to specific categories of diagnosis. These are identified in an appendix (Appendix 4), but are still relatively minor, compared to the big differences between DSM-II and DSM-III.

One of the major problems with the DSM series is that they are basically designed to be used by psychiatrists. Psychiatrists rely on medical examinations and interviews as their chief source of information. To be sure they do utilize the services of psychologists, but their information and decision base is radically different from that of psychologists. Psychologists on the other hand, not having their own system to rely on, have attempted to take personality tests and relate them to the DSM categories. But this does not work very well, because psychiatric diagnoses as reflected in the system of

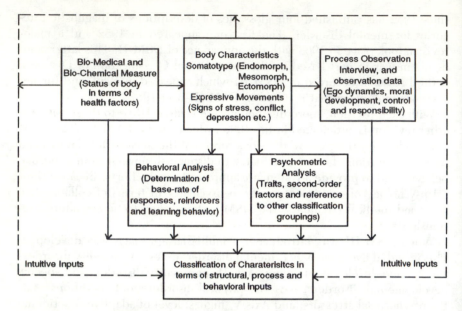

Figure 12-2   **Conceptual Linkages Between Alternative Classification Systems**

DSM-III are atheoretical and based chiefly on the consensus of psychiatry groups convened to consider specific problems. In addition, the DSM-III system disavowed specific connections with earlier systems. What the DSM series seem to indicate is the consensus of psychiatrists about the factors present or not present in a specific syndrome or condition. The problems that psychologists have in fitting psychological profiles to DSM-III-R categories relate to the fact that psychological tests are based on a psychometric procedure and are designed to be objective, which does not necessarily fit with a system based primarily on collective intuition.

Examples of this problem are multiple. Widiger and Frances (1985) point out that this cumulative intuition approach does not work equally well with personality disorders. As they state: "as only five of the eight criteria are necessary to meet the diagnosis of axis II borderline personality disorder, there are 93 different combinations of criteria that would qualify as a borderline personality disorder" (p. 616). Meyers (1983) has attempted to relate MMPI and 16 PF summary profiles to DSM-III categories, but there is so much overlap that it is possible for many profile analyses to be related to each DSM-III category.

Unfortunately, from a scientific point of view, the entire system of DSM categories is suspect. According to Eysenck, Wakefield, and Friedman

(1983), in a research review of DSM-III, the reliability of classification efforts by professionals is mixed. Validity estimates are similary judged, and there is no evidence that the system as used by psychiatrists can truly distinguish between normals and abnormals. Thus in view of the continuity of some elements between DSM-II and DSM-III, the study of Rosenhan (1973) in which eight normals were admitted to 12 different mental hospitals simply by indicating that they heard voices may still be possible to replicate. In addition, Widiger and Frances (1985) point out that inter-rater reliabilities for diagnostic classification in the area of antisocial, borderline, compulsive and schizotypal personality disorders are generally poor, chiefly, as they argue, because of the monothetic diagnostic criteria that are subject to so many different interpretations and the subjective weights used by many. Some of these problems may have been modified and ameliorated by the new DSM-III-R, but at this time no evidence is available.

In summary, the DSM series, particularly in recent revisions, represent a set of criterion judgments to aid individuals in reaching a diagnostic classification. The system is impressive, and the decision trees carry a lot of weight with individual clinicians. The classification system is itself impressive. But there are two besetting problems: (1) there are no suggestions for treatment for the various categories, and (2) the system does not stand still long enough for appropriate research to establish the validity of categories. Ideally, from the psychologists' point of view, the system would be much improved if diagnostic tests could be related to the decision-making process.

This chapter has summarized the major methods of classifying assessment data. Empirical assessment has included not only interview data, but also some consideration of constitutional characteristics. Behavioral data provide concrete levels of estimating functioning. Psychometrics are classified by profile analysis and in some instances by codes. Finally, abnormal phenomena are classified by contrasts with formalized criteria, the most popular of which is currently the DSM series.

CHAPTER XIII

Pseudoscientific Assessment Systems

This chapter deals with a class of assessment information that may be called pseudo-intuitive. Intuitive classification involves a correspondence between some kind of believed structure and individual differences. In this chapter the focus is on a number of techniques that might be termed pseudosciences. What is referred to here is not the same as that clinical insight often found in relationship to empirical or psychometric data, but rather to a number of specific assessment approaches that are widely used in society and are often accorded as much validity as scientifically-derived assessment data or projective techniques. Because they are so widely used, and from years of experience in teaching assessment, I am including this chapter to explain to students just what these systems are and what is the basis of their intuitive judgments.[1]

Intuitive assessment systems are based on an inferred correspondence between individual behavior and cosmic determinants. They posit an influence relationship between unknown (magnetic?) forces in the universe and individual thinking and behaving. The purpose of this section is to explain a number of methods of assessment which are typically classified in scientific assessment as pseudosciences. They are classified this way because many scientists do not recognize the causal linkages which they suggest. For some scientists these methods represent a kind of vestige of man's early belief in "magic." In addition, they are frequently associated with "fortune telling." Many scientists have argued that these systems meet the psychological need for security or prediction of the future. Regardless of the arguments against these systems, it is a fact that millions of human beings believe in them. They also are closely related to religious beliefs in many of the existing religious systems.

Ordinarily these systems are simply dismissed in assessment books, but because they represent a form of assessment which is accepted by many people, and because elements of these systems have been around for at least three thousand years, they cannot be ignored. In the following sections, I have attempted to review these approaches as objectively as possible to provide readers with an overview of the systems, both from the point of advocates of the techniques and from a critical point of view by opponents.

Contemporary scientific thinking often rejects in one period what is acceptable in a future period. Typically, the paradox which is faced in discussing these approaches is that the scientific establishment rejects them as pseudoscientific while they continue to last and prosper. Scientists attack them as not based on principles of scientific inquiry. And yet, it is well known that other scientists at the time of Kepler and Gaileo opposed their findings, and physicists at the end of the nineteenth century thought that all physics had been explained just before Einstein presented his theory of relativity. Two illustrations may make the above argument clearer. Very often we ascribe to superstitions or unscientific reasoning, phenomena which later are found to be based on scientific explanations. Second, we are often as scientists subject to a psychological "set" or predisposition as to what we consider within the realm of science. Thus Goodstein and Brazis (1970) prepared two virtually identical abstracts of presumably empirical research in the area of astrology, one with positive findings and the other with negative findings. The data collected by mail from a random selection of professional psychologists indicated that those psychologists receiving the negative abstract rated the study as better designed, more valid, and as having more adequate conclusions than those receiving the positive abstract. The authors concluded from the many emotionally charged spontaneous comments included with the responses that strong affective reactions are involved as well as prejudgments in the evaluation of objective data.

Again, with regard to the former argument about our ascribing to folklore certain effects which we do not understand, one can consider the "Chihuahua effect." Years ago, a remedy for children with severe asthma was related to what was called the "Chihuahua effect." Briefly, the observation was that small dogs with lots of short hair should be kept very close to children with asthma. Typically, this was interpreted from a psychoanalytic point of view as a psychological strategy since asthma was often viewed as the physiological consequence of a psychological need for intimacy. Later it was found through the use of electrostatic field meters that such dogs because of a high metabolism and short hair generate up to 400 microvolts of positive charge and about double the usual earth potential of 200 V/m. Negative voltage is said to be related to illness and is also said to be characteristic of large glass and steel buildings. Thus, what was interpreted as a psychological strategy at best, and an old wives tale at worst, appears to have a scientific explanation (Beal in Llaurado, 1974).

In the following sections, an attempt will be made to provide as objective an analysis of these pseudoscientific approaches of the classification of individual differences as is possible. In the summary analysis of the alternative systems, their approach to the meeting of objective criteria will be discussed. The focus in this discussion will be on Western manifestations of intuitive assessment, though one of the most extensive systems is that of the Chinese which was discussed in some detail in Chapter 3.

Chirognomy. Characteristics of the hand are thought to reflect personality and health. Chirognomy has a history rooted in ancient philosophy and a theory of both cosmic and personal relationships. Chirognomy is the more scientific name for palmistry. It is derived from a Platonist theory suggesting that what exists within is clearly demonstrable without. The hand as the principal tool of man is viewed as particularly sensitive to biological and behavioral characteristics of the individual. There are then biological and behavioral traces found in hand characteristics which are indicative of both constitutional factors and actual events which have occurred. What man does consciously or unconsciously is displayed in his hand. This is quite obvious in the sense that hard labor would induce callouses, but it is not so obvious relative to physical and medical disorders as such. However, there are those who do argue hand analysis is relevant to medical diagnosis.

Gettings (1965) provides a comprehensive analysis of chirognomy from ancient days to the present. He argues that medical technology confirms that many diseases can be observed in the configuration of the hand, citing rheumatism and heart disease as two examples. According to Gettings, the hand is divided into three sections corresponding to the Platonic and medieval theory of personality. The upper section is considered the rational part of man, the middle section the sensible portion and the lower section the vegetative. The rational is represented by the fingers and is sometimes called the mental or ideal world, relating to the spiritual nature of the individual. Thinner fingers are considered more spiritual and shorter thicker ones more material. The sensible area relates to the interplay of emotions and practical aspects of life. If this area is particularly large, then the individual's life is said to be identified within the emotional plane. The vegetative or lower level is related to the unconscious and basic instincts of the individual.

Hands are classified quantitatively by type and configuration, and qualitatively by line and mound characteristics. From the quantitative point of view hands are classified as elementary (large, thick, heavy in appearance associated with workmen and farmers usually with a strict earthy common sense and under the influence of Saturn); motoric (wherein fingers tend to be longer, more flexible and associated with practical vocations such as engineering, sports, business and the military and under the influence of Jupiter); sensitive (distinguished by a long palm and long fingers, associated with emotional unstable and sensitive personalities, artists, musicians, etc., and under the influence of the moon); and the intellectual (characterized by a square palm and relatively long but strong fingers, associated with scientists, researchers and others, and under the influence of Mercury).

With the internal dimensions of the hand both lines and mounds must be considered relative to the general form. The basic lines are the life line (indicating the extent and quality of life), the heart line (indicating the extent and quality of emotional structures), the head line (indicating the quality of intellectual abilities), and the fate line (indicating the destiny of the individual). The interpretation of the form of the hand together with lines, mounds, and other specific characteristics is tied strongly to the influence of the basic elements of air, fire, water, and earth, along with influence of the planets. The combinations and interpretations are almost infinite.

In modern days, at least one medical doctor (Scheimann, 1969) has maintained that medical examination should consider some of the forensic evidence from this area. Scheimann argues at some length that specific tremors of the hand are related to Parkinson's disease, cerebellar problems in multiple sclerosis and toxic conditions due to barbiturates, narcotics, and alcoholism. Skin texture, temperature, and color are indicative of conditions of glandular problems. Thus smooth satin-like and warm hands suggest overactive thyroid glands, and doughy, dry, cold and coarse hands of hypothyroidism (Scheiman, 1969, p. 29). Conditions in blood circulation are also reflected in skin color, and coronary heart disease is reflected by palmar changes below the little finger and ring finger. Past violent heart attacks are indicated by lumps of hardened tissue in the palm of the hand due to previous swollen conditions. Pearly and yellowish formations on the palm which are often translucent are associated with signs of malignancy and cancer. Scheiman also discusses at length how middle age crises can be ascertained from the analysis of the various lines of the palm, as well as what are the signs of both vital and diminishing capacity.

Unfortunately, though Dr. Scheiman cites many personal examples of the documentation of his allegations, and some references to other professionals who also think the same, there is virtually no independent documentation of research supporting the more esoteric aspects of chirognomy. Certainly, that the hand does reflect illnesses is something no physician would deny, but the causal inferences associated with such observations needs further documentation.

Astrology. Astrology posits a cosmic-individual relationship that reflects predispositions of personality, character, and vocation. A very perplexing topic to consider in a book on assessment is that of astrology. Typically, it would be ignored or discarded after a brief sentence or two, but a system which has existed for at least twenty-five hundred years, even if superstition, cannot simply be dismissed. Watson (1973) states that it can be traced back to the building of the first pyramid in Egypt about 2870 BC and that over half of the world's population believe in some aspect of it.

There is probably no older system for assessing individual differences than that of astrology. Just as medicine grew out of the tribal witch doctor practice, and psychology had its roots in the same source, so astrology was related closely to astronomy from the early days. The ancient Egyptians, the Chaldeans, the Mayans, the inhabitants of India, and the Chinese all seem to have had a body of knowledge about astrology. The Greeks and Romans adopted much of the literature about astrology and particularly the Ptolemaic view of the heavens and earth. In the Middle Ages there were formal courses in astrology. Aquinas indicated that he could see no problem in astrology as long as it focused on human characteristics and did not get into the prediction of future behavior. Newton and Kepler believed strongly in astrology and so did a host of other scientists concerned with the expansion of physical science.

Today, the number of individuals who consult horoscopes or employ astrologers to provide them with specific trends and information is unknown, but from publicity in the newspapers it may be that even high policy decisions in government have some relationship to astrology. In view of the quantity of professional astrologers listed in telephone directories throughout the nation, it is most likely that there are a great many people who consult astrologers. In addition, computer technology exists with astrological computations, programs can be run on microcomputers that will provide a twelve page report on all aspects of an individual charted from the exact position of the planets, the houses, and the signs of the zodiac in relationship to their mutual aspects. This includes even daily computations (Astrological services, 1980). Such programs are known to be used by professional psychiatrists and psychologists. They represent the programming of the old complex laws and interpretations of astrology into a specific set of descriptors.

Professional spokesmen for astrology inveigh against both the popularized newspaper columns and the idea of prediction itself. Rudhyar (1963) suggests that the very concept of prediction is inappropriate to astrology. He also indicates that astrology cannot become a positivistic science because it relies on intuition. Rudhyar distinguishes between what he terms positivistic approaches (presumably psychometry) and actuarial approaches. The actuarial approach deals in probabilities and takes into consideration many factors. It attempts, according to Rudhyar, to mobilize cumulatively a set of factors that relate to the probability of an occurance. He states that zodiac signs, and planetary aspects do not predispose anyone to anything, but operate as a celestial frame of reference basically related to the ebb and flow of life. Rudhyar specifically indicates that contextual factors and social cultural variables, as well as other personality characteristics must be added to the total actuarial approach. In short, Rudhyar acts as an apologist for the consideration of naturalistic observations (which are the basis of what he believes is the origin of astrological study) and intuitive judgment in the question of assessment and integration of data.

Though Rudhyar believes that astrology originated through naturalistic observations and intuition about them, possibly from studies of astronomy, Watson (1973) points out that some astronomical events have occurred only 29 times in recorded history (such as the conjunction of Uranus and Neptune) and that observations to include multiple and replicated events would then have to extend over a period of about 35,000 years (p. 65).

Astrology is a complex system which needs to be considered in terms of a large body of laws, beliefs, and techniques. But as Jenkins (1974) pointed out, this statement can also be applied to psychology—with this difference: that psychology attempts to base its judgments on scientific fact. The easiest way to conceptualize the system is to view it in terms of three concentric wheels. These wheels represent in each case the plane of the skies above and the earth below at the location and moment of an individual's birth. One of the wheels is related to the location of what are called houses. Six of these are above the horizon at the moment of birth and six are below the horizon. The twelve houses can be briefly described as referring to the following personal areas: (1) personality, appearance to others, (2) possessions, wealth, finances, values, (3) learned habit patterns and close relatives, (4) home, family and security, (5) creative self-expression, fun, and children, (6) work, duty, responsibility, and service, (7) one-to-one relationships, marriage, (8) possessions, (9) concern with broad expansive issues such as travels, (10) career, life goals, sense of social status, (11) ideals, friends, and group identity, and (12) last things and issues which are buried.

The second wheel superimposed on the first relates to the constellation or sign in which the houses are found. These are 12 in number and roughly correspond to mid-month periods with Aquarius representing a period from about mid-January until mid-February, Pisces from mid-February until mid-March and so on. Each of these signs is also described in certain characteristics which relate to individual differences. Moreover, the 12 signs are also divided into elements of fire, earth, air, and water. The third wheel which is superimposed on the other two represents the position of each of the planets at the exact time of birth as determined by exact degrees of longitude and latitude. Finally, the angles between the planets represent positive and negative aspects. Thus planets can be essentially in conjunction with each other or more commonly at 60, 90, 120 and 180 degree relationships. Other angular relationships in between the above ones are also categorized. The task then is to determine the location of the houses, the position of the planets and the signs in which both houses and planets are found. Obviously, the interactions between planets, signs and houses can lead to an almost infinite set of comparisons and interpretations.

The assumptions upon which astrology rest are basically Platonic. It is believed that there is a totality of meaning in the universe and that man is a part of the larger cosmos. The particular arrangement of planets in houses, signs, and their favorable or unfavorable aspects at the moment of birth are all considered a part of a system to describe the characteristics of individuals in all portions of their lives.

Far more research has been done with the system than is often recognized. Jung experimented with astrological data in relationship to the similarity and differences in married couples. He also related the topic to his consideration of the concept of synchronicity (Jung, 1973). Jung was particularly adept at bridging cultural motifs and in interpreting symbols, and ascribed a good deal of the meaning of astrology to symbols which were intuitively interpreted and related to a collective unconscious.

Many efforts have been made to compare astrological and psychological data in terms of assessment. Some of these studies have looked at the correspondence between psychological characteristics and sun sign (the month in which a person is born). A few of these studies are those of Orme (1962) who looked at intelligence and season of birth; Metzner, a Stanford psychologist who reviewed a number of studies with astrology and used it in counseling(1970); Silverman and Whitmer (1974) who examined peer ratings as related to the *Eysenck Personality Inventory* and sun signs, and Pellegrini (1973) who compared sun signs with CPI dimensions for 412 college students.

One of the problems with this correlational approach is that psychometric characteristics are grouped by month of birth and birth sign. The implicit reasoning is that there should be some correspondence between the psychometric characteristics of individuals born under a certain sign and the characteristics attributed to that sign. This is tantamount to suggesting that if astrology is true there should be 12 psychometric types which emerge from this procedure.

The argument of correlations of this nature can be countered both from psychometry and astrology. In the first instance, it is unreasonable to believe that one testing of an individual—no matter how sophisticated the instrument may be—is not influenced by situational characteristics (weariness, poor testing conditions, anxiety, etc.). Minimally, repeated multiple observations of the individual are required for a valid psychometric assessment. From the other approach of astrology, professional astrologers point out that subtle changes are taking place within each sign and that individuals born at the very beginning of the sign and at the very end of the sign show some characteristics similar to the previous or next sign. In addition, given the earlier discussion relative to the interaction between signs, planets, and houses, it is obvious that correlations based only on signs do not adequately validate or refute the system.

Another approach has been to examine the specific set of planetary aspects which occur at the moment of birth. The most noteworthy of these studies is the work of Michael Gaugelin, a psychologist at Strasbourg University in France. Examining over 25,000 births in several European countries, he found that the birth dates of successful physicians were concentrated in periods when Mars or Saturn were either rising or culminating in the sky (1967) Gaugelin has recently revised his original calculations, and expanded them using computer technology to verify his original calculations.

Jenkins (1974) in a psychology doctoral dissertation made an effort to relate astrological characteristics to psychological dimensions by taking into account the angular relationships of planets at the time of birth determining whether they are complementary or oppositional. Reasoning that individuals with oppositional or predominantly negative aspects should be more maladjusted on some standardized personality tests, he placed an ad in a college newspaper and recruited 200 respondents. After computing their horoscopes he identified 25 subjects who had very positive aspects and 25 who had very negative ones and administered to all subjects the *MMPI* and the *16 Personality Factor Test*. Using a two-way analysis of variance and multiple discriminant analysis he found that a number of *MMPI* scales distinguished significantly between harmonious and discordant aspect groups with the discordant group appearing to have more negative indicators on the *MMPI*. Some marginal results occurred on the *16 Personality Factor Test* (Jenkins, 1974).

On the other hand, in a thorough study of lunar phases, psychiatric hospital admissions, suicides and homicides, Campbell and Beets (1978) conclude that the evidences of causal relationships to lunar phases, etc., may well be examples of type 1 errors. But they suggest that researchers might well look at the effect of the natural environment including meterological variables such as temperature, turbulence, and air-ion concentrations. According to Campbell and Beets, it is well known and established by research that a variety of behaviors are related to cosmic ray activity including ratings of psychiatric patient behavior, season of birth, automobile accidents, mental test scores, and criminal behavior. Thus they suggest that scientists and students of human behavior should not rule out these areas as potential sources of variability in individual differences.

Recently, Rotton and Kelly (1985) take to task the work of Campbell and Beets by reporting results of a meta-analysis of 37 published and unpublished studies to examine relationships between phases of the moon, type of lunar cycle, sex, admissions to mental hospitals, psychiatric disturbances, homi-

346 PSYCHOLOGICAL ASSESSMENT

cides and other criminal offenses. The results of their meta-analysis are confirmatory in certain ways of some lunar influence, but are judged by the authors under the most rigorous scientific interpretation of effect-sizes to be nonconfirming of such influences. Both of these studies, however, focus on one aspect of astrological research, i.e., lunar effects and cannot be representative of the total impact of astrological inferring.

The current level of research studies does not establish astrology as a scientific classification system though there have been a number of quite sophisticated statistical analyses reported in the new journal *Correlation* published in Great Britain since 1981. From the partial efforts that have been made to relate psychology to astrology it would seem very difficult to make such comparisons. Psychological data usually refers to observations made at one point in time, whereas astrological data seems to be related to more pervasive general tendencies. Thus to make a valid comparison between the two systems it would be necessary to have repeated psychometric or behavioral measures of individual characteristics, and it would be necessary to have some method of converting the general rubrics of astrology into quantitative indices which reflect the technique. Most important there is a need for replication of findings over many studies.

There is no doubt that astrology bothers scientists very much. In 1975, 186 leading scientists signed a document condemning astrology (Bok, 1975). They insisted that astrology is a collection of myths and quackery. They believe it maintains its hold on individuals through general descriptions which may apply more or less to everyone. Reading this document and the exchanges between scientists and astrologers provides one with a good deal of understanding of how limited is the common base of the two groups. Eysenck, however, believes these areas should be examined further and suggests that replicability of results over different studies and methods for countering self-fulfilling prophecies (i.e., most people know the sign they are born under and whether they believe in astrology or not, tend to assimilate consciously or unconsciously some of the characteristics of that sign) need to be done (1976). Eysenck remains on the editorial board of the scientific journal *Correlation* and participates in scientific research efforts regarding astrology and psychology. He participated in the first scientific research meeting on astrology in the United States in 1986 and states that we should have an open mind to the investigation of these phenomena.

Jung in his studies of synchronicity (simultaneous and unexplained occurrence of events on levels of consciousness and unconsciousness) tends to see a connection between the two which is not directly susceptible to causal inferring, but may be related to some kind of intuitive bridge. He writes:

If—and it seems plausible—the meaningful coincidence or cross-connection of events cannot be explained causally, the connecting principle must lie in the equal significance of parallel events. If therefore, we entertain the hypothesis that one and the same (transcendental) meaning might manifest itself simultaneously in the human psyche and in the arrangement of an external and independent event, we at once come into conflict with the conventional scientific and epistemological views. We have to remind ourselves over and over again of the merely statistical validity of natural laws and of the effect of the statistical method in eliminating all unusual occurrences. The great difficulty is that we have absolutely no scientific means of proving the existence of an objective meaning which is not just a psychic product. We are, however, driven to some such assumption if we are not to regress to a magical causality and ascribe to the psyche a power that far exceeds its empirical range of action. Psychology, of all the sciences, cannot in the long run afford to overlook such experiences. These things are too important for an understanding of the unconscious, quite apart from their philosophical implications. (Jung, 1973, pp. 66–67)

In summary, no firm conclusions can be drawn at this point about astrology as a classification system. It exists, and apparently is based on some combination of empirical observations and intuition. To those who accept the premises of cosmic-individual influences and the validity of intuition as a method of classification, it may make sense, but at present the evidence does not establish it as a scientific system for classifying individual differences.

Color Analysis. The choice of colors is thought to be related to personality characteristics. Color analysis is another fairly recent addition to assessment which has become very popular as a kind of parlor game, although the author of the technique admonishes against this use. Lüscher (1969) has devised a system for analyzing personality traits via color preferences. Through the presentation of a series of cards with basic colors, he draws conclusions about the nature of personality. For example, a preference for dark blue represents a depth of feeling and is concentric, passive, incorporative, heteronomous, sensitive, perceptive, and unifying. Its affective aspects are considered to be tranquillity, contentment, tenderness, love, and affection. Blue-Green stands for elasticity of will and is concentric, passive, defensive, autonomous, retentive, possessive, and immutable. Its affective aspects are persistence, self-ascription, obstinacy, and self-esteem. Orange-red represents force of will and is active, offensive-aggressive, autonomous, locomotor, competitive, and operative. Its affective characteristics relate to desire, excitability, domination and sexuality. Bright yellow represents spontaneity and is active, projective, heteronomous, expansive, aspiring, and investigatory. Its affective aspects are variability, expectancy, originality and exhilaration. The other combination colors such as violet (blue and red) and brown (orange-red and black) are looked at as mixtures. Black, gray or brown are seen as indicative of a predominantly negative attitude towards life (Lüscher, 1969, pp. 27–28).

Lüscher's system involves the presentation of the color cards to individuals. The sequencing of the cards represents, according to him, a basic personality type, and combinations of cards represent desired objectives, the existing situation, characteristics under restraint, rejected or suppressed characteristics, and the actual problem at hand. A number of reference tables are provided by Lüscher for interpretation of the alternate functions and combinations. Although Lüscher provides many references, for the most part these studies were written in German. Thus it is comparatively difficult to evaluate his system without the ability to read German which would enable a detailed examination of the references.

In part, the analysis of color preferences relates to information provided by Vance Packard in the *Hidden Persuaders* (1957) and Wilson Bryan Key (1974) in his book *Subliminal Seduction*. Both argue that sales center around objects which have sex appeal to individuals and that color is part of the total package. The extent to which these contentions are valid is questionable.

Circadian Rhythms and Low-Frequency Magnetic Fields. Circadian rhythms and/or low-frequency magnetic fields may influence human moods and behavior. It is noteworthy to mention here that very likely some of the intuitive observations which have been held for centuries may have a foundation in circadian rhythms or low-frequency magnetic fields. Because this area of scientific exploration appears to impinge on questions of human behavior, it is appropriate to summarize some of the findings on circadian rhythms and low-frequency magnetic fields.

The term "circadian" comes from the Latin *"circa dies"* which means "about a day." It refers to the rhythmic periodicity of physical forces which appear to govern all forms of life on this planet. Thus just as plants through time photography can be seen to open and close their petals during certain times of the day, so ants, crayfish, and bees show specific feeding times which are governed by the daily cycle. According to Luce (in a work published in 1971 and summarizing a Public Health Service Publication of the U.S. National Institute of Mental Health in 1970 No. 2088 under the title *Biological Rhythms in Psychiatry and Medicine*) human behavior is strongly influenced by circadian rhythms in, for example, body temperature, blood pressure and pulse, respiration, blood sugar, hemoglobin levels, levels of adrenal hormones in the blood, urine output, and many other physiological measures. Individuals who rapidly cross time zones in jet flight, or who suddenly have to work nights and sleep days show a real disturbance in their physiological characteristics such as jet lag. Disorganized bodily rhythms appear to be related to mental disorders, such as when depression may interrupt the regular phases of REM sleep. The relationship of disorientation to space studies and isolation also indicate the basic dependence which the human being has on cyclic rhythms.

The reasons for such a close dependency to circadian rhythms are suggested by Luce thus: "It is probably fair to say that many of the scientists now studying biological rhythms believe that inherited mechanisms give earth organisms the propensity to synchronize themselves with certain periodicities in the environment. A roughly 24 hour oscillation within living cells may help the creature to survive by acting in tune with its changing environment" (p. 12).

The influence of solar flare activity and geomagnetic disturbances, on frequencies of excitement and periodic outbursts in mental hospital wards has also been documented (Luce p. 14). Luce records a study done in Douglas Hospital in Montreal which involved round-the clock observation of patients over periods of several months:

> Correlations between increased aggression and staff on duty, changes in menu, medication, or visiting days were too weak to explain the group behavior. Barometic pressure, temperature, humidity and other environmental factors were juxtaposed against the hospital calendar of aggressive behavior. When no explanation could be found Dr. Heinz Lehmann compared his hospital data against data from the U.S. Space Disturbance Forecast Center in Boulder, Colorado. There appeared to be a correlation between solar flare activity (sun spots) geometric disturbances and excitement on the ward. Since sun flares are bursts of gaseous material, high energy particles that influence the ionosphere, causing changes in magnetic fields on earth, a relationship is not impossible. Sun storms sometimes cause a noticeable deflection in a compass needle. Perhaps, since the brain is at least as sensitive as a fine compass, it also responds to large magnetic disturbances. (Luce, p. 14)

The evidence that some people can and do respond to very small changes in magnetic fields was provided by Rocard (1962) who followered dowsers on their sensing missions. (Dowsers are alleged to be able to locate water by holding their arms straight and taut, balancing before them a long hickory stick.) Rocard found that such dowsers could respond with sensitivity to very tiny changes in the earth's magnetic field (3–5 milligauss). By planting electric coils underground to simulate changes in magnetic strength similar to nature, he was able to condition their ability to detect 3–10 milligauss changes in magnetic field.

Brown (1966a, 1966b) found similar results with planaria. Knowing the planaria periodically change the direction in which they swim in response to magnetic fields, he controlled their changes by a weak magnetic field under them. Brown has suggested that variations in terrestrial magnetism, electric field and background radiation may provide cues for an internal timing system of rhythms. Luce commenting on Brown's studies states: "Brown believes that all living organisms gain information about time and orientation in space from weak electromagenetic fields in the environment. In his terms, these fields are used by the central nervous system and provide a kind of medium enabling the bioelectric activity of the brain. Presumably, the full use of the atmospheric media could give man unusual sense information including abilities to detect weather changes" (Luce, p. 13).

It has been known from many decades of observations that animals have the unusual ability to recognize impending weather conditions. For example, fiddler crabs have been reported to disappear into inland burrows two days before an oncoming hurricane. Keen observers of nature note that elk in the Northwest gather in the shelter of trees two or three days before a blizzard. The nature of animal coats of hair has been studied to determine what might be the characteristics of the coming winter. When they are thick and shaggy, the winter is seen as a hard one. Conversely, when they are thin, the winter is forecast as mild. In Kentucky, the texture of the hair on "woolly worms" (caterpillars) is inspected in the fall. If there is a good deal of hair and it is thick, then the winter will be tough, but if the texture is thin, it will be an "easy" winter.

The relationship of geomagnetic forces to behavior of horses, dogs, and other animals has also been noted in terms of impending earthquakes. Animals are "nervous" before such events. According to Beal, the magnetic field of the earth averages about 0.5 gauss and has a particular configuration, intensity, and mode of behavior. Beal points out that the pressure buildup which triggers an earthquake can result in the release of large amounts of energy just before the quake which is markedly different from the regular and continuous pulsations of low magnitude frequencies given off by the earth. Approaching storm fronts can show an increased frequency of 3 to 5 Hz (Beal, 1974, p. 14).

Human Biorhythms. Biorhythm analysis suggests three different patterns within each human life: emotional, intellectual, and physical curves that reflect high and low conditions. Around the turn of this century, Dr. Hermann Swoboda, professor of psychology at the University of Vienna and Dr. Wilhelm Fliess, a nose and throat specialist at Berlin, and a friend of Freud, arrived at the conclusion that human behavior was strongly influenced by cyclic swings in human energy (Swoboda, 1904; Fliess, 1906, 1925). The observations they made were based in part on some earlier speculation of Herbart who seemed to report changes in mental states relating to rhythmic cycles, and to studies of family births and illnesses. Swoboda continued his observations over many years culminating in his last work in 1954 which was called: *The Meaning of the Seven Year Rhythm in Human Heredity*. Much of this latter work is devoted to providing biorhythm theory through a mathematical analysis of the timing of births within families over a period of time, and the charting of illnesses, heart attacks, and other critical events. Fliess concentrated mainly on the illnesses of children and male-female differences. Ultimately three rhythm patterns were identified: (1) the physical rhythm which was viewed on a 23 day cycle; (2) an emotional rhythm observed on a 28 day cycle, and (3) an intellectual rhythm thought to operate on a 33 day cycle. Much research has been accumulated regarding such rhythms in human life and behavior—considered to start on the day of birth. Accidents have been related to low cycles. Sports activities have been related to team curves in biorhythms, and many case histories have been documented relative to critical areas (see Bernard Gittelson, *Biorhythm: a Personal Science*, third edition, Arco Publishing Co., 1977 for details).

The Swiss and the Japanese tend to place considerable reliance on biorhythms. According to Gittelson, Swissair has had no accidents for almost a decade and it charts the biorhythms of the pilot and co-pilot and does not allow both to fly when they are jointly experiencing critical days (either the day of a dual low or days before or afterwards). In addition, it is reputed that more than 5,000 Japanese companies now use biorhythm analysis to control their accident rates (Gittelson, 1977, pp. 52–53).

Critique. Intuitive methods of assessment are unquestionably popular. Distinctions need to be made between popularized versions of these techniques and more scholarly approaches. On Chinese streets one finds many vendors who will "tell your fortune," and in large American newspapers there are columns read by many people giving the astrological forecast for each 12th of the population. If one is to examine seriously these systems, it is necessary to rule out those practitioners who are obviously in it for a "fast buck." Those who criticize these systems suggest that they are based on a kind of "magic" and are the residue of man's ancient thinking. They point out rightly that there is a kind of "aunt Fannie effect" in what they say. "You are usually a balanced person, but sometimes you are depressed, and sometimes you act irrationally." The "aunt Fannie" effect is "so does my aunt Fannie!" Thus, through a psychological "set" many people accept those aspects of the system which are congruent with their own self-perception and ignore those which are not. Others point out that the scientific basis for prediction has not been established adequately. Still others indicate that there is no proof that distant planets exert any kind of magnetic effect on human beings, suggesting that the "magnetic force field" of the delivering physician in birth is far greater than all of the planets together. Research findings are ambiguous, sometimes providing statistical significance and at other times being nonsignificant. However, because of the popularity of these systems, critical well-designed studies need to be done, and findings replicated. Many who study the logic of inference suggest that there is an unwarranted leap in positing a correspondence between empirically observed behavior in individuals and cosmic conditions. However, some efforts have been made to document the efficacy of certain procedures (see for example Lu and Needham's review of medical research supporting acupuncture and ancient Chinese pressure points). Other research tends to show a connection between meteorological data such as sun spots, lunar time periods, and erratic human behavior. The subsequent verification of some old folklore accounts through modern research, suggests that perhaps some of the ancient systems have a basis in scientific principles which have not yet been discovered or enunciated. Certainly the increased recognition in Western society of the effects of stress on the human body and the bad consequences of certain diets and drugs on human behavior, suggests possible wisdom in the ancient homeopathic approach.

In summary, the use of intuitive methods in psychological assessment is still an issue which has not been resolved satisfactorily. **More research of a rigorous nature is needed to determine the validity and utility of inferences drawn from intuitive methods.** In addition, even if there are minor effects established for some intuitive methods, the ultimate question for those concerned with assessment research is this: to what extent do the addition of these techniques of assessment and their data base increase the validity of assessment with known techniques? In brief do these techniques account for a substantive portion of the variance associated with individual differences? At this point there is no affirmative answer and, though research may continue, these techniques are clearly not within the standard repertory of approved psychological assessment methods.

CHAPTER XIV

Typology, Temperament, and the Regulation of Behavior

> *"Wanted a good cookbook"*
> *Paul Meehl, 1955)*
> *"Validity is not a commodity that can be purchased with techniques. Validity, as we will treat it, is a concept designating an ideal state . . . validity has to do with truth, strength, and value. The discourse of our field has often been in tones that seem to imply that validity is a tangible 'resource,' and that if one can acquire a sufficient amount of it, by applying appropriate techniques, one has somehow 'won' at the game called research. We reject this view. In our view, validity is not like money—to gain and lose, to count and display. Rather validity is like integrity, character, or quality, to be assessed relative to purposes and circumstances"* (Brinberg & McGrath, 1985, p. 13, italics theirs).

In Chapter 12 the question of classification was reviewed. Classification is important in assessment because it provides us with a method of analyzing individual differences in accordance with certain criteria. Nonetheless, the problem of synthesizing data from a variety of sources remains a problem of considerable magnitude in psychology. Some of these efforts have been related to the idea of a cookbook, others have relied on the consensus of clinical accumulation of validity data from experience, such as the DSM series, and still others have implicitly, if not explicitly, relied on a typology. At present, the use of computer analyses has become a kind of informal typology relating to classification.

In this chapter typology as an integrating tool will be discussed, both as it has been used in the past, and as it may be logically conceptualized for the future. Temperament will be reviewed as a construct that is most applicable to the development of a typology appropriate to psychological assessment. Finally, some implications of temperament as a typology will be applied to treatment selection.

TYPOLOGY ANALYSIS

The integration of assessment data has been a topic of concern for many decades. Some of the earliest efforts were outlined by Meehl (1955) in contrasting what he termed the "rule of thumb" method with the "cookbook" method. Meehl described the rule of thumb method thus:

> Here we sit, with our Rorschach and Multiphasic results spread out before us. From this mess of data we have to emerge with a characterization of the person from whose behavior these profiles are a highly abstracted much-reduced distillation. . . . You look at the profiles, you call to mind what the various test dimensions mean for dynamics, you reflect on other patients you have seen with similar patterns, you think of the research literature; then you make inferences. . . . It requires no systematic study, although some quantifiable data have begun to appear in the literature, to realize that there is a considerable element of vagueness, hit-or-miss, and personal judgment involved in this approach. Because explicit rules are largely lacking, and hence the clinicians's personal experience, skill and creative artistry play so great a role, I shall refer to this time-honored procedure for generating personality descriptions from tests as the rule-of-thumb method. (Meehl in Megargee, 1966, pp. 640–641)

Meehl contrasted this typical approach to the cookbook method. He did not mean that some kind of automatic reference system could be established that would cover all circumstances, but rather a more limited approach in which a configuration of data could be arrived at in which "psychometric data are associated with each facet of a personality description and the closeness of this association is explicitly indicated by a number. This number need not be a correlation coefficient—its form will depend upon what is most appropriate to the circumstances. It may be a correlation, or merely an ordinary probability of attribution" (Meehl in Megargee, pp. 640–641).

What Meehl was concerned about was that the end result of assessment should be the formulation of a set of hypotheses about what can be done relative to the problems of an individual. Not only do all relevent characteristics of the individual play an important part in this process, but specifically how these characteristics relate to a treatment plan.

The integration of multiple sets of data in assessment usually refers to the term typology. **Typology may be defined as an integrative method of classifying individual differences into a system.** A typology should not only classify adequately, but should provide guidelines for intervention. **Criteria for an effective typology are: logical coherence as expressed both by formal logic and research findings, parsimony, universality, multimethod equivalence, experimental validation and practicality.**

Logical coherence signifies that the system for classification has a solid basis in the logic of its propositions and their extension, and a similar basis in correlative and corroborating chains of acceptable research. **By parsimony** is meant that classification categories manifest a limited number of major variables that truly discriminate between individual differences, and that the categories are comprehensive in their extension. **Universality** denotes that the classification system reflects both qualitative and quantitative differences in individuals as manifested in human cultures. There are two considerations here: that the system be relevant to all kinds of individual characteristic, i.e., not limited exclusively to psychopathology, and that there be strong evidence of cross-cultural generalizability.

Multimethod equivalence refers to those variables or categories so distinguished that should be capable of being verified by empirical, behavioral, psychometric and intuitive observations. **Experimental verification** indicates that the typology provides diagnostic information possessing power potential for treatment and change. This means that there is significant information available from the system to aid psychologists in determining how the characteristics of the individual relate to possible interventions. It also means that change effected in individuals through treatments or therapy are reflected in changes in the typology. Finally, **practical** means that the system is usable in a limited amount of time and can be taught to a wide range of professionals in a reasonable manner.

At present there would seem to be only two major candidates for a typology. One is the DSM series and the other is temperament theory. The DSM series has been discussed in the previous chapter. It does not meet any of the major criteria outlined above. It is atheoretical in origin, it does not possess logical coherence in terms of corroborating chains of acceptable research; it does not possess parsimony in the sense that major categories are identified that possess multimethod equivalence, there is no evidence that the system possesses universal validity, it is primarily designed to classify psychopathology rather than normal behavior, and above all it has little relevance to differential approaches to therapy or treatment—at least as specified in the manuals. Further it is a categorical system that places individuals, but does not provide methods of effecting change. It is therefore ruled out in this chapter as a relevant typology.[1]

The other candidate for a typology, temperament, through the progress of investigations into social learning aspects of personality, behavior modification patterns, the influence of heredity on environment, and many other lines of research has come into focus more and more in recent decades. There is a growing recognition that underlying interview data, psychometrics, and even naive inferences about personality are a set of templates, largely hereditary in origin, that manifest a continuing influence on individual reactions towards environmental influences. These dispositions tend to manifest a parsimonious but universal base for human behavior as identified in many different studies using different methods.

It is the purpose of this chapter to review the construct of temperament as it has begun to emerge from various research studies, and to examine its relevance as a typology. Because the topic is recognized as important there have been marked efforts to more clearly define temperament. For example, a round-table discussion including the majority of American researchers in this field (Goldsmith, Buss, Plomin, Rothbart, Thomas, Chess, Hinde and McCall, 1987) examine the major constructs of temperament. Some of their conclusions were: (1) the construct is helpful despite the inability to define precisely how it interacts with environmental influences. (One reviewer pointed out that we have no final definitions of intelligence either, but accept it without hesitation.) Another conclusion (2) was that temperament included elements of **activity** energy, intensity, vigor, and pace of movement in both speech and thought, but not their contents), **reactivity** in terms of approach or withdrawal from stimuli, **emotionality**, and **sociability**. A third conclusion (3) was that the origins of temperament were in biological predispositions, but the extent to which this was true was not agreed upon. Finally, (4) there was a recognition that there was a higher degree of stability manifested in temperament expressions through the life span than for other features of personality.

Given the plenary nature of this conference and the continuing need for clarification of the construct, temperament will be considered in the context of a number of research studies including the historical continuity that has existed from early times. **There are five major foci for such a discussion: (1) logical, empirical and psychometric studies; (2) statistical and factor-analytic evidence; (3) neurophysiological and neuropsychological evidence; (4) temperament-aptitude treatment interactions, and (5) behavioral studies.** Finally, the conclusions drawn from these sources will be related to the regulation of human behavior and how temperament may relate to psychological interventions.

THE NATURE OF TEMPERAMENT

The concept of temperament forms a basic typology for classifying individual characteristics on a meta-theory level. By typology is meant an integrative system for diagnostic evaluation and treatment planning that transcends individual methods of data analysis. Temperament is viewed as a control hierarchy reflecting dimensions of biological arousal, intentionality, and volitional execution.

Temperament theory has had a long tenure in the house of assessment. Hippocrates enunciated his homeopathic version of it about 500 BC. Ptolemy saw it related to celestial components of astrology and astronomy at the beginning of the Christian era. Galen extended it to encompass a wide variety of personality characteristics including physiology, exercise, and dietetics. The medievalists even used it as a basis for preparing food, and also found it helpful for spiritual advising and counseling (Tanquery, 1930 and Barta, 1956). It was endorsed by Kant as representing examples of categorical imperatives applied to individuals and held by Wundt to be verifiable through observation and experience forming the basis of character analysis (character was considered the interaction of temperament dispositions with learned patterns of behavior). In addition, temperament along with various characteristics of physiognomy formed the basis of classification systems developed by Kraepelin (1913), Kretschmer (1925) and Sheldon (1954). According to Strelau (1983) it also formed a central component of Pavlov's thinking wherein personality types were thought to represent different mixes of central nervous system characteristics.

Because the construct of temperament has been around for a long time, there are some notable problems in discussing it. First of all, many psychologists feel that because it existed in ancient times, it must be pre-scientific. Again, others believe that temperament really divides the world into extroverts and introverts, and this seems to be a simplistic category system. In addition, others tend to identify temperament with trait.

These three ideas are wrong. First of all, though temperament theory has been around for a long time, there is nothing wrong with examining an ancient construct in terms of modern research and redefining it in current terms. Because an idea is old does not mean it is wrong. Although we reject the humoural theory of Hippocrates and Galen, it may be that they recognized something empirically that they explained in accordance with the then known state of knowledge. Second, though extroversion and introversion both are valid concepts relating to neurological characteristics, it is obvious that there are many gradations of these categories. Finally, temperament is a much larger construct than trait. Traits are rather derivatives of temperament. Most trait characteristics are based either on rational empirical generalizations or factor-analytic solutions. Temperament has its foundations in physiological characteristics and is therefore not an identical construct to trait.

Increasingly in recent decades the construct of temperament has been defined as a cluster of biologically inherited dispositions which immediately and directly interact with environmental elicitations and subjective conditions of the organism such as stress (Allport, 1961). Temperament has been viewed as a coherent grouping of hereditary dispositions primarily related to the limbic system of the brain that tend to serve as a template that restricts the total possible range of behavior in individuals. This restriction of the range of behavior is the by-product of learning. Individuals differ in reactions to stimulation, arousal, speed of arousal, and duration of arousal. Buss and Plomin explain this process by comparing the development of an individual's life from infancy to adulthood as an ever-narrowing funnel. Thus individuals born with a tendency towards extroversion become gradually more extroverted in their behavior by reason of how they react to environmental stimulation and their learned responses. Similar judgments might be made for introverts, disruptive-impulsive individuals, etc., (Buss & Plomin, 1975).

Strelau (1983) summarizing the Soviet and Eastern Bloc studies relative to temperament also views it as the biological base which interacts with physical and social environment components to form what we refer to as personality.

TEMPERAMENT AS AN INTERNAL MEDIATOR

The concept of temperament forms a necessary and functional link in the development of a comprehensive and adequate theory of assessment of individual differences.

This proposition needs further explanation. The terms necessary and functional link refer to the role temperament plays in relationship to other assessment phenomena. In assessment theory, one can distinguish an hierarchy of measurable phenomena. The most basic one is the response. Responses are unified through learning into skills. Psychometric representations of skills or behavior have been designated as traits—particularly when these characteristics can be verified by longitudinal analysis. Aptitude tends to be evaluated as a larger construct directly reflecting intelligence, achievement, and skills. It can therefore be primarily related to cognition. Temperament, on the other hand, tends to represent a construct closely related to emotions and survival. It thus has a direct and mediating influence on all of the rest.

The influence of temperament is particularly related to the filter it places on perception. In terms of causal relations, temperament acts as formal causality within the forum of consciousness, and particularly with regard to the phenomenon of perception. Temperament provides the intentionality to the act of perception. It is therefore closest to the executive functions of individuals that we may term either will or ego. Temperament through its biological etiology is the filter through which reality is viewed, traits developed and cognitive aptitudes evolved. It provides the qualities of individual differences that relate to formal intentionality, or goal-centered activities, and is the scaffolding upon which much assessment data are based. This relationship between other levels of assessment data and temperament is not clearly an efficient causal relationship between temperament and cognition, skills or aptitude, but rather a predisposition towards certain kinds of actions and behaviors that are congruent with the individual goals of arousal-reduction and survival and the level of intelligence.

By the term **comprehensive** is meant an approach that is both equal to the explanation of interaction effects of individuals differences and environmental stimulation, and which provides a **parsimonious and adequate** understanding of human differences.

In terms of assessment itself, it is obvious that responses, skills, traits, and aptitudes all play an important role in understanding individual differences. No real assessment can avoid these components. To a large extent these assessment phenomena are covariates of cognition as permeated by intelligence. But to understand these components, and particularly the intentional perception that underlies consciousness, to probe motivation and goals, temperament is indispensable as the component of personality most closely related to emotionality.

COGNITION, VOLITION, AND TEMPERAMENT; A LOGICAL ANALYSIS

Assessment in virtually all instances involves the forum of consciousness. Functions that occur within it are grouped under the general term of "mind." Mind is not synonymous with brain. In the nineteenth century a great debate was initiated over whether psychology was a biological science or a science of consciousness. Considerable development has taken place in the biological arena over the past hundred years, but it is evident today that consciousness is still the *terra incognita* of psychology and that its analysis must proceed by careful logical analysis of the phenomena themselves rather than by efforts to tie neuronal activity as such to psychic phenomena of thinking, willing, and choosing.

To understand consciousness it is necessary to identify the components that exist and operate within it. We cannot study the contents of consciousness as we study biological phenomena, because consciousness has no extension. It is filled with representations derived from perception. It is unitary and successive in terms of a continual flow of mental phenomena, and is virtually always emotionally toned. How then can we study it? One way is to determine its functions, since it is axiomatic that function proceeds from structure. What an entity does or can do tells us something about the nature of its structure. When this axiom is applied to the products of consciousness, it becomes at once evident that consciousness operates as a vehicle in which two major entities are functioning continually. These are cognition and volition.

Consciousness involves awareness, understanding and decision making. Both cognition and volition relate to these dimensions. Cognition provides the data for decision making, and volition provides the actual decisions. Consciousness is the forum for the control of human behavior. In human beings consciousness reflects an organization dictated by a control hierarchy. This control hierarchy extends from the top down, even as in corporate affairs management extends its control from the corporate suites to the branch offices and individual salesmen. By logical inference, the greater the management control, the more central the component.

The two major functions of consciousness are cognition and volition. Cognition has a biological reference in intelligence, a largely inherited structural component. But it also includes attention, perception, and judgment with subcategories of memory and imagination. Volition is the executive aspect of conscious process. It too has a biological component anchored in what has been globally termed emotion.

Unfortunately, common sense and history tell us that cognition does not hold the chief executive position in human consciousness. If it did, knowledge would determine behavior, studying philosophy would make one wise, knowing theology would make one virtuous, and understanding the consequences of atomic war would lead nations to disarm. Cognition serves in the human cabinet of conscious activity as the controller, i.e., the conservator of resources. It has the programmatic function of amassing the facts, and the intellectual resources for **making decisions.**

Volition, on the other hand, has extensive control over the nature and products of consciousness because of its very close relationship to emotions of love and hate and the primary biological directives of self-survival and species survival. Derangement of normal emotions can have extensive and lasting influences on both consciousness and bodily functions. Thus depression acts as an impediment to cognition. Depression can also influence bodily states through changes in chemistry within the brain itself. Depression often has widespread consequences on the organism both in spatial and temporal dimensions. The same situation may exist with regard to passion. States of tension within the biological organism not only can make needs aware to volition, but perception can respond to such needs by creating the imagery necessary for bodily arousal.

Regardless of academic controversies over the priority of cognition versus volition, the role of direct and subliminal arousal from ads, television, and other sources play a great role in selling liquor, vacations, and countless other items. Although the physiological status of the organism can act as a cause in altering states of consciousness as well as impeding cognition and volition, the converse is also true, i.e., that volition itself can make the decision that sets physiological forces in action or it can choose to shut them down.

A recognition of the importance the volitional control system plays in human behavior is a moot fact in psychological assessment. How, when, what and even why people do certain things in life is related to how they perceive, how they feel, and the extent to which they believe they are in control of themselves or not in control. To estimate these feelings we have to ask them to describe them. Such impressions are important to the process of therapy and they exist in accessible form only via consciousness. Thus we cannot ignore consciousness, even though it can be analyzed at present only through logical analysis.

If volition constitutes the major controlling feature of consciousness, then a recognition of those forces that relate to arousal and inhibition is important. To continue our corporate analogy further, if volition is the chief executive and cognition the controller, the emotions form the balance of the management team and temperament is the caucus leader.

EMPIRICAL AND PSYCHOMETRIC STUDIES OF TEMPERAMENT

Empirical studies of individual differences provide evidence regarding the impressionistic organization of characteristics related to temperament classification. Empirical documention of temperament theory has developed slowly, beginning first in the eighteenth and nineteenth centuries with observational data related to physiognomy and phrenology. Individual character analysis was believed to be related to nose, chins, eyes (for example, note the expressions "a weak chin" and a "tricky eye"). Phrenology attempted to relate skull characteristics to personality problems and looked at bumps on the head to indicate such characteristics. Later on, a considerable mass of information was assembled that included physiognomy, elements of Darwininian evolution, and character analysis that extended into the first decades of the twentieth century. (See for example, Stanton's book on face and form reading published in 1920.)

Lombroso argued that there were physical characteristics associated with criminality. These beginnings cannot be called scientific. They were simply first attempts to relate physical features to temperament characteristics. More research momentum built up as Nacarrati (1921) found correlations of about $+.23$ between body build and intelligence. Ernst Kretschmer (1925) then attempted to correlate psychiatric characteristics to body build, and Sheldon during the 1940s and 1950s developed an entire typology of physiological development that related to personality characteristics, medical problems, and life expectancy (Sheldon, 1954).

A systematic examination of the theoretical positions of Adler, Horney, Dreikurs, Lewin, Sheldon, Kefir, Borgatta, and Jung was done by Kefir and Corsini (1974). Though they admit terminology differs between the theorists, they found evidence that all of these theorists employed the construct of temperament in terms of classification of types of people.

But of all these theorists, Carl Gustaf Jung provided the most direct analysis of temperament characteristics from an analytic standpoint. Jung (1971) developed two broad personality types: the introverted and extroverted. For the introverted, subjective and psychological processes are primary, while for the extroverted object relations and external behavior is the focus. "The psychological result of these two standpoints is two totally different orientations: one sees everything in terms of the objective event (extraverted); the other sees everything in terms of his own situation (intraverted). This broad classification does not exclude the existence of a second set of psychological types determined by the four basic psychological functions: thinking, feeling, sensation, and intuition, found within both intraverted and extraverted personalities" (*Jung Abstracts*, 1976, p. 45).

Jung utilized his typology to discuss the development of doctrine in Christian theology, viewing early crises in the church and conflicts in doctrine as the result of basic personality differences in proponents. Interestingly enough, Michael and Norrisey (1984) using Myers-Briggs classifications suggest that the Apostle Peter was a sensing-perceiving type, Paul an intuitive type, John a thinking type and James a sensing type. Thus Peter and Paul are seen as extroverts, and James and John as introverts.

Jung also points out that temperament typology was central to the Reformation, the nature of poetry, psychopathology and various problems of philosophy. Jung also shows how the symbol represents a collective unconscious in man, how this aspect as well as personal aspects of unconsciousness coincide with objective events to form what he calls a principle of synchronicity. Based on experimental studies, he suggests that synchronicity may be related to both astrological studies and to the use of various divining approaches such as the I Ching.

More important to research in recent decades has been the combination of empirical observation with psychometric studies. Perhaps foremost among those who have attempted to identify some of the properties of temperament have been Thomas and Chess (1977). Over a 20 year period these researchers observed children. They began their observations with birth and extended them into the elementary school. They concluded from their research that children show temperament characteristics right from birth. They identify nine categories of observable behavior that form the basis of three temperament groupings. These characteristics are: (1) activity level, (2) regularity and rhythmicity, (3) approach-withdrawal, (4) adaptability, (5) intensity, (6) sensory threshold, (7) mood, (8) distractibility, and (9) attention span.

Using factor analysis and qualitative analysis of their data they define major temperament groups: (1) the easy child is characterized by "regularity, positive approach responses to new stimuli, high adaptability to change and mild to moderately intense moods which are preponderantly positive. These children quickly develop regular sleep and feeding schedules, take to most new foods easily, smile at strangers, adapt well to a new school, accept most frustration with little fuss, and accept the rules of new games with no trouble. Such a youngster is aptly called the Easy Child and is usually a joy to his parents, pediatricians and teachers" (Thomas & Chess, p. 23). Thomas and Chess indicated that this type of child comprised about 40% of their sample.

On the other hand, the Difficult Child (2) was described by Thomas and Chess as a "group with irregularity in biological functions, negative withdrawal responses to new stimuli, non-adaptability or slow adaptibility to change and intense mood expressions which are frequently negative. These children show irregular sleep and feeding schedules, slow acceptance of new foods, prolonged adjustment periods to new routines, people or situations, and relatively frequent and loud periods of crying. Laughter also is characteristically loud. Frustration typically produces a violent tantrum. This is the Difficult Child, and mothers and pediatricians find such youngsters difficult indeed" (Thomas & Chess, p. 23). Thomas and Chess indicate that about 10% of their sample falls into the Difficult Child category. In addition to these categories there is another group that ranges between these two polar types.

Thomas and Chess have observed the consistency of these temperament clusters from initial contact with parents as infants up to the preschool setting. They find remarkable internal consistency in the behaviors of children classified by types. They believe that some of the disorders identified by psychoanalytic theory may have their origins in interactions between temperaments of children and that of their parents. For example, Difficult Children create aversive responses even from well-educated parents. The coping with such a child, without the reinforcent of smiling or any degrees of placidity, results in parent frustration with the infant that then starts a coercive-demanding type of relationship between them. Though the Thomas and Chess studies are well documented through case studies and questionnaires, the conclusions about temperament are based on varying samples.

Martin (1982) developed a temperament assessment battery derived in large part from the Thomas and Chess findings. Lisa Barclay (1987) administered this battery to a group of American preschool children and had it translated into Chinese. It was then also administered to Chinese preschool children in Taiwan. Utilizing in both samples an early-childhood kindergarten screening tool that identifies deficit areas in motor, social, auditory, and cognitive skills (Barclay and Barclay, PACE, 1986), she found that children with more skill deficits at the 4, 5, and 6 year old levels also showed more negative scores on Martin's temperament assessment battery. These studies suggest a clear linkage between skill deficits in early children and maladaptive temperament characteristics.

Other studies with the Martin inventory have shown a variety of relationships to early childhood problems, academic achievement, and other observational data (Pullis & Cadwell, 1982; Martin, Nagle, and Paget, 1983; Martin, Drew, Gaddis and Moseley, 1988).

Considerable research has been reported for many developmental time periods. Perhaps the greatest concentration has been in the area of early childhood and has been reported in the basic journals of that area (*Child Development*, the *Merrill-Palmer Quarterly*, and *Developmental Review*). For example, the *Merrill-Palmer Quarterly* (vol. 30, 1984) is virtually devoted to the topic of temperament studies. This research is too voluminous to report here, but the number of research studies of an empirical and psychometric nature support current enthusiasm about the construct of temperament.

Windle, Hooker, Lenerz, East, Lerner and Lerner (1986) using the *Dimensions of Temperament Survey* (Lerner, Palermo, Spiro, and Nesslroade, 1982) have provided data regarding characteristics of early and late adolescents.

Burkes and Rubenstein (1979) have applied the Thomas and Chess system to the evaluation and counseling-treatment of adults. They use the same basic dimensions as Thomas and Chess and describe an interesting method of client appraisal using an inventory they devised for adults. On the basis of the results from this inventory, feedback can be made to the client and different emphases in treatment devised. To this point, however, no research has been reported using the adult version.

Perhaps the most impressive methodological support for a temperament theory of personality has been provided by the work of Buss and Plomin (1975, 1984). UItilizing Allport's definition of temperament (Allport, 1961), they postulate the existence of four temperament components. **These are: activity (referring to total energy output) emotionality (referring to intensity of reaction), sociability (defining the desire for affiliation), and impulsivity (involving the tendency to respond quickly rather than in an inhibited manner to responses).**

What is most important in their work is the careful methodological approach for setting up criteria for deciding which personality dispositions should be called temperaments. The crucial one is inheritance leading to stability of development expectations during childhood and retention into maturity. They postulate that inheritance is the most important criterion. This means that any theory of temperament must demonstrate a genetic component in human dispositions. A second criterion is stability during development. This is important because if there is a genetic component, this should not be eliminated during development or environmental learning, but should be part of a differential susceptibility to environmental stimulation. One might expect an analogous comparison in temperament development to those anatomical components, obviously inherited, but also modifiable by diet, such as height and weight. A third criterion is that of adaptiveness. Adaptiveness is important, state Buss and Plomin, because all temperament characteristics are subject to a degree of social modification. However, they believe this may be a weaker criterion. The final criterion is seen as presence of temperament characteristics in animals also.

In the pursuit of evidence to demonstrate the validity of their findings against the criteria that they establish, Buss and Plomin emphasize the first one, i.e., heritability. This was demonstrated by the construction of a questionnaire relating to temperament characteristics (EASI—emotionality, activity, sociability, impulsivity). This questionnaire was administered to 139 mothers of same-sexed twins. Zygosity of these children was determined independently via a questionnaire of Nichols and Bilbro (1966) without knowledge of the EASI results. The results indicate high correlations for identical twins and much lower correlations for fraternal twins. A factor analytic study of these data indicated the presence of four temperament factors. These findings are consistent with other twin studies.

Buss and Plomin not only consider the evidence they amass for the use of EASI with college and adult samples, but review the literature relating to temperament characteristics. They believe the evidence is strong for the existence of three temperament factors: emotionality, activity and sociability. The evidence is weaker, in their judgment, for impulsivity. Nonetheless, they provide a good case for the manner in which environmental effects bring about the gradual narrowing of the range of temperament characteristics over the course of development. They suggest that the initial parameters of temperament characteristics are modified by interactions of the individual with environmental stimulation and learning. This results in a gradual narrowing of the initial parameters much in the manner of a funnel. Thus with increased development, learning and behavior, the individual's initial range of behaviors, attitudes and views tend to become more restricted and limited.

In summary, logical, empirical, and psychometric studies of some duration and complexity have suggested strongly that certain clusters of behaviors can be identified as relating to temperament.

FACTOR ANALYSIS AND STATISTICAL INFERENCE

Factor analysis and other statistical studies confirm the existence of groupings of traits under higher-order structures. Factor analysis is a common method for attempting to determine the underlying common structure of a number of items, traits, scales, or tests. This procedure for determining the nature of traits and organizing them was originally tried by Bernreuter (1935) who found hundreds of traits, all very confusing in nature as identified by many researchers and test developers. Prior to the development of factor analysis as a tool, the confusion about how traits related to each other was essentially unanswerable.

Factor analysis basically attempts to determine the amount of variance that various items, scales, or traits have in common and identify those clusters that load on common factors. This has been no easy task even with modern computers because unless items, scales, or traits have been carefully studied both from a logical definition and internal consistency, factor analysis will do little to improve the situation.

There have been, however, careful studies of well-defined traits. The results of these studies are often arranged in a circular model. Another approach is an hierarchical tree model. The circumflex approach generally represents a model in which all components are deemed to be equal and opposing traits are placed at 180 degrees from each other. The tree or hierarchical model suggests the priority and power of earlier and more primary factors vis-a-vis subordinate ones.

Comte and Plutchik (1981) provide examples of the circumflex model and report two studies that attempted to develop a higher-order model of traits. The first places 171 traits rated by three judges in a similar scaling procedure. The second selected 40 major characteristics that were rated by 10 new judges on a semantic differential. Similar circular configurations are reported by Widiger and Frances (1985) with reference to DSM-III categories.

Of particular interest to temperament are the extensive studies of Royce and his colleagues (Royce, 1973; Royce and Buss, 1974; Royce and Diamond, 1980; and Royce and Mos, 1980). These studies are generally directed at the search for invariant higher-order factors across other factor analytic studies. They do this in an hierarchical fashion identifying fourth-order factors (which are often equal to the trait characteristics identified elsewhere), third, second and first-order components that are more all inclusive. They suggest that a few major components act as independent variables to all the rest.

For example, one of the major third-order factors of affective type is emotional stability. The second-order components of emotional stability are identified as energy mobilization, anxiety, and excitability. These second-order factors load differently on emotional stability. Thus energy mobilization loads positively, while anxiety and excitability load negatively. A high factor score on emotional stability would ordinarily mean a high score on energy mobilization (defined as good avoidance, appropriate territoriality and escape usage). It would also mean a low score on anxiety (defined in terms of low scores on guilt, fearfulness, ergic tension, and high scores on autonomic balance). Finally, in terms of excitability (which would also load negatively on emotional stability), high excitability would mean high cycloid mood swings, whereas low excitability would relate to positive dimensions of trust and ego strength.

Royce's many studies require much effort to comprehend, but essentially he posits a set of cognitive variables and another set of emotional or affective ones. Since most of his studies were based on other factor-analytic studies, **his major thesis is that one can determine a set of invariant factor characteristics across valid factor analytic studies that provides a nomological network of descriptive systems adequate to the definition of a meta-theory of individual differences.** Royce concluded out of his analyses that both cognitive and affective systems are biologically anchored and are composed of clusters of traits that combine in specific ways with learning and human development to form individual differences. In the cognitive area he sees the major characteristics as related to perceiving, conceptualization, and symbolizing. In the affective area the major components are emotional stability, emotional independence, and introversion-extraversion. For purposes of this paper, these basic ideas are highly consistent with other approaches to the identification of temperament.

Another approach is to look at the major similarities between the factor structures of well-accepted tests. Stroup and Manderscheid (1977) in three studies using large samples of college students tested on the *California Psychological Inventory* and the *Sixteen Personality Factor Test* found that a common factor structure emerged for the two instruments. The major factors were (1) a general adjustment (represented by the CPI components of conformity versus neurotic anxiety, and the 16 PF ones of adjustment versus anxiety), (2) extraversion, (3) intellectual resourcefulness, (4) emotional sensitivity, and (5) superego strength.

The findings of Stroup and Manderscheid are highly confirmatory of Royce's findings, noting that emotional stability or adjustment appears to be a major component. They are also important in view of the fact that the CPI is a rationally determined system based on empirical observation and distilled from the MMPI, and the 16 PF is an instrument based on factor analysis.

J. Barclay (1987) in a study with the 16 PF and Strelau's Temperament Inventory (Strelau, 1983) found that these two instruments when factor-analyzed together have an identical structure to that reported by Stroup and

Manderscheid for the CPI and 16 PF. Since Strelau's inventory was derived in part from physiological studies including reaction-time and other methods, it would appear that whether one uses a good empirically derived test, a factor-analytically derived test, or a physiologically based test, the second-order factors are identical. The figure following provides a schematic ordering of variables found in these analyses.

NEUROPSYCHOLOGY AND PHYSIOLOGY

The ultimate source of temperament differences resides in neurological susceptibility to arousal and inhibition, as derived from heredity and modified by environmental elicitation and learning.

One of the besetting problems in relating temperament to brain functioning is a methodological one. Powell (1979) states that one can view brain functioning on five levels: (1) inherited differences in anatomical and physiological structures (visceral brain, reticular-activating system, neocortex); (2) psychophysical differences (EEG, EMG, GSR, uric acid and catecholamines); (3) observed differences from experimental studies (conditioning, learning, sensory thresholds, perception and motivation); (4) personality (extraversion, introversion, neuroticism and stability); and (5) special phenomena (neurosis, crime, accident proneness, sexual behavior etc.). Different methods are utilized at each level and very often direct measures between levels are difficult to come by. "The point being made is that if one wishes to relate two parameters of distant levels of analysis then there is no substitute for a study in which the two parameters are simultaneously measured. Such studies are, however, rare in the field of brain and personality. Instead we often have to fiddle around with results pertaining to shorter causal chains that have to be spliced together to give what we hope is a reasonable representation of the relationship" (Powell, 1979, p. 4).

Of current Western personality theories, that of Eysenck (1957) is most often cited as appropriate for exploration between brain and temperament. This is because Eysenck's theory postulates direct neural actions related to extroversion and introversion, and because Eysenck has found that factor-analytic studies of his own scales yield characteristics directly parallel to the older Galen temperaments (Eysenck & Eysenck, 1964).

Eysenck maintains that extroverts (individuals preferring sociable outgoing and gregarious activities) differ from introverts (individuals preferring to keep their own company) with respect to the speed with which excitation and inhibition are produced, the strength of the excitation and inhibition produced, and the speed with which the inhibition is dissipated. These differences are related to stimulus-response connections and properties of the physical structure of the brain. Individuals in whom excitatory potential is generated slowly and in whom excitatory potentials so generated are relatively weak, are predisposed to develop extroverted patterns of behavior; individuals in whom excitatory potentials so generated are strong, are predisposed to develop introverted patterns of behavior (Eysenck, 1957).

Crucial to an understanding of Eysenck's theory is an understanding of what is meant by excitation and inhibition. Powell's clarification is particularly succinct. "Excitation concerns the ease with which impulses can travel from neuron to neuron in a very general sense (and hence is easily linked with the non-specific facilitative effects on neural transmission or activation in the ascending reticular formation). It also includes the growth of facilitatory connections between specific neurons (learning). Inhibition includes both Pavlov's distraction by an external source or an internal gradual build up of resistance to a conditioned reflex, and Hull's concepts of reactive inhibition and conditioned inhibition. (For example, the acquisition of a conditioned eye-blink response is taken as an obvious facilitatory or excitatory process whereas its extinction would be an inhibitory phenomenon, as would be taking a rest pause during a boring task)" (Powell, 1979, pp. 8–9).

Powell demonstrates the relationship of Eysenck's theory to brain functioning on three chains of evidence. The first source relates to matching results of classification as extrovert or introvert to excitation-inhibition responses. He cites 27 studies that relate to the establishment of this link. For example, extroverts condition poorly, show more reminiscence, show greater work deterioration, see flickers at a higher frequency, pause more frequently, are less vigilant, tolerate pain better, are poorer at rote learning, and show fewer after-effects on the spiral after-effect.

The second source of evidence relates to the consequences of drugs on excitation and inhibition. Here Powell cites 14 studies that indicate depressant drugs increase cortical inhibition, decrease cortical excitation and thereby produce extroverted behavior patterns. On the contrary stimulant drugs decrease cortical inhibition, increase cortical excitation and thereby produce introverted patterns of behavior. Where individuals are already high on internal cortical excitation (such as is the case with introverts), depressants tend to make them more extroverted. Thus alcohol can make an introvert who is unwilling to go to a party, more extroverted and relaxed. Conversely, stimulants may increase cortical excitation, particularly in extroverts and possibly make them more task-ordered. Powell also cites the work of Barkley (1977) who reported research with hyperactive children (N = 915). He found that 75% of these children who received amphetamine treatments showed a reduced level of attention deficits.

Aside from these arguments, Powell also examines the results of various surgical procedures on patterns of extroversion and introversion. It is known that the hypothalamus and the amygdala both have a relationship to the

Table 14-1 Schematic Coordination of Major Traits

Royce Model	Descriptor	Thomas & Chess	Buss & Plomin	Thorndike Temperament	Guilford Zimmerman	Holland VPI
General Intelligence Verbal Non-Verbal Speed	Task-Order Achievement Energy Activity	+1. Activity +5. Intensity +9. Attention	+Activity	+Activity-Lethargy +Reflective-Practical +Responsive-Casual	+1. General Activity +3. Ascendancy	+Int +Co
Psycho-Motor & Sensory Integration	Sociability Affiliation	+2. Regularity +3. Approach-Withdrawal +4. Adaptibility	Sociability	+Social-Solitary +Responsive-Casual +Accepting-Critical	+4. Sociability +7. Friendliness +8. Thoughtfulness	+Soc +Conv −msReal
Emotional Reactivity	Impulsivity-Control	+6. Sensory Threshold +8. Distractibility	Impulsivity	−Placid-Irritable +Impulsive-Planful	−5. Emotional Stability	−Co +Art
Cortical Excitation Inhibition	Extroversion Introversion	+7. Mood +3. Approach-Withdrawal +9. Attention	+Emotionality	+Cheerful-Gloomy +Placid-Irritable −Reflective-Practical	−2. Restraint +9. Personal Relations	+Ent −Art +St

Table 14-1 Continued

Royce Model	Descriptor	Eduards	CPI	16PF	Barclay BCCI
General Intelligence Verbal Non-Verbal Speed	Task-Order Achievement Energy Activity	+ Ach Achievement + Ord Order + End Endurance + Aut Autonomy	+ Wb Well Being + Ac Achievement by conformity + Ai Achievement by independence + Ie Intellectual efficiency + Re Responsibility	+ B Gen. Int. + C Ego Strength + N Shrewdness + Q₁ Rebelliousness	+ I. Task-Order Achievement + V. Cognitive Motivation + IV. Energy
Psycho-Motor & Sensory Integration	Sociability Affiliation	+ Aff Affiliation + Suc Succourance + Nurt Nurturance	+ Sy Sociability + So Socialization + Sp Social Presence + Cm Communality	+ II Boldness + A Warmth + I Tender-mindedness + Q₂ Self-Sufficiency	+ V. Sociability Affiliation
Emotional Reactivity	Impulsivity Control	− Cha Change + Int Intraception + Agg Aggression	− Sc Self-Control − To Tolerance − Fx Flexibility	− G Super-ego + F Impulsivity + Q₃ Ability to Bind Anxiety + Q₄ High Ergic Tension − C Ego Strength + O Guilt Proneness	+ II. Impulsivity Control
Cortical Excitation-Inhibition	Extroversion Introversion	+ Exh Exhibition − Def Deference + Dom Dominance − Aba Abasement	+ Do Dominance − Fe Feminity + Gi Good Impression	+ A Warmth + F Impulsivity + H Boldness + Q₂ Self-Sufficiency	− III. Introversion Extroversion + VI. Enterprising Dominance

Note: Traits are defined + or − in terms of agreement with underlined descriptions.

arousal and emotional level of the organism. When surgical procedures such as amygdalotomy and hypothalamotomy have been done, there are some changes in basic patterns of extroversion or introversion. Similar changes have been noted in operation or damages to the frontal lobes. Powell argues that most likely the reasons for such changes are related to disconnection of redundant fibre connections in the brain. What would appear to be evident here is that introverts seem to have a higher level of redundant connections in the brain that tie together the reticular-activating system, the limbic system, and the frontal lobes. **Severing some of these connections often creates a diminishing of overriding anxiety and increases in extroverted behavior.**

The neurological basis of temperament has also been a primary target of Soviet and Eastern Bloc research. The directions of Pavlov's early research were based on some major assumptions about temperament theory. Pavlov felt that central nervous processes relating to reactivity, inhibition, and mobility were related to properties of the nervous system (NS). Much research has focused on these properties. Strelau (1983) in summarizing the research identifies three major properties of the nervous system that relate to whether it should be considered "strong" or "weak." The first of these is the level of energy and activity demonstrated by excitation; the second generally corresponds to the notion of inhibition as utilized in Western research; and the third is mobility reflecting ability to shift from one area to another.

Strelau defines the components of the strength of the nervous system to be related to the strength of excitation, the strength of inhibition, and the mobility of the nervous system itself. Strength of excitation is defined by Strelau as "the ability to do long-lasting intensive work, speed of recovery after fatigue and intensive activity, persistence and ease in coping with obstacles." Strength of inhibition is defined as "the ability to regain control, the ability to refrain from a given activity, and restrained speech." Finally, mobility of the nervous system is defined as "ease of passing from one activity to another, ability to organize behavior in situations requiring different kinds of activity, and uninhibited social contacts" (Strelau, 1983, p. 116).

Because most of the Eastern Bloc studies employed physiological measures that are time-consuming and often difficult to use outside of laboratories, Strelau developed an inventory, in part based on physiological research, called the *Strelau Temperament Inventory* (STI). The inventory consists of 150 items to which responses are made by "yes," "no," and "don't know." Four scores are obtained from the inventory: an excitation score, an inhibition score, a mobility score, and a ratio score (E/I). A number of studies relative to this instrument are reported by Strelau (1983). In addition, Barclay (Barclay, J., 1987) administered an Americanized form of the STI to a sample of

80 college students in Kentucky along with the 16PF, and factor analyzed the results.

He also analyzed results from a Chinese version of the STI that was administered to 200 junior-high school students along with the *Barclay Classroom Assessment System* (BCAS) (Barclay, 1983). The results suggest a convergence of excitation scores from the STI with positive sociometric scores, and significant positive correlations between the BCAS reticent nominations and the STI inhibition scores.

In summary, from both British and Eastern Bloc studies, it would appear that there is a basic consensus on the involvement of neurological components in the determination of temperament. Specific differences between Eysenck's ideas and those of the Eastern Bloc psychologists still remain unresolved.

APTITUDE-TREATMENT INTERACTIONS

Interactions between aptitudes or temperaments and alternative treatments provide experimental evidence of the utility of the concept of temperament.

Another set of evidence relating to temperament is drawn from the work on aptitude-treatment interaction studies. Though this technique has been around for some time and has been seen as a promising but unfulfilled approach to interaction studies (Hunt, 1975), the most succinct review of the literature relating to it has been that of Cronbach and Snow (1977).

What is meant by the acronym ATI is the analysis of interactions between aptitudes and treatments. An interaction in this sense is an effect that results in a different set of outcomes for one individual (or group) as against others. The basic assumption is that individual differences constitute a set of characteristics that react uniquely to alternative treatments.

Cronbach and Snow indicate that a decade or more of ATI research has shown few outstanding examples of promising findings. They suggest that at least part of the problem for the paucity of findings with such a potentially powerful technique may have been the questionable ways in which aptitude and treatment have been defined by researchers. In discussing these two key terms, they write: "to keep the problem as open as possible, aptitude is here defined as any characteristics of a person that forecasts his probability of success under a given treatment. We emphatically do not confine our interest to aptitude tests. Personality, as well as ability, influences response to a given kind of instruction. Nontest variables (social class, ethnic background, educational history) may serve as proxies for characteristics of the learner that are not directly measurable. Attention ought to go to variables that were neglected in aptitude tests developed under selection models, since tests that predict outcomes under a standard treatment may not be differentially predictive of success when more than one treatment is considered. New kinds of aptitude probably need to be detected and measured" (Cronbach and Snow, 1977, p. 6).

Three ideas are important here: (1) the identification of the construct of aptitude as something larger than a score on a standardized test; (2) the need to utilize a larger complex of characteristics that are more representative of the organism; and (3) the need to identify this cluster possibly by new methods not traditionally associated with previous tests.

With regard to the construct of treatment, Cronbach and Snow give to this notion a broad meaning. "It covers any manipulable variable. Instructional studies vary the pace, method, or style of instruction. Classroom environments and teacher characteristics are also treatment variables of interest. Even where a characteristic cannot be manipulated (e.g., teacher sex), the student's experience can be manipulated by an assignment policy" (p. 6).

Part of the overall critique evident in this evaluation of ATI by Cronbach and Snow concerns the difficulty of establishing a cluster of predictors that relate differentially to treatment conditions. Particularly with human beings in either educational or life settings, it is difficult to establish precisely the nature of the treatment itself. And yet as they state: "the whole process of seeking order in behavioral and biological science is one of partitioning a grand matrix of organisms and situations into blocks in such a manner that a single generalization applies to all the organisms and all the situations classified within a block. The science of human behavior is built up by identifying a class of persons who respond similarly to some particular range of situations" (p. 3).

The need to take into consideration some parsimonious grouping of individual characteristics for use with alternative treatments is also highlighted by the authors when they point out that it is simply not possible to look for uniform differences from treatments. Thus the typical approach of studies that have attempted to apply "open education" to all, or to use a specific reading method, or a specific curriculum applied to all children must necessarily fail since individuals do not respond to alternative treatments in a uniform manner. In similar ways, classroom environment affects children with varying individual characteristics in different ways.

Cronbach and Snow state: "Genetics has established a multi-variant conception of environments and of heredities and recognizes that the ecology that benefits one genotype blocks the development of another. A similar complexity is required in thinking about social environments" (p. 10). It is therefore imperative, particularly in learning, to ascertain the kind of environment that will enhance a specific set of individual differences. Practically speaking this means that the same method of teaching and/or curriculum materials that will aid mentally retarded or slow learners will prove to be boring and therefore detrimental to gifted children.

The point of this discussion is simply that a treatment may be excellent in conception and execution, but without a relevant classification system for individual differences, it is unlikely that results will be obtained. Harootunian (1978) has stated: "Not using an ATI model in doing research on teaching may almost insure the finding of nonsignificant results because of what might be termed the cancelling effects of individual differences. As the results accumulate, the bases for matching will become more clear and would benefit not only the learner but the teacher" (Harootunian in Goldstein, 1978, p. 402).

Comparatively few studies have used personality variables in ATI interactions. Domino (1971) used personality variables drawn from the *California Psychological Inventory* in an ATI study. Hypothesizing that achievement would be better for college students when the instructor facilitated the students' natural learning styles, he tested sophomores in an introductory psychology course on the CPI with specific reference to the scales AI (achievement via independence) and AC (achievement by conformity). Identifying 50 individuals high on AI and 50 high on AC, Domino then divided each group in half, assigning 25 to a section compatible with their learning style and half to a section not compatible. An instructor who did not know on what basis students were assigned agreed to teach two sections emphasizing independence learning, and two sections utilizing conformity. The results of the study indicated that students with high AI did better in the classes where this was emphasized. Similar results were found for those high on AC, who did better when conformity was emphasized.

McCord and Wakefield (1981) reported a study in which arithmetic achievement in fifth graders was seen to be a function of introversion-extroversion and teacher use of reward and punishment. Following Eysenck's theory, they hypothesized that the arithmetic achievement of extroverts would be better than that of introverts in classrooms where teacher-presented rewards were predominant. Conversely, they hypothesized that introverts would do better under conditions of threat or mild punishment. After administering the *Junior Eysenck Personality Questionnaire* to a total of 101 fourth and fifth grade students, they identified samples of introverts and extroverts, and classified teachers in accordance with their predominant style of teaching (i.e., reward and reinforcement, or threat and/or mild punishment). They then covaried original arithmetic achievement scores and observed consequent gains over a 40 day period on an arithmetic post-test. They found significant changes in gains on arithmetic scores that supported their hypotheses.

Barclay (1983b) completed another study based on the ATI format. Drawing individuals from a number of studies that had used the BCAS (*Barclay Classroom Assessment System*, Barclay, 1983a), he classified them according to the second-order factor structure of the BCAS (i.e. high energy-high sociability, high energy-low sociability, low energy-high sociability, and low-energy-low sociability). These groups are described in sequence to the above factor scores as leaders, thinkers, followers, and agitators. The children were all in third through sixth grades.

Various educational and counseling treatments had been administered in these different studies. Four of them related to the curriculum, i.e.: (1) a traditional approach; (2) an open approach; (3) a behavioral approach and (4) the use of mastery learning. Three counseling approaches involved: (1) a humanistic one using group discussion and projects approach (DUSO); (2) a discipline-confrontive approach modeled on rational-behavior therapy; and (3) a teacher consultation model that involved working individually with children targeted from the assessment.

Utilizing meta-analysis and effect size scores from pre-post comparisons, an analysis of the four polar groups based on temperament was made against the seven treatments. Though there were many significant findings to this study and the reader is referred to the article reporting them in detail (Barclay, 1983b), some of the major conclusions were:

1. Children who have higher ability and are characterized by an adequate or above average level of achievement and social support systems from teachers and peers do well in the comparatively unstructured "open" classroom. They also appear to be able to excel in the traditional approach, but they do not do as well in the behavioral approach;

2. Children who had lower ability and who are characterized as impulsive and uncontrolled do best through mastery learning, and show some moderate gains in behavioral approaches. But they did very poorly in the "open" classroom and did not do well in traditional classrooms.

Perhaps the most striking result of this study was what happened when all effect sizes for all groups were pooled and the methods were looked at separately. The results were insignificant effect size scores. The same finding occurred when all treatments were pooled and tried against each temperament. Again absolutely insignificant effect size scores. This confirms what Harootunian said earlier, i.e., that individual groups may react differently to alternative treatments and averaging all results will then cancel out the actual differences. It was only when the pre-post results were analyzed in a temperament x treatment paradigm that significant positive and negative results were obtained.

The three studies that have been reviewed here suggest strongly that temperament characteristics form a viable focus for the ATI format. The results are confirmatory of Hunt's ideas that learning style, conceptual level and degree of structure are the primary variables influencing learning (Hunt, 1975). They also support Cronbach and Snow's contention that personalogical variables may be crucial to successful ATI studies.

BEHAVIORAL CONFIRMATION

The analysis of repeated behavioral observations confirms psychometric trait charcteristics. One of the besetting problems with the construct of trait in general, and the clustering of traits in temperament in particular, is the relationship found between behavioral observations and psychometric characteristics.

Much criticism has been directed at tests by behaviorists on the grounds that one-time sets of behavioral observations do not show high correlations with psychometric measures. Mischel (1968, 1969, 1972, 1973) has been a primary advocate of abandoning psychometric traits because he has maintained that there is little evidence for the consistency of behavior and much more evidence for the specificity of behavior. He has also stated that traits are in the mind of the observer and not really there (though if this occurs with many individuals viewing the same types of behavior, there is at least a consistency on what is being seen). Finally, he has suggested that there is little or no predictability from such psychometric traits.

Epstein (1979) in reviewing the arguments against trait theory states that observational data made on a one-time base can hardly be considered evidence for the existence or the denial of a trait, and that in analysis of variance procedures "the proportion of variance attributable to any one factor such as individuals, is always influenced by the range of variability represented by the other factors" (p. 1102), and therefore the null hypothesis cannot be demonstrated by the failure of many studies to demonstrate stability in personality traits.

Epstein reports three studies that provide evidence relative to the stability of behavior. His hypothesis for these three studies is phrased thus: "Stability can be demonstrated over a wide range of variables as long as the behavior in question is averaged over a sufficient number of occurrences. This applies equally to data derived from the direct measurement of objective behavior, from self-reports, and from ratings by others" (p. 1105). In addition, he maintains that behavioral ratings and psychometric traits derived from tests

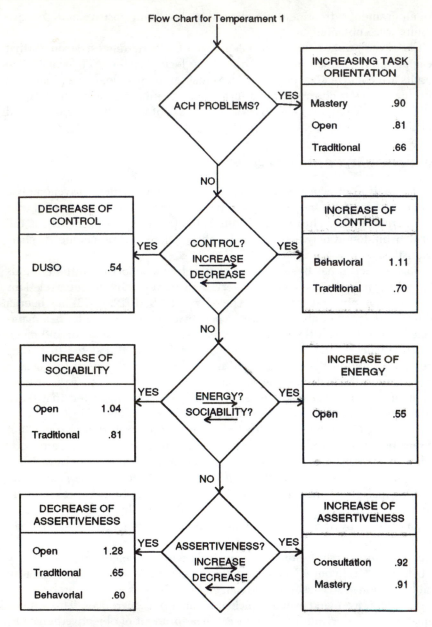

Note: A large effect size is estimate at .80 and above, and a moderate one from .50 to .79

Figure 14-1 Results of Temperament-Treatment Interaction for "Thinker" Students

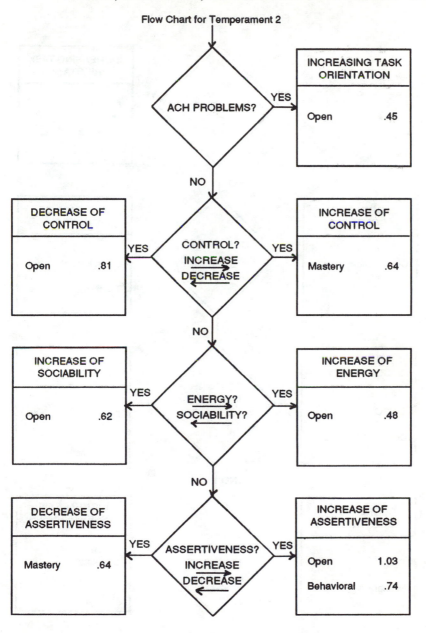

Flow Chart for Temperament 2

Note: A large effect size is estimate at .80 and above, and a moderate one from .50 to .79

Figure 14-2   Results of Temperament-Treatment Interaction for "Leader" Students

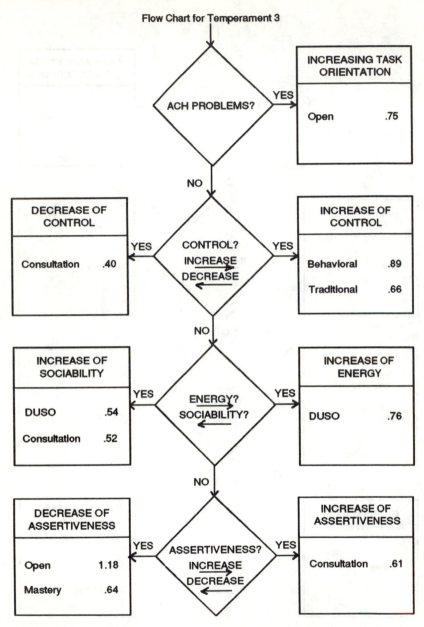

Figure 14-3   Results of Temperament-Treatment Interaction for "Follower" Students

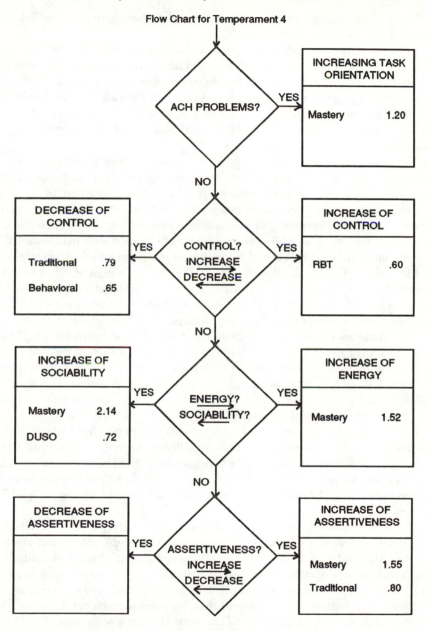

Flow Chart for Temperament 4

Note: A large effect size is estimate at .80 and above, and a moderate one from .50 to .79

Figure 14-4   Results of Temperament-Treatment Interaction for "Agitator" Students

will also show appropriate correlations provided that there are a sufficient number of behavioral observations.

Epstein documented his hypotheses by showing that the initial behavioral observation had a low but insignificant correlation with test traits. However, as multiple observations were made, these correlations rose in significance. For example, heart rate range correlated significantly with disturbed hostile feelings and uncontrolled anxiety, as well as with the *Eysenck Neuroticism Scale*. The same was true for headaches and a variety of other physiological measures.

The implications of Epstein's studies are clear. Obviously, not every person is as predictable as the next one, but some are clearly quite predictable in their behavior. Self-report behavior is related to observations by others and to standardized personality assessment instruments. But the crucial determinant is the frequency of observation. The stability of self-report and behavioral measures, as well as the correlations obtained with psychometric instruments, are directly related to the frequency of repeated observations.

Block also (1975) has dealt with some of the objections that Mischel raised earlier. Is there a consistency of personality over time? Block points out that, in a study with the CPI in which adult subjects were administered this inventory over a 10 year period and four independent samples were involved, the discriminant validity (e.g., whether the specific scale correlates higher with itself over the period or with other scales) was for each of the samples very high: 89% for sample one (16 out of 18 scales); 100% for sample two (18 out of 18 scales); 89% for sample three (16 out of 18 scales); and finally 100% for sample four (18 out of 18 scales). According to Block the mean covergent validities for the samples were .68, .70, .72, and .73.

In addition, Block reports data that span a 25 year period from senior high school to middle adulthood in which significant correlations are obtained between an inventory designated by Block as the WILTD questionnaire and the CPI administered 25 years later. For the CPI Ego control scale correlations with the WILTD scale of overcontrol were .52, and .50 with the CPI self-control scale.

One of the classical studies that has been cited as adverse to test traits is the series on honesty done by Hartshorne and May (1928, 1929), and Hartshorne, May and Shuttlework (1930). This was a project of great magnitude that involved over 8000 children tested nationally. There were a number of behavioral items relating to cheating and honesty, and when correlations were obtained with tests it was found that the average intercorrelation of 23 subtests that were used as a part of the total character score was .23. This apparently resulted in a conclusion by Hartshorne and May that honesty in any particular setting does not generalize to others.

Epstein (1979) in commenting on these findings points out, however, that when Hartshorne and May combined several tests of honesty (in effect combining observations) the reliability coefficient of the single score increased to .73. In addition, a later factor analysis of the same data by Burton (1963) resulted in a conclusion that a factor of honesty accounted for nearly 50% of the total variance (Epstein, 1979, p. 1101).

In short, it would appear that different methods of observation can relate to each other, providing they are reliable measures and based on repeated observations. Parenthetically, it is probably because sociometric nominations are based on prolonged observation of others that such outcome data have such robustness in predicting future behavior (Barclay 1983a).

TEMPERAMENT AS A REGULATIVE THEORY OF BEHAVIOR

Recently, Strelau (1988) has enunciated a regulative theory of temperament based on his own research relating to Pavlovian concept of types of the central nervous system (CNS), theories of arousal and arousability, and a theory of action. The regulative theory of temperament is drawn from both East and West influences. It holds as a main thesis that temperament primarily acts as a set of regulative principles of relatively stable nature that serve as a control mechanism for the flow and intensity of activity in human beings. Strelau suggests that reactivity and activity are the two basic dimensions responsible for individual differences. **"Reactivity is a temperament trait that reveals itself in relatively stable and characteristic intensity or magnitude of reactions. It co-determines sensitivity and endurance. Activity is a temperament trait that reveals itself in the amout and range of undertaken actions, i.e., goal-directed behaviors of a given stimulative value. By means of activity the individual regulates the level of arousal in order to attain or maintain the optimal level of arousal."**

Strelau states that there is a relationship between reactivity and activity. Reactivity is directly determined by physiological mechanisms, whereas activity is an outcome of the level of reactivity and socialization. Reactivity refers to reactive behavior, whereas activity refers to operant (goal-directed) behavior. As a consequence, Strelau suggests that high reactive individuals (high sensitivity and low endurance) show low levels of activity, and low reactive individuals (low sensitivity and high endurance) show high levels of activity. The categories of high and low reactive individuals broadly correspond to the earlier classifications of introversion and extroversion with high reactives being more disposed towards introversion, and low reactive individuals more disposed towards extroversion.

Strelau suggests that there are performance and style of action charac-

Table 14-2 **Summary of Evidence for a Temperament Typology of Dimensionality**

Clinical Synthesis	Traditional	Psychiatric Dispositions or Tendencies	Body Type		Psychometric
Accord	Sanguine (Activity-Approach)	Manic	—	Easy Child	Activity
Conflict	Choleric (Activity-Withdrawal)	Paranoid	Mesomorph (Assertive)		Impulsivity
Evasion	Melancholic (Passivity-Depression)	Depressive	Ectomorph (Retiring-Sensitive)	Difficult Child	Emotionality
Neutral	Phlegmatic (Passivity-Pleasant)	Hebephrenic Schizophrenic	Endomorph (Pleasant)	Sociability	
		Authors			
Keifer & Corsini	Hippocrates/Galen Wundt Barta		Sheldon (Kreschmer)	Thomas/Chess	Buss/Plomin
		Basis of Classification			
Clinical synthesis of 8 systems	Homeopathic observations	Psychiatric matching	Body Type (somatotyping)	Longitudinal Follow-up Studies	Co-twin & other studies

Table 14-2 Continued

Clinical Synthesis	*Traditional*	*Psychiatric Dispositions or Tendencies*	*Body Type*	*Psychometric*
	Factor Analytic Studies		*Method and Approach*	*Physiological Studies*
Stable Extrovert	Mature, Stable Talkative, Cheerful	Efficient, Forceful Dominant	Sociable Energetic Stable	Slow excitation Weak inhibition Stable affect*
Unstable Extrovert	Adventurous, Jealous, Suspicious	Aggressive, Manipulative, Opportunistic	Impulsive Unstable	Slow excitation Weak inhibition Unstable affect*
Unstable Introvert	Silent, Introspective, Shy, Anxietous	Apathetic, Awkward, Distrustful	Passive Individualistic, Unstable	Fast excitation Strong inhibition Unstable affect*
Stable Introvert	Mature, Calm, Aloof, Self-Confident	Conscientious, Unassuming, Mild	Retiring	Fast excitation Strong inhibition Stable affect*
Authors				
Eysenck	Cattell	Gough	Barclay	Powell, Eysenck, Gray & many others
Factor analysis of old Galen model	16 Personality Factor Test	California Psychological Inventory	Barclay Classroom Assessment Systems	Medical & Physiological studies

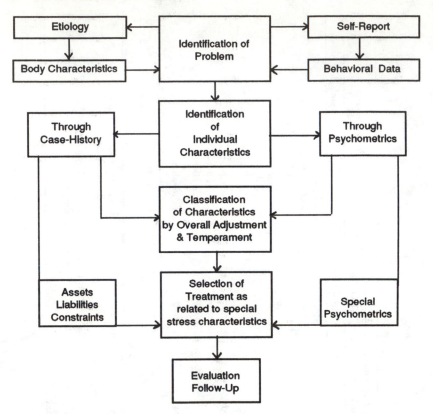

Figure 14-5   Summary of Integration Process

teristics for high and low reactives. **In highly stimulating situations the efficiency of performance decreases in high reactives as compared with low reactives; however in deprivation situations, the performance of high reactives increases and that of low reactives decreases.** In terms of style of action, high reactives aim at lowering the stimulative value of activity, and low reactives do not. **High reactives prefer situations of low stimulative value whereas low reactives prefer situations of high stimulative value.** These findings of Strelau relative to high and low reactives can be described best in graphic form. In the following figures and tables, an integrative effort has been made to provide a model for such an integration. In addition, Strelau has identified the major constructs that are associated with the regulative theory of temperament, and those surveys, psychometric instruments and behavior schedules that appear to facilitate such measurement. He graciously agreed to my inclusion of this list of instruments in this chapter.

Table 14-3 **Temperament Traits and Measuring Instruments***

ACTIVITY
> Barclay (BCAS); Buss & Plomin (EASI); Carey & McDevitt (ITQ); Fullard, McDevitt & Carey (TTS); Goldsmith (TBAQ); Guilford & Zimmerman (GZTS); Hegvik, McDevitt & Carey (MCTQ); Martin (TAB); McDevitt & Carey (BSQ); Rothbart (CBQ, IBQ); Thomas & Chess (NYLSQ); Windle & Lerner (DOTS-R).

ADAPTABILITY
> Carey & McDevitt (ITQ); Hegvik, McDevitt & Carey (MCTQ); Fullard, McDevitt & Carey (TTS), Martin (TAB); McDevitt & Carey (BSQ), Thomas & Chess (NYLSQ).

AFFECT INTENSITY
> Larsen & Diener (AIM).

AGGRESSION
> Klinteberg, Schalling & Magnusson (KSP).

ANGER
> Godmith (TBAQ); Rothbart (CBQ).

APPROACH
> Carey & McDevitt (ITQ); Fullard, McDevitt & Carey (TTS); Hegvik, McDevitt & Carey (MCTQ); Martin (TAB); McDevitt & Carey (BSQ); Rothbart (CBQ), Windle & Lerner (DOTS-R).

AROUSABILITY
> Mehrabian (SSQ).

ASCENDANCE
> Cattell (16PF, A +, E +); Gough (CPI DO +); Guilford & Zimmerman (GZTS).

ATTENTION FOCUSING
> Rothbart (CBQ)

ATTENTION SPAN
> Thomas & Chess (NYLSQ).

BALANCE OF NERVOUS PROCESSES
> Strelau (STI).

BOREDOM
> Zuckerman (SSS IV & V).

CHOLERIC
> Barclay (BCAS); Cruise, Blitchington & Futcher (TI).

CONTROL
> Barclay, (BCAS); Balleyguier (BD); Rusalov (QST).

DISTRACTIBILITY
> Carey & McDevitt (ITQ); Fullard, McDevitt & Carey (TTS); Hegvik, McDevitt & Carey (MCTQ), Martin (TAB); Thomas & Chess (NY-LSQ).

EMOTIONALITY
> Barclay (BCAS), Buss & Plomin (EASI), Caprara, Cinanni, et al. (IESS); Cattell (16PF, C −), Feij (ATL), Martin (TAB); Rusalov (QST).

EXTRAVERSION
> Barclay (BCAS); Cattell (16PF, Q3+, Q4−, L−, A+, F+); Eysenck & Eysenck (EPI, EPQ); Gough (CPI, WB+, RE+, SC+, AC+, GI+)

*Note: the majority of these instruments were catalogued by Professor Strelau who gave me permission to cite the list. I have also added to the list some common instruments discussed in this book.

Table 14-3 **Continued**

FLEXIBILITY-RIGIDITY
  Windle & Lerner (DOTS-R).
FRIENDLINESS
  Guilford & Zimmerman (GZTS).
IMPULSIVITY
  Barclay (BCAS), Barratt (BIS); Eysenck, Easting & Pearson (Junior); Eysenck, Pearson, Eastling & Allsopp (Questionnaire) Feij (ATL); Klinteberg, Schalling & Magnusson (KSP); Rothbart (CBQ).
INHIBITORY CONTROL
  Rothbart (CBQ).
INTENSITY
  Carey & McDevitt (ITQ), Fullard, McDevitt & Carey (TTS), Hegvik, McDevitt & Carey (MCTQ), McDevitt & Carey (BSQ), Thomas & Chess (NYLSQ).
IRRITABILITY
  Caprara, Cinanni et al. (IESS); Klinteberg, Schalling & Magnusson (KSP).
MELANCHOLIC
  Barclay (BCAS Check-list); Cruise, Blitchington & Futcher (TI).
MOBILITY
  Gorynska & Strelau (TTI).
MOBILITY OF NERVOUS PROCESSES
  Strelau (STI).
MONOTONY AVOIDANCE
  Klinteberg, Schalling & Magnusson (KSP).
MOOD
  Balleyguier (BS), Carey & McDevitt (ITQ); Fullard, McDevitt & Carey (TTS); Hegvik, McDevitt & Carey (MCTQ); McDevitt & Carey (BSQ); Thomas & Chess (NYLSQ); Windle & Lerner (DOTS-R).
MOTIVATION
  Janke, Erdmann & Netter (APS).
MUSCULAR TENSION
  Klinteberg, Schalling & Magnusson (KSP)
NEUROTICISM
  Cattell (16PF, Q3−, O+, Q4+, L+); Eysenck & Eysenck (EPI), (EPQ); Gough (CPI, WB−, RE−, SC−, AC−, GI−).
PERSISTENCE
  Barclay, (BCAS); Bates (ICQ-IC); Carey & McDevitt (ITQ); Fullard, McDevitt, & Carey (TTS); Gorynska & Strelau (TTI); Hegvik, McDevitt & Carey (MCTQ); Martin (TAB); McDevitt & Carey (BSQ), Thomas & Chess (PTQC), (TTQC).
PERSONAL RELATIONS
  Guilford & Zimmerman (GZTS).
PHLEGMATIC
  Barclay (BCAS-check-list); Cruise, Blitchington & Futcher (TI).
PLASTICITY
  Ruslov (QST).
PLEASURE
  Goldsmith (TBAQ); Rothbart (CBQ).

Table 14-3 **Continued**

REACTIVITY
    Friendensberg & Strelau (RRS1,2,3); Kohn (RS), & Rothbart (CBQ).
RESTRAINT
    Guilford & Zimmerman (GZTS).
RHYTHMICITY
    Carey & McDevitt (ITQ), Fullard, McDevitt & Carey (TTS); McDevitt &
    Carey (BSQ), Netter & Othnmer (PS); Thomas & Chess (NYLSQ); Windle &
    Lerner (DOTS-R).
SANGUINE
    Barclay (BCAS-Check-List); Cruise, Blitchington & Futcher (TI).
SENSATION-SEEKING
    Zucherman (SSS IV & V).
SOCIABILITY
    Barclay (BCAS); Buss & Plomin (EASI); Gough (CPI, RE+, SC+, SO+);
    Guilford & Zimmerman (GZTS).
SOCIAL TEMPO
    Rusalov (QST).
SPEED
    Gorynska & Strelau (TTI).
STRENGTH OF EXCITATION & INHIBITION
    Strelau, (STI).
TASK-ORIENTATION
    Barclay (BCAS); Windle & Lerner (DOTS-R).
TEMPO
    Gorynska & Strelau (TTI); Rusalov (QST)
TENSION
    Balleyguier (BD); Feij (ATL).
THRESHOLD (SENSORY)
    Carey & McDevitt (ITQ); Fullard, McDevitt, & Carey (TTS); Hegvik,
    McDevitt & Carey (MCTQ); McDevitt & Carey (BSQ); Thomas & Chess
    (NYLSQ).
THRILL AND ADVENTURE SEEKING
    Zuckerman (SSS IV & V).
VENTURESOMENESS
    Eysenck, Easting & Pearson (Junior); Eysenck, Pearson, Eastling & Allsopp
    (Questionnaire).

SUMMARY

In this chapter the evidence for considering temperament as a typology of human behavior has been reviewed. Historical, clinical, empirical, psychometric and neurological studies support temperament as a meta-theory. In addition, aptitude-treatment interactions, and behavioral studies confirm the validity of the construct in research. Most recently, a regulative theory of temperament enunciated by Strelau has provided a linkage between Eastern and Western approaches. Temperament theory is a system that involves a few major biologically-anchored components that tend to specify the direction and intensity of human development. It is therefore parsimonious in identifying activity, sociability, impulsivity and emotionality as the core ingredients. Second it is based on comprehensive evidence including presence in animals, and consistency across methods of assessment, and third it possesses power potential for change as can be witnessed from the ATI results. Fourth, and finally, temperament is a dimensional and hierarchical system of classification that has many potentials for integrating diagnosis with treatment. It therefore qualifies as a typology appropriate for psychological assessment.

Endnote

1. By ruling out DSM-III-R as a candidate for a typology, I am sure that I will be offending some readers. Aside from the reasons indicated in the text, DSM-III-R is a consensus of psychiatric thinking about the nature and extent of *mental illness*. It conveys the process of decision making through a series of decision trees. These decision trees are useful in arriving at a diagnosis relating to the presence or absence of mental illness. The fact, however, that the basic intent of these decision trees is to help individuals in an organized manner to reach a conclusion about the extent of mental illness *is precisely the major reason why the DSM-III series is rejected as a candidate for an effective typology of assessment with normals.*

A good typology of assessment ought to be focused primarily on normals since the vast amount of assessment studies relate to individuals who are functioning one way or another in society. It is this population that counseling and school psychologists and many clinical psychologists deal with. When an individual does not meet the criteria of any given decision tree in DSM-III-R where does this leave him or her? Can the judgment be made that there are no relevant diagnostics without pathology? I think not.

Psychologists need a typology of assessment that will enable them to both evaluate diagnostically individuals in a normal setting and to provide them with some relevant treatment procedures. The development of such a typology will take much time and research. The existence of a typology used primarily for assessing pathology in accordance with both political and financial criteria of reimbursement can be accepted as a political and financial reality, but hardly an example of good research and moral responsibility to individuals falling within the broad ranges of normal human behavior. For the reasons indicated in the text and also in this footnote, I cannot accept the DSM-III-R as a relevant candidate for a typology of assessment.

CHAPTER XV

Epilogue

The last chapter of this book will deal with three topics: (1) a review of the model of assessment that has been presented sequentially in this book; (2) a discussion of other forms of specialized assessment that need further attention; and (3) some speculations about the future.

TOWARD AN INTEGRATIVE MODEL OF ASSESSMENT

In the preface, I mentioned that writing this book was a personal challenge. The effort was undertaken because somehow assessment seem very tangled up, and though one could read extensive reviews of psychometric instruments, interview techniques, behavioral methods, and projective instruments, it seemed virtually impossible to put them all together into a common framework. For the most part, the flow of this book has been related to developing a scaffolding for this endeavor by using logical analysis rather than statistical integration. Thus the thrust of this book has not been to demonstrate either clinical or statistical prediction, but rather to describe each of the components of assessment and how they fit together.

Another task that became evident as the book developed was to provide for readers the theoretical background of each of the methods that were to be discussed. Somehow, the relationship of various personality theories to assessment and the assumptions made by theorists relative to methods never seemed to be clearly demonstrated in traditional testing books or interview manuals.

Assessment in the model that has been presented relates to methods, content, and diagnostic outcomes. The first and primary method discussed is that of empirical observation. Empirical information includes body characteristics and movements as well as information processed in identifying client problems, and the relationship to a host of background etiology and present functioning. Imbedded within these dimensions are elements of personal history relating to learning, achievement, past experience in modeling and reinforcement along with specific current states of personal stress, physiological as well as mental, and estimated levels of cognitive and emotional functioning.

The second method described was that of psychometrics. Major emphases in psychometric testing include both intelligence-achievement and various aspects of emotional functioning as determined from a variety of personality test. Both group and individual tests were discussed as adjuncts to empirical assessment.

The third method was that of intuitive inferring in which projective techniques were utilized to assess higher levels of executive decision-making and ego functioning.

Each of these methods differ in the level of epistemological certitude associated with them. The primary level of certainty is related to empirical observation; psychometrics are based on a set of assumptions relative to normal distribution of characteristics and are therefore more valid for groups than for individuals; and finally, intuitive methods are based on a further set of assumptions about the nature and meaning of specific responses to stimuli presented by the assessor to the client.[1]

All three methods make an assumption of correspondence between what is observed and what is realized through the method. Thus it is assumed that observations in the interview are valid judgments of what is occurring. It is likewise assumed that test scores correspond in a general way to what exists in thinking and behaving. Finally, depending on the assumptions made about projective techniques, it is likewise believed that responses made by a client reflect some set of ordering of internal dynamics, resistances, and methods of thinking. The fact remains, however, that behaviors, traits, and dynamic entities such as ego differ in level of complexity and ambiguity. A complete assessment, however, requires ideally all three methods.

Each of these methods in turn can be applied to content problems or needs areas that center on cognition-learning, emotional behavior, and conation-willing. Some problems are primarily cognitive in nature, i.e., information-seeking about study methods, and vocational alternatives. Others are primarily related to emotional responses such as impulsivity, self-control, frustration, and gratification of personal needs. Another large group of problems relate to decision making, willing, motivation, planning, and goal seeking.

In the interaction between methods and content areas one must always be aware of the continuing interaction between hereditary components and environmental effects on these components. No single one of the content areas is free from the others. Cognition is always mediated by emotional

I. Individual Assessment

Methods
1. Empirical [Impressionistic
                Behavioral
                Content-Analysis]

2. Psychometric
     [Cognition-Learning
     Affect-Behavior
     Conation-Willing]

3. Intuitive
     [Projective & Other]

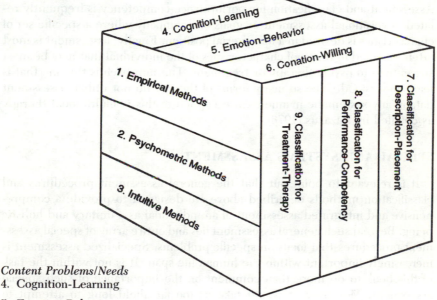

Content Problems/Needs
4. Cognition-Learning

5. Emotion-Behavior

6. Conation-Willing
     [Integrative Decision-Making

Diagnostic-Outcomes
7. Classification for Description,
     Evaluation, Placement
8. Classification for Performance-
     Competency
9. Classification for Treatment-
     Therapy

II. Special Assessment

As Related to
Special Assessment

[Learning Disabilities,
Depression, Alcoholism,
Sexual Disorders, Aging
etc.]

*III. Systems
        Assessment*

As Related to
Group Assessment

[Family, Business,
Military and other
systems]

Figure 15-1   **Integrative Model of Assessment**

response, and conation or willing is a continual interaction between levels of past response and estimates of the future.

Finally, the manner in which methods and content areas interact is relevant to the focus of classification. We may classify such interactions in terms of description-placement and evaluation functions, or in terms of performance-competency criteria, or in a classification mode for treatments, counseling and psychotherapy. An example of the first form of classification is that used in placing children in a school setting such as a class for gifted children, or for handicapped ones, or for special remediation of learning disabilities. This form of classification is also often utilized to determine whether an individual is psychotic and should be placed in an institution. Assessment and classification for performance-competency is frequently related to vocational assessment or goals of a company where a specific set of characeristics is desired in a managerial position. Finally, assessment is most often classified in terms of characteristics of the individual that may be most susceptible to psychotherapy or treatment. This approach is the one that is least understood since so many forms of therapy do not utilize assessment data in any systematic manner. An exception to this is multimodal therapy as detailed by Lazarus (1976).

SPECIAL AND SYSTEMS ASSESSMENT

It is relevant to point out that the general assessment procedures and classification methods described above are designed to provide a comprehensive and integrated assessment of an individual as a unitary and holistic being. Beyond such general assessment lies and entire array of special assessment procedures that focus on specific problems. Specialized assessment is increasingly important within the human life span. It is not within the task of this book to do more than comment on the importance of such special assessment. Moreover, it would take us too far afield long to attempt to discuss what should be included in each of these special areas. However, the main point that should be made here is that these special assessment areas build upon the general assessment theory that has been discussed in this book. It is the fundamental assumption of this book that a knowledge of general assessment quickly transfers to problems of special assessment. Conversely, special assessment without general assessment is often misdirected. Once the overall assessment is understood, then focus on a specific problem can be undertaken.

This assumption is illustrated time and again by students who want to find a measure of depression, alcoholism, sexual disorder, values, type A behavior, bulimia, or some other specific area, rather than relating these ancillary measures to overall personality characteristics. What is ignored in this search is the fact that depression or type A behavior, or sexual disorders are often by-products of overall personal characteristics, not just some isolated entities in themselves.

Specialized assessment procedures are relevant within the entire life-span. Early childhood assessment, learning disabilities, adolescent problems such as bulimia and drug abuse, juvenile delinquency, vocational decision making, mid-career crises, aging, death and dying, are all areas of assessment that call for specialized tools and techniques. Each of these areas has much research published relative to tools, methods, etc.

In addition, some aspects of assessment require a systems analysis in terms of dyads or more individuals such as in family counseling, marriage problems, dual career families, crisis interventions, medical diseases, business situations, military applications, and many other areas.

NEEDED FUTURE DEVELOPMENTS

Assessment plays an important role in any form of classification, or intervention. In the recent decade there have been considerable developments with instruments such as the MMPI and MMPI-2, the CPI, Millon's diagnostic instruments, and particularly Krug's codification of 17,000 cases with the 16 PF (Krug, 1981). In each of these instances diagnostic evaluation has moved more and more towards reliance on computer reporting systems. However, the integration of these testing systems with each other is not known. Moreover, none of these systems at the present lead to clearly defined treatment alternatives.

In this book, temperament has played a central role because it relates primarily to emotional responses, appears to be related to primary factors of personality in both Eastern and Western psychological thinking, and is at the bedrock foundation of much of personality. Though the arguments can be and have been developed for this contention, the linkage between both environmental factors and other forms of assessment has not been completed. Some pioneering work with developing strategies of intervention from multimethod assessment of children in classrooms has been done by Barclay with the BCAS (1983a, 1983b), but these formulations have not been tested out on large-scale follow-ups of intervention.

Though temperament theory provides the distinct possibility for a true psychological classification scheme, there is still much work to be done with it before it can attain status similar to that of the DSM series.

The complexity of such development and the integration of many aspects of assessment that are still left up to the individual, call for the development of computer programs that will estimate characteristics of the individual, taking into consideration all or many of the components of assessment that have been described in this book. Once such a computer system can be developed (and the problems of doing this are formidable beyond the present generations of computer programs for analyzing test results), there may be an opportunity to match diagnoses with alternative treatments. Through this latter process we may eventually develop a diagnostic-treatment system that estimates relatively accurately the nature of the problem, the best treatment available, and the probability of successful outcomes.[2]

Tied in with such continuing development may be opportunity to provide invaluable feedback to individuals from elementary school through the life span of human development as to what kinds of strategies they need to develop self-help activities that maximize their abilities and minimize their liabilities. This type of feedback can be of tremendous value to all levels of education and the workforce. It cannot develop, however, without much collective effort on the part of researchers and practitioners.

Notes

Chapter 1.

1. One of the major issues of the late nineteenth century was related to whether psychology was a science and an adjunct to physiology or whether it was primarily focused on the nature and contents of consciousness. In assessment one must examine both the physiological data relating to human behavior and the contents of consciousness. Thus assessment must include both structural and process components.

2. There are many accounts of out of body experiences. Moody (1975) describes accounts drawn from 150 cases and examines issues relating to medicine, pharmacology, dreams and other phenomena. He also provides a historical account of these phenomena from ancient times to the present.

Chapter 2.

1. Unquestionably these statements could be the source of much philosophical controversy. For example, Descartes argued we could only make inferences of a scientific nature on entities that had extension (e.g., form, weight, texture). Locke argued that observations themselves formed the nature of generalizations about reality. However, since the time of Darwin, the role of perception as a construct characterized by meaningfulness through inferring reflects the structural imprint of thinking. Leibnitz's view that environmental information provided the grist for the mill of the human mind seems consistent with thinking today.

Chapter 3.

1. Social behavior is learned in very specific ways. One major determinant according to Bandura (1978) is related to the systematic process of shaping human behavior through modeling and reinforcement by parents. Parents thus form the first role models and later peers contribute to the development

of social behavior whether appropriate or not. Our approach to our culture is thus related to the process of social learning that takes place in relationship to our basic inherited tendencies.

2. Although other anthropologists may not subscribe to White's particular theories, they do recognize the force of his arguments. Moreover, in recent decades the study of the theory of culture has been joined to an understanding of how a culture effects its transmission. Certain cultural control mechanisms exist in every society. The primary one is the family itself in which the entire substance of cultural transmission is usually found. In addition, in the early tribe as well as in modern society, there must be those who set the laws of the culture. These people in tribal and earlier societies were the chieftan, the medicine-man, and the council of elders. Often when there were crucial matters to discuss all of the adult men of the community were brought together. In later society, the chieftan became the king or noble. The heirs of the medicine-man became the priest. This functional arrangement exists today utilizing modern technology. The president of the United States can now address all of the people in the nation on television, and religious evangelists can enter every home for their diverse purposes using the same media.

3. Egypt has had a very long history. There are records of 30 ruling families which extend before 3000 BC until the beginning of the last one that was founded by Ptolemy in 323 BC. Egypt is the story of a place in which earlier settlers formed two kingdoms and later a single unified kingdom under the rule of the pharaohs who were viewed as god-kings. The Nile acted as a great green highway between the Mediterranean at one end and the mountains of Ethiopia at the other. Over a period of several thousand years an urban civilization grew up here that was secured by the desert on both sides, blessed with alluvial floods that allowed multiple crops, and experienced an unparalled explosion in architecture, sculpture, and all kinds of learning.

About the same time (3500–2500BC) on the vast plain joined by the Tigris and Euphrates rivers, another urban civilization developed, that of Sumeria. Although the alluvial flooding created a good environment for agriculture, this land was not as protected as Egypt and as a consequence, the entire history of that area is one of warfare and conquests. However, warfare led to the recognition that conquered people could become slaves and could be a source of increased economic advantage. Sophisticated developments in metallurgy with the invention of hard metals were all probable consequences of continued warfare. In addition, the need to keep reports led to the development of writing and arithmetic. Our present system of dividing the year into twelve months, the days into two sets of twelve hours, the hour into sixty minutes, and the minute into sixty seconds is a product of Sumerian thinking.

4. In the light of subsequent discoveries, the Hebrew dietary laws were eminently rational and correct in their formulations of what was potentially clean or safe food. Vegetarianism was permitted except for the fruit of newly planted trees. With regard to meat, fowl and fish, only herbivorous animals which had parted hooves were considered acceptable (*Lev. 11:3–8, Deut. 14: 4–8*). All insects except locusts, rapacious aquatic and predatory birds, and fishes without fins or scales were forbidden. The beneficial nature of these ordinances is demonstrated by the fact that under subtropical conditions, meat from vegetarian animals is much less likely to contain food poisoning agents than those of carnivores. Restrictions against pork were especially severe, but for good reasons. The pig is subject to infestation by Trichenella Spiralis and tapeworms. The Egyptians also had a prohibition against pork.

Other features in Hebrew medicine were related to hygiene and personal cleanliness. Hebrew laws considered all body discharges as unclean (*Lev.15: 1–5*). These regulations incorporated into the purification framework extended to both abnormal body discharges as might be found in gonorrhea and normal emissions of semen. Women were subject to special restrictions regarding their menstrual period and also following parturition. Detailed laws existed relating to the removal of wastes, refuse, and the burial of the dead. Comprehensive regulations existed for leprosy and other skin diseases.

5. Some of these assessments were done by actual testing, and others were done by judgments of proficiency. The tests were administered at three levels. Any individual could apply to take the test in his district capitol. If he did well, he would be permitted to take another battery of tests at the provincial capitol. Usually some 20 or so individuals would be picked out to attend the testing sessions at the provincial capitol which took place each third year under the supervision of scholars sent from Peking. A handful of scholars were then picked from the provincial examinations and registered in the national competition. If a scholar was successful in the national competition, he was easily given access to the political and governmental positions available throughout the empire. Meanwhile provincial and district posts were available to those who had passed the examinations at the other levels. Examinations were scored by two or more independent examiners and the candidates' names were carefully concealed. Scores were obtained on the basis of rank-order.

A similar system existed within the Roman Empire and was established by Augustus in the first years of the Christian era. This system which was in all effects a national civil-service system lasted almost intact up to the period of Diocletian, some 300 years later. Unfortunately, the system failed because of debased currency, population loss, poor communications, increased forced responsibility on this class, and invasions.

These two examples point out that assessment was used in a very widespread manner in the ancient world and affected politics, medicine, and all forms of governmental jobs.

6. There is a recurring theme in psychological thought which suggests that at various times in the history of psychology, there have been those who preferred to seek more precise and definable knowledge of human behavior through careful, logical, or experimental analyses of behavior, as against those who recognize the complexity of mental phenomena. With Plato and Aristotle we observe the first clash between a system based on empirical observation of facts (Aristotle) and humanistic considerations of internal phenomena (Plato). In medieval times, Thomas Aquinas attempted to reduce complex mental processes to a set of orderly and logical judgments. Duns Scotus rejected such methods in favor of a specific individuality that later influenced Luther and existentialism. Still later, Hermann Helmholtz proclaimed that psychology was essentially the study of physiology and that there was no room for a soul or psyche. Franz Brentano opposed this view indicating that a natural science of psychological phenomena could be established on the basis of the analysis of the contents of consciousness. Most recently, American psychology has seen the clash between structuralism and functionalism in the 1920s, and then the debate between B. F. Skinner and Carl Rogers. Thus there appears to be within various time periods, a clash between those who accent and value the external forms of behavior versus those who look at the complexity of human thinking and consciousness.

7. There is some evidence that the Greeks knew something about experimental methods and used them to amass scientific proofs. From the manner in which the Pythagorean theorem was demonstrated and from other findings about the circumference of the earth, many commentators on the development of science believe that the Greeks used experimental methods. What is important to realize, however, is that they considered these methods a trade secret and kept them as a part of the mysteries relating to scientific studies and initiations into what they termed philosopher status. For this reason, there is little or nothing written down about the process.

8. Within the whole medieval period, and extending up to modern times, there was a form of counseling and advising that was done under the title of "spiritual advising." This was an effort to develop spiritual aspects of "character" through a one-to-one effort of an advisor to help a neophyte.

Chapter 5

1. What happens from observations made under each of these methods is that inferences are drawn, usually of a causal nature. Sociable and affiliative relationships towards people are judged to be indicators of a trait of socia-

bility by virtually all observers. Likewise, aloofness, withdrawal and reticence are seen as indicators of a trait of introversion. The concept of trait is then viewed by many psychologists as a rather stable set of characteristics which are consistent over long periods of time with the temperament disposition of the individual. Behaviorists generally do not view inferences thus drawn as indicative of stable enduring dispositions, but, rather see them as temporary states that are situation specific. In their position, a state of anxiety if generarated by a combination of circumstances and learning that lead to such a condition of the organism disappear when the state of the organism changes.

2. Lewin's premature death resulted in a kind of Zeigarnik effect on many of his colleagues. His theoretical system had not been completed, and his effort to operationalize phenomological concepts was still in need of extensive development. His contributions to dynamic psychology and the social aspects of learning were enormous.

Chapter 6

1. Obviously there is much more to be said about temperament, but I have relied here on the most basic and most agreed upon elements that combine to make up the construct of temperament.

Chapter 10

1. Parts of this section were presented at the **Fifth International Conference on Temperament** at Athens, Georgia, November 2, 1988. It should be noted that the rather extensive coverage given to the BCAS has not been done for self-serving reasons, but is reported because after 25 years of research with this tool, the writer believes that the findings provide evidence of the utility of sociometrics and the basis that they have in good assessment.

2. On a personal note I should indicate that 33 years ago when this was being done, there were no guidelines for interventions or even consultation. It is difficult for the modern reader to understand that the words themselves were not even in the vocabulary of psychologists, i.e., interventions and consultation. My reasoning at that time was that something could be done. The configuration of the grid itself suggested that children in cell 7 needed to develop a support system, and that children in cells 1 and 9 needed different types of help. For the main part, I chose curriculum alternatives, worked with the school district to regroup children in new settings, and tried out a number of group discussion and group intervention processes. Some failed miserably. However, enough seemed to work to have teachers request testing year by year. It was, however, extremely time-consuming to do all this research by hand, without any clerical help, and in most instances without calculators.

3. A further commentary of a personal nature needs to be made on this matter. I was in England at the time the Bennett report was published. Because of the highly similar findings, I contacted Bennett who immediately invited me to visit him at the University of Lancaster. When I arrived there, he had the earlier manuals of the BCAS and a number of research studies on a work table and pointed them out to me. He indicated that he modeled his own system on that of the BCAS. He had considered using my system, but because of funds, and the possibility that some items were not relevant to English students, he developed his own similar system.

Chapter 13

1. A note should be made here about what is referred to as intuitive. The word intuitive comes from the Latin word *intuor*, that means to look into or beyond. Intuitive inferences are those which are made about empirical or psychometric data that include judgments or leaps in judgments that do not find their necessary basis in logical-scientific criteria. Sometimes individuals who have great skills in a specific method such as the Rorschach, can make such intuitive judgments. For example, as a student intern, I worked with a psychologists who claimed he could tell what country an individual's grandparents came from by the individual's responses on the Rorschach. Another example can be found in astrology that postulates a cosmic relationship which influences or at least provides certain inclinations towards ways of thinking and behaving. For example, if an individual does not like to go to parties, is introverted, and prefers to spend free time in the pursuit of hobbies, how is this related to the configuration of planets and houses found at the moment of this individual's birth?

2. It is relevant for me to here to indicate why I am devoting so much space to the topic of intuitive assessment because these approaches are often considered aspects of pseudoscience. The reasons for this inclusion in the text relate to four facts. First of all, in 30 years of teaching graduate courses in testing and assessment, I have found that virtually all students are highly curious about these methods. When they are simply dismissed by instructors as superstition, there is no real opportunity for students to examine the theoretical bases of these approaches. In addition, recently Rotton and Kelly (1985) reported that nearly half of 165 undergraduates surveyed in a study stated that they believed in lunar influences and that such belief was common among psychiatric nurses surveyed. Second, even very fair-minded psychologists either ignore or choose to omit relevant information about some of these techniques. For example, Sundberg in his book on assessment (1977), mentions that Gaugelin (1967) did not establish a relationship between Aries or Mars and military birth dates (Gaugelin is a French statistician). But he fails to mention that Gaugelin did establish a significant

relationship between the rise of Saturn and the birth of physicians and that this relationship was confirmed by independent studies in Belgium. Third, very reputable psychologists such as Hans Eysenck, have called for more rigorous and intensive studies of astrology to determine what are the facts involved in the variability of individual differences ascribed to these intuitive variables (Eysenck, personal communication). For that reason he continues to serve on the editorial board of a new journal of research on astrology published in England (*Correlation, Journal of Research into Astrology*). Finally, it is a fact that there are a number of studies of astrological nature present in current psychological literature on assessment. A recent research of APA abstracts yielded 69 abstracts, and a search of *Dissertation Abstracts* listed 29 doctoral dissertations done on some aspect of astrology and psychology.

Chapter 15

1. Although I have placed these dimensions in a cube arrangement to denote their mutual interaction, it is possible to consider each of them as separate assessment axes. In this way they would each provide an approach similar to the DSM series axes.

2. I am not convinced that a statistical, linear, or regression relationship of significant magnitude exists between the various components or axes of individual assessment to justify a profile analysis. The ordinary method of presenting these components might be in a profile analysis. Such a graphic representation, however, would postulate some kind of efficient causal relationships between components or axes, or the assumption of equal variance relating to each component. Given the present status of assessment, it would seem to me that it would be rash to believe that a comprehensive assessment of various axes or methods would yield results that would fit a regression equation. Sometimes very minor events in life result in great changes on some or all of the axes over time. Moreover, the effects of living through various stages of the life-span of individuals must also be examined. Thus, it would appear to me that longitudinal studies of diagnostics and outcomes as related to the several and collective arrays of assessment data need to be done. The ultimate outcomes of this type of research might yield probability estimates of the effectiveness of placements or treatments over a period of time. Something similar to this proposal was done by Hartl, Monnelly and Elderkin (1982) in a thirty-year follow-up of the initial diagnostics of 200 men whose youthful biographies were assembled by Sheldon in 1949.

Bibliography

Adams, H. E., Doster, J. A. & Calhoun, K. S. (1977). A psychologically based system of response classification. In Ciminero, A. R., Calhoun, K. S. & Adams, H. E. (Eds.), *Handbook of behavioral assessment*. New York: Wiley-Interscience.

Albee, G. W., (1982). Preventing psychopathology and promoting human potential. *American Psychologist, 37*, #9, 1043–1050.

Allport, G. W. (1961). *Pattern and growth in personality*. New York: Holt, Rinehart & Winston.

American Psychiatric Association (1980). *Diagnostic and statistical manual of mental disorders*. Washington D.C.

American Psychiatric Association (1988). *Diagnostic and statistical manual of mental disorders*, third edition, revised. Washington, D.C.

American Psychological Association (1985). *Standards for educational and psychological testing*. Washington, D.C.

Amidon, E. (1963). The isolate in children's groups: changing his sociometric status. Chapter in J. M. Seidman (Ed.), *Educating for mental health*. New York: Thomas Y. Crowell.

Anastasi, A. (1976). *Psychological testing* (fourth edition). New York: Macmillan Co.

Anderson, G. J. (1970). Effects of classroom social climate on individual learning. Paper presented AERA National Meeting, Minneapolis.

Anderson, G. W. (1968). Effects of classroom social climate on individual learning. Unpublished doctoral dissertation, Harvard University.

Anderson, H. A. & Anderson, G. L. (1951). *An introduction to projective techniques*. Englewood Cliffs: Prentice-Hall, Inc.

Astin, A. (1965). *Who goes where to college*. Chicago: Science Research Associates.

Astrographic Services Inc. (1980). *Computer programs for astrological computation*. Orleans, Mass.

Atkinson, J. W. (1964). *An introduction to motivation*. Princeton, N.J.: Van Nostrand.

Ausubel, D. P. (1963). *The psychology of meaningful verbal learning*. New York: Grune & Stratton.

Backus, D. W. (1969). The seven deadly sins, their meaning and measurement. Ph.D. dissertation, University of Minnesota.

Bandura, A. (1969). *Principles of behavior modification*. New York: Holt, Rinehart & Winston.

Bandura, A. (1972). *Modeling theory: some traditions, trends, and disputes, in Recent trends in social learning theory*, Park, R. D. (Ed.), New York: Academic Press.

Bandura, A. (1978). *The self system in reciprocal determinism*. American Psychologist, 33, #4, 344–358.

Bandura, A. & Walters, R. H. (1963). *Social learning and personality development*. New York: Holt, Rinehart & Winston.

Barbe, W. B. (1954). Peer relationships of children of different intelligence levels. *School and Society*, 60–62.

Barclay, J. R. (1956). Unpublished data, Redford Union School District, Detroit, Michigan.

Barclay, J. R. (1964). Studies in sociometry and teacher ratings: a diagnostic and predictive combination for school psychology, lithographed. Pocatello: Idaho State University.

Barclay, J. R. (1966a). Sociometric choices and teacher ratings as predictors of school dropouts. *Journal of School Psychology*, 33, #4, 344–358.

Barclay, J. R. (1966b). Interest patterns associated with measures of social desirability: some implications for dropouts and the culturally disadvantaged. *Personnel and Guidance Journal*, 45, #1, 56–60.

Barclay, J. R. (1966c). Variability in sociometric scores and teachers' ratings as related to teacher, age and sex. *Journal of School Psychology*, 5, #1, 52–58.

Barclay, J. R. (1966d). Sociometry: rationale and technique for effecting behavior change in the elementary school. *Personnel and Guidance Journal*, 44, #10, 1067–1076.

Barclay, J. R. (1967a). Effecting behavior change in the elementary classroom: an exploratory study. *Journal of Counseling Psychology*, 14, #3, 240–247.

Barclay, J. R. (1967b). Approach to the measurement of teacher "press" in the secondary curriculum. Monograph, *Journal of Counseling Psychology*, 14, 550–567.

Barclay, J. R. (1968a). *Counseling and philosophy: a theoretical exposition.* Boston: Houghton-Mifflin.

Barclay, J. R. (1968b). *Controversial issues in testing.* Boston: Houghton-Mifflin.

Barclay, J. R. (1970) Expectancy and social interaction in classroom learning. Paper presented at APA Symposium, "What experimental psychology has to offer—donor learning theory and principles: recipient, the classroom," APA National Convention, Miami.

Barclay, J. R. (1971a). Measuring the social climate of the classroom. Monograph #40, *Educational Technology.*

Barclay, J. R. (1971b). *Appraising individual differences in the elementary classroom: a manual of the Barclay Classroom Climate Inventory.* Lexington, Ky.: Educational Skills Development Inc.

Barclay, J. R. (1971c). Descriptive, theoretical and behavioral characteristics of sub-doctoral school psychologists. *American Psychologist, 26, #3,* 257–280.

Barclay, J. R. (1971d). *Foundations of counseling strategies.* New York: John Wiley.

Barclay, J. R. (1972). *The Barclay classroom climate inventory: a research manual and studies.* Lexington, Ky.: Educational Skills Development Inc.

Barclay, J. R. (1974a). A preliminary evaluation of Elyria's experiment in affective education. Unpublished report, University of Kentucky.

Barclay, J. R. (1974b). What teachers, parents, students and professionals say about the Barclay Classroom Climate Inventory. Unpublished paper, University of Kentucky.

Barclay, J. R. (1974c). System-wide analysis of social interaction and affective problems in schools. In Park O. Davidson, Frank W. Clark, and Leo A. Hamerlynck (Eds.), *Evaluation of behavioral programs in community, residential, and school settings.* Champaign, Illinois: Research Press.

Barclay, J. R. (1974d). Needs assessment in the elementary school. In H. J. Walberg (Ed.), *Evaluation of educational performance: a sourcebook of methods, instruments and examples* (pp. 47–56). Berkeley, California: McCutchan Publishing Co.

Barclay, J. R. (1980). Classroom motivation. In R. Woody (Ed.), *Encyclopedia of clinical assessment* (Vol. 2, pp. 766–775) San Francisco: Jossey-Bass.

Barclay, J. R. (1982). Meta-theory and meta-analysis: the possible contribution to measurement and evaluation. *Measurement and Evaluation in Guidance, 11, #4,* 370–376.

Barclay, J. R. (1983a). *Manual of the Barclay Classroom Assessment System,* Los Angeles: Western Psychological Services.

Barclay, J. R. (1983b). A meta-analysis of temperament-treatment interactions with alternative learning and counseling treatments. *Developmental Review*, #3 (November), 410–443.

Barclay, J. R. (1983c). Moving toward a technology of prevention: a model and some tentative findings. *School Psychology Review*, 12, #3, 228–239.

Barclay, J. R. (1987). The Strelau temperament inventory as a broad classification system. *Archives of Clinical Neuropsychology*, 2, 307–327.

Barclay, J. R. (1988a). Temperament as a typology. Unpublished paper, University of Kentucky.

Barclay, J. R. (1988b). The computer as a diagnostician for interventions: implications for school psychology. Paper in preparation, University of Kentucky.

Barclay, J. R. (1988c). *The student adjustment inventory*, Champaign, Ill.: Metritech Inc.

Barclay, J. R., Stilwell, W. E., Barclay, L. K. (1972). Influence of paternal occupation on social interaction measures in elementary school children. *Journal of Vocational Behavior*, 2, 433–446.

Barclay, J. R., Covert, R. M., Scott, T. W. & Stilwell, W. E. (1975). *Some effects of schooling: a three-year follow-up of title III project*. Lexington, Ky.: Educational Skills Development.

Barclay, J. R. & Kehle, T. J. (1979). The impact of handicapped students on other students in the classroom. *Journal of Research and Development in Education*, 12, 80–91.

Barclay, J. R., Montgomery, R., & Barclay, L. K. (1971). Measuring the effectiveness of intensive teacher training in social learning and behavior modification techniques. *Measurement and Evaluation in Guidance*, 4, #2, 79–89.

Barclay, J. R. & Soldahl, T. A. (1966). Student characteristics of success and failure in a vocational education follow-up. Unpublished paper, California State University at Hayward.

Barclay, J. R., Stilwell, W. E., Santoro, D. A. & Clark, C. M. (1972). Correlates of behavioral observations and academic achievement with elementary patterns of social interaction. Unpublished study, University of Kentucky.

Barclay, J. R. & Wu, W. (1980). Classroom climates in Taiwanese and American elementary classrooms: a cross-cultural study. *Contemporary Educational Psychology*, 5, 65–82.

Barclay, J. R., Phillips, G. & Jones, T. (1983). Developing a predictive index of giftedness. *Measurement and Evaluation in Guidance*, 16, #1, 25–35.

Barclay, L. K. (1987). Skill development and temperament in kindergarten children: a cross-cultural study. *Perceptual and Motor Skills*, 65, 963–972.

Barclay, L. K. & Barclay, J. R. (1965). Measured indices of perceptual distortion and impulsivity as related to sociometric scores and teacher ratings. *Psychology in the Schools, 2,* #4, 372–375.

Barclay, L. K. & Barclay, J. R. (1986). *PACE: A computer-based instrument for assessing and developing learning skills.* Champaign: Metritech, Inc.

Barkley, R. A. (1977). A review of stimulant drug research with hyperactive children, *Journal of Child Psychology and Psychiatry, 18.* 137–165.

Barlow, D. H. (1977). Assessment of sexual behavior. In A. R. Cimenero, K. S. Calhoun & H. E. Adams (Eds.) *Handbook of behavioral assessment.* New York: Wiley-Interscience.

Barnes, G. E. (1985). The Vando R-A Scale as a measure of stimulus reducing-augmenting. In J. Strelau, F. H. Farley, & A. Gale (Eds.), *The biological bases of personality and behavior: theories, measurement techniques and development* (Vol. 1, pp. 171–180). Washington: Hemisphere.

Barratt, E. S. (1985). Impulsiveness subtraits: arousal and information processing. In J. T. Spence & C. E. Izard (Eds.), *Motivation, emotion, and personality* (pp. 137–146). Amsterdam: North-Holland.

Barta, F. R. (1956). *The moral theory of behavior.* Springfield, Illinois: Charles C. Thomas.

Baron, J. (1982). Personality and intelligence. Chapter in Sternberg, R. J. (Ed.), *Handbook of human intelligence.* Cambridge: Cambridge University Press.

Barrett, R. L. (1968). Changes in accuracy of self-estimates. *Personnel and Guidance Journal, 47,* #4, 353–357.

Bates, J. E. (1984a). Information on the infant characteristics questionnaire (ICQ-IQ), unpublished manuscript, Department of Psychology, Indiana University, Bloomington, Indiana.

Bates, J. E. (1984b). Information on the infant characteristics questionnaire (ICQ-CC), unpublished manuscript, Department of Psychology, Indiana University, Bloomington, Indiana.

Bates, J. E. (1984c). Information on the infant characteristics questionnaire (ICQ-IC), unpublished manuscript, Department of Psychology, Indiana University, Bloomington, Indiana.

Bauman, I. & Angst, J. (1972). Die marke-nyman temperamentskala (MNT). *Zeitschrift fuer Klinische Psychologie, 1,* 189–212.

Baumrind, D. (1971). Current patterns of parental authority. Monograph supplement, *Developmental Psychology, 4,* #1, Part 2.

Beal, J. B. (1974). Electrostatic fields, electromagnetic fields, and ions—mind/body environment interrelationships. Chapter in J. G. Llaurado, A., Sances, J. R. & Battocletti, J. H. (Eds.), *Biologic and clinical effects of low-frequency magnetic and electric fields.* Springfield, Illinois: Charles C. Thomas.

Beck, A. T. (1967). *Depression: causes and treatment*. Philadelphia: University of Pennsylvania Press.

Becker-Carus, C. (1971). Relationships between EEG, personality and vigilance. *Electroencephalography and Clinical Neurophysiology, 30*, 519–526.

Bedoian, V. H. (1953). Mental health analysis of socially over-accepted, socially under-accepted, over-age and under-age pupils in the sixth grade. *Journal of Educational Psychology, 44*, 366–371.

Beemer, L. C. (1972). Developmental changes in the self-concept of children and adolescents. Dissertation Abstracts, 32 (A), March, 5031–5032.

Bellak, L. (1954). *The thematic apperception tests and the children's apperception test in clinical use*. New York: Grune & Stratton.

Belous, V. V. (1968). Type of temperament as a function of type of the nervous system. *Voprosy Paikhologii, 14*, #8, 77–80.

Bender, L. (1964). *Instructions for the use of the visual motor gestalt test*. New York: American Orthopsychiatric Association.

Benjamin, L. S. (1974). Structural analysis of social behavior. *Psychological Review, 81*, 392–425.

Benjamin, L. S. (1977). Structural analysis of a family in therapy. *Journal of Consulting and Clinical Psychology, 45*, 391–406.

Benne, K. D. (1976). The processes of re-education: an assessment of Kurt Lewin's views. *Group and Organizational Studies, 1*, #1, 26–42.

Bennett, N. (1976). *Teaching styles and pupil progress*. London: Open Books.

Bergan, J. R. (1977). *Behavioral consultation*. Columbus: Charles E. Merrill Co.

Bergin, A. E. & Garfield, S. L. (1973). *Handbook of psychotherapy and behavioral change*. New York: John Wiley.

Bernreuter, R. G. (1935). *The personality inventory*. Stanford: Stanford University Press.

Berlyne, D. E. (1967). Arousal and reinforcement. Chapter in Levine, D. (Ed.), *Nebraska symposium on motivation*. Lincoln, Nebraska: University of Nebraska Press.

Bidwick, A. J. (1972). A study of the effectiveness of meaningful adult contacts on the self-concept, behavior and achievement of junior high school disciplinary problems. *Dissertation Abstracts, 32* (A), February, 4339–4340.

Bilby, R. W. (1972). Current and future characterizations of self: a theoretical model for analyzing the sources and functions of self-conception. Dissertation Abstracts, 33 (A) November, 3024.

Binder, D. M., Jones, J. G. & Strowig, R. W. (1970). Non-intellective self-report variables as predictors of scholastic achievement, *Journal of Educational Research, 63*, #8, 364–366.

Birdwhistle, R. L. (1970). *Kinesics and context*. Philadelphia: University of Pennsylvania Press.

Bjerstedt, N. (1956). The interpretation of sociometric status scores in the classroom. *Nordisk Psychologi, 8*, 1–14.

Bledsoe, J. C., & Wiggins, R. G. (1973). Congruence of adolescents' self-concepts and parents' perceptions of adolescents' self-concepts. *Journal of Psychology, 83*, #1, 131–136.

Block, J. (1961). *The Q Sort method in personality assessment and psychiatric research*, Springfield, Ill.: Charles C. Thomas.

Block, J. (1975). Recognizing the coherence of personality. Paper presented at the American Psychological Association symposium: the future of personality assessment, Chicago.

Block, J. & Haan, N. (1971). *Lives through time*. Berkeley, CA: Bancroft.

Bloom, B. J. (1968). *Learning for mastery*. Evaluation Comment, Los Angeles: Center for the Study of Evaluation of Instructional Programs, 1, #2.

Bloom, B. S. (1956). *Taxonomy of educational objectives: handbook I., cognitive domain*. New York: David McKay Co.

Bok, B. J. (1975). Objections to astrology. *The Humanist, September-October*, 4–9.

Bonney, M. E. (1943a). The constancy of sociometric scores and their relationship to teacher judgments of social success and to personality self-ratings. *Sociometry, 6* , 409–424.

Bonney, M. E. (1943b). The relative stability of social, intellectual and academic status in grades II to IV and the interrelationships between these various forms of growth. *Journal of Educational Psychology, 34*, 88–102.

Bonney, M. E. & Powell, J. (1953). Differences in social behavior between sociometrically high and sociometrically low children. *Journal of Educational Research, 46*, 481–495.

Bordin, E. S. (1946). Diagnosis in counseling and psychotherapy. *Educational and Psychological Measurement, 6*, 169–184.

Boring, E. G. (1950). *A history of experimental psychology*. New York: (2nd edition), Appleton-Century-Crofts.

Bouchard, R. P. (1971). An experiment in student self-concept change through teacher interaction, *Dissertation Abstracts, 32* (A), August, 660.

Bowes, S. & Gintis, H. (1973). I.Q. in the U.S. Class Structure, a Warner Modular Publication Reprint #296 (reprinted from Social Policy, 3, #4 & 5).

Boyko, G. W. (1970). Effect of methodology on the self-concept of students. *Dissertation Abstracts International, 31*, December, 2607A.

Bradley, R. W. (1982). Using birth order and sibling dynamics in career counseling. *Personnel and Guidance Journal, 61*, #1, 25–30.

Brady, R. P. (1972). An examination of selected variables affecting the vocational development of elementary school children. *Dissertation Abstracts 32* (A), January, 3681–3682.

Brammer, L. & Shostrum, E. (1977). *Therapeutic psychology*. Englewood Cliffs, New Jersey: Prentice-Hall.

Brauer, S. L. (1971). Reappraisal of the self through knowledge of the performance of others, identification vs. social comparison processes. *Dissertation Abstracts, 32* (A) September 1618–1620.

Brentano, F. (1876 & 1924). *Psychologie vom empirischen*. Standpunkt, Vols I, II, Leipzig: Meiner.

Brigham, C. C. (1923). *A study of American intelligence*. Princeton: Princeton University Press.

Brimberg, D. & McGrath, J. E. (1985). *Validity and the research process*, Beverly Hills: Sage Publications.

Bringman, W. C. & Bringman, N.J. (1980). In W. C. Bringman & R. D. Tweney (Eds.), *Wundt studies: a centennial collection*. Toronto: C. J. Hogrefe Inc.

Broadhurst, A. & Glass, A. (1969). Relationship of personality measures to alpha rhythm of the electroencephalogram. *British Journal of Psychiatry, 115*, 199–204.

Brock, A. J. (1963). *Galen on the natural faculties*. Cambridge, Mass.: Harvard University Press.

Brophy, J. E. & Good, T. L. (1974). *Teacher-student relationships: causes and consequences*. New York: Holt, Rinehart & Winston.

Brown, F. A. (1966). Effects and after-effects on planarians of reversals of the horizontal magnetic vector. *Nature, 211*, (5051), 533–535.

Brown, F. A., Park, Y. H. & Zeno, J. R. (1966). Diurnal variation in organismic response to very weak gamma radiation. *Nature, 211*, (5051), 830–833.

Brown, S. R. (1968). Bibliography on Q techniques and its methodology, *Perceptual and Motor Skills, 26*, 587–613.

Bruner, J. S. (1963). *On knowing*. Cambridge, Mass.: Harvard University Press.

Bruner, S. R. (1966). *Toward a theory of instruction*. Cambridge Mass.: Harvard University Press.

Buffery, A. W. H. & Gray, J. A. (1972). Sex differences in the development of spatial and linguistic skills. In C. Ounsted and D. C. Taylor (Eds.), *Gender differences: their ontogeny and significance*. London: Churchill-Livingston.

Burks, J.& Rubenstein, M. (1979). *Temperament styles in adult interaction*. New York: Brunner/Mazel.

Buros, O. K. (Ed.) (1972). *The seventh mental measurements yearbook*. Highland Park, N.J.: Gryphon Press.

Bush, R. N. (1954). *The teacher-pupil relationship*. Englewood-Cliffs: Prentice-Hall.

Buss, A. H. & Plomin, R. (1975). *A temperament theory of personality development*. New York: Wiley.

Buss, A. R. (1975). The emerging field of the sociology of psychological knowledge. *American Psychologist, 30*, #10, 988–1002.

Buss, A. R. & Royce, J. R. (1975). Ontogenetic changes in cognitive structure from a multivariate perspective. *Developmental Psychology, 11*, #1, 87–101.

Butcher, J. N., Graham, J. R., Williams, C. L. & Ben-Porath, Y. S. (1990). *Development and use of the MMPI-2 content scales*. Minneapolis: University of Minnesota Press.

Cairns, R. B. (1983). Sociometry, psychometry and social structure: a commentary on six recent studies of popular, rejected and neglected children. *Merrill-Palmer Quarterly, 29*, #4, 429–438.

California Test Bureau (1958). *The S-O-Rorschach Test* (SORT) Los Angeles.

Campbell, D. E. & Beets, J. L. (1978). Lunacy and the moon. *Psychological Bulletin, 85*, #5, 1123–1129.

Campbell, D. P. (1971). *Handbook for the strong vocational interest blank*. Stanford: Stanford University Press.

Campbell, D. T. & Fiske, D. W. (1959). Convergent and discriminant validation by the multitrait-multimethod matrix. *Psychological Bulletin, 56*, 81–105.

Canty, J. J. (1970). Personality and behavior correlates of extreme positive regard. *Dissertation Abstracts International, 31* (5-B), November, 2978–2979.

Caprara, G. V., Cinanni, V., D'Imperio, G., Passerini, S., Renzi, P., & Travaglia, G. (1985). Indicators of impulsive aggression: present status of research on irritability and emotional susceptibility scales. *Personality and Individual Differences, 6*, 665–674.

Carey, W. B., & McDevitt, S. C. (1978). Revision of the infant temperament questionnaire. *Pediatrics, 61*, 735–739.

Carkhuff, R. R. (1969). *Helping and human relations*. (2 vols.) New York: Holt, Rinehart & Winston.

Carlson, R. (1971). Sex differences in ego functioning, *Journal of Consulting and Clinical Psychology, 37*, 267–277.

Carroll, J. B. (1982). The measurement of intelligence. In R. J. Sternberg (Ed.), *Handbook of human intelligence*. Cambridge: Cambridge University Press.

Cattell, R. B. (1946). *Description and measurement of personality*. New York: World Book Co.

Cattell, R. B. (1966). *Handbook of multivariate experimental psychology*. Chicago: Rand-McNally.

Catterall, C. D. & Gazda, G. M. (1978). *Strategies for helping students*. Springfield, Ill.: Charles C. Thomas.

Cautela, J. R. (1981a). *Organic dysfunction survey schedules*. Champaign: Research Press.

Cautela, J. R. (1981b). *Behavior analysis forms for clinical intervention*. Champaign: Research Press.

Cheney, C. & Morse, W. C. (1972). Psychodynamic interventions in emotional disturbance. In William C. Rhodes & Michael L. Tracy (Eds.), *A study of child variance, study of mental retardation and related disabilities* (Vol. 2). Ann Arbor: Institute for the Study of Mental Retardation.

Chicago Board of Education (undated). Measures of self-concept.

Ciminero, A. R., Calhoun, K. S. & Adams, H. E. (Eds.) (1977). *Handbook of behavioral assessment*. New York: Wiley-Interscience.

Clark, K. B. (1955). *Prejudice and your child*. Boston: Beacon Press.

Clark, K. B. & Clark, M. P. (1947). Racial identification and preference in Negro children. In T. L. Newcomb & E. L. Hartley (Eds.), *Readings in social psychology*. Boston: Holt.

Coan, R. W. (1968). Dimensions of psychological theory. *American Psychologist, 23*, October, #10, 720.

Cohen, D. W. (1983). The relationship of temperament clusters to causal attribution of academic success and perceived self-competence in fourth, fifth and sixth grade children. Unpublished doctoral dissertation, University of Kentucky.

Coie, J. D. & Dodge, K. A. (1983). Continuities and changes in children's social status: a five-year longitudinal study. *Merrill-Palmer Quarterly, 29*, 261–282.

Coleman, J. S. (1961). *The adolescent society*. New York: The Free Press of Glencoe.

Coleman, J. S. (1966). Equality of educational opportunity. Washington D.C.: U.S. Dept. of Health, Educational, and Welfare, U.S. Office of Education, OE-38001.

Conley, J. J. (1984). Longitudinal consistency of adult personality: self-reported psychological characteristics across 45 years. *Journal of Personality and Social Psychology, 47*, #6, 1325–1333.

Conte, H. R., & Plutchik, R. (1981). A circumplex model for interpersonal personality traits, *Journal of Personality and Social Psychology, 48*, #4, 701–711.

Conway, W. J. (1972). Parents' use of behavior modification to enhance their children's self-concept of ability and academic achievement. *Dissertation Abstracts, 32*, (A), March, 5034.

Coopersmith, S. (1967). *Antecedents of self-esteem*. San Francisco: W. H. Freeman, Co.

Cormier, W. H. & Cormier, L. S. (1979). *Interviewing strategies for helpers*. Monterey, Ca.: Brooks-Cole.

Cotler, S., & Palmer, R. J. (1970). The relationships among sex, sociometric, self, and test anxiety factors and the academic achievement of elementary school children, *Psychology in the Schools, 7*, #3, 211–216.

Crandall, R. (1972). On the relationship between self-esteem, coping and optimism. *Psychological Reports, 30*, #2, 485–486.

Crandall, R. (1973). Measures of self-esteem. In J. R. Robinson & P. R. Shaver (Eds.), *Measures of social psychological attitudes*. Ann Arbor, Michigan: Institute for Social Research, University of Michigan.

Crandall, V. J., Katkovsy, W. & Preston, A. (1960). A conceptual formulation for some research on children's achievement development. *Child Development, 31*, 787–797.

Crites, J. O. (1969). *Vocational Psychology*. New York: McGraw-Hill.

Cronbach, L. J. (1970). A possible hierarchical structure of abilities. Cited in N. D. Sundberg, *Assessment of persons*. Englewood Cliffs: Prentice-Hall.

Cronbach, L. J. & Gleser, G. C. (1965). *Psychological tests and personnel decisions*. Urbana: University of Illinois Press.

Cronbach, L. J. & Snow, R. E. (1977). *Aptitude and instructional methods*. New York: Irvington Press.

Cruise, R. J., Blitchington, W. P., and Futcher, W. G. A. (1980). Temperament inventory: an instrument to empirically verify the four-factor hypothesis, *Educational and Psychological Measurement, 40*, 943–954.

Crumbaugh, J. C. (1980). Graphoanalytic cues. In R. H. Woody (Ed.), *Encyclopedia of clinical assessment* (Vol. 2). San Francisco: Jossey-Bass.

Cucelogu, D. M. (1967). A cross-cultural study of communication via facial expressions. Doctoral dissertation, University of Illinois.

Cunningham, M. (1979). Weather, mood and helping behavior: quasi experiments with the sunshine samaritan. *Journal of Personality and Social Psychology, 37*, #11, 1947–1956.

Cunningham, W. G. (1975). The impact of student-teaching pairings on teacher effectiveness. *American Educational Research Journal, 12*, #2, 169–189.

Dahlstrom, W. G. & Welsh, G. S. (1960). *An MMPI handbook: a guide to use in clinical practice and research*. Minneapolis: University of Minnesota Press.

Dana, R. H. (1982). *A human science model for personality assessment with projective techniques*. Springfield, Ill.: Charles C. Thomas.

Dangaard, C. (1974). Ten thousand hands. *Psychic, 6*, #1, 40–43.

Darley, J. G. & Hagenah, T. (1955). *Vocational interest measurement.* Minneapolis: University of Minnesota Press.

Davis, D. (1967). The validity and reliability of a sociometric device. Unpublished master's thesis, Idaho State University.

Deakin, J. F. W. & Exley, K. A. (1979). Personality and male-female influences on the EEG alpha rhythm. *Biological Psychology, 8,* 285–290.

deCharms, R. (1976). *Enhancing motivation.* New York: Irvington Publishers.

DeFries, J. C., Kuse, A. R. & Vandenberg, S. G. (1979). Genetic correlations, environmental correlations and behavior. In J. R. Royce & L. P. Mos (Eds.), *Theoretical advances in behavior genetics.* Alphen aan den Rijn, Netherlands: Sitjthoff & Noordhoff.

D'espagnat, B. (1979). The quantum theory and reality. *Scientific American, 241,* #5, November, 158–181.

Diamond, S. (1957). *Personality and temperament.* New York: Harper Bros.

Dineen, M. A. & Garry, R. (1963). Effect of sociometric seating on classroom cleavage. In J. M. Seidman (Ed.), *Educating for mental health.* New York: Thomas Y. Crowell.

Dodge, K. A., Schlundt, D. C., Schocken, I., & Delugach, J. D. (1983). Social competence and children's sociometric status. The role of peer group entry strategies. *Merrill-Palmer Quarterly, 29,* 309–336.

Doll, E., & Barclay, J. R. (1988). The development of a brief screening instrument for assessing temperament in elementary school children. Study in progress.

Dollard, J. & Miller, N. E. (1950). *Personality and Psychotherapy.* New York: McGraw-Hill.

Domino, G. (1971). Interactive effects of achievement orientation and teaching style on academic achievement. *Journal of Educational Psychology, 62,* 427–431.

Dubois, P. (1964). A test-dominated society: China 1115 B. C.–1905 A. D. In A. Anastasi (Ed.), *Testing problems in perspective.* Washington D.C.: American Council on Education.

Duckworth, J. (1990). MMPI-1 and MMPI-2: a comparison for counseling psychologists, APA National Convention, Boston, August 10–13.

Earl, W. B. (1971). A study of the relationship between frequence of use of independent study behaviors and student self-concept. *Dissertation Abstracts 32* (A) March, 4918.

Easch, M. J. & Waxman, H. C. (1983). *Our class and its work,* published by the authors, University of Chicago.

Edinger, A. L. (1954). *Ego and archetype.* New York: Penguin Books.

Edwards, A. L. (1953). *The Edwards personal preference schedule.* New York: Psychological Corporation.

Ekehammer, B. (1974). Interactionism in personality from a historical perspective. *Psychological Bulletin, 81,* #12, 1026–1048.

Ellis, A. (1962). *Reason and emotion in psychotherapy.* New York: Lyle Stuart.

Epstein, S. (1979). The stability of behavior 1. On predicting most of the people most of the time. *Journal of Personality and Social Psychology, 37,* #7, 1097–1126.

Erikson, E. H. (1959). Identity and the life cycle. *Psychological Issues,* Monograph 1, Vol. 1, 102.

Erikson, E. H. (1968). *Identity: youth and crisis.* New York: W. W. Norton & Co.

Evans, M. (1969). Convergent and discriminant validities between the Cornell Job Description Index and a measure of goal attainment. *Journal of Applied Psychology, 53,* 102–106.

Exner, J. E. Jr. (1974). *The Rorschach: a comprehensive system.* New York: Wiley-Interscience.

Eysenck, H. J. (1957). *Dynamics of anxiety and hysteria.* London: Routledge & Kegan Paul.

Eysenck, H. J. (1967). *Behavior therapy and the neuroses.* Oxford: Pergamon Press.

Eysenck, H. J. (1970). *The structure of human personality.* London: Methuen Co.

Eysenck, H. J. (1976). Personal communication.

Eysenck, H. J. (1981). The importance of methodology in astrological research. Correlation: *Journal of Research in Astrology, 1,* #1, 11–14.

Eysenck, H. J. & Eysenck, S. B. G. (1964, 1968, 1975). *Manual of the Eysenck Personality Inventory,* London: University Press and San Diego: Educational and Industrial Testing Service.

Eysenck, H. J. & Rachman, S. (1965). *The causes and cures of neurosis.* San Diego: Robert Knapp & Co.

Eysenck, H. J., Wakefield, J. A., & Friedman, A. F. (1983). Diagnosis and clinical assessment: the DSM-III. *Annual Review of Psychology, 34,* 167–193.

Eysenck, S. B. G. (1965). *Junior Eysenck personality inventory* (British Edition). London: University of London Press.

Eysenck, S. B. G., Easting, G., & Pearson, P. R. (1984). Age norms for impulsiveness, venturesomeness, and empathy in children. *Personality and Individual Differences, 5,* 315–321.

Eysenck, S. B. G., Pearson, P. R., Easting, G., & Allsopp, J. F. (1985).

Age norms for impulsiveness, venturesomeness and empathy in adults. *Personality and Individual Differences, 6,* 613–619.

Feij, J. A. & Kuiper, C. D. (1984). *ATL handleiding: adolescenten temperament lijst.* Lisse: Swets & Zeitlinger.

Felker, D. W., & Stanwyck, D. J. (1971). *General self-concept and specific self-evaluation after an academic task.* Psychological Reports, 29, #1, 60–62.

Felker, D. W., & Thomas, S. B. (1971). Self-initiated verbal reinforcement and positive self-concept. *Child Development, 42,* #4, 1285–1287.

Felsenthal, H. (1972). Parental role in self-concept, chapter in Yamamoto, K. (Ed.). *The child and his image: self-concept in the early years.* Boston: Houghton-Mifflin, 178–203.

Fenichel, O. (1945). *The psychoanalytic theory of neurosis.* New York: W. W. Norton.

Ferris, A. (1968). A descriptive analysis of the characteristics of elementary reticent males. Unpublished master's thesis, California State University at Hayward.

Fiske, D. W. (1971). *Measuring the concepts of personality.* Chicago: Aldine Publishing Co.

Fitts, W. (1964). *Tennessee self-concept scale.* Nashville: Counselor Recording and Tests.

Fitts, W. (1965). *Manual: Tennessee self-concept scale.* Nashville: Counselor Recording and Tests.

Flach, F. F. & Draghi, S. C. (Eds.) (1975). *The nature and treatment of depression.* New York: John Wiley.

Flammer, D. (1971). Self-esteem, parent identification, and sex-role development in preschool age boys and girls, *Child Study Journal, 2,* 39–45.

Flanders, N. A. & Havumaki, S. (1963). The effect of teacher-pupil contacts involving praise on the sociometric choices of students. In J. M. Seidman (Ed.), *Educating for mental health.* New York: Thomas Y. Crowell.

Fliess, W. (1906). *Der ablauf des lebens.* Leipzig-Vienna: Deuticke.

Fliess, W. (1925). *Zur periodenlehre.* Leipzig: Ebenda.

Forer, B. R. (1950). A structured sentence-completion test, *Journal of Projective Techniques, 45,* #15.

Forsythe, F. & Jackson, E. (1966). A comparison of upper elementary school childrens' responses on a vocational preference inventory and a semantic differential in relationship to a social desirability grid. Unpublished master's thesis, California State University at Hayward.

French, J. W. (1953). *The description of personality measurements in terms of rotated factors.* Princeton, N.J.: Educational Testing Service.

Freud, S. (1953). *Collected Papers* (IV). Toronto: Clark Irwin Ltd.

Friedensberg, E., & Strelau, J. (1982). The reactivity rating scale (RRS): reliability and validity. *Polish Psychological Bulletin, 13*, 223–237.

Frieze, I. (1979). Beliefs about success and failure in the classroom. In J. H. McMillan (Ed.), *The social psychology of school learning.* New York: Academic Press.

Fullard, W., McDevitt, S. C. & Carey, W. B. (1984). Assessing temperament in one-to-three-years-old children. *Journal of Pediatric Psychology, 9*, 205–217.

Gabel, P. S. (1971). A study of the self-concepts of high school seniors and their post high school plans. *Dissertation Abstracts, 32* (A), October, 1852.

Gage, N. L. (Ed.) (1963). *Handbook of research on teaching.* Chicago: Rand-McNally.

Gale, A. (1983). Electroencephalographic studies of extraversion-introversion: a case study in the psychophysiology of individual differences. *Personality and Individual Differences, 4*, #4, 371–380.

Gale, A., Coles, M. & Blaydon, J. (1969). Extraversion-introversion and the EEG. *British Journal of Psychology, 60*, #2, 209–223.

Gale, A., Coles, M., Kline, P., & Penfold, V. (1971). Extraversion-introversion, neuroticism and the EEG: basal and response measures during habituation of the orienting response. *British Journal of Psychology, 62*, #4, 533–543.

Gallagher, J. J. & Crowder, T. (1957). The adjustment of gifted children in the regular classroom. *Exceptional Children, 23*, 306–312, 317–319.

Galton, F. (1972). *Hereditary genius.* Gloucester, Mass.: Peter Smith.

Gaugelin, M. (1967). *The cosmic clocks.* Chicago: Henry Regnery.

Gazda, G. M. (1971). *Group counseling: a developmental approach.* Boston: Allyn Bacon.

Gazda, G. M. (1973). *Human relations development: a manual for educators,* Boston: Allyn & Bacon.

Gazda, G. M., Walter, R. P. & Childers, W. C. (1975). *Human relations development: a manual for health sciences.* Boston: Allyn Bacon.

Gecas. V. (1972). Parental behavior and contextual variations in adolescent self-esteem. *Sociometry, 35*, #2, 332–345.

Geisler, J. S. (1968). The effects of a compensatory education program on the self-concept and academic achievement of high school age youth from low income families. *Dissertation Abstracts International, 29*, (8-A), 2525–2526.

Gettings, F. (1965). *The book of the hand.* Prague: Hamlin Publishing Co.

Giannitrapani, D. (1985). *The electrophysiology of intellectual functions.* Basel, Switzerland: S. Karger Inc.

Gittelson, B. (1977). *Biorhythm: a personal science*. New York: Arco Publishing Co.

Glass, G. V., McGaw, B. & Smith, M. L. (1981). *Meta-analysis in social research*. Beverly Hills: Sage Publications.

Glazer, V. I. (1972). The relationship of high approval motivation to differences in reported self-esteem. *Dissertation Abstracts, 33*, (B), January 3301–3302.

Glueck, S. & Glueck, E. (1950). *Unraveling juvenile delinquency*. New York: Commonwealth Fund (Hildreth Press).

Glueck, S. & Glueck, E. (1956). *Physique and delinquency*. New York: Harper Bros.

Gobar, A. (1968). *Philosophic foundations cf genetic psychology and gestalt psychology*. The Hague: Martinus Nijhoff.

Golden, C. J., Hammeke, T. A. and Purisch, A. D. (1984). *Luria-Nebraska Neuropsychological Battery*. Los Angeles: Western Psychological Services.

Goldman, L. (1972). Tests and counseling: the marriage that failed. *Measurement and Evaluation in Guidance, #4*, 213–220.

Goldsmith, H. H. (1987). The toddler behavior assessment questionnaire: a preliminary manual. Technical report, Department of Psychology, University of Oregon, Eugene: Oregon.

Goldsmith, H. H., Buss, A. H., Plomin, R., Rothbart, M., Thomas, A., Chess, S., Hinde, R. A. and McCall, R. B. (1987). Roundtable: what is temperament? Four approaches. *Child Development, 58*, 505–529.

Goodenough, F. L. (1926). *Measurement of intelligence by drawing*. Yonkers, New York: World Book Company.

Goodstein, L. D. & Brazis, K. L. (1970). Psychology of the scientist: credibility of psychologists, an empirical study. *Psychological Reports, 27*, #3, 835–838.

Gordon, T. (1974). *Teacher effectiveness training*. New York: David McKay Co.

Gorynska, E. & Strelau, J. (1979). Basic traits of the temporal characteristics of behavior and their measurement by an inventory technique, *Polish Psychological Bulletin, 10*, 199–207.

Gottfredson, G. G. (1984). *The effective school battery*, Odessa Fl.: Psychological Assessment Resources Inc.

Gottschalk, L. A. & Gleser, G. C. (1969). *The measurement of psychological states through the content analysis of verbal behavior*. Berkeley & Los Angeles: University of California Press.

Gottschalk, L. A., Winget, C. N. & Gleser, G. C. (1969). *Manual of instructions for using the Gottschalk-Gleser content analysis scales*. Berkeley & Los Angeles: University of California Press.

Gough, H. G. (1960). The adjective check list as a personality assessment research technique. *Psychological Reports, 6,* 107–122.

Gough, H. (1964). *California psychological inventory manual.* Palo Alto: Consulting Psychologists Press.

Gough, H. G., & Heilbrun, A. B. Jr. (1980). *The adjective check list manual* (Revised), Palo Alto: Consulting Psychologists Press.

Gray, S. W. (1963). *The psychologist in the schools.* New York: Holt, Rinehart & Winston.

Greenblatt, S. L. (1979). Individual values and attitudes in Chinese society: an ethnomethodological approach, Chapter 3 in Richard W. Wilson, Amy Auerbach Wilson and Sidney L. Greenblatt (Eds.) *Value change in Chinese society,* New York: Praeger.

Gronlund, N. E. (1951). The accuracy of teacher judgments concerning the sociometric status of sixth grade students. *Sociometry Monographs, No. 25* , New York: Beacon House.

Gronlund, N. E. (1955). Generality of sociometric status over criteria in the measurement of social acceptability. *Elementary School Journal, 56,* 173–176.

Gronlund, N. E. (1959). *Sociometry in the classroom.* New York: Harper Bros.

Gross, M. J. (1962). *The brain watchers.* New York: McGraw-Hill.

Guilford, J. P. (1959). *Personality.* New York: McGraw-Hill.

Guilford, J. S., Zimmerman, W. S., & Guilford, J. P. (1976). The Guilford-Zimmermann *Temperament Survey handbook: twenty-five years of research and application.* San Diego: Edits Publishers.

Guinouard, D. E. & Rychlak, J. F. (1962). Personality correlates of sociometric popularity in elementary school children. *Personnel and Guidance Journal, 40,* 438–442.

Guttman, L. A. (1944). Basis for scaling qualitative ideas. American *Sociological Review, 9,* 139–150.

Guttman, L. (1947). The Cornell technique for scale and intensity analysis. *Educational and Psychological Measurement, 7,* 247–280.

Hamacheck, D. E. (1969). Self-concept as related to motivation and achievement, chapter in H. F. Clarizio (Ed.) *Mental health and the educative process.* Chicago: Rand-McNally Co.

Hare, E., Price, J., and Slater, E. (1974). Mental disorder and season of birth: a national sample compared with the general population. *British Journal of Psychiatry, 124,* 81–86.

Harman, H. H., (1968). Factor analysis. In D. K. Whitla (Ed.), *Handbook of measurement and assessment in behavioral sciences* (pp. 142–170). Reading, MA: Addison-Wesley.

Harootunian, B. (1978). Teacher training in A. P. Goldstein (Ed.) *Prescriptions for child mental health and education*. New York: Pergamon Press.

Harre, R., Clarke, D., and DeCarlo, N. (1985). *Motives and mechanisms*. London: Methuen.

Harris, D. B. (1963). *Children's drawing as measures of intellectual maturity*. New York: Harcourt, Brace and World.

Harrow, A. J. (1972). *A taxonomy of the psychomotor domain*. New York: David McKay Co.

Harrower, M. R. & Steiner, M. E. (1951). *Large scale Rorschach techniques*. Springfield, Ill.: Charles C. Thomas.

Hart, J. W. (1980). An outline of basic postulates of sociometry. *Group Psychotherapy, Psychodrama & Sociometry, 33*, 63–70.

Hart, J. W. & Nath, R. (1979). Sociometry in business and industry: new developments in historical perspective. *Group Psychotherapy, Psychodrama & Sociometry, 32*, 128–149.

Hartl, E. M., Monnelly, E. P., & Elderkin, R. D. (1982). *Physique and delinquent behavior: a thirty-year follow-up of William H. Sheldon's varieties of delinquent youth*. New York: Academic Press.

Hartlage, J. (1973). *Mental development evaluation of the pediatric patient*. Springfield, Ill.: Charles C. Thomas.

Hartschorne, H., & May, M. A. (1928). Studies in the nature of character: vol. 1. *studies in deceit*. New York: Macmillan.

Hartschore, H., & May, M. A. (1929). Studies in the nature of character. vol 2. studies in service and self control. New York: Macmillan.

Hartschore, H., May, M. A. & Shuttleworth, F. K. (1930). Studies in the nature of character: vol. 3. *studies in the organization of character*, New York: Macmillan.

Hathaway, S. R. & Meehl, P. E. (1951). *An atlas for the clinical use of the MMPI*. Minneapolis: University of Minnesota Press.

Hebb, D. O. (1968). Concerning imagery. *Psychological Review, 6*, 7–12.

Heckhausen, H. (1968). Achievement motivation research: current problems and some contributions towards a general theory of motivation. In William J. Arnold (Ed.), *Nebraska symposium on motivation* (103–174). Lincoln: University of Nebraska Press.

Hegvik, R. L., McDevitt, S. C., & Carey, W. B. (1982). The middle childhood temperament questionnaire. *Journal of Developmental and Behavioral Pediatrics, 3*, 197–200.

Heider, F. (1958). *The psychology of interpersonal relations*. New York: John Wiley.

Hess, R. D., & Shipman, V. C. (1965). Early experiences and the socialization of cognitive modes in children, *Child Development, 36*, 869–886.

Higgins, J. C. (1972). A pupil personnel services program to develop self-esteem. *Dissertation Abstracts, 32* (A) February, 4351.

Hill, E. F. (1972). *The Holtzman inkblot technique.* San Francisco: Jossey-Bass Co.

Hock, C. (1950). *The four temperaments.* Milwaukee: Bruce Publishing Co.

Holland, J. L. (1958). A personality inventory employing occupational titles. *Journal of Applied Psychology, 42,* 336–342.

Holland, J. L. (1959). A theory of vocational choice. *Journal of Counseling Psychology, 6,* #1, 35–44.

Holland, J. L. (1964). Personal communication.

Holland, J. L. (1966a). A psychological classification scheme for vocations and major fields. *Journal of Counseling Psychology, 13,* 278–288.

Holland, J. L. (1966b). *The psychology of vocational choice.* Waltham, Mass: Blaisdell.

Holland, J. L. (1971). *Counselor's guide for the self-directed search.* Palo Alto, CA: Consulting Psychologists Press.

Holland, J. L., Viernstein, M. C., Kuo, H., Karweit, N. L. & Blum, Z. D. (1970). A psychological classification of occupations. Baltimore: Center for Social Organization of Schools, Report No. 90, John Hopkins University.

Holland, J. L. (1982). Planning for alternative futures. *Counseling Psychologist, 10,* #2, 7–14.

Hollander, E. P. & Marcia, J. E. (1970). Parental determinants of peer-orientation and self-orientation among pre-adolescents, *Developmental Psychology* (2), 292–302.

Holtzbert, J. T., & Taylor, J. L. (1947). Contributions of clinical psychology to military neuro-psychiatry in an army psychiatric hospital. *Journal of Clinical Psychology, 3,* #24.

Homme, L. (1965). Control of coverants, the operants of the mind. *Psychological Record, 15,* 501–511.

Horton, J. & Walsh, W. B. (1976). Concurrent validity of Holland's theory for college degree working women. *Journal of Vocational Behavior, 9,* 201–208.

Hull, C. L. (1943). *Principles of behavior.* New York: Appleton-Century-Crofts.

Humphries, L. C. (1960). A note on the multitrait-multimethod matrix. *Psychological Bulletin, 57,* 86–88.

Hunt, D. E. (1975). Person-environment interaction: a challenge found wanting before it was tried. *Review of Educational Research, 45,* #2, 209–320.

Hunter, J. E. (1978). Dynamic sociometry. *Mathematical Sociology, 6,* 87–138.

Hutt, M. L. (1945). The use of projective methods of personality measurement in army medical installations. *Journal of Clinical Psychology, 1,* 134–140.

Hymel, S. (1983). Preschool children's peer relations: issues in sociometric assessment. *Merril-Palmer Quarterly, 29,* 237–260.

Jackson, D. (1969). Multimethod factor analysis in the evaluation of convergent and discriminant validity. *Psychological Bulletin, 72,* 30–49.

Janke, W., Erdmann, G., & Netter, P. (1976). Activity preference scale, unpublished manuscript, University of Duesseldorf, Department of Psychology, Duesseldorf.

Jaynes, J. (1973a). In M. Henle, J. Jaynes & J. J. Sullivan (Eds.), *Historical conceptions of psychology* (p. ix). New York: Spring.

Jaynes, J. (1976). *The origin of consciousness in the breakdown of the bicameral mind.* Boston: Houghton-Mifflin.

Jencks, C. Smith, M., Ackland, H., Bane, M. J., Cohen, D., Gintis, H., Heyne, B. & Michelson, S. (1972). *Inequality: a reassessment of the effect of family and schooling in America.* New York: Basic Books.

Jenkins, R. R. (1974). Comparisons between an ancient instrument and modern instruments for assessing personality: a pilot study. Ph.D. Dissertation, University of Houston. Ann Arbor, Michigan: University Microfilms.

Jennings, H. H. (1950). *Leadership and isolation.* New York: Longmans, Green & Co.

Jensen, A. R. (1969). How much can we boost I.Q. and scholastic achievement? *Harvard Educational Review, #1,* 1–123.

Johnson, E. L. (1961). The relationship between certain propositions of client-centered theory and certain tenets of philosophy. Unpublished doctoral dissertation, Indiana University.

Jones, W. H. S. (1923). *Hippocrates.* Cambridge, Mass.: Harvard University Press.

Jung, C. G. (1971). *Psychological types* (2nd edition). Princeton, N.J.: Princeton University Press.

Jung, C. G. (1973). *Synchronicity.* Tans. R. F. C. Hull. New York: Bollingen Press.

Jung, C. G. (1976). *Abstracts of the collected works of C. G. Jung.* Rockeville, Maryland: Information Planning Associates Inc.

Kamin, L. I. (1975). Social and legal consequences of I.Q. tests as classification instruments: some warnings from our past. *Journal of School Psychology, 13, #4,* 317–323.

Kaplan, H. I., Freedman, A. M. & Sadock, B. J. (1980). *Comprehensive textbook of psychiatry/III, Vol. 1.* Baltimore, Waverly Press Inc.

Kefir, N., and Corsini, R. J. (1974). Dispositional sets: a contribution to typology, *Journal of Individual Psychology, 30, #2,* 163–178.

Kehle, T. J. (1972). Effect of the student's physical attractiveness, sex, race, intelligence, and socio-economic status on teachers' expectations for the student's personality and academic performance. Unpublished dissertation, University of Kentucky.

Kehle, T. J. & Guidubaldi, J. (1978). Effect of EMR placement models on affective and social development. *Psychology in the Schools, 15,* 275–282.

Kelly, G. A. (1955). *A theory of personality: the psychology of personal constructs.* New York: W. W. Norton & Co.

Kelly, G. A. (1966). A brief introduction to personal construct theory. Unpublished manuscript, Brandeis University.

Kennedy, D. (1969). Sociometric assessment, a validity study. Paper presented at the 1969 American Personnel and Guidance Association convention, Las Vegas.

Kent, G. H. & Rosanoff, A. (1910). A study of association in insanity, *American Journal of Insanity, 67,* 37–96 and 317–390.

Kerr, M. (1945). A study of social acceptability. *Elementary School Journal, 45,* 257–265.

Key, W. B. (1974). *Subliminal seduction.* Englewood Cliffs: Prentice-Hall.

Keyser, D. J. & Sweetland, R. C. (1984). *Test critiques* (Vols. 1–5). Kansas City: Test Corporation of America.

Kidd, J. W. (1951). An analysis of social rejection in a college men's residence hall. *Sociometry, 14,* 266–234.

Kifer, E. (1975). Relationships between academic achievement and personality characteristics: a quasi-longitudinal study. *American Educational Research Journal, 12,* 191–210.

Kikuchi, T. (1968). Decline in self-concept, *Tohoku Psychologica Folia, 27,* 22–31.

Kinsbourne, M. (1972). Contrasting patterns of memory span decrement in ageing and aphasia. *Journal of Neurology, Neurosurgery and Psychiatry, 35,* 192–195.

Kirkendall, D. R., & Gruber, J. J. (1970). Canonical relationships between motor, personality, and intellectual achievement domains in culturally deprived high school pupils. Paper presented at the National Convention of American Association of Health, Physical Education, and Recreation, Seattle, Washington, April 6, 1970.

Kirkpatrick, S. (1979). A Maslovian counseling model. *Personnel and Guidance Journal, 57,* #8, 386–391.

Kohlberg, L. (1976). Moral stages and moralization: the cognitive-developmental approach. In T. Lickona (Ed.), *Moral development and behavior theory, research and social issues.* New York: Holt, Rinehart & Winston.

Kohn, P. M. (1985). Sensation seeking, augmenting-reducing, and strength of the nervous system. In J. R. Spence & C. E. Izard (Eds.),

Motivation, emotion and personality (pp. 167–173). Amsterdam: North-Holland.

Koppitz, E. M. (1975). *The Bender Gestalt test for young children: research and application 1963–1973.* New York: Grune & Stratton.

Kounin, J. S. (1970). *Discipline and group management in classrooms.* New York: Holt, Rinehart & Winston.

Kounin, J. S., Gump, P. V. (1961). The comparative influence of punitive and nonpunitive teachers upon children's concepts of school misconduct. *Journal of Educational Psychology, 52,* 44–49.

Kounin, J. S., Gump, P. V. & Ryan, J. J. (1961). Explorations in classroom management. *Journal of Teacher Education, 12,* 235–247.

Kraepelin, E. (1913). *Psychiatrie: ein lehrbuch* (9th Edition), vol. 3, Leipzig: Barth.

Kranzler, G. D., Mayer, G. R., Dyer, C. O. & Munger, P. F. (1966). Counseling with elementary school children: an experimental study. *Personnel and Guidance Journal, 44,* 944–949.

Krathwohl, D. R., Bloom, B. S. & Masia, B. B. (1956). *Taxonomy of educational objectives: the classification of educational goals. Handbook II: affective domain.* New York: David McKay Co., Inc.

Kretschmer, E. (1925). *Physique and character: an investigation of the nature of constitution and of the theory of temperament,* New York: Harcourt-Brace.

Krug, S. E. (1981). *Interpreting 16 personality factor profile patterns.* Champaign, Ill.: Institute for Personality and Ability Testing Inc.

Krug, S. E. (1984). *Test Plus (computer application of the adult personality inventory),* Champaign, Ill.: Metritech.

Krupszak, W. P. (1973). Relationships among student self-concept of academic ability, teacher perception of student academic ability and student achievement. *Dissertation Abstracts, 33,* (A), 3388–3389.

Kuhlen, R. G. & Collister, E. G. (1952). Sociometric status of sixth and ninth graders who fail to finish high school. *Educational and Psychological Measurement, 12,* 632–637.

Kuhn, T. S. (1969). *The structure of scientific revolutions.* Chicago: University of Chicago Press.

Kuo, Z. Y. (1967). *The dynamics of behavior development.* New York: Random House.

LaChance, A. I. (1972). A study of the correlation between humor and self-concept in fifth grade boys and girls. *Dissertation Abstracts, 33* (B), 424.

Ladd, G. W. (1983). Social networks of popular, average, and rejected children in school settings. *Merrill-Palmer Quarterly, 29,* 283–307.

La Mettrie, J. O. (1943). *Man a machine.* Translated by Margaret W. Calkins. LaSalle, Ill.: Open Court Publishing Co.

Langeheine, R. (1978). Computer aided data analysis in sociometry. *Educational and Psychological Measurement, 38,* 189–191.

Larrabee, H. A. (1964). *Reliable knowledge.* Boston, Houghton-Mifflin.

Larsen, R. J. & Diener, E. (1987). Affect intensity as an individual difference characteristic: a review. *Journal of Research in Personality, 21,* 1–39.

Laryea, E. P. (1972). Race, self-concept and achievement. *Dissertation Abstracts, 33* (A), 2172–2173.

Lavater, J. C. (1855). *Essays on physiognomy designed to promote the love of mankind.* London: William Tegg.

Lazar, I. & Darlington, R. (1982). Lasting effects of early education, a report from the consortium for longitudinal studies. *Monographs of the Society for Research in Children, 47,* Nos. 2–3. Chicago: Society for Research in Child Development, University of Chicago Press.

Lazarus, A. A. (1976). *Multimodal behavior therapy.* New York: Springer.

Leary, T. (1957). *Interpersonal diagnosis of personality: a functional theory and methodology for personality evaluation.* New York: Ronald Press.

Leary, T. & Coffey, H. S. (1955). Interpersonal diagnosis, some problems of methodology and validation. *Journal of Abnormal and Social Psychology, 50,* 110–124.

Lefebvre, A. (1971). The relationship between self-concept and level of aspiration with Negro and White children, *Dissertation Abstracts, 32* (B), 3056.

Lekarczyk, D. T., & Hill, K. T. (1969). Self-esteem, test anxiety, stress and verbal learning. *Developmental Psychology, 1,* #2, 147–154.

Lerner, R. M., Palermo, M., Spiron, A., & Nesselroade, J. R. (1982). Assessing the dimensions of temperament individuality across the life-span: the dimensions of temperament survey (DOTS), *Child Development, 53,* 149–159.

Lester, D. (1976). Preferences among Sheldon's temperament. *Psychological Reports, 38,* #3, 722.

Lester, D. (1977). Deviations in Sheldonian physique, temperament match and neuroticism. *Psychological Reports, 41,* #3, 442.

Levy, P. (1973). On the relation between test theory and psychology. In P. Kline (Ed.), *New approaches in psychological measurement.* New York: Wiley.

Lewin, K. (1935a). *A dynamic theory of personality.* New York: McGraw-Hill.

Lewin, K. (1935b). *A dynamic theory of personality; selected readings.* Translation, Donald K. Adams & Karl E. Zener. New York: McGraw-Hill.

Lewin, K. & Grabbe, P. (1945). Conduct, knowledge and acceptance of new values. *Journal of Social Issues, 1,* #3, 56–64.

Lewin, P. (1970). Home and self-concept factors related to differential academic achievement of teen-agers in one parent, father-absent families from two social classes. *Dissertation Abstracts, 30* (A) 5240.

Lindzey, G. & Borgatta, E. F. (1954). Sociometric measurement. In G. Lindzey (Ed.), *Handbook of social psychology.* Cambridge: Addison-Wesley.

Llaurado, J. G., Sances, A. Jr. & Battocleti, J. H. (1964). *Biologic and clinical effects of low-frequency magnetic and electric fields.* Springfield, Ill.: Charles C. Thomas.

Locke, E., Smith, P., Smith, C., Kendall, L., Hulin, C. & Miller, A. (1964). Convergent and discriminant validity for areas and methods of rating job satisfaction. *Journal of Applied Psychology, 48,* 313–319.

Loevinger, J. (1976). *Ego development.* San Francisco: Jossey-Bass.

Lovaas, I. (1973). Informal commentary on the follow-up of autistic children over a ten year period of time. Fourth International Conference on Behavior Modification, Banff.

Lu, G. & Needham, J. (1980). *Celestial Lancets.* Cambridge: Cambridge University Press.

Luce, G. G. (1970). *Biological rhythms in human and animal physiology.* New York: Dover Publications.

Lumsden, J. (1976). Test theory. *Annual Review of Psychology, 27,* 251–280.

Luria, A. R. (1973). *The working brain.* New York: Basic Books.

Lüscher, M. (1969). *The Luscher colour test.* Translated, J. A. Scott (Ed.). London: Jonathan Cape Ltd.

Maccoby, E. E. & Jacklin, C. N. (1974). *The psychology of sex differences.* Stanford: Stanford University Press.

Machover, K. (1953). Human figure drawings of children. *Journal of Projective Techniques, 17,* 85–91.

Madaus, G. F., Scriven, M. S. & Stufflebeam, D. L. (1983). *Evaluation models.* Boston: Kluwer-Nijhoff.

Magnusson, D. (1986). Individual development and adjustment (technical report no. 64). Stockholm: Department of Psychology, University of Stockholm.

Mahoney, M. J. & Thoresen, C. E. (1974). *Self-control: power to the person.* Monterey, CA: Brooks/Cole.

Marrow, A. J. (1969). *The practical theorist: the life and work of Kurt Lewin.* New York: Teachers College Press, Columbia University.

Martin, R. P. (1984). *The temperament assessment battery: interim manual.* Athens: Developmental Metrics.

Martin, R. P. & Holbrook, J. (1985). Relationship of temperament characteristics to the academic achievement of first-grade children. *Journal of Psychoeducational Assessment, 3,* 131–140.

Martin, R. P., Paget, K. & Nagle, R. (1983). Relationships between temperament and classroom behavior, teacher attitudes, and academic achievement. *Journal of Psychoeducational Assessment, 1*, 370–386.

Martin, R. P., Drew, K. D., Gaddis, L. R. & Moseley, M. (1988). Prediction of elementary school achievement from preschool temperament: three studies. *School Psychology Review, 17*, 125–137.

Maslow, A. H. (1954). *Motivation and personality*. New York: Harper.

Mason, E. Teacher expectancy: what does it mean? In G. R. Gredler (Ed.), *Ethical and legal problems of school psychology*. Harrisburg, Pa.: State Department of Education.

Matarazzo, J. D. (1978a). Heredity and environmental correlates of I.Q. *Journal of Continuing Education in Psychiatry*, January, 35–46.

Matarazzo, J. D. (1978b). *Wechsler's measurement and appraisal of adult intelligence* (5th edition). New York: Oxford University Press.

Matarazzo, J. D. & Wiens, A. M. (1977). Black intelligence test of cultural homogeneity and Wechsler Adult Intelligence Scale scores of black and white police applicants. *Journal of Applied Psychology, 62*, 57–63.

Mayer, G. R., Kranzler, G. D. & Matthes, W. A. (1967). Elementary school counseling and peer relations. *Personnel and Guidance Journal, 46*, #4, 360–365.

McClelland, D. C. (1965). Toward a theory of motive acquisition. *American Psychologist, 20*, 321–333.

McClelland, D. C. & Altschuler, A. S. (1971). Achievement motivation development project. Final Report, Project #7–1231, Grant #0–8–071231–1746. Washington D.C.: U.S. Office of Education, Bureau of Research.

McClelland, D. C., Atkinson, J. W., Clark, R. A. & Lowell, E. L. (1953). *The achievement motive*. New York: Appleton-Century-Crofts.

McCord, R. R. & Wakefield, J. A. Jr. (1981). Arithmetic achievement as a function of introversion-extraversion and teacher-presented reward and punishment. *Personality and Individual Differences, 1*, 145–152.

McDevitt, S. C. and Carey, W. B. (1978). The measurement of temperament in 3–7 year old children. *Journal of Child Psychology and Psychiatry, 19*, 245–253.

McGee, S. E. (1972). Fifth grade boys' self-esteem as a function of teacher expectations. *Dissertation Abstracts, 32* (A), 6211–6212.

McIsaac, D. N. (1974). Trend surface analysis. In H. J. Walberg (Ed.), *Evaluating educational performance*. Berkeley, Ca.: McCutchan Publishing Co.

McLenmore, C. W. & Benjamin, L. S. (1979). Whatever happened to interpersonal diagnosis? a psychological alternative to DSM-III. *American Psychologist, 34*, #1, 17–34.

McMillan, J. H. (Ed.) (1980). *The social psychology of school learning.* New York: Academic Press.

Meacham, M. L. & Trione, V. (1967). The role of the school psychologist in the community school. In J. F. Magary (Ed.), *School psychological services in theory and practice, a handbook.* Englewood Cliffs: Prentice Hall.

Meehl, P. E. (1962). Schizotaxia, schizotypy, schizophrenia. *American Psychologist, 17,* 827–838.

Meehl, P. E. (1966). Wanted a good cook book, chapter in E. L. Megargee (Ed.) *Research in clinical assessment.* New York: Harper and Row Publishers (Originally presented as the presidential address, Midwestern Psychological association, Chicago, April 29, 1955).

Megargee, E. I. (Editor), (1966). *Research in clinical assessment,* New York: Harper and Row.

Mehrabian, A. (1977). A questionnaire of individual differences in stimulus screening and associated differences in arousability, *Environmental Psychology and Nonverbal Behavior, 1,* 89–103.

Mehrabian, A. & Ksionzky, S. (1972). Categories of social behavior. In Speer, D. C. (Ed.), *Nonverbal communication.* Beverly Hills: Sage Publications.

Meichenbaum, D. & Cameron, R. (1981). Issues in cognitive assessment. In T. V. Merluzzi, C. R. Glass & M. Genest (Eds.), *Cognitive assessment* (pp. 3–15). New York: Guilford Press.

Mercer, J. R. & Lewis, J. F. (1979). *System of multicultural pluralistic assessment: technical manual.* Cleveland: Psychological Corporation.

Metzner, R. (1970). Astrology: potential science and intuitive art. *Journal for the Study of Consciousness, 3,* #1, 70–91.

Meyer, R. G. (1983). *The clinician's handbook.* Boston: Allyn & Bacon.

Michael, C. P. and Norrisey, M. C. (1984). *Prayer and temperament.* Charlottesville, Virginia: The Open Door.

Mill, J. S. (1950). *Philosophy of the scientific method.* New York: Hafner Publishing Co.

Miller, G. A. & Buckout, R. (1973). *The science of mental life* (2nd edition). New York: Harper & Row.

Miller, R. V. (1956). Social status and socio-empathic differences among mentally superior, mentally typical, and mentally retarded children. *Exceptional Children, 23,* 114–119.

Miller, T. W. (1971). Differential response patterns of parents as they affect the child's self-esteem. *Dissertation Abstracts, 32* (B), 1827

Millon, T. (1981). *Disorders of personality, DSM III Axis II.* New York: John Wiley & Sons.

Millon, T. (1982). *Millon clinical multiaxial inventory* (2nd edition). Minneapolis: National Computer Systems Inc.

Mischel, W. (1968). *Personality and assessment.* New York: Wiley.

Mischel, W. (1972). Direct versus indirect personality assessment: evidence and implication. *Journal of Consulting and Clinical Psychology, 38,* 319–324.

Mischel, W. (1973). Toward a cognitive social learning reconceptualization of personality, *Psychological Review, 80,* 252–283.

Mischel, W. (1975). Symposium on the future of personality assessment. Chicago: American Psychological Association Convention.

Mischel, W. (1981). A cognitive-social learning approach to assessment. In T. V. Merluzzi, C. R. Glass & M. Genest (Eds.), *Cognitive assessment* (pp. 479–498). New York: Guilford Press.

Mitchell, J. V. Jr. (1985). *The ninth mental measurements yearbook.* Lincoln: Buros Institute of Mental Measurements, distributed by the University of Nebraska Press.

Moody, R. A. Jr. (1975). *Life after life.* Covington, Georgia: Mockingbird Press.

Moos, R. H. (1974). *Family work and group environment scales.* Palo Alto, Ca.: Consulting Psychologists Press, Inc.

Moos, R. H. (1978). A typology of junior high and high school classrooms. American *Educational Research Journal, 15,* #1, 53–68.

Moreno, J. L. (1934). *Who shall survive?* Washington D.C.: Nervous and Mental Disease Publishing Co.

Moreno, J. L. (1947). Sociometry and Marxism. *Journal of Sociometry, 12,* 106–144.

Moreno, J. L. & Moreno, Z. T. (1976). A sociometric view of recent history: the rise and fall of leadership. *Group Psychotherapy, Psychodrama and Sociometry, 29,* 63–69.

Morse, W. C. (1965). Intervention techniques for the classroom teacher of the emotionally disturbed. Presented to the First Annual Conference on the Education of Emotionally Disturbed Children.

Mouton, J. S., Blake, R. R. & Fruchter, B. (1955a). The reliability of sociometric measures. *Sociometry, 18,* 7–48.

Mouton, J. S., Blake, R. R., & Fruchter, B. (1955b). The validity of sociometric responses. *Sociometry, 18,* 181–206.

Murphy, G. (1949). *Historical introduction to modern psychology,* New York: Harcourt-Brace.

Murray, H. (1943). *Thematic apperception test manual,* Cambridge Mass.: Harvard University Press.

Murray, H. A. (1938). *Explorations in personality.* New York: Oxford University Press.

Murstein, B. I. (1963). *Theory and research in projective techniques.* New York: John Wiley.

Naccarati, S. (1921). The morphologic aspect of intelligence. In T. S. Woodworth (Ed.), *Archives of Psychology, 6,* #45, 1–44.

Nay, R. W. (1979). *Multimodal clinical assessment.* New York: Gardner Press.

Netter, P. and Othmer, E. (1967). Periodicity scale, unpublished manuscript, University of Hamburg, Department of Psychosomatic Medicine, Hamburg.

Newman, J. R. (1956). *The world of mathematics* (four volumes). New York: Simon & Schuster Inc.

Nichols, R. C. & Bilbro, W. C. (1966). The diagnosis of twin zygosity. *Acta Genetica, 16,* 265–275.

Northway, M. L. (1952). *A primer of sociometry.* Toronto: University of Toronto Press.

Orme, J. E. (1962). Intelligence and season of birth. *British Journal of Medical Psychology, 35,* 233–234.

Osgood, C. (1966). Dimensionality of the semantic space for communication via facial expressions. *Scandinavian Journal of Psychology, 7,* 1–30.

Osgood, C. E., Suci, G. J. & Tannenbaum, P. H. (1957). *The measurement of meaning.* Urbana, Ill.: University of Illinois Press.

Pace, C. R. & Stern, G. G. (1958). An approach to the measurement of psychological characteristics of college environments. *Journal of Educational Psychology, 49,* 269–277.

Packard, V. (1959). *The hidden persuaders.* New York: Pocket Books.

Pavlov, I. P. (1927). *Conditioned reflexes.* London: Oxford University Press.

Pawlik, K. (1973). Right answers to the wrong questions? a reexamination of factor analytic personality research and its contributions to personality theory, in J. R. Royce (Ed.) *Multivariate analysis and psychological theory,* pp. 17–43, New York: Academic Press.

Pearson, K. (1901). On lines and planes of closest fit to systems in space. *Philosophy Magazine, 6,* 559–572.

Pellegrini, R. J. (1973). The astrological "theory" of personality: an unbiased test by a biased observer. *The Journal of Psychology, 85,* 21–28.

Pepinsky, H. B. (1948). The selection and use of diagnostic categories in clinical counseling. *Applied Psychological Monographs,* #15 (American Psychological Association).

Peters, R. S. (1965). *Brett's history of psychology.* Cambridge Mass.: Massachusetts Institut of Technology Press.

Piaget, J. (1952). *The origins of intelligence in children.* New York: International Universities Press Inc.

Piers, E. & Harris, D. (1969). *The Piers-Harris children's self-concept scale.* Nashville: Counselor Recordings and Tests.

Piotrowski, C., & Keller, J. W. (1983). Psychodiagnostic testing in APA approved clinical psychology programs, paper presented at the meeting of the Southeastern Psychological Association, Atlanta.

Piotrowski, Z. A. (1957). *Perceptanalysis*, New York: Macmillan.

Porkert, M. (1979). *The theoretical foundations of Chinese medicine*. Cambridge: Massachusetts Institute of Technology.

Powell, G. (1979). *Brain and personality*. New York: Praeger.

Pullis, M. & Cadwell, J. (1982). The influence of children's temperament characteristics on teachers' decision strategies. *American Educational Research Journal, 19, #2*, 165–181.

Raimy, V. C. (1950). *Training in clinical psychology*. Englewood Cliffs: Prentice-Hall.

Rainwater, G. D. (1983). *Psychological/social history computer program and manual*. Indialantic, Fl.: Psychologistics.

Rapaport, D., Gill, M., & Schafer, R. (1946). Diagnostic psychological testing: the theory, statistical evaluation and diagnostic application of a battery of tests. Chicago: *Yearbook Publishers*, vol. 2.

Ratner, C., Weissberg, R. & Caplan, M. (1986). *Ethical considerations in sociometric testing: the reactions of preadolescent subjects*. Washington D.C.: Presentation, APA National Convention.

Ratner, J. (commentator) (1927). *The philosophy of Spinoza*. New York: Random House (Modern Library).

Redl, F. & Wineman, D. (1952). *Controls from within: techniques for the treatment of the aggressive child*. Glencoe: The Free Press.

Reitan, R. M. (1966). A research programe on the psychological effects of brain lesions in human beings. In N. R. Ellis (Ed.), *International review of research in mental retardation* (Vol. 1). New York: Academic Press.

Reschley, D. J. (1982). Assessing mild mental retardation: the influence of adaptive behavior, sociocultural status, and prospects for nonbiased assessment, in C. R. Reynolds & T. B. Gutkin (Eds), *The handbook of school psychology*. New York: Wiley.

Reynolds, C. R. (1985). Review of the system of multi-cultural pluralistic assessment, in J. V. Mitchell (Ed.). *Ninth mental measurements yearbook*. Lincoln: University of Nebraska Press.

Richmond, B. O. & White, W. F. (1971). Sociometric predictors of self-concept among fifth and sixth grade children, *Journal of Educational Research, 64, #9*, 425–429.

Rickers-Ovsiankina, M. A. (Ed.) (1960). Rorschach psychology, New York: Wiley.

Rim, D. & Masters, J. (1974). *Behavior therapy*. New York: Academic Press.

Rocard, Y. (1962). *Le signal du Sourcier*. Paris: Dunod.

Roe, A. (1956). *The psychology of occupations*. New York: Wiley.

Rogers, C. R. (1951). *Client-centered therapy*. Boston: Houghton-Mifflin.

Roman, K. G. (1961). *Handwriting: a key to personality*. London: Routledge & Kegan, Ltd.

Rorschach, H. (1942). *Psychodiagnostics* (translated by Hans Huber). Bern: Bircher.

Rosenthal, R. (1982). Evaluating of social importance: a framework for meta-analytic procedures. Paper presented as part of a symposium, Recent Developments in Meta-analysis, at the annual meeting of the American Psychological Association, Washington D.C.

Rosenthal, R. & Jacobson, J. (1966). Teacher expectancies: determinants of pupils' I.Q. gains. *Psychological Reports, 19*, 115–118.

Rosenthal, R. & Jacobson, J. (1968). *Pygmalion in the classroom: teacher expectation and pupil's intellectual development*. New York: Holt, Rinehart, and Winston.

Rosenzweig, S., Fleming, E. E., and Rosenzweig, L. (1948). The children's form of the Rosenzweig picture-frustration study, *Journal of Psychology, 26*, 141–191.

Rothbart, M. K. (1981). Measurement of temperament in infancy. *Child Development, 52*, 569–578.

Rothbart, M. K. (1986). Longitudinal observation of infant temperament, Developmental Psychology, 22, 356–365.

Rothbart, M. K. (1987). Children's behavior questionnaire: version 1. Unpublished manuscript, Eugene: Department of Psychology, University of Oregon.

Rotter, J. B., & Rafferty, J. E. (1950). *The Rotter incomplete sentences blank*. New York: The Psychological Corporation.

Rotton, J. & Kelly, I. W. (1985). Much ado about the full moon: a meta-analysis of lunar-lunacy research. *Psychological Bulletin, 97, #2*, 286–306.

Royce, J. R. (1973). The conceptual framework for a multi-factor theory of individuality. In J. R. Royce (Ed.), *Multivariate analysis and psychological theory*. New York: Academic Press.

Royce, J. R. (1974). Cognition and knowledge: psychological epistemology. In E. C. Carterette & M. P. Friedman (Eds.), *Handbook of perception* (Vol. 1). New York: Academic Press.

Royce, J. R. (1979). The factor-gene basis of individuality. In J. R. Royce & L. P. Mos (Eds.), *Theoretical advances in behavior genetics*. Alphen aan den Rijn, Netherlands: Sitjthoff & Noordhoff.

Royce, J. R. & Buss, A. R. (1974). The role of general systems and information theory in multi-factor individuality theory, paper 160A-74, Edmonton: Center for Advanced Study in Theoretical Psychology, University of Alberta.

Royce, J. R. & Diamond, S. R. (1980). *A multifactor-system dynamics theory of emotion: cognitive-affective interaction*. Alberta: Center for Advanced Study in Theoretical Psychology, University of Alberta.

Royce, J. R. & Mos, L. P. (Eds.) (1979). *Theoretical advances in behavior genetics*. Alphen aan den Rijn, Netherlands: Sitjthoff & Noordhoff.

Royce, J. R. & Mos, L. P. (1980). *Manual psycho-epistemological profile*, Edmonton: Center for Advanced Study in Theoretical Psychology, University of Alberta.

Royce, J. R. & Powell, A. (1979). *An overview of multifactor-system theory*. Edmonton: Center for Advanced Study in Theoretical Psychology, University of Alberta (mimeographed).

Rubin, K. H. & Daniels-Beirness, T. (1983). Concurrent and predictive correlates of sociometric status in kindergarten and grade one children. *Merrill-Palmer Quarterly*, *29*, 337–351.

Rudhyar, D. (1963). *The astrology of personality*. Hague, Netherlands: Servire-Wassenaar.

Ruedi, J. & West, C. K. (1973). Pupil self-concept in an "open" school and in a "traditional" school, *Psychology in the Schools*, *10*, #1, 48–53.

Rusalov. V. M. (1987). Questionnaire for the measurement of the structure of temperament (QST). Moscow: unpublished manuscript, Academy of Sciences, Institute of Psychology.

Ryan, T. A. & Zeran, F. R. (1972). *Organization and administration of guidance services*. Danville, Ill.: Interstate Printers & Publishers.

Rychlak, J. F. (1977). *The psychology of rigorous humanism*. New York: John Wiley, 1977.

Sallade, J. B., (1973). A comparison of the psychological adjustment of obese vs. non-obese children, *Journal of Psychosomatic Research*, *17*, 89–96.

Sattler, J. M. (1980). *Assessment of children's intelligence* (2nd edition). Philadelphia: W. B. Saunders Co.

Scarr, S. & Carter-Saltzman, L. (1982). Genetics and intelligence. In R. J. Sternberg (Ed.), *Handbook of human intelligence* (pp. 792–879). Cambridge: Cambridge University Press.

Scheiman, E. (1969). *A doctor's guide to better health through palmistry*. West Nyack, N.Y.: Parker Publishing Co.

Schludermann, S., & Schludermann, E. (1970). Personality correlations of adolescent self-concepts and security-insecurity. *Journal of Psychology*, *74*, #1, 85–90.

Schneideman, E. S. (1966). Problems of research in clinical assessment, in E. J. Megargee (Ed.), chapter in *Research in clinical assessment*, New York: Harper and Row, 7.

Sehestead, O. H. (1976). *The basics of astrology*. Woodland Hills, Ca.: Uranus Publishing Co.

Shapiro, E. S. (1987). Intervention research methodology in school psychology. *School Psychology Review, 16*, #32, 290–305.

Shaw, M. E. & Wright, J. M. (1967). *Scales for the measurement of attitudes*. New York: McGraw-Hill.

Sheldon, W. H. (1943). *Varieties of temperament*. New York: Harper.

Sheldon, W., Dupertuis, C. W. & McDermott, E. (1970). *Atlas of men: a guide for somatotyping the adult male at all ages*. Darien, Conn.: Hafner (originally published by Harper & Row, 1954).

Shertzer, B & Linden, J. D. (1979). *Fundamentals of individual appraisal*. Boston: Houghton-Mifflin.

Shertzer, B. & Stone, S. C. (1980). *Fundamentals of counseling* (third edition). Boston: Houghton-Mifflin.

Shostrum, E. (1968). *Manual for the personal orientation inventory*. San Diego: Educational and Industrial Testing Service.

Silverman, B. I. & Whitmer, M. (1974). Astrological indicators of personality. *The Journal of Psychology, 87*, 89–95.

Singer, E. (1969). *A manual of graphology*. London: Gerald Duckworth & Co.

Smith, D. L. (1951). *A manual of sociometry for teachers*. Ann Arbor: University of Michigan School of Education (mimeographed).

Smith, G. M. (1967). Usefulness of peer ratings of personality in educational research. ERIC document, ED 012 494.

Snow, R. E. (1969). Unfinished Pygmalion. *Contemporary Psychology, 14*, #4, 197–199.

Snow, R. E. & Yalom, I. D. (1982). Education and intelligence. In R. J. Sternberg (Ed.), *Handbook of human intelligence* (pp. 493–559). Cambridge: Cambridge University Press.

Snygg, D., & Combs, A. W. (1949). *Individual behavior: a new frame of reference for psychology*. New York: Harper.

Soares, A. T. and Soares, L. M. (1971). Comparative differences in the self-perceptions of disadvantaged and advantaged students, *Journal of School Psychology, 9*, #4, 424–429.

Soares, A. T. and Soares, L. M. (1972). The self concept differential in disadvantaged and advantaged students. Proceedings of the Annual Convention of the American Psychological Association, Part 1, 195–196.

Spearman, C. (1904). General intelligence objectively determined and measured. *American Journal of Psychology, 15*, 201–293.

Speisman, L. (1973). Relative effectiveness of short term facilitative communication training on secondary students' self-concept. *Dissertation Abstracts, 33* (A), 3309–3310.

Spuck, D. W. (1974). Geocode analysis. In H. J. Walberg (Ed.), *Evaluating educational performance*. Berkeley, Ca.: McCutchn Publishing Co.

Stanescu, H. (1971). Young Freud's letters to his Rumanian friend, Silberstein, *The Israel Annals of Psychiatry and Related Disciplines*, 9, 3, 195–207.

Stangl, D., Pfohl, B., Zimmerman, M., Bowers, W. & Corenthal, C. (1985). A structured interview for the DSM-III personality disorders. *Archives of General Psychiatry*, 42, #6, 615–624.

Stanton, M. O. (1920). *The encyclopedia of face and form reading* (sixth edition). Philadelphia: F. A. Davis Publishers.

Steger, H. (1975). Dimensions and correlates of children's self-concept. Unpublished Ph.D. dissertation, University of Kentucky.

Stephenson, W. (1953). *The study of behavior: Q technique and its methodology*. Chicago: University of Chicago Press.

Stephenson, W. (1980). Newton's fifth rule and Q-methodology: application to educational psychology. *American Psychologist*, 35, 882–889.

Stern, D. (1972). Effect of level of self-concept, type of feedback, and internal-external locus of control of reinforcement upon performance on a digit symbol task. *Dissertation Abstracts*, 32 (A) 4432.

Sternberg, R. J. (1982). *Handbook of human intelligence*. Cambridge: Cambridge University Press.

Sternberg, R. J. & Salter, W. (1982a). Conceptions of intelligence. In R. J. Sternberg (Ed.), *Handbook of human intelligence*. Cambridge: Cambridge University Press.

Sternberg, R. J. & Salter, W. (1982b). The nature of intelligence and its measurement. In R. J. Sternberg (Ed.), *Handbook of human intelligence* (pp. 3–24). Cambridge: Cambridge University Press.

Stickel, N. (1968). A descriptive analysis of the characteristics of elementary reticent females. Unpublished master's thesis, California State University at Hayward.

Stilwell, W. E. (1975). Recent efforts in planned interventions for affective education, paper presented AERA Annual Convention, Washington, D.C., March 31, 1975.

Stilwell, W. E. & Barclay, J. R. (1976). Effects of education through developmental guidance services: a one-year study. Stuttgart, AR: Stuttgart School district, ERIC Document No. ED. 133 077.

Stilwell, W. E. & Barclay, J. R. (1977). Effects of an affective-social education program over two years. Stuttgart, AR: ERIC Document No. ED. 143 425.

Stilwell, W. E. & Barclay, J. R. (1979). Effects of affective education in the elementary school. *Psychology in the Schools*, 16, 80–87.

Strelau, J. (1983). *Temperament, personality, activity*. London: Academic Press.

Strelau, J. (1988). The regulative theory of temperament, address delivered at the University of Kentucky, November 7, 1988.

Strong, E. K. Jr. (1943). *Vocational interests of men and women*. Stanford, Ca.: Stanford University Press.

Stroup, A. L. and Manderscheid, R. W. (1977). CPI and 16PF second-order factor congruence. Journal of Clinical Psychology, 33, #4, 1023–1026.

Sundberg, N. D. (1977). *Assessment of persons*. Englewood Cliffs: Prentice-Hall.

Sunqvist, V. B. (1975). Potential relationships between body-build and personality characteristics in a student population. *Nordisk Psykiatrisk Tilsschrift, 24*, #8, 634–646.

Swoboda, H. (1904). *Die perioden des menschlichen lebens in ihrer psychologischen und biologischen bedeutung*. Leipzig-Vienna: Deuticke.

Swoboda, H. (1954). *Die bedeutung des siebenjahn rhythmnus fuer die menschliche verebung*. Florence, Italy: Industria Tipografica Fiorentina.

Takacs, G. G. (1973). A comparison of selected self-concept variables of tenth grade students and their course of study. *Dissertation Abstracts, 33* (A), January, 3410.

Tanquery, A. (1930). *The spiritual life: a treatise on ascetical and mystical theology*. Trans. H. Branderis. Tournai, Belgium: Desclee & Co.

Tapp, G. S. & Barclay, J. R. (1974). Convergent and discriminant validity of the Barclay Classroom Climate Inventory. *Educational and Psychological Measurement, 34*, 439–447.

Tendler, A. D. (1945). Significant features of disturbance in free association, *Journal of Psychology, 20*, 65–89.

Terman, L. M. (1916). *The measurement of intelligence*. Boston: Houghton-Mifflin.

Terman, L. M. (1917). Feeble-minded children in the public schools of California. *School and Society, 5*, 161–165.

Thiessen, D. (1979). Biological trends in behavior genetics. In Jr. R. Royce & L. P. Mos (Eds.), *Theoretical advances in behavior genetics*. Alphen aan den Rijn, Netherlands: Sitjhoff & Noordhoff.

Thistlethwaite, D. L. (1959). College environments and the development of talent. *Science, 130*, 71–76.

Thistlethwaite, D. L. (1960). College press and changes in study plans of talented students. *Journal of Education Psychology, 51*, 224–234.

Thomae, H. (1973). Determinants of consistency and change in personality development. *Revista de Psicologia General y Aplicada, 28*, 3–16.

Thomas, A. & Chess, S. (1977). *Temperament and development*. New York: Brunner-Mazel.

Thoresen, C. E. & Mahoney, M. J. (1974). *Behavioral self-control.* New York: Holt, Rinehart & Winston.

Thorndike, R. L., Hagen, E., & Sattler, J. (1986). *Technical Manual: Stanford-Binet Intelligence Scale,* Fourth Edition. Chicago: The Riverside Publishing Co.

Thurstone, L. L. (1929). Theory of attitude measurement. *Psychological Bulletin, 36,* 222–241.

Thurstone, L. L. (1931). *The measurement of social attitudes.* Chicago: University of Chicago Press.

Thurstone, L. L. (1935). *The vectors of the mind.* Chicago: University of Chicago Press.

Thurstone, L. L. (1947). *Multiple factor analysis.* Chicago: University of Chicago Press.

Tiebout, H. M., Jr. (1952). Philosophy and psychoanalysis: theories of human nature and conduct in Freud's psychology. Unpublished doctoral dissertation, Columbia University.

Tindall, R. H. (1955). Relationships among indices of adjustment status. *Educational and Psychological Measurement, 15,* 152–162.

Tomkins, S. S. (1962). *Affect, imagery, consciousness.* New York: Springer.

Travers, R. M. W. (Ed.) (1973). *Second handbook of research on teaching.* Chicago: Rand-McNally.

Trickett, E. V. (1969). Stability and predictability of children's self-concept and perception by others. *Dissertation Abstracts International, 29* (8-A), 2577.

Trowbridge, N. (1972). Self-concept and socio-economic status in elementary school children. *American Educational Research Journal, 9,* #4, 525–537.

Tryon, W. W. (1979). The test-trait fallacy. *American Psychologist, 34,* 402–406.

Uhlenberg, D. M. (1971). Provisional perspective on the self with a summary of pertinent research, 1959–1969. *Dissertation Abstracts International, 29,* (8-A), 2577.

Uhr, R., Thomae, H. & Becker, J. (1969). Entwickungsverlaufe im kindes und jugen-alter. *Zeitschrift fuer Entwicklungspsychologie und Padogogische Psychologie, 1,* 151–164.

U.S. Office of Strategic Services Staff (1977). *Assessment of men.* New York: W. W. Norton Co.

Vygotsky, L. S. (1962). *Thought and language,* translated by E. Hanfmann and G. Vakar. Cambridge Mass.: Massachusetts Institute of Technology Press.

Wade, E. (1970). *Astrology.* New York: Arco Publishing Co.

Wahlsten, D. (1979). A critique of the concepts of heritability and heredity in behavioral genetics. In J. R. Royce & L. P. Mos (Eds.), *Theoretical advances in behavior genetics.* Alphen aan den Rijn, Netherlands: Sitjthoff & Noordhoff.

Wainwright, J. C. (1980). A framework for the observation of movements and sounds. *Group Psychotherapy, Psychodrama and Sociometry, 33,* 6–24.

Walberg, H. J. (Ed.) (1974). *Evaluating educational performance.* Berkeley, Ca.: McCutchan Publishing Co.

Walberg, H. J. & Anderson, G. J. (1968). Classroom climate and individual learning. *Journal of Educational Psychology,* 59, 414–419.

Walsh, K. W. (1978). *Neuropsychology, a clinical approach.* Edinburg, London: Churchill Livingstone.

Watson, L. (1973). *Super nature.* New York: Doubleday.

Wechsler, D. (1939). *The measurement of adult intelligence.* Baltimore: Williams and Williams.

Wechsler, D. (1944). *The measurement of adult intelligence* (3rd edition). Baltimore: Williams and Williams.

Weiner, B. (1974). *Achievement motivation and attribution theory.* Morristown: Silver Burdett.

Weiner, B., Frieze, I., Kukla, A., Reed, L., Rest, S. & Rosenbaum, R. M. (1971). *Perceiving the causes of success and failure.* New York: General Learning Press.

Welch, G. S. & Dahlstrom, W. G. (Eds.) (1956). *Basic readings on the MMPI in psychology and medicine.* Minneapolis: University of Minnesota Press.

Wells, L. E. & Marwell, G. (1976). *Self-esteem: its conceptualization and measurement.* Beverly Hills, Ca.: Sage Publications.

Werts, C. E. & Watley, D. J. (1970). Paternal influence on talent development. Evanston, Ill.: National Merit Scholarship Corporation, Research Report No. 4.

White, W. F., and Allen, R. (1971). Art counseling in an educational settings: self-concept change among pre-adolescent boys, *Journal of School Psychology,* 9, #2, 218–225.

White, L. A. (1949). *The science of culture.* New York: Grove Press.

Widiger, T. A. and Frances A. (1985). The DSM-III personality disorder, *Archives of General Psychiatry,* 42, 620.

Wiggins, J. S. (1969). Content dimensions in the MMPI, in J. N. Butcher (Ed.) *MMPI: research developments and clinical applications* (127–180). New York: McGraw-Hill.

Williams, R. L. (1972). The Black Intelligence Test of Cultural Homogeneity (BITCH): a culture-specific test. Paper presented at APA meeting, Honolulu.

Williamson, E. G. & Darley, J. G. (1937). *Student personnel work*. New York: McGraw-Hill.

Windle, M., Hooker, K., Lenerz, K., East, P. L., Lerner, J. V., & Lerner, R. M. (1986). Temperament, perceived competence and depression in early and later adolescents. *Developmental Psychology, 22*, #3, 384–392.

Windle, M. and Lerner, R. M. (1986). Reassessing the dimensions of temperament individuality across life span: the revised dimensions of temperament survey (DOYS-R). *Journal of Adolescent Research, 1*, 213–230.

Witelson, S. F. & Paillie, W. (1973). Left hemisphere specialization for language in the newborn: neuroanatomical evidence of asymmetry. *Brain, 96*, 641–646.

Wolff, W. (1943). *The expression of personality*. New York: Harper & Bros.

Wooster, A. D. & Harris, G. (1972). Concepts of self and others in highly mobile service boys. *Educational Research, 14*, #3, 195–199.

Wu, W. T. (1975). Comparative climates of Chinese and American classrooms, unpublished doctoral dissertation, University of Kentucky.

Wundt, W. (1903). *Grundzuge der Physiologischen Psychologie* (5th edition, Vol. III). Leipzig: W. Engelmann.

Wylie, R. C. (1961). *The self-concept*. Lincoln: University of Nebraska Press.

Wylie, R. C. (1974). *The self-concept: a review of methodological considerations and measuring instruments*. Lincoln: University of Nebraska Press.

Yamamoto, K. (1972). *The child and his image: self-concepts in the early years*. Boston: Houghton-Mifflin.

Zajonc, R. B. (1976). Family configuration and intelligence: variations in scholastic aptitude scores parallel trends in family size and the spacing of children. *Science, 192*, 227–236.

Zajonc, R. B. (1980). Feeling and thinking: preferences need no inferences. *American Psychologist, 35*, #32, 151–175.

Zuckerman, M. (1979). *Sensation seeking: beyond the optimal level of arousal*. Hillsdale, New Jersey: Erlbaum.

Author Index

441

Subject Index